THE
RAILWAY
DICTIONARY

4th EDITION

WORLDWIDE RAILWAY FACTS
AND TERMINOLOGY

ALAN A. JACKSON

First published in the United Kingdom in 1992 by
Sutton Publishing Ltd · Phoenix Mill · Stroud · Gloucestershire

Fourth edition 2006

British Library Cataloguing in Publication Data

A catalogue record for this book is available from the British Library.

ISBN 0-7509-4218-5

Typeset in Plantin 9/11 pt.
Typesetting and origination by
Sutton Publishing Limited.
Printed and bound in England by
J.H. Haynes & Co. Ltd, Sparkford.

CONTENTS

PREFACE TO FOURTH EDITION

This new edition becomes necessary to provide some record of the host of additions to the railway acronyms and terms which have emerged in the past five years, not least those arising from substantial rearrangement of the constituents of the controversial privatized regime launched in 1996. Parts of the original structure have already disappeared, to be replaced by new ones, while an additional authority was formed by the political successors of the original privatizers. This enjoyed only a brief life before seeing much of its remit assumed by the Department for Transport, itself the proud owner of yet another new name and acronym.

For their part, the Train Operating Companies have been shifted around and renamed, often several times, and in an increasingly desperate search for novelty we have seen the arrival of curious brand titles such as C2C and ONE, duly noted herein. Southern, trading name of New Southern Railway Ltd, came along to replace Connex South Central but was not to be confused with the Southern Railway Company of 1923–47. Inevitably this restless activity has had repercussions for the Dictionary compiler, as has the rapid advance of technology appropriate to improving the efficiency, performance and safety of rail transport in the interval since the last edition.

One consequence of the introduction of a privatized railway regime in Britain has been the arrival in the industry of many who have little or no previous familiarity with railway work and its internal language. In some cases this has encouraged the emergence of new words and acronyms, a feature particularly apparent in a very necessary increased emphasis on the safety of those whose work or duties take them out on the track.

To make room for the many new entries and amplification of some existing definitions, the layout of the Dictionary has been rearranged while maintaining convenience of access and clarity. Coverage of the nomenclature and language of rail transport outside the United Kingdom has been further strengthened in this edition, and for the first time there is some mention of each of the major national networks across the whole world. At the same time we have increased the detail given on British nomenclature and practice. In total there are around 1,550 new and expanded entries.

Fellow members of the Railway & Canal Historical Society have given this work valued support since it was first published in 1992. Michael Robbins, who died in 2002, and H.W. (Harry) Paar, who died in 2005, will be greatly missed; both again contributed helpful and constructive suggestions which have been included in this new edition. I am also grateful this time for useful comments and additional material supplied by Graham Bird, Grahame Boyes and Brian Hardy, and for the generous practical help and encouragement given by Gerald Jacobs.

As always, suggestions for new entries or changes to the existing ones will be carefully considered for any future editions and should be addressed to me, care of the publishers.

Alan A. Jackson
Dorking, 2006

NOTES ON USING THE DICTIONARY AND ITS ARRANGEMENT

Order of dictionary entries: Entries are made in strict alphabetical order by letter, ampersand and the abbreviation 'St' being treated as 'and' and 'Saint' respectively. Company names will be found under their initials, including ampersand, where one applies. For example, the *Stratford-upon-Avon & Midland Junction Rly* appears under **S&**MJR not **SMJ**R. Definite articles are ignored for the purposes of placing in alphabetical order. Headwords are printed in bold type, with an initial capital.

Named trains: With one or two exceptions, only those names bestowed officially by the operating railway are given.

For those named trains operating in Britain, the dates when the name was first and last *officially* used (i.e. in timetables and/or on the trains themselves) are noted, as are any major changes in route. It should, however, be borne in mind that the name may have been applied to a service that already existed and that the service may have continued after the name had been discarded.

In general it may be assumed that named trains ran in both directions between the places given in the entry, but a very small number did work in one direction only.

Again as a general rule, it should be noted that most named trains in Britain and mainland Europe ceased to operate as such during both world wars; where they were resumed afterwards, this is normally clear from the entry. As always there are exceptions, and in Britain, for example, in the Second World War, the Aberdonian, Cornish Riviera, Flying Scotsman and Night Scotsman continued to run as named trains. During the preparation of the Second Edition, it became apparent that the official naming of trains in Britain had by the 1990s become increasingly ephemeral and undervalued. For this reason the coverage of recent British train names makes no claim to be comprehensive.

Outside Britain, the aim has been to include all the *CIWL* 'Grand Expresses', the *TEE* and *EC* names and other *major* named services.

Terms capable of more than one interpretation: Some generic terms such as 'tramway' have had several meanings over the period of their use. In such cases each definition is given a number, and any reference elsewhere in the dictionary to the word repeats the relevant number, e.g. 'tramway *(4)*' indicates that in the context of the entry it is a tramway of the type defined at '**Tramway** *(4)*'.

National variations: Unless otherwise noted by the presence of an abbreviation such as '(US)' or '(Fr)', the definition given relates to British/Irish usage and practice. Where an entry is annotated '(US)', the usage explained can generally be taken to flow over into Canada. Foreign words and phrases are shown in italics.

British and Irish railway companies: These normally appear in the main dictionary under their *full initials*, including any '&' in the title (see Order of dictionary entries above).

No attempt has been made to list every railway company that ever existed in Britain and Ireland, but all the major companies are shown, as well as all others owning rolling stock. In addition, many other companies have been included, particularly those whose title offers little or no indication of the location of their lines. An effort has been made to include all jointly owned or jointly worked lines of significant length.

The notes against each company entry do not attempt to summarize its history and geography but merely give the date of incorporation (normally that of the first Act of Parliament or LRO), the extent of the main system, the opening date of the first lines and the date of any disappearance into the maws of a larger concern. In the case of those small companies which remained independent after the grouping of 1923, and light railways, closure dates are normally given.

Gauge: This is noted only when it differs from the British standard (4 ft 8½ in, or in Ireland 5 ft 3 in).

Slang, colloquialisms and nicknames: In some cases usage did not, and does not, stray far from the place of origin, but it is always difficult to be dogmatic about this, so no regional distinctions are noted other than those for the London Underground system (marked '(LTRS)'), and even some of these may have gained currency in parts of the main railway system. Some very localized and transient terms have been omitted. For these, the user is referred to the three works on railway slang noted in the list of sources below.

Difficulty also arises in distinguishing between the language of railway officers and staff and that of railway amateurs or enthusiasts. This occurs partly because so many of the latter are to be found in the ranks of the former but also because there has always been a certain cross-fertilization. For this reason, although we began with the intention of distinguishing between these two categories of slang, colloquialisms and nicknames, it soon appeared that the boundary was too often ill defined, and all has therefore been classified as '(RS)'. This general classification also includes terms and expressions used in relation to tramways (3). As well as distinguishing slang words peculiar to the London Underground, we have also annotated the often colourful North American railway expressions as '(USRS)'.

The derivations of slang, colloquialisms and nicknames are sometimes obvious, but where they are not, the origins are often obscure. If a derivation is of particular interest or can be given with reasonable certainty it has been noted; but on the whole, we have preferred not to make intelligent guesses. It should also be noted that certain terms which may now be considered offensive are included in the Dictionary because of their historical and specific relevance to railways. Their appearance here in no way reflects the views of either author or publisher.

Obsolete and obsolescent terms: The annotation '(obs)' has been omitted where the entry makes it clear that the company, etc. no longer exists. Although most of the telegraphic codes (TC) noted are no longer in daily use, these words continue to have currency among modellers and others and in many cases have survived to become the convenient accepted names of the type of rolling stock mentioned in the entry. In all other cases, although many words, abbreviations and expressions have fallen out of everyday use on the main railway systems, they do remain current among those fascinated by railways, most notably among modellers and those working with old railway and tramway equipment in museums and on preserved lines, both in the UK and overseas. For these reasons the annotation '(obs)' has been used somewhat sparingly.

Place-names: These are usually given in the form current in Britain at the time to which the entry relates, e.g. Portmadoc rather than Porthmadog, but should always be recognizable. For most of the period covered by this dictionary it was customary to use Anglicized versions of some foreign place names, e.g. Venice and not Venezia; Cologne, not Köln; Hook of Holland, not Hoek van Holland, etc. Again these English forms have been used here and should offer no difficulty.

Other proper names, companies, societies, etc.: These usually appear under their *initials* when consisting of more than one word.

Trade and proprietary terms: Inclusion in this dictionary of some words or trade marks does not imply that they have acquired non-proprietary or general significance; no judgment of any kind concerning the legal status of these words is intended by such inclusion.

Institutes/Institutions: These are shown under their initials, e.g. 'ICE, IEE'.

Periodicals: Except where the title consists of a single word, periodicals are usually entered under the initials of their titles, thus *Railway Magazine* appears in alphabetical position as '*RM*'. Some modern periodicals which have had only a brief life have been omitted. All the more important periodicals are included, along with many others of less value for historical and technical reference, together with brief details of dates and title changes. Those seeking further information about periodicals published before 1900 are recommended to consult *Victorian Periodicals and Victorian Society*, pp. 179–96 (*see* **Sources**).

Permanent way terms: Some terms whose meaning is obvious or those which relate to minor components of trackwork have been omitted for space reasons. These may be found in the more comprehensive lists in the *Vocabulary of Terms used by the Permanent Way Department* (UIC, 1975) or in I.W. Ellis,. *British Railway Track*, vol. 9 (see **Sources**).

National Railway Systems: These are listed in the Dictionary under their UIC (qv) code or other headings as shown below. Track gauge is only given if other than standard gauge (qv) predominates in the country concerned. Route length figures, given in kilometres (multiply by 0.6214 to convert to miles), are only approximate since the sources consulted were often found to give disparate totals. In general, only those countries with over 1,000 km of route have received entries.

Albania: HSh
Algeria: SNTF
Angola: CFA (2)
Argentina: FA
Australia: AUS/Ghan
Austria: OBB
Bangladesh: BAN
Belarus: BZD
Belgium: B-Rail
Bolivia: ENF
Bosnia: ZBH
Brazil: RFFSA
Bulgaria: BDZ
Burkina Faso: SCFB
Burma – *see* Myanmar
Cameroon: RNCFC
Canada: VIA Rail
Chile: EFE; A&BR (2)
China: CR (11); KCRC; TRA
Colombia: FNC
Congo (Democratic Republic of): SNCRDC
Corsica: CFC
Croatia: HZ
Cuba: FdeC
Czech Republic: CD
Denmark: DSB
Egypt: ENR
Estonia: EVR
Finland: VR
France: SNCF
Germany: DB/DEBAG
Ghana: GRC
Great Britain: Network Rail

Greece: CH/OSE
Hungary: MAV
India: Indian Rlys
Indonesia: PJKA
Iraq: IRR
Iran: RAI
Ireland (Irish Republic): IE
Israel: IR
Italy: FS
Ivory Coast: SICF
Japan: JR (2)
Jordan: ARC; Hedjaz
Kenya: KR (6)
Korea: KNDR; KNR
Latvia: LDZ
Lebanon: CEL
Lithuania: LG
Luxembourg: CFL
Macedonia: MZ
Malawi: CEAR
Malaysia: KTM(B)
Mexico: FNM
Moldova: CFM (2)
Mongolia: MNR
Morocco: ONCFM
Mozambique: CFM (1)
Myanmar: MRC
Namibia: NVK
Netherlands: NS
New Zealand: TRANZRAIL
Nigeria: NRC
Northern Ireland: NIR
Norway: NSB
Pakistan: PAR
Panama: FCP

Paraguay: FCCP
Peru: ENAFER/ Perurail
Philippines: PNR
Poland: PKP
Portugal: CP
Romania: CFR
Russia: RZD
Saudi Arabia: SRO
Senegal: SNCS
Serbia/Montenegro: ZS
Slovakia: ZSR
Slovenia: SZ
South Africa: SARCO; Spoornet
Spain: RENFE
Sri Lanka: SLG
Sudan: SRC
Sweden: BV
Switzerland: CFF; FFS; SBB; SFF
Syria: CFS
Taiwan: TRA
Tanzania: TRC
Thailand: SRT
Tunisia: SNCFT
Turkey: TCDD
Turkmenistan: TDZ
Uganda: URC
Ukraine: UZ
United States: USA
Uruguay: AFE
Viet Nam: DSVN
Zambia: ZR
Zimbabwe: NRZ

ABBREVIATIONS

Aus	Australia/Australian
BR	British Rail
BSI	British Standards Institution
cctv	closed circuit television
Co./co.	company
EC	The European Commission
EU	European Union
Fr	France/French language
Ger	Germany/German language
h	hours
inc	incorporated
Ire	Ireland (usually Republic of Ireland)
It	Italy/Italian language
Junc	Junction
kph	kilometres per hour
loco	locomotive
LT	London Transport and predecessors (London Underground railways). For simplicity, LT is also used in the Dictionary for references to the successor organization, London Underground (TfL)
LTRS	slang or colloquialism used by staff of London's underground railways
m	miles
min	minutes
mph	miles per hour
NI	Northern Ireland
NZ	New Zealand
obs	obsolete
OED	*Oxford English Dictionary*
qv	*quod vide* – refer to the main entry under this name, term or word
rly	railway
RR	Railroad
RS	slang or colloquialism used by railway and tramway/light rail staff and transport amateurs
S	general British slang or colloquialism
Sp	Spain/Spanish language
TC	telegraphic code
tph	trains per hour
US	United States of America
USRS	railway slang or colloquialism in the US and Canada
vdu	visual display unit
WW1	First World War (1914–18)
WW2	Second World War (1939–45)

All other abbreviations used are defined in the main dictionary.

SOURCES

Of the wide variety of sources consulted, the following proved particularly helpful:

Books and Articles
Anon., *British Railways Glossary of Terms*, 1966 (limited circulation).
Anon., *The Railroad Dictionary of Car and Locomotive Terms*, USA, 1980.
Anon., *The Railway Yearbook/Railway Directory & Yearbook*, various issues.
Beck, James H., *Rail Talk: A Lexicon of Railroad Language*, USA, 1978.
Beebe, Lucius, *Mixed Train Daily*, USA, 1961.
Behrend, G., *The History of Wagons-Lits 1875–1955*, 1959.
Body, G., *The Railway Language*, 1972, and *Supplement* [on slang] (n.d.).
Botkin, B.A., and Harlow, Alvin F. (eds.), *A Treasury of Railroad Folklore*, USA, 1954.
Charlton, E. Harper, *Railway Car Builders of the United States & Canada*, USA, 1957.
Cole, W.H., *Permanent-Way Material, Platelaying and Points and Crossings with a few remarks on Signalling and Interlocking*, 8th edn., revised by Lt.-Col. G.R. Hearn, 1920.
Davies, W.J.K., *Light Railways, their Rise and Decline*, 1964.
Ellis, I.W., *British Railway Track* vol. 9: Track Terminology, 2004.
Gale, P.R., *The Great Western Railway*, 1926.
Humm, Robert, *Catalogues*, Robert Humm & Co. Transport Booksellers, *passim*.
McKenna, F., *The Railway Workers 1840–1970*, 1980.
Marshall, J., *A Biographical Dictionary of Railway Engineers*, 2nd edn., 2003.
——, *Guinness Book of Rail Facts & Feats*, 1979.
Mitchell, N.H.G., 'A Dictionary of Underground Slang', published in *Underground*, no. 6 (July 1980).
O'Dell, A.C., *Railways and Geography* 1956.
Price, J.H., *A Source Book of Trams*, 1980.
Rowsome, Frank, *Trolley Car Treasury*, 1956.
Sekon, G.A., *Sekon's Dictionary of Railway Words & Phrases* 1901.
Sheppard, H., *Dictionary of Railway Slang*, 2nd edn., 1970.
Stones, H.R., *British Railways in Argentina 1860–1948*, 1993.
Vane, J. Don, and Van Arsdel, Rosemary T. (eds), *Victorian Periodicals and Victorian Society*, University of Toronto Press, 1994.

Periodicals
Various issues of the following:
  Modern Railways
  Modern Tramway
  Modern Transport
  Railroad Magazine [USA]
  The Railway & Travel Monthly
  The Railway Magazine
  Railways/Railway World
  Railway Gazette
  Trains Illustrated
  Transport & Travel Monthly
  La Vie du Rail [France]

A

A&BR
1. Aylesbury & Buckingham Rly:
   Aylesbury–Verney Junction (junc with
   L&NWR) inc 1860, opened 1868,
   worked by GWR, part of Metropolitan
   Rly, 1891, worked by Metropolitan
   from 1894.
2. Antofagasta (Chile) & Bolivia Rly
   (FCAB): First section opened 1873,
   2 ft 6 in/762 mm gauge; completed
   1892; converted to metre gauge 1928.

A&N Jt
Ashby & Nuneaton Joint, Nuneaton to
Overseal & Moira/Coalville, inc 1866,
1867, opened 1873, jointly vested in
Midland and L&NWR, part of LM&SR
from 1923.

A&ST
Alford & Sutton Tramway, Alford to
Sutton-on-Sea, 2 ft 6 in gauge steam
tramway (*4*), inc 1880, opened 1884,
renamed Great Northern Steam Tramways
Co. 1886, closed 1889.

A&TER
Athenry & Tuam Extension Rly (Ire), inc
1890, opened 1894, worked by G&SWR,
part of GSR 1924.

A&WCR
Aberystwyth & Welsh Coast Rly,
Machynlleth– Aberystwyth/Pwllheli/Dolgelley,
inc 1861, opened 1863, 1864, 1865, 1867,
1869, part of Cambrian from 1865.

AAR
Association of American Railroads;
established 1934, a consolidation of the
American Railway Association and other
organizations dating back to 1867. The
central coordinating and research agency of
the US rly industry. Canadian and
Mexican rlys also participate.

Aardvark (RS)
BR Class 89 loco; from the shape of its
nose. *See also* Anteater.

AAT
Amalgamated Association of Tramway &
Vehicle Workers. *See also* UVW.

ABAC
*Association Belge des Amis des Chemins de
Fer*; formed 1929, published *Ferrovia* from
October 1931. Now known as *ARBAC* (qv).

Abadan (RS) (obs)
Loco driver who makes excessive use of oil.
From the Iranian oil port.

ABB
ASEA Brown Boveri: manufacturers of
railway rolling stock, a 1988 merger of
ASEA (Sweden) and Brown–Boveri
(Switzerland/Germany). In 1992 ABB
acquired a majority shareholding of BREL
(qv) which became ABB Transportation
Ltd. In 1995 ASEA Brown Boveri merged
with Daimler Benz (Germany) to form
ABB Daimler–Benz Transportation.

Abbey Tanks (RS)
GCR 4–6–2T.

ABC
ABC or Alphabetical Railway Guide; a rly
timetable, published monthly, set out in
alphabetical order of places served from
London, showing services from and to
London; first published in 1853. Guides
arranged on similar lines were also
published for some other British cities and
towns. 'I would sooner lose a train by the
ABC than catch it by *Bradshaw*' – Oscar
Wilde. Renamed *OAG Railguide* (qv).

ABCs
Booklets of loco numbers published by Ian Allan for the use of train spotters (qv). When a loco was seen, the user crossed out the printed number. *See also* Number cruncher; Ref.

ABCL
Automatic half Barrier level Crossing Locally monitored. Monitored from a signal box adjacent to the crossing. *See also* Automatic level crossings.

ABCR
Automatic half Barrier Crossing Remotely monitored. Monitored by cctv from a signal box or signalling centre (qv) at some distance from the site. *See also* Automatic level crossings.

Aberdares (RS)
GWR inside-cylinder 2–6–0 locos of 1900. From their use on coal trains between Aberdare and Swindon.

Aberdonian, The
Express between London (Kings Cross) and Aberdeen, introduced 1927, name dropped 1971. Reintroduced 5.1982, ceased 5.1987. *See also* Night Aberdonian.

Abermule
Station on the Cambrian Rlys near the scene of a 1921 head-on collision caused by the issue of the wrong tablet, which was not checked by the driver. Some locos in India later carried the words REMEMBER ABERMULE inscribed in their cabs.

Abnormal Load/s
see Exceptional load; Out of gauge load.

Abonné (Fr)
Season ticket holder, commuter.

ABP
Associated British Ports (formerly BTDB (qv)).

ABS
1. Automatic Brake System.
2. Air Braked Service.
3. (Ger) *Ausbaustrecke/n* (qv).
4. (US) Automatic Block Signal, in use from 1900s. Positioned at loops and junctions to show occupation of a single line section and prevent collisions.

Absent rider (RS)
An engineman who has failed to report for duty.

Absolute block
see Block system.

Abt
see Rack railway.

Abteilwagen (Ger)
Compartment coach (qv).

Abutment
Supporting structure at the ends of an arch or bridge usually carrying both horizontal and vertical loads.

Abzweigstelle/Abzw (Ger)
A junction or connection with other lines which is not situated in a station area.

ACC
American Car Co., St Louis, Mo, US, established 1891, bought by Brill (qv) 1902. Builders of all types of electric traction rolling stock. Plant closed 1931.

Accelerato (It) (obs)
Stopping Train; 'Somewhat faster than the Treno Omnibus' – Baedeker.

Accessible toilet
One accessible to MIP (qv). This rather uncertain description (are all others inaccessible?) replaced from 2004 the ambiguous 'Disabled toilet'.

Accommodation bogie
A simple truck with railway wheels for moving car bodies during overhaul whilst the normal bogies are receiving separate attention.

Accommodation crossing/bridge
A private bridge or level crossing provided for the use of the landowner or his tenants when a parcel of land under single ownership has been severed by construction of a rly.

Accommodation train (US)(obs)
A slow or local train.

ACE
1. Area Civil Engineer (BR)
2. Atlantic Coast Express (qv).

Ace, The (RS)
The Atlantic Coast Express (qv).

Acela
Brand name for the Amtrak (qv) high-speed services in the North East Corridor (qv), introduced in 2000–1 (New York–

Washington in 2 h 30 min, New York–Boston 3 h). An invented word 'evoking acceleration and excellence', 1999.

ACF
American Car & Foundry Co., manufacturers of rly and tramway rolling stock, established 1899 following a merger of thirteen companies. British works functioned at Trafford Park, Manchester 1904–9. From 1954 known as ACF Industries Inc.

ACFI
A form of feed-water heater (qv) evolved by the French organization *Association des Chemins de Fer Industrielles. See also* Hikers.

ACI (US)
Automatic Car Identification. A set of modules on each side of locos and rolling stock which, when read by an optical scanner as the train passes (at up to 80 mph), identifies ownership, number, classification, etc. *See also* AEI (2); AVIS.

ACL (US)
Atlantic Coast Line RR Co.

ACLG
AC Locomotive Group founded 1996 to ensure the preservation and restoration of BR (qv) electric locos.

ACM
Axle Control Module, a module which simplifies the interface between SSI (qv) and an axle counter.

ACoRP
Association of Community Rail Partnerships, 2000, representing small local rail improvement projects, funded by the Countryside Agency, ATOC (qv) and other sponsors under the government's Community Rail Initiative.

A–Co–Tra–L
Operators of the Rome Metro and Rome–Ostia Rly.

ACPF
Asociacion del Congreso Panamericano de Ferrocarriles; Pan-American Railway Congress Association.

ACSES
Advanced Civil Speed Enforcement System of Alstom (qv). Fitted to braking equipment and designed to control and enforce train movement at different speeds. Capable of imposing speed limits and deceleration and full braking where required for safety.

ACTO
Association of Charter Train Operators.

ACV/ACV Sales Ltd
Associated Commercial Vehicles, a combination of AEC (*1*) (qv), Crossley Motors and the Maudslay Motor Co., formed *c.* 1949. In 1952 ACV produced an experimental 3-car diesel unit which was tried on several BR lines, preceding the BR decision to order its first diesel railcar sets.

Adelante
A Spanish word meaning 'forward' or 'future', adopted by First Great Western (qv) for its fleet of Class 180 high-speed trains, introduced 2001–2. *See also* Coradia.

ADEMAS
Association d'Exploitation du Matériel Sprague: an organisation which arranges night tours of the Paris *Métro*, including closed stations and sections not normally used, in the classic Sprague trains (qv) of 1908–33.

Adex (obs)
TC for an advertised excursion.

Adriatic (US)
A steam loco with 2–6–4 wheel arrangement.

Adriatico
TEE Milan–Bari, introduced 1973, IC 1987.

ADtranz
Title of ABB Daimler Benz Corporation in which the rly activities of ABB (qv) and AEG (qv) were merged from 1996. *See also* Schindler. Acquired by Bombardier (qv) 2000.

Advance, in
Signalling term denoting anything beyond a given point on the rly when facing the direction of travel.

Advanced starter
Stop signal placed more than a train length in advance (qv) of the starting signal, indicating a point to which trains can draw up after completing station platform work if the block section ahead is not clear, thus allowing a following train to use the platform.

Advenza
Rail freight services begun 2004 as FreightBus.

Advertised, on the (USRS)
see On the Advertised.

AEA Technology
Successors to BR(1) Research, from 1996.

AEC
1. Associated Equipment Co., a subsidiary of the UERL (qv), formed in 1912, became independent in 1933.
2. American Electric Co., formed jointly by Professor Elihu Thomson and Edward J. Houston in 1880; suppliers of electric traction equipment. Became known as Thomson–Houston (qv) in 1881.

AEG
Allgemeine Elektrizitäts Gesellschaft, manufacturers of electrical equipment. Founded 1881 as German Edison Co., became AEG 1887, merged with *Union Elektrizitäts Gesellschaft*, the German subsidiary of GE(2) (qv), 1903 to form *AEG–Union*, later AEG again. From 1995 part of ABB Daimler-Benz.

AEI
1. Associated Electrical Industries Ltd, successors to BTH (qv) and MV (qv) 1959–67; part of GEC (qv) 1967.
2. Automatic Equipment Identification. A system in which transponders fitted to locos and rolling stock transmit to lineside readers and thence to a central computer to show the location and status of all vehicles and data on their loadings, thus optimising use. *See also* ACI (US); AVIS.

Aerial rlys/ropeways
Not really rlys in the strictest sense but sometimes known as such. Also called Telphers or Telpherways. With cars or buckets suspended from cables strung between towers and hauled by a continuous cable, these installations normally serve industrial requirements such as carriage of minerals between mines and quarries and factories, ports or road/rail transfer facilities. Some traverse considerable distances, and intervening obstacles and severe gradients present little or no difficulty. Passengers may also be carried, usually in mountainous areas. *See also Luftseilbahn, Seilbahn,*

Seilschwebebahn, Teleferica, Télépherique, Telpher.

Aero
A GWR (qv) wagon designed to carry three-blade aircraft propellers, 1935.

AET
Automatic Equipment Technician (LT).

AFAC
Association Française des Amis [originally *Amateurs*] *des Chemins de Fer*; founded 1929; has published *Chemins de Fer* since 1933.

AFC
1. Automatic Fare Collection [system].
2. Area Freight Centre.

AFE
Administración de Ferrocarriles del Estado: State Rlys of Uruguay, *c.* 2,000 km.

African Village, The (RS)
Muddle of buildings in the forecourt area of Kings Cross station, London, not finally cleared away until 1972–3.

Agent (obs)
Scottish alternative term for stationmaster (which was also used). *See also* Station Agent.

Aguila Azteca
Express between Mexico City and Nuevo Laredo.

AGV (Fr)
Automotrice de Grande Vitesse, high speed (350kph) articulated (qv) train sets, SNCF (qv), 2005.

AHBC
Automatic Half Barrier Crossing with barriers obstructing the nearside half of the roadway at a level crossing when actuated by an approaching train, returning to raised position automatically after the train has passed. Road traffic warned by traffic lights. Fitted with a telephone to the responsible signal box. *See also* Automatic level crossings.

AICCF
Association Internationale du Congrès des Chemins de Fer; International Rly Congress Association, established at Brussels 1885 to facilitate the progress and development of rlys by holding periodical congresses and issuing publications.

AIR
Association of Independent Railways. A

retitling of AMRC (qv). *See* AIRPS.

Air Artist (USRS)
A driver skilful in the use of the air brakes.

Air brake
A braking system in which brakes are held off by compressed air acting on a piston and applied by the controlled release of pressure.

Air cons (RS)
Air conditioned coaches.

Air dump (US)
A car which tips its body by use of air pressure to ease loading and unloading.

Airey's Maps and Junction Diagrams
Published by John Airey and Zachary Macaulay of the RCH (qv) from 1854; they show the distances between stations and junctions and the ownership of each section of rly. They became official publications after the RCH purchased the business in 1895.

Air giver (USRS)
Brakeman.

Air jammer/jumper (USRS)
Rlyman who connects train air hoses.

Air line (US)
Term indicating a rly providing the most direct route between two places, e.g. Seaboard Air Line, following the Atlantic coast from Richmond to Florida by the shortest and straightest route.

Air monkey (USRS)
Air brake fitter/mechanic.

AIRPS (obs)
Association of Independent Railways and Preservation Societies; an amalgamation from 1 April 1996 of ARPS (qv) and AIR (qv). Renamed HRA (qv) 1998.

Air slide (US)
Car whose contents can be unloaded by use of air pressure and a sliding interior section.

Air-Track
A consortium and forum headed by Surrey County Council from 2003 to investigate and sponsor a direct rail link between London Airport (Heathrow), Woking and Guildford via Staines.

Aisle (US)
Gangway through a coach.

AJR
see Axholme.

Akropolis
Through service between Munich and Athens via Salzburg and Belgrade, introduced 1968.

AL
Chemin de Fer de l'Alsace-Lorraine [France]; part of *SNCF* (qv), 1938.

ALA
Same as SANAL (qv).

Aladdin (LTRS)
A handlamp.

ALAF
Asociacion Latino Americana de Ferrocarriles; Latin American Railways Association.

Albert Schweitzer
TEE Dortmund–Strasbourg, introduced 1980, ceased 1983.

ALC
Accommodation Level Crossing. *See* Accommodation crossing.

Alco
Alco Products Inc, 1955 renaming of the American Locomotive Co. (formed 1901). Loco production ceased in 1970.

Ale
GWR TC for a wagon used for carrying casks.

Alexandria, The (obs)
Unofficial name for the 11.00 London (Waterloo)–Plymouth L&SWR express in the 1890s, probably after the Pullman car in its consist.

Alice
The service between Sydney and Alice Springs (Australia).

Alignment
The course of a rly as determined by the final surveys; a ground plan of a rly route.

Alive
Code word used in WW2 for a special train used by Prime Minister Winston Churchill, ministers and British and US service commanders; also (in France, Holland and Germany) for the special train used by General Eisenhower as his mobile headquarters.

Allegheny (US)
A loco with 2–6–6–6 wheel arrangement.

Alleluia! (RS)
A signal to shut the tap when washing out the boiler of a steam locomotive.

Alley (USRS)
An unobstructed track in a marshalling or shunting yard.

Alliance Approach
An arrangement which ties all or some contractors for a specific major project to pre-defined budget figures. If costs rise above these levels, all participating contractors pay penalties; likewise all share any financial incentives if performance proves to fall below the budget.

All system timetable
A single volume containing details of all BR passenger services, first issued by BR in 1974. After privatization superseded by National Rail Timetable (qv).

Alpazur
A Geneva–Digne service, later Grenoble–Digne. The seasonal railcar service from Digne to Nice of the *Chemins de Fer de Provence* also carried this name 1974–89.

Alpen Express
Through service between Copenhagen and Rome via Brenner, introduced 1957, became a day train Munich to Rome. *See also* Michelangelo.

Alphaline
Name used from 1994 by Regional Railways South Wales & West for trains with trolley refreshment services, telephones, reserved seat accommodation and air-conditioning.

Alps/over the Alps
1. (RS) Several routes with pronounced undulations received this description, notably Alton to Alresford, Carlisle to Stranraer via Castle Douglas, and Barnstaple to Torrington.
2. (LTRS) The raised sidings at Neasden and Ealing Common depots.

ALR
Ashover Light Rly, Ashover to Clay Cross, 60 cm gauge, opened 1925, closed to passengers 1936, to freight 1950.

Alsace-Lorraine, Chemin de Fer de l'
see AL.

Alsthom
Société Alsacienne–Thomson–Houston, formed 1928, successor to *CFTH* (qv) and *SACM* (qv). Now part of GEC–Alsthom. *See* **Alstom.**

Alstom
Renaming from June 1998 of GEC–Alsthom (*see* Alsthom, GEC). Acquired 51 per cent shareholding in *Fiat Ferroviaria* (qv) 2000.

Alternate layout
Parallel tracks arranged in pairs, Up and Down, Up and Down.

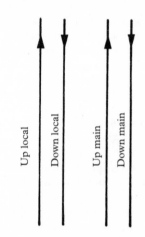

Alternate layout

Alweg
A monorail system in which the cars straddle a reinforced concrete beam. After the inventor, Dr Axel L. Wenner-Gren.

AM
1. Area Manager.
2. (obs) BR prefix for alternating current mu sets (AM6, etc.).

Amain (RS) (NE England)
Runaway (qv). A usage derived from the normal meanings 'at full speed; in or with full force' (*Shorter Oxford English Dictionary*).

AM&EE
Area Mechanical & Electrical Engineer.

Ambrosiano
TEE Milan–Rome, introduced 1974, lost TEE status 1987.

Ambulance (USRS)

A caboose (qv).

Ambulance Train

A train specially equipped to carry invalids, principally soldiers wounded in battle, or taken sick at the front. Accommodation is provided for stretcher cases, doctors and nurses. There is usually a dispensary, operating room and kitchen, etc. First used in the American Civil War and much refined and extensively deployed in WW1 and WW2. *See also* CET, HAT, Hospital Train.

Ambulant (Fr)

A postal sorter on a mail train.

Américain, chemin de fer

see Chemin de fer Américain.

American

A loco with 4–4–0 wheel arrangement. From its wide adoption by American rlys in the nineteenth century.

American devils (RS)(obs)

Steam-driven excavators used in rly construction, originally developed in the US in the 1840s. *See also* Steam navvy.

American–European Express

Luxury club, sleeper and dining cars available at supplementary fares, attached to Amtrak (qv) expresses and segregated from the rest of the train. First adopted on the Capitol Limited (qv) in 1989.

American Express

An express freight (qv) company, formed in US 1850, a consolidation of competing operators. *See also* Wells Fargo.

American Specials/American Boat Specials

L&NWR trains between London (Euston) and Liverpool connecting with Atlantic liner sailings and arrivals.

AMRC

Association of Minor Railway Companies, founded 1938 to replace ARLI (qv). Became AIR (qv).

Amshack (USRS)

A contraction of Amtrak (qv) and shack = a small station.

Amtrak

Brand name for the US National Railroad Passenger Corporation (NRPC), a public corporation set up in 1970 with authority to support the operation of inter-city and some other passenger trains using federal funds. Began to operate train services May 1971. A contraction of 'American Track'.

Anadolu Express

Service between Istanbul (Haydarpasa) and Konya.

A(N&SW)D&R

Alexandra (Newport & South Wales) Dock & Rly Co., inc as dock and dock rlys undertaking 1865, renamed A(N&SW)D&R, 1882. Pontypridd to Penrhos, opened 1884, absorbed 1897. Part of GWR from 1922.

Anatolian Rly Co.

See CFDA.

Anatolie Express

A *CIWL* all-sleeper service between Istanbul (Haydarpasa) and Ankara, introduced 1927.

Anchor (USRS)

1. A handbrake

2. A caboose (qv)

Anchor length

Component placed at each end of CWR (qv) to resist the effects created by rail tensor (qv).

Anchor sole plate

A reinforcing 'I' section steel beam or piece of inverted rail placed beneath a rail joint on tramways (3) to reduce loosening of the joint by vibration.

Anchors, to release (USRS)

To release handbrakes.

Anchor them, to (USRS)

To set handbrakes.

Ancient lights (RS)

Modern rly employees' term for semaphore signals (qv).

Andalucia Pullman Express

A Pullman car train between Seville and Granada operated by the *CIWL* 1929–39 (Malaga was also served in 1929–30).

ANF

Ateliers de Construction du Nord de la France, Blanc-Misseron and Raismes.

Angel's seat, the (USRS)

The cupola (qv) in a caboose (qv).

Angel Train Contracts
A ROSCO (qv).

Angle bar (US)
Fishplate (qv).

Angle iron
US for fishplate (qv).

Anglia (obs)
BR region formed in 1988 out of Eastern region and embracing all lines east of the axis London (Fenchurch St.)–Hertford East–Meldreth–Whittlesea–Kings Lynn (all inclusive).

Anglia Electrics (obs)
NSE brand name from 1989 for services between London (Liverpool St.) and Cambridge, Kings Lynn, Southend, Southminster, Braintree, Colchester, Clacton/Walton, and Harwich.

Anglia Rlys
A TOU (qv), 1994. A TOC (2) (qv), 1996, operating the franchise for the London (Liverpool Street)–Norwich main line and local services in East Anglia from 1997. Part of National Express Group's Greater Anglia TOC (qv) from 1 April 2004.

Anglo-Scottish Car Carrier
A restaurant car train for motorists and their cars between London (Holloway), Newcastle and Edinburgh, introduced 1960. Name dropped in 1966 when the London terminal became Kensington (Olympia) and the term Motorail (qv) came into use.

Animal car (USRS)
A caboose (qv).

Ann Arbor (US)
Toledo, Ann Arbor & North Michigan RR, eventually known as the Ann Arbor Co.

Annett's Key
Key and lock for little-used siding connections, invented by J.E. Annett, L&SWR signal superintendent, in 1875. When the siding is out of use the key is kept in the controlling signal box and cannot be removed from its housing in the signal locking frame until all conflicting signals are set at danger. These signals remain locked until the key is replaced. At the siding, the key unlocks the lever controlling the access points and cannot be removed until that lever is relocked. On single lines, the key is normally incorporated in the train staff (qv).

Annunciator
A device in a signal box which gives audible indication that a train has stopped at the home signal (qv) when it is showing a danger aspect.

Anorak (RS/S)
A trainspotter (qv), from the garment often favoured by the genus in the years 1950–95. Subsequently the term has been used more widely by those not sharing the relevant fixation, to denote anyone showing an obsessive interest in the minutiae of any sport or other leisure activity.

ANR or AN Rail
Australian National Rlys, formed 1975. An amalgamation of Commonwealth Rlys, Tasmanian Government Rlys and the non-metropolitan lines of South Australian Rlys. *See also* **GSR** *(2)*.

Anschlusstelle/Anst (Ger)
A siding, usually with manually worked points, unlocked with a key held at the nearest station; the through line is blocked until the key is returned. *See also* Annett's Key.

Ant
GWR TC for six-wheel composite coach.

Anteaters (RS)
Another name for Class 89 locos; from the shape of its nose. *See also* Aardvark.

Antwerp Continental
see Continental Express.

AOCL
Automatic Open Crossing Locally monitored; a level crossing without road barriers and fitted with flashing lights for road users. Correct operation of the road lights is shown by white lights exhibited to the train driver at the approach to the crossing. *See also* ABCL, Automatic level crossings.

AOCR
Automatic Open Crossing Remotely monitored by cctv; a level crossing without road barriers and fitted with flashing lights for road users. Correct operation of the road lights is proved in the controlling signal box.

There is a telephone to the responsible signaller. *See also* Automatic level crossings.

APB (US)
Absolute Permissive Block Signal; allowing a following train to enter a single line section and move along it two block sections behind the preceding train (in use from 1920s).

Ape wagon (USRS)
A caboose (qv).

Apex
Advance Purchase (Excursion) ticket. Special cheap InterCity return fares only available if purchased seven days in advance of travel, introduced 1990. Subsequently extended to other services.

Appendix [to the Working timetables]
An official publication containing instructions on the working of sidings, stations, etc., also particulars of signal boxes, gradients, tunnels and other matters not varying frequently enough to justify inclusion in the Working timetables (qv).

Applesauce (US)
Nickname for New Orleans, Opelousas & Great Western RR, later part of Southern Pacific RR.

Apply the rule, to (LTRS)
To pass a signal at danger under 'stop and proceed' rule (qv).

Approach control
A colour-light signal (qv) at a junction which shows red, irrespective of whether the line ahead is clear, until the train is within a short distance, in order to require drivers to slow down over a speed-restricted turnout.

Approach light
A colour-light signal (qv) which is illuminated only when a train is approaching it.

Approach locking
Electric locking effective while a train is approaching a signal displaying a clear (proceed) aspect and designed to prevent alteration to the route set should the signal be replaced to danger in face of the train.

Approach release
A system of electrical control preventing clear or caution aspects being displayed by a signal until the approaching train is within a predetermined distance.

Apron (US)
A metal platform between loco and tender or between passenger cars.

APS (Fr)
Alimentation par le Sol a system of ground-level electric traction supply to modern tramways (3) using a third rail with a succession of 8 metre-long powered sections and 3-metre neutral sections, the former actuated by skates under the tram as it moves along and always only energised when under the vehicle. Pioneered in Bordeaux 2003/4.

APT
Advanced Passenger Train. An unsuccessful BR tilting train project of 1969–86 designed to achieve high speed running without the expense of altering existing track alignments. APT-E was the APT-Experimental gas-turbine train completed in 1972; this was followed by the electrically propelled APT-P (APT-Prototype).

APTA
American Public Transit Association; formed 1974, incorporating the American Transit Association and the Institute for Rapid Transit.

APTIS
All Purpose Ticket Issuing System (BR); introduced from 1984. *See also* PORTIS; SPORTIS.

APTO
Association of Public Passenger Transport Operators, inc 1970, became part of CPT (qv).

Aquilon
Express between Paris and Marseilles, introduced 1959. Now an unnamed *TGV* service.

Aquitaine
TEE Paris–Bordeaux, introduced 1971, journey time 4 h and then the fastest train in Europe, lost *TEE* status 1984, ceased 1990.

ARBAC
Association Royale Belge des Amis des Chemins de Fer. Renaming of *ABAC* (qv) following its receipt of a royal charter.

Arbalète
TEE Paris–Basle–Zurich, introduced 1957, lost TEE status 1979, EC from 1987.

Arbeiterzug (Ger)
Workmen's train.

Arbor lights
Junction route indicators or lunar lights (qv). Arbor = Latin for 'tree'.

ARC
1. Automatic Revenue Control (BR).
2. Amey Roadstone Co.
3. Aqaba Rly Corporation, Menzil-Ma'an-Aqaba (Jordan), a 293 km,1,050 mm gauge southern extension of the *Hedjaz* Rly (qv) completed in 1976 and operated from 1998 by WCTC (qv).

Arc roof
A coach roof profile forming a perfect unbroken curve, the radius varying with the owning body.

AREA
Association of Railroad Engineers of America; its main objective is to develop and maintain standards for all aspects of rly infrastructure and rly operation.

Argyle Line
Partick to Rutherglen via Glasgow Central (LL). Former steam underground service, reopened with electric trains in 1979.

Ark, The (RS)(obs)
The loco lifting shop at Stratford, London.

ARL
Above Rail Level; a vertical measurement usually for the height of a vehicle (qv), often expressed in millimetres.

Arlberg Express/Arlberg–Orient Express
A *CIWL* service of through sleepers from Paris to Athens and Bucharest with Calais–Bucharest portion, running via Basle, Zurich, Vienna and Arad, introduced 1924. Re-introduced after WW2. Paris to Vienna only from 1962, when it became known as the *Arlberg Express*.

ARLI
Association of Railways of Local Interest; formed 1912 as the Association of Railways; an organization of those fifty or so small companies not parties to the RCA (qv). Replaced by AMRC (qv).

Armistice Coach
A 1913 *CIWL* dining car in which the Armistice marking the end of WW1 was signed on 11 November 1918. After exhibition at the Invalides Museum in Paris, it was moved back to a building on the site of the signing in the Forest of Compiègne in 1927. On 22 June 1940 Hitler obtained a French surrender in the same coach, after which it was exhibited in Berlin. It was destroyed by the Germans in 1944, probably to prevent its use for a third time. A replacement car of the same type was installed at Compiègne in 1950.

Armourclads (RS)
SR Merchant Navy and West Country 4–6–2 locos in their original form. From their outer casing.

Armstrong (USRS)
Any manually operated device for which there is no power-driven alternative.

Armstrong gear (RS)(obs)
A combined lever and screw loco reversing gear introduced by William Bouch, loco superintendent of the S&DR in 1865. It required considerable effort to operate, hence the name.

Armstrongs (RS)
LM&SR 4F class locomotives used on the S&DJR. From the builders, Armstrong, Whitworth.

Armstrong, Whitworth
Sir W.G. Armstrong, Whitworth & Co. Ltd, Newcastle, loco and railcar builders, 1919–37.

ARO
Army Railway Organisation, administering all military railways in the UK. Disbanded July 1992.

ARPS
Association of Railway Preservation Societies, founded 1960. See AIRPS.

Arrestors/Arrestor buffers
See Buffer stops.

Arrêt pipi (FrRS)
A comfort stop (qv).

Arriva
A bus company which took over operating Merseyrail (qv) and Northern Spirit (qv) in 2000 as Arriva Trains Merseyside and

Arriva Trains Northern. Awarded franchise for Wales & Borders (qv) as Arriva Trains Wales (*Trenau Arriva Cymru*) (qv) 2003. Merseyside franchise transferred to Merseyrail (Serco/Ned) 2003. Arriva Trains Northern other urban and rural services transferred to new Northern Rail (qv) franchise 2004 and its longer-distance interurban services to new franchise TransPennine Express (qv) 2004.

Arriva Trains Northern
See Arriva.

Arriva Trains Wales
See Arriva.

Arrow of Indecision
A cynical nickname for BR double arrow logo introduced in 1965, arising from a wilful misinterpretation of its meaning.

ARS
Automatic Route Setting. First installed by BR at Three Bridges 1983. A computerized system which enables signalmen to control large areas by setting up the signalling and precise track routes over long distances, ensuring that trains operate to schedule. Operated by train describers (qv) on SDS (qv).

Artesia
A jointly owned subsidiary of *SNCF* (qv) and *FS* (qv) operating luxury sleeping-car trains between Paris and Rome, Paris and Milan, and Paris and Lyon.

Articulated stock
Rolling stock in which vehicles share one bogie at adjacent ends. *See also* Quad-arts.

Arun Valley Line
Ford Junc–Arundel–Horsham–Three Bridges. *See also* Mid-Sussex Line.

Asbestos (USRS)
Poor quality loco coal.

Ash blower/ejector
A perforated pipe on the floor of a steam loco smokebox (qv) which, when filled with steam by use of the blower handle, allows ejection of deposited ash and hot cinders upwards through the chimney.

Ashbury
Ashbury Railway Carriage & Iron Co. Ltd, 1862–1902, became part of MCW (qv).

Ashcat/ash eater (USRS)
A steam loco fireman.

Ash pit engineer (USRS)
A steam loco fitter.

Asia Express
A streamlined steam train introduced 1935 by South Manchuria Rly between Dairen and Changchun. Ceased *c.* 1944.

ASLEF
Associated Society of Locomotive Engineers & Firemen, founded 1880. Now the trade union for all types of train driver.

ASLRA
American Short Line Railroads Association.

ASM
Assistant Station Master/Manager.

Asmo
GWR TC for covered motor car-carrying wagon.

Aspect
The indication given by a signal which is seen by drivers approaching it at any given time.

ASRS
Amalgamated Society of Railway Servants; the first enduring rly trade union in the UK, founded 1871, registered as a trade union 1872, amalgamated with UP&SS (qv) and GRWU (qv) to form NUR (qv), 1913.

Assisting engine
A loco attached to the front of a train engine (qv) to provide additional power on a steep gradient or for working a heavy train, or simply as a convenient means of returning it to its home depot.

ASTRIDE
Acronym for ASynchronous DrivE and TRI-voltage locos, built 1999 by Alstom (qv) for working international freight trains in Europe.

Astrodome
Upper deck section of a passenger car with large glazed areas to allow passengers to view scenery.

ASTT
All System Timetable (qv), BR.

ATAC
Azienda Tramvie e Autobus del Commune di Roma; Tramways and Bus Agency for the Commune of Rome, formed 1929.

AT&SF (US)
Atchison, Topeka & Santa Fe Railway Co. *See also* Santa Fe (*1*).

ATB
Automated Ticketing & Boarding System.
ATC
1. Automatic Train Control. A general term for any system designed to check the driver's reaction to signals, etc, ranging from cab warning systems to complete automatic control. *See also* ATO; ATP; AWS.
2. Army Transportation Corps, US. *See also* USA TC.
3. Angel Train Contracts, a ROSCO (qv).

ATCS
Advanced Train Control Systems; incorporating a radio data link between an on-board controller unit and a central computer.

ATH
American Thomson–Houston Co.; became part of the General Electric Co. of America.

ATIS
Advance Traffic Information System for freight services, fully operational on BR from 1970. Eventually included in TOPS (qv).

Atlantic
US, and later British, term for steam loco with 4–4–2 wheel arrangement. From the Atlantic Coast RR, which ordered the first one.

Atlantic Coast Express, The
An express between London (Waterloo) and Padstow, also serving Ilfracombe, Bude, Torrington and Plymouth, introduced by the SR in 1926. Re-introduced 1947, ceased 1964. Name revived by BR for London (Paddington) to Newquay summer service, 1988.

Atlantic Coast Line
Brand name for the Newquay (Cornwall) branch line (from 2004).

Atmospheric railway
A system of traction tried in the first half of the nineteenth century. Trains were usually drawn by a small four-wheeled vehicle fitted with a piston which engaged in a continuous pipe between the rails or by other means of creating a vacuum in front of the train. As air was exhausted, usually by stationary steam engines, the vacuum created was sufficient to pull the truck and its train forward. The problems encountered could not be overcome by the technology of the period and were not in any case pursued after *c*. 1850 owing to the successful development of the steam loco. Atmospheric propulsion for tube rlys (qv) was, however, considered as a possibility for a further thirty years or so. *See also* Pneumatic rly.

ATO
Automatic Train Operation. Term used by LT for system in which all train movement control is automatic apart from door operation and starting from stations. Safety information is continuously transmitted to the train in the form of electrical codes in the running rails which tell the train its permitted speed. If codes are absent or incorrect, the brakes are applied. For signal stops, a brake command signal in the running rail causes the brakes to be applied and restarts the train automatically when the signal is cleared. Similarly, speed reduction and braking instructions are given by electrical impulses as the train approaches a station. Lineside signals are not provided except at junctions and for station starters. After trials in 1963–4, the new Victoria Line tube rly was equipped with ATO from 1968 onwards.

ATOC
Association of Train Operating Companies, formed 1995. Manages NRES (qv), Railcards (qv), licenses travel agents (qv), allocates revenue from ticket sales to TOC (*2*) (qv). Communicates with passengers, Government and the rail industry on behalf of TOC (*2*) and helps them to work together.

ATP
Automatic Train Protection. A system which will stop a train automatically or regulate its speed if a driver fails to respond to signal indications or speed restrictions.

ATS
Automatic Train Supervision. A system for maintaining adherence to timetable and headways, and imposing coasting to save electrical energy, over-riding the driver's manual controls in these respects.

Attika
A sleeping car service between Munich and Athens, introduced 1989.

ATWS

Automatic Track Warning Systems, using ultrasound sensors under rails which transmit audible and visual warnings to track workers of approaching trains. Adopted in UK from 2004. Similar arrangements also operate warning lights at level crossings.

Aubiner (Fr)

To replace a signal at danger automatically, after Aubine, inventor of a treadle for reversing mechanical signals, especially the outer red disc signals.

AUR

African Union of Railways, founded 1972.

Aurora

1. *TEE* Rome–Reggio di Calabria, introduced 1974, lost *TEE* status 1975, continued as Rapido service, extended to Syracuse 1979, name dropped 1987.
2. A fast day service between Moscow and Leningrad, so named 1964–77.

AUS

Australian Rlys. 42,711 route km of 1,600 mm,1,435 mm and 1,067 mm gauges.

Ausbaustrecken (Ger)

DB lines upgraded for high speed operation in the 1980s and '90s.

Austerities (RS)

WW2 Ministry of Supply steam locos; also Bulleid Q1 0–6–0 locos.

Austin Sevens/Austins (RS)

LM&SR Fowler 7F 0–8–0 locos, introduced 1929 when the famous 'baby car' was becoming popular.

Austria Express

An express between Hook of Holland (connections with sailings to and from Harwich), Amsterdam and Klagenfurt, introduced 1953. Hook portion withdrawn 1989.

Austrian Goods (RS)

G&SWR 2–6–0 locos of 1915, built by North British, which incorporated parts originally intended for an Austrian contract.

Ausweich Anschlusstelle (Ger)

Same as *Anschlusstelle* (qv) but with equipment which allows a train to take refuge in the siding protected by points locked in the straight position using a key. When this is done, the points are electrically locked by the appropriate signal box/control, allowing trains to pass on the through line.

Auto (LTRS)

Automatic signal/ticket machine/internal telephone.

Autobuffet (obs)

A BR coach fitted with self-service coin-in-the-slot machines dispensing snacks, cigarettes and drinks, introduced 1962.

Auto button

A button on an entrance/exit signal panel placed alongside the entry button for a controlled route which enables the signaller to set a junction signal to work automatically when it is set for the principal route.

Auto-car(s) (obs)

A railcar (qv); also used to describe an auto-train (qv).

Auto coach/trailer

The passenger vehicle in an auto train (qv).

Auto dropper

Same as pan-catcher (qv).

Autoflat

A rail wagon designed to carry large private cars such as 4x4s and Peoplecarriers, as well as small vans and trucks. Introduced 2002 by Autoliner (qv).

Autoliner

The automotive transport arm of Freightliner (qv) Heavy Haul.

Automatic brakes

Continuous brakes (qv).

Automatic level crossings

Level crossings with roads in which audible and light warnings to road users are given when approaching trains actuate a treadle (qv) fixed to a running rail at a designated distance from the crossing. Full-width or half-width barriers may also be lowered and raised across the roadway. See also: ABCL; ABCR; AHBC; AOCL; AOCR; MWL.

Automatic Section

A section of line signalled by automatic signals (qv).

Automatic signal[ling]

A system in which signals, normally in the 'clear' mode, are activated and changed to 'stop' by the passage of the train itself, affording protection to the track section it occupies while it remains on it. Treadle devices were formerly used but these were superseded by the use of track circuits (qv).

Automatic train
Train without an active driver, entirely controlled by electronic systems during normal operation. *See also* ATO.

Automotrice (Fr)
An electric railcar (qv).

Autorail (Fr)
A railcar (qv).

Autos-Express
SNCF motorcar-carrying service, using fast freight trains.

Auto-train
1. (obs) A semi-permanently coupled train of one to six coaches, capable of being driven from either end, usually with steam tank locomotive at one end and at the other a control driving cab fitted with connections to the loco regulating handle, reversing gear, brake valve and whistle. In some cases there were control driving cabs at each end with the steam loco in the centre of the train. Also known as 'auto-cars' and 'motor trains'.
2. A sleeping car train, carrying the passengers' cars; US equivalent of Motorail (qv).

Auto-Train (Fr)
The *SNCF* equivalent of Motorail (qv), 1994, formerly *TAC* (qv). The term Motorail is also used by the *SNCF*.

Autowagon (obs)
A BR experimental project of 1971 involving self-propelled, unmanned container wagons operating over the rly system in a computer-planned movement pattern. It included automatically controlled transfer of the containers from road to rail vehicles and vice versa.

Auxiliary catenary wire
See: Compound catenary.

Auxiliary signal (obs)
Old name for distant signal (qv).

AV (It)
Alta Velocità, a new railway constructed for high speed running (Rome–Naples,

Florence–Milan, Milan–Turin, etc).

AVE (Sp)
Alta Velocidad Española, Spanish high-speed line and service, built to standard gauge; alternatively interpreted as *Ancho de Via Europeo*, European Gauge; or in Castile, a bird (as reflected in the logo). First section of the *AVE* network opened 1992 between Madrid and Seville.

Aveling & Porter
Established 1850 at Rochester as Messrs Aveling; works located at Strood from 1861; became A&P 1862. Manufactured small industrial locos from 1866. Later merged with Barford & Perkins to become Aveling–Barford of Grantham.

Average throughout trainload
The number of passengers averaged over the complete journey or train service; usually calculated by dividing passenger miles by loaded train miles.

AVIS
Automatic Vehicle Identification System; introduced 1989–91 for MGR (qv) trains. Each wagon is fitted with a transponder coded to represent its number and as it moves around the rly system, it is detected by lineside reading equipment which passes the data to TOPS (qv) and the computer installations of major customers. A later version uses bar codes. *See also* ACI (US); AEI (*2*).

Avocet Line
Brand name for the Exmouth branch, 2003.

Avoiding line
Tracks provided to allow trains to bypass a station or some other location specified in its full title.

Avonside
Avonside Engine Co., 1866 (formed from Stothert, Slaughter & Co., loco builders, established at Bristol in 1841, name changed to Slaughter, Gruning & Co. 1858). Goodwill purchased by Hunslet (qv) 1935. *See also* LH Plant Engineering Co.

Avon Valley
A preserved rly on former BR Bath–Bitton–Bristol line, opened from 1991.

Awanst (Ger)
Ausweich Anschlusstelle (qv).

Awayday (obs)
Cheap day return tickets in London and south east England, introduced 1972, hence (LTRS) a day's unauthorized absence from duty.

AWB
Advance Warning Board; a lineside board bearing a St George Cross warning drivers to regulate speed over an OLC (qv).

AWS
Automatic Warning System (BR); gives driver an audible and visual confirmation of clear and caution indications of signals and applies brake if the caution warning is not acknowledged.

Axholme
Axholme Joint Rly, Haxey Junc to Marshland Junc/Fockerby/Hatfield Moor, promoted as Goole & Marshland Light Rly and Isle of Axholme Light Rly (LROs 1898). Opened 1900, 1903, 1904, passenger traffic from 1905. Hatfield Moor branch (freight only) opened 1909. Purchased by L&YR and NER jointly 1902 and renamed AJR; owned by L&NWR and NER 1922, LM&SR and L&NER 1923, BR from 1948.

Axle counter
Equipment placed at entrance and exit to a block section which electrically records the number of axles which have passed over it. Signalling apparatus which is locked to protect a train in the corresponding block section is not unlocked until the exit counter has registered the same number of axles as leaving the section.

Axle load
The load placed on the track by a single wheelset (qv), described as 'static' if the vehicle is stationary or 'dynamic' if it is in motion.

B

B

1. BR gangwayed bogie brake coach.

2. Bogie van.

Babe/Baby (RS)

Baby Scot (qv).

Baby Bongos (RS)

L&NER Thompson K1 2–6–0 steam locos.

Baby Deltics (RS)

English Electric BR class 23 1,100 hp
diesel-electric locos, 1959.

Baby lifter (USRS)

A brakeman on a passenger train.

Baby load (USRS)

Freight load requiring great care in handling.

Baby Scots (RS)

LM&SR 4–6–0 5XP steam locos; Patriot
class of 1930 rebuilt from LNWR 1913
Claughton class. Also known as Babes or
Babies.

Bacchus

TEE Munich–Dortmund, introduced
1979, ceased 1980, replaced by Albert
Schweitzer (qv).

Back board (RS)

1. A distant signal (qv). So called because
   it is the signal at the back of others
   (Home and Starter) in the section, in
   the direction of running.

2. A white painted board placed behind a
   semaphore signal (qv) to heighten its
   visibility.

Back down, to

To move a loco backwards towards its
train.

Back edge

The outside face of an installed rail. Also
known as Back face, Back of the head,
Field face/side and Outside edge.

Back edge corner

The outside curve of the head (qv) of a rail
between the running surface (qv) and the
back edge (qv).

Back face

See Back edge.

Backhead (US)

Back plate (qv).

Backing signal

A semaphore signal (qv) with two circular
holes in a short arm or an arm of scissors
outline which when cleared authorizes a
wrong line (qv) movement as far as any
obstruction.

Back light

The light shown by a semaphore signal
lamp at the back allowing signalman to
check whether signal is 'on' or 'off' and
whether lamp remains lit.

Back Load

A remunerative load for a freight train
which would otherwise return empty from
its destination to its point of departure.

Back of the Head

See Back edge.

Back plate

The plate at the back of the boiler and
firebox of a steam loco on which the
regulator, gauges and other controls are
mounted.

Back porch yardmaster (USRS)

A switchman in a yard.

Back shift (RS)

Late turn (14.00 to 22.00)

Back shunt, to (LTRS)

To propel a train.

Back signal (RS)

see Back board (qv).

Back slotting

A GWR signalling system controlling stop and distant signals with one lever.

Back stick (RS)

see Back board (qv).

Back Track

An illustrated magazine devoted to loco and rly history/nostalgia, first published in 1987.

Back tripped (LTRS)

A train irregularly tripped by operation of rear tripcock (qv).

Back 'un (RS)

see Back board (qv).

Bacon slicer (RS)

A large wheel in a signal box for manual operation of level crossing gates. From its resemblance to the bacon slicing machines formerly seen in grocers' shops.

Badge porter (obs)

A man working at a rly station, under supervision of the rly staff but paid by the passenger, according to an agreed scale, for carrying luggage outside the station area. Also known as an outside porter.

Bad Order (USRS)

A vehicle or loco in need of repair or attention.

Bad order track (USRS)

A siding reserved for bad order (qv) stock.

Bag (RS)

1. The leather sleeve of a water crane (qv). Hence 'to put the bag in', to take water into the tank of a loco using a water crane.
2. A flexible vacuum hose used for connecting brake pipes between vehicles.

Bag, to (RS)

see Cop, to (qv).

Baggage (US)

Luggage.

Baggage car (US)

Luggage van.

Baggage master

An official at US rly stations, usually in the baggage room, who takes charge of passengers' luggage, issuing a 'check' in exchange which is used to reclaim the item(s) at the destination. Also: the official in charge of the luggage car.

Baggage Smasher (USRS)

Baggage master (qv).

Baghdad Rly

(Also known as Berlin–Baghdad Rly.) Planned to connect Mesopotamia (now Iraq), then part of the Turkish Empire, with the main European network. Originally a German expansionist project, aimed at securing influence over Turkey and pushing out towards British imperial interests, it was financed mostly by the *Deutsche Bank*. A start was made with a line eastwards from Konya, opened in 1904. Further work then proceeded under a new co., with a German majority on its board. Progress was accelerated under German auspices in WW1, so that by 1918 the main line had reached as far east as Nisibin, 684 miles from Konya. In 1928 the Turkish government purchased the rights of the old co. and the rly reached the Iraq frontier in 1935, with Iraq Rlys motor services covering the remaining gap. A continuous standard gauge rly between the Bosphorus and Baghdad was finally achieved in July 1940. *See also CFDA*; Taurus/Toros Express.

Bagnall

W.G. Bagnall & Co. Ltd, Stafford, loco builders, established 1875. Part of EE (Vulcan Foundry) (qv) 1961.

Bagpipe (RS)

BR class 31 diesel loco with nose end air and control pipes.

BAGS

Buenos Aires Great Southern Rly (*Ferrocarril Gran Sud de Buenos Aires* (GS)), the largest British-owned rly in Argentina, inc 1862, 5 ft 6 in gauge, first section opened 1865, acquired by Argentine Government 1948, then 4,902 route miles (7,889 km), and renamed *FC Nacional General Roca*.

Bag tenders (obs)

Royal Mail and other rly vehicles used for carriage of mail in bags or sacks but with no facilities for sorting en route.

Baguley

Baguley Cars Ltd, loco and railcar builders, Burton on Trent from 1911, became Baguley Engineers Ltd 1923, E.E. Baguley Ltd 1932. Amalgamated with Drewry (qv) as Baguley-Drewry Ltd 1967. Ceased production 1984.

Bahn Card (Ger)
A railcard which after purchase secures half-price travel on any day of the week over *DB* (qv), introduced 1992.

Bahnhofsmission (Ger)
A German organization similar to Travelers' Aid (qv) offering help to the disabled and the needy.

Bahn 2000
Development plan to provide Switzerland with more frequent and faster direct train services with increased comfort. Voted by referendum 1987, planned for completion by 2005. Renamed *Rail 2000* (qv).

Bail, to (USRS)
To fire a steam loco.

Baileys (RS)
see Bill Baileys.

Bailing out (Ire RS)
Stopping a train between stations to raise steam from poor quality fuel (current in WW2).

Bait (RS)
A rlyman's packed lunch.

Bake a cake, to (USRS)
To build up a good head of steam on a loco.

Bakehead (USRS)
A fireman on a steam loco.

Bakerloo
A London tube rly owned by a US co., so called by the journalist G.H.F. Nichols ('Quex') because it linked Baker St. and Waterloo stations. The tag was adopted officially from 1906. '. . . for a railway itself to adopt its gutter title, is not what we expect from a railway company. English railway officers have more dignity than to act in this manner.' – The editor of the RM (Sekon), 1906. *See also* BS&WR.

BAL (Fr)
Block Automatique Lumineux, automatic colour-light signalling (qv) with track circuits (qv).

Balaclava Rly
The first military rly, built out of Balaclava port by the British, to serve the Crimean Front in 1855.

Bala Lake
Bala Lake Rly, a 1 ft 11$\frac{1}{2}$ in/597 mm gauge pleasure rly over the former BR line

between Bala Junction and Llanuwchllyn. First section opened 1972.

Balcony car/Open Balcony car (obs)
A type of tramcar (qv) with roofed but otherwise open ends on the upper deck, usually fitted with curved seats.

Bald facing (USRS)
Propelling a train

Bald wheels (USRS)
Loco wheels without flanges, to facilitate negotiation of sharp curves.

Baldwin (US)
Baldwin Locomotive Works, Philadelphia; founded by Matthias W. Baldwin in 1832.

Balise (Fr)
Trackside TCS (qv) transmitter providing drivers with precise location information which is then passed back to the NMC (qv).

Balkan Express/Balkanzug
A service between Vienna, Graz and Belgrade, with coaches for Athens and Istanbul, introduced 1955, ceased 1965.

Balkanzug (GerRS)
Any lengthy East European international train made up with vehicles from several countries or a train carrying migrant workers to or from Germany. The original train so-named linked Berlin, Sofia and Istanbul from 1916 and included Mitropa (qv) sleeping cars.

Ballast
Small stones used as a bed for sleepers (*1*) (qv). Clinker, slag, shingle and other substitutes are sometimes used. The rly (as distinct from the original marine) usage of the word appears to have started with the Thames gravel carried by collier brigs returning to the north-east. Piles of this gravel accumulated at north-east ports, eventually finding a use as a foundation for new rly lines. *See also* Top ballast; Bottom ballast.

Ballast engine
Originally (1830s/1840s) a loco used in rly construction, or such locos subsequently retained for light work on the completed rly. Later, any loco allocated to permanent way trains.

Ballast scorcher (RS) (USRS)
A loco driver fond of high speed.

Ballast train
A train designed for bringing in new ballast and from which ballast is distributed over the formation. On LT, the term was formerly used to describe any type of engineer's train.

Ballet master (USRS)
A section foreman, in charge of gandy dancers (qv).

Ball of fire (USRS)
A very fast run.

Balloon (RS)
Foreman. ('Don't let me down, lads!')

Balloon stack (USRS)
The wide chimney of a wood-burning loco.

Balloon stock/Balloons (RS)
LB&SCR (qv) coaches of 1905, distinguished by their high elliptical roofs; a name suggested by the prominent roof profile.

Ball the jack, to (USRS)
To build up the speed of a loco or train.

Ballycastle
see BR (2).

Baltic
US, and later British, term for steam loco with 4–6–4 wheel arrangement.

Baltimore & Ohio (US)
A steam loco with 4–4–4–4 wheel arrangement, after the first had been delivered to that rly in 1938.

Balt–Orient Express
A service from Stockholm to Bucharest, introduced 1948; operated between Stockholm and Sofia via Bucharest from 1950. From 1954 the name was applied to the Berlin–Bucharest–Sofia service with its connecting Stockholm–Sassnitz–Berlin sleeping cars. From 1956 the train again ran to Sofia via Belgrade. Later ran Berlin–Bucharest.

BAM
Baikal–Amur–Magistral; a relief line for the Trans-Siberian Rly (qv), completed 1974–89.

Bamboo
A lightweight hooked pole used to move the trolley pole of a tramcar, originally made of bamboo.

BAN
Bangladesh Rly (Pakistan Eastern Rly 1947–71), 2,706 km of 1,676 mm gauge and metre gauge. Physically connected to the Indian Rlys. See also PAR.

Banalisation (Fr)
A double track line in which each track is available for reversible working (qv), thus allowing a one-way, double capacity flow in either direction according to traffic requirements.

Banana boats (RS)(obs)
IC-125 HST sets in their original livery.

Bananas (RS)
see Flying Bananas.

Banana van (RS)
A coach or van with distorted frame, sagging in the middle.

B and B gang (USRS)
Building and bridge maintenance men.

B&A
Boston & Albany RR USA; became a subsidiary of NYC (qv).

B&CDR
Belfast & County Down Rly, NI; Belfast–Downpatrick–Ardglass; Downpatrick–Newcastle–Castlewellan; Comber–Donaghdee; Ballynahinch; Belfast– Bangor; inc 1846, first section opened 1848. Purchased by UTA 1948. All except Belfast–Bangor and Newcastle–Castlewellan closed 1950, latter closed 1955.

B&ER
Bristol & Exeter Rly, inc 1836, opened 1841, 1842, 1843, 1844, 1847, 1848, part of GWR from 1876.

B&FT
Blackpool & Fleetwood Tramroad, inc 1896, electric tramway (3), opened 1898, taken over by Blackpool Corporation 1920 and then connected to that town's tramway system.

B&LR
Ballymena & Larne Rly, inc 1873, 3 ft gauge, opened 1877, 1878, part of B&NCR from 1889.

B&M (US)
Boston & Maine RR. See also GTI.

B&M&RR
Beira & Mashonaland & Rhodesian Rlys. Renamed Rhodesia Rlys 1927. See RR (6).

B&MTJR
Brecon & Merthyr Tydfil Junction Rly,
Bassaleg–Rhymney; Bargoed–Dowlais–
Brecon; Pontsticill–Merthyr, inc 1859, first
section opened 1863. Merthyr line joint
with L&NWR from 1875. Part of GWR
from 1922. *See also* BMR.

B&NCR
Belfast & Northern Counties Rly, formed
in 1860 of Belfast & Ballymena Rly,
Ballymena Rly, Coleraine & Portrush Rly,
and the Londonderry & Coleraine Rly.
Absorbed BC&RBR (qv) 1884. 201m on 5 ft
3 in gauge, 48m on 3 ft gauge. Absorbed
by Midland Rly, 1903. *See also* NCC.

B&NSR
Bristol & North Somerset Rly, Bristol to
Radstock and Camerton branch, inc
1863, opened 1873, 1882, part of GWR
1884.

B&NT
Bessbrook & Newry Tramway (NI), inc
1884, 3 ft/914 mm gauge, electric tramway
(*4*) on private right of way, opened 1885,
closed 1948.

B&NWR
Bengal and North Western Rly, India,
formed 1882.

B&O (US)
Baltimore & Ohio RR.

B&PCR
Brompton & Piccadilly Circus Rly, London,
tube rly inc 1897, part of GNP&BR, 1902.

B&SWUR
Bristol & South Wales Union Rly, Bristol
(Lawrence Hill) to New Passage with steam
ferry across River Severn and line from
Portskewett Pier to P. Junc, inc 1857, opened
1863, worked by GWR, part of GWR from
1868. New Passage Ferry discontinued 1886
on the opening of Severn Tunnel. Part
reopened by GWR 1900 for use as a section
of its new Pilning–Avonmouth line.

Bandwagon (USRS)
A coach from which men are paid.

B&WR
see Bodmin & Wenford Rly.

B&WVR
Brynmawr & Western Valleys Rly,
Nantyglo Junc to Brynmawr, inc 1899,

opened 1906, vested in L&NWR & GWR
1902, LM&SR & GWR 1923, BR 1948.

Banestyrelsen
(Danish) Infrastructure authority of DSB
(qv).

Banger (RS)
Detonator placed on the line as a warning.

Bang road (RS)
Wrong line, opposite to normal direction
of working.

Bang them up, to (LTRS)
To shunt loose-coupled or uncoupled
vehicles.

Banjo (RS)
Anything vaguely banjo shaped, thus:
1. Fireman's shovel on steam loco.
2. Vacuum brake handle in loco cab.
3. (LTRS) A shunt signal.
4. Tripcock (qv) on steam loco.

Banjo player (RS)
A fireman on a steam loco: *see* Banjo (*1*).

Bank
1. A steep incline (usually in northern
    England).
2. A raised platform in parcels or goods
    depot or goods shed.

Banker, banking engine
An additional loco attached at front or rear
of a train to assist it up a bank (qv).

Bank foot
Base of a steep incline.

Bank head
Same as Bank top (qv).

Bank rider (obs)
A man employed to control trains on steep
banks and inclined planes (e.g. on the
S&DR (qv) and the cable-worked Camden
Bank in north London.

Bank top
Summit (top) of a steep incline.

Banner, to carry the (USRS)
To flaunt Brotherhood (qv) emblems.

Banner repeater
A small illuminated centrally pivoted
semaphore arm in a circular glass case or a
similar electronic representation, showing
the indication of a signal which may be
hidden from view when a train is at a
station platform; usually placed 50–200
yards in rear of the relevant signal.

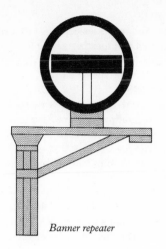

Banner repeater

Banner signal

Similar to a banner repeater (qv) but with a red instead of a black banner and a signal in its own right, not simply repeating the indication of another.

BAP

Buenos Aires & Pacific Rly, *Ferrocarril de Buenos Aires al Pacifico*, inc 1882, first section opened 1885. The third-largest British co. in Argentina with 2,788 route miles (4,487 km) of 5 ft 6 in gauge (including lines worked for separate cos) when acquired by the Argentine Government in 1948 and renamed *FC Nacional General San Martin*.

BAPR (Fr)

Block Automatique à Permissivité Restreinte, automatic colour-light signalling (qv) using axle counters (qv) and non-continuous track circuits (qv) for control of lightly trafficked lines.

BAR (Ger)

Berlin Aussenring; a belt line around Berlin. *See also GAR*.

Bar and Circle

See Bull's-eye.

Barbed wire badge (RS)

The BR double-arrow logo introduced in January 1965.

Barbel

A 27 ton ballast and spoil wagon used by BR engineers.

Bar boys (RS)(obs)

Slim and nimble youths able to enter a steam loco firebox to clean the firebars and remove clinker.

Barcelona Express

A *CIWL* night train, Paris–Port Bou with connection to Barcelona, 1903–14, re-introduced 1929, renamed *Paris–Côte Vermeille* 1974.

Barcelona TALGO

A sleeping car express between Paris and Barcelona with *TALGO* (qv) stock, introduced 1974.

Barclay

Andrew Barclay, Sons & Co. Ltd, Kilmarnock. Loco and rolling stock builders established 1859. Merged with Hunslet (qv) 1972 to form Hunslet–Barclay. Assets and rights of Hunslet Engine Co. sold to LH Plant Engineering Co. (qv) 2004.

Bardic lamp

A battery-powered hand lamp with white, green, red and yellow filters introduced by BR (1) in the 1960s to replace the similar oil lamps previously used by train crews and others for hand signalling.

Barefoot (USRS)

A loco with brakes on tender only.

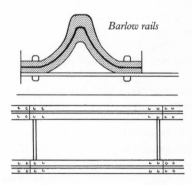

Barlow rails

Barlow rails (obs)

Rails with profile which enabled them to be supported continuously on the ballast, dispensing with sleepers, the exact gauge maintained by tie bars. Patented in 1849 by the engineer W. H. Barlow (1812–1902).

Barn (USRS)

A loco shed. *See also* Carbarn.

Barn, railroad in a (USRS)
A line protected by snow sheds (qv).

Barneys (RS)
Highland Rly Drummond 0–6–0 locos.

Barnums (RS)
1. GWR double-framed Dean 2–4–0 locos
   of 1889 after Barnum's Circus
   appearing in London that year.
2. GCR 1910 excursion open saloons with
   matchboarded straight sides, resembling
   vehicles in Barnum's Circus train.

Barracks (RS)(obs)
1. An enginemen's overnight hostel.
2. A terrace or series of terraces built by a
   railway company to house employees
   and their families.

Barred train
Any train on which rly employees' passes
and privilege tickets are not usable.

Barrel (USRS)
A cylinder on diesel-electric loco.

Barrier vehicles
Vans, empty coaches or wagons placed
between a dangerous load and the loco or
between the loco and the brake van, or at
each end of a passenger train.

Barrow crossing
A crossing at track level between station
platforms, used by authorized pedestrians.
From its use by station staff wheeling
barrows.

Barrow-way (obs)
Wooden tracks, later iron plates, laid in
underground workings to facilitate
movement of trams (1)/wagons.

Barry
Barry Dock & Rly, inc 1884,
Barry–Bridgend/Coity; Barry–St Fagans–
Pontypridd/Trehafod; Cadoxton–Cardiff
(Cogan); St Fagans–Penrhos Junc with
B&MJR. First section opened 1888, renamed
Barry Rly 1891, part of GWR from 1922.

BART
Bay Area Rapid Transit; rail system,
linking San Francisco with Oakland and
other communities on the east side of the
Bay, opened 1972.

BASA (Ger)
Bahn-Selbst-Anschluss; the internal rly
telephone network.

Base plate
A plate fixed under a sleeper (1) to form a
bearing pad and locating device for
flatbottom (qv) rail. The rail is secured to
the base plate by spring clips.

Bash, to (RS)
To visit a local depot or other rly facility,
usually without permission. Also to travel
behind a certain type of loco.

Basher (RS)
Abbreviated form of haulage basher (qv) or
track basher (qv).

Basic rly
A BR concept for lightly-used lines featuring
unmanned stations stripped of all structures
except bus type shelters, tickets issued on
trains by conductors, minimal signalling,
automatic level crossing systems, etc. First
introduced on ER rural lines in 1966.

Bass
A 31 ton general minerals wagon used by
BR engineers.

Bassett-Lowke
A firm of model-makers and model-
engineers based in Northampton, founded
by Wenman ('Whynne') Joseph Bassett-
Lowke (1877–1953) about 1900. Limited
company 1910. *See also* MRGB, NGR (1).

Bathgate Line
Edinburgh (Waverley)–Bathgate–
Airdrie–Glasgow.

Baton-pilote (Fr)
Train staff (qv).

Baton, train starting
A white disk with a handle, resembling a
table tennis bat, used by platform staff to
indicate to train crews that a train is ready
to start; introduced on BR *c.* 1991.

Bat out, to (USRS)
To shunt or classify wagons and vans very
quickly.

Battering
Rail wear caused by wheels skidding on
curved track.

Battery end (RS)
1. A buffer stop.
2. That end of a 1972 BR emu (qv) set
   fitted with control batteries.

Bat the stack [off her], to (USRS)
To work a loco hard, making fast time.

Battlefield Line

Preserved operation on former BR Coalville–
Nuneaton line between Shackerstone,
Market Bosworth and Shenton. First section
reopened (as The Shackerstone Rly), 1978.

Battleship (USRS)

Any very large and ponderous loco or
interurban car.

Battlewagon (USRS)

A coal wagon.

Baulk road (obs)

A form of permanent way (qv)
construction adopted by the engineer
I.K. Brunel for the early lines of the GWR
(qv) consisting of bridge rails (qv)
supported on 'baulks', longitudinals of
heavy pine faced with hardwood, which
were braced by cross ties or 'transoms'
spiked to piles sunk into the road bed (qv).

Bavaria

TEE Zurich–Munich, introduced 1969,
lost *TEE* status 1977, EC from 1987.

BAW

Buenos Aires Western Rly, *Ferrocarril Oeste
de Buenos Aires*, inc 1890, fourth-largest
British-owned rly in Argentina, 1,925 miles
(3,098 km) in 1948 when acquired by
Government and renamed *FC Nacional
Domingo Faustino Sarmiento*.

Bay

1. A short platform with buffer stops at
   one end, usually in a through station
   and normally set into opposite side
   (and sometimes at opposite ends) of a
   full length platform. Used for branch
   line or stopping services terminating at
   the station.
2. A group of seats either side of the
   gangway in an open coach (qv), in pairs
   with a table between.

Bay line

A track in a bay (qv).

BB&CIR

Bombay, Baroda & Central India Rly,
formed 1855, taken over by government
1905. Mostly part of Western Rly of India
from 1951.

BB&TJR

Birmingham, Bristol & Thames Junc Rly,
inc 1836, became WLR (qv) 1840.

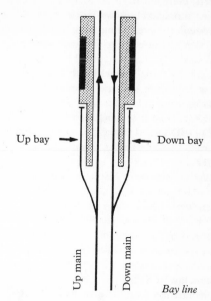

Up bay →   ← Down bay

Up main   Down main   *Bay line*

BC

British Coal. *See also* NCB.

BC&RBR

Ballymena, Cushendall & Red Bay Rly
(NI), inc 1872, 3 ft/914 mm gauge,
Ballymena–Retreat, opened 1875, 1876,
part of B&NCR 1884, closed 1940.

BCC

Bureau Centrale de Compensation. Central
Office for rly Compensation questions,
established at Brussels, 1925.

BCK

BR Brake Corridor Composite coach.

BCK (obs)

*Cie. de Chemin de Fer du Bas-Congo au
Katanga*; inc 1906.

BCM

Ballast Cleaning Machine.

BCR

1. Bishop's Castle Rly, inc 1861, Craven
   Arms & Stokesay (Stretford Bridge
   Junc) to Lydham Heath and Bishop's
   Castle, opened 1866, closed 1935.
2. Border Counties Rly, inc 1854, 1859,
   Riccarton Junc–Bellingham–Hexham.
   First section opened 1858, part of NBR
   1860.

BD&R

see Barry.

BDE (Ger)
Bundesverband Deutscher Eisenbahnen, an association representing minor railways physically connected to the main system and operating under national railway legislation. Amalgamated with *VÖV* (qv) to form VDV (qv), 1991.

BDM
Battery Driving Motor [car].

BDT/BDTS
Battery Driving Trailer/Standard Class.

BDZ
Bulgarski Durzarni Zeleznici, Bulgarian State Rlys, 4,294km.

Beanery (USRS)
Mess room. Hence *beanery queen*, a waitress in a mess room.

Beans, to go to (USRS)
To go for a meal.

Bear law (USRS)
A federal law limiting loco and train crews to a maximum of twelve hours' continuous duty. *See also* Dog law; Hog law, Monkey, caught by the.

Bearcat (USRS)
Any rlyman disliked by his colleagues.

Beardmore
William Beardmore & Co. Ltd, Glasgow, loco builders 1919–30.

Beardmores (RS)
GER/L&NER N7 0–6–2T locos. From the builders, William Beardmore & Co. Ltd.

Bearers
Timber, concrete or hollow steel beams supporting trackwork, notably special work (qv).

Beaver
GWR TC for flat trucks of various types (Beaver A, B, C, D & E).

BEC
British Electric Car Co. Ltd, Trafford Park, Manchester, suppliers of electric tramcars, established 1900. Production ceased 1904. Purchased by Castle Car Syndicate on behalf of UEC (qv).

Bed
The space usually filled with ballast (qv) between adjacent sleepers (qv), timbers or bearers (qv). Also known as crib.

Bedbug (USRS)
A Pullman car porter.

Bed house (USRS)
A caboose (qv).

BEE
see Brush (2).

Beeching/Beeching Era
The traumatic period (1961–5) in which BR was drastically 're-shaped', reduced, modernized and 'rationalized' under the chairmanship of Dr (from 1965 Lord) Richard Beeching (1913–85). The cuts made in mileage, services and staff were referred to as the 'Beeching Axe'. The associated 'Beeching Report', *The Reshaping of British Railways*, was published in 1963.

Beedler (USRS)
A driver who works his loco to the limits of its performance.

Beehive (USRS)
A yard or control office.

Beer trains (RS)(obs)
The Garden Cities & Cambridge Buffet Car expresses (qv).

Beetle crusher (RS)(Scottish)
Shunting loco; from its slow, ponderous movements.

Beetles
1. GWR TC for continuously braked cattle wagons or boxes, with attendant's compartment.
2. (RS) LM&SR Sentinel 0–4–0 locos.

BEF
British Electrical Federation, a joint purchasing subsidiary of the BET (qv).

BEL
1. Battery Electric Locos.
2. SR five-car all-Pullman emu open-corridor sets for Brighton Belle (qv); two motor brake parlour Second/Standard class cars, two kitchen First class cars, and one Second/Standard class parlour car; 5-BEL, 1933.

Belfast Boat Express
1. A GWR express between London (Paddington) and Birkenhead, connecting with Liverpool–Belfast night sailings, introduced 1928.

2. A BR express between Manchester (Victoria) and Heysham, connecting with Belfast sailings, ceased 1976.

Belfast Express
A Londonderry–Belfast express with 2 h15 min timing introduced in 1949 by the UTA (qv). *See also* Derry Express.

Bellamy roof (obs)
A covered double-deck tramcar with unroofed open end balconies, first introduced by the Liverpool tramways general manager, C.R. Bellamy.

Bellowers (RS)
Football supporters, or gricers (qv) who windowhang (qv) and shout at all and sundry from trains.

Bell ringer (USRS)
A loco fireman.

Bells (RS)(obs)
see On the bells.

Belpaire
A type of steam loco firebox invented in 1860–4 and refined in 1884 by the Belgian engineer A.J. Belpaire (1820–93).

Belt line (US)
A rly around or within a city or town linking up different companies' lines and facilitating interchange of freight, etc.

Bench, the (RS)(obs)
The cab road side of the old South Station at London (Waterloo). So named from the steps leading down to the cab road which formed a seat for the waiting cab drivers.

Bend the iron/the rails/the rust, to (USRS)
To change the position of points.

Benguela Rly
Caminho de Ferro de Benguela; Benguela Rly, Angola, SW Africa, 3 ft 6 in (1,067 mm) gauge, from Lobito (Angola)–Congo frontier and extended thence to Tenke (Congo); opened 1928–31. *See also CFA (2)*.

Bennie Railplane
A suspended monorail system invented by George Bennie, employing a lightweight car propelled by airscrews. A test installation erected at Milngavie (Glasgow) in 1930 was dismantled in 1956.

Bent dart (RS)
Long steel poker with an arrow head and a bend at its centre, used for dislodging clinker from the firebox of a steam loco.

BEP
BR (SR) four-car emu corridor sets with Buffet car and Electro-Pneumatic brakes, 1956 and 1958–9; two motor brake Second/Standard Class, one trailer composite, and one buffet trailer; 4-BEP.

Be ready! (RS) (obs)
Term used by signalmen to signify the offer or acceptance of a train on block indicators (qv).

Bergbahn (Ger)
Any type of mountain climbing rly.

Berks & Hants
Inc 1845 as Berkshire & Hampshire Rly, Hungerford to Reading and Basingstoke, opened 1847, 1848, amalgamated with GWR 1846.

Berks and Hants Extension
Hungerford to Devizes, inc 1859, opened 1862, worked by GWR, part of GWR 1882.

Berks & Hants Line
Reading–Newbury–Westbury.

Berkshire (US)
A steam loco with 2–8–4 wheel arrangement. The first were made for the Boston & Albany RR which traversed the Berkshire Mountains of New England.

Berliner
The unofficial name for the British military restaurant car train operated daily from 1945 until 1990 to and from Braunschweig across the former German Democratic Republic territory, to serve the British zone in Berlin.

Berlin–Baghdad Rly
see Baghdad Rly.

Berne Conference/Convention
See UT.

Berne [Convention] Gauge
A loading gauge (*1*) (qv) standardized for general use on the European mainland standard gauge lines and laid down by the Berne Convention to come into force in 1914. Officially known as the *Gabarit Passe-Partout International* or PPI, it was superseded by various *UIC* (qv) standards.

Berne Key
A standard carriage key (qv) for use on rlys of mainland Europe, as agreed by the Berne Convention.

Berne rectangle

A space to be left clear between the buffers and couplers of adjacent vehicles for the safety of rly employees, as agreed by the UT (qv).

Berthing/berth, to

Movement of empty rolling stock to a suitable place where it can stand ready for further use, hence 'berthing sidings'.

Berth track circuit

A track circuit (qv) on the approach side of a stop signal.

Berts (RS)

Ordinary passengers, those interested only in getting from A to B, not in the rly as such. From 'Bert 'n' Ada'.

BET

British Electric Traction Co. Ltd.

Betuwelijn/Betuweroute

New electrified freight-only line Rotterdam port–Zevenaar–[Emmerich, Germany], first section opened 2004.

Bexleyheath Line

London (Charing Cross/Cannon St.)–Bexleyheath–Dartford.

Beyer–Garratt

A Garratt (qv) steam loco built by Beyer, Peacock.

Beyer, Peacock

Beyer, Peacock & Co. Ltd, Gorton Foundry, Manchester, loco builders 1853–1966.

Bf/Bhf (Ger)

Bahnhof; an ordinary railway station, as distinct from *Haltepunkt* (qv), *Haltestelle* (qv), or *Hauptbahnhof* (qv).

BFB

Bulleid-Firth & Brown: a double disc wheel for steam locos on the Boxpok (qv) principle designed by O.V. Bulleid in conjunction with the Sheffield firm of Firth & Brown.

BFK

BR Brake Corridor First class compartment coach.

BFO

Brake First Open coach (BR).

BG

BR bogie brake van, gangwayed, with open stowage area and guard's brake compartment.

BGZ

BG (qv) with six wheels.

BH&BR

Belfast, Holywood & Bangor Rly, 12½ miles, first section Belfast–Holywood opened 1848, extended to Bangor 1865, part of B&CDR (qv) 1884.

BHC

Belfast Harbour Commissioners.

BHR

Bexley Heath Rly, inc 1883, opened Blackheath (London) to Slades Green, 1895, part of SER 1900.

Bh rail

Bullhead rail (qv).

BI/BICC

British Insulated Wire Co., Prescot, Lancs, manufacturers of overhead line fittings for railways and tramways (3), later BICC (British Insulated Callender's Cables Ltd), then BICC Group.

Bible (RS)

The rule book for rly employees.

BIC

Bureau International des Containers; International Office for Container Traffic, established at Paris 1933.

Bicester route

London (Paddington)–High Wycombe–Bicester–Banbury.

Bicycle (RS)

A steam loco with 4–2–2 wheel arrangement.

Bicycles (RS) (obs)

Alternative name for 'Single' (qv) locos.

Bi-directional line

A single track signalled for traffic in both directions.

Bifur (Fr)

Bifurcation, a junction.

BIG

1. BR (SR) four-car emu sets with Buffet car and Interconnecting Gangway, 1965–6, for London to Brighton services. Formation as CIG (qv) but with buffet car instead of Second/Standard Class trailer, 4-BIG.

2. Business Infrastructure Group, formed 1999, a part of the RFG (qv), organized to campaign for enhanced rail freight infrastructure and against deterioration of existing facilities.

Big Bertha (RS)
Midland Rly 0–10–0 no. 2290 built 1920
for use as a banking engine on the Lickey
Incline. *See also* Big Emma.

Big Boys (USRS)
Union Pacific RR articulated Mallet (qv)
4–8–8–4 locos of 1941–4.

Big brain (RS)
Control (qv).

Big dipper (RS)
An exceptionally tall semaphore signal to
give visibility over the tops of bridges, etc.

Bi-directional line
A single track, signalled for traffic in both
directions.

Big-E (USRS)
Brotherhood of Locomotive Engineers,
hence any loco driver.

Big Emma (RS)
Another name for Big Bertha (qv).

Big end
The end of a connecting rod (qv) of a
steam loco, adjoining the crank axle or pin.

Big Four, the
1. The companies formed in the
   'grouping' of 1 January 1923, i.e.
   LM&SR, L&NER, GWR, SR.
2. (US) Nickname of Cleveland,
   Cincinnati, Chicago & St Louis RR.
3. (US) Brotherhood of Locomotive Engineers;
   Brotherhood of Railway Conductors;
   Brotherhood of Railway Firemen and
   Brotherhood of Railway Trainmen.

Big handle man (RS)(obs)
A steam loco driver using mainly two
positions on the regulator – wide open and
slammed shut.

Big hole
1. (RS) The Severn Tunnel.
2. (USRS) The emergency position (qv) of
   a Westinghouse brake control lever.

Big hook (RS)(USRS)
A breakdown train. From the hook on its
large crane.

Big Lizzies (RS)
LM&SR 4–6–2 locos of 1937. An enlarged
version of 1933 Princess Elizabeth class.

Big Mets (RS)
L&NER N2 0–6–2T used over the
Metropolitan Rly CWL (qv).

Big–O (USRS)
Order of Railway Conductors (a guards'
trade union).

Big ox (USRS)
A conductor (*3*).

Big penny (RS)
Overtime or bonus payment.

Big pike (USRS)
A major rly co. or system.

Big smoke (USRS)
A loco fireman.

BIL
SR two-car emu sets of 1935 for semi-fast
services, with side corridors to give access
to lavatory but no gangway connection
between cars, hence BI-Lavatory; one
motor brake Second/Standard Class and
one driving composite; 2-BIL.

Bi-level cars (US)
Double-deck coaches.

Bill Baileys (RS)
L&NWR 1903 four-cylinder compound
4–6–0 locos 1400 class. After the
contemporary song 'Come Home, Bill
Bailey'.

Billy (RS)
A ground signal.

Binder (USRS)
A hand brake.

Bin-liners (RS)
Trains carrying domestic refuse to landfill sites.

Bionics (LTRS)
LT 1973 stock.

Birdcage
1. (RS) A signalbox resting on a gantry or
   girders.
2. (RS) A spark arrester on a loco chimney.
3. (USRS) A brakeman's oil lamp.
4. Air pipe compartment of a diesel loco.
   From the open arrangement of the
   pipes, resembling a birdcage.

Birdcage brake/coach (RS)
1. A coach design incorporating an open
   air verandah type side corridor
   protected by ironwork.
2. A passenger train brake van or
   brake composite coach with raised
   glazed section in guard's compartment
   projecting above roof level to allow
   observation of signals, etc.

Birds, to join the (USRS)
To jump from a moving train.

Birkenhead Joint
Inc as Birkenhead Rly 1859, Chester to
Birkenhead, opened 1840, 1848, 1850.
Vested in L&NWR and GWR jointly 1861,
LM&SR & GWR from 1923, BR from 1948.

Birmingham
BRCW (qv).

Birmingham Pullman
A BR eight-car dmu air-conditioned
Pullman train painted medium blue,
introduced between London (Paddington),
Birmingham and Wolverhampton in 1960.
Withdrawn 1967. Also a BR Pullman
service between Birmingham (New St.)
and London (Euston) introduced 1988.

Birney car
A tramcar design patented by Charles O.
Birney, first produced in USA, 1916. A
lightweight, one-man-operated, single-
truck, single-deck car with important safety
features which included door interlocks
which prevented the car from moving when
the doors were open and also a deadman's
handle (qv).

Birth control engine (RS)(obs) A steam
loco consuming large quantities of coal, thus
making very heavy work for the fireman.
According to railway legend, firing such locos
in the early hours of the morning rendered a
man impotent for a lengthy period.

Birth control hours (RS)
Night work after midnight.

Birth Controllers (RS)
LM&SR Beyer–Garratt locomotives
(2–6–6–2T) of 1927–30. From the supposed
effect of their rough riding on the enginemen.

Biscuit (RS)
1. An insulator.
2. A token (*see* Train staff/tablet/token and
   ticket).

Bissell truck
A two- or four-wheel radial truck in which
the pivoting point is located at some
distance from its transverse centre.
Invented in US in 1857 by Levi Bissell.

Bittern Line
Brand name for the Norwich–Cromer–
Sheringham line, 1996.

Bk (Ger)
Abbreviation for *Blocksignal*; *see* Block signals.

Black Art Fraternity (RS)
Railway signal engineers.

Blackboard (RS)
An oblong ground signal.

'Black box'
See OTMR.

Black box recorder
An electronic device of the 1970s allowing a
fuller record of track condition and quality to
be made than was possible with the Hallade
track recorder (qv). It was in turn superseded
by track geometry recording vehicles (qv).

Black diamonds (USRS)
Company coal.

Black Eights (RS)
Latter day term for LM&SR Stanier class
8F 2–8–0 freight locos.

Black Fives (RS)
LM&SR Stanier class 5 4–6–0 mixed traffic
locos.

Black hole (USRS)
A tunnel.

Blackies
1. (RS) Another name for Black Fives (qv).
2. (USRS) Loco firemen.

Black Isle branch
Muir of Ord to Fortrose.

Black light (RS)
An empty electric light bulb socket; also a
lamp unlit at night.

Black Motors (RS)
L&SWR Drummond 700 class 0–6–0 locos
of 1897, rebuilt 1923–9. Name probably
derived from the contemporary arrival of
the motor car.

Black oil (RS)
An unlit semaphore signal lamp.

Black Pigs (RS)
1. GCR 4–6–0 locos, L&NER class B7.
2. LM&SR class 4MT 2–6–4T of 1945.

Black Princes (RS)
Steam loco cleaners.

Black snake (USRS)
A train consisting entirely of coal wagons.

Black Staniers (RS)
Another name for Black Fives (qv).

Black Tanks (RS)
LB&SCR Stroudley E1 tank locos.

Black wagon
Another name for a chaldron wagon (qv).

Blackwall
see L&BR (*3*).

BL&CJR
Birkenhead, Lancashire & Cheshire Junction Rly, Chester to Walton Junction (Warrington), inc 1846, opened 1850, name changed to Birkenhead Rly (qv), 1859.

Blank card ticket
An Edmondson ticket (qv) with a blank space to allow the destination and fare to be written in by the booking clerk in cases where no pre-printed ticket for the journey was available. Used for journeys to stations on the issuing rly. *See also*: Paper tickets.

Blanket
A separation layer of sand or stone dust (often sandwiched in impervious plastic as a sand blanket) placed between the subgrade (qv) and ballast (qv) to counter upward migration of underlying wet clay or silt.

Blanketing
Excavation and dumping of an existing track bed to a depth of about 1.5 metres, with renewal of the drainage system and the laying down of a blanket of stone dust before reballasting.

Blanket stiff (USRS)
A vagrant who steals rides on trains.

Blast pipe
A hollow pipe, narrowing towards its top, situated inside the smokebox (qv) of a steam loco. Its function is to eject the expanded steam from the pistons and also the air drawn through the ashpan and fire grate by the suction of the escaping steam, forcing the burning gases, smoke and steam upwards through the chimney.

Blauer Eisenbahner (Ger)(obs)
DR (qv) railwaymen transferred to military duties on the railways in wartime but retaining their civilian railway grade and *blau* (blue) uniforms.

Blauer Enzian
A service between Hamburg and Munich, *TEE* from 1965, extended to Klagenfurt 1970, lost *TEE* status 1979, EC Dortmund–Klagenfurt 1987.

Blazer (USRS)
A hot axle box which has set the packing alight.

Bleed, to (USRS)
To drain air from a brake reservoir.

Bleeder (RS)
Bulleid Leader class 0–6–6–0T of 1948. Rhyming slang, referring to the very poor operating environment afforded to the fireman.

Blind baggage (USRS)
Any vehicle at the front of a train without through gangway access to the rest of train.

Blind rider (USRS)
A vagrant riding in a blind baggage car.

Blind tires (USRS)
see Bald wheels (qv).

Blinkers (RS)(obs)
Smoke deflectors; fitted to front end of steam locos to lift smoke away from the cab windows and sides.

Blister (RS)
Any request from management for information; also drivers' report form explaining lateness, etc.

Blizzard lights (USRS)
Auxiliary lamps on a loco.

Bloater
GWR TC for fish van.

Block
1. Closure of a line in an emergency.
2. (RS) Engineer's possession of a section of track for maintenance, renewal or repairs.

Blockade
1. TC for 'all lines blocked'.
2. (USRS) A yard so choked with wagons that shunting is almost or completely impossible.
3. Total closure of a section of railway by Network Rail (qv) for an extended period while infrastructure is replaced or removed on a large scale (from *c.* 2003).

Block bell
A bell in a signal box used to convey the bell codes between adjacent boxes. *See also* Block System.

Block book (RS)
A signalbox train register.

Block controls

Additional links from track circuits (qv) or treadles (qv) to block indicator circuits to ensure the elimination of mistakes by signallers in block working.

Blocked

BR term for a line taken over by one department (usually an Engineer's possession), with signals, etc. maintained in working order. *See also* Mothballed.

Blocked line

A section of line temporarily closed to normal traffic. *See also* BTET.

Blockhead (RS)

A brakeman.

Block indicators

Instruments in a signal box which show the signalmen the state of the Up and Down (qv) lines between any two adjacent manual boxes, i.e. 'Train on Line', 'Line Clear' or 'Line Blocked'.

Blocking back

Protecting a train or shunting movement within the clearing point (qv) by indicating 'line blocked' to the signal box in the rear. A secondary meaning implies trains queueing behind a congested junction or obstruction on the line.

Block instruments

see Block system.

Block load (obs)

A group of wagons, less than a trainload, remaining in the same formation between point of origin and destination which may be marshalled as a unit in different trains en route.

Blockman

British Army term for a rly signalman.

Block marker board (LT)

A square plate showing signal number and red diagonal stripe placed in station platform areas which is the equivalent of a signal without aspects (qv).

Block, on the (RS)

see Blocking back; On the block.

Block post

British Army term for signal box. Also any signal box equipped with block instruments. *See also* Block system.

Blocks

Buffer stops. *See also* On the blocks.

Block section

see Block system.

Block shelf

The space in a signal box (normally above the levers) occupied by the block instruments (qv block system) together with signal, lamp and point repeaters and plungers, etc.

Block signals

The beats on the bells and the indications given on block instruments in signal boxes.

Block switching

The operation of a switch in a signal box which brings together the block circuits of the boxes on each side of it, enabling the intervening box to be closed.

Block system

Widely adopted signalling arrangement in which the rly is divided into absolute intervals of space known as 'block sections'. Only

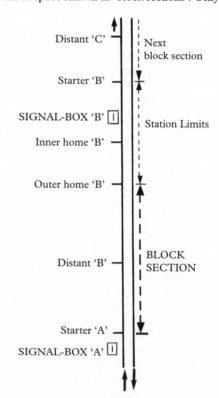

Block system

one train is allowed into each block section at a time. The sections are controlled by signal boxes at each end. A block section extends from the most advanced starting signal (qv) under the control of one box to the first (outermost) home signal (qv) controlled by the next. In the traditional system, signalmen communicate with colleagues in adjacent boxes regarding all train movements, using electric block telegraph instruments which indicate 'train on line', 'line clear' or 'line blocked', and by single stroke bell signals (bell codes) which are sent forward in conjunction with the block telegraph indications to describe the type of train. Also known as 'Absolute Block'. *See also* Moving block; Permissive block; Station limits.

Block système (Fr)
An apparatus with a measure of dependence on interlocking (qv) placed between the mechanism operated by the signaller and the lineside signals, thus constituting a partial lock and block (qv) system. *See also Cantonnement*.

Block train
1. A train which is not normally uncoupled, i.e. always runs as an integral unit.
2. A freight train whose formation remains unaltered between point of origin and destination. Often a complete consignment between consignor and consignee.

Blood and custard (RS)
BR's first passenger coach livery (carmine and cream).

Blood spitters (RS)
NER/LNER B16 4–6–0 locos.

Bloomers (RS)
L&NWR 2–2–2 steam locos. They were contemporary with the activities of Mrs Amelia Bloomer, a US propagandist for feminine dress reform.

Blow, to give it/her a (LTRS)
To apply the air brake.

Blowback
The dangerous situation in which flames and hot gases blow on to the footplate of steam loco through the firehole. Usually the result of a sudden closure of the regulator when the engine is steaming hard and the blower is not turned on.

Blower
1. Annular lobes round the blast pipe (qv), which when supplied with steam by a valve in the driving cab, stir up the fire of a stationary loco when the action of the exhaust is not available. *See also* Ash blower; Soot blower.
2. (S) A telephone.

Blow her down, to (USRS)
To reduce the amount of steam pressure or water in the loco boiler.

Blowing off (RS)
A safety valve releasing a jet of steam.

Blow off, at (USRS)
A steam loco ready to start, its boiler at full pressure, safety valve about to blow off.

Blow through (RS)(obs)
A wagon lacking continuous brakes but equipped with pipes to connect up the braking system through the train.

Blow up, to (RS)
1. To stop to raise more pressure in a badly steaming loco.
2. To create a vacuum for braking.
3. (LTRS) To sound train whistle/hooter.

BLS
1. Branch Line Society; formed 1955, publishes *Branch Line News*.
2. Berne–Loetschberg–Simplon Rly, formed 1906.

Blue Arrow (obs)
A registered transit scheme for goods normally carried as passenger traffic (qv). Introduced January 1936.

Bluebell Line/Rly
A name given by a journalist *c*. 1955 to former LB&SCR line between East Grinstead and Culver Junc near Lewes, closed 1958. The section between Horsted Keynes and Sheffield Park was reopened in 1960 by the Bluebell Railway Preservation Society, which from 1990 extended its operations northwards towards East Grinstead over the old alignment. The name 'Bluebell & Primrose Line' was also current in the 1960s but has now fallen out of use.

Blue Book (RS)
Requirements for Passenger Lines and Recommendations for Goods Lines of the Minister of Transport in Regard to Railway

Construction and Operation. A publication of the MoT (qv) and its successors, periodically revised, each edition superseding its predecessors. From the colour of the cover of some editions. Subsequently retitled *Railway Safety Principles & Guidance* (qv).

Bluebottles (RS)
GWR 14XX 0–4–2T locos.

Blue Danube
A train between Ostend, Vienna and Budapest chartered by Dean & Dawson Ltd for holiday travel, 1933. From 1934 it was replaced by special reserved coaches in the Ostend–Vienna express.

Blue Electrics (RS)(obs)
Glasgow suburban electric trains and services of BR when first introduced. From the livery. *See also* Blue Trains.

Blue Engine
see Red Engine.

Blue flag/light (US)
Displayed at each end of a loco, car or train when receiving attention from workmen and not able to be moved.

Blue Flashes (RS)(obs)
25 kV 50 Hz BR electric locos, when first introduced.

Blue Lagoons (RS)(obs)
Nightrider (qv) coaches. From the dimmed lighting.

Blue liner (USRS)
A rly employee who steals from trains.

Blue One/'un (RS)
A green signal indication.

Blue Pullmans
see Blue Streaks.

Blue Streaks (RS)(obs)
BR 'Blue Pullman' dmu trains introduced in 1960 (Midland Pullman, Bristol Pullman, Birmingham Pullman (qv)). From the contemporary Blue Streak rocket.

Blue Train
1. Colloquial term (also, in Fr, *le Train Bleu*) for the *CIWL* Calais–Méditerranée Express and Paris–Méditerranée Express to San Remo and Ventimiglia. These trains were combined in the 1930s and the title was adopted officially in 1949 for the Calais/Paris–Ventimiglia sleeping car service. The service was reorganized in 1980, when the name was transferred to a new overnight Paris–Ventimiglia service.
2. Name given to new blue and cream coaches introduced on the SAR Union Express (Cape Town–Johannesburg) when introduced in 1939. In 1946 the name was officially adopted for the luxury service between Cape Town, Johannesburg and Pretoria. New stock was introduced in 1972, featuring accommodation entirely in private rooms, some with en suite bathrooms.

Blue Trains (RS)(obs)
1960 emu sets for Glasgow area suburban services. From the original livery. *See also* Blue Electrics.

Blue 'uns (RS)
L&NER A4 4–6–2 locos. From the livery.

Blunderbuss (RS)
A train incorrectly signalled.

BM (obs)
BR Braked Milk van.

BM (Fr)
Block Manuel, absolute block working under the block system (qv).

BMAG
Berliner Maschinenbau Aktien-Gesellschaft: loco builders established in 1852. By 1910 it had 3,500 employees and an annual output of around 400 locos.

BMR
Brecon Mountain Rly. A pleasure line on a section of B&MTJR from Pant (Merthyr) to Torpantau 1 ft 11¾ in/603.25 mm gauge, opened 1980. *See also* B&MTJR.

BN
Belgian rly and tramway equipment manufacturers, originally *La Brugeoise*, Bruges. Merged with *Nicaise et Delcuve* of la Louvière, 1913, to form *La Brugeoise et Nicaise et Delcuve* (*BND*). Merged with *les Ateliers Métallurgiques* of Nivelles, 1956, to form *La Brugeoise et Nivelles* (*BN*). Sold to Bombardier group (qv) 1986–88. *See also* Bombardier–Eurorail.

BND
see BN.

BNFL
British Nuclear Fuels Ltd; operated own locos and nuclear flask trains. Became DRS (qv), 1995, effectively a state-owned FOC (qv).

BNR
Bengal–Nagpur Rly, formed 1887, taken over by Government of India 1944. From 1952 part of ER (5).

BNSF
Burlington Northern Santa Fe RR, a merger (1970) of CB&Q (qv), GN (qv), NP (qv) and the Spokane, Portland & Seattle Rly, also subsequently acquiring Santa Fe (1) (qv) to become the second largest US rly in terms of mileage. Amalgamated with CNR (qv) 2000 to become NA Rly (qv), the largest system in North America.

BNW&SR
Birmingham, North Warwickshire & Stratford-upon-Avon Rly, Birmingham (Tyseley) to Bearley, inc 1894, powers transferred to GWR 1900, opened 1907, 1908.

BO (US)
Bad Order (qv).

'Bo (USRS)
Abbreviation of hobo, US (S) for tramp or vagrant.

Board
1. (RS) Originally the arm of a semaphore signal, but later any type of signal.
2. (USRS) Any fixed signal, e.g. slow board, order board, clear board, etc.
3. (USRS) A list of employees available for service.

Boarding card
see Regulation [of passenger traffic].

Board of Trade Stop (obs)
A compulsory stop on a tramway (3), as required by the Board of Trade Inspector, to ensure that a tramcar is brought to a stand in the interests of safety, e.g. during the descent of a steep hill or before a busy intersection.

Boat train
A train operated exclusively for passengers travelling by shipping services, connecting with the sailings and arrivals of specific services at ports. Originally so-named because the first ones connected with *packet boats* crossing the English Channel.

Boat Train Routes
see BTR.

Bobbing signal (RS)
A defective colour-light signal with aspects repeatedly changing.

Bobby (RS)
A signalman. From Sir *Robert* Peel, founder of the police force; signalling was originally a responsibility of the rly police, so the popular nickname adhered.

Bob hole donor (RS)
A wagon door which only opens halfway.

Bobol
TC for bogie bolster wagon.

Bobtail bounce (USRS)
A short train.

Bobtails
1. (RS) LC&DR Kirtley 'R' Class locos of 1891.
2. (US)(obs) Colloquial term for tramcars without a rear platform and designed for one-man operation and haulage by a single horse or mule.
3. (USRS) A shunting loco.

Bocar
GWR TC for van with canvas cover used for carrying motor car bodies.

'Bo chaser (USRS)
A rly policeman or security man.

Bodmin & Wenford Rly
Bodmin & Wenford Rly plc; preserved rly on former BR Bodmin (Parkway)–Bodmin–Boscarne Junc line, first section opened to passengers and freight 1990. Operates a freight service in connection with BR.

Body Pits (LTRS)
Suicide pits (qv).

Boff vans (RS)(obs)
L&NWR guard's van of c. 1900 fitted with cycle racks designed by a guard named Boff.

BOG (RS)
A Battery-Operated Guard or FRED (qv).

Bogie
1. A short-wheelbase four-wheeled vehicle.
2. An alternative term for truck (3) (qv).
3. A trolley manually propelled along the line by track maintenance staff.

4. In India, a term for any passenger coach
fitted with bogies (2).

Bogie blocks (RS)
L&SWR four-coach suburban sets of
c. 1906.

Bogie centre
The pivot point of a truck (3) (qv).

Bogie man (RS)
Passenger stock repair man. Pun on bogie.

Bog unit (RS)
A dmu with lavatory/wc (bog = (S) for wc).
Also used to describe all types of DMMU
(qv) and DHMU (qv).

Boiler ascension (RS)(obs)
A loco boiler explosion.

Boiler head (USRS)
A steam loco driver.

Boiler header (USRS)
Any person riding in a steam loco cab.

Boiler wash (USRS)
A nervous, ultra-cautious steam loco
driver.

Boiler washer
A steam loco driver.

Bolero
USA 2–8–0 locos, USATC (qv) type S160,
used in Britain from 1942–3 (Bolero was
the code name for the build-up of US
armed forces in Britain in preparation for
the liberation of mainland Europe).

Bolster
A transverse member of a truck normally
carrying the weight of the car body and
usually separated from the bogie frames by
springs and other shock-absorbing devices.

Bolster wagon
An open wagon with raised transverse
beams to hold a load clear of the floor, thus
easing loading and unloading.

Bolt hole (RS)
1. A refuge (qv).
2. (LTRS) A cross passage between
running tunnels on underground rlys.

Bombardier–Eurorail
European acquisitions of Bombardier Inc.
(qv). Rly and tramway/LRV
manufacturers, formed 1991,
incorporating BN (qv), *ANF Industrie
(Ateliers du Nord de la France)* and
Bombardier–Rotax, Vienna.

Bombardier Inc
Manufacturers of rly rolling stock, etc.,
based at Montreal, Canada and Barre VT,
US. *See also Bombardier–Eurorail*;
Bombardier Pro Rail.

Bombardier Pro Rail
New name of Procor (qv) after its purchase
by Bombardier Inc. in 1990.

Bomber (RS)
A 16-ton oil tank wagon.

Bombs (RS)
BR class 20 diesel electric locos.

'Bo money (USRS)
Money collected by freight train crews from
vagrants allowed to ride on the train. Usually
a fixed amount for each division traversed.

Bon Accord
An express between Glasgow (Buchanan
St.) and Aberdeen, introduced 1937,
ceased 1939, re-introduced 1949.

Bonding/Bonds
Electrical connection (usually copper
wires) attached to the ends of the running
rails and ends of the conductor rails (qv) to
permit the passage of electric current along
the track of an electric rly or in a signalling
track circuit (qv). *See also* Impedance
bond.

Bone out, to (RS)
To carry out a survey of a section of rly to
adjust levels.

Bone yard
1. (RS) British Army (Royal Engineers)
term for a cripple (qv) siding.
2. (USRS) A rip track (qv) or scrap yard.

Bongos (RS)
L&NER B1 4–6–0 locos.

Boning rods (RS)
Boards used for sighting when surveying.

Bonnet (RS)
Any loco with a front end resembling a
road vehicle bonnet (e.g. class 37).

Bonus mileage (obs)
The device of charging fares above the
standard mileage rate by assuming the
distance was greater than the actual
mileage. Applied to section of railway
particularly costly to construct and operate.
Required specific permission by an Act of
Parliament authorising the works.

Book, the (RS)
The Working Timetable (qv).

Booked service
A train appearing in the Working timetable (qv), for which loco, rolling stock and crew are diagrammed.

Booking clerk
An employee who issues passenger tickets. From the early practice of entering each passenger transaction in a book. *See also* Booking office.

Booking constable (obs)
In the early days of rlys, a rly policeman who acted as the sole member of staff at a small station, performing all duties including that of booking clerk.

Booking lad
A trainee signalman, employed in busy signal boxes to enter information in train register (qv). *See also* Box boy.

Booking office
A ticket office. From the road coaching and early rly practice of entering each passenger transaction separately in a book.

Booking on (RS)
Reporting for duty.

Boom
The pole carrying the trolley (qv) of an electric tramcar or simple electric loco or car.

Boomer
1. (USRS)(obs) Rly worker who wandered from system to system and job to job at will, staying only a short time, and often going south in the winter. From boom camps.
2. (USRS) Any item of rolling stock which has been owned by more than one rly co./system.

Boomerang (RS)
A return ticket.

Boomer pike (USRS)
A rly using a high proportion of boomer (qv) labour.

Booster
A small steam engine driving the wheels of a loco tender or the trailing pony truck or bogie between the footplate and the tender. Originally manufactured by Franklin Railway Supply Co. Inc, USA.

Booster/retarder
A device which automatically accelerates or slows down wagons, moving by gravity in a marshalling yard. It works by reference to a pre-arranged (latterly computer-calculated) optimum speed, acting to bring the wagon to rest at the correct position in the sorting siding. Also used for the flywheel control on BR class 74 locos.

Boosters (RS)
BR class 71 locos.

Bootlegger (USRS)
A train running over more than one rly system.

Boozer (RS)
Any late night train. *See also* Vomit Special.

BOP
Booking On (qv) Point for BR footplate staff.

'Bo park (USRS)
Any place at which vagrants (hobos) assemble to seek illicit free rides on freight trains, usually a rly yard.

Boplate
TC for bogie freight wagon.

Borail (TC)
Long bolster wagons (qv); 4 types.

Border Counties Line
Riccarton Junc to Reedsmouth and Hexham.

Borderer, The
A Glasgow (Central)–Kilmarnock–Carlisle–Newcastle service, so named in 1992.

Bord-na-Mona
Irish Turf Board, operators of narrow gauge rlys in peat bogs.

Bosh (RS)
A mixture of water and chemicals used to clean grease and oil from locomotive underframes.

Boshing/bosh, to (RS) (obs)
A very thorough cleaning of steam loco parts at Swindon Works (GWR) and possibly elsewhere.

Boss key (LTRS)
Driver's control switch key (with raised boss).

Boss man (LTRS)
A station manager.

Bostwick gates
Lattice steel folding gates used for lifts, at entrances to platforms, etc.

BoT
Board of Trade; the government department with responsibility for rly and tramway matters from 1840 until formation of the MoT (qv) in 1919.

Bothie/Bothy (RS)
Scots for cabin used by shunters or permanent way staff.

Bottle (RS)
The LB&SCR (qv) London train service to and from Wimbledon either via Merton Abbey or via Haydons Road, from the shape of the two routes.

Bottom ballast
The layer of stone, slag or ashes packed closely over the formation (1) (qv) to provide an even bed for the track. Sometimes called the lower ballast. *See also* Ballast; Top ballast.

Bottomside (obs)
The bottom rail of the body side of a wooden railway carriage.

Boulton's Siding
The premises of Isaac Watt Boulton at Ashton-under-Lyne; Boulton bought up old locos, restored them to working condition and hired them out. He also built small industrial locos. The workshops were sold off in 1898 and he died the following year. *See The Chronicles of Boulton's Siding*, Alfred Rosling Bennett, Locomotive Publishing Co., 1927.

Bouncer (USRS)
A caboose (qv).

Bourbonnais (Fr)(US)
Term for loco with 0–6–0 wheel arrangement. The original design was built for work over the Massif Central.

Bouré (Fr)
A key type interlocking (qv) system, easily and economically applied to simple forms of ground levers without modification. Named after its inventor.

Bournemouth Belle
A Pullman car express between London (Waterloo) and Bournemouth (West), introduced 1931, reintroduced 1946, ceased 1967.

Bournemouth Limited
A service between London (Waterloo) and Weymouth, non-stop to Bournemouth, introduced 1929, ceased 1939.

Boviduc (Fr)
Cattle creep (qv).

Bow collector
A uni-directional sliding current collector in the form of a bow, sprung to press its top surface against the overhead wire carrying the traction current. Used for both rlys and tramways (*3*).

Bowes Rly
From near Pontop to Jarrow, first section opened as Springwell Colliery Waggonway 1826, incorporating rope-worked inclines; operated by colliery owners John Bowes & Partners from 1850, renamed Bowes Rly 1932. Worked by NCB until 1974. Section between Blackhams Hill and Springwell operated as a preserved rly since 1981.

Bowl (USRS)
The fan of tracks at the base of a hump (qv).

Bowled (LTRS)
An employee run down by train.

Bowler hats/bowler hat brigade (RS)
Inspectors and foremen not in uniform. Until recent years, the bowler hat was a symbol of middle-management authority on the rlys.

Bowling alley (USRS)
A manually fired loco. From the motion of throwing lumps of coal through the fire hole.

Bowling green (RS)
A line laid out for fast running, the fast roads.

Box (RS)
1. An intermodal container.
2. Alternative term for Locker (qv).
3. Any electric or diesel loco.

Box boy (RS)
A booking lad (qv).

Box car/wagon (US)
A covered freight wagon or van.

Box car tourist (USRS)
Vagrant (hobo (qv)) who hitches illicit free rides on freight trains.

Boxer (RS)
1. Any untimetabled train proceeding at short notice from one signal box to the next.
2. Message passing between signal boxes.

Boxes (RS)
Diesel or electric locos. From their shape.

Boxing (RS)

1. The effect on rails of sideways movement of bogies.
2. Completion of work on track.

Boxing-in

1. (obs) The practice of covering the sleepers with ballast (qv) when returning it to the track after removal during opening out or when arranging fresh ballast.
2. (obs) The formation of the ballast shoulders.
3. The rearrangement by manual work of ballast unloaded from ballast wagons.

Boxing-in ballast

Ballast unloaded onto a track ready for ballasting; Top ballast (qv).

Boxing up

Placing ballast (qv) in the correct profile between and around the sleepers.

Box on wheels (RS)(obs)

Derogatory term used by steam loco enthusiasts for early diesel locos.

Box, out of the (S)

Condition of newly manufactured items on delivery, before any inspection and testing, as in 'nothing ever works out of the box'.

Boxpok (US)

A disc-type wheel designed for steam locos by Baldwin (qv) embodying a cast steel centre and indentations or holes instead of the usual spokes. These and similar wheel designs (*see* BFB) aimed to reduce wheel weight and eliminate hammer blow to the track, maintaining an even pressure on the tyre.

Box Tanks (RS)

L&NWR (qv) 0–6–0 'Coal Engines' (qv) which were rebuilt as 0–6–0 ST (qv ST), the last one withdrawn 1948. From their box-like appearance.

Boy driver (RS)

A newly-passed out guard/motorman or motorman.

Boys' club (LTRS)

British Transport Police.

Boys' Line (LTRS)

Metropolitan Line.

BP (obs)

A bogie gangwayed brake vehicle with racks for racing pigeon baskets (BR).

BP&GVR

Burry Port & Gwendraeth Valley Rly, inc 1865 as Kidwelly & Burry Port Rly, first section, Burry Port to Cwmmawr opened 1869. Part of GWR from 1922.

BPR&P

Bristol Port Rly & Pier; Bristol (Hotwells) to Avonmouth Dock, inc 1862, opened 1865. Clifton Extension, Bristol (Ashley Hill Junc) to Avonmouth (Sneyd Park Junc), inc 1867, vested in GWR and Midland 1871, opened 1874. GWR & LM&SR 1923–47. Original line vested in GWR and Midland 1890, closed 1922.

BR

1. British Rail/ways. General title of the nationalized rly system from its formation on 1 January 1948. Operated initially by the Railway Executive (qv) as an agent of the BTC (qv) and divided into six regions (London Midland; Western; Southern; Eastern; North Eastern and Scottish). From 1963 managed by the BRB (qv). Short title 'British Rail' and double arrow logo in use from 1 January 1965. Regional organization discarded in favour of 'business sectors' and 'profit centres' from 1990–2. *See also* BRB. Term ceased to be used from 7 January 1996. *See also* Railways Act, 1993.
2. Ballycastle Rly (NI); Ballymoney–Ballycastle, 3 ft/914 mm gauge, inc 1878, opened 1880, absorbed by NCC 1924, closed 1950.
3. Buckinghamshire Rly; formed 1847 as an amalgamation of Buckingham & Brackley Junction (Claydon–Brackley) and Oxford & Bletchley Junction Rlys (both inc 1846) opened 1850, 1851, Bletchley–Banbury/Oxford. Worked by L&NWR, part of L&NWR from 1879.
4. Barry Rly; *see* Barry.
5. Bangladesh Rly, *see* BAN
6. Bowes Rly; *see* Bowes.
7. Burma Rlys; metre gauge, nationalized 1948. *See* MR (*19*).
8. Berwickshire Rly; inc 1862, opened Duns to Earlston 1863 and to Ravenswood Junc 1865. Part of NBR 1876.
9. Brampton Rly (qv).

Brabant
TEE Paris (Nord)–Brussels, introduced 1963, lost *TEE* status 1984, became EC 1987.

Bracket arm
A straight or curved tubular steel arm fixed at right angles to a traction pole to suspend the overhead wire of a tramway (*3*).

Bradford Executive
An express between London (Kings Cross) and Bradford, introduced in 1973.

Bradford Pullman
BR Bradford–Leeds–London (Kings Cross) service, introduced 1991.

Bradshaw
Bradshaw's General Railway & Steam Navigation Guide for Great Britain and Ireland. A comprehensive volume of public rly timetables, published monthly from December 1841, originally compiled by George Bradshaw (1801–53), Quaker printer and engraver of Salford. Publication ceased after the issue of May 1961. Also *Bradshaw's Continental Railway Guide*, from June 1847 until August 1939 and *The General Directory & Shareholders' Guide*, 1847 until 1923. *Bradshaw's Air Guide* was published from November 1934 until May 1961 and *Bradshaw's Manchester ABC Railway Guide* from 1861 until May 1961. An Indian *Bradshaw* is still published ten times a year by Newman of Calcutta. However, to the British public in general, *Bradshaw* signified the monthly national rly timetables. 'The vocabulary of *Bradshaw* is nervous and terse, but limited.' – Sir Arthur Conan Doyle.

Bradshaw's Railway Gazette
Published in London and Manchester 1845–6, retitled *Railway Gazette* 1846–72, retitled *Joint Stock Companies Journal, Railway Gazette and Mining Chronicle* 1872; ceased 1882.

BRAG
Better Rail Advisory Group, launched 2002 to represent 23 regional passenger groups.

B-Rail
As a wholly owned subsidiary of the Belgian Railways holding co. (the 2004 successor to *SNCB* (qv)), B-Rail is

responsible for operating all passenger and freight services in Belgium over 3,471 route km.

Brain cage (USRS)
Caboose (qv).

Brain plate (USRS)
A badge worn by a rly employee.

Brains
1. (RS) Traffic Control Office/staff.
2. (USRS) A conductor (*3*) of a passenger or freight train (qv).

Brains car (USRS)
A caboose (qv).

Brake club (USRS)
A hickory stick about 3 ft/914 mm in length used to tighten hand brakes on freight trains.

Brake compo[site]
A coach with accommodation for two classes of passengers and also compartment for guard, luggage, etc.

Brake, First/Second/Third
A passenger coach incorporating accommodation for the guard, luggage, parcels, bicycles, etc., and the guard's equipment including handbrake.

Brakeman (US)
An auxiliary working with a train crew or in a yard.

Brake pin
An iron pin holding wagon brake secure after brake lever handle has been pushed down.

Brake road
A siding allocated to storage of brake vans.

Brakes (RS)
A fully fitted (qv) freight train.

Brakesman
A freight train guard.

Brake staff (obs)
A vertical spindle on the driving platform of a tramcar (qv) with ratchet handle and base for operating the wheel brakes through a system of chains and levers.

Brake stick/pole
Used by shunters for forcing down wagon brake handles.

Brake tender (obs)
A four-wheeled 35-ton vehicle equipped with continuous brakes, introduced by BR

in the 1960s and '70s to provide adequate braking power on unfitted or partly-fitted trains hauled by diesel locos.

Brake tri-compo[site] (obs)
Coach with accommodation for three classes of passenger and compartment for guard, luggage, etc.

Brake van
Alternative term for Guard's van (qv).

Brakie (USRS)
A brakeman (qv).

Braking distance
Distance required to bring the fastest trains on a given route to a halt, taking into account such factors as gradients and signal spacing.

Brampton Rly/s
A group of rlys serving collieries south-east of Brampton, Cumberland, originating as horse-worked waggonways (qv) in the late eighteenth century. Steam locos were introduced in the 1830s and all lines were worked by steam by 1881. Passenger services were provided by a Dandy (qv) from 1836–81 between Brampton and Brampton Junc (NER), then replaced by steam-hauled trains 1881–90. These services were resumed 1913–17 by the NER (qv) and again in 1920–3. Freight workings, latterly by the NCB (qv), continued over the remaining trackage until 1953.

Brass (USRS)
A bronze bearing on which the weight of a rly vehicle rests.

Brass buttons (USRS)
A tramcar conductor or a member of a passenger train crew. From the uniform.

Brass collar/hat (USRS)
A middle-ranking rly official. From the gold braid on uniform collar and brass plate worn on cap.

Brass pounder (USRS)
A rly telegraph operator.

BRB
British Railways Board. Formed in 1963 under Transport Act, 1962, to take over from the BTC (qv), with virtually complete commercial freedom, the responsibility for running the nationalized rly system.

Abolished by Transport Act, 2000; residual functions and responsibilities transferred to SRA (qv).

BRCW
Birmingham Rly, Carriage & Wagon Co., Smethwick, 1855–1963.

BRE
see BREL.

BR (E) (obs)
British Railways, Eastern Region. Absorbed former BR (NE) from 1966. *See also* Anglia; BR (NE).

Bread & Onion Line (RS)(obs)
Wansford to Stamford branch.

Bread Bins (RS)
GCR 4–6–2T locos.

Breakaway
A train accidentally divided.

Breakdown train
A train with heavy lift crane, tool vans, kitchen and other accommodation for breakdown gang, maintained in a state of readiness at depots for attendance at any accident, breakdown or derailment.

Breaker (RS)
A circuit breaker.

Bream
A runner (qv guard truck) used by rly engineers.

Breast beam (US)
A buffer beam.

Breather (RS)(obs)
An evening excursion working to the seaside.

Breeze (RS)
A short physical (qv).

Breeze (USRS)
Service air in the brake system.

Breidsprecher wagen (Ger)
A freight wagon with interchangeable wheel sets designed to accommodate movement between different gauges primarily between standard gauge (Germany) and 5 ft (1.524m) (Russia). Named after the inventor.

Breitspurbahn (Ger)
Plans drawn up in 1942–5 at the wish of Adolf Hitler for a system of 3 metre (9 ft 10.1 in) gauge rlys in the Third Reich. Also known as *Gigantenbahn*.

BREL

Formed 1970 as British Rail Engineering to take over management and operation of the various railway workshops; subsequently incorporated as a limited company (British Rail Engineering Ltd). Sold off in 1989 as an independent undertaking manufacturing all types of railway rolling stock. ABB (qv) acquired majority control 1992 as ABB Transportation Ltd.

Brenner Express

A night service Munich–Milan/ Venice/Florence, introduced 1954.

BRH

British Rail Hovercraft Ltd; formed 1966, brand name 'Seaspeed'. Initial service was to the Isle of Wight. A subsidiary of BRB until merged with Hoverlloyd Ltd as Hoverspeed (qv) 1981.

BRI

1. British Rail International Inc; a BTC subsidiary formed to sell technical advice to overseas administrations. Taken over by BRB 1963. *See also* Transmark.
2. British Rail International. Specialized marketing and promotional organization for rail travel between Britain and mainland Europe. *See also* EPS; BRIL (*2*).

BRI

British Railways Illustrated; a magazine devoted to British rly and loco history/nostalgia, first published in 1991.

Brick, the (RS)(obs)

Bricklayers' Arms loco depot, Bermondsey, London.

Brick, to/bricked, to be (S)

The action of throwing bricks or other hard objects at trains or road vehicles with intent to cause injury or damage/to be the object of such an attack.

Bridge bashing (RS)

Damage caused to underline rail bridges by drivers of road trucks and buses from forgetfulness or lack of awareness of the size of their vehicle. Such incidents, which may seriously disrupt rail services and require costly repairs to structures, are frequently not even reported by the culprits.

Bridge hog (USRS)

A bridge maintenance engineer/worker.

Bridge rails (obs)

Bridge-shaped in cross section, with wide bottom flanges or wings, these rails were secured to longitudinal sleepers by fang spikes and bolts. Used by GWR for many years.

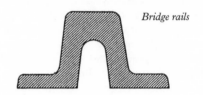

Bridge rails

Brigade of cars (US)(obs)

An early expression for a rly train. *See also* Car.

Brighton, the (RS)

LB&SCR (qv).

Brighton Belle

1934 renaming of Southern Belle (qv) all-Pullman car express between London (Victoria) and Brighton, re-introduced 1947, ceased 1972.

Brighton [Pullman] Limited

A Sunday all-Pullman car train between London (Victoria) and Brighton, introduced 1898, running October to June. Name dropped 1908. *See also* Southern Belle.

BRIL

1. British Rail Investments Ltd, a subsidiary of BR, 1980–4, subsumed in reorganized BRPB (qv).
2. British Rail International Ltd, a subsidiary of EPS (qv), formed 1992, to manage sales of rail tickets between UK and mainland Europe, also included Britrail Travel International (marketing BR travel in North America) and Asia–Pacific (marketing BR travel in Asia and Australasia). A subsidiary of EPS (qv) from 1992.

Brill

1. J.G. Brill, Philadelphia, established 1868, J.G. Brill Co. 1887, Brill Corporation 1926. Builders of rly and tramway (*3*) cars. Ceased rail vehicle production 1941.
2. 58-ton bogie bolster wagon used by engineers.

Bristol
Bristol Wagon & Carriage Works Ltd,
1866–1920.

Bristolian
An express between London (Paddington)
and Bristol, introduced 1935, ceased 1939.
Name restored 1951, dropped 1965,
restored 1971, dropped 1973.

Bristol Pullman
BR eight-car dmu air-conditioned Pullman
trains painted medium blue, introduced
between London (Paddington) and Bristol
in 1960, withdrawn 1973.

British Railway Journal
see BRJ.

British Railways
see BR (1).

British Railways Magazine
see BRM.

British Railways Press Bureau
A retitling from 1928 of the British
Railways Information Bureau. From 1929
it published RN (2) (qv).

British Westinghouse
see BWE&M.

BRITRA
British Road/Rail Intermodal Trunk Route
Association.

Brits (RS)
BR standard class 7P 4–6–2 locos. The
first in the class was named Britannia.

Brittany Express
A summer service between London
(Waterloo) and Southampton Docks in
connection with St Malo sailings, 1954–64.

BRJ
British Railway Journal, an illustrated
magazine devoted to rly history, first
published 1983.

BR (LMR) (obs)
British Rail, London Midland Region.

BRM
British Railways Magazine, issued in
monthly regional editions from 1950 until
1963. *See also Railnews.*

BR (M) (obs)
British Railways, London Midland Region.

BRML (obs)
British Rail Maintenance Ltd. A division of
BREL (qv) retained in BR ownership.

BR (NE) (obs)
British Railways, North Eastern Region.
Merged with BR (E) 1966.

Broad gauge
Any rail gauge wider than standard (qv). The
early lines of the GWR were 7 ft/2,134 mm
gauge, later altered to 7 ft 0¼ in/2,140 mm.
A broad gauge of 5 ft 6 in/1,676 mm is used
in India, Pakistan, Sri Lanka, Spain, Portugal,
Argentina, and Chile; 5 ft 3 in/1,600 mm in
Ireland, South Australia, Victoria, and Brazil;
and 1,520 mm (originally 5 ft) in Russia.

Broadlands Line
Brand name adopted in 1990 for BVR
(qv).

Broadsman
An express between London (Liverpool
St.), Norwich, Cromer and Sheringham, so
named 1950. Name dropped 1962.

Broad Street Rattlers (RS)
NLR 4–4–0T.

Broadway Limited
An overnight Pennsylvania Railroad express
between New York and Chicago, via
Pittsburgh. Began 1902 as all-Pullman
Broad Way Limited, the name arising from
the six-track formation between New York
and Philadelphia, not the famous New York
street, although that was soon changed.
18 h in 1932. New loco and train designs
by Raymond Loewy and a 16 h schedule
from 1938. After wartime relaxation, the
16 h timing was resumed in 1946 and
reduced to 15 h 30 min in 1954. Name
dropped 1967. Name adopted by Amtrak
New York–Chicago service from 1972.

Broca rail
A grooved rail designed for street tramways.

Brogden joint
A joint used in laying long rails, in which
a vertical cut is made along the centre
line of the rail for about 9 in (228 mm) and
half the rail cut away, the other half
overlapping the corresponding half of the
adjoining rail, thus preserving a continuous
bearing surface for the wheel tread.
Each rail end is supported by a 'joint
chair'.

Broken rail (USRS)
An experienced, long service rlyman.

Brotherhood (US)
Equivalent of trade union.

Brother in law (RS)(obs)
A device concealed in the clothing of conductors on tramways (*3*) to imitate the bell which denoted a ticket had been cancelled by punching, deceiving passengers into believing their fare had been registered as paid.

Brown House (RS)(obs)
BR headquarters. A distortion of *das braunes Haus* (the Nazi Party headquarters).

Brownie box (USRS)
A coach used by the superintendent of the railroad and so-called because it was sometimes used to inform staff of award or imposition of Brownies (qv).

Brownies/Brownie points (USRS)
Demerit points, graded according to the seriousness of the offence, which would be entered in a railwayman's career records. Named after George R. Brown, the General Superintendent of the Fall Brook Rly, who in the late nineteenth century introduced a system of rly staff discipline which included this feature. His scheme was widely adopted in the USA and Canada, often with modifications, sometimes with merit points which could be used to reduce the demerits.

Brown, Marshalls
Brown, Marshalls & Co. Ltd, Birmingham, rolling stock manufacturers 1870–1902. Became part of MCW (qv).

Brown one/'un (RS)
A distant signal showing yellow.

BRP
Babcock Rail Projects, 1989, part of Babcock International Group based at Rosyth Dockyard and specialising in refurbishment and conversion of railway rolling stock.

BRPB
British Rail Property Board. Set up 1970 as a professionally managed property company to replace the BRB Property Committee. Its purpose was to control all property matters for the whole of the BRB undertakings, notably commercial development and sale of surplus railway lands,

exploitation of air space over rly stations, etc. Reorganized 1984 with additional responsibilities for exploiting BR assets. Sold to private sector, 1997.
See also RSL.

BRSA
British Railways Staff Association, formed 1952 and functioned during the nationalization regime.

BR (S) (obs)
British Railways, Southern Region.

BR (Sc) (obs)
British Railways, Scottish Region. *See also* Scotrail.

BRT
1. British Railway Traffic & Electric Co., established 1902 as rolling stock hirers. Acquired by Procor (qv), 1974.
2. BR Telecommunications plc; BR subsidiary formed 1994 to operate BR's radio and telecommunications network and to market and develop surplus capacity and offer facilities on a commercial basis. Sold to Racal Electronics, 1995.

Bruffs
Vehicles capable of running on both rails and roads using a modification of road trucks devised by the Bruff Engineering Co.

Brugeoise, la
see BN (*2*).

Bruiteur (Fr)
Paris Métro equivalent of hustler (qv).

Brush
Brush Electrical Engineering Co. Ltd, Falcon Works, Loughborough. The original co. was established in 1879 by Charles F. Brush; became Brush Electrical Engineering following a merger with Falcon (qv) in 1889. Manufacturers of steam, electric and diesel locos, rly coaches, electric tramcars, wagons and road transport vehicles. Steam loco production ceased 1912. Amalgamated with Bagnall (qv) as Brush–Bagnall Traction Ltd, 1951. Renamed Brush Traction 1956. Part of Hawker Siddeley Group (qv), 1957.

Brush (RS)
A guard.

Brushes (RS)

BR class 47 locos; after the manufacturer, Brush (qv).

BRUTE (obs)

British Railways Universal Trolley Equipment; large manually-propelled or tractor-hauled open wire net-sided trucks (for parcels, luggage, etc. at stations), introduced 1964. Out of use by 1995.

BRV

Brake release valve.

BR (W) (obs)

British Railways, Western Region.

BS (obs)

BR Brake Second/Standard class compartment coach, non-gangwayed, with luggage and guard's sections.

BS&WR

Baker Street & Waterloo Rly, inc 1893. A tube rly connecting these two London stations, eventually extending from Elephant & Castle to Queens Park. First section opened 1906. Part of LER (qv) from 1910. *See also* Bakerloo.

BSK (obs)

BR Brake Corridor Second/Standard class Compartment coach.

BSO

BR Brake Second/Standard class Open coach.

BSOT

Brake Standard class Open, Trolley [coach], BR.

BT

Back Track (qv).

BTA

British Transport Advertising Ltd; BTC subsidiary, handling commercial advertising rights on stations, etc. A wholly owned subsidiary of BRB and THC 1963; sold to a group of BTA managers, Ironlook Ltd, 1987.

BTB

Burgdorf–Thun Bahn, Switzerland.

BTC (obs)

British Transport Commission, formed under Transport Act, 1947, as a public authority to control and administer all nationalized inland transport, including the rly system. Took over the rlys of Great Britain from 1 January 1948; first chairman Sir Cyril (from 1950 Lord) Hurcomb. Reorganized 1953–4 with the abolition of the Railway Executive (qv). Management then delegated to the LTE (qv) and (from 1955) to BR Area Boards for the six rly regions, whose CROs (qv) became General Managers. The BTC was effectively dissolved in 1963 though did not peter out formally until 1 January 1964. The rlys then passed to BRB and LTB (qv).

BTCP (obs)

British Transport Commission Police [Force], formed 1948 to take over responsibility for policing all BTC (qv) undertakings, assuming the duties of the police forces of the former railway companies. Absorbed London Transport Police Force 1958. *See* BTP.

BTDB

British Transport Docks Board. Originated as Docks & Inland Waterways Executive of the BTC, inheriting the rly companies' docks and ports in 1948 and also the rly-owned canals, which were later transferred to the British Waterways Board. Reorganized 1953 as a division of the BTC. BTDB formed under Transport Act 1962 as a separate undertaking, 'privatized' as ABP (qv) 1982.

BTET

A section of line Blocked To Electric Traction/Trains but otherwise open to traffic.

BTFU or BTF

British Transport Films Unit. Formed by the BTC in 1949 to make documentary films for general distribution and instruction films for the staff of the BTC undertakings. Soon abbreviated to British Transport Films (BTF). Wound up 1986.

BTH

1. British Thomson-Houston Ltd, Rugby, formed 1894 as British subsidiary of GE (2) (qv). Became British Thomson-Houston Co. Ltd, 1896. Manufacturers of electric traction equipment for rlys and tramways (3). Controlled by the International General Electric Co. (USA) 1929–58. Part of AEI (qv), 1959.
2. British Transport Hotels. Originated 1948 as the Hotels Executive of the

BTC, which inherited the rly companies' hotels. From 1953 became BTH & Catering Services, a division of the BTC, responsible in 1958 for 36 hotels, 350 refreshment rooms and 700 daily restaurant and buffet car services. Registered as BTH Ltd 1962 with continuing responsibility for station catering facilities, restaurant car services, and rly and hotel laundry services. In this capacity it became a wholly owned subsidiary of the BRB from 1963. Following the 'privatization' policy of the 1980 Conservative administration, by the end of 1983 all the rly hotels had been sold to private companies outside the BRB. Station catering was separated from BTH in 1982 (*see* Travellers-Fare) and train catering became a direct responsibility of the BRB at the same time. These changes enabled BTH to be dissolved in 1984.

BTHR

British Transport Historical Records. Responsible for the care of the archives of the constituents of the BTC undertakings and for making them available for historical research. The records were transferred to the Public Record Office in 1972 and BTHR ceased to exist.

BTOG (obs)

British Transport Officers Guild. Staff association for railway officers (qv) during the nationalization regime.

BTP

British Transport Police, a 1962 renaming of BTCP (qv). Responsibility for the BTP was transferred to the BRB 1963, with a separate area force assigned to LT. BTP ceased to police the former railway docks and ports after 30 June 1985. Remained intact after privatization of Britain's rlys but became an independent police authority from 2000 under Railtrack (qv) then under the SRA (qv). Finally separated as a fully independent police authority from 2003, having statutory jurisdiction over the national rail network and London Underground, although continuing to be funded by the railway industry .

BTR

British Transport Review, quarterly official publication of BTC (qv), April 1950–January 1964.

BTR (obs)

Boat Train Route(s); the routes used by international services between London, Folkestone, Dover and the Channel Tunnel. Now CTR (qv).

BTS

Bangkok Transit System. An elevated third rail system, first lines opened 1999, brand name 'Skytrain' (qv).

BTU

Breakdown Train Unit.

Bubble cars (RS)

BR diesel railcars capable of running as a single unit.

Buchan Line

Dyce to Fraserburgh.

Bucharest Express

A service between Zagreb and Bucharest via Subotica, 1967–78.

Buchli drive (obs)

A form of drive employed on electric locos from 1917 in which a system of levers, rods and gear sectors outside each driven wheel allowed the body-mounted motors to transmit traction to a wheel able to rise and fall slightly to accommodate track irregularities. After the inventor Dr Ing. J. Buchli.

Bucker plow (US)

A simple form of snow plough with curved blades coming to a point, designed to push snow aside from the track and propelled by one or more locos. *See also* Snowbucking.

Bucket (USRS)

The piston of a diesel-electric loco.

Buckeye

A vertical plane automatic knuckle coupling invented by Eli H. Janney, in which the coach ends are bow-shaped and thus brought close together, allowing the steel jaws of the couplers to engage firmly with each other when the vehicles are pushed close, in a similar fashion to the locking together of the curled fingers of two human hands. These couplers were the recommended practice of the MCB (*1*) (qv) from 1899 and in the US are therefore known as MCB (later AAR) couplers. They were introduced in Britain in 1897. Named after the Buckeye Steel Castings Co. of Columbus, Ohio, USA (Ohio is the 'Buckeye State').

Buckingham Palace (RS)
The former NER headquarters building, York. From its palatial and dignified architecture.

Buck Jumpers (RS)
GER J67, J68 and J69 0–6–0T locos.

Budd
Established by Edward G. Budd in Philadelphia, US, in 1912 but did not produce rail vehicles until 1932. Holders of patents for stainless steel bodywork construction for which licences have been granted to French and Portuguese firms.

Buenos Aires Great Southern Rly
(*Ferrocarril Gran Sud de Buenos Aires* (GS)), the largest British-owned rly in Argentina, inc 1862, 5 ft 6 in gauge, first section opened 1865, acquired by Argentine Government 1948, then 4,902 route miles (7,889 km), and renamed *FC Nacional General Roca*.

BUF
SR four-car emu corridor set with BUFfet car, provided for 1938 Mid-Sussex line electrification; two motor-brakes Second/Standard class, one First class trailer, one buffet trailer, the last two with open seating areas, 4-BUF.

Buffer beam/plank/plate
The horizontal component of locos and rail vehicles to which buffers and coupling gear are fixed. Also known as a headstock. *See also* Buffer stops.

Buffer kissing (RS)
see Track bashing.

Buffer locking
A phenomenon occurring on very sharp curves in which part of the flat head of one buffer of a vehicle passes behind the head of a buffer on the adjoining vehicle. Derailment may ensue when straight track is regained. Locking may also occur on ramps or sharp changes in gradient.

Buffer shrouds
Square steel plates fixed to the buffers of rolling stock (qv) by lugs to prevent buffer locking (qv).

Buffer stops
A fixed device mounted at the end of a railway siding or platform track designed to absorb the shock from contact with the buffers of vehicles or locos which have overrun. At terminal tracks in passenger stations, hydraulic buffers, sliding buffer stops with friction clamps, sand drags (qv) or other means of frictional retardation are installed to limit damage and injuries. On LT a buffer beam on the front arrestor buffers or fixed buffers is fitted to spread loads on impact.

Buffet car
A coach with a counter from which snacks, hot and cold drinks and alcoholic refreshment are served. There is a small kitchen unit and the coach may also contain benches or seats and tables. *See also* Autobuffet; Mini[ature] buffet.

Buff, rly/steam (US)(S)
Term for anyone particularly interested in rlys or steam locos. Has some currency in UK, usually among those who are not.

Bug, the
1. Combined inspection saloon and loco (F9 4–2–4T) built 1899 for the personal use of the L&SWR mechanical engineer, Dugald Drummond.
2. (USRS) A high speed telegrapher's key.
3. Name of RHDR (qv) industrial pattern 0–4–0 tender-tank two-cylinder loco built by Krauss (Munich), delivered 1926, sold to Bellevue Park Rly, Belfast 1933. Returned to RHDR 1972 and subsequently rebuilt.

Bug box (RS)(obs)
A four-wheel passenger coach.

Bug dust (RS)(obs)
Coal in very small pieces.

Buggy (USRS)
A caboose (qv).

Bugler (RS)(obs)
A driver who uses the whistle excessively. From the bugles used before the invention

of the steam whistle. *See also* Captain
Hornblower.

Bug letter (USRS)

A standard form of words used by rly co.
head offices in reply to any complaint
regularly received from passengers. From
the response to complaints about insects in
the upholstery of rly cars.

Bug torch (USRS)

A shunter's lamp. From the insects its light
attracts at night.

Bug unit (RS)

A multiple unit train (qv).

Bulgarian wheels (RS)

Poorly maintained wheel sets (qv) which in
wear have produced second 'flange' on the
outer edge of the tyres.

Bulgarski Durzavni Zeleznici

Bulgarian State Rlys.

Bulkhead

A partition extending over the full width of
a vehicle at some point between the ends,
usually fitted with a door.

Bull

see Railroad bull.

Bulldogs (RS)

1. GWR 4–4–0 locos class 3300 (1898).
2. L&SWR 415 class Adams 4–4–2T of
   1882.
3. Midland Rly Johnson 3F 0–6–0 locos
   used on the S&DJR.

Bulldozer (RS)(obs)

A steam loco used for ECS working.

Bulletin (Fr)

CIWL (qv) sleeping car ticket.

Bullet trains

Trains used on Japanese Shinkansen (qv)
high speed lines.

Bullhead rail

A development of parallel rail (qv), it has a
larger upper surface over which the train
wheels run. The lower bulge is supported
in chairs which are fastened to the
sleepers. In Britain bullhead rail is now
largely superseded by flat-bottom rail (qv).
See also Chair; Key.

Bullnose (USRS)

1. The front drawbar of a loco.
2. A clerestory (qv) sloped down at each
   end of a coach.

Bullhead rail

Bull pen (USRS)

A crew room.

Bull's-eye

Bar and circle logo adopted by the
Underground (qv) in 1908; still in use in
slightly modified form today.

Bull's Eye (RS)

A signal light.

Bump, to (USRS)

To gain another man's position by
exercising seniority.

Bumper (RS)(obs)

1. Another word for a bunk (qv).
2. (RS) A diesel shunting loco.

Bumper (USRS)

A buffer.

Bungalows (RS)

Flat-roofed substations installed by BR
(SR) 1952–8.

Bunk (RS)(obs)

A train working a short branch line, hence
the line, or its traffic. Possibly from bunker
(2) (qv).

Bunk a shed, to (RS)

To trespass in a loco depot in order to cop
(qv) locos. Current in 1920s, if not earlier,
still in use.

Bunk car (USRS)

A car fitted up with sleeping
accommodation for train crews.

Bunker

1. A coal container at back of tank loco.
2. (RS) Any small tank loco.

Bunker first

A tank loco travelling backwards.

Bunny (RS)

A locally experienced driver conducting

another over an unfamiliar stretch of line.
See also Pilotman.

Bun trains (LTRS)(obs)
Tube trains adapted in WW2 to carry
refreshments to people sheltering in
tube stations during air and missile
raids.

Bure Valley
Bure Valley Rly, 15 in/381 mm gauge light
rly between Aylsham and Wroxham,
Norfolk, over former BR Wroxham–
County School line. Opened 1990.

Bürklii
Swiss rly timetable also including aerial
rlys, (qv), funiculars and lake steamer
services. First published 1856 by David
Bürklii.

Burlington
CB&Q (qv). *See also* Q, The

Burlington Zephyr
Streamlined three-car articulated diesel-
powered stainless steel sets introduced
1934. First used on Lincoln (Nebraska)–
Omaha–Kansas City service, 250 m in 4 h
55 min. Later operated between Chicago
and Minneapolis–St Paul, also Chicago and
Denver. Renamed Pioneer Zephyr (qv).

Burma Rly/Burma–Thailand Rly
see Railway of Death.

Burma Road (RS)(obs)
Any difficult stretch of line through wild and
lonely country, e.g. Halwill–Torrington;
Carmarthen–Aberystwyth; Settle–Carlisle;
Claremorris–Collooney.

Burns Line
Brand name for Kilmarnock–Ayr–Girvan
services, 1996.

Burnt ballast
Clay soil burnt on site during construction
of a rly through an area with clay subsoil
and then spread to form a blanket over the
formation (qv).

Burrowing junction
A formation in which a diverging line is
carried beneath a main line to avoid
conflicting movements.

Burst (RS)
A loss of air pressure or vacuum in the
braking system, usually from a fault or
severance in a pipe.

Bury
Edward Bury & Co., Clarence Foundry,
Liverpool, machinery manufacturers,
established by Edward Bury (1794–1858);
built steam locos from 1829, later known
as Bury, Curtis & Kennedy. Ceased
production 1850.

Bus (USRS)
A loco.

Business car (US)
A car for use by rly officials travelling
round the system, fitted out with office,
cooking, eating and sleeping
accommodation, lavatories, etc.

Bus line
A multi-core cable providing an electrical
connection between the collecting shoes of
an emu (qv) train and between them and
the master controller/power junction box.

Bustitution
The replacement of rly passenger service
by buses; rarely a satisfactory substitute
and therefore often followed after a short
interval by complete withdrawal of the
service. A term first used in the 1960s.

Butlin's Expresses (obs)
Special trains between London (Kings
Cross) and Skegness, London (Liverpool
St.) and Clacton, and London (Victoria) and
Bognor, introduced 1950 to carry traffic
generated by Butlin's Holiday Camps.

Butterfly
1. (RS) Indicator and re-set valve at ends
   of passenger carriages. From its shape.
2. GWR TC for six-wheel tricomposite
   coach.
3. (USRS) A notice passed by a train crew
   member to a rlyman at lineside or vice
   versa. From the shape of the note, when
   tied and weighted at the centre.

Butterfly cock (LTRS)
An external door valve cock. From the
shape of the handle.

Button (LTRS)
The master controller in an electric
train.

Button pusher (LTRS)
A guard. From the door control buttons.

Buzzard's roost (USRS)
The yard office.

BV

Banverket; Swedish National Rail Administration, responsible for rly tracks and other infrastructure since 1988. Sweden has 12,621 route km of rly, physically connected to the main European network by the Oresund Link (qv). *See also SJ.*

BVB

see BVG.

BVG (Ger)

Berliner Verkehrs Gesellschaft; Berlin Public Traffic Authority, formed to manage and operate the city's trams, buses, and *U-bahn* from 1 January 1929. The East Berlin operations became *Berliner Verkehrs Betriebe* (*BVB*) after 1945 but following German reunification the whole system again became *BVG.*

BVR

Bure Valley Rly (qv).

BW (Ger)

Bahnbetriebswerk; motive power depot.

BWE&M

British Westinghouse Electric & Manufacturing Co. Ltd, Trafford Park, Manchester, formed 1899. Absorbed by MV (qv) 1919.

BWH&AR

Bideford, Westward Ho! & Appledore Rly, inc 1896; its line, opened 1901 and 1908, was not connected with main rly system. Closed 1917.

BY (obs)

BR four-wheeled passenger brake vehicle.

Bye-stand (obs)

A crossing loop on a plateway (qv) or waggonway (qv).

Byeway/Byway/Sideway (obs)

The inbound track of a plateway (qv), used by empty wagons and therefore usually of lighter construction than the outward road carrying loaded traffic.

Byset (obs)

A bye-stand (qv).

BZ (obs)

BR six-wheeled passenger brake vehicle, non-gangwayed.

BZD

Bielorrusse Zeleznue Dorogi; Belarus Rlys, 1,520 mm gauge.

C

C
BR Composite Compartment coach, non-gangwayed.

CAB
A warning (on a lineside sign) to remind drivers that they should change over to cab signalling.

Cab, to (RS)
To ride by invitation with the driver or to look at a driving cab.

Cabbage car (USRS)
A diesel loco with its engines removed to provide space for baggage but retaining its cabs.

Cab hop (USRS)
Abbreviation of caboose hop (qv).

Cabin
see Signal cabin.

Cabin car (US)(obs)
Early term for caboose (qv).

Cabin cars
Liverpool Corporation Tramways series 782–817, built 1933–4.

Cable bridge
A structure carrying cables over a rly.

Cable route
Provision for cables alongside a rly; either in pre-cast concrete troughs or above ground level supported by concrete posts, or in pre-punched metal 'Admiralty trays' fixed to retaining walls and lineside structures.

Cable stile (LT)
A set of stairs or ladders to enable staff to cross over a cable route (qv).

Caboose (US)
Since c. 1855 the accepted term for last vehicle on a freight train, accommodating the train crew and providing a vantage point (see Cupola) for inspection of the moving train.

Caboose bounce (USRS)
see Caboose hop.

Caboose hop (USRS)
Train consisting only of loco(s) and caboose(s) (qv).

Cab rank (RS)(obs)
Siding at Stratford, east London, on which Buck Jumpers (qv) lined up to work the Jazz Service (qv).

Cab secure radio (CSR)
A secure radio link between signalling centres (qv) and drivers.

Cad (USRS)
A conductor (3) (qv).

CAF (obs)
BR Cafeteria car (qv).

CAF (Sp)
Compania Auxiliar de Ferrocarriles, Spanish rolling stock builders, Beasain.

Cafeteria car (obs)
A coach fitted out to dispense self-service hot meals and other refreshments; introduced by BR 1952.

Cage (USRS)
A caboose (qv).

Cages à Poules (RS) (Fr) (obs)
Steam auto-trains (1) (qv) with a passenger coach either side of a central power unit, introduced by the Nord Rly Co. 1901–8 and initially used in the Paris area. There were no end control positions as the passenger cars were constructed to allow the driver a forward view in either direction. The name relates to the appearance of the lateral luggage containers with their metal grilles.

Cairn Valley
Cairn Valley Light Rly, Dumfries–Moniaive, LRO 1899, opened 1905, worked and owned by G&SWR and from 1923 by LM&SR. Closed 1943 (passengers), completely closed 1949.

CAL (obs)
Carted Across London; freight moved across London by rly-owned road transport.

Calais–Bruxelles Pullman Express
A *CIWL* express providing Brussels connection with cross channel sailings to and from Dover; ran 1927–39.

Calais–Méditerranée Express
see Blue Train.

Calais–Nice–Rome Express
A *CIWL* service, 1883–1914.

Calder Valley Line
Normanton–Wakefield–Sowerby Bridge–[Todmorden–Manchester].

Caledonian
Express between London (Euston) and Glasgow, 1957–1964, and again from 1994. Name ceased to be used from 2 June 2002 but was restored for London (Euston)–Glasgow Central *Pendolino* (qv) services 2004.

Caledonian Rly (Brechin)
A preserved rly between Brechin and Bridge of Dun on former BR Forfar–Bridge of Dun line.

Caley (RS)
Caledonian Rly; *see* CR (*1*).

Caley-stop (RS)
see Euston stop.

California car
A single deck tramcar in which half the passenger accommodation has open sides and the other half is fully glazed and protected from the weather.

California Zephyr
A Chicago–Denver–San Francisco service of CB&Q, D&RGW and WPRR. Introduced 1949 with Vista–Dome cars (qv), withdrawn 1970. Re-introduced 1983 as Amtrak service. *See also* San Francisco Zephyr.

Call a train over, to (obs)
To walk along a train making an announcement to all passengers in each coach.

Call boy (USRS)
Employee responsible for locating train crews when required for duty.

Caller (US)(obs)
A boy employed to rouse train crews for duty.

Caller-up (obs)
Employee who roused train crews for duty by knocking at their bedroom windows.

Callie (RS)
Caledonian Rly; *see* CR (*1*).

Calling a route (RS)
Setting up a route for a train in a panel signal box (qv) or IECC (qv).

Calling-on arm/signal
A small semaphore signal fixed to the post carrying a starting or home signal. In the 'off' position it authorizes a movement at caution to the next stop signal when the block section ahead is not clear. When fixed to a distant signal post, the 'off' indication allows a cautious advance beyond the home signal (which will also be 'off') up to the starting signal (which will be 'on'). The calling-on signal usually shows no light when 'on', green when 'off'. Such signals were also used at termini to call on light engines after the train they had brought in had left, allowing the loco to follow the train out and attach itself to another train. These signals also allow a train to enter a platform already partly occupied.

Calliope (USRS)
Steam loco. From (US) calliope = a steam organ.

Call point examiners
Rolling stock examiners located at specified points on LT rlys where they are 'on call' to attend to defects arising on trains in service.

Calmac
Caledonian MacBrayne shipping services to and from the islands off the west coast of Scotland, many of them operating in connection with rail services.

Calumet (US)
A steam loco with 2–4–2 wheel arrangement, after these had been supplied to the Chicago & Calumet Terminal Co.

Camber

Raising of one rail above the other to allow higher speeds round curves. *See also* Super-elevation.

Cambrian

Cambrian Rlys Company, inc 1864, from Oswestry, Ellesmere & Whitchurch Rly (opened 1863, 1864), Oswestry & Newtown Rly, (opened 1860, 1861, 1863), Llanidloes & Newtown Rly (opened 1859) and the Newtown & Machynlleth Rly (opened 1863). The Aberystwyth & Welsh Coast Rly (opened 1863, 1864, 1865, 1867 and 1869) was absorbed from 1865. The company operated 295 route miles by 1914, mainly in central Wales. Amalgamated with GWR 1922.

Cambrian Coast Express

GWR summer express between London (Paddington) and Aberystwyth/Pwllheli, introduced 1927. Re-introduced by BR 1951. Pwllheli working withdrawn 1966, ceased 1967. Re-introduced 1987 as London (Euston) to Aberystwyth all year round service, ceased 1991.

Cambrian Coast Line

Dovey Junction–Barmouth–Pwllheli.

Cambrian Radio Cruise

see Land cruise.

Cambridge Cruisers

Half-hourly London (Kings Cross)–Cambridge services with on-board refreshments operated by West Anglia & Great Northern (qv). *See also* Beer trains; Garden Cities & Cambridge Buffet Car Expresses.

Camels/Camelbacks

1. (USRS) Steam locos in which the driving controls and driver's cab were placed centrally, on top of the boiler, with firing cab in the normal position.
2. Any electric or diesel loco with cab in the centre.
3. (RS) An alternative term for Saddlebacks (qv).

Cammell Laird

Cammell Laird & Co. Ltd, Sheffield, manufacturers of locos and rolling stock and parts, established 1903. Rolling stock activities transferred to Metro-Cammell (qv), 1929.

Camp car (US)

Outfit car (qv).

Camping coaches

Rly coaches adapted as holiday accommodation and placed in sidings at suitable locations. Introduced 1932, withdrawn 1939, restored 1946, finally withdrawn as a public service 1971.

Can (USRS)

A tank wagon.

Canadian

A CPR express between Montreal and Toronto and Vancouver via Calgary, with 'scenic dome' cars, introduced 1955, scheduled at 70 h 20 min eastbound. Withdrawn 1990.

Canal Line

Glasgow–Paisley(Canal)–Elderslie.

Canal [vessel] haulage rlys

Rlys built alongside a canal expressly to haul barges and ships. An early trial took place on the Forth & Clyde Canal in 1839 but the most famous example is the Panama Canal Rly, opened in 1914. This uses electric locos ('mules') on 1,524 mm (5 ft) gauge tracks to tow and guide ocean-going vessels through the canal. In Europe, the most extensive installation, using 1,700 electric locos on metre and 600 mm gauge tracks to haul barges, operated alongside French inland waterways between Basel on the Swiss frontier and Dunkerque on the English Channel except for a few short breaks, reaching its maximum extent in 1949. *See also* Ship rly.

Canari (Fr)

Nickname for *Cerdagne* (qv) from the yellow livery used.

C&D (obs)

Collection & Delivery; parcels and freight 'smalls' collected from consignor and delivered after rail transit to the consignee's address, using the rly's road vehicles at each end of the journey.

C&GWUR

Cheltenham & Great Western Union Rly, Swindon–Gloucester–Cheltenham, inc 1836, opened 1841, absorbed by GWR 1844.

C&LR

Cavan & Leitrim Light Rly, (Ire) inc 1883

as Cavan, Leitrim & Roscommon Light Rly, Dromod–Ballinamore–Belturbet and Ballinamore–Arigna, 3 ft gauge, opened 1887, 1888. Renamed C&L Light Rly 1895, part of GSR from 1925. Closed 1959.

C&MR

1. Cork & Muskerry [Light] Rly, inc 1883, 3 ft/914 mm gauge, Cork–Blarney–Donoughmore–Coachford, opened 1887, 1888. Donoughmore–St Annes opened by separate co, worked by C&MR, 1893. Part of GSR from 1925, closed 1934.

2. Campbeltown & Machrihanish Light Rly, 2 ft 3 in/686 mm gauge line between these two places, inc 1905, opened 1906, partly a conversion of 1875 industrial line. No connection with main rly system. Closed 1932.

C&MDR

Cork & Macroom Direct Rly, inc 1861, opened 1866, part of GSR 1925. Regular passenger services ceased 1935, closed 1953.

C&NW

Chicago & North Western Rly Co. Purchased in 1972 by C&NW Transportation Co., which also included CGW (qv).

C&O

Chesapeake & Ohio Rly Co.

C&O Hotel Express

A Caledonian Rly weekend express between Glasgow, Callander and Oban, 1905–14.

C&O Joint

Croydon & Oxted Joint Committee, inc 1878 (part of Croydon, Oxted & East Grinstead Rly) South Croydon–Oxted–Crowhurst Junc East. LB&SCR and SER (later SE&CR) Joint from opening in 1884. Partly built on the abandoned works of the S&SJR (qv).

C&OVR

Cardiff & Ogmore Valley Rly, Llanharan–Blackmill, inc 1873, opened 1876, amalgamated with L&OR 1876.

C&PRR

Chinnor & Princes Risborough Rly. *See* Icknield Line.

C&SLR

City & South London Rly. London tube rly, inc 1884 as City of London & Southwark Subway, name changed 1890. Opened Stockwell to King William Street, City, 1890. Extended from Borough to Moorgate and also from Stockwell to Clapham Common 1900, from Moorgate to Angel 1901, from Angel to Euston 1907. Became part of UERL (qv) from 1912. *See also* Northern Line.

C&T

see D&RGWR.

C&T indicators

Illuminated lineside indicators showing the commencement and termination of temporary speed limits.

C&VBT

Castlederg & Victoria Bridge Tramway (NI), inc 1883, 3 ft/914 mm gauge tramway (4), opened 1884, closed 1933. Ordinary steam rly locos used from 1904.

C&W

Carriage & Wagon [Department/Examiner].

C&W Jc

Cleator & Workington Junction Rly, inc 1876 Cleator/Rowrah to Workington and Linefoot, first section opened 1879, part worked by FR. Part of LM&SR from 1923.

C&WT

Cavehill & Whitewell Tramway, inc 1881, opened 1882, Chichester Park, Belfast to Glengormley. Steam and horse-worked tramway (4). Electrified 1906 and in 1910 became part of the Belfast tramway system. Closed 1949.

Candy butchers (USRS)

Peripatetic salesmen offering confectionery, etc. at stations.

Candy run (USRS)

An easy trip.

Cannonball Express (USRS)

Any fast, high priority train working.

Canopy switch (obs)

A main switch mounted on the ceiling of the roof over the end platform of a tramcar (qv).

Cant

The extent to which an outer running rail is raised above the inner to compensate for some or all of the lateral forces generated as a train passes over a curved track. The acceptable amount in Great Britain is 150 mm although 200 mm has been shown to be feasible. Also known as superelevation. *See also* Cant deficiency, Negative cant.

Cant deficiency limits
The acceptable difference between the actual cant and an equal loading of both rails at a given speed. The maximum cant deficiency in Britain is 110 mm.

Canteen Cowboys (RS)
Men on duty but awaiting work.

Cantonnement (Fr)
A plain block system (qv). *See also Block système*; Lock and block.

Cantrail
The longitudinal member forming the top of the side sections of a coach body which secures the vertical pillars and forms the base of the roof; where body construction is integral, it is the point at which the profile between the body side and roof changes.

Canvasser (obs)
A member of the senior clerical staff assigned to seeking and progressing traffic for a rly undertaking. *See also* Railway Services Representative.

CAP
BR four-car emu sets formed from two 2-HAP units semi-permanently coupled and used for 'Coastway' services east and west of Brighton, 4-CAP.

Capacity Utilization
A term coined in 2003 by the SRA (qv) for elimination or reduction of train services as a means of improving the performance of those services retained.

Capacity Utilization Index (CUI)
The proportion of the theoretical maximum paths (qv) (based on the track and signalling capacity) of a particular route that are actually in use in the current service timetable.

Cape
TC for 'cancel', e.g. for a designated train, cancelled throughout its scheduled journey. This term has now become part of the general rly vocabulary.

Cape gauge
3 ft 6 in/1,067 mm gauge, as used in South Africa (beginning in Cape of Good Hope).

Cape to Cairo Rly
The dream of Cecil Rhodes – a continuous line of rails under the British flag from Capetown to Cairo. By the end of 1928 it had become possible to make this journey by rail and public bus and lake steamer services, but even today there remain two gaps in the rail link, one fairly short (El Shellal (Egypt)–Farriq (Egypt)) and the other lengthy (Waw (Sudan)–Kindu (Zaire)).

CAPI (Fr)
Cantonnement Assisté par l'Informatique, block working over a single line assisted by telephonic block messages displayed and recorded by VDUs.

Capital card
see Travel card.

Capitals Limited
An express between London (Kings Cross) and Edinburgh introduced 1949, renamed The Elizabethan (qv), 1953.

Capitals Mail
TPO (qv) London–Edinburgh, 1994.

Capitals United Express
An express between London (Paddington) and Cardiff, so named 1956, name dropped 1965.

Capitole
A First class only express between Paris and Toulouse, introduced 1960, a *TEE* 1970–84. The first European express timed at 200 km/h (from 1967). Name ceased to be used 1991.

Capitol Limited
A B&O express between Washington, New York and Chicago, introduced 1923. An Amtrak service since 1971.

Capo Stazione (It)
An official in red-topped cap who is equipped with a green baton (green light at night), responsible for controlling entry of trains to a station and allowing trains to continue to the next booked stop. His office is usually located on the main station platform, or at large stations in a separate building occupied by the signalling installation; in busy locations he has assistants who wear and carry similar badges of authority.

Captain (USRS)

A train conductor (*3*) (qv). *See also* Train captain.

Captain Hornblower (RS)(obs)

A driver using whistle excessively. *See also* Bugler.

Capuchon

A raised lip at front of a steam loco chimney intended to prevent down draught and to deflect exhaust steam and smoke, lifting it clear of the front windows of the driving cab. In France the term denotes the whole cap of the chimney and the projection is known as *la visière*.

Capuchon

CAR

1. Committee of Alpine Railways, formed 1993 to coordinate plans, briefing and lobbying in European Community and development of end-to-end route management of railways through the Alps. Members provided by the rly undertakings of France, Germany, Italy, Austria and Switzerland.

2. Central Argentine Rly; *Ferrocarril Central Argentino*, the second-largest British-owned rly in Argentina, inc 1864, first section opened 1864, 5 ft 6 in gauge. Acquired by Argentine Government 1948 and renamed *FC Nacional General Bartolomé Mitre*; 3,941 route miles (6,342 km) at that time.

Car (US)

Term for any passenger or freight rail vehicle, adopted in UK, from early 1900s, at first mainly for electric rly passenger coaches. Also used in UK from *c.* 1895 as an abbreviated term for tramcar (qv), and always used of Pullman cars (*see* Pullman). Frequently used also in UK for catering and other special types of passenger vehicle, e.g. restaurant car, dining car, tea car, sleeping car, observation car (qv).*See also* Cars.

Carbarn (US)

Tram/interurban shed or depot.

Car carrier

Train carrying motorists and their cars, later known as Motorail (qv).

Cardeans (RS)

Caledonian Rly 4–6–0 locos.

Cardiff Rlys/Cardiff Railway Co.

A TOU (qv), 1994, became TOC (*2*) (qv), 1996, operating the same Cardiff Valleys services under the brand name Valley Lines (qv). Became Wales & Borders Railways TOC (*2*) (qv) 2001.

Carfit (TC)

Carriage truck (qv).

Cargo AG (Ger)

DBAG (qv) freight sector, reorganized as a stand-alone business, 1996. *See* Railion.

Cargospeed

A road/rail intermodal system, introduced 2004, using specially designed bogie well wagons (qv) in fixed sets of 30 or 40 to carry road trucks or trailers which can be transferred to or from road level by hydraulic lifting devices positioned between rail tracks in unloading/loading areas which raise and swivel the customized interiors of each wagon to load or unload the road vehicles. The whole train can thus be emptied or loaded in a short time.

Car hop (USRS)

A brakeman (qv).

Car knocker (USRS)

A carriage and wagon fitter.

Carline

1. Transverse members supporting the roof of a wagon or car.

2. An iron strut following the roof profile, fitted to the clerestory (qv) of an open saloon and bolted to the cantrails (qv), to add rigidity and reduce roof sag.

Carman

1. (US) A fitter who maintains rolling stock.

2. (obs) A driver of a horse-drawn van delivering/collecting goods from/to rly stations or depots. The term persisted into the motorized era, not falling out of use until the 1960s.

Car mile
A measurement unit equalling one car, loaded or empty, moved over one mile of track.

Carmyllie Rly
Originally a private mineral line from Elliot Junc to Carmyllie opened 1854 and worked by SNER (qv). Absorbed by SNER 1865, LRO (qv) 1898. Passenger service from 1 February 1900 to 30 November 1929. Freight services ceased 19 May 1965.

Carp
A 27-ton ballast wagon with drop sides used by engineers.

Carpati Pullman Express
A *CIWL* express between Bucharest and Brasov, 1929–31.

Carré (Fr)
A home signal protecting a station or junction. From *un carré*, a square, this being the shape of the original signal used, which turned edge-on for clear.

Carriage
Although some consider it the preferred term, in rly terminology 'carriage' remains interchangeable with 'coach' (qv), except on the London Underground and some other electrified rlys, where the US 'car' is well-established. In common parlance, 'carriage' is often used to signify a section of a coach or a compartment. *See also* Car; Cars.

Carriage dock
A short platform with an end ramp to road level abutting on to a dead-end siding and designed to facilitate loading of road and military vehicles on to rly flat wagons or end-door vans.

Carriage key
A universal socket-end key for locking and unlocking doors of passenger coaches.

Carriage lines
Tracks used solely or mainly for movement of ECS (qv) to and from large passenger stations.

Carriage train (NZ)
A loco-hauled passenger train, as distinct from railcar/s.

Carriage truck (obs)
A flat open wagon designed to convey private horse carriages or motor cars in passenger trains.

Carriage van (obs)
A van provided to convey the more valuable private horse-drawn road carriages and (later) motor cars, usually attached to a passenger train.

Carry a white feather, to (RS)
see White feather.

Carry green, to (USRS)
To run under green flags (day) and green lights (night), indicating that a second part of the train is following immediately behind.

Carry On
A staff newspaper issued by LM&SR (qv), published October 1939–December 1947, replacing *LMS Railway Magazine* (qv).

Carry the banner, to (USRS)
To use flags for signalling (usually applied to brakeman).

Carry the mail, to (USRS)
To bring train orders (qv).

Carry white, to (USRS)
To run under white flags (day) and white lights (night), indicating that the train is an extra working.

Cars
Term used by LT&SR and GER to denote a train of ECS (qv).

Car Sleeper Limited
A summer express with accommodation for cars and their passengers, between London (Kings Cross) and Perth, introduced 1955. The first BR service of this kind. Subsequently many other similar services were added under the brand name Motorail (qv).

Cart (RS)(obs)
A steam loco (mainly used on the GER), thus 'an old cart' was a derogatory term for a loco in poor working order.

Cartage (obs)
The transport of goods, parcels, etc., using the rly's own road vehicles for collection and for delivery at each end of the rail transit; also use of rly road vehicles between rly stations/depots in large towns and cities. *See also* C&D.

Carte Orange (Fr)
Orange Card, a period ticket introduced in Paris in July 1975, allowing unlimited travel on all forms of public transport in one or more of a series of concentric zones covering

the urban and suburban areas. The inspiration for London's Travel Card (qv).

Cartic

A BR articulated wagon for transporting motor cars in quantity. Cartic 4s, introduced in 1964, carry up to thirty-four cars on two decks.

Car-tink/tonk (USRS)

A carriage & wagon inspector.

Car toad (USRS)

A carriage & wagon fitter or carman (qv).

Cartruck (TC)

Carriage truck (qv).

Car whack (USRS)

A carman (qv).

Cascade

1. TC for 'rearrange timings'.
2. The process which follows the injection of new rolling stock on to the rly, allowing older but still serviceable stock to be moved 'down' to other duties and in turn, at the bottom of the 'cascade', the withdrawal from service of outdated and worn out stock. Also used for a similar process with other items such as rails.
3. (obs) A method of controlling polyphase electric traction motors.

Casey Jones

John Luther Jones, a loco driver on the Illinois Central RR (US) who was killed in a head-on collision between his Cannonball Express and a freight train on 30 April 1900. Although his fireman jumped clear, Jones stayed on to sound his whistle, giving the crew of the freight time to escape. His sacrifice was commemorated in a folk song written by the black loco cleaner Wallace Saunders. 'Casey Jones' was then adopted to describe any loco driver in the US.

Casseyway (obs)

A Scottish term for waggonway/tramroad. Derived from 'causeway'.

Castle (USRS) (obs)

A rly station.

Castleman's Corkscrew/Snake

The Southampton & Dorchester Rly, inc 1845, opened 1847, part of L&SWR 1848. From its sinuous course through the New Forest to avoid stands of timber and the name of its promoter, a Wimborne solicitor.

CAT

1. Customer Action Teams, groups of specially-trained BR staff assigned to assist passengers en route when train services were seriously disrupted. *See also* CIRT.
2. *Conducion Automatica de Trenes* (Sp), automatic train driving, term for LZB (qv) cab signalling.

Catalan TALGO

Originated as a Geneva–Port Bou (connection to/from Barcelona) diesel service 1955–69. This was replaced by the *Catalan TALGO*, a through service between Geneva and Barcelona, a *TEE*, in 1969. Lost *TEE* status 1982, became EC 1987.

Catch points

Trailing points arranged to derail harmlessly any vehicle running in the wrong direction. Inclines are usually protected in this manner and catch points are an official requirement where the gradient exceeds 1 in 260; a second pair is also required if the gradient is lengthy. A runaway or catch siding may also be provided. They were originally self-acting (to catch vehicles running backwards) and then known as 'runaway catch points', or were worked from a signal box (to catch trains out of control on a falling gradient). *See also* Safety points; Trap points.

Catch the water, to (RS)

The priming of a steam locomotive with excess of water in boiler.

CATE

Computer Assisted Timetable Enquiries; a BR computer system.

Catenary

The supporting catenary wire and droppers or hangers from which the conductor or contact wire of an overhead wire feeder system for electric traction is suspended.

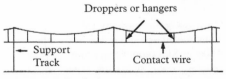

Catenary (side view)

See also Compound catenary; Contact wire; Dropper; OLE; Jumper (5); Knuckle, Stitch wire.

Catfish
A 19-ton hopper ballast wagon used by engineers.

Catford Loop
Nunhead–Catford–Shortlands [London].

Cathcart Circle
Glasgow (Central)–Langside–Cathcart–Glasgow (Central).

Cathedrals (RS)
Electrical substations erected by the L&SWR and SR for direct current electrification schemes. From their lofty appearance and tall arched windows.

Cathedrals Express
A service between London (Paddington), Oxford, Worcester and Hereford, introduced 1957. Name dropped 1965, re-introduced 1985.

Cat's eyes (RS)
A calling-on signal (qv) or the proceed aspect of a position light signal (qv).

Cattle arch/creep
A form of occupation crossing (qv), a subway provided beneath a rly when the fields of a farm are severed by its construction.

Cattle box
A van designed to convey valuable prize cattle, formerly often marshalled into passenger trains.

Cattle guard
Triangular-section timbers or similar deterrent devices installed either side of level crossings to discourage animals or humans from wandering onto the rly.

Caught for a job (LTRS)
Spare trainmen given running work to do.

Cauliflowers (RS)
LNWR Webb 0–6–0 locos. From the L&NWR crest on the wheel splashers which was thought to bear a resemblance to the vegetable.

Caution indication/signal
A distant signal (qv) in the horizontal position (if a semaphore signal (qv)) or showing an orange/yellow aspect (if a colour light (qv)).

CB&PR
Cork, Blackrock & Passage Rly, (Ire), inc 1846 as Cork, Blackrock, Passage & Monkstown Rly, opened Cork to Passage 1850. Converted from 5 ft 3 in/1,600 mm to 3 ft/914 mm gauge 1900–4 and extended to Crosshaven. Part of GSR 1925. Closed 1932.

CB&Q
Chicago, Burlington & Quincy RR. Co. *See also* Burlington; Q, The.

CB&SCR
Cork, Bandon & South Coast Rly, (Ire), Cork to Bantry, branches to Baltimore, Clonakilty, Courtmacsherry and Kinsale. Inc 1845 as Cork & Bandon Rly, first section opened 1851. Part of GSR 1925.

CBI
Computer-Based Interlocking. A signalling system still under development in 2005.

C-board
A board carrying the letter 'C' (for 'Commencement') erected at the beginning of a portion of line subject to a temporary speed restriction. To avoid misunderstanding, these boards now carry a figure showing the maximum permitted speed.

CB Rail
A ROSCO (qv) formed 2004 by Babcock & Brown and the Bank of Scotland to lease out locos and passenger stock in the European rail market.

CBTU
Companhia Brasileira de Trens Urbanos; a subsidiary of *RFFSA* (qv) operating metros (qv) and suburban rlys in Brazilian towns and cities, transferred to local State Government control 1988.

CCC
Cincinnati Car Co., Cincinnati, Ohio, US, established 1903. Builders of cars for tramways (*3*) and interurbans. Ceased production 1931.

CCCC
Cross Channel Catering Company, formed 1992 by IC (*1*), *CIWL* and Belgian Airlines (Sabena) to provide on-board catering for international rail services using the Channel Tunnel.

CCD
Coal Concentration Depot, a BR development, combining traffic formerly handled at numerous small freight yards.

CCE
Chief Civil Engineer.

CCE&HR
Charing Cross, Euston & Hampstead Rly. London tube rly inc 1892, opened Charing Cross (SER) to Golders Green and Highgate (now Archway) 1907. Part of LER (qv) from 1910. *See also* Northern Line.

CCF
Canadian Car & Foundry Co., Montreal, established 1909, manufacturers of all types of rly, tramway and interurban equipment.

CCFE (Fr)
Communauté Chemins de Fer Européens, Community of European Rlys.

CCSC
Carlisle Citadel Station Committee, formed 1857. The station and approaches north and south were the joint property of CR (*1*) and L&NWR. The NER, M&CR, G&SWR, NBR and Midland were tenants. The L&NER and LM&SR shared ownership 1923–47.

CCT
1. (obs) Covered Carriage Truck, BR; similar to PMV, with end doors and end flaps so that motor cars could be driven on board. Non-gangwayed.
2. Cook's Continental Timetable *see* Cook's Timetables.

CD
1. (obs) Carriage department.
2. *Česky Drāhy*; Czech Republic Rlys, 1993, 9,454 km, mostly standard gauge; formed following the 1992 creation of the state of Slovakia (*see* ZSR).
3. Close doors (seen on signs at stations).

CDL
Central Door Locking (qv).

CDR (obs)
Cheap Day Return fare or ticket.

CDRJC
County Donegal Railways Joint Committee, Londonderry–Strabane–Donegal–Killybegs/Ballyshannon, with branches to Glenties and Letterkenny. Opened 1863 as Finn Valley Rly,

5 ft 3 in/1,600 mm gauge, Strabane–Stranorlar. West Donegal Rly, Stranorlar–Donegal, inc 1879, 3 ft/914 mm gauge, opened 1889. Both rlys amalgamated as Donegal Rly 1892. System completed and Finn Valley line converted to 3 ft/914 mm gauge 1893–1905. Taken over by GNR (I) and Midland Rly of England 1906 and CDRJC formed. Strabane–Londonderry was wholly owned by Midland but worked by Joint Committee. Midland interests passed to LM&SR 1923. CDRJC also worked the Strabane & Letterkenny Rly, opened 1909. All CDRJC-worked lines were closed 1947–59.

CE
Country end (qv).

CEAR
Central East African Railways; privatized operation of the state-owned rly system in Malawi from 1999, a joint venture by RDC (qv), CFM (qv) and local investors. Malawi has 789 km of 1,067 mm gauge and its rlys are physically connected to those of Mozambique.

CEH
Conférence Européenne des Horaires; European Timetable Conference, established at Berne, 1872.

Ceinture, Grande, la
Outer belt line around Paris, linking all radial trunk lines.

Ceinture, Petite, la
Inner belt line around the centre of Paris. Now exists only in part.

CEJ
Clifton Extension Joint Rly; *see* BPR&P.

CEL
Chemins de Fer de l'Etat Libanais; State Rlys of Lebanon, 222 km connected to Syrian Rlys via Tripoli (*see* CFS). Former link to Haifa (Israel) severed by political problems.

CEM
Component Exchange Maintenance (BR).

CEMT
Conférence Européenne des Ministres des Transports; Conference of European Ministers of Transport, established at Paris, 1953.

CEN
Comité Européen de Normalisation. The EC body based in Brussels responsible for formulating and issuing standards which apply across the EU.

Cenotaph (RS)(obs)
A mechanical coaling plant in a steam loco depot. From the shape, like a giant version of the famous London war memorial.

Centenary stock
GWR (qv) sets for the Cornish Riviera Express (qv) placed in service in 1935, the centenary year of the Act authorizing the first section of the GWR, from London to Bristol.

Centenary, The
LM&SR restaurant car express London (Euston)–Birmingham (New Street), 1938.

Centipede (US)
1. A steam loco with 2–12–0 wheel arrangement.
2. (USRS) Baldwin 2D+D2 locos of 1945–8 from their many equal-sized wheels.

Central/Central London
see CLR.

Central door locking
A safety system of secondary door locking under the control of the guard/conductor of the train, which prevents passengers from opening manually operated doors (slam doors) while a train is in motion or temporarily stopped between stations; fitted by BR 1993–5.

Central Rly
see CRG.

Central Trains Ltd
A TOU (qv), 1994. A TOC (2) (qv), 1997, operating services within the area bounded by: Pwllheli–Aberystwyth–Hereford–Cardiff–Leamington Spa–Coventry–Leicester–Cambridge–Norwich–Skegness–Cleethorpes–Doncaster–Sheffield–Manchester–Liverpool–Chester. Franchise expired 2006. Distributed between Silverlink, Chiltern, Virgin Cross Country, Midland Mainline and Northern (all qv).

Central Wales
Central Wales Rly, inc 1859, Llandrindod Wells–Craven Arms, opened 1865, part of L&NWR 1868, LM&SR 1923. Also Central

Wales Extension Rly, Llandrindod Wells–Llandovery, inc 1860, opened 1866, 1867, 1868, part of L&NWR 1868, LM&SR 1923. *See also* Heart of Wales Line.

Central Wales Line
Shrewsbury–Craven Arms–Llandrindod Wells–Llanelly–[Swansea].

Centre bound
A sleeper supported by the ballast (qv) only at its centre rather than across its full width. *See also* Sleeper (1).

Centre, The (RS) (obs)
BRB headquarters.

Centre the key, to (LTRS)
To move the reverser key of an electric train into the central or 'off' position (this is against the rules when coasting).

Centre throw
The horizontal displacement of the centre of a truck (qv) relative to the centre line of the track as a rail vehicle passes round a curve.

Centro
The brand name of West Midlands Passenger Transport Executive, adopted 1990.

CEP
BR four-car all-steel Corridor emu sets with Electro-Pneumatic brakes, of 1956 and 1958–9; two motor brake Second/Standard class, one Second/Standard trailer and one composite trailer, 4-CEP.

CER
Community of European Rlys: a grouping of some 22 national rly undertakings. The UK is represented by Network Rail (qv) and ATOC (qv).

Cerdagne, la ligne de (Fr)
La Tour de Carol–Perpignan. *See also Canari.* Also called *le Métro des Pyrénées* and *le Petit Train Jaune.*

CERTS (obs)
Cheap Evening Return Tickets, LT.

Cess
The space between the base of the ballast (qv) shoulder and the toe of a cutting slope; or between it and the top of an embankment slope; or between it and the unworked surface when the line is at ground level. That part of the cess within three metres of the outermost rail is in the area known as 'On or near the line' (qv).

Cess strip
A strip of land 2.5–3 m wide alongside and beyond the cess (qv).

CET
Casualty Evacuation Train (WW2 in UK). *See also* Ambulance train; Hospital train.

Cévenol
A diesel railcar service between Clermont Ferrand and Marseilles, introduced 1955. 'Panoramique' railcars with Vistadome (qv) from 1959, name transferred to Paris–Clermont Ferrand–Marseilles service 1979.

CFA
1. *Chemins de Fer Algériens*; formed 1933, an amalgamation of the existing Algerian State Rlys and the *PLM* (qv) system in that country. *See also SNCFA*.
2. *Caminhos de Ferro de Angola*; Angola Rlys, formed 1975 of *CFL* (qv), Benguela Rly (qv), Namibe and Amboim Rlys; 2,761 km, mostly 1,067 mm gauge.

CFC
Chemin de Fer de la Corse; Corsican Rlys. 232 km metre gauge.

CFD (Fr)
Chemin de Fer Départementale; Departmental Railway, a secondary rly (qv), authorized and largely financed by the *départment* (local authority). Usually, but not necessarily, a light rly.

CFDA
Chemin de Fer Ottoman d'Anatolie inc 1889, Haydarpasa (opposite Istanbul)–Ankara opened 1893, and Eskesehir–Konya 1896, the first substantial lengths of main line in Asiatic Turkey. Konya was to be the starting point of the Baghdad Rly (qv).

CFE (Fr)
Chemin de Fer Économique; term for a light rly.

CFF
Chemins de Fer Fédéraux Suisses; Swiss Federal Rlys. Also known as SBB, SFF, and FFS (qv). 2,983 km, almost all electrified.

CfIT
Commission for Integrated Transport, an independent body formed 1999 to advise the government on the implementation of an integrated transport policy.

CFL
1. *Société Nationale des Chemins de Fer Luxembourgeois*; Luxembourg National Rlys Authority.
2. *Caminhos de Ferro de Luanda*; Luanda–Malange and branch to Dondo, Angola, became part of *CFA* (qv) 1975.

CFM
1. *Caminhos de Ferro de Moçambique*; Mozambique Rlys, 3,123 km, mainly 1,067mm gauge with international links to South Africa, Swaziland, Zimbabwe and Malawi.
2. *Caile Ferate Moldova*; Moldovan Rlys, 1,520 mm gauge.

CFR
Câile Ferate Romane; Roumanian State Rlys.

CfRS
Centre for Rail Skills, established 2003; an independent company formed by the rail industry in Great Britain.

CFS
Chemins de Fer Syriens; Syrian Rlys, 2,743 km; physically connected to rlys of Turkey, Lebanon and Iraq (*see* Baghdad Rly). Also a 1,050 mm gauge line from Damascus to Amman (Jordan) (*see* Hedjaz Rly).

CFTA
Compagnie Générale des Chemins de Fer et Transports d'Automobiles. A company operating various minor rlys, road services, etc. on behalf of the *SNCF* (qv).

CGC (Fr)
Compagnie Générale de Construction.

CGR
Cape Government Rlys 1863–1910, 1,067mm gauge. Became part of SAR[&H] (qv).

CGTC
Carlisle Goods Traffic Committee, formed 1873 with representatives of CR (*1*), L&NWR, Midland and G&SWR to manage and control the jointly owned goods loop from south of Citadel station, Carlisle, to Caldew and Willowholme Juncs. LM&SR was sole owner from 1923.

CGW (US)
Chicago Great Western RR Co.

CH
UIC (qv) code for Hellenic [Greek] State Rlys, formed 1962, 2,479 km; standard, metre and 750 mm gauge. *See also OSE*.

Chafer
GWR TC for invalid coach.
Chain boy (obs)
A youth who led horses from one end of a tramcar (qv) to the other at a terminus.
Chain gang (USRS)
A relief train crew.
Chain road (obs)
A rly laid with rails one chain (66 ft/20.12m) long instead of the shorter lengths previously used.
Chair
A cast iron fitting fastened to a sleeper which supports bullhead (qv) rail secured in it by a key (qv).

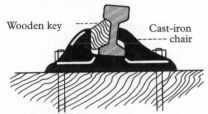

Wooden key   Cast-iron chair

Chair car (US)
Pullman (qv) type coach.
Chair, in the (RS)
At the controls of a loco.
Chair shuffle
Inadequately fastened chairs (qv) moving sideways under the action of traffic.
Chaix
The French equivalent of 'Bradshaw' (qv), *l'Indicateur Chaix*, showing the times of all trains running in France. First published April 1847. Ceased publication 1976. By the 1930s, the style of *Chaix* was standard for all French rly timetable matter and the train service posters displayed at stations were enlarged photographic reproductions of pages in the main volume. Named after the *Imprimerie Chaix*, its printers and publishers.
Chaldron [wagon] (obs)
An open wagon design dating from the late eighteenth century, developed for use at collieries in Northumberland and Durham and fitted with low dumb buffers (qv). Such wagons were still to be seen on private colliery lines to shipping staithes as late as the 1920s. Named after their capacity (one chaldron = 25½ cwt. (1 tonne 295.4kg)).

Challenger (US)
A steam loco with 4–6–6–4 wheel arrangement.
Challengers
Virgin Cross Country 2001 rebranding of ex-BR (1)(qv) HST (qv) redesignated Class 255s.
Challenger, The
Chicago–Los Angeles service introduced 1954; 2,301 miles in 39 h 30 min.
Chamber maid (USRS)
A fitter at a local depot.
Champs Elysées
Paris–Lausanne *TGV*, introduced 1984.
Change pit (obs)
see Ploughshifts.
Channel trains (obs)
BR term adopted in 1989 for trains connecting with cross-Channel marine services via Dover, Folkestone, Newhaven and Harwich.
Chaos in Excelsis (obs)
Nickname for CIE (qv).
Chariot
1. (RS)(obs) A GWR shunters' wagon.
2. (USRS) A caboose (qv).
Charlies (RS)
SR Bulleid Q1 0–6–0 locos.
Charnwood Forest
Charnwood Forest Rly, Hugglescote to Loughborough (Derby Rd), partly on site of a canal and canal tramway (1) opened 1794, closed 1799; inc 1874, opened 1883, worked by L&NWR, part of LM&SR 1923.
Charter/ed train/s
A guaranteed excursion (qv) or rail tour with seats pre-booked and payment assured. *See also* Awayday; Excursion [trains]; Special traffic.
Chartex
TC for chartered excursion train.
Chaser (RS)(obs)
Rly worker who braked wagons being shunted in a marshalling yard.
Chase red, to (USRS)
To go to the rear of a train stopped on the running line with a red flag or light to protect it.
Chasse-boeuf (Fr)
Cow-catcher (qv). *See also Chasse-pierre.*

Chasse-pierre (Fr)
Device attached to the front of a loco to deflect large stones from the track, a form of cow-catcher (qv).

Chatham, The
LC&DR or SE&CR (qv).

Chat Moss Line
Manchester–St Helen's Junction–Liverpool.

Cheap, The (RS)(obs)
A parliamentary train (qv).

Check down, to (LTRS)
To reduce speed.

Checking back (LTRS)
Blocking back (qv).

Check rail
An additional rail placed inside and parallel to running rails to guide wheel flanges at road and rail crossings and also on curves, viaducts, bridges, etc. to hold wheels to rails. *See also* Guard rail.

Check system (US)
Method of handling rly passengers' luggage. *See also* Baggage master; Transfer agent.

Cheddar Valley Branch
Yatton–Wells.

Chef du Train (Fr)
Official in charge of a train, also used for *CIWL* (qv) head conductor in charge of sleeping cars.

Cheltenham Flyer
An express between London (Paddington) and Cheltenham Spa, introduced 1923. The name never enjoyed full official status, but appeared on loco headboards from 1931. This train soon became the fastest regular service in Britain and by 1931 was officially claimed by the GWR as 'The World's Fastest Train', attaining speeds of around 90 mph at times. A year later, the average booked speed between Swindon and Paddington was raised to 71.35 mph. In 1933 its record was taken by the *Fliegende Hamburger* (qv).

Cheltenham Spa Express
A BR express between London (Paddington) and Cheltenham Spa, introduced 1956, name dropped 1973. Name revived 1985.

Chemin de fer Americain (Fr)(obs)
Tramway (*3*). By the 1870s it had been replaced by the English word.

Chemin de fer secondaire (Fr)
Secondary rly (qv).

Chemin de fer vicinal (Fr)
Local light rly line/lines, usually narrow gauge. The term is also used in Belgium and Switzerland.

Cheminots (Fr)
Rly workers.

Cherries (LTRS)
Current rail gap indicators.

Cherry picker (USRS)
A pointsman. From the red lights on his signals.

Cherwell Valley Line
Leamington–Banbury.

Chesapeake (US)
A steam loco with 2–8–8–2 wheel arrangement. First used on the C&O (qv).

Chessie
Nickname for the C&O (qv).

Chicago Bears (RS)
BR class 59 3,300 hp diesel-electric freight locos owned by Foster Yeoman, National Power and ARC. Built by General Motors at La Grange, Illinois, USA, and London, Ontario.

Chicane (Fr)
Catch points (qv).

Chicken coop (RS)
Class 153.

Chief, The
An express running daily between Los Angeles and Chicago, introduced 1926. 50 h 25 min in 1936. Ceased 1967. *See also* Super Chief.

Children's Railways
Miniature rlys (qv) established in communist countries, to serve the dual purpose of providing amusement and serious training for a rly career.

Child's control portion
Section of an Edmondson ticket (qv) which is detached and separately accounted for when a ticket is issued for a child at a reduced fare.

Chiltern Lines/Trains/Rlys
NSE brand name introduced 1989 for London (Marylebone)–Aylesbury/High Wycombe and Banbury [Birmingham] dmu services. Chiltern Rlys Co. Ltd. TOU (qv), 1994. A TOC (*2*), 1966.

Chimney petticoat
see Petticoat.
Chinese Fours (RS)
BR Class 4 2–6–0 freight locos.
Chinese labour (RS)(obs)
Part-time luggage porters at large stations, making a living solely from gratuities.
Chintz
GWR TC for family saloon.
Chip bin (RS)
A lineside ballast container.
Chippies (USRS)
Narrow gauge rolling stock.
Chipstead Valley
Chipstead Valley Rly, Purley to Tadworth, inc 1893, opened 1897, 1900, part of SER from 1899.
Chopin
A Warsaw–Vienna service with seasonal through coaches to and from Moscow, introduced 1961.
Chopper
1. A thyristor, used in electric train control, which 'chops' electric current, providing variable ac voltage by interrupting the fixed voltage supply in a controlled manner.
2. (USRS) Inspector.
Choppers (RS)
1. L&NWR Webb 4 ft 6 in 2–4–2T, some of which were fitted with 'chopper valves' in the smokebox to divert the exhaust into the side tanks to condense it when working through London Underground tunnels.
2. BR diesel locos class 20, from a sound effect resembling the intrusive row created by helicopters.
Christmas card (LT rhyming S)
A guard.
Christmas tree (RS)
1. Colour light signals on a gantry.
2. A loco or vehicle pillaged of parts or elements (i.e. cannibalized) to keep others of same type in service.
Chub
1. GWR TC for an eight-wheel Third class saloon with table and end compartment.
2. 25-ton ballast wagon used by engineers.

Chunnel
The Channel Tunnel.
Churchills (RS)
1. French rlymen's term for GWR Dean Goods locos imported into France during WW2.
2. LM&SR class 8F 2–8–0s used overseas in WW2.
Church interval
The suspension of certain London local train services for 2–3 hours during Sunday morning church services, a practice first adopted by the London & Greenwich Rly in 1836, with the intention that employees should attend church. The custom was broken by the CLR from its opening in 1900 but did not finally disappear from all London lines until 1926.
Churnet Valley Line
North Rode–Leek–Rocester.
CIE
Córas Iompair Eireann; Transport Company of Ireland, formed 1945, assuming responsibility for managing and operating rlys in the Republic of Ireland. The rlys passed to *IE* (qv) in 1986 but *CIE* continues as a government-owned co., owning IE, Dublin Bus and other transport groups.
CIG
BR (S) four-car emu sets of 1964–72 for London–Brighton services with Corridor throughout and Interconnecting Gangway. Two driving trailer composites, one trailer Second/Standard class and one non-driving motor brake Second/Standard, 4-CIG.
CIM
Convention Internationale concernant le transport des Marchandises par chemins de fer; international convention regulating rly freight transport, established at Berne, 1890.
Cinder cruncher (USRS)
A pointsman.
Cinder dick (USRS)
A rly policeman.
Cinderella (RS)
An electric train or loco on a third or fourth rail system (qv) which has discarded a current-collecting shoe.

Cinderella's coach (RS)
A special coach with an observation platform, used by District Engineers and other senior officers.

Cinder snapper (USRS)
Brakesman. Also a passenger riding on the open end platform of a passenger coach.

CIRAS
Confidential Incident Reporting & Analysis System, by which staff of Network Rail (qv) and staff of maintenance contractors and sub-contractors can telephone anonymously to report on incidents and circumstances affecting safety, rogue operators working on the railway and unsafe operating procedures.

Circle/Circle Line
see Inner Circle.

Circus (USRS)
A rly.

Circus train
A train composed of vehicles suitable for carrying all the animals, equipment, staff, performers, etc. of a circus, particularly in North America.

CIRT
Critical Incidents Response Team formed by GNER (qv) and Arriva Trains Northern 2003 to be mobilized in the event of a serious incident. *See also* CAT (1).

CIS
Customer Information Systems. Displays at stations showing passengers the expected train arrival and departure times, destinations and station calls. *See also* LICC.

Cisalpin
TEE Paris–Milan, introduced 1961, ceased 1984. Name used for Paris–Lausanne TGV 1984 and connecting EC Geneva–Milan, 1987.

Cisalpino
Dual-voltage ETR470 tilting trains used on international services between Italy and Switzerland from 1996.

Cistern wagon
British Army term for tank wagon (qv) to avoid confusion with a wagon for transporting armoured fighting vehicles.

CIT
1. *Comité Internationale des Transports par chemins de fer*; international committee for transport by rly, established at Berne, 1902.
2. SR six-car emu sets 1933, for London Bridge–Brighton commuter services with one Pullman car and a high proportion of First Class accommodation, 6-CIT.
3. *Compagnia Italia Turismo*; Italian Tourism Co., owned by *FS* (qv).
4. Chartered Institute of Transport. *See* IofL&T.

City-Bahn (Ger)
see CB.

City Express
An express between London (Holborn Viaduct) and Ramsgate, introduced 1896. To and from Cannon St. 1904, ceased 1905. In 1921–7 the name was used for various services between London and Ramsgate, some with Pullman cars.

City Limited
Businessmen's express between Brighton and London Bridge, introduced 1921, name dropped 1934.

Cityrail
Brand name of the urban/suburban rail network in Sydney, Australia.

City to City
An L&NWR service for businessmen between London (Broad St.) and Birmingham (New St.), 1910–14. A typist was available on the train.

City Widened Lines
A second pair of tracks between Kings Cross and Moorgate, Metropolitan Rly (London), mostly used by passenger and freight services to and from Midland Rly and GNR (LM&SR and L&NER from 1923–47, then BR (M) and BR (E)). Used by Thameslink (qv) cross-London passenger services since 1988.

CIV
Convention Internationale concernant le transport des Voyageurs et des bagages par chemins de fer; international convention regulating transport of passengers and luggage by rail, established at Berne, 1923.

Civils (RS)
Engineers responsible for rly structures as

distinct from those involved with permanent way and signalling.

CIWL

Compagnie Internationale des Wagons-Lits; International Sleeping Car Company, founded 1876, '*et des Grands Express Européens*' added to title 1883. Title altered to *CIWL et du Tourisme* (*CIWLT*) in 1967. Until 1970–1 *CIWL* operated and staffed international sleeping, dining and Pullman car services in Europe, Asia and Africa (and Russia until 1917). The last Pullman service on the European mainland (Milan–Rome) ran in 1971. National sleeping car and on-train catering services continue in Europe and Morocco as well as hotel and catering services at airports, etc. 'Discretion is the better part of *Wagons-Lits*' – Robertson Hare in the 1932 film *Rome Express*.

CK (obs)

BR Corridor Composite Compartment coach.

CK&PR

Cockermouth, Keswick & Penrith Rly, inc 1861, opened 1864, 1865, worked by L&NWR and S&DR/NER, part of LM&SR 1923.

CKD Praha Tatra

A Czech joint stock company engaged in production, repair, rebuilding and maintenance of rly vehicles and tramcars.

CL (obs)

1. Carted Luggage; system by which luggage brought to a station was carried by rail and then delivered to destination by rly road vehicle.
2. BR composite compartment coach, non-gangwayed, with lavatory reached by a side corridor, this being on opposite sides for each class.

Clactons (RS)

BR class 309 emu; mainly used on London–Clacton services.

Clacton Sunday Pullman

A L&NER service from London (Liverpool St.) to Clacton, introduced 1928.

Clag (RS)

A pronounced display of exhaust steam and smoke by a steam loco or heavy exhaust emission by a diesel loco.

Clam

A 20-ton ballast wagon used by engineers.

Clan Goods (RS)

Highland Rly Cummings 4–6–0 locos.

Clankers (RS)

L&NER K2 2–6–0 locos. From the distinctive noise made by their nickel chrome steel connecting rods.

Clansman

An express between London (Euston), Birmingham and Inverness, introduced 1974. Cut back to Edinburgh 1991. Ceased 1992.

Clarence Rly

Inc 1828, Port Clarence to S&DR at Simpasture, first section opened 1834, absorbed by WHH&R, 1852.

Class

1. A grade of rly passenger accommodation, accessed by corresponding fares and tickets. *See also* Fourth class; Second class; Standard class, Third Class.
2. A category of freight [goods] charged at the same rate. *See* Classification of Goods.
3. An indication of the relative priority to be given to each type of train, the highest being 'Class A' (later 'Class 1'), for the guidance of signallers and other operating staff.
4. A group of locos of identical or similar design.

Classification of Goods (obs)

A standardized system for UK rlys issued by the RCH (qv) 1847–1962, which for charging purposes grouped goods (freight) into five classes initially and 21 eventually.

Class, to (RS)

The train spotter's triumph – to see and note all the locos in a particular class.

Class 1 railroads (US)

A classification embracing those major undertakings with operating revenue above a certain minimum level.

Clauds/Claud Hammies (RS)

GER 4–4–0 locos, one of which was named after Lord Claud Hamilton, GER chairman from 1893 to 1923. L&NER class D15/16. *See also* Super Clauds.

Clay & Knocker
Nickname for LD&ECR.

Clay hoods (obs)
Open wagons with tarpaulins supported by a central rail, formerly used for carrying china clay.

Clayliner
A BR wagon designed for carriage of china clay, replacing clay hoods (qv) and based on MGR (qv) pattern.

Clayton
Clayton Wagons Ltd, Lincoln, later Clayton Equipment Co., manufacturing locos and railcars.

Claytons (RS)
BR class 17 900hp centre cab diesel locos built by Clayton.

CLC
Cheshire Lines Committee, Liverpool/ Southport–Warrington–Manchester; Glazebrook–Baguley–Stockport–Godley Junc; Altrincham–Northwich–Chester. Constituted 1865, with GNR and MS&LR as owners. Midland became third partner in 1866. LM&SR and L&NER joint 1923–47. First section opened 1862. The CLC possessed passenger and freight stock, but the owning companies supplied locos.

Clearance/depression bar
A bar fixed on track at junctions or platforms, interlocked to signals, which cannot be put to 'off' until the bar is lifted, thus ensuring no vehicles are present, since the bar cannot be raised when a vehicle is on it. These bars are used to define the fouling point between diverging tracks. *See also* Fouling bar; Fouling point.

Clearance card (US)
An authority to operate on the main line.

Clearance distance
see Clearing point.

Clearance gauge
Same as structure gauge (qv).

Clearing a signal
Action taken by a signalman to alter signal aspect from danger to clear.

Clearing House
see RCH.

Clearing point
In absolute block working, the point ahead of the first stop signal/outer home signal, usually a quarter of a mile distant, to which the line must be clear of obstruction before a signalman can accept a train from the box in the rear.

Clear pop (RS)
A clear signal, i.e. one showing 'off' indication.

Clear signal
A signal on the 'off' position or aspect showing green, indicating it is safe to proceed.

Clee Hill
Ludlow & Clee Hill Rly, inc 1861, Ludlow–Clee Hill (Corley), including 1 m rope incline, opened 1864, worked by L&NWR and GWR from 1877, vested in L&NWR and GWR 1893. Used only as a mineral line. Incline closed 1960, remainder closed 1962.

Clé de Berne (Fr)
Berne Key (qv).

Cleminson (obs)
Running gear for a 6-wheel carriage or wagon designed and patented by the engineer of that name.

Clerestory
A raised central section of a coach roof fitted with ventilators and deck lights, intended to give extra daylight and ventilation.

Cleveland Executive
An express between London (Kings Cross) and Middlesbrough, introduced 1981, withdrawn 1990.

Clickety, The (RS)
Grimsby & Immingham Electric Rly, GCR/L&NER/BR. From the sound made by its electric cars running at high speed.

Clifton Extension Joint
see BPR&P.

Cliftonville Express
A summer service London (Victoria/Holborn Viaduct)–Ramsgate, 1894 only. Re-introduced 1911, Victoria–Ramsgate, ceased 1915. Re-introduced 1921, name dropped 1927.

Clinker link (RS)(obs)
Men who cleaned out loco fires in loco depots.

Clip basher (RS)
Person who patrols the track to check its

condition, including the state of the clips, the fastenings used to secure flat-bottom rails (qv) to the base plates. *See also* Pandrol clip.

Clipper-shaped
A coach with sides turned inwards below and above the waist (qv), producing the profile reminiscent of a fast sailing ship.

Cloakroom/Cloakroom business
A facility at stations to deposit luggage and other items for a small fee.

Clock (RS)
A loco steam gauge. Hence 'Knock the clock back', to take action to reduce steam pressure.

Clockface service
A regular interval service providing departures from stations at the same minutes past each hour in the same sequence throughout the day (with the possible exception of peak hours). Introduced for the first L&SWR electric services (1915) and subsequently adopted for the SR electric network, and for many BR services. 'People don't like timetables, make it easy for them' – Sir Herbert Walker, general manager L&SWR.

Clock train (RS)(obs)
The LB&SCR 'Southern Belle', from the clocks in its Pullman cars.

Clockwork engines (RS)
Midland Rly 0–6–4T with a motion access aperture in the side tank which suggested the key hole of a toy clockwork engine.

Clockwork Orange (RS)
Glasgow Underground Rly as modernized in 1980. From the novel and film of that title and suggested by the new livery and circular nature of the service.

Clockworks (LTRS)
District Line trains.

Clodhoppers (RS)
LM&SR class 4 MT 2–6–0 locos of 1947.

Clog & Knocker (RS)
GCR, or GCR main line.

Clogging-on (RS)
Fixing chairs (qv) or base plates (qv) on sleepers or on timbers of special work (qv) before placing the sleepers in position.

Clogs on (RS)
A loco or vehicle with flat wheel(s).

Closed block
The normal state of a block section (qv block system) which must be cleared for a train to enter.

Closed line
Strictly the term implies a line which is closed to all normal traffic but retains its tracks and infrastructure.

Close the gate, to (USRS)
To move points back after a train has passed.

Clown (USRS)
A brakeman or switchman.

Clown wagon (USRS)
A caboose (qv).

CLR
1. Central London Rly, a tube rly, inc 1891, opened Bank to Shepherds Bush 1900, extended to Wood Lane 1908, to Liverpool St. 1912. Part of UERL (qv) from 1912.
2. Corringham Light Rly, LRO 1899, Corringham to Coryton (Kynoch Town) and Thames Haven, opened 1901. Closed to passengers 1939, reopened 1945, closed entirely 1952 except for Coryton–Thames Haven section, which was relaid to main line standards and remains in use for oil tanker traffic.
3. Carmyllie Light Rly (qv).

Club (US)
see Brake Club.

Club car (obs)
A special car for men, equipped for service of alcoholic drinks and light refreshments. Cuspidors were placed within convenient range of leather armchairs. Such cars were a regular feature of Pullman accommodation in the US for many years and were also found in British club trains (qv).

Club Train (obs)
A long distance commuter train which included private club cars, in which regular travellers (predominantly if not exclusively male) enjoyed segregation from other passengers and were provided with special facilities such as armchairs, tables, hairdresser/barber, private bar, personal lockers, etc. in return for payment of a premium over the season ticket rate. Until WW2, club train

services operated between Manchester and the North Wales coast, Manchester and the Fylde coast, Manchester and the Lake District, etc.

Club Trains, The

First class supplementary fare services between London and Dover (for Calais and Paris) inspired by the Paris Exhibition of 1889 and operated by the LC&DR, SER and *CIWL*, 1889–93. 'I'm leaving this afternoon by the Club Train' – Mrs Erlynne in Oscar Wilde's play *Lady Windermere's Fan.*

Club winder (USRS)

A brakeman. From brake club (qv).

Clyderail

Brand name for the reopened and electrified Glasgow Central Low Level or Argyle line, Partick to Rutherglen and Cambuslang, linking north and south bank suburban lines, in use from 1979.

Clydesider, The

Glasgow (Queen St.)–Perth–Dundee–Aberdeen service, so named 1992.

CM&DP Light Rly

Cleobury Mortimer & Ditton Priors Light Rly, LRO 1901, opened for passengers and freight 1908, part of GWR, 1922, closed to passengers 1938, completely closed 1965.

CM&EE

Chief Mechanical & Electrical Engineer.

CM&GIR

Croydon, Merstham & Godstone Iron Rly, inc 1803, opened from SIR at Croydon to Merstham only, 1805. Closed *c.* 1842.

CME

Chief Mechanical Engineer.

CMP

Chemin de Fer Métropolitain de Paris; Paris Métro or underground rlys. First section opened 1900. Part of *STCRP* (qv) from 1942.

CMR

Cornwall Minerals Rly, Newquay to Fowey and branches, inc 1873, and included existing tramways (*1*) dating from 1847, which were to be converted to rlys. First section opened 1874, worked by GWR from 1877. Absorbed Lostwithiel & Fowey Rly (opened 1869) from 1892. L&FR was closed in 1880 and reopened by GWR 1895. CMR became part of GWR from 1896.

CNR

Canadian National Rlys, inc 1919, to enable various rlys under federal control (including Canadian Northern, Inter-Colonial & National Transcontinental) to be operated by one company for the government. Amalgamated with Grand Trunk Rly of Canada 1923. All capital owned by the government. *See* NA Rly.

CNW (US)

Chicago & North Western RR.

Coach

Interchangeable with 'carriage' when referring to a rly passenger vehicle but *see also* Car; Cars. On the Metropolitan (1) (qv) 'coach' was reserved for compartment stock and 'car' was used for saloon stock. *See also* Carriage.

Coach (or Day Coach) class (US)

The cheapest type of accommodation on trains, broadly equivalent to British Third (later Second and Standard). Reclining seats were often provided for night use.

Coaching stock

Vehicles used in passenger trains, including those not designed to carry passengers.

Coaching traffic (obs)

Same as Passenger traffic (qv).

Coach train (obs)

Early (1830s/1840s) term for a passenger train.

Co-acting signal

A signal (normally a semaphore signal (qv)) coupled with another on the same post or bracket, one higher than the other above an obstruction to vision, to be visible at a longer distance, the lower more convenient for the driver's eye level when the train has moved closer. Also two colour light (qv) signals, one behind the other, wired to give the same indication.

Coal cell/pit

Alternative terms for coal drop.

Coal engines (RS)

L&NWR Webb 0–6–0 locos.

Coal Fish

A 32-ton ballast wagon used by engineers.

Coal heaver (USRS)

A steam loco fireman.

Coal pusher
A steam piston device to push coal forward in the loco tender, thus easing the fireman's task.

Coal stage
A platform from which locos are loaded with coal.

Coal tanks (RS)
L&NWR Webb 0–6–2T; these locos were not confined to coal traffic and were also used on passenger trains.

Coastway
BR brand name for Portsmouth–Brighton–Hastings services, introduced 1972.

Cobbinshaw Line
Cowlairs Junc, Glasgow, to Edinburgh. From the Cobbinshaw summit, west of Kirknewton.

Cobblers (RS)
Electric services between London (Euston) and Northampton.

Cobo (RS)
BR Metrovick class 28 loco fitted with one Co and one Bo bogie (*see* Notation).

Cocked hat
A triangular rly or tramway double junction at which two lines meet at right angles; from its shape when viewed from above with one line east to west joined to one running north to south.

Cockle
A 12-ton unfitted ballast brake van with plough, used by engineers.

Cock-loft (USRS)
A cupola (qv).

Cockneys (RS)(obs)
1. GWR men's name for Midland Rly lines and trains in South Wales.
2. Train crews from NLR.
3. NLR 0–6–0T locos.

Cod
A 22-ton wagon for carrying sleepers, used by engineers.

Cod's mouth, the (RS)(obs)
The effect of the streamlined front casing of L&NER A4 Pacific locos when opened up to give access to the smoke box.

COFC (US)
Container on flat car.

Coffee Pot (RS/USRS)
Any vertical-boilered steam loco; any antiquated loco, especially one with tall chimney.

Coffee Pots (RS)
GER 0–4–0T locos (L&NER class Y5).

Coffin (RS)
Any BR air-conditioned coach with sealed windows. The term arises from the frustration of those inclined to indulge in windowhanging (qv).

Cog wheeler (RS)
Midland Rly Kirtley 0–6–0 locos with coupling rods inside the frames.

Coke wagon
An open wagon with high slatted sides rising above the five-plank sides designed to carry a larger volume of the lighter-weight fuel.

Coligny–Welch signal lamp (obs)
Equipment fixed alongside signal lamps of distant signals when these signals had green and red indications, to show a white arrow at night, thus enabling a driver or fireman to distinguish the distant from other signals. From the names of the inventors. Replaced from 1924 by the use of yellow light for distants in the 'on' position.

Collar work (RS)
Any very heavy task for a steam locomotive.

Collector shoe
A device which bears down on the positive conductor rail (qv) of a third- or fourth-rail electrified rly to collect the traction current, and in the case of a fourth-rail system to return the current to earth. *See also* Paddle.

Collegamento (It)
A word appended to the name of a rly station to indicate the existence within the station of an interchange facility between the *FS* (qv) and another rly undertaking.

College Boy (RS)
An area manager imported from head office or employed direct from university.

College of knowledge (RS)
A trade union representative.

Collieries route
Huyton–St Helen's–Tyldesley–Eccles.

69

Colonel Stephens Rlys
Light rlys associated with Lt.-Col. H.F.
Stephens RE (TR) (1868–1931) and
managed from 23, Salford Terrace,
Tonbridge until 1948, viz EKR, K&ESR,
WC&PR, HofM&ST (WSR) and S&MLR
(qv).

Color blind (USRS)
A dishonest employee unable to distinguish
between his own money and property and
that of his employer.

Colosseum
TEE Milan–Rome, introduced 1984, the
Settebello (qv) re-equipped. Lost *TEE* status
1985, became EC Frankfurt–Rome, 1987.

Colour light area
Area in which the whole layout or route is
controlled by colour-light signals (qv).

Colour-light signal
A signal employing a powerful beam of
electric light by day and by night, capable
of penetrating fog and providing easy
visibility in sunshine. *See also* Multi-aspect
signal; Searchlight signal.

Columbia (US)
A steam loco with 2–4–2 wheel
arrangement.

Combination car (obs)
A single-deck tramcar (qv) incorporating
both a closed saloon and some open bench
seating.

Combination train (US)
Mixed traffic train (qv).

Combined Transport Ltd
A joint venture company formed 1991 to
offer freight services using both road and
rail for international and other traffic,
notably via the Channel Tunnel. Owned by
BR, 50 UK road haulage companies, the
Road Haulage Association, *Kombiverkehr*
(Germany) (qv) and *Novatrans* (France)
(qv).

Combine Harvesters (RS)
BR Class 9F 2–10–0 steam locos. From
their ungainly appearance.

**Come Back Amid Summer's Ceaseless
Rains**
Nickname for CB&SCR (qv).

Comeng
Loco and rolling stock builders, Sydney,

New South Wales, formerly the
Commonwealth Engineering Co.

Comet
1. A steam loco with 0–4–0 wheel
   arrangement.
2. An express between London (Euston)
   and Manchester, 1932–39. Re-
   introduced by BR 1949–62.

Comfort stop
A scheduled stop to allow train crew to use
station or depot lavatories.

Comic (RS)
Any newspaper or magazine produced
officially for consumption by rly employees,
especially *Railnews*.

Common carriers
Until 1953 the rlys of Great Britain were so
described because they were obliged to
carry any type of freight traffic offered to
them. This obligation was removed by the
Transport Act 1952.

Common user
1. Any vehicle which can be used for traffic
   purposes on any part of the rly system
   irrespective of its ownership. Such a
   scheme was introduced as a wartime
   measure in December 1915 to reduce
   wasteful use. It allowed any rly company
   receiving a wagon to load it for any
   further destination instead of returning
   it empty to the originating system. This
   reduced empty running of wagons from
   around 60 per cent of those in transit to
   around 20 per cent. This arrangement
   lasted until the arrival of nationalization
   in 1948.
2. (RS) A female child.

Commonwealth
Trade name for loco cylinders and cradles,
loco and rolling stock trucks, frames, etc.
manufactured by General Steel Castings,
Granite City, Illinois and Eddystone, Pa.,
USA.

Commonwealth Rlys
see CR (7).

**Commuted charge/commuted annual
payment arrangement** (obs)
Paid annually by traders in respect of
wagons owned by them instead of paying
daily shunting and siding rental charges.

Commuter/commute, to
Originally a US term for the holder of a rly commutation ticket (i.e. season ticket) and the associated travelling. Adopted in UK to describe rly season ticket holders *c.* 1950 and subsequently extended (principally by journalists) to cover all those travelling regularly to and from their daily workplace, by any form of transport, including private motor cars, and the action of so doing.

Company Bible (USRS)
Rly employees' rule book.

Company jewelry (USRS)
Hat badges, points keys, carriage keys, etc.

Company neutral grant
An SRA (qv) scheme introduced in 2004 to encourage more use of rail freight, under which grants were made to any rail freight operator for movement of an intermodal unit over a set distance.

Company notch (USRS)
The position of the steam loco regulator handle most likely to lead to economical coal consumption.

Company train
A freight train worked regularly for full trainload traffic associated with one customer.

Compartment
A partitioned-off section of a coach, with seats facing and opposite to direction of travel, accommodating on standard gauge two to six passengers each side, according to class and the need to provide space for a side corridor. On corridor stock there may be a door on the outside in addition to the door into the side corridor.

Compartment coach
A coach consisting entirely of compartments (qv).

Compensated gradient
An easing of gradient over curves so that resistance offered by curve and gradient together does not exceed that due to the gradient on a straight road.

Compensators
An attachment which allows for contraction or expansion of point rodding.

Composite/compo
A coach containing accommodation for two classes of passenger. *See also* Tri-composite/compo.

Composteur (Fr)
Self-service ticket-validating machine in use on the *SNCF.*

Compound
A design of steam loco in which the expansion of steam is divided into two stages. Two types of cylinders are fitted in various combinations, the high pressure ones taking steam direct from the boiler and then passing it in partially expanded state into low pressure cylinders, which complete the expansion. If the compounding is well designed, the work done in relation to the amount of coal burnt is high.

Compound catenary
A system of overhead electric traction supply in which there is an upper catenary (qv) wire insulated from the supporting structures and below it an intermediary bare stranded conductor, the auxiliary catenary wire supported by droppers (qv) and finally the traction/contact/conductor wire, which is suspended from the intermediary wire by loops which allow it to move in a direction parallel with the track.

Con (US)
Abbreviation for conductor (*3*) (qv).

Concentration depot/yard
A facility provided to replace a number of small goods depots or freight yards.

Concertina (RS)(obs)
A GWR 70 ft/21.34 metre coach of 1906 with recessed doors.

Concrete Bob
Nickname for Robert (later Sir Robert) McAlpine arising from his extensive use of concrete construction when building the West Highland Rly.

Concrete cavern, the (RS)
Birmingham New St. station as rebuilt in 1967 with a low roof over all platforms to carry station amenities, shops, etc.

Condensing loco
A loco fitted with arrangements to divert exhaust steam by means of flap valves to the upper parts of the water tanks to provide some improvement in the atmosphere when

working over tunnel rlys, principally in London, Liverpool and Glasgow.

Condor

A BR express door-to-door freight container service, London (Hendon)–Glasgow, introduced 1959 and Birmingham–Glasgow, introduced 1963. Both withdrawn 1967.

Conductor

1. An engineman accompanying a loco hauled by another.
2. An engineman or guard accompanying staff working on an unfamiliar line.
3. (US) The official in sole charge of a passenger or freight train, responsible for its safe operation, its administration, care of passengers, ticket checking, documentation, etc. The title was also current in Britain in the 1840s but was superseded by 'guard' in the 1850s. From 1988 all BR InterCity guards became known as 'conductors' or 'senior conductors', the latter undertaking a range of duties broadly equivalent to those of the US passenger train conductor.
4. Guards on London Underground electric rlys were so described from 1905 to *c.* 1920 as a consequence of US management.
5. The second crew member of a tramcar, responsible for collecting fares, turning the trolley at the end of the line, etc.
6. (obs) The senior attendant on a British Pullman car train. Derived from US usage (*3*).
7. (US) Head of a switch or yard crew (switchmen (qv)) and responsible for the shunting and marshalling of freight trains and freight cars.

Conductor-guard

Term first used by GER in 1921 to describe guards on branch line and other local services who were also required to issue and check tickets on the trains and assist passengers using steps at ground-level halts. BR adopted the term in 1963 to describe guards given ticket-issuing and revenue protection responsibilities.

Conductor rail

A rail placed in the centre or at the side of running rails to carry the positive traction

current, which is collected by shoes on the locos or emu trains. *See also* Collector shoe; Guard boarding; Paddle.

Conductor's van (US)(obs)

A caboose (qv).

Conduit blanche (Fr)

White pipe; a through pipe on an unbraked vehicle or a vehicle differently braked from the main part of the train; or a pipe conveying steam for coach heating.

Conduit track (obs)

Traction system for tramways (*3*) in which rails carrying the positive and return traction current are placed in a trench and below the running rails. Traction current is collected and returned by ploughs fixed to the tramcars and designed to pass through a continuous slot above the trench. In the 1900s and 1910s this method, though more costly to install and maintain, was favoured as more aesthetically acceptable than overhead wire trolley systems.

Cone

GWR TC for gunpowder van.

Confederation (US)

A steam loco with 4–8–4 wheel arrangement.

Conflat

GWR TC for a container flat wagon with four wheels.

CON-G

Control Governor unit in a LT Underground car.

Conger

A 51-ton concrete beam-carrying wagon set used by engineers.

Congressional

A long-lived express between New York and Washington DC, introduced 1885. Scheduled at 3 h 35 min in 1936.

Con-IC

Control Isolating Cock in a LT Underground car.

Conker (RS)

Any motor vehicle used only on rly premises, and not licensed for running on public roads.

Connecting rod

This connects the crosshead on the piston rod of a loco with the crank pin or axle. Pivoted to the crosshead, it converts the backward and forward motion of the piston into the circular motion of the wheels or crank axle.

Connection

A group of fittings (qv) such as a crossover (qv).

Connections (RS)

Points (qv) and crossings (qv).

Connex Rail Ltd

A TOC (2) (qv) owned by the French transport group CGEA; from 1996 holding Connex South Central and Connex South Eastern franchises, operating in the former TOU Network South Central (qv) and South Eastern Train Co. (qv) areas. New service Gatwick Airport–Rugby via Clapham Junction added in 1996. Replaced by South Central (qv) and SET (qv) when its franchises expired in 2000 and 2003 respectively.

Conqueror

A London (Charing Cross)–Hastings service, so named in 1987, for that year only.

Conrail

Abbreviation for Consolidated Rail Corporation, a US government enterprise formed on 1 April 1976 to take over some 15,000 m of rly from seven bankrupt private rly companies (B&M; Penn–Central; Erie–Lackawanna; LVR (3); Central of New Jersey; Reading Lines; and Lehigh & Hudson River). A private company from 1987. Dissolved and taken into CSX and NS 3 (qv), 1997.

Con rod (RS)

Connecting rod (qv).

Consigne (Fr)

A left luggage office.

Consist (US)

Train make-up/formation; also the report sent ahead with this information so that yardmasters can make plans for marshalling. Adopted by BR in 1955.

Console

That part of a power box (qv) which houses the control buttons and switches and track diagram indications. *See also* Panel.

Consolidated Signal

Consolidated Signal Co., originally the Pneumatic & General Engineering Co.; acquired majority interest in Saxby & Farmer (qv) and Evans O'Donnell & Co. Ltd (qv) in 1901–2, operating from the latter's Chippenham Works from 1903. Later acquired a controlling interest in McKenzie, Holland & Westinghouse Power Signal Co. (qv). Became part of Westinghouse Brake & Saxby Signal Co. (qv) from 1920.

Consolidation (US)

A steam loco with 2–8–0 wheel arrangement.

Construction gauge

The extreme limits used by the civil engineer building a rly, to form the space through which trains will operate, more generous than loading gauge (1) (qv).

Contact strip

The shiny strip along the rail head on which most wheels make contact.

Contact wire

A bare, solid conductor wire, the lowest component of the catenary (qv), which offers traction current (qv) to the pantographs (qv) of locos and multiple units (qv), etc. *See also* Catenary; OLE.

Container

A large storage box or tank which can be lifted on and off ships, rail and road trucks to facilitate intermodal transit.

Conti (obs)

Nickname for the former through service from Birkenhead to Dover (for the Continent) via Reading and Tonbridge.

Continental Club Train

see Club Trains, The.

Continental Express

A GER service between London (Liverpool St.) and Harwich in connection with Antwerp and Rotterdam sailings, introduced 1864; daily from 1882. Separate trains for the Antwerp and the Hook of Holland services 1893; all year round services, 1896. Withdrawn 1914. Restored 1921, with Pullman cars, as 'Continental Restaurant & Pullman Car Expresses', one for each service. The L&NER renamed the services respectively, 'The Antwerp Continental' and 'The Hook Continental' in 1927. Amalgamated as one train, 'The Hook & Antwerp Continental', in 1932. From 1938

separate trains again, both ceasing in
September 1939. 'Hook Continental'
restored 1945, name dropped 1987.

Continental notation
A system of classifying steam locos by
enumerating from left to right the number
of axles in any leading truck, the coupled
driving wheels and any trailing truck; thus
2–2–1 in Continental notation corresponds
to 4–4–2 in Whyte's notation (qv).

Continental services/traffic (obs)
A generic term for rail and sea
services/traffic between UK and European
mainland current until *c.* 1970.

Continuous blowdown valve
A device to allow a limited amount of water
to be continuously blown out of a loco
boiler while the regulator is open, thus
prolonging the period between boiler
washouts.

Continuous [automatic] brakes
Any system of braking all the vehicles in a
train simultaneously under the control of
driver or guard which is also self-applying in
the event of severance of the train or other
failure in continuity of brake action.
Vacuum and compressed air systems were
both formerly employed but the latter is
now standard on BR. Continuous automatic
brakes have been a government requirement
for passenger trains in the UK since 1889.

Contract (obs)
Term used in northern Britain for a season
ticket.

Contremarque (Fr)
The passenger's control coupon of a party
ticket (used internationally on mainland
Europe).

Control/Train or Traffic Control
A system of controlling, organizing and
reorganizing train and loco movements, staff
duties, vehicle provision, etc. over a large
defined area of rlys, working from a central
point, using telephones, diagrams, etc.
Information on the state of traffic is received
from selected signal boxes, depots, etc.
Controllers have wide powers to adjust timetables in emergencies. First introduced on
Midland Rly in 1907–12. Not to be confused
with Automatic Train Control (*see* ATC).

Under the privatized regime in Britain,
organizations to monitor and control train
operation and performance became the
responsibility of Network Rail (qv) regions
and the relevant TOC (2) (qv). From 2005
Integrated Control Centres (ICC (qv))
were established, including representatives
of both organizations. *See also* RUS.

Contrôle de l'Etat (Fr)
A central government department established
in France in the 19th century to regulate the
practices of the private rly companies. Its
remit included fares and freight rates.

Contrôleur de route (Fr)
Travelling ticket inspector.

Controlled signal
Any signal whose aspect can be altered by
the action of a signalman.

Controlled train
see Regulation [of passenger traffic].

Controller
1. A staff grade employed in Control (qv).
2. Apparatus used to control the current
   applied to the motors of electric locos,
   emu motor cars and control trailers and
   tramcars, allowing regulation of speed by
   varying the voltage, and also controlling
   starting, stopping and reversing.

Control orders
Orders issued by Control (qv) arranging
special trains, alterations to timetables or
staff rosters, or for allocating tasks to spare
locos and crews, or rearranging crew duties.

Control trailer
Unmotored car in an mu train containing
driving cab and driving controls.

Convertible car
A tramcar design in which the glazed body
sides can be fully or partly (semi-convertible)
removed for summer operation. Popular in
the US from *c.* 1890 until *c.* 1914.

Conveyor car (US)
A motorized freight car used for freight
movements on wharves, etc.

Conwy/Conway Valley Line
Llandudno Junction–Blaenau Ffestiniog.

Cook (USRS)
A brakeman.

Cook's
see Cook's Timetables; Thomas Cook.

Cook shack (USRS)

A caboose (qv).

Cook's Timetables

Cook's Continental Timetables and Tourists' Handbook, first published 1873, with the aim of providing a handy summary of European train services which could be carried by the traveller. Cook's was the first British timetable to adopt the 24-hour clock system, in 1919. *Cook's Overseas Timetable*, first published in 1981, offers a similar useful abstract of train times for all countries outside Europe.

Coolie (RS)(obs)

A loco fireman.

Coon, to (USRS)

1. To operate a train at low speed.

2. To walk along the tops of cars.

Coordonnée, une ligne (Fr)

A line open for freight but whose passenger traffic is entrusted to a 'coordinated' road service shown in the rly timetable, calling at the rly stations and making convenient connection with other rly services.

COP

Corridor Open Plan, 3-COP; class 421/7 emu introduced by Connex South Central, 1997.

Cop, to/cop, a (RS)

To see and record a loco for the first time. Also used as a noun. In use in this sense in the 1920s if not earlier. From northern English dialect, to cop = to capture, to catch. *See also* Train spotter.

Cop book (RS)

Notebook containing details of cops (qv).

Coppernobs (RS)

Furness Rly Bury 0–4–0 locos.

Coppertops (RS)

SE&CR Wainwright D class 4–4–0 locos.

Copypit Line, The

[Leeds–]Halifax–Burnley–Blackburn [–Preston–Blackpool]. *See also* Roses Line, The.

COR

SR four-car emu CORridor sets of 1937–8 for Portsmouth and Mid-Sussex electrifications, two motor brake Second/Standard class cars, one Second/Standard trailer and one composite trailer, 4-COR. Also BR six-car emu sets of

1965 made up from 6-PUL and 6-PAN units, 6-COR.

Coradia

Alstom (qv) name for a family of dmu (qv), including classes 175 and 180 delivered from 2000.

Corail

Inter-city VTU 75 centre-aisle passenger stock with two-tone grey livery used on accelerated internal services introduced by the *SNCF* from 1975 onwards. First *SNCF* standard stock with air-conditioning. Name derived from *COnfort et RAIL*.

Coral

GWR TC for four-wheel glass-carrying truck.

Cordon

GWR TC for gas reservoir truck.

Cork Express

Dublin to Cork non-stop service introduced 1953.

Corks (RS)(obs)

Boiler tubes choked with ashes.

Corner, to (USRS)

To move a car or wagon in a siding to a position in which it fouls another line.

Cornfield meet (USRS)

A head-on collision of two trains on a single line.

Cornishman, The

1. Unofficial name for an express introduced in 1890 between London (Paddington) and Penzance via Bristol. Not used after 1904.

2. A relief to The Cornish Riviera, running only in 1935.

3. An express between Wolverhampton and Torquay/Penzance, introduced in 1952 and later extended to Leeds and Bradford. Name dropped 1975.

4. An express between Edinburgh and Penzance, introduced 1986.

5. Virgin Cross Country (qv) service between Dundee and Penzance (702 miles in 12hr), the longest journey by the same train in Britain. Name ceased to be used after 2 June 2002.

Cornish Riviera Express/Limited

An express between London (Paddington) and Penzance via Westbury, introduced

1904 as Cornish Riviera Limited. 'Limited' dropped 1977.

Cornish Scot

An Edinburgh, Glasgow and Penzance service, introduced 1987. Name ceased to be used from 2 June 2002.

Cornwall Rly

see CR (*4*).

Coronation

A L&NER supplementary fare streamlined express with 'beaver-tail' observation car, and meals served at seats; ran between London (Kings Cross) and Edinburgh in 6 h, 1937–9.

Coronation Land Cruise

see Land Cruise.

Coronation Scot

A LM&SR streamlined express between London (Euston) and Glasgow, 1937–9. It carried a maximum of only 232 passengers; journey time 6 h 30 min.

Correo, tren (Sp)

A stopping train conveying mails.

Corridor

A passageway between the outer side of a coach and compartments, allowing passengers access to lavatories and, via corridor connections, to other parts of the train. *See also* Vestibuled [train/coach].

Corridor connection

Another term for gangway (qv).

Corridor, The

West Coast Corridor Express (qv).

Corridor tender

A loco tender vestibuled to its train and incorporating a side corridor which allowed engine crews to change over during non-stop runs. Introduced on the L&NER in 1928.

Corris Rly

see CR (*3*).

Corrugation

A regular pattern of alternate ridges and hollows appearing on the running surface of rails. Caused by various factors, not properly understood, and most frequently encountered on electric rlys. When present, the passage of a train is marked by a characteristic roaring noise. Cured by use of rail-grinders (qv). Also a problem on tramways (*3*).

Cosh it, to (LTRS)

To make an emergency brake application using driver's brake handle.

COSS

Controller Of Site Safety. A competent person is always appointed for this role when a person or group requires to walk or work on or near a rly track.

COT

Condition Of Track; a term used to explain the reason for a speed restriction.

Côte d'Azur Pullman-Express

A *CIWL* service between Paris, Nice and Ventimiglia, introduced 1929, ceased 1939.

COTIF

Convention on International Carriage by Rail (1980) imposing a uniform system of international law for the carriage of freight, passengers and luggage across frontiers. Implemented in the UK by the Railways and Transport Safety Act, 2004.

Cotswold & Malvern Express

A service between London (Paddington), Worcester and Great Malvern introduced 1985. Extended to Hereford and renamed Cotswold Express, 1988. Renamed Cotswold & Malvern Express 1989.

Cotswold Line

Oxford–Worcester.

Cotter

A wedge used for tightening the ends of the connecting rod of a loco.

Cotton Belt

Nickname of the St Louis Southwestern RR.

Couchette (Fr)

A coach with low-cost double- or triple-berth sleeping accommodation arranged in compartments opening on to a corridor.

Counter pressure brake

A refined version of the classic method of braking a steam loco in an emergency by opening the regulator (qv) and reversing. Introduced by L. le Chatelier in 1865 and widely adopted on the European mainland.

Count ties, to (USRS)

To reduce speed to the point at which it becomes possible to count the sleepers.

Country end

The end of a station opposite to the London end (qv).

Countrylink
Brand name of the New South Wales state rly authority (Australia) for its longer-distance and rural services.

County tanks
GWR 4–4–2T rebuilt from County Class 4–4–0 locos.

Coupé
A half-compartment with seats facing a partition, in the first or second class usually accommodating two or three passengers, sometimes with its own lavatory; in the classic British first class Pullman (qv) car it denoted a private enclosed compartment usually with four Pullman chairs around a table.

Coupe-vent (Fr)(obs)
Wind-cutter (qv).

Coupling rod
The exterior rod which couples together the driving wheels of a loco.

Coupling screw
Two iron links with right and left hand screw between them and a lever in the centre allowing the couplings of passenger coaches and fitted wagons to be screwed taut until buffers press into one another, so preventing oscillation at high speed.

Coupling stick (obs)
A shunter's pole fitted with a hook at one end, used to couple and uncouple wagons.

Coupon ticket
A ticket for a long journey valid for travel over two or more rly systems, with detachable coupons covering different sections of the journey.

Cou V
Coupler valve.

Covered way
Railway tunnel formed after cut and cover (qv) construction.

Cove roof
A carriage roof which in profile has an arc (qv) type centre but a profile of much smaller radius at the junctions with the cantrail (qv), descending almost vertically.

Cow & Calf (USRS)
Two diesel-electric locos permanently coupled, one (without a driving cab) controlled from the other.

Cowboy Line (LTRS)
The East London Line.

Cowcatcher
A metal grid fixed to buffer beam of loco, railcar or interurban car and designed to push aside any obstruction on the track.

Cow crate (USRS)
A cattle wagon.

Cow puncher (USRS)
A derisive term for a cowboy riding stock trains (qv) and prodding cattle when loading and unloading.

Cow Shed, The (RS)
The Waterloo Area Signalling Centre, Wimbledon. From its featureless, utilitarian appearance.

Cow's horn (RS)
A hook shaped like a cow's horn on which single line tokens, usually enclosed in a pouch with a loop attached, are deposited by train crews without stopping the train.

Cow's udder (RS)
A plastic sleeve for twin connections between vehicles.

CP
Companhia dos Caminhos de Ferro Portugueses; Portuguese Rly Authority. 2,850 km, mainly 1,668 mm gauge. *See also REFER.*

CPR
Canadian Pacific Rly, inc 1881, completed Montreal–Vancouver trans-Canada line in 1887, absorbed many smaller companies and became the largest ocean-steamship owning rly in the world, operating trans-Atlantic and trans-Pacific routes.

CPT
Confederation of British Road Passenger Transport, formed 1973–5 by a combination of PSTA (qv), the Public Service Vehicle Operators Association (coach and independent bus operators) and APTO (qv). Renamed Bus & Coach Council, further renamed 1995 the Confederation of Passenger Transport UK (to include light rail operators).

CR
1. Caledonian Rly, inc 1845, first section opened 1847, 1,117 route miles by 1914, mainly in central Scotland. Became part of LM&SR from 1923.

2. Cardiff Rly, inc 1897, lines in Cardiff Bute Docks; also Heath Junc, Cardiff to Rhydyfelin Halt near Treforest (intended junc with TVR not completed). Opened freight 1909, passengers 1911. Part of GWR from 1922.

3. Corris Rly, Machynlleth to Aberllefenni and Ratgoed Quarry 2 ft 3 in/686 mm gauge, inc 1858 as Corris, Machynlleth & River Dovey Tramroad, opened 1859, name changed to CR 1864, relaid and operated by locos from 1878, passenger service from 1883, absorbed by GWR 1930, passenger service ceased 1931, closed 1948. Preservation project in progress.

4. Cornwall Rly, Plymouth to Falmouth, inc 1846, leased to GWR, B&ER and SDR 1859, opened 1859, 1863. Part of GWR from 1889.

5. Cambrian Rlys; *see* Cambrian.

6. Central Rly [of India], formed 1951.

7. Commonwealth Rlys [Australia]. Part of ANR (qv) from 1975.

8. (obs) Company's Risk.

9. Cardiff Rlys (qv).

10. Chiltern Rlys (qv).

11. *Zhong Guo Tie Lui*; Chinese Rlys. 70,058 km with physical connections to the North and South Korea and Viet Nam systems.

Crab
A 20-ton ballast wagon with fixed sides, used by engineers.

Crab and Winkle
Nickname for Canterbury & Whitstable Rly and GER Brightlingsea and Tollesbury branches.

Crabs (RS)
LM&SR Hughes Class 6P/5F 2–6–0 steam locos of 1926. From the appearance of the outside motion in action.

Cracker (RS)
A detonator.

Cradle (USRS)
A gondola or hopper wagon.

Crampton
A type of loco designed by Thomas Russell Crampton (1816–88) in which a low centre of gravity was obtained by placing the driving wheels behind the boiler and firebox.

Crampton, prendre le (Fr)(obs)
Expression for taking the train, after Thomas Russell Crampton, locomotive engineer, whose designs were very popular in France. Also *M'sieu' Crampton* (obs), colloquial Fr term for a rlyman.

Crankex
TC for a special train chartered by rly enthusiasts.

Cravens
Cravens Railway Carriage & Wagon Co. Ltd, Darnall, Sheffield, established 1867. Rolling stock activities taken over by Metro–Cammell (qv) in 1965.

Crawfish
A 20-ton side-tipping ballast wagon used by engineers.

CRC
Continental Railway Circle. Catering for those interested in European mainland rlys.

CRE
Conductor Rail Equipment. The conductor rail (qv) and related items.

Crease/Creese (obs)
Flange of a wheel made entirely of wood for use on waggonways (qv).

Creaser (obs)
A man employed to clear debris from the flangeways (qv) of a waggonway (qv).

Creep
Rail creep (qv).

Creeper (LTRS)
A three-aspect draw-up signal which can be passed at low speed.

Creosote
A 22-ton creosote tank wagon used by engineers.

Crescent Limited
A Southern Rly System express between New Orleans and New York, introduced 1925. Became an Amtrak service in 1971, renamed Southern Crescent, later renamed The Crescent.

Crested Goods (RS)
Another name for Cauliflowers (qv).

Crewe goods (RS)
Early L&NWR 2–4–0 locos.

Crewe type

A loco with inclined outside cylinders set between two deep iron frames. Known in France as *le Buddicom* after its introduction there by William Buddicom. The real significance of this design, with cylinders outside the wheels, was elimination of the cranked driving axle, costly to manufacture and prone to breakage.

CRG

Central Railway Group, a private venture project to build and operate a new freight rly between Leicester, London and the Channel Tunnel, formed 1991. By 2000 a Liverpool–Lille rly for both freight and passengers and built to UIC (qv) loading gauge (qv) was being proposed.

CRI&P

see Rock Island.

Crib

1. *See* Bed.
2. The space between adjacent sleepers.
3. (USRS) A caboose (qv).

Cricket

GWR TC for eight-wheel composite coach.

Crimea

Name given (e.g. Crimea Sidings) to any rly installation broadly contemporary with the Crimean War (1853–6).

Crime sheet (RS)

The personal record of an employee, including a note of any disciplinary offences.

Criminal link (RS)(obs)

A link (qv) incorporating much trip (qv) and shunting work, to which top link drivers were posted after committing disciplinary offences.

Crimson Ramblers (RS)

Midland Rly and LM&SR 4–4–0 compound locos. From their use all over the LM&SR system.

Cripple

Any defective, damaged or worn vehicle.

Cripple siding

Siding allocated to berthing cripples (qv).

Cripple train (US)

A breakdown train (qv).

CRO (obs)

Chief Regional Officer, in charge of BR

regions under the BTC regime 1948–55. In the latter year they became general managers under the Area Boards.

Crocodile

1. GWR TC for long low truck ('trolley') for conveying rolling stock, lofty road vehicles, boilers, etc. There were thirteen types (A to M).
2. (RS) Articulated rod-driven *SBB* 1–C+C–1 electric locos; also locos of similar appearance used by Rhaetian Rly and *OBB*.

Cromer Express

A service between London (Liverpool St.) and Cromer, by-passing Norwich, introduced in 1897, renamed Norfolk Coast Express (qv) 1907.

Crompton Parkinson

Crompton Parkinson (Chelmsford) Ltd. Established as Crompton & Co. Ltd 1888, became CP Ltd 1927 after amalgamation with E. & A. Parkinson Ltd. Manufacturers of electric traction equipment. Taken over by Hawker Siddeley Group 1967, rail traction business transferred to Brush (qv).

Cromptons (RS)

BR diesel locos class 33, from the manufacturer, Crompton Parkinson. Also used for the 10 prototype Peaks (qv) as they had Crompton Parkinson electrical equipment.

Cronks (RS)

BR diesel locos class 08. Also known as Gronks.

Cross, The (RS)

Kings Cross Station, London, and associated depots.

Cross bench car (obs)

A tramcar (qv) with transverse bench seats but no gangway, obliging the conductor to collect fares by passing along the footboards at the sides.

Cross Country Trains

A TOU (qv), 1994. *See* Virgin Cross Country.

Crossing

1. The place in a set of points or diamond crossing (qv) where two lines of rail first come into contact and the wheels

following one rail cross over another. In points, the type of crossing in general use is the 'V' or frog.

2. Same as Flat crossing (qv).

3. A device used at the intersection of two trolley wires (qv) to allow passage of the vehicles' current collectors along either wire route.

Crossing keeper

A person responsible for manually closing/locking gates against road/pedestrian traffic when a train is approaching and for opening the gates when the train has passed.

Crossing place or loop

The point on a stretch of single line at which double track is provided to allow trains or tramcars proceeding in opposite directions to pass. On rlys usually sited at a station, for convenience.

Crosslink (obs)

An Anglia (qv) service, subsidised by the SRA (qv) between Norwich/Colchester/Ipswich and Basingstoke via Stratford, Highbury, West Hampstead and Feltham, 2000–2.

Crossover/crossover road

A pair of rails leading from one line to another to allow movements from up to down line or vice versa or, on a 4-track layout, from slow to fast lines or vice versa. On tramways (3) the term denotes a connection allowing reversal on double track lines. See also Ladder (1).

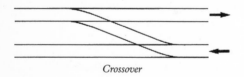

Crossover

CrossRail/Crossrail

A much-delayed scheme for full-size tube tunnels to connect existing main-line rlys across the centre of London from west to east on the pattern of the *RER* (qv), opened in Paris from 1969 onwards. It first emerged in the London Rail Study of 1974 and the concept was endorsed by the 1988–9 Central London Rail Study as 'the most effective option to relieve congestion on existing lines and cater for future growth'. Following extensive preparatory and detailed design work, legislation was put to Parliament but rejected in 1994 under a Conservative administration after £144m had been spent on planning and trial borings. Further delays ensued while more money was spent on consultants' reports and 'design development' bringing the total to around £300m. Government approval in principle was finally secured in 2003–4 and fresh legislation was sought in 2004–5 for works to connect Maidenhead/Heathrow Airport with Shenfield/Abbey Wood in the east and south-east, through new tunnels between Paddington and Stratford/Woolwich.

Cross span wire

A wire across the tracks to secure the overhead equipment in the optimum position. *See also* Headspan wire.

Crow

1. A sequence of five loco whistle signal blasts, imitating a cock's crow.

2. (RS) Abbreviation for Jim Crow (qv).

Crow, to [a rail]

To bend it; from Jim Crow (qv).

Crown, to (USRS)

To complete a train by attaching the caboose. Until this is done the train is referred to as a cut (qv) of cars.

Crow's nest (USRS)

A cupola (qv).

Croydon Tramlink

see Tramlink.

CRS

1. Computerized Reservations System (BR), linked to about 450 stations. *See also* TRIBUTE.

2. Continuous Route Signage; comprehensive highway-type lineside signage along a route detailing speed restrictions, countdown markers for stations, signals, etc., junction names and other information which enables drivers without specific knowledge of the route to use it safely.

CRTA

Chicago Regional Transportation Authority.

CRUCC

Central Rail Users' Consultative Committee, replacing CTCC (qv) from 1 April 1994. Replaced by RPC (qv).

Cruise operators/Cruise trains

Private companies (GS&WR (qv), RCS (qv) and VSOE (qv)) which provide loco-hauled trains of 'heritage' saloon coaches offering pre-booked seating for luxury recreational travel, including on-board catering, side trips and in some cases sleeping accommodation. Trains are staffed on the basis of one attendant per coach. *See also* Land cruise.

Crummy (USRS)

The commonest slang term for a caboose (qv).

Crumpet line (LTRS)(obs)

A diagonal stripe to denote season ticket issued to a female commuter, thus assisting detection of fraudulent use. From (S) crumpet = the female sex.

Crystal Palaces (RS)

GER '1300' (L&NER F7) 2–4–2T, from their disproportionately large side-windowed cabs. *See also* Glass houses.

CS

Carriage sidings; also carriage/coaching stock.

CS

International code for *ZS* (qv).

CSAR

Central South African Rlys, 1902, controlling OVGS (qv) and NZASM (qv) following the conclusion of the South African War. Part of SAR&H (qv), 1910.

CS&TE

Chief Signals & Telegraphs/ Telecommunications Engineer.

CSD

Carriage Servicing Depot. *See also* Traincare centre/depot.

ČSD

Československé Státní Dráhy; Czechoslovakian State Rlys; became *CD* (qv) and *ZSR* (qv), 1993.

CSR

Cab Secure Radio; a VHF radio system which allows direct communication

between drivers and signallers and supports DOO (qv). *See also* GSM-R.

CSX Transportation Inc

A conglomerate of shipping, rly and other companies which from 1980 included the B&O (qv) and SCL (qv).

CT

1. Control Trailer (qv).

2. Central Trains (qv).

Ct (Fr)

Cantonnement (qv).

CTA

Chicago Transit Authority.

CTAC

Creative Tourist Agents' Conference. A consortium of nine UK travel agencies and firms formed in 1932 and reconstituted in 1946. It chartered special trains for Continental holidays from 1933–9 and from 1946–68, also from the Midlands and the North to Scotland from 1952–65. Disbanded 1969.

CTC

Centralized Traffic Control. A system, first used in the US in 1927, in which the signalling of a long section of rly is undertaken from one control point, using illuminated diagrams which show the position of any trains on the line, and push buttons which can operate the signals and points and set up non-conflicting routes for any train movement. First used in Great Britain on the Metro-politan Rly's new Stanmore branch, 1932.

CTCC (obs)

Central Transport Consultative Committee, established 1948 under the 1947 Transport Act; reconstituted 1962. Represented the interests of users of BR and investigated complaints, taking a national view. Its remit excluded fares and charges. There were eight separate Transport Users' Consultative Committees (TUCC) for designated areas of Great Britain including one for London. These had a similar function but concentrated on local matters; they also had the duty of considering and reporting to ministers upon proposed withdrawals of passenger services. CTCC became CRUCC (qv),

and TUCC became RUCC (qv), 1994.
London TUCC became LRPC (qv), 1984.

CTL
Combined Transport Ltd (qv).

CTR
Channel Tunnel Routes, term used from
1994 for routes available between London
and the Channel Tunnel, viz. CTR1 via
Bromley South, Orpington and Tonbridge;
CTR2 via Bromley South, Swanley &
Maidstone East; CTR3 via Redhill &
Tonbridge; and CTR4 via Bromley South,
Swanley, Sevenoaks & Tonbridge.

CTRL
Channel Tunnel Rail Link. New direct
high speed rail line between London
(St. Pancras) and the Channel Tunnel.
Construction (Phase 1 Folkestone–
Fawkham Junction (42m)) begun for
Railtrack (qv) overseen by Union Rlys
(qv), 1998, for opening 2003. Phase 2
(26m) to London (St Pancras) planned to
open in 2007. *See also* L&CR (*2*).

CTRLDS
Channel Tunnel Rail Link Domestic
Services. Train services between London
(St. Pancras) and Kent over the CTRL
(qv) and the associated rolling stock.

CTT
1. Continental Time Tables: *see* Cook's
   Timetables; Thomas Cook.
2. *Correas Telegrafs Telefones*, Portuguese
   Postal & Telecommunications Service
   (initials seen on rail vehicles).

C2C
Market branding for LTS Rail (qv) 2000.
Open to various interpretations, e.g.
Capital to Coast, Country to Capital,
Commitment to Change. *See also* London
Lines; National Express Group plc.

Cuckoo line
Nickname for Eridge–Polegate line,
LB&SCR.

Cuffley Loop
Hertford Loop (qv).

Culemeyer (Ger)
A road vehicle designed to carry a loaded
rail wagon.

Culm Valley
Light rly from Tiverton Junc to Hemyock,

inc 1873, opened 1876, part of GWR from
1880.

Culvert
Pipe or small tunnel beneath a rly
embankment carrying water from one side
to the other.

Cu Na Mara
A service between Dublin and Galway,
introduced 1960, name dropped 1975.

Cunarder
A boat train between London (Waterloo)
and Southampton Docks, introduced
1952, to connect with sailings of RMS
Queen Mary and *Queen Elizabeth*. Ceased
1968.

Cunarders
GWR (qv) special 'Super Saloon' coaches
built 1931 for use in boat trains (qv)
serving transatlantic liners calling at
Plymouth.

Cunard Firsts
GWR 70 ft/21.34 metres eight-
compartment corridor First class coaches
built for Atlantic liner boat trains to and
from Fishguard 1909–14.

Cupboard, The (RS)
Coppermill Junction, GER (Walthamstow,
East London).

Cupboard, in the (RS)
Placed in a layby or loop to allow another
train to pass on the running line.

Cupola (US)
A covered lookout cabin raised above the
roof of a caboose (qv).

Cushions (RS/USRS)
Passenger vehicles. *See also* On the
cushions.

Customer
BR term for a passenger, introduced
1988.

Customer train
Company train (qv).

Cut
1. (US) A cutting.
2. (USRS) Two or more cars coupled
   together without a caboose.
3. (RS)(obs) A part of a train; a set of two
   or more wagons in a yard bound for the
   same destination or for the same siding
   in the yard.

Cut and cover
A method of building tunnels and underground rlys by cutting out a trench and roofing it with girder work.

Cut back, to
To remove a service, or all services, from the outer end of a branch or route. Mostly used of tramways (*3*).

Cut card (obs)
A document showing in code the cuts (*3*) (qv) into which a train must be split for marshalling, the destination siding of each cut, the number of wagons in each, and other information.

Cut lever (USRS)
Lever kept at the side of a wagon or van and used to raise a coupling pin and thus separate a wagon from its neighbour.

Cut-off
1. The period of steam admission to the cylinders of a loco as controlled by the driver when using the valve gear. At the moment of starting, cut-off is about 75 per cent but it can be reduced until the loco is cutting off in the cylinders at 25 or 20 per cent of piston stroke.
2. Term used by shunters, guards, etc. meaning to uncouple vehicles.

Cutter-up (RS)(obs)
An employee in a marshalling yard who divides a train into cuts (*3*) (qv) for various destinations.

Cut the crossing, to (USRS)
To separate the wagons of a train to allow road traffic across the rly when a train has blocked a level crossing for more than ten minutes.

CV&HR
Colne Valley & Halstead Rly, Chappel &
Wakes Colne to Halstead and Haverhill, inc 1856, 1859, opened 1860, 1861, 1862, 1863, part of L&NER 1923. Short section at Castle Hedingham now preserved as 'Colne Valley Rly'.

CV&YR
Cheddar Valley & Yatton Rly, Yatton Junc to Wells (S&DR Junc), inc 1864. In 1865 powers transferred to B&ER who built it; opened 1869, 1870. Built to broad gauge, converted 1875.

CVLR
Cairn Valley (qv).

CVR
1. Clogher Valley Rly, NI, Maguiresbridge–Tynan, 3 ft/914 mm gauge, inc 1884 as a tramway. Much of it was built as a tramway (*4*). Opened 1887, title changed to CVR 1894, closed 1941 (officially, but actually in the early hours of 1942, delayed deliberately 'to get the better of the Government').
2. Chipstead Valley Rly (qv).
3. Colne Valley Rly: *see* CV&HR.
4. Culm Valley Rly (qv).

CW/CWD
Chemical Warfare Department (WW1).

CWE
Carriage and Wagon Examiner.

CWR
Continuous Welded Rail over distances exceeding half a mile. *See also* LWR/LWT.

Cyclops (RS)
Class 67 diesel-electric locos. From the single windscreen.

Cycnus
TEE Milan–Ventimiglia, introduced 1973, lost *TEE* status 1978.

D

DA
Disturbance Allowance.

Dab Hand (RS)
A carriage painter.

Dace
A 20-ton ballast and sleeper wagon with fixed sides, used by engineers.

Dagger
TC instructing signalman to 'cease accepting [trains] without assent'.

Daisies (RS)
The 0–8–4T locos used at Wath Yards.

Daisy chain (USRS)
The type of derailment that can occur as a train negotiates a very sharp curve.

Dales Rail
A scheme started in 1975 to sponsor and organize rail services in the Yorkshire Dales area, also connecting buses for ramblers using the Settle & Carlisle and other rly services.

Dalmatia Express
A service between Ostend and Rijeka, introduced 1958, renamed Rijeka Express 1969. Dalmatia Express then became a Stuttgart–Split service, later combined with Stuttgart–Sarajevo services as Mostar–Dalmatia.

Damo
GWR TC for covered motor car truck.

Damper
A cover fixed to the ash pan of a steam loco to regulate the supply of air to the firebox.

Dance the carpet, to (USRS)
To be the subject of a disciplinary investigation or interview in a manager's or supervisor's office (cf. British (S) 'On the carpet').

Dancing (RS)
Loco wheels slipping on the rails and preventing movement.

D&A Joint
Inc as Dundee & Arbroath Rly, 1836, 5 ft 6 in/1,676 mm gauge, opened 1838, 1839, 1840. Converted to standard gauge 1847. Vested in Scottish North Eastern Rly, 1862, part of CR (*1*) 1866, jointly vested in CR (*1*) and NBR from 1880, including the Carmyllie mineral branch, opened 1854 by Lord Panmure. LM&SR & L&NER Joint 1923–47. Carmyllie branch became Carmyllie Light Rly (LRO 1898), providing a passenger service 1900–29; freight services ceased 1965.

D&B Joint
Dumbarton & Balloch Joint Rly, inc 1891 (*see* L&DR), opened 1896, joint NBR, CR (*1*) and L&DR. Vested in CR (*1*) and NBR from 1909. LM&SR & L&NER joint 1923–47.

D&BJR
Dublin & Belfast Junction Rly, inc 1845 Drogheda to Portadown. Opened 1849, 1850, 1852. Part of GNR (I) from 1876.

D&BT
Dublin & Blessington Tramway, steam tramway (*4*) between Dublin (Terenure) and Blessington, opened 1888. Extension to Poulaphouca opened 1890, closed 1928. Physical connection at Terenure with Dublin electric tramway system. Main line closed 1932.

D&CR
Devon & Cornwall Rly, a renaming of OR (*2*) (qv), inc 1865. Yeoford–North Tawton

opened 1865, extended to Sampford Courtenay 1867, to Okehampton 1871, to Lydford 1874. Leased to L&SWR, part of L&SWR from 1874.

D&D

Dean & Dawson Ltd, a travel agency owned successively from 1904 by the GCR/L&NER/BTC/THC. Part of Thomas Cook (qv) from 1969.

D&H (US)

Delaware & Hudson Rly Co. Acquired by CPR (qv) 1991.

D&KR

Dublin & Kingstown Rly, inc 1831, opened 1834, Dublin to Dun Laoghaire, first rly in Ireland, 4 ft 8¹/₂ in/1,435 mm gauge. Part of Waterford, Wexford, Wicklow & Dublin Rly (*see* D&SER), 1846. Converted to 5 ft 3 in/1,600 mm gauge, 1857.

D&LST/D&LER

Inc as Dublin & Lucan Steam Tramway 1880, opened 1881, 1883, 3 ft/914 mm gauge, tramway (*4*). Extension to Leixlip inc as Lucan, Leixlip & Celbridge Steam Tramway 1889, opened to Leixlip only 1890. Renamed D&L Electric Rly 1897 and gauge changed to 3 ft 6 in/1,067 mm. Leixlip–Lucan steam tramway closed 1897. D&LER electrically worked with double and single deck overhead trolley wire tramcars from 1900, freight wagons hauled by electric loco. Leixlip extension reopened as electric tramway by Lucan & Leixlip Electric Rly, 1910, worked by D&LER. Line closed 1925. The two undertakings became part of the Dublin United Tramways from 1927 and the tracks were rebuilt to 5 ft 3 in/1,600 mm gauge to Lucan only. Reopened as part of the Dublin city tramways system in 1928, closed 1940.

D&RGW

Denver & Rio Grande Western Railroad, a US 914 mm and standard gauge system, Denver/Pueblo–Salt Lake City/Ogden, etc. Section in Colorado State now operated by Combres & Toltec Scenic RR.

D&SER

Dublin & South Eastern Rly, Dublin, Wicklow, Waterford and Wexford, inc 1846 as Waterford, Wexford, Wicklow & Dublin

Rly, and including D&KR (qv) which had been opened in 1834. Generally known as Dublin, Wicklow & Wexford Rly. Opened 1854, 1856, 1864, 1872, 1887, 1891, 1904. Name changed to D&SER 1907. Part of GSR from 1925.

D&SR

Devon & Somerset Rly, inc 1864, Norton Fitzwarren to Barnstaple, opened 1871–3, worked by B&ER and then GWR, absorbed by GWR 1901.

Dandy (RS)(obs)

A small four-wheeled coach hauled by a horse, especially that on the Port Carlisle branch of the NBR.

Dandy cart (obs)

A wagon in which a horse travelled to descend an incline, behind a train going down under gravity, after having hauled a train up.

Dangerous goods

Traffic capable of posing a significant risk to health, safety or property when carried by rail (i.e. of an explosive, flammable, corrosive, poisonous or radioactive nature). Handled under special commercial and operating regulations.

Danger signal

A semaphore (qv) stop signal at horizontal with red lamp at night, or colour light signal (qv) with red light showing, requiring a train to come to an absolute stop.

Danubiu

A *CIWL* Pullman service between Bucharest and Galatz, 1932–9, a renaming of the *Dunarea*.

Dare Valley

Aberdare to Nantmelyn and Bwllfa Dare Colliery, inc 1863, opened 1866, worked by TVR, leased to TVR 1871, part of TVR 1889.

Dark money (LTRS)

Unsocial hours allowance.

Dark track (USRS)

Single track mileage which is not fully signalled or controlled by CTC (qv).

DART

1. Dublin Area Rapid Transit; name adopted for Dublin suburban electric services when introduced in 1984.

2. Dallas Area Rapid Transit, including light rail, 1996.

3. A high-quality Digital Advanced Radio for Trains; an international train radio system developed for installation in 2000 and beyond to replace CSR (qv) and National Radio Networks (NRN) in all situations where a secure system is required.

Dart
A catch on the inside of the smokebox door of a steam loco.

Dartford Loop
London (Charing Cross/Cannon St.)–Hither Green–Sidcup–Dartford.

Dart Valley
Totnes to Ashburton line. Section between Buckfastleigh and a point near Totnes now operated as a preserved line, first section opened 1969, under various names: Dart Valley Light Rly, Buckfast Steam Rly, Primrose Line, and (1990) the South Devon Rly. *See* SDR (2).

Dart Valley Rly plc
The owners of the preserved rly between Paignton and Kingswear from 1973. *See also* P&DSR.

Dash (obs)
A semi-circular panel extending round the end platforms of a tramcar (qv) at waist level.

Dating press
A device invented in 1837 by Thomas Edmondson (1792–1851) to stamp the date of issue on the small cardboard passenger tickets of his design, printed on a machine of his design. Tickets were consecutively numbered and kept in racks. This combined system, which replaced the laborious arrangement of writing out an individual ticket for each passenger, and recording the issue in a book, was virtually universal on British rlys for many years, not finally disappearing until the late 1980s. *See also* Edmondson ticket.

Davis wheel
A cast solid steel wheel with a disc in the centre introduced in the USA in the early twentieth century.

Day Coach (US)
see Coach (or Day Coach) class.

Day Continental
A BR boat train between London (Liverpool St.) and Harwich (Parkeston Quay) introduced 1947, name dropped 1987.

Daylight Saving (RS)
An electrical failure in a passenger carriage.

Daylight sidings
Tracks on which engine movements are forbidden after dark.

DB
Deutsche Bundesbahn, formed 1945 to take over former *DR* (*3*) (qv) lines in West Germany. Part of *DBAG* (qv), 1994.

DB (LT)
Disciplinary Board. Also (LTRS) 'to be DB'd' – to appear before a DB.

DBAG (Ger)
Deutsche Bahn Allgemeine Gesellschaft, a public limited company wholly in Federal ownership responsible for management and operation of the entire German rail system from 1 January 1994, following reunification of East and West Germany in 1990. 45,514 km, mostly standard gauge.

DBSO
A BR driving brake Second/Standard class open coach fitted with TDM (qv).

DC, The (RS)
Any section of BR or LT operated by direct current (dc) electric traction, usually to distinguish it from a nearby line operated by alternating current (ac).

DCE (obs)
Divisional Civil Engineer, BR.

DCR
Dorset Central Rly, inc 1856, Wimborne to Blandford. Opened 1860, 1862, part of S&DJR (qv) 1862.

DD (obs)
BR (S) Double Deck four-car units introduced 1949, two driving motor cars and two trailers, 4-DD.

Dead (RS)
A train or loco suffering loss of power.

Dead buffers
Buffers consisting of nothing more than square wooden beams.

Dead centre
The position in which a steam loco comes to a stand and in which, when the regulator is

opened to re-start, the valves are covering the steam ports, preventing steam from entering the cylinders. Overcome by reversing.

Dead early (LTRS)

A duty covering first train of the day.

Dead end kid (RS)

An employee refusing promotion.

Dead end siding

A siding with access at one end only.

Dead engine (RS)

A loco not in steam, or switched off.

Deadhead (USRS)

1. Empty stock or other unproductive working.
2. An employee travelling free on a pass or any other non-revenue-earning passenger.
3. A brakeman.

Dead late (LTRS)

A duty covering last train of the traffic day.

Dead load

The tare weight of a wagon or coach including all its permanent fixtures.

Deadman's handle/button/control

A safety device incorporated in the master controller of an electric train which requires the driver to exercise a continuous pressure to prevent interruption of current supply and the application of the brakes. Invented in 1902 by the American Frank J. Sprague. Originally (RS), but later adopted officially. *See also* DSD.

Dead signal (RS)

Signal permanently at the danger or 'on' position, often lettered 'STOP'.

Dead, stuck on the (RS) (obs)

A tramcar (qv) brought to a halt owing to loss of contact between its plough (qv) and the current rail owing to an electrical gap in the track layout.

Dean and Dawson

see D&D.

Dean Forest Rly

A preserved line from Lydney to Park End over part of former S&WJR. *See also* S&WR&C.

Dean Goods (RS)

GWR 0–6–0 locos, designed by William Dean, introduced 1883–99. Many served in war zones overseas in both World Wars.

Dearness Valley

Dearness Valley Rly, NER Waterhouses

branch, inc 1855, part of NER 1857, opened 1858, passenger service 1877.

Dearne Valley

DVR (*1*) (qv).

Death chamber (RS)

The high voltage cubicle in a diesel loco.

Death, Railway of

see Railway of Death.

Deauville Express

CIWL Pullman train between Paris and Deauville; ran only in 1927.

DEBG (Ger)

Deutsche Eisenbahn Betriebs-Gesellschaft; a co. owning secondary rlys, mainly in southern Germany.

Decapod

Any steam loco with ten coupled driving wheels.

Decauville line

A term used (mainly by the British Army) to describe any light rly of narrow gauge (usually 60 cm), including those not equipped with the products of this firm. *See also* Decauville track.

Decauville track

Pre-fabricated narrow gauge (usually 60 cm) track, produced in unit lengths to facilitate ease of transport and fast laying. Much used in France and French Empire for military and other light rlys. After its inventor, Paul Amand Decauville. Patented 1875.

Deccan Queen

An express between Bombay and Poona.

Decency board (obs)

A screen placed below the upper deck rails of an open-topped tramcar to protect ladies' ankles and legs from the vulgar masculine gaze.

Deck

1. (US) Footplate (qv) and also the footwalk on the roofs of freight cars.
2. *see* Bank (*2*).
3. The floor of a wagon, coach or tramcar, hence Double-deck/er (qv).

Deck, to

see Decking.

Deckhand (USRS)

Vagrant (US = hobo) who steals a free ride on the roof of a freight car.

Deckies (RS)(obs)
Persons working on goods loading decks in depots and warehouses. Usage confined to the GWR.

Decking (USRS)
Riding on the roof of a freight wagon.

Decklights
Long and narrow windows in the clerestory (qv) of a passenger coach.

Déclassement/déclassé (Fr)
A formal abandonment of a section of rly by the French government. Services may have long since ceased but until *déclassement* the trackbed cannot be used for other purposes.

Decorate, to (USRS)
To climb to the roof of a freight car.

Deepdene (obs)
TC for a royal train carrying members of the royal family but not the monarch. After Deepdene, Dorking, Surrey, site of the SR offices in WW2.

Deeplus (TC) (obs)
Code for a special party travelling in reserved accommodation on a timetabled train service.

Deerstalker Express
Unofficial name for West Highlander Sleeper train (qv), 1995.

Deeside Line/Rly
Aberdeen to Ballater.

Déferée, une ligne (Fr)
see Déposée, une ligne (qv).

Delayed Yellow
An arrangement which allows a passenger train to approach a colour-light signal (qv) without the protection of full overlap (qv) by holding the next signal in the rear at 'on' (qv) until the train is almost at it, whereupon it will clear to yellow, thus reducing the speed of the train.

Delayer (USRS)
A train dispatcher; *see* Train order.

Dels (RS)
Deltics (qv).

Deltics
BR class 55 3,300 hp diesel-electric locos introduced 1961. From the profile of their diesel engines.

Demi-car
A small single deck tramcar designed or adapted for one-man operation.

DEMU
Diesel-electric multiple unit.

Demurrage
A charge raised for the detention by consignor or consignee of wagons, wagon-sheets or containers held beyond a prescribed free period, also for wagons held up in transit to meet a trader's convenience.

Den (USRS)
A caboose (qv).

Denver Zephyr
An express diesel set running between Chicago and Denver, introduced 1936.

Departmental (obs)
A term used to distinguish locos, rolling stock, depots. train services, etc. employed or allocated to activities (e.g. engineering work) not contributing directly to revenue.

Departure siding
A siding (qv) used to hold trains before departure from a depot or yard.

Déposée, une ligne (Fr)
A line which has been closed and completely lifted.

Depot (pronounced *deepo*) (US)
A station; now largely superseded by 'train station'.

Depot, The
London Transport Museum's reserve collection, a 'working museum store', opened to the public from 1999 at Ealing Common LT rolling stock depot; rail-connected to LT system.

Depression bar
see Clearance/depression bar.

DERA
Defence Evaluation and Research Agency.

Derail (US)
Catch points (qv).

Derailer
A device which can be moved into position on top of a running rail to derail a loco attempting to back on to its train before the road is set. It requires less space than catch or trap points.

Derby (RS)
Midland Rly, later London Midland Region, BR.

Derrick car (US)
A crane wagon.

Derry Express
A UTA (qv) express introduced 1949 with new rolling stock and a timing of 2 h 15 min between Belfast and Londonderry. *See also* Belfast Express.

Derwent Valley
see DVLR (*1*).

Describer
see Train describer/indicator.

Desert Driver (RS)(obs)
A steam engineman in fear of running short of water and/or sand.

DES
Department of Explosive Supplies (WW1).

DESG (Ger)
Deutsche Eisenbahn Speisewagen Gesellschaft. A pre-1914 subsidiary of *CIWL* (qv) which operated restaurant cars in Germany.

Desiro
Name for a family of Siemens (qv) dmu (qv) delivered from 2000.

Desk Jockey (RS)
A clerk.

Det (LTRS)
A detonator.

Detainer (USRS)
A train dispatcher; *see* Train order.

Detector bar
The part of a signal interlocking mechanism which warns the signalman that points are not properly home.

Detectors, point
A mechanical system which aligns signal wire slides and point slots to ensure that signals cannot be cleared unless the point blades are fully home and have correctly responded to the lever movement.

Detonator
see Fog signal.

DETR
Department of the Environment, Transport & the Regions, formed in 1997 by incoming New Labour administration. Replaced DOT/DTp (qv). Became DTLR (qv) 2001.

DEV (Fr)
SNCF standard coach design of the late 1940s.

Devils (RS)
Coal braziers.

Devil's Arrow, The (RS)
BR double arrow logo.

Devil strip (USRS) (obs)
The road surface between the two tracks of a double-track stretch on which careless motorists could suffer serious damage to themselves, their passengers and their vehicle when two tramcars passed.

Devon & Cornwall Special
A Third-class-only express between London (Paddington) and Falmouth with through coaches to Torquay, Paignton and Newquay, operated in 1913–14.

Devon Belle
An all-Pullman summer-only express, with rear observation car, between London (Waterloo) and Ilfracombe/Plymouth, introduced 1947, Plymouth section withdrawn 1950, ceased 1954.

Devon Great Consols Mineral Rly
A mining rly running north from the River Tamar and Tavistock Canal at Morwellham, 1858–1901.

Devonian
A summer express between Bradford and Leeds and Torquay and Paignton, introduced 1927, ceased 1939. Re-introduced by BR 1949. Name dropped 1975. Revived 1987 as Leeds–Paignton, later Newcastle–Paignton. Name ceased to be used from 2 June 2002.

Devon Scot
A through service between Aberdeen and Plymouth via Birmingham, introduced 1988. Name ceased to be used from 2 June 2002.

Devon Valley
see DVR (*2*).

DF (Ger)
Deutsche Fähregesellschaft, a merging of *DB* (qv) and *DR* (qv) ferry services from 1 January 1993.

DfT
Department for Transport, formed 2002, assuming responsibility for transport from DTLR (qv).

DGS
BR driving trailer with guard's accommodation (Driving Guard Second/Standard class).

DH

Diesel-Hydraulic.

DHMU

Diesel-Hydraulic Multiple Unit.

DI

District Inspector. Still used on LT rlys, after the correct title became Area Manager.

Diagram

1. A schedule designed to obtain the best working arrangements for train crews, rolling stock and locos over a given period of time, showing the routes and services to be covered, times, etc.

2. A reference drawing maintained for each type of loco and other movable equipment, showing dimensions, weight, design details, etc.; brought together in Diagram Books.

Diamant

A Paris–Brussels–Amsterdam service introduced 1954, became Antwerp–Bonn 1962. Name then given to *TEE* Antwerp–Dortmund, introduced 1965, reduced to Brussels–Dortmund 1966, Cologne–Brussels 1968–70, Hanover–Brussels 1970–6. Name revived 1979 for a Hamburg–Munich service. Lost *TEE* status 1981.

Diameter

For rly purposes the diameter of a wheel is measured across the tread at its centre, ignoring the flange.

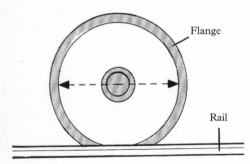

Diameter

Diamond cracker/pusher (USRS)

A loco fireman. From black diamonds = coal.

Diamond crossing

A track crossing another track diagonally, the rails so forming a diamond or lozenge shape.

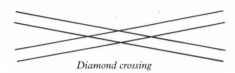

Diamond crossing

Diaphragm (US)

Flexible covered gangway connection between two coaches; a corridor connection.

DIC

Door Isolating Cock.

Dice train (USRS)

A fast train.

Dick

1. W.B. Dick & Co., Kilmarnock, builders of locos, and tramway and narrow gauge rly equipment (including cars) from 1881. Became Dick, Kerr & Co., 1883 (DK (qv)).

2. (LTRS) District Line, LT.

Diddly Dike (RS)(obs)

Cheltenham–Andover line, M&SWJR.

Diddy box (LTRS)

A small disconnection box used with signalling equipment.

Dido (RS)(obs)

A GCR and L&NER train service for rlymen, Bulwell Common to Annesley, The 'Annesley Dido'. An acronym for Day In, Day Out.

Die, to (USRS)

To bring a train to a stop on a hill, or to stall or lose motive power.

Die/d on the law, to (USRS)

To cease work after 12 continuous hours, the limit laid down in the Federal Hours of Service Act.

Diggle Route

Huddersfield–Stalybridge.

Dike, to (RS)

To signal a train into a refuge siding.

Dilly (LTRS)

Piccadilly Line, LT.

Dilly road (USRS)

A spur line.

Diner (USRS)

1. A restaurant car.

2. (US) A cheap roadside restaurant in an old rly car body or a building resembling a rly car.

Ding-ding and away (RS)

A dangerous situation which can arise if a driver starts his train from a station on hearing the guard's bell or buzzer without checking the aspect of the starting signal. *See also* SPAD.

Dinger (USRS)

A yardmaster or a conductor (*3*) (qv).

Dinky (USRS)

A four-wheel tramcar; also a small loco.

Dinting (RS)

Digging out old ballast.

Dip (LTRS)

A flyunder.

Diplodocus (Fr)

A large rail-mounted crane used by French Army Engineers.

Dippers (RS)

LM&SR Hughes 2–6–0 locos. From the 'dip' in the footplate.

Direct-Orient Express

A *CIWL* service between Paris, Milan and Belgrade, introduced 1921. Re-introduced 1950, extended to Istanbul 1962–7. Ceased to run beyond Venice 1977 and name dropped. This was the last through Paris–Istanbul service and the last of the long-distance *CIWL* European international sleeping and dining car services. *See also* Marco Polo; Marmara Express; Orient Express.

Directors (RS)

GCR 4–4–0 locos named after the company's directors.

Direct Portsmouth

see PR (*4*).

Direct, un train (Fr) (obs)

A daily service on a trunk line calling only at principal stations.

Direct stairs (obs)

Stairs to the upper deck of a tramcar (qv) which rise in an anti-clockwise half turn or quarter turn. *See also* Reversed Stairs.

Diretti (It)

Fast regional train services.

Direttisima (It)

FS line built to give faster and more direct routes between the major Italian cities.

Direttissimo, treno (It)

An express train. Originally a mail train with accommodation restricted to First and old Second class.

Diretto, treno (It)

A semi-fast train or 'ordinary express'.

DIRFT

Daventry International Rail Freight Terminal.

Dirt, in the (RS)

Derailed or driven into a sand drag.

Dirt, to hit the (USRS)

To jump or fall from a moving train.

Dirt relief (LTRS)

Trainmen's physical needs relief.

Dirty, Ragged and Greasy, The

Nickname for D&RGW (qv).

Disc

A ground signal.

Dishwasher (USRS)

A loco cleaner.

Dispatcher/dispatching

see Train order.

Dispatchers (obs)

See Loaders.

Display board

A white board fixed behind a semaphore signal to enhance its visibility.

Distant signal

The first signal of a set seen from approaching trains, usually sited 600–1,000 yd (549–915 metres) before the first stop signal (home or outer home) to which it applies. If at caution, it indicates that the home or stop signal ahead is likely to be in that position and the driver may pass it at reduced speed until he can see the indication of the stop signal. If 'off' (clear), it indicates that the subsequent signal is also 'off' and it can only be cleared if this is so. To ensure there is sufficient braking distance where signal boxes are closely spaced, the distant signal for one box may be combined with the starter signal for the box in the rear, slotted (qv) to prevent the distant signal showing a clear indication when the stop signal is at danger. Semaphore distant arms are fish-tailed in shape (i.e. a vee notch cut into the outer end of the arm). At night such signals originally showed a white light when 'on' but *c.* 1900 this was altered to red.

The MDR (qv) used yellow lights for an 'on' aspect from 1907 and orange/yellow became universal in Britain from 1924. *See also* Warning boards.

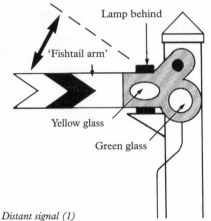

Distant signal (1)

Distress warning
See Train in distress warning.

District
Abbreviation for MDR (qv) or, after 1933, the equivalent District Line of LT.

DIT (US)
Dead In Train; the movement of an inactive loco as part of a train.

Ditch, to (USRS)
1. To derail a train [often putting it in the drainage ditch at the side of the track].
2. To throw a vagrant (hobo) off a train.

Ditch, in the (USRS)
Wrecked or derailed; see Ditch, to.

Ditch Lights
Additional train or loco headlights at the level of the top edge of the headstock (qv) which flash alternately when a horn or siren is sounded, or are used independently. They are designed to improve safety at level crossings by providing a visual indication of an approaching train at motorists' eye level.

Division (LTRS)
Divisional Manager's Office.

Dixie (US)
A steam loco with 4–8–4 wheel arrangement.

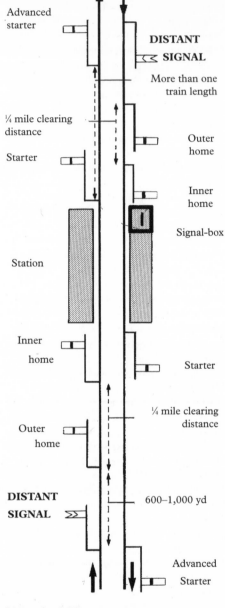

Distant signal (2)

DK
Dick, Kerr & Co. Ltd, Britannia Works, Kilmarnock. Formerly Dick (*1*) (qv); founded 1883, builders of steam tramway locos and suppliers of equipment for tramways (*3*). New works set up at Preston in

1899 for the manufacture of electric tramcars, etc. under the control of a subsidiary, ER&TCW (qv). New works built at Preston in 1900 for manufacture of electric traction and power station equipments by a subsidiary, English Electric Manufacturing Co. Ltd, which was absorbed into DK in 1903. All taken into EE (qv) in 1919.

DL&W (US)

Delaware, Lackawanna & Western RR Co.

DLR

Docklands Light Rly (London), inc 1984, 1985, Tower Gateway–Poplar–Stratford/Island Gardens [North Greenwich], largely over formation of L&BR (*3*) and MER (*2*). Opened 1987, Britain's first fully automatic computer-controlled passenger rly, with driverless trains; also London's first LRT line. Under-contact third rail traction supply. Extension to Bank 1991; to Beckton 1995; and to Greenwich and Lewisham in 1999.

DM

1. Driving Motor car in an mu set.
2. Diesel Mechanical.

DMB

BR Driving Motor Brake power car.

DMBC

BR Driving Motor Brake Composite coach.

DMBS

BR Driving Motor Brake Second/Standard class car.

DMBSO

BR Driving Motor Brake Second/Standard class Open coach.

DMC

BR Driving Motor Composite car.

DMCC

BR Driving Motor Composite Coach with lavatory.

DMLV

BR Driving Motor Luggage Van.

DMMU

Diesel Mechanical Multiple Unit.

DMO

Divisional Manager's Office.

DMR

Deferred Meal Relief allowance, paid to LT trainmen if meal relief is delayed.

DMS

BR Driving Motor car Second/Standard class.

DMSL

BR Driving Motor Second/Standard class coach with lavatory.

DMSO

BR Driving Motor Second/Standard class Open coach.

DMT(LT)

Duty Manager (Trains), officer in charge of performance of Train Operators, introduced 1998.

DMU

Diesel Multiple Unit.

DN&GR

Dundalk, Newry & Greenore Rly, NI/Ire. Inc 1863, capital raised by L&NWR, who were virtual owners, supplied the locos and rolling stock and operated a steamer service to Greenore from Holyhead. Became part of LM&SR 1923. Dundalk–Greenore opened 1873, Greenore–Newry 1876, GNR (I) (qv) took over working from 1 July 1933. Closed 1951. Company dissolved 1957.

DN&SR

Didcot, Newbury & Southampton [Junction] Rly, Didcot to Shawford Junction, Winchester, inc 1873, opened 1882, 1885, 1891. Worked by GWR, name changed to DN&SR 1883. Absorbed by GWR 1923.

DNG (TC) (obs)

Prefix for a telegraphic message warning of a dangerous occurrence (e.g. a broken axle observed in a passing train).

DO

Driver Only; a train crewed only by its driver.

Dock

A short length of track with platforms arranged to facilitate loading and unloading of cattle, horses, road vehicles, parcels, milk churns, etc. Adopted from canal usage.

Dockers' umbrella

Nickname for the Liverpool Overhead Rly, whose continuous viaduct afforded shelter for dockers in wet weather.

Dod (RS)

A ground or shunt signal.

Dodger (RS)(obs)

1. A shunting track.

2. A branch line train.

DoE

Department of the Environment.
Responsible for transport 1970–6. *See* DTp.

Dog (USRS)

A freight train operating for a short
distance only; also 'short dog'.

Dog catcher (USRS)

A member of a relief crew.

Dog catching (USRS)

The act of relieving a train crew which has
'died on the law' (qv).

Dog charts (RS)

Diagrams of mechanical interlocking in
signal boxes.

Dog collector (obs)

A large dog with a collecting box for a rly
charity strapped to its back, which
patrolled station premises unsupervised,
seeking contributions from passengers.

Dogfish

A 24-ton hopper ballast wagon used by
engineers.

Doggy (RS)

A platelayer (qv). Possibly from dog spike
(qv).

Doghouse (USRS)

1. A caboose (qv) (usually a four-wheeler).

2. A cupola (qv).

3. A brakeman's shelter on a loco tender.

Dog law (USRS)

A federal law restricting train crews to a
maximum of twelve hours' continuous
duty. *See also* Bear law; Hog law; Monkey,
caught by the.

Dogs (RS)

A tool for pulling up sleepers.

Dog Spike

A spike with a large head projecting sideways.

Do-it-yourself kit (RS)(obs)

A contemptuous term for a badly
maintained steam loco (steam enginemen
were expected to carry out minor running
repairs and adjustments).

Doll (RS)

Signal post with one or more semaphore arms.

Dolly (RS)

1. A dwarf ground or shunt signal.

2. A small shunting loco.

3. A roll of cotton waste.

Dolphin

A 40-ton bogie rail and sleeper wagon used
by engineers.

Dolly Mixture sets/trains (RS)

Trains composed of locos and rolling stock
in varying liveries. First used in 2002 to
describe one consequence of the
privatization of the British rly system.

Dome

Dome-shaped enclosure on top of the
boiler of a steam loco in which steam
collects in as dry a state as possible. It
contains the regulator (qv).

Dome car

see Vistadome.

Domed roof

A coach roof which curves downwards at
each end when viewed from the side.
'Doming' was sometimes applied to the
ends of a clerestory (qv) as well as to the
roof.

Domino (RS)

Same as Blackboard (qv).

Donauwalzer

Vienna–Ostend/Amsterdam over-night
service.

Donegal

see CDRJC.

Donegan (USRS)

An old rly coach converted to an office or
residential accommodation. From the
name of a man who specialized in such
conversions.

Donkey (RS)

1. A Westinghouse pump.

2. (obs) A branch line, or the branch line
    train, e.g. Marlow Donkey, Delph
    Donkey.

Donkeys (RS)

LM&SR 350 hp diesel shunting locos.

DOO

Driver-Only Operation (i.e. train in sole
charge of driver, no other train crew).

Doodlebugs

1. (RS) BR 4–6–2 locos. After the German
    WW2 missile.

2. (RS) LM&SR 430XX 2–6–0 locos. After the missile.
3. (USRS) A petrol railcar, especially the small type used to transport track maintenance workers.

Doorand
A 33-ton ballast wagon used by engineers.

Dope, doping it (USRS)
A chemical compound used to prevent boiler water foaming when the loco was being worked hard; the insertion of this material.

Dope monkey (USRS)
A car inspector.

Dormientes (South American Sp)
Track sleepers.

Dormy depot/shed
A small shed accommodating overnight one or two vehicles (tramcars or buses) to avoid inconvenient/uneconomic journeys back to a distant main depot.

Dorset Scot
An Edinburgh–Poole service, introduced 1990. Withdrawn 1992. Reintroduced May 1994.

Dortoir (Fr)
A staff dormitory/hostel.

DoT
Department of Transport (UK). *See* DTp.

DoT (US)
Department of Transportation. Formed in 1966, it includes the Federal Railroad Administration.

Double (TC)
Bolster wagon (qv).

Double, to (USRS)
To take a train over a steeply graded section by dividing it into two parts.

Double bedroom
A private compartment in a US long-distance train consisting of a wide settee across the width for day use, convertible to a bed at night, when a second bed is let down from the compartment wall. Introduced *c*. 1938.

Double berth
The upper or lower 'half section' in a US Pullman sleeping car.

Double block working (obs)
An operating state in which at least two block sections in front of high-speed trains were kept clear; the procedure was also used ahead of and in the rear of royal trains (qv) and also during fog when fogmen (qv) were not deployed.

Double Breasters (RS)
L&SWR '443' T14 class 4–6–0s. Notorious for oscillation; their drivers were alleged to wear double-breasted coats for protection.

Double bubble (LTRS)
A double shift (sixteen hours of duty).

Double bucket (RS)
Two class 20 diesel locos running together with cabs at outer ends.

Double champignon (Fr)
Bullhead rail (qv) in chairs.

Double-deck/er
Tramcar or rly carriage with two decks furnished with passenger seating.

Double crossing
Another name for scissors crossover (qv).

Double docking
Allowing a second train into an occupied platform at a terminus, thus trapping the first.

Double end, to (LTRS)
To use two crews, one at each end of a train, to obtain quick turnrounds. The term is also current on the Toronto metro, where two drivers are used, one acting as guard in one direction. *See also* Stepping up/back.

Double-ended tank/double ender (RS)
A tank loco with symmetrical wheel arrangement, e.g. 2–4–2T.

Double headed/ing
Two locos hauling one train.

Double home turn (RS)(obs)
A lodging turn (qv).

Double peg[ged] (RS)
Both signals in the 'off' position on a single post, indicating that two sections in advance are clear.

Double quad (RS)(obs)
Two quad-arts (qv) coupled together.

Double rest (LTRS)
Two rest days in one week.

Double shovelling (RS)
Bringing the coal forward towards the footplate.

Double shunt

A loco propelling two sets of wagons, from one line to another, each set coupled together but not to each other, or to the loco.

Double singles (RS)

Locos with two sets of driving axles, each connected to its own set of cylinders.

Double slip

A diamond crossing with connections between both tracks in both directions. *See also* Slips.

Double slip

Double stack (US)

Haulage of freight containers placed one above the other on low flat trucks.

Double yellow

see Double yoke.

Double yoke (RS)

A colour-light signal showing the double yellow preliminary caution indication.

Doubling back (RS)

Changing to an earlier shift with no intervening rest day, thus obtaining short rest period between shifts.

Doughnuts/Donuts (RS)

BR class 60 locos. From the hole in their sides.

Doves (RS)

LB&SCR 2–4–0 and outside-framed 0–6–0 locos built by Dübs & Co., Glasgow.

Down

1. Usually this denotes the line carrying trains away from London. There were some exceptions: e.g. away from the location of the rly's headquarters; or, in Scotland, away from Edinburgh; and on the TVR (qv), the term denoted a line down to the South Wales coast. The principal meaning was derived from road stage coach usage dating from the 17th century. *See also* Up (*1*).

2. (RS) Late, e.g. 'ten down' = ten minutes late. *See also* Up (*2*).

Down siding

A siding trailing off the Down (*1*) (qv) line.

Downstairs (LTRS)

East London Line, LT.

Down the hole (LTRS)

In the deep level tube system.

Down the nick (RS)(obs)

A loco short of steam.

Down the pipe (LTRS)

see Down the hole.

Down the plug (RS)(obs)

A loco running short of water.

Down the road, to go (LTRS)

To see a manager over a misdemeanour.

Down the slot/put down the s., to (RS)

To divert a freight or slow passenger train to a loop or siding to make way for a fast train.

DPU

BR diesel parcels unit.

DR

1. District Rly: MDR (qv).

2. (LTRS) District Line.

3. *Deutsche Reichsbahn*; German State Rlys, formed 1923. Continued in East Germany (GDR) after WW2 but part of system located in West Germany (FRG) became *DB* (qv). From 1994 part of *DBAG* (qv). *See also DRB, DRG*.

4. Donegal Rly *see* CDRJC.

DRA

Driver's Reminder Appliance. A cab warning system that when set indicates that the signal ahead is showing a danger aspect. Once set, the driver cannot move the train. Installed from 1998.

Drag (USRS)

1. A very slow or heavy freight train.

2. A train of empties.

Drag, to (RS)

To move an inactive loco, with or without train, by hauling it with another loco. *See also* Thunderbirds.

Drahtseilbahn (Ger)

A funicular (cable) rly.

Drain, The (RS)

1. The Waterloo & City platforms at Waterloo station, London, or the whole rly. Originally (RS), but since it was suitably depreciatory, subsequently adopted by journalists and commuters.

2. Tunnels between Metropolitan City Widened Lines and surface lines at Kings Cross.

Drain/Pump train

A train of water and sludge carriers and high-pressure water jet equipment which is marshalled to clear pipes and culverts along the rly.

Draisine (Fr) (Ger)

A motorized track inspection railcar. After *Draisienne*, an early form of bicycle invented by Baron Karl Drais.

Dram road (obs)

An alternative term used from *c.* 1790 for a Tramroad (*1*) (qv), principally current in south Wales and probably no more than a Welsh prononciation of tramroad.

Drapeau

An express between Paris and Bordeaux, introduced 1955. Replaced by unnamed TGV 1990.

Drawbar

The hooked bar fixed to the centre of the end frame of a vehicle for coupling purposes.

Drawbar pull

The force exerted on a train at the loco/tender drawbar after taking account of all resistance losses of loco and any tender. Sometimes known as 'drawbar tractive effort'. 'Equivalent drawbar pull' includes correction for gradient and acceleration on the weight of the loco and tender; on the level and at uniform speed it is the same as drawbar pull.

Drawing room

1. A private compartment on US long distance train accommodating up to four passengers; furnished with settee and two loose armchairs for day use and transverse upper and lower beds and a longitudinal bed for night use.
2. (USRS) A caboose (qv).

Draw up to the peg, to (RS)

To approach and stop at a signal.

DRB (Ger)

Deutsche Reichsbahn; *DRB* was the correct abbreviation for *DR* (*3*) (qv), the German rly undertaking during the period 1937–45,

but *DR* continued to be used informally and on some documents.

DRE

Defence Rail Executive; an organization formed in 2001 working for all branches of the armed services, which is tasked with operating the military rlys and arranging military movements over the national network. It is also responsible for partnership deals with the private sector involving use of rail-connected military storage facilities when these are not required for military purposes.

Dreadnoughts (RS)

1. GWR (qv) Churchward corridor coaches of 1904, 70 ft/21.3 m long, 9.5 ft/2.9 m wide.
2. L&YR 4–6–0 locos of 1908–9.
3. Metropolitan Rly compartment coaches with round-topped doors, introduced 1910–12.
4. Open-top Blackpool tramcars of 1898–99 with twin staircases each end, to speed up loading and unloading.

All were named after the contemporary Royal Navy battleships introduced from 1906.

Drewry

Drewry Car Co. Ltd, Burton on Trent, railcar and loco builders from 1911. Amalgamated with Baguley (qv) as Baguley-Drewry Ltd, 1967.

Drewry (RS)

BR class 03 and 04 diesel-mechanical locos.

DRG (Ger)

Deutsche Reichsbahn-Gesellschaft. Full title of *DR* (*3*) (qv) from 1924–37. *See also DRB.*

DRICO (obs)

DRIver to COntroller tunnel wire communication system formerly used on LT Rlys.

Drift, to (USRS)

To run a loco downhill without working steam.

Drifting throttle (USRS)

Running with the regulator cracked open to keep air and dust from being sucked into the steam cylinders.

Drill (USRS)

Operations in a shunting yard.

Driving Trailer

A car devoid of traction equipment but fitted with a driving cab. Also known as a control trailer.

Drone

GWR TC for six-wheel Third class coach.

Drone A

GWR TC for Third class bogie coach with luggage compartment.

Drone B

GWR TC for four-wheel Third class coach with luggage compartment.

Drone cage (USRS)

A private rly car (qv).

Drooping arm/signal (RS)

Lower quadrant semaphore arm not in the precise horizontal position but dropping slightly down. Has to be treated as being a danger signal (qv).

Drop, to (USRS)

To shunt by uncoupling wagons from the loco and allowing them to roll into position by their own momentum.

Drop a track, to (LTRS)

The process whereby a train de-energizes a track circuit (qv) on entering a section.

Drop coach (obs)

The early term for slip coach (qv).

Drophead Buckeye Coupler

A form of central automatic coupler adopted by BR consisting of a drawhook and drophead. When one coach is shunted against another, the claw of one coupling passes and engages with the claw of the other. In the engaged position, the coupling is secured with a pin. Introduced specifically to allow vehicles with buckeye couplers (qv) to be coupled up with others still fitted with screw coupler gear (qv coupling screw).

Drop lever frog

An automatic frog (2) (qv).

Droplight

That part of a coach door window which can be lowered and secured with leather strap, or in more modern stock by a spring clutch.

Drop off, to (of a signal) (RS)

To change from 'on' to 'off' (clear) indication.

Drop off-Drop on signal (LTRS)

A signal that illuminates and clears as a train approaches it.

Drop on, to (of a train) (LTRS)

To appear on the signalman's track diagram or train describer.

Drop out, to (of train motors) (LTRS)

To cease to function owing to action of circuit breakers.

Dropped ends (LTRS)

Ends of cars bent downwards by clumsy shunting or coupling up.

Dropper

A fitting in electric railway overhead gear which holds the contact/conductor/traction wire below the catenary (qv).

Droppers (USRS)

Brakemen riding on a wagon and jumping off during shunting operations.

Dropping a short (LTRS)

Evading fares by buying two short-distance season tickets covering only the end sections of a long journey. Also known as the dumb-bell fraud/trick.

Dropping back (LTRS)

1. *see* Doubling back.

2. *see* Stepping up/back.

Dropping the consist (USRS)

Passing down a consist [form] (qv) to a telegraph operator from a train.

Drop the button/the deadman's/the handle, to (RS)

To release pressure on the deadman's handle, so stopping the train.

Drop the lever, to (RS)

To advance the cut-off on a steam loco to provide more power when starting, accelerating or climbing.

Drop the lot, to (RS)

To make an emergency stop.

DRS

Direct Rail Services, a subsidiary of BNFL (qv), an FOC (qv) formed in 1995 to handle BNFL freight flows and other business. Uses its own rolling stock and locos. Operates all nuclear material movements by rail in Great Britain.

DRT

Diesel Railway Traction. Supplement to *RG* (4) (qv) from 1931, separate monthly publication from 1946, incorporated in *RG* (4) from January 1964.

Druid (RS)
A Welsh rlyman.

Drum (RS)
Tea can.

Drumm battery cars
Battery electric railcars using an improved alkaline battery with high rates of charge and discharge, patented by Prof. James Drumm in 1929. Ran on the GSR/CIE 1930–49.

Drunkard (USRS)
A late Saturday night service carrying drunks home from a town or city.

Dry seat (obs)
A wooden flap which could be turned to cover a seat on the upper open deck of a tramcar (qv) to protect it from rain.

Dry turn (RS)
A duty with a guard or driver who rarely, if ever, brews tea.

DSB
Danske Statsbaner; Danish State Rlys. 3,164 km. *See also* Oresund link.

DSD
Driver's Safety Device, ensuring that the train stops if the driver collapses. Usually a plate depressed by a foot. *See also* Deadman's handle/button/control.

DSDC
Defence Storage and Distribution Centre.

DSG
Deutsche Schlafwagen und Speisewagen Gesellschaft; German Sleeping Car and Restaurant Car Company, formed 1950 to undertake all internal sleeping and restaurant car services on the *DB*. Renamed *Deutsche Service Gesellschaft der Bahn*, 1990.

DSO (obs)
Divisional Superintendent's Office.

DSVN
Duong Sat Viet Nam; Viet Nam Rlys, 2,430 km of metre gauge and 400 km of standard gauge.

DTBS
BR Driving Trailer Brake Second/Standard class.

DTBSO
BR DTBS (qv) with Open plan seating.

DTC
BR Driving Trailer Composite.

DTC (US)
Direct Train Control; an operating system used for long stretches of dark track (qv) in which train crews receive and repeat back train orders (qv) by radio.

DTCL
BR DTC (qv) with Lavatory cubicle.

DTCO
BR DTC (qv) with Open plan seating.

DTCOL
BR DTCO with Lavatory cubicle.

DTCSOL
BR DTC (qv) with Open plan seating but also some Compartment seating and a Lavatory cubicle.

DTFSOL
BR Driving Trailer with First class Open plan seating and Compartment seating and Lavatory cubicle.

DTLR
Department of Transport, Local Government and the Regions, replaced DETR (qv), 2001; transport responsibilities moved to new DfT (qv), 2002.

DTMA
Defence Transport & Movement Agency, Ministry of Defence; organizes Defence transport services, including rail, for the Royal Navy, Army and Royal Air Force.

DTp
Department of Transport. Re-formed 1976 as a separate department of state (between 1970 and 1976 the relevant rly and road functions had been the responsibility of the Department of the Environment). For earlier history *see* MoT. Also abbreviated DoT. Replaced by DETR (qv), 1997.

DTPMV
BR Driving Trailer Parcels and Mail Vehicle.

DTS
BR Driving Trailer Second/Standard class.

DTSL
BR DTS with Lavatory cubicle.

DTSO
BR DTS (qv) with Open plan seating.

DTSOL
BR DTSO (qv) with Lavatory cubicle.

Dual electrified line
A rly electrified on two different systems; in Britain, 650/750 V dc conductor rail and 25kV ac with catenary overhead.

Dual-fitted (obs)
A loco or vehicle equipped with both air and vacuum brake systems.

Dub Ds (RS)
BR 2–8–0 locos ex Ministry of Supply and War Department (hence WD, 'Dub D'); introduced 1943.

Dublos (RS)
BR standard 2–6–4T (80000–80130) from their alleged resemblance to Hornby (qv) Dublo 00 gauge model locos.

Dübs
Dübs & Co., loco builders, Glasgow from 1863. Amalgamated with Neilson (qv) and Sharp (qv) to form North British (qv) in 1903.

Duchesses (RS)
LM&SR 4–6–2 locos introduced in 1937.

Duckbill roof
US version of royal clerestory (qv). *See also* Bullnose.

Duck eggs (RS)(obs)
Coal briquettes in ovoid form.

Duck eights (RS)
L&NWR 0–8–0 locos.

Ducket
A small projecting window at the side of a coach to provide the guard with view along the train and the line.

Dud (LTRS)
A defective train.

Dudding Hill Loop
Acton to Cricklewood (London).

Dude (USRS)
A passenger train conductor, especially on the more important trains. From his smartly uniformed presence (dude = dandy).

Dude wrangler (USRS)
Brakeman on a passenger train, apt to wrangle (argue) with the dude (qv).

Duewag (Ger)
Short title (originally *Düwag*) of *Waggonfabrik Düsseldorf AG*, manufacturers of rly, light rly and tramcar rolling stock. Established 1916/1919 as *Gebruder Schöndorff AG*; new ownership, new name and combination with *Waggonfabrik Verdingen AG* of Krefeld,

c. 1935. Designers of KSW tramcar (qv). Wholly owned by *Siemens AG* since 1994.

Duffield Bank
Pioneer 15 in/381 mm gauge rly built by Sir Arthur Heywood on his estate on the outskirts of Duffield, near Derby, to demonstrate the potential of the gauge. This line was operated from 1874 until 1916.

Duff (RS)(Ire)(obs)
A coal dust mixture used to fire steam locos in Ireland during the WW2.

Duffs (RS)
BR class 47 diesel electric locos.

Dukedogs (RS)
GWR class 90XX 4–4–0 locos, built with parts from Duke and Bulldog classes.

Dukeries Route (obs)
Brand name of the LD&ECR line from Chesterfield to Lincoln.

Dulas Valley
see DVMR.

Dumb-bell Fraud (RS)
Same as 'Dropping a short' (qv).

Dumb buffer
A buffer which does not compress when in contact with another buffer. Banned on main-line rlys from 1915 (England and Wales) and 1916 (Scotland).

Dumb end
Head shunt (qv).

Dumb irons (RS)
Iron prongs extending vertically below loco or driving unit buffer beam ahead of the leading wheels to deflect any obstruction from the track.

Dummy
1. (obs) A small steam loco used to haul tramway (*3*) trailer cars; often disguised as a passenger car to avoid frightening the horses in the streets.
2. A grip car (qv).
3. (RS) A ground or shunt signal. Mainly SR and BR (S) usage.
4. (USRS) (obs) A shunting loco.
5. (GWR) (obs) Broad gauge truck or coach with buffers arranged to allow it to run with either broad or standard gauge vehicles or locos. (During conversion from broad to standard gauge, it was the practice to mix locos and stock of either gauge in trains.)

Dummy chucker (RS)
A shunter.
Dummy coach
An empty vehicle placed between loco and train for safety reasons.
Dummy crankshaft drive
A type of loco in which inside cylinders drive onto a shaft having cranks on the outer ends which hand the power to the wheels by connecting rods.
Dummy point (obs)
Point through which vehicles could not be run at horse and steam tramway (*3*) passing places. It consisted of one groove raised ¼ in to ¾ in, which sent the vehicle to the left hand track; in running out, the vehicle 'dropped off' into the running track. *See also* Open point.
Dump car (US)
A wagon designed to discharge its load through doors or by tipping of its body.
Dumpling
A method of construction under streets in which trenches are first excavated on both sides of the street and the side walls of the rly tunnel are built in them. The road surface is then replaced by timber baulks and the area below these dug out to enable steel cross girders to be inserted, to rest on the walls and form the permanent roof of the tunnel. The remaining soil ('the dumpling') is then removed to complete the tunnel.
Dunalastairs (RS)
McIntosh Caledonian Rly 4–4–0 locos, introduced 1896–1914.
Dunarea
A *CIWL* Pullman train between Bucharest and Galatz, introduced 1929. Renamed the *Danubiu* (qv) in 1932. Ceased 1939.
Dundee gauge (obs)
5 ft 6 in, as adopted for rlys in the Dundee region before the area was connected to the national network in the 1840s.
Dunnage
Straw pads or other packing materials used to protect freight in transit.
Duorail
A term used by planners and architects to distinguish the conventional rly from monorail or other unconventional forms.

Not found in the vocabulary of those professionally involved in rly transport.
Duplex
A development of the Roomette (qv) a private compartment on a US long-distance train with corridor at one side and transverse beds, upper and lower. The several duplex sections in a coach are arranged to dovetail into each other to make the optimum use of available space.
Duplex fog signal
A single detonator with two sets of explosives providing two fog signals in one case.
Duplex TGV (Fr)
TGV (qv) with double-deck passenger accommodation.
Duplex ticket
A two-part ticket divided by perforation.
Duplicate locos (obs)
Locos replaced in the capital accounts of a rly company were entered on the 'duplicate list'. As such they received no further heavy repairs but often remained in service for several years until thoroughly worn out. They could usually be identified by special numbers or a prefix to their original number.
Duster (USRS)
A loco.
Dust her out, to (USRS)
To put sand through the fire door of an oil-burning steam loco while working it hard, to reduce soot in the flues and assist steaming.
Dust raiser (USRS)
A loco fireman.
Dusty bin (RS)
BR class 321 emu.
Dutch clock (USRS)
A speed-recording device on a loco.
Dutch drop, to (USRS)
To shunt a wagon from the front of a loco to behind it.
Dutchman
Flying Dutchman (qv).
Dutton
Dutton & Co.; manufactured signalling equipment at Worcester from 1888. Dissolved 1899, assets passing to J.E. Pease & Co.

DV
Door valves.

DVA
Digitized Voice Announcer. Automatic station announcements as in London Underground trains.

DVLR
1. Derwent Valley Light Rly, standard gauge line from York (Layerthorpe) to Cliffe Common, LRO 1907, opened 1913. Passenger service ceased 1926, finally closed 1980.
2. Dart Valley Light Rly: *see* Dart Valley.

DVMR
Dulas Valley Mineral Rly, inc 1862, Cadoxton (Neath) to near Drim Colliery (Onllwyn), opened 1864, name changed to N&BR (qv) 1863.

DVR
1. Dearne Valley Rly, Black Carr Junction (south of Doncaster)–Cadeby–Grimethorpe–Brierley Junction (east of Barnsley). Inc 1897, opened throughout, 1909, passenger service began 1912; worked by L&YR, part of L&NWR 1922, LM&SR from 1923.
2. Devon Valley Rly, inc 1858, Tillicoultry–Kinross, opened 1863, 1869, 1871. Worked by NBR. Part of NBR 1875.
3. Dart Valley Rly Co., owners of the preserved former BR (1) (qv) line from Paignton to Kingswear (for Dartmouth).

DVT
Driving Van Trailer. A guard's van with driving cab designed for BR main line push-pull working in combination with electric locos, using TDM (qv), introduced 1989.

DWA (Ger)
Deutsche Waggonbau AG; rly and tramway (3) vehicle builders, Berlin. Sold to Bombardier (qv), 1997.

DW&WR
Dublin, Wicklow & Wexford Rly, formed 1860, became D&SER (qv) 1907.

Dwarf (RS)
A ground or shunt signal.

Dwarf frame
A small frame for working points and signals, set apart from normal signalbox.

Dwell time
The length of time occupied by a station stop.

Dynamiter (USRS)
A coach or wagon with defective air brakes which have locked into the full emergency position.

Dynamometer Car
A coach specially adapted to carry instruments and recording devices for measuring loco performance when working a train on the line. When in use, it is marshalled between the loco and the rest of the train.

D-Züge (Ger) (obs)
Durchgangszüge; fast corridor trains, usually with supplementary fare, on *DB, DR, OBB*. Replaced by IR (*1*) (qv).

E

E

Eilzug (qv).

Eagle eye (USRS)
A loco driver.

Eagle stock (RS) (obs)
L&SWR coaches for American Line boat trains, 1892.

E&CHR
Easton & Church Hope Rly, Easton and Inmosthay Quarries to Church Hope Cove and Portland (junction with Admiralty Portland Breakwater Rly). First section inc 1867, further acts 1884, 1887, 1890. Opened 1900. Worked by GWR and L&SWR jointly, as were the Admiralty line (opened for through running 1900) and the Weymouth & Portland Rly (inc 1862, opened 1865), the whole forming a continuous line. Passenger traffic (Weymouth–Portland) 1902. GWR and SR joint from 1923–47. BR 1948. Closed to passengers 1952, closed completely 1965.

E&CVR
Ely & Clydach Valleys Rly, Pen-y-Graig to Clydach Vale, Blaenclydach, inc 1873, opened 1878, worked by GWR, part of GWR from 1880.

E&HR
Edgware & Hampstead Rly (London), inc 1902, Edgware to junction with CCE&HR at Golders Green, part of LER (qv) 1912, opened 1923, 1924 as an open air extension of the CCE&HR tube rly.

E&MR
Eastern & Midlands Rly, inc 1882, amalgamation of Lynn & Fakenham, Yarmouth Union and Yarmouth & North Norfolk Rlys. Opened Melton Constable–Norwich 1882, Melton–Cromer (Beach) 1887. Absorbed M&ER and Peterborough, Wisbech and Sutton Bridge Rlys, 1883. Became M&GNJC 1893.

E&NR
Edinburgh & Northern Rly, inc 1845, Burntisland to Perth, purchased Edinburgh, Leith & Granton Rly 1847 and renamed Edinburgh, Perth & Dundee Rly. Opened 1847, 1848. Part of NBR 1861.

E&SBR
Ealing & Shepherds Bush Rly, Ealing Broadway to junction with WLR near Kensington (Olympia). Inc 1905 (part of GWR), connections with CLR at Shepherd's Bush authorized 1911 and built by GWR. Opened to freight traffic 1917, passenger service of CLR electric tube trains between Wood Lane Junction and Ealing Broadway started 1920.

E&SHR
Ealing & South Harrow Rly (London), inc 1894, North Ealing to South Harrow [Roxeth], part of MDR 1900, completed 1901 but not opened. Used as test bed for MDR electrification 1903 and public electric services begun. Piccadilly Line tube service was extended over it in 1932.

E&V
Engine & Van. A light engine (qv) working with a brake van and no other rolling stock.

E&WID&BJR
East & West India Docks & Birmingham Junction Rly, inc 1846, Camden Town (London & Birmingham Rly) to West India Docks at Blackwall, opened 1850, 1851, 1852; became NLR (qv) 1853.

E&WJR

East & West Junction Rly, inc 1864, from junction with N&BJR near Towcester to Stratford-upon-Avon. Opened 1871, 1873. Part of S&MJR from 1909.

E&WYJR

East & West Yorkshire Junction Rly, inc 1846, Poppleton Junction to Knaresborough, opened 1848, 1851, worked by the York, Newcastle & Berwick Rly. Absorbed by Y&NMR 1851.

E&WYUR

East & West Yorkshire Union Rly, Stourton Junc (Leeds)–Rothwell–Robin Hood–Lofthouse/Newmarket Collieries (Silkstone), inc 1883, opened 1891, part of L&NER 1923.

EAR

1. East Anglian Rly, Ely–Kings Lynn/ Wisbech–Dereham; St Ives– Huntingdon; an 1847 amalgamation of Lynn & Dereham, Lynn & Ely and Ely & Huntingdon Rlys, all inc 1845. Worked by ECR from 1852, part of GER 1862.
2. East African Rlys and Harbours Administration (operating all rlys in Kenya, Uganda, and Tanganyika), formed 1948, EA Rlys Corporation 1969; split into three separate national rly organizations 1975–7. *See* KR; TRC; URC.

Earl of Carlisle's Rly

See Brampton Rly.

Ears

Metal fittings attached to a contact/trolley wire on tramways (*3*) for the purpose of suspending it in position.

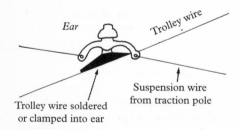

Trolley wire soldered or clamped into ear

Easingwold

see ER (*1*).

Eason's Specials (obs)

Cheap excursion trains organized by the Grimsby travel agent, J.W. Eason over the GNR and L&NER, 1905–39: Eason's slogan was 'Good for the Public. Good for the Railway'.

East Anglian

An express between London (Liverpool St.) and Norwich, introduced 1937, ceased 1939, re-introduced 1946, name dropped 1962. Name used in 1980 for a London (Liverpool St.)– Norwich–Yarmouth service. From 1987 a London (Liverpool St.)–Norwich service.

Eastbound (US)

Term for a train or train service travelling in a generally easterly direction. 'Northbound', 'southbound' and 'westbound' were similarly used. This terminology was adopted on London underground rlys from 1905 in place of the traditional British 'Down' and 'Up' (qv). Later adopted on certain BR lines and more recently, for motorways.

East Coast

InterCity East Coast (qv).

Easterbrook

Easterbrook, Hannaford & Co., signalling contractors, exploiting the patent frames and interlocking of Walter Easterbrook (1842–1914) from 1868–85.

Easterling

A summer-only express between London (Liverpool St.) and Yarmouth, so named 1950. Name dropped from 1959.

Eastern & Oriental Express

Luxury tourist service between Singapore and Bangkok, introduced 1993.

Eastern Belle [Pullman Limited]

L&NER all-Pullman excursion trains from London (Liverpool St.) to East Anglian resorts, introduced 1929.

Eastern and Western Valleys Line

Newport to Blaenavon, South Wales [Eastern]; Newport–Aberbeeg–Ebbw Vale/Blaina [Western].

East Fife Line

Leuchars Junc–St Andrews–Leven– Thornton Junc.

East Gloucestershire

see EGR.

East Lancashire
see ELR (*1*) and (*2*).

East Lincs Line
Peterborough–Boston–Grimsby.

East Norfolk Line
see ENR.

East Somerset
see ESR (*1*).

East Suffolk Line
Ipswich–Beccles–Lowestoft. *See also* ESR (*3*).

Easy sign (USRS)
Any signal requiring reduction of speed.

EBR
Eastern Bengal Rly; renamed Pakistan Eastern Rly 1961, from 1971 part of Bangladesh Rlys (*see* BR (*5*)).

EC
1. Euro-City Express (qv).
2. L&NWR term for ECS (qv).

EC&TJR
Eastern Counties & Thames Junction Rly, inc 1844, Stratford (London) to Thames Wharf and Canning Town, opened 1846. Part of ECR from 1847.

ECC
Electric Construction Co., suppliers of electric traction equipment, Bushbury, Wolverhampton, 1889. Became part of Hawker-Siddeley Group (qv).

ECJS
East Coast Joint Stock; passenger coaches jointly owned by NBR, NER and GNR and operating between London (Kings Cross) and Edinburgh/Aberdeen, introduced 1860.

ECML
East Coast Main Line, London (Kings Cross) to York, Newcastle, Edinburgh, Dundee and Aberdeen.

ECMR
East Cornwall Mineral Rly, inc 1869 as Callington & Calstock Rly, 3 ft 6 in/1,067 mm gauge, Calstock Quay, Gunnislake and Callington. Name changed to ECMR 1871, opened 1872. Part of PD&SWJR from 1891. Converted to standard gauge and connected to PD&SWJ at Bere Alston, 1908, with wagon lift from Calstock Quay to the new connecting line.

ECR
1. Eastern Counties Rly, inc 1836, London to Norwich and Yarmouth via Colchester and Ipswich, first section opened London (Devonshire St.) to Romford, 1839, 5 ft/ 1,524 mm gauge, converted to standard gauge 1844. Part of GER from 1862.
2. Electrical Control Rooms. These contain equipment for remote control of substations (qv) and track paralleling huts (qv) and the related staff.

ECRJC
East Coast Rlys Joint Committee (NER, NBR, GNR).

ECS
Empty Coaching/Carriage Stock.

ED
1. Engineering/Engineers' Department.
2. Electro-diesel (BR).

Edelweiss
1. A *CIWL* Pullman express between Amsterdam and Zurich, 1928–39. There were modifications at each end of the route over the life of this train.
2. A railcar service Brussels–Basle 1955, Brussels–Zurich 1956.
3. TEE Amsterdam–Zurich 1957; electric working throughout, completing electrification of *TEE* services, 1974. Lost *TEE* status 1979, IC/EC 1979, name dropped 1987. Name subsequently used for a Brussels–Basle service.

Edenham & Little Bytham Rly
See Lord Willoughby's Rly.

Eden Valley Line
Penrith–Appleby–Kirkby Stephen. *See also* EVR (*3*).

EDER
Epsom Downs Extension Rly, inc 1892, 1897, part of SER from 1899, opened Tadworth–Tattenham Corner 1901. *See also* Chipstead Valley.

Edge rails/rly (obs)
Early nineteenth-century term used to distinguish rails/rly accommodating flanged wheels from tramplates/tramroad (*1*) (qv).

Edgeway (obs)
A rly with edge rails (qv).

Edinburgh Pullman
Unofficial name for an all-Pullman service
between London (Kings Cross), Leeds,
Harrogate, Newcastle and Edinburgh,
introduced 1925 (extension of Harrogate
Pullman). Became Queen of Scots (qv) 1927.

Edinburgh Suburban Line
Gorgie–Duddingston.

EDL
Electro-Diesel Locos, BR class 73 or 74.

EDLR
Egyptian Delta Light Rlys Co. Ltd
(Alexandria), 2 ft 6 in gauge, carrying
freight and passenger traffic in the Nile
Delta, taken over by Egyptian State 1953,
600 route miles; closed 1960–1.

Edmondson ticket
A cardboard ticket, in Britain $1^3/_{16}$ in by
$2^1/_4$ in/5.7 cm by 3 cm, numbered
consecutively, pre-printed with journey
details, station of issue and price, date-
stamped at moment of issue by a dating
press (qv). Named after its inventor,
Thomas Edmondson (1792–1851). In
general use on British rlys for some 150
years, the Edmondson ticket system was
finally displaced on BR in 1989. It survives
on some British preserved lines and
overseas rlys.

EDS (Ger)
Eisenbahn Dienstsache, internal mail of the
rly undertaking. *See also* OCS.

EE
English Electric Co. Ltd, an amalgamation
in 1918–19 of DK (qv), Siemens Bros,
Stafford (qv), Phoenix Dynamo
Manufacturing Co. Ltd and Willans &
Robinson (Rugby). Suppliers of large
electrical generating plant and switchgear,
electric and diesel-electric locos and
railcars, tramcars, buses and trolleybuses,
also radio valves. Electric traction activities
were concentrated at Preston. Merged with
GEC (qv), 1968.

Eel
A 51-ton bogie rail wagon used by
engineers.

EFB
Electric Fouling Bars. Provided on the
track to protect places where light engines

and other vehicles may stand. *See also*
Fouling bar.

EFCR
East Fife Central Rly, inc 1893, from a
point near Cameron Bridge to Lochty,
opened 1898. Part of NBR from 1895.

EFE
Empresa de los Ferrocarriles del Estado;
Chilean State Rlys. 6,585 km, mostly
1,676 mm and metre gauge.

EFK
Initials of German title of European
Timetable Conference. *See also* CEH.

Egg Timers (RS)
BR class 58 diesel electric locos. Suggested
by their outlines.

EGR
1. East Gloucestershire Rly, Witney to
   Fairford, inc 1862, opened 1873, worked
   by GWR, part of GWR from 1890.
2. East Grinstead Rly, inc 1853, Three
   Bridges to EG, opened 1855, worked by
   LB&SCR, part of LB&SCR from 1865.

Egret
A 20-ton ballast and sleeper wagon with
fixed sides and ends and steel floor, used
by engineers.

EH
Engineering Hours (qv).

EH&LR
Edgware, Highgate & London Rly, inc
1862, Edgware to Finchley and Finsbury
Park; High Barnet to Finchley, inc 1866;
part of GNR from 1867; opened Finsbury
Park–Edgware 1867, Finchley to High
Barnet 1872.

EHLR
Edge Hill Light Rly, Burton Dassett
S&MJR to ironstone workings on Edge
Hill, including $^1/_2$ m cable-worked incline,
LRO 1919, opened 1920, closed 1925.

EHO
Extra Heavy Overhaul.

Eight Freights (RS)
LM&SR Stanier class 8F 2–8–0 locos.
From the power classification. Also
abbreviated to 'Eight Fs'.

Eight wheel switch[er] (US)
A steam shunting loco with 0–8–0 wheel
arrangement.

Eilzug (Ger) (obs)
A train stopping at most stations on its route.

EIR
East Indian Rly; purchased by the government 1879. From 1952 part of Eastern Rly (of India) and Northern Rly (of India).

EIR (Fr)
Express d'Interêt Régional, cross country service.

Eisenbahn betriebsleiter (Ger)
Rly Operating Manager.

Ejector
A part of steam loco which, by means of a continuous jet of steam, creates the vacuum for keeping the brakes released.

EJL
Extended Jubilee Line: Green Park–Waterloo–North Greenwich–Stratford, opened 1999.

EKLR
East Kent (Light) Rly: Canterbury Road (Wingham)–Shepherdswell/Sandwich Road. Sandwich Road–Richborough extension built but not opened. LROs 1911, 1912. Opened 1912, passengers 1916. Part of BR (S) and closed to passengers 1948. Last section out of use 1984. There is a preservation project, based at Shepherdswell.

EKR
East Kent Rly; St Mary Cray–Chatham–Faversham–Canterbury–Dover; inc 1853, first section opened 1858. Renamed LC&DR (qv) 1859.

El, The (US)(S)
Elevated rly (qv).

Elan Valley
A construction rly for building Birmingham Corporation Reservoir; ran west from Mid-Wales Line near Rhayader to Craig Gôch, inc 1892, opened 1894, 1896, closed 1917.

Electric Railway and Tramway Journal
see LR&TJ.

Electric Scots (obs)
Brand name for Anglo-Scottish WCML services when first electrified, 1974.

Electric token block
see Train staff.

Electric train staff
see ETS (*1*); Train staff.

Electronic token
see RETB.

Electrostar
Adtranz (qv) name from 2000 for a family of emu (qv) including classes 357 and 375.

Electrotren (Sp)
A fast emu service.

Elephant car (USRS)
A passenger coach marshalled behind the loco for use of the front brakeman.

Elephant's ears (RS)
Loco smoke deflectors (qv).

Elettrotreni (It)
The fastest services, electrically worked, usually First class only, with supplementary fare.

Elevated [rly]
An urban passenger rly rapid transit system running over and along the line of city streets on elevated steel structures. Such systems were built in New York, Chicago, Boston, Philadelphia, Hamburg and Berlin. *See also* LOR.

Elevated Electric (obs)
Brand name for LB&SCR electric services on South London Line (qv) when introduced in 1909. Derived from the route, which is largely on viaducts and embankments.

Elham Valley Line
Cheriton Halt–Canterbury. *See also* EVLR.

Elizabethan
A renaming of Capitals Limited, 1953. Name dropped 1963.

Elk (LTRS)
A device on a flat wagon, used for lifting rails.

Ellen
Nickname for the Louisville & Nashville RR (US). *See also* Old Reliable, The.

Elliptical (High elliptical/Full elliptical) roof
A carriage roof half-oval in profile, its shape formed by setting-out a series of arcs linked together.

Ellofamess
Nickname for LM&SR.

Ellson rail joint (obs)
A rail joint devised *c.* 1940 by George
Ellson, chief engineer SR, which was
suitable for bullhead (qv) and flat-bottom
(qv) rails, in which the outside ends of the
rails were recessed to receive an angle
bridging piece of rail-quality steel which
formed the outer fishplate (qv), a standard
fishplate being used on the inner side. By
using a cast iron baseplate, rail end
deflection, sleeper pounding and noise at
joints were almost eliminated.

Elmer (RS)
A North American travelling on BR,
usually with a Britrail go-as-you-please
ticket.

ELNA
Engerer Lokomotiv–Normen–Ausschuss. A
committee set up to design standard steam
locos for German rlys after WW1.

ELR
1. East Lancashire Rly; Manchester
   (Clifton Junc)–Bury–Blackburn/
   Burnley/Colne/Bacup. Inc 1844 as
   Manchester, Bury & Rossendale Rly,
   renamed ELR 1845, opened 1846.
   Absorbed Blackburn & Preston;
   Blackburn, Burnley, Accrington & Colne
   Extension; and Liverpool, Ormskirk &
   Preston Rlys in 1846. Extended to Bacup
   1852, part of L&YR 1859.
2. A preserved rly operating over parts of
   (*1*) from 1987.
3. East London Rly, inc 1865, opened
   1869 Wapping to New Cross (LB&SCR)
   via the existing Thames Tunnel. Worked
   by LB&SCR. Extended to Shoreditch
   and Liverpool St. (GER) 1876. SER
   services 1880 and connection at New
   Cross in use. Metropolitan and MDR
   through services to New Cross SER and
   LB&SCR via connection at Whitechapel,
   1884. GER services from 1887. MDR
   services ceased 1905, Metropolitan
   1906. LB&SCR, SER and GER
   passenger services ceased 1913.
   Electrified 1913 with passenger services
   operated by Metropolitan Rly. Managed
   by Metropolitan from 1921 and
   maintained by it from 1924, vested in SR

1925. Managed and operated by LPTB
from 1933. Part of BTC 1948, managed
and controlled by LT. With the cessation
of through freight and parcels traffic over
the ELR in 1966, all connections with
BR were severed (the last, in sidings at
New Cross Gate, in 1975), and the line
became a part of the London
Underground system. *See also* ELRJC.
4. East Lincolnshire Rly, inc 1846,
   Grimsby to Louth and Boston, opened
   1848. Leased by GNR 1846. Part of
   L&NER from 1923.
5. Engineer's Line Reference (qv).

ELRJC
East London Rly Joint Committee, inc 1882
to lease ELR in perpetuity, lease operated
from 1884. Composed of Metropolitan,
MDR, LB&SCR, LC&DR, SER (later
SE&CR). The GER joined in 1885. SR,
Metropolitan, MDR and L&NER were the
lessees from 1923, the SR, L&NER and
LPTB from 1933. The Committee was
dissolved in 1949 following formation of the
BTC, which became the owner.

Elver
Former Freightliner flat wagons used by
engineers for carrying concrete sleepers.

Ely Valley
see E&CVR; EVER; EVR.

Em (USRS)
One thousand tons load. From the Roman
M = 1,000.

Embedded track
A type of track in which pre-coated or
grooved rails are set in concrete slabs with
the tops of the rails level with the upper
surface of the slabs. Used for street
tramways and in rly tunnels.

Embsay
see ESR (*5*).

EMC (LT)
Escalator Machine Chamber.

EMD Inc
Electro Motive Diesel Corporation
(USA), purchasers of GM (EMD) (qv)
loco building plants in USA and Canada,
2005.

Emerald Isle Express, The
Express between London (Euston) and

Holyhead, in connection with Dunlaoghaire (Dublin) night sailings, introduced 1954, named dropped 1975. Name revived 1993 for a Birmingham International–Holyhead service.

Emergency application
A brake application at maximum reduction in air pressure, to stop a train as quickly as possible. Occurs automatically if a brake pipe is severed.

Emergency [TSR] Indicator
A special sign erected at the lineside to warn drivers of an emergency TSR (qv) of which no notice has been given.

EML
BR (S) term for a train of emu (qv) stock hauled or propelled by a loco under power.

Emmett
GWR TC for Third class six-wheel brake coach.

Emmett A
GWR TC for Third class bogie brake coach.

Emmett B
GWR TC for Third class four-wheel brake coach.

Empire Builder
A Great Northern RR express between Chicago, Tacoma and Seattle, introduced 1929. Now an Amtrak express of double-decker 'Superliner' cars between Chicago and Seattle, introduced 1980, covering the 2,287 m in 46 h.

Empire State Express/Limited
An express between New York and Buffalo, introduced 1891 and later extended to Cleveland and Detroit. Featured on a US postage stamp in 1901. In 1947 it was covering the 637$\frac{1}{2}$ m from New York to Detroit in 13 h 15 min. Later withdrawn but the name has been adopted by Amtrak for its New York–Buffalo–Niagara Falls service.

Empress Voyager
A boat train between London (Euston) and Liverpool (Riverside) in connection with Canadian Pacific sailings, 1953–66. Name was also used for the contemporary Glasgow (Central)–Gourock (Princes Pier) boat trains for Canadian Pacific.

EMU
Electric Multiple Unit.

ENAFER
Empresa Nacional de Ferrocarriles SA; Peruvian National Rlys, 1,610 km, formed 1972 from various state and other rlys. *See also FCCA*; Peru Rail; RDC (3).

End board
A board fitted to the end coach of a corridor (qv) train which completely covers and secures the unusable gangway opening.

Endeavour Rail
A ROSCO (qv), formed 2000.

End dock
A dock (qv) which provides end as well as side loading/unloading facilities.

End man (USRS)
The rear end brakeman on a freight train.

End steps
Steps, usually three each side with a fourth fixed centrally above, fastened to the ends of passenger coaches and fitted with handrail to enable rly staff to reach the roof.

ENF
Empresa Nacional de Ferrocarriles, National Rlys of Bolivia, metre gauge. 3,519 km of metre gauge.

Engadine Express
An express between Calais (connections with UK) and Chur for St Moritz, introduced 1901. Revived after WW1 as a winter sports train. Ceased 1939. Revived 1946–7 only.

Engerth
Loco design (usually a tank loco) incorporating an auxiliary powered bogie/truck. Named after its German inventor.

Engineer (US)
Loco driver, adopted in UK by ASLEF (qv), but not generally.

Engineering Hours (LT)
The normal, regular night hours interruption of public train services when traction current is switched off to allow access for routine maintenance, inspection of track, tunnel cleaning, etc.

Engineer's Line Reference
A code of three or four alpha-numeric

characters allocated to a route or section of a route between major stations or junctions. The code is then used to identify all relevant structures and features and track features.

Engineer's possession
An arrangement in which a section of rly is temporarily closed completely to normal traffic to enable major engineering work to proceed; movements are restricted to engineer's trains (qv), railborne cranes and other railborne plant.

Engineers' trains/traffic
See Infrastructure traffic; Possession trains.

Engineman
A driver (usually of a steam loco). In the plural also used as a collective term for driver and fireman/second man.

Engine turner
see Turner, engine.

Englaenderen Express
Copenhagen–Esjberg service connecting with Esjberg–Harwich sea route.

Englische Weiche (Ger)
English points, a double slip (qv).

Englishman (RS)
An inside double slip. See Double Slip.

ENR
1. East Norfolk Rly, inc 1864, Whitlingham to North Walsham, inc 1872 to Cromer, inc Reepham to County School 1879. Opened 1874, 1876, 1877, 1882. GER running powers Norwich to North Walsham 1874, part of GER 1881.
2. Egyptian National Rlys, 5,105 km. *See also* EDLR; ERR (1); ESR (4).

Enterprise
1. An express between Dublin and Belfast, introduced 1947. Extended to Cork 1950–3 only.
2. Less than trainload service introduced by EWS (qv), 1997.

Entrance-exit control panel
see NX.

Entrance–exit system
See NX system.

EofFR
East of Fife Rly, inc 1855, 1856, Leven to Kilconquhar; opened 1857, worked by

Edinburgh, Perth & Dundee Rly. Amalgamated with LR as Leven & East of Fife Rly 1861, extended to Anstruther 1863, part of NBR 1877.

EOLE (Fr)
Est–Ouest Liaison Express, a main line link from east to west across Paris, opened 1999.

EOS
see ENS.

EP
Electro-Pneumatic [brake].

EP&DR
Edinburgh, Perth & Dundee Rly *see* E&NR.

EPB
BR (S) emu two- and four-car Second/Standard class sets of 1951–5 and 1960 with EP Brakes. Motor brake open and driving trailer open cars, 2-EPB. Two motor brake open cars, one open trailer and one trailer with compartments, 4-EPB.

EPBIC (LT)
Electro-Pneumatic Brake Isolating Cock.

EP Blow (LTRS)
Audible warning of an electrical defect in EP brake.

EPS
European Passenger Services Ltd, a BR subsidiary formed 1990 to provide international passenger services via the Channel Tunnel. Renamed Eurostar (UK) in 1996 (*see* Eurostar) and forming part of L&CR (qv).

ER
1. Easingwold Rly, inc 1887, opened 1891, closed passengers 1948, closed 1957.
2. Exeter Rly, inc as Exeter, Teign Valley & Chagford Rly, 1883, Exeter to Christow (junction with TVR (2)) and branch to Chagford. Name changed to ER 1898, and Chagford branch dropped; opened 1903, worked by GWR, part of GWR from 1923.
3. Eyemouth Rly, inc 1884, Burnmouth to Eyemouth, opened 1891, worked by NBR. Part of NBR from 1900.
4. Eastern Region, BR.
5. Eastern Rly [of India], formed 1952. Part of it became SER (2) in 1955.

ER&SJR

Evesham, Redditch & Stratford-upon-Avon Junction Rly, inc 1873, from E&WJR at Stratford to Midland Rly at Broom, opened 1879, completing the cross country link between Broom and Blisworth. Worked by E&WJR. Part of S&MJR from 1909.

ER&TCW

Electric Railway & Tramway Carriage Works Ltd, a subsidiary of DK (qv), established at a new works at Preston for the manufacture of electric tramcars and rly rolling stock, 1898. Name changed to UEC (qv), 1905.

ER&TJ

Electric Railway & Tramway Journal; *see LR&TJ.*

Erasmus

TEE The Hague–Munich, introduced 1973. Amsterdam–Frankfurt 1979. Lost *TEE* status 1980. EC Amsterdam–Munich 1987, extended seasonally to Innsbruck.

ERC

European Rail Catering Ltd, a 1997 renaming and relaunch of OBS (qv), using the brand name 'Prego'. Sold in 1998 to S Air Group (SwissAir) and name changed to Rail Gourmet (UK) Ltd (qv).

Erewash Valley

Trent–Clay Cross (Midland Rly).

ERFA

European Rail Freight Association, formed 2003.

ERIC

Enhanced Railfreight Intermodal Control. A computer system designed to control the movement of containers (qv) and swap bodies (qv), linked to TOPS (qv) to provide information on these items as loaded and moved.

Erie

New York, Lake Erie & Western RR, eventually renamed Eries RR Co., then Erie Lackwanna RR Co. from 1960 following merger with DL&W (qv).

ERO (obs)

Executive Research Office, established 1929 by the LM&SR (qv) to overhaul the arrangements for forms and other printed matter, including timetables; also responsible for purchase of paper and stationery in bulk and for supervision of all non-urgent printing requirements.

EROS (LT)

London Underground acronym for Estimated Resumption/Restart/Restoration of Service after temporary interruption of train operation or station closure.

ERR

1. Egyptian Republic Rlys, a renaming of ESR (*4*) (qv) from 1954. Became ENR (qv).
2. *European Railway Review*, established 1995, a quarterly review of rly technology, published in London.

ERRI

European Rail Research Institute, Utrecht, replacing *ORE* (qv) 1990, undertaking research projects to an agreed cost and timescale.

ERS

1. Electric Railway Society, established 1946. Published *The Electric Railway*, until 1955 and from 1956 the *Electric Railway Society Journal*.
2. Emergency Replacement Switch, allowing a signalman to put an automatic signal to the danger aspect in an emergency.

ERTMS

European Rail Traffic Management System, integrating ticketing, operating and information systems of the national rly systems of the European Community. Includes European Train Control System (ETCS), a form of TCS (1) (qv).

ERU

Emergency Response Unit, LT, providing six-person 24-hr standby teams capable of tackling incidents anywhere on the London Underground system. Their objective is to restore normal service as quickly and as safely as possible.

ES

Engineering Supervisor (for work on the track).

ES&SR

Edinburgh Suburban & Southside Rly, inc 1880, St Leonards Junc to Haymarket and Niddrie spur, opened 1884, part of NBR from 1885.

Eskdale
see R&ER.

Esk Valley Line
Whitby–Grosmont–Battersby
(–Middlesbrough).

ESL (LT)
Electric sleet loco.

Espee
Nickname of Southern Pacific RR. From
initials.

ESR
1. East Somerset Rly, Witham Junction to
   Wells, inc 1856, opened 1858, 1862,
   worked by GWR, absorbed by GWR
   1874 and in same year converted from
   broad to standard gauge. *See also* (*2*).
2. A steam rly preservation centre at
   Cranmore on part of (*1*), opened 1973.
3. East Suffolk Rly, inc as Halesworth,
   Beccles & Haddiscoe Rly 1851,
   opened Beccles to Haddiscoe 1854,
   worked by ECR. Name changed
   to ESR 1854. Extension to Woodbridge
   and branches to Leiston, Framlingham
   and Snape; inc 1854, opened
   1859. Leiston–Aldeburgh opened 1860.
   All worked by ECR. Yarmouth &
   Haddiscoe and Lowestoft &
   Beccles Rlys absorbed 1858. Leased to Sir
   Morton Peto 1855–61. Part of GER 1862.
4. Egyptian State Rlys, formed 1905.
   Retitled ERR 1954.
5. Embsay Steam Rly. A preserved rly on
   part of former BR Embsay Junc–Ilkley
   line. First section opened (as Yorkshire
   Dales Rly), 1979. Name changed to
   ESR 1988.
6. Emergency Speed Restriction.

Essex Coast Express
A commuter express between London
(Liverpool St.) and Clacton, 1 h 26 min,
introduced 1958. Name dropped 1968.

Essex Continental
A service between London (Liverpool St.)
and Harwich in connection with sailings to
the Continent, calling at principal
intermediate stations, 1986–8.

Est
Chemin de fer de l'Est, France. Part of
SNCF (qv) from 1938.

Estate agent (RS)(obs)
Second man (qv).

ETA
Estimated/Expected Time of Arrival.

État, Chemins de Fer de l'
French State Rlys, incorporating from
1909 the former *Chemin de fer de l'Ouest*.
Part of *SNCF* (qv) from 1938.

ETB
Electric Token Block. *see* Train staff.

ETCS
European Train Control System, for
international high speed trains, including
cab signalling and ATP (qv).

ETD
Electric Traction Department/Depot.

ETD (US)
End of Train Device, replacing caboose
(qv) and incorporating a strobe light and a
motion detector; linked up with the train's
brake air line, it relays radio messages
regarding brake pressure and motion to the
train crew in the loco cab.

Étendard
An express between Bordeaux and Paris,
introduced 1968. *TEE* from 1971 with 4 h
25 min timing. Extended to Irun, with
Madrid connection, 1973–5. Lost *TEE*
status 1984. Fastest train in Europe
1973–81 (jointly with *l'Aquitaine* (qv)
1973–6). Ceased 1990.

ÉTG (Fr)(obs)
Élément de Turbine à Gaz. The first type of
SNCF gas turbine train, 1970.

ETH (obs)
Electric Train Heat. A system involving an
additional generator fitted to locos to
supply heating to passenger coaches.

ETHEL (obs)
Electric Train Heating Locos; mobile
generators, converted from BR class 25
diesel locos, to supply power for ETH.

Étoile du Nord
A *CIWL* Pullman express between Paris
(Nord), Brussels and Amsterdam,
1927–39. Revived 1946, *TEE* 1957. Lost
TEE status 1984, EC 1987.

ETS
1. Electric Train Staff, patented 1888; *see*
   Train staff/tablet/token and ticket.

2. Electric Train Supply; the use of power output from locos to supply electricity to passenger trains for lighting, air conditioning, catering equipment, tail lamps, safety systems, heating, etc. *See also* HEP.

ETT

1. Electric Train Tablet, patented 1878; *see* Train staff/tablet/token and ticket.
2. (obs) Experimental Tube Train, LT. Two three-car sets of 1973 stock used in 1983 to try out chopper (qv) control. Later converted to standard 1973 stock.

ETY

Empty; a train not in passenger service.

EUR

1. Eastern Union Rly (Colchester–Ipswich–Norwich/Bury St Edmunds) inc 1844, opened 1846. Absorbed Eastern Union & Hadleigh Rly 1848 and Ipswich & Bury St Edmunds Rly 1849. Extended to Norwich (Victoria) 1849. Worked by ECR from 1854, part of GER 1862.
2. East Usk Rly, Newport along east bank of River Usk to Uskmouth, inc 1885, opened 1898, part of GWR 1892, completed 1901.

Eurailpass

A ticket available for a period of unlimited First or Second class travel on all railways in Western Europe except BR. Sold only outside Europe and North Africa. Introduced 1959.

EuroCargo Rail

A wholly owned subsidiary of EWS (qv) 2005, to operate freight services over the European rly system including traffic via the Channel Tunnel.

Euro-City Express

A brand name introduced 1987 for two-class, high-quality international trains in Europe which meet criteria set by the UIC (qv). Replaced most *TEE* (qv) and international IC (qv) services.

Eurodomino

A ticket offering five days' rail travel in any one month in any one of seven West European countries. Introduced (for UK residents), 1991.

Eurofima

European Company for the financing of rly rolling stock, founded 1956.

Euro-400

Brand name for BR marketing arrangement relating to international rail journeys to popular destinations originating in the UK. Provided information and fares to facilitate ticket issue. Introduced 1990.

European

A service in connection with Continental sailings, Glasgow/Edinburgh–Manchester–Sheffield–Harwich (Parkeston Quay), introduced 1983. Replaced 1987 by Rhinelander (qv).

Europ Wagon Pool

Established 1951; formed of common user wagons conforming to UIC standards circulating on European rail systems.

Euro-Scot (obs)

An Edinburgh–Harwich–Felixstowe Freightliner service introduced 1968.

Eurostar

Brand name for the class 373 international high-speed train sets operated by EPS (qv), *SNCF* (qv) and *SNCB* (qv) between London and Lille, Paris and Brussels via the Channel Tunnel from 1994. From 1998 operated by a consortium of National Express, British Airways, SNCF (qv) and SNCB (qv). *See also* Eurostar (UK) Ltd.

Eurostar Italia (It)

FS (qv), Pendolino (qv) and other high-speed electric services linking major cities.

Eurostar (UK) Ltd

A renaming of EPS (qv) after its transfer to the private sector in 1996, when it became part of L&CR (2) (qv). Owns the Eurostar (qv) trains, the International stations at London (Waterloo) and Ashford (Kent), the CTRL (qv) station at Ebbsfleet and the Eurostar maintenance depots.

Eurotram

ADtranz (qv) modern light rail car with SFE (qv) built at Derby for Strasbourg, Milan and NET (qv).

Eurotunnel

Anglo-French company owning the Channel Tunnel (Folkestone–Calais (Fréthun)) also operating its own drive-on services for road vehicles, using specially designed rail wagons [*le shuttle* (qv)], from 1994. Leases 50 per cent of Channel Tunnel capacity to Eurostar (UK) (qv) and *SNCF* (qv).

Euston Square Confederacy, The
L&NWR, Midland Rly and MS&LR acting in concert, 1850–7.

Euston Stop (RS)
A rough, jolting stop, often said to consist of three applications: the first to lift the passenger to his feet, the second to jerk his luggage on to his head, and the third to assist him unceremoniously through the door. Also known as a 'Caley Stop'.

Evans, O'Donnell
Evans, O'Donnell & Co. Ltd, established a signalling equipment works at Chippenham in 1894. Effectively taken over by the Pneumatic & General Engineering Co., later the Consolidated Signal Co. (qv), in 1901–2.

Even time
Sixty miles an hour.

EVER
Ely Valley Extension Rly, inc 1863 from junc with EVR (*1*) near Hendreforgan to Gilfach, opened 1865, part of OVR 1865.

Eversholt
A ROSCO (qv); acquired by Forward Trust, 1997; *see* HSBC Rail.

EVEX (obs)
TC for evening excursion train.

EVLR
Elham Valley Light Rly, inc 1881, Cheriton–Elham–Canterbury, part of SER from 1884, opened 1887, 1889.

EVR
1. Ely Valley Rly, Llantrisant to Pen-y-Graig, with branches, inc 1857, opened 1860, 1862, 1865. Leased to GWR 1861, part of GWR 1903.
2. Exe Valley Rly, inc 1874, opened Tiverton–Stoke Canon 1885, part of B&ER from 1875.
3. Eden Valley Rly, inc 1858, Kirkby Stephen–Clifton (near Penrith). Opened 1862, worked by S&DR, part of S&DR from 1863.
4. Esk Valley Rly, inc 1863; Esk Valley Junc NBR to Polton. Opened 1867, leased by NBR, part of NBR from 1871.

EVR
Eesti Vabariigi Raudtee; Estonian Rlys, 1,520 mm gauge.

EWD
Every/Each Week Day. A train service running every day of the year except Saturdays and Sundays.

EWP
Europäische Wagenbeistellungsplan; European through coach working book. Issued yearly to regulate balancing mileage between the various railway systems on a basis of axle-kilometres.

EWS
English, Welsh & Scottish Railway, a FOC (qv) formed in 1996 by Wisconsin Central (qv) to take over the former BR freight businesses Res (qv), Mainline (qv), Transrail (qv) and Loadhaul (qv). The co. also took over Railfreight Distribution (RfD) (qv), 1997. Inherited by CNR (qv) when it took over Wisconsin in 2001. *See also* WCTC.

EWS International
The former Railfreight Distribution (qv), so renamed in 1998 after acquisition by EWS (qv).

Examination of line
Use of loco or train to run slowly over a section of line to check for damage, obstruction or other risks to safety.

Exceptional load
An indivisible out-of-gauge load (qv) or one of exceptional length or weight which has to be moved by special authority under special working arrangements. *See also* Out of gauge load.

Excess fare ticket
A paper ticket usually made out by a ticket inspector/conductor/collector as a receipt for payment of a fare by a passenger unable to produce a valid ticket.

Exchange sidings
Tracks on which inwards and outwards traffic is exchanged between private siding (qv) owner and the main rail system.

Excursion [trains]
Traditionally the term covered cheap tickets available on ordinary services or special trains, subject to conditions (e.g. no

luggage allowed) and normally classified 'Day', 'Half-Day' or 'Evening'. This facility faded away in the late 1960s and early 1970s under BR (1) to be replaced by charter trains (qv). *See also* Awayday; Special traffic.

Executive
Express between London (Euston), Birmingham and Wolverhampton, 1967–72.

Exe Valley Line
[Exeter]–Stoke Canon–Tiverton–Morebath Junction[–Dulverton]. *See also* EVR (*2*).

Exhibition coach/train
A coach or complete train which tours around the rly system, fitted out to display products and services, demonstrate processes, techniques, etc. for the Government, public bodies and commercial firms. *See also* TrainEx.

Expansion joint/switch
A long scarfed joint, allowing considerable longitudinal movement between adjacent lengths of long or continuously welded rails to allow for thermal movement.

Expreso, tren (Sp)
Fast trains, sometimes restricted to First class.

Express
A term in use in Britain from around 1840 to denote the fastest train on any main route.

Express fares (obs)
Fares above normal rates charged for travel on the fastest trains of the day. Largely abolished in the UK by the end of the nineteenth century; reintroduced from

1935 for high-speed trains such as the Silver Jubilee (qv) and Coronation (qv) and survived on SR boat trains until 1940.

Express freight
A system, unique to North America, and first established in 1839, by which private companies independent of the rlys undertook the care and handling of luggage and many types of freight consignment, using fast passenger train services and collecting and delivering at each end of the journey. Special trains were also operated by the rly companies for this traffic, running at passenger train speeds. Express freight companies included Wells Fargo (qv) and American Express (qv). *See also* REA.

Express poste, un train: (Fr) (obs)
A fast mail train carrying passengers.

Express, train (Fr)(obs)
A term in use in France for about 100 years from the mid-nineteenth century, denoting the fastest trains on any line apart from a *rapide* (qv), if one were available. Originally not accessible to third class (qv) passengers.

Extended London Area (obs)
All stations within 80 m radius of London termini.

Extension Line (LTRS)
The section of the Metropolitan Line between London (Baker St.), Harrow and beyond.

Extra board (USRS)
see Board (*3*).

Eye (USRS)
A fixed signal at the side of the running line.

E-Züge (Ger) (obs)
see Eilzug.

F

F
First class (BR)

FA
Ferrocarriles Argentinos; Argentinian Rlys.
34,463 km of 1,676 mm, 1,435 mm and
metre gauge. *See also BAGS; BAP; BAWR;
CAR.*

Face
That part of a platform alongside a track.

Facing point bar
A lifting or clearance bar (qv) arranged to
prevent movement of facing points when a
train is passing over them.

Facing point detector
A device which ensures that the relevant
signals cannot be moved to the 'off'
indication unless the point movement has
been fully and properly completed.

Facing point locks
Bolts securing points to be run over in the
facing direction before the signal for a
train or route can be placed in 'off'
indication.

Facing points
Points facing a train in its direction of
travel, giving a choice of route, and over
which the train will move from the toe to
the heel of the points before reaching the
crossing. Facing points are 'like good
dinners, the fewer one has of them, the
better'. – Henry Oakley, GNR general
manager.

Facing points

FACS (Fr)
*Fédération des Amis des Chemins der Fer
Secondaires*; League of Friends of
Secondary Railways.

FACT
Full Automatic Control of Trains (LT).

Factory, The (RS)
Swindon Works, GWR, BR (W).

Facultatif (Fr)
An optional vehicle, an extra coach, for use
as required.

Fahrzeug (Ger)
An indivisible two-bodied coach or other
vehicle.

Faidherbe
TEE Paris–Tourcoing, introduced 1978.
The last *TEE*, with Watteau (qv).

Fail-safe
A design feature which ensures that any
mechanical or electrical failure results in
signal aspects reverting to danger.

Failte
A service between Dublin and Cork, so
named 1960, name dropped 1975.

Fairlie
An articulated steam loco invented in 1863
by Robert Francis Fairlie (1831–85).

Fair Maid (obs)
An express between London (Kings Cross),
Edinburgh and Perth; an extension and
renaming of Morning Talisman from 1957.

Fairy glen (RS)
A wc.

Fairyland (RS)
Multiple-aspect colour light signals; also
such signals when malfunctioning.

Falcon
Falcon Engine & Car Works Ltd,

Loughborough, originally Henry Hughes, and Hughes' Locomotive & Tramway Works Ltd, manufacturers of rly and steam tramway locos. Loughborough Foundry (Falcon Ironworks) established 1874. Falcon Engine & Car Works Ltd established 1882. Merged with Brush (qv), 1889.

Fall-plate

A hinged steel plate covering the gap between loco and its tender; also a similar plate between two coaches with open end balconies.

Falmouth coupé (obs)

A type of GWR non-corridor coach designed to be detached from main line trains at junctions to serve branch lines (e.g. Falmouth). Self-contained with accommodation for First and Third class, lavatories, and luggage compartment.

Family saloon (obs)

A special coach (usually on six wheels) which could be added to a timetabled passenger train at additional payment above the normal fares on prior notice being given. It was fitted with lavatories, tables and chairs and had separate accommodation for servants, smoking and luggage.

Fan

1. A complex of sidings diverging from one track.
2. (USRS) The blower on a steam loco.

F&BR

Formartine & Buchan Rly, inc 1858, Aberdeen (Dyce)–Peterhead/Fraserburgh, opened 1861, 1862, 1865, worked by GNofSR, part of GNofSR 1866.

F&CJR

Forth & Clyde Junction Rly, inc 1853, Stirling to Balloch, opened 1856, worked by NBR, leased by NBR 1875, part of L&NER 1923.

F&KR

Fife & Kinross Rly, inc 1855, Ladybank to Kinross, opened 1857, part of NBR from 1862.

F&MJR

Furness & Midland Joint Rly, inc 1863, Wennington Junc–Carnforth, opened 1867, part of LM&SR from 1923.

F&RR&H

Fishguard & Rosslare Rlys & Harbours Company, inc as Fishguard Bay Rly & Pier, 1893, name changed to F&RR&H 1894 and Waterford & Wexford Rly and Rosslare Harbour Commissioners taken over. Waterford–Rosslare and Fishguard & Goodwick station to Fishguard Harbour lines opened 1906 together with connecting steamer service, giving a 13 h timing London to Cork. Rlys worked by GWR (later BR) in Wales, by GS&WR (later GSR, CIE, IE) in Ireland. Steamer service suspended 1941–7. F&RR&H remained a separate company, jointly owned by the BTC and CIE, from 1948. British properties vested in BRB 1967.

F and S

Full and Standing; the official description of a well-loaded train.

Fang bolt

A screw bolt which passes through the lower flange of an FB rail and is secured to the sleeper by a nut.

Fang spike

A metal spike driven into a sleeper to secure FB rail.

Fan table (obs)

A movable (pivoted) section of track placed at the end of two converging lines which could be used to transfer vehicles or locos from one line to the other.

Far North line

Inverness to Wick and Thurso.

Fasser (RS) (obs)

Engine cleaner (on the LB&SCR (qv) and possibly elsewhere). From 'fass', the colloquial name for the mixture of accumulated coal dust, dirt, oil and grease that had to be removed from a steam locomotive after daily use.

Fast [lines]

BR term for the primary pair of tracks where there are four or more passenger lines in parallel.

Fast trotter (RS)(obs)

A smartly timed local service.

Fat box (RS)(obs)

An axle grease box.

Fat boys (RS)(obs)

Wagon-greasers.

'Father of British railways'
George Stephenson (1781–1848). The term has also been applied to the L&MR (qv) and to its secretary, Henry Booth.

'Father of Railways'
William James (1771–1837), solicitor, surveyor and first protagonist of rly construction.

Fat Nancy (RS)
A saddle tank (qv).

Fat Nannies (RS)
L&YR 0–6–0 saddle tank locos.

Fayle's Tramway
An industrial rly, 3 ft 9 in/1,143 mm gauge, operated by Messrs Fayle to carry excavated ball clay from Norden, Corfe Castle, to Goathorn Pier and Middlebere Wharf on Poole Harbour. First lines opened with animal haulage c. 1806. Lines to Poole Harbour closed by 1936. Some remaining trackage at Norden converted to 1 ft 11½ in/597 mm gauge 1948. Finally closed 1972. *See also* Middlebere Plateway.

FBR
Forth Bridge Rly inc 1873 and 1882, opened 1890. Bridge and rly owned jointly by NBR, Midland Rly, GNR and NER. Worked by NBR, and from 1923 the L&NER.

FB rail
Flat Bottom rail (qv).

FC
Foot Crossing; a level crossing of a rly for pedestrians, protected only by warning notices.

FCAB
see A&BR (2).

FCCA
1. *Ferrocarril Central Andino*; the former Central Rly of Peru, later part of ENAFER (qv), now operated by RDC (qv).
2. *Ferrocarril Central Argentino*; *see* CAR.

FCCP
Ferrocarril Central del Paraguay; a British-owned system, acquired by the state 1961, closed 1996.

FCE
Ferrocarriles del Estado, State Rlys of Chile. *See* EFE.

FCM
Ferrocarriles de Mallorca; 3 ft gauge rlys in Majorca opened from 1875. Part of *FEVE* (qv) 1981 and converted to metre gauge. Renamed *SFM* (qv)1981.

FCP
Ferrocarril de Panama; Panama Rlys. 355 km of 1,524 and 914 mm gauge. *See also* Canal haulage rlys.

FD&R
Felixstowe Dock & Rly, inc 1879, opened 1886. Still an independent company.

FdeC
Ferrcarriles de Cuba ; Cuban National Rlys, 3,442 km.

FD-Züge (Ger)
Ferndurchgangzüge or *Fernschnellzüge*; long distance fast trains usually serving holiday resorts not on the *IC-netz* (qv).

Feathers (RS)
1. Lunar lights (qv).
2. Crossed bars placed over signals to indicate they are not in use.

FEBA
Full Emergency Brake Application. *See also* Emergency application.

FEC
Florida East Coast Rly, formed 1892. *See also* Flagler's Folly.

FEDECRAIL
European Federation of Museum and Tourist rlys, formed 1994.

Feeder (RS)
An oil can, usually one with a long and thin spout.

Feeder boxes/pillars
Also known as section boxes, these are spaced at convenient (usually half-mile) intervals alongside tramways (3) (qv). The traction current is routed through them via switches which enable insulated sections of the traction supply to be safely isolated when emergency repairs become necessary. Telephones to the control room may be included.

Feeders
Insulated copper conductors feeding traction current to the trolley wire (qv). On tramways (3) the wire is fed at intervals of about half a mile, forming sections which

can be isolated, if required, by closing switches in the feeder boxes.

Feed pipe
The means of conveying water from tank or tender to the boiler of a steam loco. *See also* Injector.

Feed-water heater
A device for heating water to a high temperature before it enters the boiler of a steam loco.

Feldbahn (Ger)
A military narrow gauge light rly, or a contractor's narrow gauge temporary line using similar equipment.

Fell
A system for mountain rlys employing the friction between a wheel of the specially designed locos and an additional central rail. Invented by J.B. Fell (1815–1902). First used for line over Mont Cenis Pass, Switzerland, in 1868.

Fell loco
BR experimental 2,000 hp 4–8–4 diesel-mechanical loco no. 10100 of 1950. Named after Lt.-Col. L.F.R. Fell, inventor of the transmission and various ancillary features.

Felthams
Nickname for all-enclosed, double-deck, front-exit, rear-entrance tramcars built 1930–31 by the UCC (qv) at Feltham, Middlesex for the London United Tramways and the Metropolitan Electric Tramways. The name was also used in some official publications.

Fender (US)
A horizontal metal bar fitted at the front of a loco, rly car or tramcar to absorb shock and limit damage in collisions.

Fenman
An express between London (Liverpool St.) and Hunstanton/Bury St Edmunds, introduced 1949. Name dropped 1968.

Fercam (Fr)
Fer+camion, rail+road truck, a rail trunking and road collection/delivery service, *SNCF*.

Fernando's Hideaway (RS)
A remotely situated lineside hut.

Fernbahn (Ger)
Main line rly.

Fernschnellzug (Ger)(obs)
Long-distance fast train with mandatory supplementary fares.

Ferro-equinology/ist
The study of rlys, strictly the study of *steam locos* (iron horses)/one who studies these.

Ferrophiliac (US)
Classically inelegant term for a person seriously interested in rly matters.

Festiniog/Ffestiniog Rly
See FR (1).

Festival land cruise
see Land cruise.

Fettle, to/fettling
To arrange and secure rly track in its optimum position for safe and satisfactory running of trains up to the maximum speeds appropriate for the traffic it carries; also minor maintenance, especially tensioning of fastenings.

Fettler (obs)
An alternative term for platelayer (qv) or lengthman (qv).

Feu clignotant (Fr)
A flashing aspect in a signal.

FEVE
Ferrocarriles de Via Estrecha; established 1965 to operate Spanish narrow gauge (metre gauge) rlys.

FFS
Ferrovie Federali Svizzere, Italian language designation since 1944 for Swiss Federal Rlys, replacing *SFF* (qv). *See also CFF, SBB.*

FGS
Ferrocarril Gran Sud de Buenos Aires. See BAGS.

Fiat Ferroviaria
Italian locomotive, rly rolling stock and tramcar manufacturer; producer of *Pendolino* trains (qv). Majority shareholding acquired by Alstom (qv), 2000.

FIC
Freight Integration Council, formed 1968.

Ficelle (Fr)
A funicular rly.

Field (USRS)
A classification (freight marshalling) yard.

Fielder (USRS)
Brakeman in a field (qv).

Field face/side
See Back edge.

Field man (USRS)
The brakeman (qv) working at the furthest point from the loco.

Field to field crossing
Accommodation crossing (qv).

Fife Coast Express
Summer service between Glasgow (Queen St.) and St Andrews, 1949–51.

Fife Coast Line
Thornton Junc–St Andrews–Leuchars Junc.

Fifeshire Coast Express
A summer service between Glasgow (Queen St.) and St Andrews, 1912–39.

Fifty Five Broadway
Headquarters offices of the Underground Co., London, and later of the LPTB, LTE, LTB, and LRT (all qv). Situated at 55 Broadway, Westminster, London, SW1 and completed in 1929 to the designs of the architect Charles Holden.

Figurehead (USRS)
A timekeeper.

Fill (US)
An embankment.

Fingerboards
Boards showing destination and calling points of the next train at a platform, slotted into a socket on a post by platform staff. Almost extinct by 1995.

Fireboy (USRS)
A steam loco fireman.

Fire devil
A brazier lit at water cranes in cold weather to prevent the supply freezing; or one used by fogmen.

Fireless loco (obs)
A small steam loco without firebox, fed with steam from an external source and therefore suitable for use in high fire risk locations.

Fireman (obs)
The second member of crew of a steam loco, with the duty of maintaining the fire to produce the required quantity of steam; also attended to injectors and coupling up loco with train, etc.

Fire train (obs)
A train equipped with steam pumps, water tank wagons, etc., maintained at loco depots in a state of readiness to fight fires on or alongside the rly.

First A
GWR TC for eight-wheel First class coach.

First Great Eastern
TOC (2) from 1997, formerly GE Rlys (qv), so named 1994 after acquisition by First Group (qv). Became part of Greater Anglia (qv) 1.4.2004.

First Great Western
A TOC (2) (qv) formerly Great Western Trains (qv), so named in 1998 after acquisition by First Group (qv). Took over Thames Trains Ltd (qv) franchise from 1.4.2004, using brand name First Great Western Link, both becoming part of new 2006 franchise Greater Western (qv).

First Group plc
Originally First Bus, owners of all TOC (2) (qv) named 'First . . .' (qv).

First North Western
A TOC (2) (qv) formerly North Western Trains (qv), so named after acquisition by First Group in 1998. Operating local and regional passenger services in north-west England and North Wales and some longer-distance interurban services, receiving substantial financial support from Merseytravel, Greater Manchester and West Yorkshire PTEs (qv). North Wales services transferred to Wales & Borders franchise 2004 (*see* Arriva). Longer-distance interurban services to new franchise TransPennine Express (qv) and urban and rural services to new franchise Northern Rail (qv) 2004.

First Reader (USRS)
A conductor's train book.

First Scotrail
TOC (2) for Scotland's rlys 2004–11.

Fish
GWR TC for fish van.

Fish and chip van (RS)(obs)
A Sentinel steam railcar.

Fish bellied rails (obs)
An early form of cast iron rail with concave under-section to add strength.

Fish engines (RS)
GCR 4–6–0 locos (L&NER class B5), often seen on fast fish trains.

Fish horn (USRS)
An electric horn on a railcar.

Fishing
Placing rails together end to end.

Fishplates
Steel or wrought iron plates placed in pairs at rail joints to bring the rail heads together, strengthen the joint and form a continuous running surface. In their original form, when the two halves were held together, the shape suggested that of a fish. The patentee, William Bridges Adams, used this name when describing his invention in 1847. May be *skirted*, i.e. of increased depth to provide extra strength at ends of bullhead (qv) rail, or *insulated*, to connect rail ends when one rail is electrically isolated from another. *See also* Night caps.

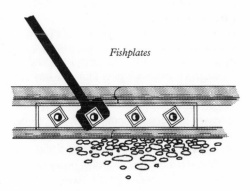

Fishplates

Fish tail (RS)
A distant signal (qv). From the notched arm, resembling a fish's tail.

Fish Tanks (RS)
BR standard 2–6–4T locos.

Fitted freight/goods
A freight train with continuous brakes.

Fitted head (obs)
A group of continuously braked wagons or vans at the head of an otherwise unfitted freight train.

Fitter's cap (RS)
A type of fault caused by unnecessary or over-conscientious interference. From the apocryphal blocking of the feed to a loco's injectors by a cloth cap left behind by a fitter when inspecting a tender water tank.

Fitting
A generic term for points and crossings of all kinds.

Fittings
A layout of points/switches and crossings of any degree of complexity.

Fixed distant
An unworked distant signal (qv) permanently in the 'on' mode. Located to mark a speed restriction or the approach to a passenger platform or a passing loop on a single line.

Fixed lights
Rly carriage windows which cannot be opened.

Fixed signals
Signals placed at fixed points along the rly line to give instructions to drivers, as distinct from Block signals (qv) and Hand signals (qv). See Fixed distant; Fixed stop signal.

Fixed stop signal (obs)
Placed in a position to prevent the movement of passenger trains at points where further advance of freight trains or ECS (qv) could only be achieved at low speeds under control of subsidiary or position light signals (qv). In at least one place, such a signal was sited at a point where further advance by any type of train or loco could have taken it to a watery grave.

FK
BR Corridor First class Compartment coach.

Flag docket (obs)
A document handed to a guard by booking clerk or other official indicating that passengers have been booked to stations at which his train stops 'conditionally', i.e. only when there are passengers to be set down on request (or waiting to be picked up).

Flagging
Controlling train movements by means of red and green flags during signal failure, track repairs, etc.

121

Flaggy (RS)

A flagman or look-out man.

Flagler's Folly

FEC (qv) between Miami and Key West, across the Florida Keys, a chain of small islands. Completed 1912 and destroyed by a hurricane in 1935. After its builder, Henry M. Flagler.

Flagman

An employee engaged in flagging (qv).

Flagman (US)

The passenger train brakeman (qv) responsible for protecting the rear of a train in an emergency.

Flag halt/station/stop (obs)

An optional stop at which trains called only when there were definite indications of passengers wishing to be picked up or set down (the guard would be notified of the latter at the previous station) (*see* Flag docket). Also known as a conditional stop. To indicate to the driver that he should stop, a red flag was exhibited (or at night, a raised lamp). In some cases the train was stopped by placing a semaphore signal in the 'on' position.

Flaman

A design of speedometer and speed recorder for locos, named after its inventor. Its use has long been a legal requirement on French rlys.

Flamer (RS)

A hot box (qv), well alight, usually when seen at night.

Flanch/Flanche (obs)

The original term for a wheel flange; also (obs) the original term for the foot (qv) of a rail.

Flandres–Riviera

A Calais–Ventimiglia service, avoiding Paris. So named 1970.

Flange lubricators

Equipment fixed to the rails to lubricate wheel flanges and reduce wear on rails and wheels.

Flange rail

Another term for Flat bottom rail (qv).

Flange squeal

The noise made by wheels as the flanges vibrate when negotiating sharply curved

track or turnout roads of switches and crossings.

Flangeway

Any groove or space in track construction or special work (qv) to allow the free passage of wheel flanges (e.g. where check rails (qv) or wing rails (qv) are fitted and over the road surface of a level crossing in the four foot (qv)).

Flank protection

Supplementary signalling and point locking at junctions to ensure safety.

Flannel Jackets (RS)

SR Bulleid Merchant Navy 4–6–2 locos of 1941 (rhyming slang: the first locomotive of this class was 'Channel Packet').

Flashbox (RS)

An emu (qv).

Flashing blade (RS)

A fireman's shovel.

Flashing green

A colour light signal permitting very-high-speed running.

Flashing yellow

A signal aspect warning drivers that trains are routed over a speed-restricted turnout.

Flat

1. (USRS) A flat wagon.
2. (USRS) A rail-carrying wagon.
3. (RS) A wheel surface partly worn flat by harsh braking or skidding.

Flat bottom rail

A rail with a flat base at its foot which is wider than the head (qv). Since the 1840s in general use in North America and elsewhere but not adopted as a standard by BR to replace bullhead (qv) until 1949. Invented along with the fixing spike and fishplates (qv) in 1830 by Robert Livingston Stevens (1787–1856), an American mechanical engineer. *See also* Vignoles (qv).

Flat car (US)**/wagon**

Freight wagon with a flat floor, no sides, ends or roof.

Flatcase

GWR TC for a wagon designed to carry goods in cases.

Flat crossing

Tracks crossing on the level.

Flat curve

A large-radius curve.

Flat irons (RS)

Midland Rly 0–6–4T. From their shape.

Flat junction

A junction on the level, as distinct from flying junction (qv) and burrowing junction (qv).

Flat rail

A worn-down rail running surface (qv).

Flat yard

A yard in which all movements require use of locos.

Fleabox (RS)

Guard's van, usually in Scotland.

Flèche d'Or, La (Fr)

Golden Arrow; a *CIWL* all-Pullman service between Calais and Paris, in connection with Dover sailings and UK Golden Arrow (qv) service. Introduced 1929, ceased 1939, re-introduced 1946. Pullmans withdrawn 1969, ceased 1972.

Fliegende Hamburger

Flying Hamburger; *DR* service Berlin–Hamburg using pioneer streamlined articulated two-car diesel-electric sets, introduced 1933. Became the world's fastest train at that time. Name revived 1997 for 2 h 14 min electric service between the same points.

Fliegende Kölner

A *DR* service Berlin–Hannover–Cologne using four-car streamlined articulated diesel-electric sets, introduced 1935.

Fliegende Münchener

A *DR* service Berlin–Leipzig–Munich, using streamlined articulated diesel-electric units, introduced 1935.

Fliers (obs)

A 1930s term for a limited service of fast trains often at extra fares, usually a single train each way daily, composed of dedicated rolling stock.

Flighting

Grouping of trains travelling at similar speeds to increase line capacity.

Flimsy (USRS)

A train order (qv). From the thin paper used.

Flip, to (USRS)

To board a moving train, hence 'flipper', a hobo stealing a ride.

Flirt, The

Nickname for MS&LR. From its many overtures to other companies.

Floater (USRS)

Boomer (qv).

Florence Nightingale (RS)(obs)

A shunter carrying his oil lamp after dark.

Florida Special

A long-established winter season express between New York and Miami, introduced 1887. In the 1930s its consist included a bathing pool and a gymnasium. In the 1970s its passengers enjoyed fashion shows, colour television and bingo sessions.

FLT

Freightliner (qv) Terminal.

Fluff (RS)

Gratuities.

Fluffer (LTRS)

A tube rly tunnel cleaner, usually a female.

Fluffing

1. (LTRS) The work of a fluffer (qv).
2. (RS)(obs) An off-duty porter picking out wealthy passengers at a large station and offering to carry their luggage in the hope of receiving fluff (qv).

Fluffy link (LTRS)(obs)

Neasden train crews on a separate duty roster from which men were drawn to cover all the odd jobs such as stock transfers, stores trains, test runs, sick absences, etc. 'Like a piece of fluff, they never settled down anywhere . . .' – Harry Luff.

Flushing Continental

An express between London (Liverpool St.) and Harwich (Parkeston Quay) in connection with sailings to Vlissingen (Flushing), introduced 1926.

Fly

1. (RS)(obs) GWR and BR (W) shunter's truck.
2. GWR TC for six-wheel slip coach.
3. (RS)(obs) A pick-up goods train (qv).
4. (RS)(obs) A branch line train.

Flyers (RS)

L&SWR Adams 4–4–0 locos.

Flying Angel (RS)(obs)
A travelling ticket inspector.
Flying Bananas
1. (RS)(obs) GWR diesel railcars. From their shape.
2. (RS) BR HST/IC 125 trains, from their shape and their original livery.
Flying Bedsteads (RS)
SE&CR Wainwright rebuilt Stirling 4–4–0 locos.
Flying Bufferbeam (RS)
A Peckett tank loco with low overall height, giving prominence to buffer beams.
Flying Duck (RS)
A section insulator.
Flying Dutchman
The unofficial title of GWR expresses between London (Paddington) and Exeter, after a famous racehorse. Particularly applied to the 11.45 'Down', introduced 1862, which from 1871–84 was claimed to be the fastest train in the world. Obs by the 1900s.
Flying Hamburger
see Fliegende Hamburger.
Flying junction
A branch line carried over main lines by a bridge, thus avoiding the conflicting movements of a flat junction.
Flying pigs (RS)
1946 Ivatt 2–6–0 locos of the LM&SR.
Flying Sausage (RS)(obs)
Early form of BR station name totem.
Flying Scotsman
The unofficial title (sometimes given as 'Flying Scotchman' or 'Flying Scot') for the principal day express between London (Kings Cross) and Edinburgh (Waverley), current from soon after its inauguration in 1862. Adopted officially by the L&NER in 1923 and still in use. Ran non-stop to New-castle from 1927 and non-stop to Edinburgh with corridor tender (qv) from 1928. The journey of 392.7 m took 8 h 15 min in 1901, 8 h 8 min in 1927, 7 h in 1937, and 3 h 29 min with electric traction in 1991.
Fly[ing] shunt (obs)
A prohibited method of shunting, in which the loco spurts ahead into one track after the wagons it was hauling have been uncoupled, leaving them to run on, switched into another siding. Also incorrectly applied to any form of loose shunting (i.e. with uncoupled wagons).
Flying Snail (RS)(obs)
The CIE emblem as adopted in 1943.
Flying Squad (RS)
Travelling ticket inspectors.
FM Rail
A merger (12.2004) of Fragonset (qv) (a ROSCO (qv)) and Merlin Rail (qv) (a TOC (qv)), offering locos and rolling stock on hire (with crews if required), as well as maintenance and engineering services.
FNC
Ferrocarriles de Colombia; National Rlys of Colombia, 2,611 km, 914 mm gauge.
FNM
Ferrocarriles Nacionales de Mexico; National Rlys of Mexico, a 1987 merger of the several state-owned systems. From this date *FNM* operated all common carrier rlys in Mexico, but in 1999/2000 the rlys of Mexico were broken up and privatized as part of the economic restructuring associated with the North American Free Trade Agreement. *c*. 20,000 km. *See also N de M.*
FO
BR First class open coach with 2 + 1 seating.
Foamer (USRS)
Trainspotter (qv) or any kind of anorak (qv).
FOC
1. Freight Operating Companies. *See* DRS; EWS; Freightliner; GB Railfreight; Mendip Rail; Railways Act, 1993.
2. Free Of Charge; carried at the cost to the rly operator, not the consignee. *See also* FOR.
Fog
1. (RS) A detonator.
2. (USRS) Steam.
Fogger (LTRS)
A fog repeater (qv).
Foggeys (RS)
Fogmen (qv).
Fogging (RS)
Fog signalling duty.
Fogging machine
A device which automatically places detonators on the rail surface when a signal

is 'on', removing them when it changes to clear.

Fog gongs
Electric gongs attached to signal posts to warn drivers of the location of signals in foggy weather and to prevent overrunning should they be 'on'.

Fogmen
Rlymen called out in foggy weather to signal trains by flags and hand lamps and place detonators on tracks when fog is obscuring semaphore signals in the 'on' position.

Fog pit
A pit between rails in which a fogman stands to place detonators on the line.

Fog repeater
A colour-light signal only switched on during periods of poor visibility to repeat the indication of the next normal signal in advance.

Fog service
A pre-arranged reduced train service to be operated in bad weather conditions.

Fog signal
Disc-shaped detonators with pliable metal clips which are placed on the surface of the rails in pairs to warn drivers that a signal obscured by fog is at danger or that there is an obstruction ahead.

Fog signalmen
Fogmen (qv).

Foot [of a rail]
That part of a rail section at the base below the web (qv).

Footboard yardmaster (USRS)
A freight conductor (3) acting as a yard switchman.

Foot boards
Wooden boards fixed to run continuously along the sides of a rly carriage/coach, or alternatively simply fitted below door openings, designed to allow exit and access when a train is not standing at a station platform.

Footex
TC for football supporters' excursion or special train.

Footplate
The platform behind the firebox of a steam loco on which the enginemen stand. Still

current for cabs of diesel and electric locos and trains.

Footplate staff
Enginemen (drivers, firemen, second men).

Footwarmers (obs)
Metal cylinders filled with very hot water or chemicals at stations and placed on the floor of coaches not fitted with any form of heating system. Steam and electric heating had rendered them obsolete by the mid-1920s.

FOR
Free On Rail; carried on the rly free of charge. *See also* FOC.

Forcing a path (RS)
Allowing an untimetabled train or a train running early to proceed forward on a signal box-to-signal box basis. *See also* Path.

Fordell Rly
St David's Harbour to Inverkeithing, 4 ft 4 in/1,321 mm gauge, opened *c.* 1770, horse-worked, carrying coal from pits to harbour. It had three self-acting inclined planes and wooden rails. Rebuilt with iron rails 1833–8 and again relaid, for steam locos, in 1867. Closed 1947.

Foreign (obs)
Any rly other than that of the person using the term; the locos and rolling stock of such a rly; traffic arrived from or despatched to such a rly.

Foreign engine (RS)
A loco from another depot, even one on the same rly system.

Foreign Legion (RS)
Men on loan outside their usual base.

Forest of Dean Central Rly
Awre to Howbeach Slade and New Fancy Colliery, inc 1856, opened 1868. Worked by GWR. Part of GWR from 1923.

Forest of Dean Rly
Bullo Pill Junc. to Churchway/Cinderford Junc. Inc 1809 as Bullo Pill Rly (horse), Churchway Hill–Bullo Pill, renamed FofD Rly 1826, purchased by SWR 1847, opened with loco traction 1854, Cinderford Loop 1908.

Forever Amber (RS)
A signal showing yellow indication consistently (fixed distant). After the title of a 1940s novel and film.

Formation

1. The graded and prepared ground over which the blanket (qv) ballast (qv) and tracks are laid.
2. Composition of a train. *See also* Consist.

Formsignal (Ger)

A semaphore signal.

Forney/Forney Engine (US)

Term for 0–4–4T steam loco type widely used on suburban and city elevated rlys. After its designer, M.N. Forney (1835–1908), US inventor and rly engineer. Came to be used for any tank loco without a leading truck.

Forth & Clyde

see F&CJR.

FO(T)

BR First class Open vehicle with Trolley refreshment and counter accommodation for sleeping car services, 1992.

Fouling bar

A bar placed alongside a rail which is depressed by the weight of a vehicle or loco, and is connected with the signals, which it prevents from being put to 'off' indication when it is pushed down.

Fouling point

The point on converging tracks beyond which a vehicle on one line will obstruct anything passing on the other line. On Network Rail, a minimum clearance of 200 mm between the kinematic envelopes (qv) of vehicles occupying converging tracks; on London Underground, the point at which the space between the structure gauges (qv) on two converging tracks reduces to 75 mm.

Four (RS)

LM&SR class 4F 0–6–0. From its power classification. Also 'Four F'.

Four aspect section/territory

Lines equipped with colour-light signals (qv) which show red, one yellow, double yellow and green aspects.

Four-foot

The space between the inside edges of the two running rails, or, if there is an electric conductor rail outside one of the running rails, the space between the inside edge of the exterior conductor rail and the inside edge of the other running rail. *See also* Conductor rail; Six-foot [way].

Four Slide Slide (RS)

BR class 455 emu; a corruption of the class number.

Fourteen wheelers (RS)

LB&SCR 4–6–4T locos.

Fourth class

The most inferior type of passenger accommodation, offered by several British cos in the 1840s and 1850s, but withdrawn after a few years. On the European mainland, Fourth class accommodation, with very cheap fares and more standing space than seats, survived into the twentieth century, not being abolished in Germany, for example, until 1928.

Fourth rail

The negative or return current rail in a ground conductor insulated return system of electrification, usually placed in the centre between the running rails and is near earth potential.

Four wheel switch[er] (US)

A steam loco with 0–4–0 wheel arrangement.

Fowler's Ghost

Nickname of the unsuccessful prototype steam loco designed by Sir John Fowler to eliminate steam and smoke as far as possible when running in the Metropolitan Rly tunnels. Built by Robert Stephenson & Co. in 1861.

Foxfield Rly

A preserved industrial line from Blythe Bridge, Staffs to Dilhorne Park, opened 1968.

FPL

Facing point lock (qv).

FR

1. Festiniog Rly, Portmadoc–Blaenau Festiniog. Inc 1832, for transport of slate from quarries to port, 1 ft 11½ in/597 mm gauge. Opened 1836, passenger service 1865. Closed passengers 1939, freight 1946. Reopened as preserved/tourist line from 1955.
2. Furness Rly, inc 1844, Barrow to Lindal, opened 1846, subsequent extensions made to Carnforth, Whitehaven,

Lakeside, Coniston. 158 route miles in 1914. Part of LM&SR 1923.

3. Fairbourne Rly, Fairbourne (Cambrian Rlys)–Penrhyn Point (Barmouth Ferry), 2 ft/609 mm gauge horse tramway, opened 1890 for freight, passengers carried from c. 1895. Converted to 15 in/381 mm gauge steam miniature rly 1916 by NGR (qv). Closed 1940, reopened 1947. Converted to 12 in/305 mm gauge 1986 and renamed F&Barmouth Steam Rly.

FRA (US)
Federal Railroad Administration; that part of the DoT (qv) which coordinates US federal government business relevant to rail safety, research and development, etc.

Fragonset Rlys Ltd
A ROSCO (qv) company based at Derby which purchases withdrawn locos and rehabilitates them for spot hire to freight and passenger operators. Merged with Merlin Rail (qv) to become FM Rail (qv) 2004.

Frame, mechanical
The apparatus, usually within a signal box, but occasionally found on station platforms or elsewhere, which includes the levers and interlocking for manual operation of points and signals.

Franchising Director
see OPRF.

Franco-Crosti boiler
A loco design incorporating a bank of tubes in a secondary drum or drums through which the exhaust gases pass before being released from a final chimney, the heat being used to raise the temperature of the feed water to a level almost as high as that in the main boiler. The chimney in the normal position is used only for lighting up when the loco is being steamed. Developed by *SA Locomotive a Vapore Franco* (It). Originally designed by A. Franco and built in Belgium in 1932 but improved by Ing. Piero Crosti and first built in Italy in 1940 and 1954. BR introduced ten 9F 2–10–0 locos with this feature in 1955.

Frankensteins (RS)
SR 0–6–0 locos class Q1 designed by O.V.S. Bulleid, introduced 1942. From their hideous appearance.

FR&P
Felixstowe Rly & Pier, inc 1875, Westerfield–Felixstowe, opened 1877, worked by GER 1879, part of GER 1887. *See also* FD&R.

Franz Liszt
An EC between Dortmund and Budapest, introduced 1989.

Freaks (RS)
L&YR 4–6–0 locos.

FRED
Flashing Rear End Device, BR. A continuously flashing red lamp attached to the last vehicle of a train. Also known as a BOG (qv).

Freds (RS)
Class 66/5 locos; acronym from FReightliner (qv) and ShEDS (qv).

Free-hauled traffic
Rly service materials carried on revenue-earning trains.

Free trucking
Free conveyance of scenery, stage properties and costumes for theatrical companies travelling by rail. Withdrawn after 1964.

Freezer (USRS)
A refrigerator wagon.

Freight
A generic term for all types of non-passenger traffic; originally US but imported to UK by the NER in the 1900s. By c. 1960 the term had replaced the former UK usage of 'goods' and 'minerals'.

Freightliner
A system for moving marine and road transport containers in dedicated trains of low-platform bogie wagons, with related transfer facilities from road to rail vehicles and vice versa. Developed by BR from 1963, the first service ran in 1965. Transferred in 1969 to Freightliners Ltd, a separate self-accounting company jointly owned by the NFC (qv) and the BRB. By 1974 there were 150 daily services carrying over 500,000 containers annually, including those to and from container

ports. In 1978 this activity was returned to direct BR control. It was merged with Speedlink (qv) to form Railfreight Distribution (qv) in 1988. Separate business again 1995, Freightliner Ltd, a FOC (qv), the biggest intermodal freight operator in the UK. *See also* Speedfreight.

Freight standards [route]
A goods line (qv).

French notation
Continental notation (qv).

Frequency
The number of trains, or tramcars/LRVs in a service per unit of time, e.g. 5 tph (trains per hour). Not to be confused with headway (*1*) (qv).

Fresh, The
Nickname for FY&NR (qv).

Fresher (RS)
Station refreshment rooms/buffet.

Fret SNCF (Fr)
The freight division of *SNCF* (qv), providing three levels of service which reflect, in descending order, the speed of delivery to the customer: *Fret express; Fret rapide; Freteco*.

Fried eggs (RS)
Poached eggs (qv).

Friedrich Schiller
A winter season *TEE* Stuttgart–Dortmund, 1979–82.

Frisco (US)
The St Louis–San Francisco Rly System.

Frog
1. The 'V' type of crossing (qv) in general use. In the US, a crossing.
2. A device used on trolley/contact wires of tramways (*3*) to allow the passage of current collectors along either the main or a branch wire where routes diverge. At facing junctions the frog is fitted with a moveable tongue. The tongue of a two-way switch frog is maintained in one position by a spring and moved to the other by a wire operated by the pointsman or point controller. Automatic frogs are designed so that their tongue is set for the branch line by the trolley pole engaging a weighted lever at the side of the frog which is then

released to allow the tongue to return to its normal 'through line' position.

Front coupled (RS)
A loco with 0–4–2 wheel arrangement.

Front garden (RS) (obs)
The area around the smokebox (qv) and front buffer beam of a steam loco.

Frontier Mail
An express between Bombay, Delhi and Peshawar, so named from 1928. Bombay to Dehli, 950 m in 23 h in 1968. Now runs between Bombay and Amritsar.

Front shift (RS)
An early turn, as opposed to back shift (qv).

Frost devil (RS)
A brazier used for melting ice in a water crane or to prevent a water crane from freezing. *See also* Fire devil.

Frothblowers (RS)
LM&SR 2–6–0 locos.

Fruit
GWR TC for fruit van.

FS
Ferrovie dello Stato; Italian State Rlys, formed 1905–7. 19,466 km. Reorganized 1999–2001 as a holding company with four principal subsidiaries: *RFI* (qv); *Trenitalia* (qv);*GS* (qv); and *Metropolis* (qv). A fifth, Metropark, manages car parks on rly lands.

FSD (obs)
Field Supply Depots: British Army installations, mostly in WW1, sited behind the battle fronts, at which ammunition and other military supplies were transferred from standard gauge rlys to military light rlys or other means of transport.

FTA
Freight Transport Association.

FTE
Forum Trans-Europe. Established 1997 to administer UIC (qv) directives and finalize international timetables in Europe.

Fudge, to (RS)
The action of a fudger or deceitful train spotter – to count a loco as 'spotted' or 'copped' when it has not been seen.

Fulger Regele Carole 1er
A *CIWL* Pullman service between Bucharest and Constantza, introduced 1933.

Full brake

A coach used in a passenger train which contains no passenger accommodation but only the guard's compartment including handbrake and space for luggage, mail, cycles, etc. *See also* Passenger full brake.

Full load siding (obs)

LM&SR (qv) term for Mileage siding (qv).

Fully fitted train

A train in which there is a continuous air or vacuum brake pipe connection throughout and on which at least 90 per cent of the vehicles are equipped with continuous brakes, including vehicles at the rear of the train.

Funnel

A less usual alternative to chimney (of a loco); at one time used officially by GWR. *See also* Smokestack.

Furloughs (RS) (obs)

Cheap tickets for Navy, Army and RAF personnel proceeding on leave. Regulations required that if the applicant was not in uniform, a sight of the leave authorization was to be requested by the booking clerk.

Furness Railway Magazine

Monthly house and staff journal of FR (2)(qv) 1921–2.

Further North Express

An express between Inverness, Dornoch and Wick, introduced 1906. *See also* John o' Groat.

Furzebrook Tramway

An industrial rly, 2 ft 8½ in/825 mm gauge, operated by Pike Bros for carriage of fire clay from Furzebrook to Ridge on Poole Harbour, opened 1840, extended west from Furzebrook to Povington 1920, main lines all closed by 1957.

Fusible plug

A plug formed of a readily fusible metal compound which will melt to allow escape of boiler pressure if the top of the inner firebox of a steam loco is not covered with water.

FY&NR

Freshwater, Yarmouth & Newport Rly (Isle of Wight), inc 1881, opened 1888, 1889, worked by IofWCR until 1913. Part of SR from 1923.

Fylde Coast Express

A service between London (Euston) and Blackpool with through coaches for Blackburn/Colne, introduced 1934.

F-Zug (Ger)(obs)

Fernschnellzug; express train, usually First class only. Replaced by IC (qv). *See also* FD-Züge.

G

Gabarit (Fr)
Loading gauge (*1*) (qv).
Gabarit Passe-Partout International
Berne Gauge (qv).
Gadfly
GWR TC for flat wagon used for carrying small aircraft.
Gadgets (RS)
L&NWR Webb 0–6–2T.
Gainsborough Line
Marks Tey–Sudbury, so-named, after the artist, from 1999.
Galileo
A Paris–Venice–Florence service introduced 1989. Paris–Florence 1990. *See also* Rialto.
Gallery (US)
1. A signal gantry.
2. The upper deck of a double deck suburban coach with upper seating in galleries flanking the high ceiling of the central aisle of the lower deck.
3. (RS) A crowd of enthusiasts all taking the same photo from a favoured lineside viewpoint.
Gallery car (US)
1. A freight car with two or three floor levels or decks.
2. A double-deck passenger car with passenger seating in 'galleries' on the upper deck either side of a central well gangway.
Galloping Goose (USRS)
Any improvised rail vehicle, especially a self-propelled van.
Galloping rod (USRS)
The connecting rod of a diesel-electric loco.

Galvaniser (USRS)
A car inspector.
Gambrinus
A Munich–Hamburg service introduced 1952, *TEE* 1978. Stuttgart–Bremen from 1980, Münster–Stuttgart 1981, Dortmund–Stuttgart 1982–3. Lost *TEE* status 1983.
G&AR
Greenock & Ayrshire Rly, inc 1865, Greenock to Bridge of Weir, opened 1869. Part of G&SWR from 1872.
G&DFR
Gloucester & Dean Forest Rly, inc 1846, Gloucester to Grange Court, opened 1851, leased to and worked by GWR. Part of GWR from 1874.
G&KER
Garstang & Knot (*sic*) End Rly, inc 1864, Garstang to Pilling, opened 1870. Closed 1872, reopened 1875; Knott End Rly inc 1898, Pilling to Knott End, opened 1908, acquired the G&KER 1908, absorbed by LM&SR 1923.
G&LT
Glenanne & Loughgilly Tramway (NI). Tramway (*4*) 1 ft 10 in/559 mm gauge, horse traction. Opened 1897, closed 1919.
G&P Jt
Glasgow & Paisley Joint (CR & G&SWR), Glasgow (Bridge Street)–Cardonald–Paisley and branches to Govan, Shieldhall and Renfrew, formed 1837, main line opened 1840, LM&SR from 1923.
G&SWR
Glasgow & South Western Rly, inc 1850, a fusion of Glasgow, Paisley, Kilmarnock & Ayr Rly and Glasgow, Dumfries & Carlisle

Rly, many other lines built subsequently; 492 route miles by 1914, serving south-west Scotland. Part of LM&SR from 1923.

G&WR
Gloucestershire & Warwickshire Rly. Preserved rly on former BR line between Cheltenham and Toddington. First section opened 1984.

Gandy dancer (USRS)
A track surfaceman. From the motion of men using track tongs or claw bars supplied by the Gandy Manufacturing Co. of Chicago when carrying rails from stockpiles to the track formation.

Gane
GWR TC for 40-ton bogie bolster truck used by Engineers' Department.

Gang car (US)
Track inspection car.

Ganger (obs)
A man in charge of a track maintenance gang, chargehand. Now known as track chargeman. A ganger would be expected to walk his length (qv) at least once a week to check the track was in a safe condition.

Gang road (obs)
A horse-worked plateway (qv).

Gangway
A flexible bellows connection affording a safe covered passage over a metal plate or deck from one passenger coach to another (or from a passenger coach to a corridor tender (qv)). Also the metal plate or deck between a steam loco and its tender. *See also* Fall-plate; Pullman gangway.

Gangwayed
A coach with a means of access from one end to the other and to adjacent vehicles.

Gannet
A 25-ton unfitted hopper ballast wagon with centre discharge used by engineers.

Gantlet (US)
A length of gauntletted track (qv).

Gantry
A structure carrying signals which spans two or more tracks.

Ganz Electric
A Hungarian state enterprise manufacturing rly electrical equipment, founded as the Ganz Electrical Co. and by 1901 the largest industrial firm in Hungary, with 6,400 employees.

Ganz–Hunslet
An Anglo-Hungarian firm partnering the Telfos-owned Hunslet (qv) and Ganz–Mavag (qv).

Ganz–Mavag
A Hungarian state enterprise manufacturing rly mechanical equipment.

Gapped (RS)
An electric train unable to move because its collector shoes are over a gap in the conductor rail.

GAR (Ger)
Güteraussenring; a freight belt line round Berlin.

Garage (Fr)
Berthing/stabling siding/s.

Garda
An EC service between Munich and Verona, introduced 1989.

Garden
1. (RS)(obs) Ashpit and fire cleaning area in a loco depot.
2. (USRS) A freight yard.

Garden Cities & Cambridge Buffet Car Expresses
A L&NER service between London (Kings Cross), Welwyn Garden City, Letchworth and Cambridge, introduced 1932, restored 1948, withdrawn 1978. *See also* Beer Trains.

Garden seats (obs)
Transverse slatted seats on open-top tramcars.

Garé/Garée (Fr)
Stored out of use.

Gares Betteraves (Fr)
'Beetroot field stations'; intermediate stations on dedicated *TGV* (qv) routes erected in open country to avoid slow-running diversion onto the historic network to reach existing stations in important urban centres.

Garex
TC for guaranteed excursion.

Garratt
A steam loco type invented in 1907 by H.W. Garratt (1864–1913). It has two independent sets of driving wheels, carrying

wheels, cylinders and motion, each mounted on a separate chassis, and each chassis carrying at its inner end one end of a central heavy girder frame supporting the boiler, which supplies steam to both sets of motion. This central unit also contains the controls and driving cab. Pivoting at each end of the central section allows negotiation of sharp curves and the general arrangement spreads the weight over a considerable length of track. The Whyte notation copes by using a plus sign, thus a Garratt might be a 4–8–2 + 2–8–4 or a 2–8–0 + 0–8–2.

Gas (RS)
Steam.

Gas buggy (USRS)
Any petrol or diesel-driven rail vehicle.

Gas house (USRS)
A yard office.

Gas up, to (RS)
To raise steam on a loco.

Gate (USRS)
A set of points.

Gate box
A signal box with the sole purpose of controlling a level crossing.

Gatwick Express/Rly Co.
Regular and frequent non-stop service between London (Victoria) and Gatwick Airport, using air-conditioned Inter-City stock, introduced 1984. Gatwick Express Rly Co. Ltd, TOU (qv), 1994. A TOC (2), 1996. New trains from 2000.

Gauge
The distance between the rails of a track; measured from inside edge to inside edge of the rail heads. *See also* Broad gauge; Construction gauge; Loading gauge; Narrow gauge; Standard gauge.

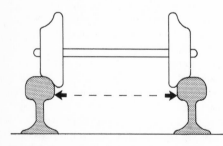

Gauge measurement

Gauge/gauging bar (obs)
Tool carried by lengthmen/gangers to check distance between running rails was correctly to gauge.

Gauge corner
The curve on the inside of the head (qv) of a rail between the running surface (qv) and the running edge (qv).

Gauge corner cracking
Rail failure beginning with sub-surface cracks parallel to the railhead (qv) which subsequently turn downwards into the railhead causing a fracture. *See also* Rolling contact fatigue.

Gauge face
See Running edge.

Gauge glass
A tube in the cab of a steam locomotive which shows the height of the water in the boiler; also a similar device showing the water level in tender.

Gauge point
The point on the inside of the railhead (qv) at the running edge (qv) from which gauge measurements are taken; on Network Rail 14 mm below the rail crown (qv), on London Underground 13 mm.

Gauntletted track/Gauntletting
In which rails or parallel tracks are arranged so that the inner rail of one set is between the rails of the other. Normally adopted to allow additional working space on a viaduct or in a tunnel under lengthy repair. Effectively reduces the section concerned to single track without the expense of installing full points but must be signalled accordingly. Also used on tramways (3) when street width becomes insufficient for double track for a short distance. Also known as interlaced track or interlacing.

Gayant
TEE Paris–Tourcoing 1978. Lost *TEE* status 1983.

GB&K Jt
Glasgow, Barrhead and Kilmarnock Joint, G&SWR and CR, formed 1869, LM&SR from 1923.

GB Rail Freight Ltd
A FOC (qv) from 2001, using locos based at Crewe.

GBNRPT
See NRT.

GBPRT
Great Britain Passenger Railway Timetable, issued twice-yearly, showing times of all public passenger train services in Great Britain. First published 1974. Retitled 1999, *see* NRT.

GB Railways
Owner of Anglia (qv) and a major stakeholder in Hull Trains (qv).

GBRf
See GB Rail Freight Ltd.

GC&DR
Glasgow City & District Rly, inc 1882, first section opened 1886, worked by NBR, part of NBR 1887. Popularly known in Glasgow as 'The Underground', from its Finnieston–Queen St. (Low Level)–High Street underground section, it comprised at its fullest extent a circular line from Queen St. via Great Western Road, Maryhill, Springburn and Bellgrove back to Queen St., with branches to Hyndland, Bridgeton Cross and Victoria Park.

GC & Midland Rly Joint Committee
Formed 1869 and inc 1872 as Sheffield [MS&LR] & Midland Committee, to administer jointly vested lines Manchester & Stockport, Hyde to Marple, and Marple, New Mills and Hayfield Junction; became GC & Midland JC 1897, LM&SR and L&NER joint 1923–47.

GC&NS Rlys Joint Committee
Formed 1871 as Macclesfield Committee, to administer the jointly vested MS&LR and NSR line Marple to Macclesfield. Name changed 1897, LM&SR and L&NER joint 1923–47.

GCGR (obs)
Gold Coast Government Rlys, first line opened 1901; GRC (qv) from 1957.

GC, H&B & Midland Rlys Joint Committee
Inc 1907, Aire Junc–Doncaster–Braithwell Junc–Thurcroft–Brantcliffe Junc/Don Bridge Junc; became LM&SR and L&NER joint 1923–47.

GCP&BVR&T
Giant's Causeway, Portrush & Bush Valley Rly & Tramway, inc 1880, Portrush–Giant's Causeway, 3 ft/914 mm gauge, opened 1883, 1887 with electric traction. First rly to use hydro-electric power. Closed 1949.

GCR
1. Great Central Rly; an 1897 renaming of the MS&LR (qv), 824 route miles by 1914, mainly in central England, but also between Sheffield and London. Became part of L&NER from 1923.
2. Great Central Rly; a preserved section of (*1*) between Loughborough and Leicester. First section opened 1973.
3. Glasgow Central Rly; inc 1888, part of CR (*1*) 1889, opened 1894, 1895, 1896, Dalmarnock (Strathclyde Junc)–Stobcross–Maryhill and Dawsholm via Central (Low Level), almost all underground. Part of LM&SR 1923. Closed 1964, reopened with electric trains 1979 (*see* Clyderail).

GCR Journal
Monthly house and staff journal of GCR (1) (qv) July 1905–June 1918.

GE
1. The GER (qv).
2. General Electric Co. [of America], formed 1892, suppliers of electric traction equipment. Based at Schenectady, N.Y. *See also* Thomson–Houston.

GEC
General Electric Co. Ltd [UK], 1889 to date. Used initials WT (qv). Absorbed AEI (qv) 1967, absorbed EE (qv) 1968. GEC-Alsthom 1989. *See* Alsthom.

GEC stock (RS)(obs)
GEC-built emu stock for LM&SR London suburban services, 1927.

General, The
Name of a 4–4–0 loco built for Western & Atlantic RR (US) in 1855. On 12 April 1862, during the Civil War, it featured in a raid into Confederate territory led by Capt. James J. Andrews, and was recaptured by Capt. W.A. Fuller after an exciting 100-mile chase. The loco, which has been the

subject of films, ballads and books, has been preserved.

General merchandise (obs)
Freight traffic other than coal and minerals; usually divided into wagonload (qv) and sundries (qv).

Generators (RS)
BR class 47 diesel-electric locos (47401–20) fitted with modified electrical equipment.

Genevois
A Paris–Geneva *TGV*, introduced 1982.

Genial menial (RS)(obs)
A labourer in loco depot.

Gentlemen's court/yard (obs)
Urinals and wc for men on stations.

Geordies (RS)(obs)
NER locomotives and men.

GER
1. Great Eastern Rly, formed 1862 of the ECR, EAR, NR, EUR, Newmarket Rly, and ESR (*3*) together with some smaller companies. 1,191 route miles by 1914, mainly in East Anglia. Part of L&NER from 1923. *See also* Great Eastern.
2. Gatwick Express (qv).

GE Rly
Great Eastern Rly Ltd, a TOU (qv), 1994. Replaced 1997 by a TOC (*2*) (qv) of the same title. Operated services London (Liverpool St.)–Southend (Victoria) and branches Romford–Upminster and Wickford–Southminster, also London (Liverpool St.)–Ipswich, Harwich, Clacton and Walton, and branches to Braintree and Sudbury. Renamed FGE (qv) 1998.

GEJ
Great Eastern Journal; the illustrated journal of the GERS (qv), first published 1974.

GERM
Great Eastern Rly Magazine, the official staff journal, published 1911–23.

Germans (RS)
SE&CR L 4–4–0 locos built by Borsig, Berlin.

GERS
Great Eastern Railway Society, formed 1973. Devoted to the serious study of all aspects of the GER (*1*) (qv), also the rlys in its territory before its formation and those operating in the area since 1923.

Get Wets (RS)
GWR 2–4–0T and 0–6–0T without cabs.

Ghan, The
Rly between Maree, Australia and Alice Springs, 3 ft 6 in/1,067 mm gauge, completed 1929. Rebuilt to standard gauge on new route from Port Augusta, via Tarcoola 1980. Also a train running over these lines, between Adelaide and Alice Springs. From April 1999 operated between Sydney and Alice Springs. Extended north to Darwin, 2004. From the Afghan immigrants who operated camel trains over the route before the rly was completed.

Ghost (LTRS)
Pop-up (qv).

Ghost Train
1. Title of a play by Arnold Ridley, first performed 1925, made into a film, 1931.
2. (RS) A nocturnal de-icing train used on electric rlys equipped with conductor rails.

Ghoul (RS)(obs)
A buckeye coupling (qv).

Ghoul, to (RS)(obs)
To couple a train by use of automatic couplers.

Giant
GWR TC for 50 ft/15.24 metres bogie van.

Giesl ejector
An oblong ejector invented by Dr Adolph Giesl-Gieslingen of Vienna for the front end of steam locos. First used in Britain on the Talyllyn Rly in 1958.

GIF
Ente Publica Gestor de Infraestructuras Ferroviarias; Spanish Railway Infrastructure Authority, 1997, also responsible for the expansion of the Spanish rly system.

Gigantenbahn (Ger)
see Breitspurbahn.

Gigs (RS)(obs)
GWR shunter's wagons.

Gin and Toffee
Nickname for the Elsenham to Thaxted branch, GER. From its association with the Gilbey family and the confectioners, Messrs. Lees.

Ginger 'un (RS)

A distant signal showing cautionary yellow.

Ginney tracks (obs)

Plateways (qv) operated by endless chain haulage.

Gippo (LTRS)

An outside telephone, as distinct from rly internal system. From GPO (General Post Office), the former telephone monopoly.

GIP(R)

Great Indian Peninsula Rly; formed 1853. Purchased by Government 1900. Part of the Central Rly of India from 1951.

Girl/old girl (RS) (USRS)

An affectionate term for a loco or train. *See also* She.

Giving on/ give on, to (RS)

The act of communicating 'train entering section' on block instruments (*see* Block system).

Giving out/give out, to

The act of communicating 'train out of section' on block instruments (*see* Block system).

GJR

Grand Junction Rly, inc 1833, Birmingham–Warrington (Newton) (junction with L&MR), opened 1837, freight 1838; amalgamated with other companies to form L&NWR (qv) in 1846.

Glacier Express

A metre-gauge service between Zermatt and St Moritz, introduced 1930. Summer only until 1981; all year round (Zermatt–Chur) from 1982.

Gladhand (USRS)

The metal coupling fitting at the end of an air brake hose; capable of causing serious injury as it jumps upwards if the hose is suddenly filled with compressed air.

Gladstone's Act

see Parliamentary fares/trains.

Glanding

Strapping sleepers together with rails in the four-foot (qv) to give extra strength to the track in situations where the subgrade (qv) is weak.

Gläserne–Zug (Ger)

Glass Train; an electric observation railcar with roof, sides and ends largely of safety-glass; introduced by *DR* in 1935, rebuilt by *DB* 1949 and based at Munich.

Glasgow District Subway

A circular underground 4 ft/1,219 mm gauge cable rly in centre of Glasgow with fifteen stations, inc 1890, opened 1896, renamed GDS Rly 1914, purchased by Glasgow Corporation 1922, electrified 1935, modernized 1980. *See also* Clockwork Orange.

Glassback (RS)

A lazy fireman, not happy about bending his back.

Glass car (USRS)

A passenger coach.

Glass Coach (RS)

The District Engineer's Inspection Saloon.

Glass houses (RS)

GER F7 2–4–2T, from their disproportionately large side-windowed cabs. *See also* Crystal Palaces.

Glaszug (Ger)

see Gläserne–Zug.

Gleiskraftwagen (Ger)

Track inspection car.

Gleiswechselbetrieb/GWB (Ger)

A facility for wrong line working/reversible working (qv).

Glenmutchkin

A mythical Scottish rly company set up to defraud Victorian investors.

Glider Pilot (RS)

An engineman riding on a dead loco being hauled by another loco.

Glimmer (USRS)

A loco headlight.

Globe strainers

Spherical insulators hung between bracket arms and ears (qv) of tramway (*3*) overhead to prevent electric current from passing between the two.

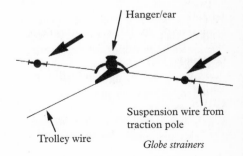

Hanger/ear

Suspension wire from traction pole

Trolley wire

Globe strainers

Glory (USRS)
A string of empty vehicles.
Glory hunter (USRS)
A reckless driver.
Glory wagon (USRS)
A caboose (qv).
Glossies (RS)
Weekly Engineering/Traffic/Operating
Notices (qv).
Gloucester
Gloucester Wagon Co., founded 1860.
Also manufactured signalling equipment
from the 1870s. Became Gloucester
Railway Carriage and Wagon Co. Ltd,
1888. Ceased production of rly equipment,
apart from trucks, 1968. Merged with
PDWCL (qv), 1986.
Glow worms (LTRS) (obs)
Circle Line trains (from their headlights).
GLV
Gatwick Luggage Vans, BR (S), fitted with
gangway at one end. *See also* MLV.
GLW
Gross Laden Weight of a vehicle, shown in
metric tonnes.
GM
General Manager.
GM(EMD)
General Motors (Electromotive Division);
US and Canadian loco builders. *See* EMD
Inc.
GMML
Greater Manchester Metro Ltd. Founded
1990 as the operating company for
Metrolink (qv).
GMPTA/E
Greater Manchester Passenger Transport
Authority/Executive.
GN (US)
Great Northern RR.
GN&CR
Great Northern & City Rly, main line
loading gauge tube rly between Moorgate,
London and a terminus under Finsbury
Park (GNR). Inc 1892, opened 1904,
absorbed by Metropolitan Rly 1913.
Passed to LPTB 1933 and was operated by
its successors (normal LT tube rly stock
used from 1939). Closed 1975. Reopened
1976 and integrated with BR Great

Northern suburban lines by new
connections at Drayton Park/Finsbury
Park, BR taking over operation.
GN&ELR
Great Northern & East Lincolnshire Rly, a
preserved rly using former Louth to
Grimsby line.
GN&GEJC
Great Northern & Great Eastern Joint
Committee, formed 1879 to manage
existing lines Huntingdon–St
Ives–March–Spalding and
Lincoln–Doncaster. Spalding–Lincoln
opened 1882. Ramsey & Somersham Rly
purchased 1896. All part of L&NER from
1923.
GN&L&NWR JC
Great Northern and L&NWR Joint
Committee, inc 1874, to manage lines
between Welham and Drayton Juncs near
Market Harborough and Melton Mowbray
and Bottesford/Saxondale Junc nr
Nottingham, opened 1879. L&NER &
LM&SR joint 1923–47.
GN&SR
Great Northern & Strand Rly, tube rly,
London, inc 1899, Finsbury
Park–Aldwych, absorbed (before opening)
into GNP&BR (qv) 1902.
GN&WR
Great Northern & Western Rly, Athlone to
Westport, inc 1857. Opened 1860, 1861,
1862, 1866. Branch Manulla to Ballina
opened 1868, 1873. Part of MGWR from
1890.
Gnat
GWR TC for slip coach (three types).
Gnat's blood (RS)
Tea.
GNER
Great North Eastern Rly: TOC (2) (qv)
awarded franchise in 1996 for operating
the InterCity East Coast (qv) services
London to Leeds/Bradford/Harrogate/
Hull, Edinburgh, Glasgow, Aberdeen and
Inverness.
GNofE, C&HJR
Great North of England, Clarence and
Hartlepool Junction Rly, inc 1837,
Wingate–Ferryhill, opened 1839, 1846,

leased to York, Newcastle & Berwick Rly 1848 and lease passed on to NER from 1854. Became part of L&NER 1923.

GNofER
Great North of England Rly, inc 1836, 1837, Darlington to York, opened 1841. Worked by Newcastle & Darlington Junction Rly from 1845 and purchased by it 1846, becoming the York & Newcastle Rly. Latter amalgamated with Newcastle & Berwick to form York, Newcastle & Berwick Rly in 1847, this forming part of the new NER from 1854.

GNofSR
Great North of Scotland Rly, inc 1846, Aberdeen to Huntly, first section opened 1854. Other lines added and absorbed; 334 route miles by 1914. Became part of L&NER from 1923.

GNP&BR
Great Northern, Piccadilly & Brompton Rly, tube rly, London, inc 1902, an amalgamation of the B&PCR (qv) and GN&SR (qv). South Kensington–Hammersmith section used powers of District Railway Deep Level scheme of 1897 between South Kensington and Earls Court, then rising to surface near West Kensington to run along the MDR alignment into separate platforms at Hammersmith. Opened Finsbury Park–Hammersmith 1906, Holborn to Strand (Aldwych) 1907. Became part of LER (qv) from 1910.

GNR
Great Northern Rly, inc 1846, London to Shaftholme Junc with York line (near Doncaster), etc., first sections opened 1848, 1849, 1850, 1852. Many other lines subsequently built and absorbed; 1,032 route miles by 1914. Became part of L&NER from 1923.

GNR (I)
Great Northern Rly (Ireland), inc 1876 as Great Northern of Ireland Rly but usually referred to as GNR (I). An amalgamation of the Ulster Rly (opened 1839 with 6 ft 2 in/1,879.6 mm gauge) and the Northern of Ireland Rly (a combination of the Dublin & Drogheda Rly (opened 1844) and the Dublin & Belfast Junction Rly) and

other smaller lines. 616 route miles by 1914. Purchased by Northern Ireland and Republic of Ireland Governments 1953 and managed by Great Northern Rly Board. In 1958 the trackage in the Republic became part of the CIE, and that in Northern Ireland part of the UTA (qv).

GO/GO Transit
Government of Ontario-financed scheme for development of the CNR suburban services in the Toronto area, inaugurated 1967.

Goat (USRS)
Any shunting loco. Also 'yard goat'.

Goat herder (USRS)
A loco driver in a shunting yard.

Go back, to (of a signal) (LTRS)
To change from green to red. When the driver of an approaching train sees this, he will describe the signal as having 'gone back in my face'.

GOB, The:(RS)
The Gospel Oak–Barking line.

Gobblers (RS)
1. GER Worsdell '650' 2–4–2T locos, from their large appetite for coal when first fitted with Joy valve gear.
2. Rly staff regularly working excessive overtime.

Goblin
Acronym for the Gospel Oak–Barking line, 1998.

God (RS)
The Line Controller.

Go dead, to (USRS)
To work twelve hours continuously.

Go devil (USRS)
A manually operated rail car.

God's Wonderful Railway (RS)
Nickname for the GWR. The term persisted into the early days of BR (W).

Goethe
TEE Paris–Frankfurt, introduced 1970. Lost *TEE* status 1975. Name used for *TEE* Dortmund–Frankfurt 1979–83 and an EC Paris–Frankfurt 1987. Extended to Dresden 1991.

Gold Coast, The (RS)(obs)
The Didcot–Newbury line.

Golden Arrow
A Pullman express between London

(Victoria) and Folkestone/Dover in connection with sailings for Calais and *La Flèche d'Or* (for Paris) (qv). Introduced 1929, ceased 1939, restored 1946, withdrawn 1972.

Golden Hind/Executive/Pullman

An express between London (Paddington), Plymouth and, from 1972, Penzance, introduced 1964. 3 h 50 min London–Plymouth in 1964, 3 h 13 min in 1982. Renamed GH Executive 1986, GH Pullman 1987.

Golden Mountain Pullman Express

A *CIWL* service Montreux–Zweisimmen (metre gauge) and thence to Interlaken by standard gauge train with same name, ran summer 1931 only.

Golden Rail

BR holiday packages, introduced 1971, renamed Gold Star Holidays 1988, sold outside BR, 1989.

Golden Sands Express

A Llandudno–Rhyl summer service, introduced 1930.

Golden Spike

A ceremony on 19 May 1869 at Promontory Point, Utah, when the final sections of the UP and Central Pacific Railroads were laid, establishing a continuous rly across the USA between the Atlantic and Pacific coasts. A spike of California gold and another of Nevada silver were driven home by distinguished officials. The original Golden Spike is now displayed at Stanford University, California.

Golden Valley

Golden Valley Rly, inc 1876, Pontrilas to Hay-on-Wye, opened 1881, 1889. Closed at various periods, part of GWR from 1899, reopened 1901.

Golfers' Express

A Belfast–Portrush service, introduced 1934.

Goliath

GWR TC for 50-ft open theatrical scenery wagon.

Gon (USRS)

A gondola (qv).

Gondelbahn (Ger)

Chair lift with enclosed cabins.

Gondola (US)

Any type of open freight wagon.

Gone Completely

Nickname for GCR, following its change of name from MS&LR ('Money Sunk & Lost') and the heavy expenditure on the London extension. Also appropriate as GCR is the only large pre-grouping rly whose main line has been completely closed.

Gone to bed (RS)

A stabled train.

Gong Iron (RS)(obs)

A lamp iron or bracket on a loco tender, situated near the cab for the driver's use, notably on the LCDR.

Good Old England! (RS)

Exclamation uttered at a derailment.

Goods line

A line normally used only by freight trains and maintained to a reduced standard accordingly. Usable by passenger trains at slow speeds in an emergency. Entry and exit controlled by separate signal boxes. *See also* Goods loop.

Goods loop

BR term for an additional running line not authorised for passenger train working, entry and exit controlled from the same signal box. *See also* Goods line.

Goose

TC for 'Stop accepting [trains] until further notice'.

Goose, to (USRS)

To make an emergency stop.

Got Nowhere

Nickname for GNR, because its main line from London ended nowhere in particular, at Shaftholme Junc, with the NER, north of Doncaster.

Gottardo

TEE Zurich–Milan, introduced 1961, extended to Basle 1965–82; extended to Geneva 1974–80. Lost *TEE* status 1988, and was the last of the *TEE* international services. Name used for a Zurich–Milan EC 1988.

Gotthard Oberland Pullman Express

A *CIWL* seasonal service Paris–Basle–Milan (with portion for Berne and Interlaken), ran 1927–31.

Gotthard Pullman Express

A *CIWL* seasonal service Basle–Milan, ran 1927–31.

Gov/Government, The (RS)(obs)

A parliamentary train (qv).

Govia Ltd

A combination of the Go Ahead Group plc and *SNCF* (qv). *See also* Southern, Thameslink; Thames Trains.

Go When Ready

Nickname for the GWR.

Goyle (RS)

Any train or loco considered to be ugly or unappealing. Applied in particular to BR class 31 diesel-electric locos. From gargoyle.

Gozunda/er (RS)

A rail-mounted device for inspecting the undersides of viaduct and tall bridge arches from track level, introduced 1974; 'goes-under'.

GPS

Global Positioning System. Satellite navigation equipment which allows the exact position of a train to be ascertained in terms of latitude and longitude.

GP-TRAMM

See TRAMM.

Grabber (USRS)

A conductor (*3*) or a ticket collector.

Grab iron (USRS)

The hand rail on a loco or other rail vehicles.

Grade (US)

Formation (*1*), also gradient and ground level.

Grade, crossing at

A crossing on the level.

Gradient measure/inclination

In Britain, South America, South Africa and Australasia this is usually quoted as a direct proportion: e.g. 1 in 50 = a rise of 1 ft in 50 ft of line measured horizontally on the level. In mainland Europe it is normally given as per thousand (pro mille) and expressed as 0/00. In North America and elsewhere gradients are expressed as percentages, 1 per cent equalling 1 in 100, 5 per cent 1 in 20, etc. Thus the British 1 in 10 is the same as 100 0/00 or 10 per

cent. Except in very dry tunnels rail vehicles need some special device to tackle gradients steeper than 1 in 10.

Gradient posts

Lineside signs indicating whether a gradient is up or down and its measure/inclination.

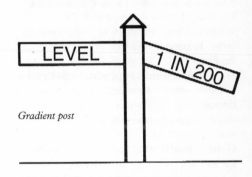

Gradient post

Grampian

A 3-hour express between Glasgow (Buchanan St.) and Aberdeen, introduced 1962.

Grampian Corridor Express

An Edinburgh–Glasgow–Aberdeen service of the CR (*1*), introduced 1905.

Grampus

TC for civil engineer's 20-ton dropside wagons.

Grand confort (Fr)

Luxury First class coaches introduced by the *SNCF* from 1969.

Grand Ducal

A Brussels–Luxembourg service, introduced 1973.

Grandes lignes (Fr)

Main lines, the principal trunk lines. The historic network as distinct from the *LGV* (qv). *see also* VFE.

Grande Vitesse (Fr)

Freight carried at premium rates on fast trains; usually small-bulk high-value items such as: flowers, fruit and perishables and other quality foods.

Grandi Stazioni

See GS.

Grand Junction Line

Stechford–Bescot–Bushbury. From GJR (qv).

Grand union (obs)
A US term, adopted in UK, and mainly applied to tramways (*3*), signifying a right-angled intersection of two sets of double track with double track connections at *all four* corners.

Granite City
An express between Glasgow (Buchanan St.) and Aberdeen, introduced 1933, restored, 1949.

Granite City Express
An Edinburgh–Glasgow–Aberdeen service, introduced 1906. Re-introduced 1933 for a Glasgow–Aberdeen service.

Grano
GWR TC for hopper wagon carrying grain.

Granville & Westgate-on-Sea Special Express
A LC&DR express between London (Victoria) and Ramsgate, introduced 1878. Title underwent various changes, name eventually dropped 1904. Reappeared as Granville Express 1921, name dropped 1927. Name derives from the Granville Hotel, St Lawrence-on-Sea, Ramsgate.

Granville Special Express
A SER First class 'Special Private Express' service between London and Ramsgate, introduced 1876 in connection with the Granville Hotel, St Lawrence-on-Sea, Ramsgate, which offered the SER a guarantee. Arguably Britain's first officially named train. Title dropped 1880, revived at various periods with title in various forms between 1884 and 1904.

Graphiste (Fr)
A timetable compiler. From his use of train graphs (qv).

Grasshoppers
1. (RS) LB&SCR Billinton B2 4–4–0 locos. Also GWR 90XX 'Dukedog' 4–4–0s. From a tendency to rough riding or wheel slip on starting. *See also* Hopper.
2. (USRS)(obs) A vertical-boilered loco. From its appearance when in motion.

Grass track
Urban and suburban light rail/tramway tracks landscaped by infilling the four-foot

(qv) and margins with topsoil which is then seeded.

Grass wagon (USRS)
A tourist coach.

Gravedigger (USRS)
A section hand.

Graveyard (RS)
Sidings accommodating condemned locos or rolling stock.

Graveyard shift (USRS)
Midnight to 08.00.

Gravitation/Gravity sidings/yard
Sidings or a yard arranged on a gradient so that shunting and marshalling can be done by gravity, minimizing use of locos. *See also* Hump.

Gravity shunting
Shunting (qv) by use of gravity in a graded yard or a hump (qv) yard.

Grazing ticket (USRS)
A meal voucher.

GRC
Ghana Railway Corporation, formed 1977; 947 km of 1,067 mm gauge. *See also* GCGR.

Grease monkey (RS)
An employee designated to oil rolling stock or (USRS) to pack grease into axle boxes; a carman (qv).

Grease the pig, to (USRS)
To oil a loco.

Greater Anglia
TOC (2) owned by National Express Group plc, replacing from April 2004 Anglia Rlys (qv), First Great Eastern (qv), WAGN (qv) (Liverpool Street services). *See also* ONE.

Greater Western
TOC (2) 2006, combining First Great Western (qv), First Great Western Link (see First Great Western) and Wessex Trains (qv).

Greathead shield
A tunnelling shield invented by J.H. Greathead (1844–96). Extensively used in construction of deep level tube rlys.

Great North
Abbreviation for GNofSR (qv).

Great Northern
Former WAGN (qv) services into Kings Cross acquired by National Express Group plc 2004. *See also* London Lines.

Great Orme

A 3 ft 6 in/1,067 mm cable tramway at Llandudno, north Wales, opened 1902, connecting the town with the summit of Great Orme.

Great Uhuru Rly

Tanzam Rly (qv).

Great Way Round

Nickname for GWR.

Great Western Trains

Great Western Trains Co. Ltd, TOU (qv), 1994. A TOC (2) (qv), 1996, operating services between London, Cardiff and Fishguard; London, Oxford, Worcester and Hereford, Swindon, Gloucester and Cheltenham; and London and Bristol/ Taunton, Exeter, Paignton and Penzance. Purchased by FirstGroup 1998 and renamed First Great Western (see FGW).

Greek Line

A boat train between London (Waterloo) and Southampton Docks in connection with GL sailings, 1954–66.

Green Arrow (obs)

A system of registered consignment fast freight transit, formerly available on payment of a premium for a package or train load. Introduced by GWR in 1930 and subsequently by the other British rly companies. Ceased 1939. Re-introduced 1953 to expedite export consignments; fully restored 1957 but subsequently withdrawn. Also L&NER V2 2–6–2 locomotives, introduced 1936 and used on trains carrying Green Arrow freight.

Greenball (USRS)

A train solely composed of fruit or vegetable vans.

Greenbat

Greenwood & Batley Ltd, Leeds, manufacturers of electric locos. Part of Hunslet (qv) from 1981.

Green card/green carding

The procedure of placing a green card into the card holder of a wagon, van or coach to indicate that although it is defective and requires attention by maintenance staff, it is considered safe to run until the end of the working day. See also Red card.

Green carrier (USRS)

The first section of a train which is running in two parts.

Green caterpillars (RS)(obs)

The original L&SWR electric trains as introduced in 1915.

Green eye (USRS)

A clear signal.

Green fire (RS)

A part of loco fire which is unburnt.

Green Goddesses (RS)

Nickname for 770 class of double-decked tramcars of Liverpool Corporation Tramways, introduced 1933. From the title of a play then being performed in the city.

Greenhouses (RS)

GER 1300 (later L&NER F7) 2–4–2T locos. From their disproportionately large side-windowed cabs.

Green pastures (RS)

High earnings from overtime/bonus payments.

Green tanks (RS)

L&SWR Urie H16 4–6–2T locos.

Green zone

An area near a rly designated as not subject to interruption of work by train movements, with the possible exception of slow-moving track plant or engineer's trains.

Greyhounds (RS)

1. L&SWR small Drummond T9 4–4–0 locos of 1899–1901. From their high speed on down gradients.
2. CIG (qv) emu sets (Class 421/4) upgraded for 90 mph running on the London (Waterloo)–Guildford–Portsmouth line.

GRG (Fr)

Grande Revision Générale, a major overhaul.

GRI

BR (SR) four-car emu corridor set with griddle (qv) cars converted from restaurant cars 1964, formation as BUF (qv) with griddle car instead of buffet car, 4-GRI.

Grice, a (RS)

A good cop (qv). Derived from gricer (qv).

Grice, to (RS)

To exhibit the characteristics of a gricer

(qv), i.e. any or all of the following: to travel enthusiastically over a particular rly line for the first time, or to ride with enthusiasm behind a particular locomotive for the first time, or to see or photograph it for the first time etc.; to watch trains obsessively; to enthuse fanatically over a locomotive, item of rolling stock or rly line; to go on a trip in pursuit of rly interests.

Gricer (RS)

The most fanatical and extreme type of rly enthusiast, intent on travelling over all existing rly track, seeing all existing locos, etc. Often used in a derogatory sense to denote the scruffily dressed, camera-, binocular- and notebook-carrying rly voyeur and collector of useless information. The origins of the term are obscure and beset with false trails, but it seems to have emerged in northern England during the 1940s, spreading into general use in the late 1950s and early '60s; it was not used in the popular rly periodicals until *c.* 1970.

Grid (RS)

Class 56 diesel loco.

Griddle car

A BR catering vehicle with bar and buffet saloons and central kitchen fitted with griddle plates, introduced 1961.

Gridiron (RS)(obs)

A marshalling yard, usually gravity-worked.

Gridirons (RS)

BR class 56 diesel locos.

Griever (USRS)

A trade union official at an investigation or inquiry.

Gril Express (Fr)

SNCF cafeteria cars (qv), introduced 1970.

Grind (USRS)

A Shay loco (qv).

Grip car

A tramcar equipped with a device to grip and release hold on moving cables beneath the track. Sometimes with passenger seating to supplement that in its trailer car.

Grip man

The driver of a grip car (qv).

Gronk, to (RS)

To travel over rlys normally difficult of public access. Also gronkage, such lines; and gronker, one who indulges in gronking. In use from *c.* 1980.

Gronks (RS)

Same as cronks (qv).

Grooved girder rail

The conventional type of tramway (3) rail used for running on road surfaces, flat-bottomed, with a groove to accommodate wheel flanges. *See* illustration at Tramway (3) entry.

Grooved rail

Flat bottom (qv) rail with an integral check rail used by tramways (3) (qv) and also by rlys laid along hard-top roads and yards.

Grossraumwagen (Ger)

High capacity tramcars designed by *VÖV* (qv) from 1951. Also a rly saloon coach. *See* Saloon.

Ground disc

A small disc-shaped signal with banner indicator, placed on the ground to control movements in sidings or over crossovers.

Ground frame

A small mechanical frame set apart from a signal box, often in the open, to control signals in sidings. Unlocked electrically from the nearest signal box, or by a release key. *See also* Annett's Key.

Ground hog (USRS)

A brakeman or yardmaster.

Ground signal

Any type of signal placed at ground level to control movements in sidings or shunting, usually one with miniature semaphore arms and spectacles. *See also* Dummy (3).

Groupie (LTRS)

A group manager.

Grouping

The amalgamation of most British rly companies into four groups (LM&SR, L&NER, GWR and SR), which took place following the Railways Act, 1921, effective from 1 January 1923.

Group station tickets (obs)

Scheme tickets (qv).

Grouting

The process of stabilizing a subgrade (qv), an embankment or a cutting by injecting a cementitious grout.

Grove (obs)

TC for royal train carrying the monarch. From The Grove, Watford, LM&SR & BR offices from 1939 to 1995.

Growler (RS)

Class 37 loco; from its sound.

Growlers (RS)

BR diesel locos.

Grunt (USRS)

A loco driver.

Grunts (RS)

BR class 08/09 diesel locos.

GRWU

General Railway Workers' Union; formed 1890, amalgamated with ASRS (qv) and UP&SS (qv) to form NUR (qv) in 1913.

GS (It)

Grandi Stazioni; a FS (qv) subsidiary managing the 13 largest stations in Italy; 40 per cent owned by *Eurostazioni SpA*, a non-FS co. partly owned by *SNCF* (qv).

GS&WR

1. Great Southern & Western Rly (Ireland), inc 1844, Dublin to Cashel and later, Cork. Blackpool, just outside Cork, reached 1849, Cork (Penrose Quay) 1855. Many small lines absorbed and others built until it became the largest rly system in Ireland with 1,130 route miles in 1914, mainly in southern Ireland. Part of GSR from 1924.

2. Great Scottish & Western Rly Co., a cruise operator (qv) in business since 1985, offering luxury tours in a loco-hauled train which includes an observation car (qv), sleeping cars, on-board showers and restaurant cars with 'gourmet cuisine'. The train is also available for private hire.

GSM

Group Station Manager, LT.

GSM-R

Groupe Speciale Mobile-Rail; Global System for Mobile Communication (Rail), a digital radio system enabling drivers to communicate with signallers from moving trains, replacing CSR (qv) and NRN (qv). *See also* ERTMS and TCS (1).

GSR

1. Great Southern Rlys Co. (Ireland), formed 1924–5, to include GS&WR, CB&SCR, MGWR, D&SER and various smaller undertakings. 2,187 route miles in 1927. Part of CIE from 1945. (GSR)

2. Great Southern Rly [Australia], a private company which in 1997 purchased the ANR (qv) passenger business.

GSRPS

Great Southern Railways Preservation Society; preserved line Tralee–Fenit, on former GS&WR/GSR Fenit branch.

GTI (US)

Guilford Transportation Industries Inc; includes B&M and Maine Central RR.

GTS

Guard's trailer Second/Standard class, a BR HST coach with guard's compartment and parcels area.

GTW (US)

Grand Trunk Western RR Co.

Guard

1. Railwayman/woman in charge of a train, but from 1988 on BR, initially on InterCity (qv) services, many passenger train guards were designated conductors, and given additional duties.

2. A tramcar conductor in north-west England.

Guard boarding/boards

Protective boarding placed along one or both sides of conductor rails (qv) in certain locations to minimize accidental contact by persons on the track.

Guard irons

Metal posts suspended vertically from the corners of the buffer beams of locos and tenders to sweep obstructions from the rails. Also sometimes used until *c.* 1914 for fastening snow brooms (qv). *See also* Life guards.

Guard rail

A type of check rail (qv) fitted on tracks over viaducts, bridges and level crossings to reduce the risk of derailments.

Guard's bedroom (RS)(obs)
A freight train brake van.
Guard's Journal
See Journals.
Guard's van
The vehicle in a passenger or freight train containing accommodation for the guard (qv) and braking and emergency equipment for use by the guard.
Guard truck
An additional low-bodied wagon marshalled next to wagons containing long items which overhang, or between two flat wagons carrying a long load.
Guard wires (obs)
Wires formerly erected above the running overhead wire of Tramways (3) to prevent traction current leaking into adjacent telegraph and telephone circuits. A BoT (qv) requirement.
Gudgeon
A 20-ton unfitted ballast and sleeper wagon used by engineers.
Guichet (Fr)
Ticket office window.
Guildford New Line
Surbiton–Effingham Junction–Guildford. Still so called to distinguish it from the original line to Guildford via Woking, although it dates from 1885.
Gumshoe (USRS)
A rly policeman. *See also* Yard bull; Cinder dick.
Gunboats
1. (RS) SER Mansell 0–4–4T locos.
2. (USRS) Steel hopper wagons.
Gunnel
A 38-ton ballast hopper wagon used by BR engineers.
Gustav Eiffel
An EC service between Paris and Frankfurt, introduced 1989. Extended to Leipzig 1991.
Gut (USRS)
The brake air hose.
Gutter running
Tramway (3) tracks placed close to the edges (kerbs) of a roadway instead of along the centre.

GUV
BR General Utility Van; no guard's compartment, side and end doors, non-gangwayed.
GVR
Gwendraeth Valley Rly, inc 1866, Kidwelly to Mynydd-y-garreg, opened 1871, worked by BP&GVR 1886–1905. Part of GWR 1923.
GVT
Glyn Valley Tramway, Chirk to Glyn Ceiriog, tramway (4), inc 1870, opened with 2 ft 4¼ in/717.55 mm gauge, 1873, 1874. Horse worked until 1886, passenger traffic then ceasing until resumed in 1891. Gauge converted to 2 ft 4½ in/723.9 mm for start of steam working in 1887–8. Closed passengers 1933, freight 1935.
GW&BR
Great Western & Brentford Rly, inc 1855, Southall to Brentford Dock, opened 1859, 1860, leased to GWR, part of GWR 1872.
GW&GCJC
Great Western & Great Central Rlys Joint Committee formed 1899, to manage Northolt Junc–Princes Risborough–Aylesbury/Ashendon Junc, opened 1906 (except for existing High Wycombe– Princes Risborough–Aylesbury line). GWR and L&NER from 1923. Part of BR from 1948.
GW&TVJ
Great Western & Taff Vale Joint, inc 1867, Merthyr, Brandy Bridge Junc to Mardy Junc, opened 1877, part of GWR from 1922.
GW&UR
Great Western & Uxbridge Rly, inc 1846, West Drayton to Uxbridge, opened 1856, part of GWR from 1847.
GWB (Ger)
Gleiswechselbetrieb (qv).
Gwili Rly
Preserved rly on former BR Carmarthen–Aberystwyth line just north of Carmarthen (Bronwydd Arms–Llwyfan Cerrig). First section opened 1978.
GWM
The GW Magazine, published unofficially from July 1862 to June 1864 by five GWR (qv) employees; possibly the first of the UK rly staff periodicals.

GWR

Great Western Rly, inc 1835, 1837, London to Bristol, opened 1838, 1839, 1840, 1841. Many other lines subsequently built and absorbed. 3,025 route miles in 1914. Re-formed by inclusion of many smaller companies 1922–3, bringing total route miles to 3,820. Part of BR from 1948.

GWR Journal

An illustrated magazine devoted to the serious study of all aspects of the GWR (qv) and BR (W) (qv), first published 1991.

GWR Magazine

House journal of GWR, published 1888–1947.

GWT

see Great Western Trains.

GySEV

Gyor-Sopron-Ebenfurt-Vasuti; an independent rly between Austria and Hungary, operating since 1879.

H

H

Handbrake fitted vehicle (BR).

HA

BR (S) code for class 71 locos.

HABD

Hot Axle Box Detector, a lineside apparatus for detecting and reporting hot boxes (qv) on passing trains.

Hack (USRS)

A caboose (qv).

Hackney Gurkhas (RS)(obs)

Rlymen in Army rly units.

Haddock

A long 12-ton wagon with drop sides used for carrying sleepers.

Hairspring, as tight as a (RS)

A mean or greedy individual.

Hairy (RS)

A rly enthusiast somewhat less fanatical and single-minded than a gricer (qv), but including those intent on seeing and/or photographing unusual rolling stock or motive power.

Hake

A 24-ton general materials wagon used by engineers.

HAL

SR two-car emu set with lavatory in one car only (hence HAlf Lavatory); Second/ Standard class compartment brake motor car and side corridor driving trailer composite with lavatory, introduced 1939 and 1948, 2-HAL.

Halcrow Transmark

Title of Transmark (qv) from December 1995.

Halesowen Joint

Inc 1865 as Halesowen and Bromsgrove Rly, Halesowen Junc to Northfield Junc, name changed to Halesowen Rly 1876, opened 1883, worked and maintained by GWR and Midland Rly, vested in GWR and Midland jointly from 1906, GWR and LM&SR 1923–47.

Hale's tours

A US invention of 1904 to simulate rly journeys. Replicas of rly cars were equipped with machinery to provide the sensation and noises of movement and cine films of scenery taken from the front or rear of actual trains were projected. Some installations were sponsored by rly companies. Named after the inventor, a Kansas City fire chief.

Half cock (RS)

Semaphore signal (qv) arm halfway between horizontal and the full 'off' (qv) aspect (upper or lower quadrant (qv)). It must be taken as showing danger.

Half dirties (RS)(obs)

Train crews employed on both steam and electric traction in the period when both existed on BR main line services. *See also* Mixed traffic men.

Half Englishman (RS)

A single slip (qv).

Half section

An upper or lower 'double berth' in a US Pullman sleeping car.

Half-snip (obs)

To snip a small piece from the base of an Edmondson (qv) ticket to indicate that its issue is related to a child fare. Later such tickets were cut in half vertically, or 'semi-diagonally' in the case of return tickets.

Halibut
A 56-ton bogie ballast wagon used by engineers.

Hallade runs
Runs made over a stretch of railway to produce recordings with the Hallade track recorder (qv).

Hallade track recorder
A portable instrument which indicates to civil and mechanical engineers the degree of smoothness of the running of a locomotive or coach and shows up irregularities or defects in the track. There are three pendulums which respond to lateral and vertical movement and any rolling, each recording a trace on a paper roll which passes through the machine at a constant speed. Used in UK since 1922, made in France, and named after M. Hallade, the French engineer responsible for the original design. Replaced in 1970s by Black box recorder (qv).

Hall's Tramroad
A horse-worked tramroad built by Benjamin Hall from Hall's Road, Risca to Abercarn Ironworks and Manmoel and branches, first section opened 1809. Leased to GWR for 1,000 years from 1877 and opened as a rly 1886 and 1912. GWR opened an extension at Manmoel 1905, and Cwmcarn branch 1911.

Halt (obs)
A minor stopping place without full station facilities, usually unstaffed, serving an area of light traffic, platforms usually of timber and amenities confined to a simple shelter and lighting. The term came into general usage in the 1900s with the introduction of railmotors and auto-trains. The GWR originally made a special distinction between a halt and a 'platform' (qv), the latter having sufficient length to accommodate an ordinary branch line or stopping train.

Halte
French and Belgian term for a minor stopping place, briefly adopted in UK by GWR and Metropolitan Rly from 1903 but very soon discarded for the anglicized version.

Haltepunkt/Hp Ger)
A stopping place with platforms and plain line (qv).

Haltestelle/Hst (Ger)
A stopping place with platforms also having *Abzweigstelle* (qv), *Überleitstelle* (qv), *Anschlusstelle* (qv), *Ausweichanschlusstelle* (qv); usually unstaffed (*unbesetzte*).

Ham
1. (RS) Overtime; hence 'fatty ham', excessive overtime work. *See also* On the ham.
2. (USRS) A learner rly telegrapher.

Hamlet
EC Hamburg–Copenhagen, introduced 1991.

Hammer, to (RS)
To delay a train.

Hammersmith & City [Rly]
Inc 1861, opened 1864, Hammersmith–Green Lane Junc, Westbourne Park, and curve Latimer Road–Uxbridge Road WLR. Vested in GWR and Metropolitan Rly 1867. Worked by Metropolitan Rly. Electrified 1906. Joint GWR and LPTB 1933–47, BR and LT 1948–69, then wholly LT.

Hampstead/Hampstead Tube
see CCE&HR.

Hand Bomber/Grenader (USRS)
A steam loco not fitted with a mechanical stoker.

H&BR
Hull & Barnsley Rly, inc 1880 as Hull, Barnsley & West Riding Junction Rly & Dock Co., first line opened, with Alexandra Dock, Hull, 1885. Renamed H&BR 1905. 92 route miles by 1914, Hull to Cudworth and Wath. Absorbed by NER 1922.

H&C (obs)
Horse & carriage traffic (qv).

Hand car (US)
A pump trolley (qv).

H&C[R]
Hammersmith & City [Rly] (qv).

H&HR
Hull & Holderness Rly, inc 1853, Withernsea to Hull, opened 1854, worked by NER 1860, part of NER 1862.

Handle (LTRS)
The master controller in the cab of an electric train. *See also* On the handle(s).

Handle winder (LTRS)
The motorman of an electric train.

H&MR
Hounslow & Metropolitan Rly, inc 1880.
Hounslow Town to Mill Hill Park (now
Acton Town) opened 1883. Worked by
MDR. Branch Osterley to Hounslow
Barracks (now Hounslow West), 1884.
Terminal at Hounslow Town closed
1886, reopened 1903, finally closed
1909. Part of MDR from 1903. Electrified
1905.

H&OJR
Halifax & Ovenden Junction Rly, inc 1864,
opened Holmfield–Halifax 1874, passenger
service 1879, jointly vested in GNR and
L&YR 1870; LM&SR and L&NER
1923–47.

Hand (of points/switch)
The direction (right or left), viewed from
the toe (qv), to which traffic will be
diverted.

Hand-on (USRS)
A train order (qv) taken up by a member of
the train crew on a moving train.

Hand points
Points independent of signalling controls,
worked manually by lever; usually found in
a yard or sidings. *See also* Unworked points.

Hand signalman/Hand signalling
Emergency signalling using signals given
manually by coloured flags or lamps.

Hand signals
Signals given to drivers when normal
signalling not available, using recognized
movements of flags in daylight or
handlamps at night.

H&SYER
Hull & South Yorkshire Extension Rly, inc
1897 Wrangbrook Junc–Wath, opened
1902. Part of H&BR from 1898.

H&WNR
Hunstanton & West Norfolk Rly, an 1874
merger of Lynn & Hunstanton Rly and
WNJR. Part of GER 1890.

Hanger
A fitting in the overhead wiring of tramways (*3*) (qv) and the simpler forms of
electric rly OHL (qv), often incorporating
insulators, which hangs from a transverse

wire or structure to support the trolley
(traction current) wire. *See also* Ears.

Hanging bar
GWR term for valance (*2*) (qv).

Hanging buffers
Vertical wooden buffers on a wagon to
permit coupling with wagons having
buffers at lower levels.

Hanging sleeper(s)
see Voiding.

HAP
BR (SR) two car EPB emu set with
lavatory in only one of the cars (HAlf
corridor electro-Pneumatic brakes); motor
brake Second/Standard class and driving
trailer composite with lavatory, introduced
1957–8, 1961–2; 2-HAP.

Harbour lights (RS)
Arbor lights (qv).

Hard class
Term used on certain overseas rlys to
describe the most inferior form of
passenger accommodation, 'hard' being
related to the quality of the seating. On the
SZD (qv), the equivalent of Second class,
with leathercloth seating. *See also* Fourth
class; Soft class.

Hard hat man (RS)
An inspector. From his once obligatory
bowler hat.

Hard road (RS)
A lack of resilience in the track due to frost
in the ground.

Hard-up (RS)(obs)
A lack of steam in a loco.

Harness (USRS)
The uniform of passenger train crews.

Harpic signals (LTRS)
Round The Benders (qv). From the
famous lavatory-cleaning product and its
advertising slogan.

Harrogate Pullman
An unofficial name for an all-Pullman
service between London (Kings Cross),
Leeds, Harrogate, Ripon, Darlington and
Newcastle, introduced 1923, extended to
Edinburgh, 1925, but still not officially
named, though known as Edinburgh
Pullman or Harrogate–Edinburgh Pullman.
Became Queen of Scots 1927 (qv).

Harrogate Sunday Pullman
An all-Pullman train between London (Kings Cross) and Harrogate/Bradford (Exchange), introduced 1927, restored 1950.

Harrovian
MDR London commuters' 'express', South Harrow to Mansion House (non-stop Hammersmith–Sloane Square), introduced 1915, ceased 1932.

Harton Electric Rly
The Harton Coal Co. operated colliery lines at South Shields connecting Harton Low Staiths, Westoe Colliery and Harton Colliery; these were electrified in 1908 on the overhead system at 550V dc. Harton was the only British standard gauge surface colliery rly with electric traction. Part of NCB Rlys from 1947. Electric traction replaced by diesels 1989. *See also* SSM&WCR.

Harvey Girls/Eating Houses (US)
Fred Harvey's chain of 'eating houses' originated in the 1870s on the AT&SFRR (qv). These railway restaurants, which existed for some 100 years in the USA, were staffed by carefully screened waitresses, accommodated in closely supervised dormitories. Many 'Harvey Girls' ended up by marrying customers. The eponymous film musical celebrating the Harvey Girls was released in 1946.

Hasler
A speed indicator and recorder for steam locos patented by the Hasler Telegraph Works, London.

Hastings Car Train
A service operated with US-built Pullman-type cars, rebuilt at Ashford Works, and introduced by the SER in 1906 between London (Charing Cross and Cannon St.) and Hastings.

HAT
Home Ambulance Train (qv). *See also* Ambulance train.

Hat (USRS)
An incompetent rlyman (useless except as a resting place for his hat).

Hat check (USRS)(obs)
A receipt issued in exchange for a collected ticket.

Haughley Mail (RS)
East Anglian TPO (qv). So called because the Norwich and Peterborough trains originally joined/divided at Haughley Junc.

Haulage basher (RS)
A gricer (qv) with an obsession to ride behind as many different types of loco as possible or every loco of a particular class.

Haul dead, to
To haul an inoperative loco.

Haulmark
Haulmark European Transport. A wholly owned BR subsidiary responsible for the collection and delivery of international freight and supply of containers and swap-bodies (qv), purchasing train space from ACI (qv) or CTL (qv). Ceased trading 1994.

Hauptbahnen (Ger)
Main lines.

Hauptbahnhof (Ger)
The central/main station in a city or large town.

Hauptlinie (Ger)
A main (or trunk) line.

Hawker Siddeley Group
Absorbed Brush (2) (qv) 1957, Crompton Parkinson (qv) 1967, Westinghouse (qv) 1979; Hawker Siddeley Rail Projects then formed to bring together the Group's related rly activities. Part of BTR Electric Power Group 1991; BTR EPG sold to FKI plc, 1996.

Hawkeye (RS)
A messroom attendant.

Hawk's/Hawkes' eye board (RS)
A type of station nameboard introduced by the LM&SR in 1934 in which the name (in black letters on a yellow ground) was placed between two parallel lines interrupted at the centre by semi-circles. From the trade mark of the manufacturers, G.C. Hawkes, Birmingham.

Hawthorn, Leslie
R & W Hawthorn, Leslie & Co. Ltd, loco builders, Newcastle upon Tyne, established 1831 as R & W Hawthorn. Amalgamated with Robert Stephenson & Co. as Robert Stephenson & Hawthorns, 1937. Part of EE, 1955.

Hayburner (USRS)

1. An antiquated loco, little better than a horse.

2. A horse used for traction on a rly or tramway.

3. A handlamp.

Haycock fire (RS)

A steam loco fire built up by feeding coal to centre of firebox and thus forming a cone.

Haystacks (RS)

Steam locos with very high fireboxes.

Haytor Granite Tramroad

Haytor Rocks quarries to Stover canal near Teigngrace, 4 ft 3 in/1,295 mm gauge on granite block 'rails'. Opened 1820 with horse traction. Carried stone used for the 1831 London Bridge, the National Gallery (1832–8) and other public buildings in London. Disused from *c.* 1858. M&SDR (opened 1866) used part of alignment between Teigngrace and a point near Brimley.

Hay wagon (USRS)

A caboose (qv). From (S) 'hit the hay' = to go to bed.

HB (obs)

1. BR abbreviation for a horse box (qv).

2. BR (S) code for class 74 locos.

H-Bahn (Ger)

Hochbahn; an elevated rly (qv).

HBTR

Haifa–Beirut–Tripoli Rly. A military line completed by South African and New Zealand army engineers, closing the final standard gauge gap between the Egyptian and Turkish rly systems, opened in 1942. A victim of post-war political upheaval, it was severed at the Israeli/Lebanon frontier in 1947 and has remained closed ever since, along with the link to Egypt across the Sinai Desert. *See also* CEL.

HCR&D

Humber Commercial Rly & Dock, inc 1901, 1904, Ulceby–Immingham Docks, opened 1910 and leased by GCR; completed 1912. In 1912 it absorbed the Barton & Immingham Light Rly (completed 1910–11), which was also leased to GCR. Part of L&NER 1923.

Head

The top or running surface of a rail.

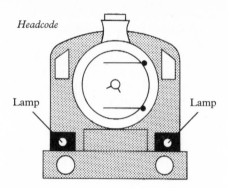

Headcode

An arrangement of boards, discs, or lights exhibited at the front of a loco or train to indicate the nature of the train and/or its route. In more recent years stencils, roller blind indicators and latterly dot matrix displays have been used, showing letters and/or numbers, combinations of both, or the full destination.

Head end

That end of a train nearest the loco/front cab.

Head end car (USRS)

The mail/baggage car, normally coupled between loco and remainder of train.

Head ender (USRS)

A head-on collision.

Head end revenue/traffic (USRS)

Mail, express, newspaper, luggage and milk traffic (carried in the head end car(s) (qv)).

Head in, to (USRS)

To take a loop road when meeting a train coming in the opposite direction on a single track.

Head lights

see Headcodes.

Head man (USRS)

The head end or front brakeman on a freight train.

Head shack (USRS)

A conductor (*3*). *See also* Shack.

Head shag/twit (LTRS)

The Headquarters Controller.

Head shrinker (RS)

A doctor paid to examine rly staff.

Headshunt

A length of track allowing shunting movements to be made into a group of sidings without fouling the running lines, to which it may have a connection.

Heads of Valleys Line

Merthyr to Abergavenny; originally the Merthyr, Tredegar & Abergavenny Rly, inc 1859, first section opened 1862. Leased to L&NWR, part of L&NWR 1866.

Headspan

A type of overhead (qv) in which the traction supply line is supported by wires suspended from masts on each side of the track. *See also* Catenary.

Headspan wire

A wire suspended across the tracks from which the traction supply line is suspended. *See also* Cross span wire.

Headstock

The transverse end of vehicle frame, to which buffers, couplings, etc. are attached.

Headwall

The wall at the end of a tube rly station tunnel surrounding the entrance to the running tunnel.

Headway

1. The service interval (usually stated in minutes) between trains, trams or LRVs on the same line. Not to be confused with frequency (qv).
2. The clear height from the top of the rails to the underside of any fixed structures over the track.

Headway chart

A recorder used on London Underground, originally worked by headway clocks (qv), which marks against a time dial the passage of each individual train past certain points on the system throughout each 24-hour period.

Headway clock (obs)

A dial on the end of certain station platforms showing a driver the number of minutes since the preceding train left the station. Introduced on the London Underground in 1907.

Hearse (USRS)

A caboose (qv).

Heart of Midlothian

An express between London (Kings Cross)

and Edinburgh (Waverley), so named 1950. Extended to Perth 1957. Name dropped 1968.

Heart of Wessex Line

Promotional name for Bristol–Weymouth line, 1999.

Heater (RS)

A hot box (qv).

Heathrow Connect

A local stopping, regular interval service for air passengers and staff between London Airport Heathrow and Paddington, 2005.

Heathrow Express (HeX)

A fast, frequent and direct electric rail service between London Airport (Heathrow) and London (Paddington), introduced 1998. A wholly owned subsidiary of BAA (formerly British Airports Authority).

Heavy rly

A conventional rly; used only where necessary to distinguish such from a light rly (qv) or light rail transit (qv).

Heavy stop (RS)

A train brought to stand with hard braking, rapidly decelerating. *See also* Caley stop; Euston stop.

Hebden Bridge route

Healey Mills/Bradford–Hebden Bridge–Rochdale–Rose Grove.

Hebridean/Hebridean Heritage

A service between Inverness (through coach from Glasgow) and Kyle of Lochalsh in connection with Skye sailings, introduced 1933. Re-introduced 1966; renamed Hebridean Heritage and equipped with observation car, 1988.

***Hedjaz* Rly/*Hijaz* Rly**

A 1,050 mm gauge line from Damascus to Amman and Medina, with branches to Haifa, Nablus and Bosra, built 1901–8 primarily to carry Moslem pilgrims to Medina (for Mecca). Severely damaged by Col. T.E. Lawrence's campaigns inWW1. The section south of Ma'an (Jordan) was left derelict after 1924. The Damascus–Amman–Ma'an section remains in use. Work in the 1960s to restore the link to Medina was suspended in 1971 after considerable progress had been made. The line featured in the epic 1962 film *Lawrence of Arabia*.

Heel (USRS)
A wagon or coach left at end of a track with brakes on.

Heel [of points]/switch heel
The pivoted end of points/switch (qv) at which the rails carrying a train on to the diverging line begin.

Heinrich Heine
TEE Frankfurt–Dortmund, introduced 1979. Ceased 1983. Re-introduced as Paris–Frankfurt EC service 1987.

Heisler
A design of geared loco suitable for working very hilly lines at low speeds.

Hellas Express
A Dortmund–Athens service 1963–88, combined in winter with a Munich–Istanbul service, the *Hellas–Istanbul Express*, in 1965–88.

Hellenic Rlys [Greece]
see CH.

Helvetia
A Zurich–Hamburg service introduced 1954, *TEE* 1957, lost *TEE* status 1979. EC 1987.

Hemmschuh (Ger) (obs)
A shoe placed on rails to arrest moving wagons when marshalling or shunting.

Hendre–Ddu Tramway
Hendre–Ddu Quarry–Gartheiniog–Aberangell [MR (*1*)] and branches, 1 ft 11 in/584 mm gauge, opened *c.* 1868; mostly closed *c.* 1940; last section lifted 1954. Worked by horses and gravity, and from *c.* 1920 by petrol tractor. Farmers, quarrymen and tourists were carried.

Henri Dunant
A Paris–Geneva *TGV*, introduced 1986.

HEP
Head End Power; same as ETS (qv).

HER
Hammersmith Extension Rly, inc 1873, Earl's Court–Hammersmith Broadway, opened and amalgamated with MDR 1874.

Herapath
Herapath's Railway Magazine, full title *Herapath's Railway Magazine, Commercial Journal and Scientific Review*, a renaming of *The Railway Magazine* (*see RM (1)*)in 1841. Further renamed *Herapath's Railway & Commercial Journal* in 1845 but usually called *Herapath's Railway Journal*, a shortened title officially adopted in 1894. Incorporated in *The Railway Times* in 1903. After the proprietor, John Herapath (1790–1868).

Herder (USRS)
A switchman (qv) who couples and un-couples locos and guides locos and trains into and out of a yard, moving point levers and giving a highball (qv) when appropriate.

Heritage fleet (US)
Amtrak passenger cars inherited from pre-1971 company fleets and mostly steam-heated.

Heritage Stock
BR standard Mark 1 and early Mark 2 coaches and first generation BR dmus retained for special workings after the early 1990s fleet modernization.

Heron
A 34-ton ballast and sleeper wagon with steel floor, used by engineers.

Herring
A 20-ton hopper ballast wagon with centre discharge used by engineers.

Herringbone (rhyming S)
A telephone.

Hertford Loop
London (Bounds Green)–Enfield–Hertford North–Langley Junc (Stevenage). Also known as the 'Cuffley Loop'.

Heusinger's valve gear
See Walschaert's valve gear.

HeX
Heathrow Express (qv).

HHA (Ger)
Hamburger Hochbahn Aktiengesellschaft, Hamburg Elevated Rly Co., now part of the regional transport undertaking.

HHL&N&SJR
Halifax High Level & North & South Junction Rly, inc 1884, opened Holmfield–Pellon–Halifax (St Paul's) 1890, vested jointly in GNR and L&YR 1894, closed passengers 1917; LM&SR and L&NER 1923–47.

HHR

Hemel Hempstead Rly, Boxmoor L&NWR
to Hemel Hempstead, inc 1863, extension
to Harpenden authorized 1866, opened
1877, worked by Midland Rly. Part of
Midland Rly 1886. Passenger service
extended from Hemel Hempstead (Mid) to
Heath Park Halt [Hemel Hempstead],
1905.

Hiawatha

Milwaukee RR steam-hauled streamlined
express between Chicago and
Minneapolis–St Paul, introduced 1935.
Diesel-hauled from 1941. Now an Amtrak
service.

Hibernian

A service between London (Paddington)
and Fishguard Harbour, connecting with
Rosslare sailings, introduced 1987.

High, to go (USRS)

see Decorate, to

Highball, to (USRS)

To drive at high speed.

Highball, to give a (USRS)

To make a signal by raising a lamp,
indicating that a train should be started:
also any other 'proceed' signalling
indication. From an early type of signal in
which a ball was hauled to the top of a
mast to indicate the line ahead was clear.

Highball artist (USRS)

A loco driver with a reputation for skilful
fast running over a clear road.

High cube wagons

Wagons with additional capacity between
the bogies/trucks. Originally a US term but
now in general use.

High Fliers/Flyers (RS)

1. L&NWR Singles.
2. L&YR Aspinall 4–4–2 locos, from the
   high-pitched boiler.
3. L&SWR Adams 4–4–0s of 1853
   (445–456), so-called from their 7 ft 1 in
   diameter driving wheels.

High grass [line] (USRS)

A little-used rly line. From the tall grasses
that grow between and along its tracks.

High Iron (USRS)

Through running lines, as distinct from
sidings and yard tracks.

Highland Chieftain

An HST between Inverness and London
(Kings Cross), introduced 1984.

Highland Line

Inverness–Perth.

Highlandman

A summer-only night express between
London (Kings Cross) and Inverness, so
named 1927.

High level passenger car (US)

A double-deck coach with seating and
dining facilities on upper deck, and
lavatories, vestibules and baggage storage
at lower level. First introduced by
AT&SFRR in 1957.

Highliner (USRS)

A fast passenger train.

High wheeler (USRS)

A high-speed loco designed for fast
passenger trains.

***Hijaz* Rly**

see Hedjaz.

Hikari

see Shinkansen.

Hikers (RS)

1. GER 1500 class 4–6–0 (L&NER B12)
   fitted (in 1927–32) with *ACFI* (qv) feed-
   water heaters mounted on top of the
   boiler and resembling a hiker's back-pack.
2. Scottish name for Black Fives (qv).
   They went everywhere.

Hiking (LTRS)

A train crew learning a depot (by 'hiking'
around it).

His Master's Voice (RS)

A deputy foreman, usually an ex-
footplateman. Also applied to any 'crawler'
or sycophant. From the famous
gramophone trade name.

Hispania

A Copenhagen–Basle–Port Bou service,
introduced 1963, later Hamburg–Port
Bou, then Basle–Port Bou.

Hit a stick, to (LTRS)

To overrun a signal at danger and be tripped.

Hitler salute (RS)(obs)

An upper quadrant semaphore in the 'off'
position.

Hit the dirt, to (RS)

see Dirt, to hit the.

Hi Vi (LTRS)

A high-visibility orange-coloured vest.

HJR

Hampstead Junction Rly, inc 1853, promoted by L&NWR, Camden Road–Hampstead Heath–Willesden Junc–Acton Wells Junc. Opened 1860, worked by NLR. Part of L&NWR 1867. Managed by NLR 1867–72 and always carried NLR passenger services.

HL

High Level.

HLP (Fr RS)

Haut Le Pied; trotting; applied to light engine working.

HMRI

Her Majesty's Railway Inspectorate, formerly RI, so titled from 1991. *See also* HSC/HSE; RI (*1*).

HMRS

Historical Model Rly Society, formed 1950 for those interested in the construction, operation and preservation of models relating to British rlys before 1948.

HN

Hurst, Nelson (qv).

HNC

Home Normal Contact. A device which ensures a Home signal (qv) lever is replaced in position in the signal frame before the 'line clear' signal code can be given by the signalman.

HOBC

High Output Ballast Cleaner.

HofM&ST

Hundred of Manhood & Selsey Tramway. A light rly between Chichester and Selsey, opened 1897, 1898; name changed to West Sussex Rly 1924, closed 1935.

Hog (USRS)

A loco, hence yard hog, etc.

Hog-backed/Hogging

The tendency of an underframe (qv) to droop at each end, rising in the centre, sometimes deliberately introduced to counteract sagging, the opposite tendency. Also used of rails vertically displaced above the ends following stresses during machining, rolling, straightening or cooling.

Hogger (USRS)

A loco driver. *See* Hog.

Hoghead (USRS)

Alternative for Hogger (qv).

Hog law (USRS)

A federal regulation preventing train crews from working more than twelve hours at a stretch. *See also* Bear law; Dog law; Monkey, caught by the.

Hog mauler (USRS)

A loco driver.

Holding siding

A siding (qv) on which motive power units and rolling stock, particularly diesel and electric locos, are held between workings.

Hole, The

1. (RS) The Severn Tunnel.
2. (RS) Any steeply graded descent into a tunnel.
3. (USRS) A passing loop.
4. The Waterloo & City Line. *See* W&CR.

Hole, in the (USRS)

On a siding or loop, to allow other trains to pass.

Holland–Scandinavia Express

Hook of Holland–Copenhagen, introduced 1958, Schiphol Airport–Copenhagen from 1988.

Holland–Wien Express

An Amsterdam–Vienna service introduced 1960.

Holy City, the (RS)

St Albans.

Holytown route

Glasgow (Central)–Holytown–Midcalder–Edinburgh (Waverley).

Home Ambulance Train

Ambulance train (qv) moving sick and wounded service personnel within Great Britain.

Home guard (USRS)

A rlyman who has long service with a particular company; opposite of a boomer (qv).

Home normal contact

see HNC.

Homer

GWR TC for 30-ton 43 ft/13.1 metres bogie open wagon.

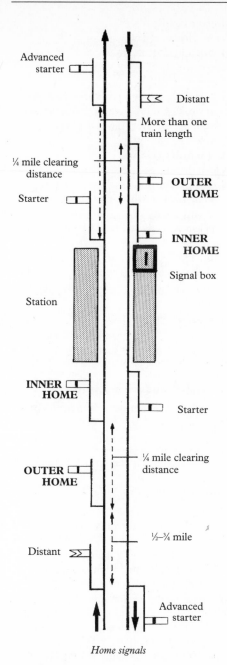

Home signals

Home signal
The stop signal which controls entry to a block section; usually placed on the approach side of the associated signal box. Normally protects a station or junction. *See also* Inner home signal; Outer home signal.

Hondekop (Dutch RS)
A type of emu with a front end resembling a dog's head.

Honeymoon compartment (RS)
A coupé (qv).

Hoo branch
Hoo Junc–Grain.

Hook (USRS)
A breakdown train. From the large crane hook.

Hook Continental
see Continental Express.

Hooker (RS)
A shunter.

Hooker-on (RS)
An additional loco to assist a train engine. *See also* Pilot engine (*4*).

Hook off, to
To uncouple vehicles.

Hook on/up, to
1. To couple up vehicles.
2. (USRS) To set regulator lever high for fast running.

Hoovers (RS)
BR class 50 diesel electric locos. From a characteristic noise, later modified.

Hope Valley Line
[Sheffield–]Dore–Hope–Chinley[–Manchester].

Hoppers
1. (RS) L&SWR Drummond 4–4–0 locos (K10 class of 1901–2 were 'small hoppers'; the L11 class of 1903–7 'large hoppers'). From grasshoppers.
2. Wagons with hinged base allowing load to fall out quickly.

Hoptoad, to (USRS)
To derail.

Hornbies (RS)
The three prototype SR electric locos, CC1–3, (20001–3); also BR diesel locos class 08. From their supposed resemblance to engines of Hornby Trains (qv).

Hornby Dublos (RS)
see Dublos.

Hornby Factor, The
An expression coined in 2002 by Deborah Pester, Head of Communications at Connex Rail Ltd (qv) when seeking to explain the relatively small number of

women in senior posts in the British rly industry. *See also* Hornby Trains.

Hornby Trains
Clockwork and electric toy trains, gauge 'O' and (later) 'OO', produced from 1920 onwards by Frank Hornby's factory at Binns Road, Liverpool.

Hornet
GWR TC for a timber wagon.

Horse, to (RS)(obs)
To haul a train, e.g. 'The 1.15 pm express was horsed by a Six Foot Compound loco'.

Horse & carriage traffic (obs)
Conveyance by passenger train of private horse-drawn carriages, with or without horses, a horse box (qv) being provided for the latter. Special loading platforms were available at many stations for this traffic, and 24 hours' notice was required. Owners were allowed to remain in their private carriages during the journey if they so wished. 'This traffic requires prompt attention to prevent delay to the passenger service' – Jenkinson, Lamb & Travis, in *The Passenger Station and Signalling*, 1914.

Horse & carriage workings (obs)
Trains carrying horse & carriage traffic (qv), and later, trains composed of miscellaneous vans and empty coaches etc.

Horse & cart (RS)
Train consisting only of a loco and brakevan.

Horse box (obs)
A van (usually four-wheeled) designed to carry horses, with passenger half-compartment (coupé) at one end for the person or persons accompanying the animals on the journey.

Horse over, to (USRS)
To reverse a loco.

Horse unit (RS)
BR class 210 DEMUS (qv) converted to de-icing cars.

Hose jumper (obs)
A very small steel bridge, with grooves, temporarily put down to enable street tramcars to avoid fire hoses laid across the tracks.

Hospital train
US term for Ambulance train (qv).

Hostile territory (RS)
Any area away from the speaker's own; another region of BR.

Hostler (US)(obs)
Term for employee who takes charge of a loco for cleaning, replacing fire, lighting the new fire, etc. Adopted from horse transport usage.

Hot and cold (LTRS)
Hammersmith & City line LT. From the initials.

Hot [Axle] box detector
see HABD.

Hot box
Overheated axle journal or bearing caused by poor lubrication, admission of sand or grit, etc., or overtight fit of axle ends.

Hot foot (USRS)
A conductor (3) engaged in shunting operations and always in a hurry.

Hot jewel (USRS)
A hot box (qv).

Hot loco (USRS)
A loco with steam up, ready to move off.

Hot pot (RS)(obs)
A loco blowing off steam from safety valve.

Hot rail (RS)
Positive rail (qv).

Hot shot (USRS)
A fast train (usually freight).

Hot standby
Any back-up system which comes into operation at once and automatically in the event of failure of a signalling installation, etc. (A **cold standby** requires human intervention to bring it into operation.)

Hot weather/heat patrols
Special inspections of the track organized at periods when rail temperatures may be rising to a point which could cause buckling or reduced stability in the track.

Hot worker (USRS)
A fitter who carries out adjustments or repairs on a hot loco (qv).

Hounslow Loop
Barnes–Hounslow–Feltham Junc/Whitton Junc. L&SWR/SR/BR(S).

House cars (US) (obs)
Rail-wheeled dormitories positioned at the end of completed stretches of track and used to accommodate rly construction gangs.

Housetops (RS) (obs)
Roofs of steam loco cabs.

Houston Control (LTRS)(rhyming S)
Cobourg Street Control Centre. From its location near Euston.

Hoverspeed
Brand name for Seaspeed (qv) after its merger with Hoverlloyd Ltd in 1981. Hoverspeed was sold to its management in 1984.

Hp (Ger)
Haltepunkt (qv).

HPSS
High Performance Switch System. A special type of electric point motor used with hollow steel bearers (qv) and a torsion secondary drive.

HR
1. Harborne Rly, Harborne to Edgbaston (Monument Lane), Birmingham, inc 1866, opened 1874, worked by L&NWR, part of LM&SR from 1923.
2. Hayle Rly, Hayle to Redruth and Tresavean and branches, inc 1834, opened 1837, 1838, passenger traffic 1843 (passengers conveyed on an irregular basis in mineral wagons from 1841). Part of WCR from 1846.
3. Hayling Rly, inc 1860, Havant–Hayling Island, opened 1865, 1867. Leased to LB&SCR 1872, part of SR 1923.
4. Hay Rly, inc 1811, 3 ft 6 in/1,067 mm gauge tramroad, Eardisley to the Brecknock & Abergavenny Canal at Brecon via Hay. Opened 1816, 1818. Purchased by Hereford, Hay & Brecon Rly 1860. Section south of Three Cocks became part of MWR and B&MJR.
5. *Hedjaz* Rly or *Hijaz* Rly, see *Hedjaz*.
6. Helston Rly, Gwinear Road (GWR) to Helston, inc 1880, opened 1887, worked by GWR, part of GWR from 1898.
7. Highland Rly, formed 1865, a merger of Inverness & Aberdeen Junction Rly (Inverness–Nairn–Keith) and Inverness

& Perth Junction Rly (Forres–Dunkeld). Other lines added subsequently. 432 route miles by 1914, all in northern Scotland. Part of LM&SR from 1923.
8. Holywell Rly, inc 1864 Holywell–Holywell Harbour, but not completed, the finished sections used for quarry traffic for some years. Purchased by L&NWR and opened throughout Holywell Town–Holywell Junc, 1912.
9. Horncastle Rly, inc 1854, Horncastle & Kirkstead Junction, opened 1855, worked by GNR. Part of L&NER 1923.
10. Hoylake Rly, inc 1863, opened 1866 Hoylake–Birkenhead (Bridge Rd), closed 1869. Purchased and re-opened 1872 by Hoylake & Birkenhead Rail & Tramway Co. (inc 1872). Hoylake–West Kirby extension opened 1878. In 1879 the H&BR&T's street tramway in Birkenhead was sold to the Birkenhead Tramways Co. and the rly was renamed the Seacombe, Hoylake & Deeside Rly in 1881. Wallasey and New Brighton branch opened 1888. Part of the WR (qv) 1891.

HRA
Heritage Railway Association, a 1998 renaming of the AIRPS (qv).

HS
Holland Spoor; an abbreviation for *HSM* (qv). The initials remained in use after 1938 to distinguish its former station at The Hague.

HSBC Rail (UK) Ltd
Renaming of the ROSCO (qv) Eversholt (qv) after acquisition, from December 1997, by Forward Trust.

HSBV
High Speed Barrier Vehicle, BR. *See* Barrier vehicles.

HSC/HSE
Health & Safety Commission/Executive; independent public entities including HMRI (qv) 1991–2004. Responsibilities for Rail Safety and HMRI passed to ORR (qv) 2005.

HSE
Health & Safety Executive: *see* HSC/HSE.

HSh

Hëkurudhë Shqipërisë; Albanian State Rlys. 378 km.

HSM (Dutch)

Hollandsche (Ijezeren) Spoorweg Maatschappij; Holland (Iron) Rly Co. inc 1838, first line 1839, worked in association with NS (1) (qv) from 1917, part of NS 1938.

HSS Express

Rail service connecting London (Liverpool St.) with the High Speed Sea link between Harwich International and Hook of Holland, 1997.

HST

High Speed Trains (BR); very successful fixed-formation train sets with integral diesel-electric locos at each end, one pulling, one pushing, later known as IC 125. Introduced 1976.

Hst (Ger)

Haltestelle (qv).

HSTRC

High Speed Track-Recording Coach.

Hudd/Strowger-Hudd ATC

A form of ATC (1) (qv) using magnetic induction. Invented by A.E. Hudd, trial on SR 1931, installed on London, Tilbury & Southend lines by the LM&SR from 1947. Converted to BR standard AWS (qv) 1962.

Hudson (US)

A steam loco with 4–6–4 wheel arrangement, from the Hudson River Line of the New York Central RR, where they were first used.

Hudson Tubes

Hudson & Manhattan RR, electric lines connecting New York (Manhattan) to Jersey City and Newark by means of tube tunnels under the Hudson River, opened in 1908–10. Taken over by PATH (qv) 1962.

Hudswell, Clarke

Hudswell,Clarke & Co. Ltd, Railway Foundry, Leeds, loco builders from 1860. Acquired by Hunslet (qv), 1972. *See also* LH Plant Engineering Co.

Hull Executive

A renaming of the Hull Pullman, 1978.

Hull Pullman

An all-Pullman train between London (Kings Cross) and Hull, introduced 1967, renamed Hull Executive 1978.

Hull Trains

A TOC (2) (qv) 2000, operating fast services between Hull and London (King's Cross).

Humber Lincs Executive

Name given to a through HST between London (Kings Cross), Grimsby and Cleethorpes, 1984.

Hump

An artificial mound in a marshalling yard arranged so that uncoupled wagons may run down by gravity from its summit and be directed by points movements to the appropriate sorting siding, hence hump yard, hump shunting. First used in Britain at Feltham Yard, L&SWR in 1922.

Hump back run (USRS)

A local freight working.

Humpies (RS)

L&NWR 0–6–0ST. From their appearance.

Humping the bricks/coal (RS)(obs)

Working a brick/coal/etc. train.

Humpties (RS)

GWR 0–6–0ST. From their appearance.

Humpty-Dumpties (RS)

GER 2–4–0 express locos. From their ungainly appearance after 1902–4 rebuilding.

Humpy (RS)

A lineside hut providing shelter from the weather and refreshment place for track maintenance personnel. From its shape.

Hunch-backs (RS)

SDR 4–4–0ST. From their appearance.

Hundred of Hoo Rly

Inc 1879, part of SER 1881, opened 1882, Hoo Junc (near Higham) to Port Victoria. *See also* Hoo branch.

Hunslet

Hunslet Engine Co. Ltd, Leeds, loco builders, founded 1864. Later Hunslet (Holdings) plc, and Hunslet GMT. Also Hunslet TPL, Hunslet Transportation Projects Ltd, Birmingham, founded 1989, suppliers of passenger rail vehicles. *See also* Barclay (Hunslet–Barclay). Hunslet GMT, Hunslet TPL and Hunslet–Barclay became part of the Telfos Group, bought by *Jenbacherwerke* (Austria) in 1991. *See also* Ganz–Hunslet.

Huns, set of (RS)(obs)
Enginemen from another depot.

Hunting
The side-to-side motion of wheelsets
in vehicle bogies/trucks in which the
flanges hit the rails. It occurs at high speeds
when the bogies/trucks are severely worn,
with ineffective dampers and defective
conicity.

Hurdy gurdy (RS)
A hand generator for working electric point
motors.

Hurry (RS)
A particularly steep gradient.

Hurst, Nelson
Hurst, Nelson & Co. Ltd, established
1880, public company 1909, works at
Motherwell, builders of railway rolling
stock and tramcars. Acquired by Roberts
(qv) 1958, ceased production 1959.

Hush-hush (RS)
L&NER 4–6–4 (strictly 4–6–2–2) four-
cylinder compound loco 10000, built 1929
with marine water tube boiler generating
steam at 450 lb per sq in. A failure, it was
rebuilt in 1937 as a three-cylinder simple
4–6–2. From the secrecy surrounding its
construction.

Hush Puppies (RS)
Silencers on dmus. After the famous shoe
trade name. Also used for second
generation BR DMUs.

Hustle alarm
An audible warning sounded on sliding
and plug-door trains that the doors are
about to close.

Hustler
An audible warning sounded to alert staff
and passengers on a crowded platform (on
London Underground) that the train has
spent the appropriate interval in the station
and should be despatched. *See also Bruiteur.*

Hut (USRS)
A caboose (qv), also a brakeman's shelter
built on to a loco tender.

HV
Heating Van. Used on CIE/IE (qv) in the
absence of electric or steam heating from loco.

HV clothing
The High Visibility Vest (HVV), an
overgarment in a specific orange colour, is
required wear for all with work or business
on the rly outside areas normally accessible
to the public.

HWst (Ger)
Hauptwerkstatt; a main overhaul works.

Hydra
GWR TC for well-trucks for carrying road
vehicles.

Hymek
Name of a co. formed by Beyer, Peacock,
J. Stone & Co. (Deptford) and Bristol–
Siddeley Engines Ltd to act as designers
and main contractor for diesel-hydraulic
and diesel-electric locos. Hence the name
for the 101 class 35 B-B diesel-hydraulic
locos supplied to BR (W) in 1961.

Hytwin (TC)
High-sided twin bolster wagon (qv).

HZ
Hrvatske Zeljeznice; Croatian Rlys, formed
1991 out of part of *JZ* (qv), 2,296 km.

I

I&AJR

Inverness & Aberdeen Junction Rly, inc 1856, Nairn to Keith, opened 1857, 1858. Absorbed Inverness & Nairn Rly (opened 1855) in 1861 and Findhorn Rly (opened 1860) in 1862. Part of an amalgamation to form HR (7), 1865.

I&FA Rly

Invergarry & Fort Augustus Rly, Spean Bridge–Fort Augustus-Loch Ness Pier, 24 miles, inc 1896, opened 1903, worked and maintained by HR (7) (qv) until 1907 and then by NBR (qv) until closed 1911. Reopened 1913, worked and maintained by NBR; bought by NBR 1914. Part of L&NER (qv) 1923. Regular passenger and parcels traffic ceased 1933 but coal traffic continued for many years. Completely closed at end of 1946.

I&RR

Inverness & Ross-shire Rly, inc 1860, Inverness–Invergordon, opened 1862, 1863, part of I&AJR from 1862. Extended from Invergordon to Bonar Bridge 1864.

IARA

International Air Rail Association, formed 1997 to bring together groups and companies with an interest in rail links to airports with the object of furthering best practice and sharing new ideas.

Iavanic

A steam loco with a 2-12–2 wheel arrangement. *See also* Whyte's notation.

Iberia Express

A Paris–Irun service, with Madrid connection, 1957–88, replacing the *Pyrénées–Côte d'Argent Express*. Through couchettes Paris–Madrid from 1969.

IBJ

Insulated Block Joints.

IBS

Intermediate Block Section/Signals, usually with electrically-controlled colour lights, installed to replace an intermediate box.

IC

1. InterCity, or Inter-City, term used by BR from 1966 to describe its fast trunk services connecting major population centres. Also, from 1982, a 'business sector' of BR. Ceased to exist as a separate unit of BR 31 March 1994 but the term 'Inter City' continued in use for publicity purposes (*see* ICMU) and in the names of some TOUs (qv). From 1994 IC services were operated by Anglia Rlys, Cross Country Trains, Great Western Trains, InterCity East Coast, InterCity West Coast, and Midland Main Line. Use of the term InterCity had disappeared from British timetables by 1999.

2. Internal inter-city services introduced by *DB* 1968, hourly from 1979. *See also* ICE (*1*) and *IC-Netz*.

3. Internal inter-city services introduced by *FS* 1985.

4. (US) Illinois Central RR, merged 1972 with Gulf, Mobile & Ohio RR to form IC Gulf RR. Name changed back to IC 1988.

ICC

1. Interstate Commerce Commission, formed in 1887 to regulate rlys, etc. operating across state boundaries in the US, controlling operating rights, rates and charges, services, accounting and valuation.

2. Integrated Control Centre; combining Network Rail (qv) and TOC (2) (qv) controllers. First installation at London Waterloo, 2004. *See also* Control; RTCC; RUS.

ICE

1. Inter-City Express; *DB* high speed (300 km/h) electric trains and lines. Operating at hourly intervals between major city centres, some over newly built lines.

2. Queensland Rlys Inter-City Electric express mu trains.

3. Interlogic Control Engineering (qv).

4. Institution of Civil Engineers, established 1818, inc 1828.

ICEC

InterCity East Coast (qv).

Ice cream jackets (RS)

Light summer jackets formerly worn by LT railway staff. From their resemblance to those worn by ice cream salesmen.

ICF

Intercontainer-Interfrigo, formed 1993 from Intercontainer (qv) and Interfrigo (qv).

Icknield Line

Preserved line over part of the former GWR Watlington branch (Princes Risborough-Chinnor).

ICM

A multi-voltage version of ICE (*1*) (qv).

ICMM

InterCity Midland Main Line, TOU (qv). 1994; TOC (*2*) (qv) 1996 as Midland Mainline (qv).

IC-Netz

A term used from 1971 for lines carrying *DB* high speed inter-city services (IC (*2*)), some of them newly built rlys.

ICOBS

InterCity On Board Services, BR, supplying train catering to IC (*1*). *See* OBS.

IC-125

BR diesel-electric train sets running at up to 125 mph, introduced 1976.

IC-225

225km/h trains of BR IC Mark IV coaches and class 91 electric locos, introduced on ECML in 1989 and London (Kings Cross) to Edinburgh in 1991.

ICT

International trains in Europe fitted with Fiat underfloor tilt equipment.

ICWC

InterCity West Coast (qv).

Idlers (USRS)

Unused flats (qv) positioned to accommodate overhang loads on adjacent wagons.

IE

Iarnród Eireann (Irish Rail), Republic of Ireland Rlys, formed 1986. 1,944 km of 1,600 mm gauge.

IECC

Integrated Electronic Control Centre. A signalling control centre based on SSI (qv), and a computer programmed with the WTT (qv), which sets up non-conflicting routes, the first at Liverpool St., London, BR, in 1989. In IECC the panoramic SDS (qv) is replaced by vdus reproducing track layout and the description and location of trains in occupation. Operators oversee the computer's activity and set up routes for special trains and trains running out of normal course by the use of a tracker ball and push buttons.

IEE

Institution of Electrical Engineers, established 1871 (as Society of Telegraph Engineers), inc 1921.

Igloos (RS)

Platform shelters with transparent walls and barrel-shaped transparent roofs adopted by BR from *c.* 1985.

IK

Infrastruktura Kolejowa, Polish Rlys Infrastructure Co.

IL

Island Line (qv).

ILE

Institution of Locomotive Engineers, founded 1911.

Île de France (Fr)

1. A division of the *SNCF* (qv) passenger business responsible for services in the Paris region.

2. *TEE* Paris–Amsterdam, introduced 1957. EC (1) from 1987.

Ilfracombe Goods

W.G. Beattie 0–6–0 locos of 1873–80, built by the L&SWR for the steeply graded Ilfracombe branch and initially largely confined to it.

Illuminated diagram

Signalbox diagram showing the exact layout of the area controlled, also location of signals and position of trains.

ILS

Industrial Locomotive Society. Formed 1937 as the Industrial and Road Locomotive Society. The two interests were split into independent societies in 1946.

Immunization

Measures taken to protect signalling and telecommunications equipment from interference from electric traction currents.

Impedance bond

A device which makes electrical connections, permitting the free flow of traction current while impeding track circuit (qv) currents.

Imperial Indian Mail

A Bombay–Calcutta service introduced 1926 by the EIR and GIPR in connection with sailings of P&O ships to and from Britain.

Impériale, à l' (Fr)(obs)

Any double-deck rly or tramway car, or the top deck of one. Also applied to the railed-in luggage enclosure on the roofs of early rly coaches.

Improved Engine Green

A yellow livery adopted by the LB&SCR soon after William Stroudley became its Locomotive, Carriage & Marine Superintendent in 1870.

IMR

1. Isle of Man Rly; see IofMR.
2. Interlocking Machine Room.
3. (obs) Imperial Military Rlys of South Africa. British military regime controlling OVGS (qv) and NZASM (qv) during the South African (Boer) War of 1899–1902.

IMV

Internal Movements Vehicles; unlicensed tractors, etc. used within rly premises.

Incident

A term used by BR to describe any accident or dislocation of service, from a coach door found open on a moving train to a major collision.

Inclined plane (obs)

A short length of rly too steep for early loco haulage over which trains were hauled by cables operated by stationary steam engines.

Inclined rail

A rail inclined (at a maximum of 1 in 20 in Great Britain) towards the centre of the track.

Independent line

A track provided to allow non-stop trains to avoid a congested area, usually a station; normally qualified as Up (qv) or Down (qv) independent [line].

Independent line/s

Track/s paralleling the main through lines to carry trains in the same direction as the adjacent main line track and mostly used for slow traffic. *See also* Slow lines.

Indian country (RS)

'Foreign' (qv) rlys, particularly Eastern Region BR for any rlyman from another region.

Indian Pacific

A through trans-Australian (Sydney–Melbourne–Perth) standard gauge service with air-conditioned coaches, introduced 1970 with a 64 h 15 min schedule. Route changed to serve Adelaide from 1986.

Indian Rlys

Formed 1950–1 to integrate all main rly systems in India. Abbreviated to IR. Between 1951 and 1966 nine zonal units were established: Central; Eastern; North Eastern; North East Frontier; Northern; South Central; South Eastern; Southern; and Western. The total length of this intensively used network approaches 64,000 km, mostly of broad (1,676 mm) and metre gauge.

Indian Valley Railroad (USRS)

An imaginary rly, on which all is perfect.

Indicators

1. The route and destination information displays on the front of trains, tramcars and LRV; also sometimes on the sides of the last two.
2. The information displayed on rly platforms or on the concourses of large

stations, showing destinations, intermediate stopping points, departure times, etc. of the next trains.

3. Devices used to measure changes of pressure in loco cylinders.

Indicator shelter (obs)

A temporary wooden shelter placed on the front end of a steam loco to protect indicators (3) and other recording instruments, and the men attending them, when a loco was under test on the line. Later developments made it possible to provide indicator diagrams and other information remotely in a dynamometer (qv) car.

Indusi (Ger)

Induktive Zugsicherung; a form of ATP (qv).

Industrial rly

A rly system solely devoted to serving the needs of quarries, mines, factories, brick works, public utilities, etc. and quite separate from the national network, though often linked to private sidings (qv). In some cases passenger trains were operated for employees and visitors. The term may be also be used for temporary rail systems used in conjunction with large construction projects. *See also* ILS, IRS; Jubilee track.

Informatique (Fr)

Any On-board (qv) computer system.

Infrabel

A subsidiary of the Belgian Rlys holding co., responsible for providing all infrastructure services, timetabling and train path allocation from 2004. Ownership rests half with the Belgian state (exercising control by having 80 per cent of the voting rights) and half with the holding co.

Infraco/InfraCo

Infrastructure Companies (Tubelines (qv) and Metronet (qv)) undertaking from 2002 maintenance and renewal ('modernization') of the existing infrastructure and rolling stock of the TfL (qv) London Underground Railways under PPP (qv) with the aim of improving standards and performance. They are paid an ISC (qv) by the OPSCO (qv).

Infrastructure traffic

Movement of rly materials (track, ballast, etc.) around the system, including possession trains (qv) and railborne

machinery. The trains and railborne machinery are known as engineer's trains.

Injector

A part of a steam loco which employs a jet of steam to force water into the boiler.

Inner Circle

A shallow subway line around the edge of inner London, Paddington–Kings Cross–Liverpool St.–Charing Cross–Victoria–South Kensington–Notting Hill Gate–Paddington, completed 1884, partly MDR, partly Metropolitan Rly, partly jointly owned by those companies. Jointly operated by Metropolitan and MDR until 1933. Electrified 1905. LPTB, etc. from 1933. Now known as the Circle or Circle Line.

Inner home signal

A designation used when an outer home signal is also installed. On the LM&SR/ BR (M) this signal was known as Home no. 2. *See also* Home signal; Outer home signal.

Inner Rail

A term used to describe the tracks of the London Underground's Circle Line (formerly the Inner Circle (qv)) which carry trains proceeding in an anti-clockwise direction. *See also* Outer Rail.

Inox

Stainless steel coach construction, normally under the Budd (qv) patents.

In running

A contact wire (qv) positioned to provide traction power to an upraised pantograph (qv) is said to be 'in running'.

Insects (RS)

Occasional or seasonal rly enthusiasts, liable to 'swarm' at certain special events such as open days, or at certain times of the year.

Inside

The lower deck or saloon of a double-deck tramcar (qv). Use of this term persisted (e.g. in the conductor's cry 'Pass down Inside!') until the 1960s, long after the unroofed top decks had become completely enclosed. *See also* Outside.

Inside rail

The inner running rail on a curve.

Inside tracks (US)

The central pair of tracks allocated for fast running in a four-track layout.

Insixfish (obs)
Insulated six-wheel van for fish traffic,
BR(W).

Instanter (obs)
A three-link coupling with the central link
in the form of a triangle which allows
adjustment to long or short length, the
latter bringing the two sets of buffers
close together, reducing the snatching of
loose couplings on an unfitted (qv) train.
Use of instanters also allowed brake pipes
to be connected in a partially fitted (qv)
train.

Institute, Rly
A social and educational centre for rly
employees, usually with library, reading
room, meeting hall, and games room. Such
facilities were provided at London (Euston,
Nine Elms, Kings Cross), Crewe, Derby,
Eastleigh, Gateshead, Swindon, York and
other rly centres.

Intelligentsia Brainbox (LTRS)
A facetious term for LT Headquarters
staff.

Interavailability
An arrangement in which a ticket is
honoured by an alternative route, especially
another company's route.

Inter-City
A label for named trains in Canada and
Australia as early as 1930. For BR and
other modern usage *see* IC.

InterCity Anglia
see Anglia Rlys.

InterCity East Coast
A TOU (qv), 1994; TOC (*2*) 1996 as
GNER (qv).

InterCity Executive
An express between Manchester and
London (Euston), introduced 1983.

Inter-City [Express]
A service between London (Paddington)
and Birmingham, so named 1950; to and
from Chester 1962, name dropped 1965.

Inter-City expresses
Name adopted by NBR (qv) in 1906 for
Edinburgh–Aberdeen services. Probably
the first use of the term.

InterCity Midland
see ICMM.

InterCity Shuttle
Brand name for regular-interval
Monday–Friday InterCity services on key
routes to and from London, introduced
1993. Features included staffed reception
desks and at-seat refreshment services.

InterCity West Coast
A TOU (qv), 1994; TOC (*2*) (qv) 1997 as
Virgin West Coast (qv).

Intercontainer
International Company for Transport by
Transcontainers. A centralized commercial
agency representing the interests of major
European rly systems in the international
transport of containers, founded 1967.
Owned by European rly undertakings and
Interfrigo. Became ICF (qv) 1993.

Interfrigo
International Society for the Carriage of
Refrigerated Goods by Rail/*Société
Ferroviaire Internationale de Transports
Frigorifiques*. Founded 1949 to rationalize
rail movement of commodities requiring
temperature control in transit, and to make
good wartime losses of wagons. It is
grouped with Intercontainer and owns a
large fleet of wagons which operate
throughout Europe. Became ICF (qv) 1993.

Interlaced track
see Gauntletted track/Gauntletting.

Interlinking
A means of proving to a signaller that a
distant signal is showing caution and its
home signal is showing danger before he
can place the rear section block instrument
to 'line clear'. *See also* Welwyn control.

Interlocking
A mechanical and/or electrical means of
ensuring that when a signal or point lever is
moved to admit a train on to a section of
line, all other signals and points which
might allow conflicting movements are
locked. Interlocking also prevents signals
from being cleared from the 'on' or danger
indication until the points to which they
apply are correctly set and facing points are
locked.

Intermediate block home signal
A stop signal at the exit from an
intermediate block section (qv).

Intermediate block section

A section of track-circuited (qv) line between an intermediate block home signal (qv) and a section signal (qv) with both signals operated from the same signal box.

Intermediate box

A signal box which is provided to break up a long block section and allow the operation of a more intensive train service. Such boxes, which are manned as required, usually only control distant and home signals for each line. In modern practice often replaced by IBS (qv).

International Express

A service between Bangkok (Thailand) and Butterworth (for Penang, Malaysia).

International Limited

A Grand Trunk RR, later CNR, express between Montreal, Toronto and Chicago, introduced 1900. 6 h 30 min schedule in 1935. Now an Amtrak service between Toronto and Chicago.

Inter-Rail

A railcard allowing unlimited travel for one month in twenty-four countries for persons under twenty-six. Introduced 1972 to mark the 50th anniversary of the UIC. The age limit was abolished in 1991 and a fifteen-day ticket available in twenty-one countries was introduced.

Inter Regio

see IR (*1*).

Intersection bridge

A bridge which carries one rly line over another.

Intersection point

Point at which two different gradients meet.

Interurban (US)

A form of electric rly linking cities and towns, or urban centres with distant suburbs and extra-urban communities, primarily passenger-carrying, running in the streets in inner urban areas and on private right of way or alongside the highway elsewhere. Rolling stock was heavier and much faster (65–75 mph maximum) than that of conventional tramways (*3*), while in the US, ticketing and luggage arrangements followed those of ordinary rlys, and freight traffic was often interchanged with the latter. Most services were worked with single cars but trains of two, three, four or more cars were also found. Traction supply was almost universally by overhead wire and trolley pole or pantograph. A small number of lines of this type were also built in Canada, Europe and elsewhere. The US interurbans were mainly constructed between 1890 and 1908 and the largest mileage was in the state of Ohio (2,798). Reaching its zenith around 1916, the US interurban had almost entirely succumbed to road competition by the 1950s.

Interval

1. The space between any two tracks on the same route. *See also* Six-foot; Ten-foot.
2. The time between consecutive trains on the same running line. *See also* Headway (1).

In the chair (RS)

see Chair, in the.

In the dirt (RS)

see Dirt, in the.

In the slough (RS)

see Slough, in the.

In track

Any track component correctly placed and secured is said to be 'in track'.

Invalid carriage (obs)

A special coach, fitted out with bed, armchairs, wheelchair, etc., which could be chartered for the carriage of invalids.

Invensys

The largest UK-based engineering co., formed 1999. Took over Westinghouse Brake & Signal (qv), but sold Westinghouse Brakes to *Knorr-Bremse AG* (qv) in 2000 to concentrate on rly automation (automatic signalling and control systems).

Invert

The base section of a tunnel lining, its lowest visible surface, forming an arch that is concave upwards. Tunnels are sometimes built without inverts.

INWR

Irish North Western Rly, formed 1862 from Dundalk & Enniskillen Rly (inc 1845) and Londonderry & Enniskillen Rly (inc 1845). Part of GNR (I) 1876.

IOAR

Isle of Anglesey Rly, operating the Amlwch branch with steam- and diesel-hauled 'heritage' and commuter services from 2000.

IofALR

Isle of Axholme Light Rly: *see* Axholme.

IofL&T

Institute of Logistics & Transport, established 1919, inc 1926, as Institute of Transport, covering all means and methods of transport; renamed Chartered Institute of Transport 1971, renamed IofL&T, 1999.

IofMR

Isle of Man Rly, 3 ft/914 mm gauge system on the Isle of Man, connecting the principal towns with Douglas, inc 1870. Opened 1873, 1874, 1879. Closed 1965. Reopened 1967–8 only. Douglas–Port Erin line reopened again 1969. Taken over by Manx Government and amalgamated with MER (qv) as Isle of Man Rlys, 1978.

IofT

see IofL&T.

IofWCR

Isle of Wight Central Rly, inc 1887, an amalgamation of Ryde & Newport (opened 1875), Cowes & Newport (opened 1862) and IofW (NJ) Rlys. Absorbed Newport, Godshill & St Lawrence Rly (opened 1897, extended to Ventnor West 1900) in 1913. Part of SR from 1923.

IofW (NJ) Rly

Isle of Wight (Newport Junction) Rly, inc 1868 Sandown–Merstone–Newport, opened 1875, 1879, became part of IofWCR (qv) when that was formed in 1887.

IofWR

Isle of Wight Rly, inc 1860 as Isle of Wight Eastern Section Rly, Ryde to Ventnor, opened 1864, 1866, renamed IofWR 1863, purchased Brading Harbour & Rly (Bembridge branch, opened 1882) in 1898. Part of SR from 1923.

IPCS (Fr)

Installation Permanent de Contre-Sens. A system providing full and permanent control of signalling in both directions over one stretch of single track.

IR

1. *Inter-Regio Netz* (Ger); Rail and bus feeder services to *IC-Netz* (qv). The trains have a distinctive appearance and operate at speeds up to 200 km/h at two-hourly intervals between regional centres and key points on the *IC-Netz* (qv) network.
2. Irish Rail: *see IE*.
3. Indian Rlys (qv).
4. Israel Rlys. 647 km over PR (5) (qv) and new lines. Until 1948, the rlys were connected both to Egypt in the south and Lebanon in the north; Haifa was also served by the *Hedjaz* Rly (qv). IR is now isolated.

IR

Indian Railways. An illustrated monthly magazine published by the IRB (qv), first issue 16 April 1956.

IRC

International Rly Congress.

IRCA

International Rly Congress Association. *See AICCF*.

IRCH

Irish Railway Clearing House, established 1848, inc 1860; role similar to that of RCH; dissolved 1974.

Iris

1. *TEE* Brussels–Zurich, introduced 1974, lost *TEE* status 1981.
2. EC Brussels–Chur, introduced 1987.

Irish Mail

Day and night services between London (Euston) and Holyhead connecting with sailings for Kingstown (Dun Laoghaire) for Dublin, and carrying the Post Office mail traffic as well as passengers. So described from 1848 but name not officially adopted until 1927. Winter day service withdrawn 1947.

Irishman

An express between Glasgow (St Enoch) and Stranraer Harbour in connection with sailings to Larne, Northern Ireland, introduced 1933, restored 1949. Name dropped 1967.

Irish Mancunian, The

A Manchester (Victoria)–Holyhead service, so-named 1993.

IRB

Indian Railway Board, formed 1905, reconstituted 1922–4 and again, after independence, in 1951. The IRB exercises the powers of central government regarding the rlys and is responsible for overall planning and control of rly matters but not for day-to-day operation. *See also* Indian Rlys.

IRC

International Rly Congress.

IRCA

International Rly Congress Association. *See AICCF.*

IRCH

Irish Railway Clearing House, established 1848, inc 1860; role similar to that of RCH; dissolved 1974.

Iris

1. *TEE* Brussels–Zurich, introduced 1974, lost *TEE* status 1981.
2. EC Brussels–Chur, introduced 1987.

Irish Mail

Day and night services between London (Euston) and Holyhead connecting with sailings for Kingstown (Dun Laoghaire) for Dublin, and carrying the Post Office mail traffic as well as passengers. So described from 1848 but name not officially adopted until 1927. Winter day service withdrawn 1947. Name ceased to be used after 2 June 2002.

Irishman

An express between Glasgow (St Enoch) and Stranraer Harbour in connection with sailings to Larne, Northern Ireland, introduced 1933, restored 1949. Name dropped 1967.

Irish Mancunian, The

A Manchester (Victoria)–Holyhead service, so-named 1993.

IRJ

International Railway Journal, professional rly journal, first published 1961.

IRO

Institution of Railway Operators, founded 2000.

Iron (USRS)

Rly track, as in high iron (qv), single iron (qv), etc.

Ironclads (RS)

1. GER Adams 4–4–0 locos of 1876–7.
2. SER Ramsbottom 2–4–0 locos of 1875.
3. L&SWR 4–4–0T of 1879.
4. L&SWR steel-panelled corridor coaches of 1921.

All from the naval vessels of this type, introduced in the 1860s.

Iron horse, the (obs)

A popular metaphor for a steam loco until *c.* 1950; also current in US.

Iron horses/men (RS)

Pairs of portable rail-wheeled gantries with lifting tackle used to move rails and special work (qv) to and from sites.

Iron lungs (RS)

Austerity 2–8–0 locos of the Second World War. Also used for Franco-Crosti (qv) Class 9F BR locos of 1955, whose exhaust was emitted from a chimney halfway along the right hand side of the boiler, polluting the fireman's supply of air. From the popular name for the artificial respirators introduced for medical treatment in the 1930s.

Iron man (RS)

An IBS (qv) post.

Iron road

An early name for a rly, which outlived the nineteenth century despite the fact that malleable iron rails were replaced by steel from the 1860s. Several European languages adopted this as their word for rly, e.g. *strada ferrata* (It), *chemin de fer* (Fr), *eisenbahn* (Ger), *järnvag* (Swedish), *iarnród* (Irish).

Iron work (LTRS)

The complicated parts of trackwork at junctions.

Iron worm (LTRS)

A tube (qv) train.

IRR

Iraq Republic Rlys. 2,422 km, physically connected to Syrian (*CFS* (qv)) and Turkish (*TCDD* (qv)) rly systems. *See also* Baghdad Rly.

IRRS

Irish Railway Record Society, formed 1946.

IRS

Industrial Railway Society. Formed 1949

as the Industrial Locomotive information section of the Birmingham Locomotive Club. The IRS title was adopted in 1968.

IRSE
Institute of Railway Signalling Engineers, founded 1910, inc 1912.

ISC
Infrastructure Service Charge, paid every four weeks to the Infraco (qv) by the Opsco (qv) under the PPP (qv) for renewing and maintaining the infrastructure assets and rolling stock of the London Underground.

ISG (Ger)
CIWL (qv).

Island Line
A TOU (qv) 1994, TOC (2) (qv) 1996, operating and owning infrastructure of former BR electrified line Ryde Pier Head–Shanklin (Isle of Wight).

Island platform
A platform with two faces for through lines, i.e. accommodating trains each side, and only accessible by footbridge or subway or by walking across the tracks.

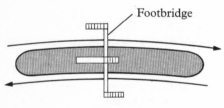

Island platform

Isle of Wight Steam Rly
A preserved rly on the former BR Ryde–Newport line between Smallbrook Junc (near Ryde) and Wootton. First section opened 1971; connection with BR at Smallbrook, 1991.

ISR
Iraqi State Rlys, now IRR (qv).

Istanbul Express
A Munich–Istanbul service, introduced 1965; Frankfurt–Istanbul from 1977.

Italia Express
A Hamburg–Rome service, introduced 1960; Frankfurt–Rome from 1977.

IT&TCC
International Timetable & Through Carriage Conference (originally titled The European Timetable Conference). Held annually since 1872, the TCC was added from 1922. All European and Asian rlys handling international traffic attended, as well as the *CIWL* (qv). The conference agreed timetables and routes for international passenger services for the ensuing year, plus any arrangements necessary to serve special events. Replaced by FTE (qv) from 1997.

IU
Internal Unit/User. BR rolling stock used only within certain closely defined premises.

Ivanhoe Line
The name given to the Leicester–Burton-on-Trent line when it was reopened to passengers in 1994–5.

Ivory Tower, The (LTRS)
Facetious term for LT headquarters, 55 Broadway, Westminster.

IWA
An Individual Working Alone on the rly.

IWS
Intermodal Wagon Systems: Formed 1993 as a subsidiary of CTL (qv) to provide rolling stock for CTL operations. Ownership 75% CTL, 25% BR.

J

Jack (USRS)
A loco.
Jack-in-the-Box (RS)(obs)
A freight brake van with its guard in residence.
Jacko (RS)
A small shunting loco on GWR and BR (W).
Jack catches/Jack traps (RS)
Catch points.
Jack points (RS)
The third pair of points at the entrance to a yard from a hump (qv), the first and second being King and Queen points (qv).
Jack rail (obs)
Check rail (qv).
Jackshaft drive (obs)
A type of transmission used in early electric and diesel-electric locos in which a rotating shaft ran across the loco with cranks at each end. The shaft was driven by gearing from one or two electric motors and the cranks carried connecting rods to transmit the motion to the wheels.
Jaffa cake (RS)(obs)
An orange and brown livery adopted by BR(S) in the mid-1980s, after the popular orange-flavoured chocolate comestible.
Jaffas (RS)
Chunks of coal too large to go into a loco firebox without being broken up. From Jaffa oranges.
Jam buster (USRS)
An assistant yardmaster.
Jam roller (LT rhyming S)
The Line controller.
Janata (India)
People's expresses. All third-class accommodation.

Jane's World Railways
A periodical reference work containing details of the principal features of the rly systems of the world, including locomotives and rolling stock and all urban metro (1) (qv) and major light rail transit (qv) systems. First published 1951 by Henry Sampson of Sampson, Low publishers as *World Railways 1950–51*. Publication under the present title and publisher began in 1972.
Janney Coupler (US)
An automatic coupler patented in 1863 by Eli Janney. Its use was made mandatory in the US in 1893.
Janney, to (USRS)
To couple up. From the Janney auto-coupler.
Janus (RS)
An electric or diesel loco with a central cab. From the Roman god with two heads, facing opposite ways.
Jaune, le petit train (Fr)
Cerdagne, la ligne de (qv).
Javanic (US)
A steam loco with 2–12–2 wheel arrangement.
Jaw
The inner vertical spaces of a chair (qv).
Jawbone shack (USRS)
A pointsman's hut.
Jay rod (USRS)
A hook for breaking up clinker in a loco firebox. From its shape.
Jazzers (RS)
GNR/L&NER K3 2–6–0 locos. From their rough riding characteristic.
Jazz trains/service (obs)
A journalist's nickname for the GER

'intensive service' introduced in 1920 as a cheap alternative to electrification for the Liverpool St. West Side suburban services.

J-door

The door between driving cab and passenger accommodation on LT trains, normally kept locked. From the letter it is allocated to distinguish it from other doors in the car.

JDS

Joint Distribution System, a continuous on-line ticket and reservation system with air line style tickets, including itineraries, introduced by BR for InterCity and European services, 1993.

Jean Jacques Rousseau

A Paris–Geneva *TGV*, so named 1983.

Jeeps (RS)

NCC WT class 2–6–4T locos. Like the famous US Army vehicle, they were said to be 'usable for many sorts of task'.

Jellicoe Specials (obs)

Coal trains worked through from English and Welsh coalfields to Thurso in WW1 to bunker naval vessels moored in Scapa Flow. The term was also applied to special through trains between Scotland and London (Euston) operated for naval personnel in WW1. A similar service was operated for RN, Army and RAF personnel in WW2, when the name was resurrected. After Admiral of the Fleet Earl Jellicoe.

Jenners (RS)

GNR locos and men. From the initials GN.

Jenny Lind

A steam loco with 2–2–2 wheel arrangement. From a Midland Rly loco given this name in 1847, the year when the singer first appeared on the London stage.

JER

Jersey Eastern Rly, St Helier–Gorey Pier, inc 1872, opened 1873, 1891. Closed 1929.

Jerk a drink, to (USRS)

To take up water from water troughs at speed.

Jerkwater town (USRS)

A small, unimportant town where trains stopped to allow the loco to take water from an overhead water tower from which a long nozzle was pulled down over the tender, an action described as to 'jerk water'. *See also* Tank town.

Jersey Central

Central RR of New Jersey (US).

Jersey Lillies (RS)

GCR 4–4–2 locos. After their graceful lines – 'Jersey Lily' was the nickname of a contemporary beauty, Lillie Langtry, a favourite of Edward VII.

Jewellery line

A rly reopened in 1995 to provide a new passenger service between Birmingham (Snow Hill) and Smethwick (Galton Bridge) via the Jewellery Quarter.

Jewett

Jewett Car Co., builders of electric interurban and tramcars at Jewett, Ohio, US, from 1894, and, from 1900, at Newark, Ohio. Ceased production 1917.

JGR

Jamaica Government Rly, 1879–80 and 1900–60. See also JRC; WIIC.

Jigger (USRS)

A fully loaded train.

Jim Crow (RS)

A manual tool used for bending rails, hence also a platelayer.

Jim Crow car (USRS)

A coach set aside for the use of black people in those US states where they were obliged to travel separately from white people. From Jim Crow Regulations, defining racial segregation, and the 1828 'nigger minstrel' song of that name.

Jimmy

1. (RS)(obs) A piece of metal (sometimes a coupling drawbar) illicitly placed in blast pipe of a steam loco to increase draught, and thus obtain a brighter fire and better steaming.
2. (USRS) A four-wheeled ore wagon.
3. (RS) (obs) A railborne trolley used by track workers. *See also* Pump trolley; Hand car.

Jinties (RS)

LM&SR 3F 0–6–0T locos introduced 1924. Its origins are obscure but it dates from the 1930s, if not earlier, and may derive from earlier usage to describe Midland Rly 0–4–0T. 'This beastliest of locomotive nicknames was certainly not coined by any railwayman and I have no doubt we have some misbegotten gricer to thank for it' – George Dow in the RM, 1973.

JNR

Japanese National Rlys. From 1987 JR (2) (qv).

Job (LTRS)

A generic term for the whole rly or the train service on a particular line (e.g. 'The job's up the wall' = the train service is badly disrupted).

Jock (RS)

Food, hence Jock tin.

Jockos (RS)

LM&SR 3F 0–6–0T locos, introduced 1924, otherwise known as Jinties (qv). Also, later, a generic term for any shunting loco.

Johannes Keppler

An EC Frankfurt–Linz, introduced 1991.

Johann Strauss

A Vienna–Frankfurt service introduced 1968. Became EC Vienna–Cologne, 1987.

John o' Groat

The unofficial name for a restaurant car train between Inverness and Wick between the wars, officially adopted by the LM&SR in 1939.

Johnson Bar (USRS)

The reversing lever of a steam loco.

Joint circular

see TC (2).

Join the birds, to

see Birds, to join the.

Joint (USRS)

A coupling between two wagons or coaches, hence to make a joint.

Joint line

A section of rly owned by two or more companies.

Joint Line, The (obs)

This could be applied to any joint line, but was most often heard to describe:

1. March–Lincoln–Doncaster (GER and GNR Joint) and
2. Northolt Junc–High Wycombe–Ashendon Junc (GWR and GCR Joint).

Joint men (RS)

Employees of a jointly owned line or joint committee.

Joint sleeper

A sleeper (qv) next to a rail joint.

Joker (USRS)

Loco brakes as distinct from those in the train.

Jolly Fisherman

Loco-hauled summer services between Leicester/Nottingham and Skegness from 1993. After the famous Hassall poster advertising GNR services to Skegness.

Jones Goods (RS)

Highland Rly 4–6–0s, introduced 1894; the first of this wheel arrangement in Britain. After their designer, David Jones, Locomotive Superintendent, HR.

Journal

That part of an axle inside the axle box.

Journal box (RS)

Axle box.

Journals

A book kept by guards (1) (qv), reporting train running times, reasons for delays, etc.

JR

1. Jedburgh Rly, Roxburgh to J, inc 1855, opened 1856, worked by NBR, part of NBR 1860.
2. UIC code for Japan Rail, formerly JNR (qv). 23,654 km mainly of 1,067 mm gauge. Privatized 1987, with six regional companies and a freight co. (JR Freight) operating over the whole network. The cos also maintain the infrastructure, which they own. Japan also has a number of small private rly cos, mostly operating electric passenger trains in densely populated areas. *See also Shinkansen*.

JR&T

Jersey Rlys and Tramways, St Helier–St Aubin–Corbière, inc 1869, opened 1870/1884–5, 1899. Converted to 3 ft 6 in/1,067 mm gauge 1885. Winter services ceased after 1928, closed 1936.

JRC

Jamaica Rly Co. 1843–79; also Jamaica Rly Corporation 1960–92. *See also* JGR; WIIC.

JTH

Journal of Transport History. First published (twice yearly) from May 1953 by the University College of Leicester. The current (third) series is published in March and September each year by the Manchester University Press.

Jubilee
A steam loco with 4–4–4 wheel arrangement.

Jubilee Line
A London tube rly between Baker St. and Charing Cross. It took over the Stanmore service of the Bakerloo Line when it was opened in 1979. Originally designated the River Line, then the Fleet Line, it was planned to run beyond Charing Cross to Fenchurch St. and Thamesmead but the necessary capital could not be obtained. Named at the suggestion of a Conservative Greater London Council administration, after the Silver Jubilee of Elizabeth II (1977) but not ready until two years later. When asked what he thought of the renaming, Prince Philip is alleged to have replied: 'Does that mean the trains will run every twenty-five years?'. An extension (EJL (qv)) to Waterloo, London Bridge, North Greenwich and Stratford was opened in 1999.

Jubilees (RS)
1. L&SWR A12 0–4–2 locos. After the 1887 Golden Jubilee of Queen Victoria.
2. Metropolitan Rly Cravens coaches of 1887. After the 1887 Golden Jubilee of Queen Victoria.
3. GER passenger 0–6–0T and 2–4–2T locos. After the 1897 Diamond Jubilee of Queen Victoria.
4. LM&SR 6P 4–6–0 express passenger locos. After the 1935 Silver Jubilee of King George V.

Jubilee track
A form of light prefabricated track for portable rlys (qv), normally consisting of steel rails on pressed steel sleepers.

Jubilee wagon
A small tipper wagon used on Jubilee track.

Juggler (USRS)
A freight handler.

Juggle the circle, to (USRS)
To fail to catch a train order when it is proffered from a hook or fork at the lineside to a crew member on a moving train.

Juice (RS)
Traction current.

Juice box (LTRS)
A current rail indicator box.

Juice bug/hog (USRS)
An electric loco.

Juice hogger (USRS)
The driver of a petrol, diesel or electric loco.

Juice rail (RS)
A conductor/live rail.

Juicers (RS)
Electric trains or locos.

Juice wagon (RS)
An electric loco.

Jules Verne
TEE Paris–Nantes, 1980–7. Now an un-named *TGV* service.

Jumbos (RS)
1. A generic term for L&NWR 2–4–0 locos. 'Big Jumbos' had 6 ft 9 in/2.06 metres diameter driving wheels; 'Little Jumbos' 6 ft 3 in/1.9 metres.
2. SE&CR B1 and F1 4–4–0 locos.
3. Caledonian Rly 0–6–0s.
4. L&SWR Beattie 4–4–0s.
5. NBR 4–4–2 locos.

In each case usage derives from a famous circus elephant so named, and accidentally killed in the US in 1882.

Jump a train, to (RS)
To cadge a ride, or take one unofficially, on a train not in passenger service.

Jumper
1. (RS) A travelling ticket inspector.
2. A ticket inspector on tramways (*3*).
3. (LTRS) An overhead trolley lead for moving cars inside a depot.
4. (LTRS) An attempted suicide by jumping in front of an Underground train, usually from a station platform. *See also* One under; Suicide pits.
5. A flexible conductor, part of the OLE (qv), which connects the parts together electrically.

Jumping point (LTRS)
Any undesirable job given to a newly promoted employee while waiting for something better.

Junction Diagrams

Originally published semi-officially at intervals from January 1867 by John Airey, an RCH (1) (qv) employee, and designed to replace hand-drawn diagrams used by RCH staff since at least 1859. From 1895 they were published by the RCH as *Official Railway Junction Diagrams*. Each book contained plans of all areas where two or more rly companies had physical connections, showing each company's lines, depots, stations and sidings in distinctive colours with the precise distances between stations and junctions. The running powers and working arrangements of each company were also listed, as were joint lines. Its primary purpose was to facilitate the calculation of mileage apportionments of traffic passing over the lines of two or more companies and to remove any basis for dispute over these.

Junction [direction] indicator

An indicator at a junction signal informing the driver of the route which has been set, three or five white lights in series (a Position Light Indicator), or an illuminated letter or digit. *See also* Arbor lights; Lunar lights; MLRI, Theatre-type indicator.

Junction signal

A signal controlling two or more routes which, if colour lights (qv), will show the route set (*see* Junction indicator) and if semaphores will have an arm for each route.

Junction work

A switch and crossing layout; special work (qv).

Junior Scotsman

An express between London (Kings Cross) and Edinburgh, introduced 1928 as a second portion of The Flying Scotsman.

Juniper

A modular emu (qv) concept developed by Alstom (qv); first applied to Gatwick Express (qv), 1999 stock. In 2000 became the name for a family of emu (qv) embracing classes 334, 390, 458 and 460.

Junk pile (USRS)

A run-down and out-of-date loco.

JZ

Jugoslovenske Zeleznice; Jugoslavia State Rlys. With the partition of Jugoslavia those lines in Serbia-Montenegro became *ZS* (qv) 2003. *See also*: *HZ*; *MZ*; *SZ*; *ZBH*.

K

K&BR
Kilsyth & Bonnybridge Rly, extension of KVR to Bonnybridge and Bonnywater Junc, inc 1882, opened 1888, jointly vested in Caledonian Rly and NBR. Co. became part of L&NER 1923 but joint working with LM&SR continued until 1947.

K&DR
Kirkcaldy & District Rly, inc 1883 as Seafield Dock & Rly, Foulford Junc near Cowdenbeath to Invertiel Junc near Kirkcaldy, renamed K&DR 1888, part of NBR 1895, opened 1896.

K&ESR
Kent & East Sussex Rly, a light rly, LRO 1896 as Rother Valley Rly, Tenterden to Robertsbridge; extension Tenterden–Headcorn authorized by LRO 1902, name changed 1904. Opened 1900, 1903, 1905. Part of BR(S) from 1948. Closed passengers 1954, freight 1961. Reopened in part under same name as a preserved line from 1974.

Kandõ
A system of electric traction adopted in Hungary, 1932–4, in which 16 kV ac single phase industrial frequency was converted on the loco to feed three, four or six phase current supply to the traction motors. Five fixed speeds were available and a liquid rheostat was used for starting. From K. Kandõ, engineer of the Ganz Electrical Co., Budapest (qv).

K&UR (obs)
Kenya & Uganda Rlys & Harbours; 1927 renaming of Uganda Rly (see UR (2)). Became EAR (2) (qv) 1948.

K&WVR
Keighley & Worth Valley Rly, Keighley to Oxenhope, inc 1862, opened 1867, worked by Midland Rly, leased by Midland Rly 1876, part of Midland Rly from 1881. Closed 1961 (passengers), 1962 (freight) but reopened to the public in 1968 by K&WVR Preservation Society, founded 1962.

Kangourou (Fr)
Kangaroo; see Piggy-back.

Kärnten Express
An Ostend–Klagenfurt summer service, 1956–8; Hamburg to Klagenfurt from 1958.

Karpaty
A Warsaw–Lvov–Bucharest service, introduced 1960. Diverted through Czechoslovakia 1988, avoiding USSR and the double change of gauge.

Katy
Nickname of MK&T (qv).

KCR
1. Kent Coast Rly, inc 1861, extension of the Margate Rly (whose name was changed to KCR) from Margate to Ramsgate. Opened Herne Bay–Margate–Ramsgate 1863, worked by LC&DR, part of LC&DR 1871.
2. Kowloon–Canton Rly, China. (UIC code KCRC), 37.3 km. Formerly a British-owned co., main line opened 1910; taken over by Hong Kong Government 1982; now virtually part of CR (11) (qv) with through trains to Beijing.

KCS
Kansas City Southern Rly (US).

Kearney
A quasi-monorail system with a single running rail and an overhead guide rail, developed by E. Chalmers Kearney from

1908. Said to be particularly suitable for use on tube rlys (qv) since it was possible to climb or descend at gradients as steep as 1 in 7, allowing stations to be constructed near the surface. No installation has so far been completed but a single demonstration car was built by Brush in 1912.

Keel board/keel board sleeper
Attached to their special concrete sleepers, keel boards are embedded in the four-foot (qv) ballast to improve the lateral stability of the track, reducing the risk of buckling and of movement away from the designed alignment.

Keel the goods, to (RS)(obs)
To code freight for loading.

Kenny Belle
Nickname for peak hours only service between Clapham Junction and Kensington (Olympia) operated by NSE. Now a regular all-day service, extended to Willesden Junction.

Kent Coast Express
A LC&DR service between Margate, Ramsgate and London, introduced 1882, ceased 1905; also SER service between same places, introduced 1888, ceased 1904.

Kentish Belle
A renaming of the summer-only Thanet Belle, 1951, with through Pullman cars to Canterbury, which ran 1951 and 1952 only. Ceased 1958.

KER
Knott End Rly: *see* G&KER.

Kerosene Castle (RS)
A GWR gas turbine loco.

Kerr, Stuart
Kerr, Stuart & Co. Ltd, loco builders, Stoke-on-Trent, 1894–1930. Goodwill purchased by Hunslet. *See also* LH Plant.

Kesselwagen (Ger)
Tank wagon (qv).

Kestrel
A 4,000 hp prototype diesel-electric loco manufactured by Hawker Siddeley Group, which worked on BR 1968–71 and was then sold to the USSR (SZD).

Kettle (USRS)
Any steam loco, especially one that is old and worn out.

Kettle-basher (RS)
One who indulges in kettle-bashing (qv); anyone sentimental about steam locos.

Kettle-bashing (RS)
Riding on special trains worked by steam locos over BR lines, or on steam-hauled trains in other countries.

Kettle on the boil (RS)
A loco in steam.

Key
1. A block of wood (usually pressed oak) or a steel block driven in to secure a rail into a chair (qv).
2. (USRS) A rly telegraph instrument.

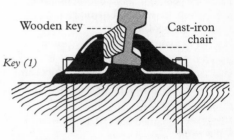

Wooden key ---- Cast-iron chair
Key (1)

Key basher (RS)
A keyman (qv).

Keyman (RS)
A maintenance man who inspects track, driving in loose keys and spikes, tightens loose bolts, replaces broken fastenings, etc.

Key token
A small key-shaped token for electric token block working. *See* Train staff/tablet/token and ticket.

Khyber Mail
A service between Karachi and Peshawar.

Kick (USRS)
To propel a wagon ahead of a loco with sufficient force so that when the loco stops, there is enough momentum to cause the wagon to roll into the required position.

Kicker (USRS)
A defective triple valve in an air brake which locks the brake into the emergency position when no air application is made.

Kick sign (USRS)
Signal given by lamp or hand movements to require loco to be driven forwards briskly.

Killarney Express

A summer service between Dublin and Killarney/Tralee 1953–6.

Killers (RS)

Diesel units. From the quietness of their approach to anyone on the track.

Kilmarnock bogie (RS)

A Glasgow Corporation tramcar design, series 1090–1140.

Kinematic envelope

Profile delineating the extreme limits permissible for trains in motion; it must be within the structure gauge (qv). When enlarged to accommodate the effects of curvature and cant (qv) on trains at speed, it is described as a 'swept envelope'. *See also* Kinematic profile; Loading gauge.

Kinematic profile (LT)

A term used on London Underground, where the kinematic envelope (qv) is enlarged to allow for enhanced vertical and horizontal movement of trains due to predictable roughness in the track at certain points.

King lever

A lever in a signal box which 'cuts out' the box and allows its signals and points to be worked remotely from another box, or to function automatically via track circuits.

King pin (USRS)

A freight train conductor.

King points (RS)

The first set of points at the entrance to a marshalling yard from a hump (qv). *See also* Jack points; Queen points.

Kings

1. (RS) Drivers, especially on SR and BR (S).
2. (USRS) A freight train conductor (*3*) or a yardmaster.

Kingston Roundabout

A service working London (Waterloo)–Richmond–Kingston on Thames–Wimbledon–London (Waterloo) and vice versa.

Kintetsu

Kinki–Nippon (central Japan) Electric Rly. Now a trading conglomerate incorporating rly operation.

Kip (obs)

1. An incline on which wagons were assembled to be run off by gravity as required, usually at a colliery to feed a loading point. A similar arrangement was also used in some places for brake vans.
2. (obs) A short and sharp change in the gradient at the head and foot of a rope-worked incline which was designed to slacken the tension in the haulage rope and facilitate its removal from the train of wagons.

Kipper trip (RS)(obs)

A special train for anglers.

Kiss'n'Ride (US)

A suburban station facility incorporating large car parks close to the platforms in which wives/partners may decant (and collect) rail commuters.

Kitchen (USRS)

The cab of a steam loco.

Kitsons

Todd, Kitson & Laird, loco builders, Leeds, established 1837, later renamed Kitson, Thompson & Hewitson, then in 1899, Kitson & Co. Ltd. Also built steam tramway locos and cars 1878–1901. Ceased production 1938. *See also* LH Plant Engineering Co.

KKOS

Kaiserlich Königliche Österreichische Staatsbahnen; Austrian State Rlys. From 1919 *ÖBB* (qv).

Kléber

TEE Paris–Strasbourg, 1971–87.

Kleinbahn (Ger)

A secondary or minor rly.

Klondyke

A name given by rlymen to rly installations or equipment broadly contemporary with the Klondyke (Canada) Gold Rush of 1898–1900, e.g. Klondyke Sidings, and the Klondykes (GNR 4–4–2 locos of 1898).

KLR

Kingsnorth Light Rly, Sharnal Street to Kingsnorth Pier, LRO 1926, 1929, applying to this existing section of the CNT (qv) after its disposal by the

Admiralty. The powers included provision for carrying passenger traffic but this was never exercised. Closed 1940.

KNDR

Zosun Minzuzui inmingonghoagug; North Korea Rlys, 5,214 km.

Knee Knockers (RS)(obs)

BR (S) 4-SUB emu. From the cramped nature of their compartments, in which the passengers' knees tended to touch those of others sitting opposite.

Kneeling cows (RS)

Any steam loco built for a steeply graded rack rly with the front portion designed to be lower than the rear in order to keep the water over the firebox. From the resemblance to the kneeling animal.

Knifeboard seat (obs)

Back to back bench seating running along a tramcar roof from one end to the other so that seated passengers faced the sides of the car, looking outwards. From its resemblance to the board used for cleaning knives in the kitchen.

Knitting (RS)

OLE (qv).

Knob (RS)

A hand lever which operates points/switches (qv). Hence to knob up.

Knobbing up (RS)

Operating points, hence knobber up, a shunter who operates points in a marshalling yard.

Knobsticked, to be (RS)

To be beaten.

Knocker (RS)

A passenger who receives assistance with luggage, etc. but fails to tip.

Knocker-up (obs)

A lad sent out from a loco depot to arouse sleeping enginemen to prepare for duty, usually by knocking at their front doors.

Knock the clock back, to (RS)

see Clock.

Knorr-Bremse AG

A Munich-based international supplier of rly brake systems and other equipment. Acquired Westinghouse Brakes (*see* Westinghouse brake) from Invensys (qv), 2000.

Knotty

Nickname for the NSR. From the armorial Staffordshire Knot appearing in the company's monogram.

Knowledge box (USRS)

A yardmaster's office.

KNR

Korean National Railroad, 3,124 km, Republic of Korea (South Korea) rlys; the two cross-border lines into North Korea (*see KNDR*) are closed owing to political dispute.

Knuckle

1. (RS) A slight raising of track to permit gravity shunting of wagons in a yard. *See also* Hump; Kip; Pimple.

2. An arrangement placed at the meeting of two sets of OLE (qv), fitted at an angle, so that one set does not cross over the other and pantographs (qv) pass smoothly from one contact line (qv) to the other without interruption of traction current (qv) supply. An *insulated knuckle* will electrically separate one set of OLE from the other, except while a pantograph passes underneath it.

Knucklehook (US)

A type of rotating coupling hook, closed by a catch or lock.

Kodama

see Shinkansen.

Kombiverkehr (Ger)

Subsidiary of *DBAG* (qv) handling intermodal traffic.

Komet

A sleeping car service between Hamburg and Basle, with through coaches to other Swiss destinations, introduced 1954. Name dropped 1995.

Königlicher Preussischer Eisenbahn Verein

Royal Prussian State Rly; DRB (qv) after 1923.

Korridorzug (Ger) (obs)

A train travelling between two parts of one country through the territory of another country, with special customs and passport arrangements for through passengers.

KR

1. Kepwick Rly, 8 m north-east of Thirsk, opened 1833 to carry limestone from Kepwick quarry in the Hambleton Hills, west to kilns near Leake church. Horse traction and a rope-worked incline. Disused from *c.* 1890.
2. Killin Rly, inc 1833 Killin Junc–Loch Tay, opened 1886, worked by Caledonian Rly, part of LM&SR from 1923.
3. Kington Rly, inc 1818, opened as 3 ft 6 in/1,067 mm gauge horse-worked tramroad, Eardisley–Kington, 1820. Extended to limeworks at Burlinjobb *c.* 1835. Virtually disused after opening of Leominster & Kington Rly in 1857. Purchased by Kington & Eardisley Rly 1862 and part of formation used for the construction of that standard gauge line (opened 1874).
4. Kinross-shire Rly, inc 1857, Kinross–Lumphinnans Junc (near Cowdenbeath), opened 1860, part of Edinburgh, Perth & Dundee Rly 1861.
5. Kircudbright Rly, inc 1861, Castle Douglas to Kircudbright, opened 1864, worked by G&SWR, part of G&SWR 1865.
6. Kenya Rlys Corporation; 2,778 km of metre gauge. *See also* EAR (2).

Kreisbahn (Ger)
A rly which is or was the responsibility of a *Kreis*, a local authority broadly equivalent to a district council.

Kremlin, The (RS) (obs)
BR headquarters.

Kriegslok (Ger)
Abbreviation of *Kriegslokomotiv*, wartime 2–10–0 locos, DR class 52. Over 6,000 were built, mostly for freight traffic, in WW2.

Krugers (RS)
GWR 4–6–0/2–6–0 locos of 1899. After the Boer leader, the national enemy of the period; probably a reflection of their ugliness.

KSR
Sleeping car services on the *JZ* (qv).

KSW (Ger)
Kriegsstrassenbahnwagen. A standard austerity wartime tramcar design manufactured 1943–50. Served as the pattern for a new standard tram in Poland.

KTM(B) (Malay)
Keretapi Tanah Melayu Berhad; operator of the 1,802 km, metre gauge Malaysian rly system, which extends from Singapore to make physical connections with the Thailand system. *See also* Eastern & Oriental Express.

Kuhlmeier (Ger)
Same as *Culemeyer* (qv).

Kunze Knorr
An air pressure braking system, largely confined to Central European rlys, which incorporates a mechanism on each wagon with a lever adjustment allowing brake pressures to be regulated according to the load being carried.

Kursbuch (Ger)
The all-lines timetable for German Rlys.

KVR
Kelvin Valley Rly, inc 1873, Maryhill [Glasgow] to Kilsyth, opened 1879, worked by NBR, part of NBR 1885.

Kylchap
A multiple jet blast pipe for steam locos invented by the engineers Kylälä and Chapelon.

Kylporta
A multiple jet blast pipe for steam locos invented by engineers Kylälä and Porta.

L

L (US)

An elevated railway (qv).

LA (LTRS)

Lengthy Absence. LA 1, 2, and 3, 3 being the most serious; also used for reprimands for lateness and/or absence.

L'aal Ratty

Alternative form of Ratty (qv). Local dialect.

Laboratory car

A passenger coach converted to a high-speed track recording vehicle.

LA&NQLR

Lampeter, Aberayron and New Quay Light Rly, LRO 1906, opened (to Aberayron only) 1911, worked by GWR, part of GWR from 1922.

Labour gain[s], one/two (RS)

Colour-light signal showing single/double yellow aspect. From the phrase used at the time of parliamentary and local authority elections when the Labour Party wins a seat from another party.

Ladas (RS)

BR class 91 locos.

Ladder

1. A layout of facing and trailing crossovers in which switches follow in sequence to allow movements across several parallel lines. This has replaced the more costly and complicated arrangement involving straight through connection with diamond crossings and double slips.
2. (US) The main track in a marshalling yard.

Lading (US)

The load in a freight car.

Lairage (obs)

Accommodation provided at a freight terminal for cattle and horses.

Lakes Express

A summer-only service between London (Euston) and Windermere/Keswick and Workington, introduced 1927; later ran on weekdays throughout the year. Ceased 1965.

Lakeside

see L&HR.

LAMA

Locomotive & Allied Manufacturers' Association. A 1956 renaming of the LMA (qv). Again renamed RIA (qv), 1971.

Lambourn Valley

see LVR (*1*).

Lambton Waggonway/Rly

Opened *c.* 1770 to connect collieries owned by J.G. Lambton (later the first Earl of Durham) at Fencehouses to the River Wear. Amalgamated with the Newbottle waggonway (opened 1813) in 1819 after which the two lines were linked and extended. Some parts of the system remained in use as NCB rlys until 1986–7.

Lamping/to lamp (obs)

To place lighted oil lamps into the purpose-built holes in coach roofs as darkness approached.

Lamp proving

A device which checks that a signal lamp is lit by measuring the current in the filament.

Lamprey

A 20-ton ballast wagon used by engineers.

Lancashire Pullman

A service between London (Euston) and Blackpool, introduced 1986.

Lancaster
Lancaster Railway Carriage & Wagon Co. Ltd, Lancaster, 1863–1902. Became part of MCW (qv).

Lancastrian
An express between London (Euston) and Manchester, introduced 1928, name restored 1957, dropped 1962.

L&A (LTRS)
Late & Absent staff return.

L&AR
Lanarkshire & Ayrshire Rly, inc as Barrmill & Kilwinning Rly, 1883, name changed to L&AR 1884 and further lines authorized. Opened Barrmill–Ardrossan 1888, Kilbirnie branch 1889, Irvine branch 1890, Newton [Glasgow]–Cathcart–Lugton–Giffen 1903, 1904. Worked and maintained by Caledonian Rly. Part of LM&SR from 1923.

L&BER
1. Leeds & Bradford Extension Rly, inc 1845, Leeds (Leeds & Bradford Rly) to Keighley, Skipton and Colne Junc (ELR (1)). Leased to Midland Rly 1846, opened 1847, 1848, 1849. Part of Midland Rly 1851.
2. Letterkenny & Burtonport Extension Rly (Ireland), 3 ft/914 mm gauge, LRO 1898, opened 1903, worked by L&LSR (qv).

L&BR
1. Listowel & Ballybunion Rly (Ireland), a Lartigue (qv) monorail line, inc 1886, opened 1888, closed 1924.
2. London & Birmingham Rly, inc 1833, opened 1837, 1838, London (Euston)–Birmingham (Curzon St.). Part of L&NWR from 1846.
3. London & Blackwall Rly, inc 1839, opened 1840, 1841, 5 ft/1,524 mm gauge, with cable haulage, London (Fenchurch St.) to Blackwall [Pier]. Converted to standard gauge and loco haulage 1849. Leased to GER 1866; part of L&NER from 1923.
4. London & Brighton Rly, inc 1837, opened 1840 and 1841, became LB&SCR 1846.
5. Lynton & Barnstaple Rly, 1 ft 11½ in/ 597 mm gauge, inc 1895, opened 1898, part of SR from 1923, closed 1935.

L&CBER
Llandudno & Colwyn Bay Electric Rly, interurban type operation between Old Colwyn and Llandudno West Shore, using ordinary single- and double-deck electric tramcars; 3 ft 6 in/1,067 mm gauge. LROs 1899, 1903, 1907, 1912. Originally promoted as L&CB Light Rly, name changed 1906 to L&CB Electric Traction Co., then L&District Electric Tramway Construction Co. Opened 1907, 1908, 1915. Name changed to L&CBER 1909. Closed 1956.

L&CR
1. London & Croydon Rly, inc 1835, opened 1839, part of LB&SCR, 1846.
2. London & Continental Rlys Ltd; privately owned co. formed 1996 to take over EPS (qv) and construct and operate the CTRL (qv). For subsequent changes *see* CTRL, Eurostar, Eurostar (UK) Ltd.

Land crabs (RS)
Another form of crabs (qv).

Land cruise
A term coined in 1925 by a New York travel agency which commissioned the construction of an 'hotel train' for special tours. Accommodation included a recreation car with gymnasium and cinema facilities, barber's shop, library, sleeping cars, lounge, dining, observation and baggage cars. In 1927 the GWR advertised so-called 'land cruises' or tours by special train and road coach for an inclusive charge, including ordinary hotel accommodation. The full US concept, involving an 'hotel train' was, however, adopted in 1933 by the L&NER – *see* Northern Belle. The term was devalued by BR to describe day circular tours by trains operated in North Wales each summer from 1950 until 1961. These started and finished at Rhyl, Llandudno or Pwllheli running via Denbigh, Corwen, Barmouth and Caernarvon in both directions. From 1955 some had radio commentaries. Various names were used: North Wales Land Cruise; Festival Land Cruise (1951); Welsh Land Cruise; Coronation Land Cruise (1953); Cambrian Radio Cruise; Welsh Chieftain Land Cruise; North Wales

Radio Land Cruise. 'Land cruises' of a similar nature, using dmus, were operated in the Lake District by BR for a few seasons from 1955. BR's Inter-City Land Cruises, introduced in 1987, were closer to the original concept.

L&DR
Lanarkshire & Dumbartonshire Rly, inc 1891, Stobcross (GCR (2))–Dumbarton–Balloch, and short lines at Partick and Maryhill. Dumbarton to Balloch jointly vested in Caledonian and NBR, worked by Caledonian. Opened 1894, 1896, 1897. Company became part of Caledonian Rly from 1909.

L&ECR
Louth & East Coast Rly, inc 1872, Louth to Mablethorpe, opened 1877, linked to the Sutton & Willoughby Rly (opened 1886) at Sutton-on-Sea in 1888. Worked by GNR, part of GNR 1908.

L&EofFR
Leven & East of Fife Rly: *see* EofFR and LR (*4*).

L&GR
London & Greenwich Rly, inc 1833, opened 1836, the first passenger rly in London. Leased to SER from 1845, part of SR 1923.

L&HCTAC
London & Home Counties Traffic Advisory Committee. Set up under Transport Act, 1919 and London Traffic Act, 1924. Issued reports of enquiries into transport in north-east, east and south-east London, 1926–7.

L&HR
Lakeside & Haverthwaite Rly. Part of former BR Ulverston–Lakeside branch (closed to passengers 1965, to freight 1967), northern section reopened as a preserved rly, 1973.

L&L Rly
Lydney & Lydbrook Rly. *See* S&WR&C.

L&LSR
Londonderry & Lough Swilly Rly, Londonderry–Letterkenny–Gweedore–Burtonport, with branch to Buncrana and Carndonagh, inc 1853, first section opened 1863. Buncrana–Londonderry altered from 5 ft 3 in/1,600 mm to 3 ft/914 mm gauge

1885, all other lines built to that gauge. Last section closed 1953.

L&MMR
Llanelly & Mynydd Mawr Rly, Llanelli–Cynheidre–Cross Hands, inc 1875, opened 1883, part of GWR from 1923.

L&MR
Liverpool & Manchester Rly, inc 1826, opened 1830; first public rly to be operated entirely by locos, first rly to operate passenger trains to a timetable and first to work all traffic itself, with its own locos and rolling stock. Part of GJR 1845.

L&MVLR
Leek & Manifold Valley Light Rly, Waterhouses–Hulme End, 2 ft 6 in/762 mm gauge, LRO 1899, opened 1904, worked and maintained by NSR, part of LM&SR from 1923, closed 1934.

L&NER
London & North Eastern Rly, formed 1923, a grouping of GCR, GER, GNofSR, GNR, NBR, NER, and various minor companies and joint lines. Part of BR 1948.

L&NER Magazine
Monthly staff and house journal of the L&NER (qv), published January 1927–December 1947.

L&NWR
London & North Western Rly, formed 1846; a merger of the GJR, L&BR (2) and the Manchester & Birmingham Rly. Many extensions and other lines absorbed subsequently; 2,063 route miles by 1914, covering area between London and Carlisle, much of Wales and central England. Absorbed the L&YR in 1922. Part of LM&SR 1923.

L&NWR Gazette
Monthly staff and house journal of the L&NWR (qv), published 1911–22.

Land of Plenty (RS)
Overtime.

L&OR
Llynvi & Ogmore Rly, inc 1866, an amalgamation of LVR (2) and the OVR. C&OVR absorbed 1876. Worked by GWR from 1876. Pencoed branch (Tondu to Bryncethin Junc) opened 1877. Extension

Nantyffyllon to Cymmer and Abergwynfi opened 1878 (Cymmer), 1880 (passengers), 1886 (Nantyffyllon). Part of GWR 1883.

L&PLW

London & Provincial Licensed Workers Union. *See also* UVW.

L&SDR

Launceston & South Devon Rly, Launceston to Tavistock, inc 1862, opened 1865, worked by SDR, part of SDR 1869.

L&SR

1. Leicester & Swannington Rly, inc 1830, opened 1832 and 1833, acquired by the Midland Rly 1847.
2. London & Southampton Rly, inc 1834, opened 1838, 1839 and 1840, renamed L&SWR 1839.

L&SROA

London & Suburban Rly Officials Association (long since defunct).

Land surveyor (RS)

Second man (qv).

L&SWR

London & South Western Rly, inc 1839; a renaming of the L&SR, which had obtained powers to extend to Portsmouth. Many other lines subsequently built and absorbed; 1,037 route miles by 1914. Part of SR from 1923.

L&TVJR

Llantrisant & Taff Vale Junction Rly, inc 1861, 1866, Treforest to Llantrisant and Common Junc, opened 1863 (passengers 1865); and Waterhall Junc (Cardiff, Ely) to Common Branch Junc (near Cross Inn), opened 1886. Leased to TVR from 1875, part of TVR from 1889.

L&WLR

Leadhills & Wanlockhead Light Rly, Elvanfoot–Wanlockhead, highest standard gauge and adhesion line in Great Britain, 1,498 ft/456.6 metres above sea level. LRO 1898, opened 1901, 1902 as part of Caledonian Rly. LM&SR 1923, closed 1938. Partly reopened as 2ft gauge tourist line from 1998.

L&YR

Lancashire & Yorkshire Rly, formed 1847, a merger of Ashton, Stalybridge &

Liverpool Junction Rly, Huddersfield & Sheffield Junc Rly, Liverpool & Bury Rly, Manchester, Bolton & Bury Canal Navigation & Rly, Manchester & Leeds Rly, Wakefield, Pontefract & Goole Rly and West Riding Union Rlys. Subsequently there were further extensions and other lines were absorbed including the ELR (*1*) in 1859. 600 route miles by 1914, mainly in south Lancashire and south Yorkshire. Part of L&NWR 1922.

Lane, The (RS)(obs)

Stewarts Lane [London] loco depot, SR, BR (S).

Langbein system

See Rollböcke.

Languish[er] & Yawn[er]

Nickname for L&YR.

Lanky, The (RS)

L&YR, its locos and trains, or its employees.

Lanky Claughtons (RS)

L&YR/LM&SR Hughes 4–6–0 locos of 1921 and 1923.

Lanky Yorky

Nickname for L&YR.

Lartigue

A species of monorail (qv), patented by Charles F.M. Lartigue in 1883, in which the single rail is carried on angle-iron trestles about 3 ft/1 metre high. A light guide or stabilizing rail is placed either side of the trestles about 1 ft 6 in/457 mm below the carrying rail. The locos and vehicles must therefore straddle the track like the panniers placed over a pack-animal. The L&BR (*1*) was constructed on this principle in 1888, as were a handful of short lines in North Africa, France, Russia and South America.

Lartigue signals, etc. (obs)

Semaphore signals and block system designed by Henri Lartigue (1830–84), brother of Charles F.M. Lartigue (*see above*), formerly used on French rlys.

Laser dozer

A bulldozer with laser equipment and capable of accurately following the plane of a laser beam emitted by a turret beacon, a combination of which allows ballast (qv) to be spread accurately.

Laser lining
Use of laser beams to align track accurately.
Lasers (RS)
BR class 87 electric locos. From the brilliance of their headlights.
Last vehicle indicator (obs)
A small board attached to the last vehicle of a train when lamps not in use, to indicate to signalmen and others that the train is complete.
Late [and] Never Early
Nickname for the L&NER.
Late fee box (obs)
A letter box at a rly station or in the side of a TPO (qv) carriage in which, for an extra charge over normal postage rates, items could be posted up to a short time before the departure of a TPO, to be carried and sorted on the TPO.
Launching pad
1. (RS)(obs) A steam loco turntable.
2. (RS) A wc seat.
LAV
SR emu sets of 1932 and 1940 for semi-fast services, comprising three Third Class compartment cars and one composite trailer with side corridor and LAVatory accommodation, 4-LAV.
Lavender Line
A short section of the former BR (S) Lewes–Uckfield line at Isfield, operated as a preserved rly.
Lawn, The (RS)
1. Fast lines.
2. The passenger concourse (formerly parcels and mails area and originally the site of the track ends and turnplates area) of Paddington station, London, possibly after a grass slope that existed here when the station was first opened.
Lay-out, to (USRS)
To side-track or delay a train.
Layover
The time a train and its crew spend at a terminus or terminating point before leaving again in the opposite direction. Also an interval between duties.
Lazarettzug (Ger)
Ambulance train (qv).

Lazy, Mucky & Slow
Nickname for LM&SR.
LB&SCR
London, Brighton & South Coast Rly, formed 1846, a combination of the L&BR (4) and L&CR. Subsequently many lines built and absorbed. 456 route miles by 1914. A great favourite with railwayacs (qv), who admired its handsome and smartly kept locos. Part of SR from 1923.
LC
Level Crossing.
LC&DR
London, Chatham & Dover Rly, inc 1853 as East Kent Rly (qv), first section opened 1858. Renamed LC&DR 1859. Other lines subsequently built and absorbed until total reached 187 miles, almost all in Kent. Fiercely competitive with the SER until 1899, from which year both lines were worked under a managing Committee as the SE&CR (qv).
LCCT
London County Council Tramways. Became part of LPTB (qv) 1933.
LCGB
Locomotive Club of Great Britain, founded 1949.
LCL (US)
Less than Carload Lot; sundries or 'smalls' traffic.
LCU
Local Control Unit (qv).
LD&ECR
Lancashire, Derbyshire & East Coast Rly, inc 1891 to build a line from Warrington to Chesterfield, Lincoln and docks at Sutton-on-Sea, with branches to Manchester and Sheffield, but opened only from Chesterfield to Lincoln, with a branch to Beighton Junction near Sheffield, in 1897 and 1898. Taken over by the GCR 1907.
LDC
Local Distribution Centre; a facility provided to assemble and break up possession trains (qv), usually provided with virtual quarries (qv).
LD Line
Chesterfield to Lincoln (LD&ECR (qv)).

LDZ

Latvijas Dzelzceli; Latvian Rlys, 1,520 mm gauge.

LE

see Locomotive Express.

Lead [of a track crossing]

The distance from the nose of a crossing to the heel of the points, measured along the straight. GWR engineers used this term as an alternative to points (qv).

Lead (LT)

The feeder cable from an overhead trolley wire, used for moving cars in depots.

Lead (USRS)

A yard track from which other tracks branch off in a series.

Leader

1. The L&NWR term for a passenger brake van or other non-passenger vehicle placed between the loco and the rest of a train to steady riding and minimize the nuisance created by any overflow when the loco was taking up water from water troughs.
2. (obs) Another word for a control trailer (qv).
3. A controversial and experimental 0–6–6–0T loco design for the SR by O.V.S. Bulleid. The project was abandoned by BR after unsuccessful trial runs in 1949 and 1950.

Leadhills

see L&WLR.

Leak down, to

To allow air to escape from the brake system until the brakes become inoperative.

Leamside Line

Ferryhill–Washington–Pelaw.

LEAP

Lifts, Escalators And Pumps, LT.

LEASCO

Same as ROSCO (qv).

Leave a train over, to (LTRS)

To hold a train, usually at a reversing point so that it omits a round trip in order to restore it to correct timing.

Lecky (RS)

Electric train. Also (in Liverpool) a tramcar.

Leeds Executive

An express between London (Kings Cross) and Leeds, introduced 1973. Name dropped 1986.

Leeds Forge

Leeds Forge Co. Ltd, Leeds, rly rolling stock builders, 1869–1923. Became part of Cammell Laird (qv).

Leeds Northern Line

Leeds–Harrogate–Northallerton. *See also* LNR.

Lee Moor

Lee Moor Tramway, a 4 ft 6 in/1,372 mm gauge horse-worked tramroad built for the carriage of china clay between Lee Moor [Cholwichtown] and Plymouth, incorporating two rope-worked inclines, opened 1858. Steam working on upper section introduced *c*. 1899. Mostly disused by 1947 and completely closed in 1960.

Leen Valley Line

Former GNR line Daybrook–Bulwell Common–Annesley North Junction–Shirebrook.

Left hand running

In which trains run on the left-hand track of a double line when viewed in the direction of travel. The normal method of operation over double tracks in the British Isles. Also in Algeria, Argentina, Australia, Austria (some lines), Belgium, Brazil (most lines), Burma, Chile, China (some lines), Egypt, France (most lines), Ghana, India, Indonesia, Italy, Japan, Kenya, Malaysia, Nigeria, Pakistan, Portugal, South Africa, Spain (some lines), Sri Lanka, Sweden, Switzerland, Tanzania, Turkey, Uganda, and Zimbabwe.

Légers, trains (Fr)(obs)

Rail motors or railcars.

LEL

Lineside Estates Ltd, a wholly owned subsidiary of the LM&SR, formed 1932 to develop land on the company's behalf.

Lemano

TEE Geneva–Milan, introduced 1958, lost *TEE* status 1982. Name used for Paris–Lausanne *TGV* 1984 and also for its Geneva–Milan EC connection, 1987.

Lemonade turn (RS)

The midday (14.00–22.00) shift, so called because there was little or no chance of obtaining alcoholic refreshment after duty.

Lemon time (RS)

An officially sanctioned refreshment/ recreation break for men engaged in shunting work. From the practice of sucking lemons at halftime during football matches.

Lempor

A multiple jet blast pipe for steam locos invented by the engineers Lemaître and Porta.

Length (obs)

A stretch of line allocated to a particular gang/crew of track maintenance workers. Average length was 2½ miles or about 6 track miles including sidings. The modern term is patrol length (qv).

Length (of rail)

See standard length rail.

Lengthmen (obs)

The track maintenance staff or gang allocated to a particular length (qv) which they normally patrolled every day. Later known as trackmen (qv) and then as patrollers (qv).

Leningrad Express

A Berlin–Leningrad service, introduced 1972, extended in summer to Paris, Cologne or Hanover.

Leonardo da Vinci

An EC service between Milan and Munich via Brenner Pass, introduced 1987.

LER

London Electric Railway, formed 1910. The legislation transferred the BS&WR (qv) and CCE&HR (qv) to the GNP&BR (qv), whose capital was rearranged and name changed to the LER, thus combining the 'Yerkes Tubes' (qv) to form a single statutory undertaking within the UERL (qv).

Let Me Sleep

Nickname for (LMS) LM&SR.

LEV (obs)

Leyland Experimental Vehicle, later interpreted as Light Economy Vehicle; a prototype for a new generation of BR light railcars, 1978–81.

Lever collar/clip

A device placed on the handle of a signal lever as a reminder that the line controlled by that lever is already occupied by a train.

The action of collar/clip engages the catch-spring, preventing the signal being moved to the 'off' position.

Lever frame

That part of a manually worked signal box which contains the levers that operate the signals by moving wires and points by movement of point rodding.

Lever jerker (USRS)

A signalman.

Leverman (US)

Signalman.

LEW (Ger)

Lokomotivbau Elektrotechnische Werke Henningsdorf GmbH, a former private firm, from 1945 nationalized by the DDR. Returned to private sector (AEG (qv)), 1992.

Lewisman

Service between Kyle of Lochalsh and Dingwall, with through Glasgow coach, introduced 1933.

Lézard Rouge (Fr)

Red Lizard; a tourist train operated between Tabeditt and Metlaoui, Tunisia.

LFK (obs)

BR Lounge Corridor First class coach, converted in 1967 from Mark 1 FK vehicles to incorporate a ten-seat lounge area.

LG

Lietuvos Gelezinkeliai; Lithuanian Rlys, 2,898 km of 1,520 mm gauge.

LGR

Lagos Government Rly, 1901. Became NR (*3*) (qv), 1912.

LGR (Fr)

Limite pour Garage Refoulement, limit of shunt.

LGV (Fr)

Ligne Grande Vitesse, high speed rly, specially built for *TGV* (qv).

LHB (Ger)

Linke-Hoffman-Busch GmbH; a rolling stock manufacturer.

LH Plant Engineering Co.

This co. has acquired the assets and design rights of Hunslet (qv) from Hunslet–Barclay (*see* Barclay); this allowed them to secure the design rights of Avonside; Hudswell, Clarke; Kerr, Stuart; Kitsons; Manning Wardle; and North British (all qv).

LiberTIN

Light Rail Thematic Network; a research programme sponsored by the EC in 2002 and actively supported by the *UITP* (qv) to investigate the potential for standardization and harmonisation across the European LRT (qv) industry.

Library

1. (RS) A messroom.
2. (USRS) A cupola (qv).

LICC

Local Information Control Centre equipped with computer servers storing and processing information on train services to feed to LED information displays (*see* CIS) on station platforms, etc.

Lickey route

Birmingham–Bromsgrove–Gloucester. In steam days, the Lickey incline, 2¼ miles at 1 in 37 between Bromsgrove and Blackwell, was a principal feature of this line for operators, engineers, and observers.

Lie-by siding (obs)

A term for a refuge siding (qv) adopted by the Midland Rly (qv).

Liegewagen (Ger)

A *couchette* (qv).

Lie up, to

see Lay over.

Life guards

1. Vertical iron bars suspended from loco frames immediately in front of the leading and rear wheels to push any obstructions off the track. *See also* Guard irons.
2. (obs). A device formerly required to be fitted to each end of electric tramcars in Britain. It consisted of a vertical gate formed of wooden slats and a horizontal tray of the same construction normally suspended just above the track. On striking any obstruction, the tray was caused to drop and scoop it up clear of the wheels.

LIFT

London International Freight Terminal, Stratford E., opened 1967.

Lift (RS)

A train; e.g. 'a lift of three wagons and two vans'.

Lift [tickets], to (USRS)

To collect tickets from passengers, usually in exchange for a 'hat check' (qv). Sometimes expressed as to 'uplift'.

Lifted line

A route on which the tracks have been completely removed.

Lifting bar

see Clearance/depression bar.

Lifting barrier

A pivoted boom lowered across a roadway at level crossings when a train is due.

Lift van

An early form of container (qv); demountable bodies developed in the second half of the nineteenth century for lifting on and off road and rail flat trucks, notably for household removals involving road and rail transport. Also known as a 'sling van' or 'pantechnicon'.

Light

1. Window in a rly carriage. *See also* Fixed lights; Decklights; Drop lights; Quarter lights; Top lights.
2. *see* Light engine for the normal sense. The NLR also used the term to indicate a train of ECS (qv), e.g. 'To return light to Acton Sidings' meant train to return empty to Acton Sidings.

Light engine

A loco moving along the line on its own, or with a brake van. *See also* E&V.

Lightning slinger (USRS)

A rly telegrapher.

Light rail/light rail rapid transit/light rail transit

Versions of a generic term in use from the early 1970s for a public transport facility using electric tramcars or light emu sets (LRV (qv)) on street tracks, segregated street or roadside alignments, shallow subways, elevated structures or surface private right of way, or conventional rly tracks and alignments, singly or in combination, to provide a flexible and environmentally friendly low-cost urban/suburban passenger transport facility constructed and operated on light rly principles. In essence an updated form of tramway (*3*). although with somewhat heavier vehicles, the description 'light' being related principally to the track and other infrastructure. *See also* Parry People Mover; Ultra Light Rail.

Light rly

A rly purposely built more simply and below the engineering standards of normal rlys, to reduce the cost of construction and attain economy in working. Gradients may accordingly be steeper and curves sharper than those normally provided. Tracks may be unfenced and placed alongside or in the centre of public roads and there may be intermingling with tramways (*3*). A narrower gauge than standard may be chosen to facilitate and cheapen construction. The constraints mentioned may result in lower average speeds than normal and signalling and safety systems may therefore be much less elaborate than on a conventional rly. In Britain the majority of such lines have been constructed under the provisions of the Light Railways Act, 1896, but the term is also applied to similar lines built before that legislation existed and to others authorized subsequently by private legislation. The term first appeared in British legislation in The Regulation of Railways Act, 1868. For convenience, some tramways (*3*) were authorized under the 1896 Act and were therefore formally entitled light rlys although wholly or mainly laid along streets and in every other respect no different from tramways (*3*). Since 1992 light rlys, including light rail systems, have been authorized under the system laid down by the Transport & Works Act (qv). *See also* Light rail/light rail rapid transit/light rail transit.

Light Railway & Tramway Journal
see LR&TJ.

Light rapid transit

A generic term embracing light rail transit (qv) and also unconventional rail and non-rail modes fulfilling a similar role at similar cost.

Ligne Impériale, la (Fr)

The rly between Paris and Marseille (the former *PLM* (qv) main line), since it led to the port serving the French overseas empire.

Ligure, le

TEE Marseilles–Milan, introduced 1957. Extended to Avignon 1969–82. Lost *TEE* status 1982.

Lijn, De

Brand name of the *VVM* (qv).

LIM

Conférence internationale des horaires des trains de Marchandises. Conference to agree timetables of international freight trains. Established at Prague, 1924.

Limited

A train on which all seats must be pre-booked and to which passengers who have no seat reservation are denied access.

Limited Mail (obs)

A train primarily for carriage of mail but with one or two coaches for passengers.

Limited, The (RS)

Cornish Riviera Express (qv).

Limits of deviation

The extreme outer boundaries within which new rlys authorized by parliament must be built.

Limpet

A 33-ton ballast wagon used by engineers.

Line-basher (RS)

Track-basher (qv).

Line behind (USRS)

To throw points back after a loco or train has passed through.

Line blocked

The normal indication of a signalling block instrument, the others being 'Train on line' and 'Line clear'.

Line capacity

The maximum number of trains which can be passed over any particular line in a given period. Constrained by the signalling system, the physical characteristics of the line (less important with electric traction), train speeds, speed restrictions, station stopping times and the required pattern of service.

Line clear

An indication on a signalling block instrument denoting that a train has been accepted into a block section but has not yet entered the section.

Line clear release
A lock which prevents the lever for the most advanced starting signal (qv) being pulled off until line clear is displayed on the block instrument and usually then locks the lever before the next pull.

Line-haul railroad (US)
Term for a rly performing main trunk line common carrier functions.

Linemen (obs)
Men responsible for repairs to and maintenance of telephone, telegraph, electrical, signalling and related equipment.

Line occupation
1. Use of a line in terms of trains.
2. Obstruction of a section of line by a train, or by engineers' plant and vehicles during maintenance and reconstruction work ('engineer's occupation').

Line of route crime
See Route Crime.

Line of sight
A method of emergency working in which the driver keeps the train in front in view but maintains a safe speed and sufficient braking distance behind it.

Line, On or near the
See On or near the line.

Liner (USRS)
A luxury passenger train.

Liner train
see Condor; Freightliner.

Lineside
The space which extends from the boundary of the rly property to the outer edge of the cess strip (qv) alongside the nearest track.

Linesider (RS)
One who enjoys watching and photographing steam-hauled special trains from bridges or the lineside but tends not to ride on them or give them other financial support.

Lineside Estates
see LEL.

Linesiding (RS)
The activities of a linesider (qv).

Line speed
The maximum speed permitted on a given stretch of rly.

Ling
A 14-ton ballast wagon used by engineers.

Linger & Die (RS) (obs)
The LB&SCR (qv) route from London to Brighton via Dorking, Horsham, Henfield and Shoreham, often used for excursion trains (qv) to relieve congestion on the main line via Three Bridges and Haywards Heath.

Linger, Crawl & Delay
Nickname for LC&DR.

Link
A combination of duties providing a sequenced pattern of work over a given period of time for a group of personnel qualified to undertake them. The 'top' or 'first' link were those engine crews enjoying the highest rates of pay and monopolizing the principal passenger express workings. *See also* Fluffy link; Long link.

Link and pin (USRS)
The traditional type of US freight wagon coupling now generally superseded. Hence (USRS) by association, any old-fashioned rlyman or practice.

Link span
A form of lifting bridge between a train ferry (qv) and the tracks on shore.

Linx
A company jointly owned by *SJ* (qv) and *NSB* (qv), formed in 2001 to operate international rail services between Denmark, Sweden and Norway. *See also* Oresund Link.

LIRR (US)
Long Island Railroad, formerly a subsidiary of the Pennsy (qv), it now operates its suburban services between Long Island and New York under contract to the MTA (qv).

Lisboa Express
A day service between Madrid and Lisbon, introduced 1967. Replaced by *Luis de Camoes* (qv) in 1989.

Littleboy (LTRS)
A surveying tool, placed next to a rail to check alignment of track. After its designer.

Little Eds/Edwards (RS)
BR electro-diesel locos, class 73. From Electro-Diesel.

Little Egberts (RS)
L&YR 0–8–2T. From a troupe of performing elephants to which they were compared by crews impressed by their versatile abilities.

Little Londons (RS)(obs)
Stopping services between London (Euston), Northampton and Birmingham (New Street).

Little North Western
The NWR (qv).

Little Ratty
Ratty (qv).

Little Sharps/Sharpies (RS)
GNR 2–2–2 locos of 1848 built by Sharp Bros & Co. (*see* Sharp) and converted to tank engines (qv) in 1852.

Little Sir Echo (RS)
His Master's Voice (qv).

Littl'un (RS)
A dwarf shunting signal.

Little Waterloo (RS) (obs)
Victorian name for Waterloo East (SER/SECR) station.

Littorina (It)
A pioneer single-unit petrol-engined light railcar (qv) with driving cab at each end manufactured by Fiat from 1933.

Live engine
A loco with steam up, ready to move.

Liver & Bacon (RS)
Nickname for the LB&SCR in the period when its locos were lettered 'L&B'.

Liverpool Executive
A service between London (Euston) and Liverpool, introduced 1984. Name dropped 1985. *See also* Merseyside Pullman.

Liverpool Pullman
A service between London (Euston) and Liverpool (Lime St.), introduced 1966 with new Pullman cars. Ceased 1975.

Livery
The manner in which locos and rolling stock are painted, including lettering and symbols.

Lizard scorcher (USRS)
The Chief Steward of the restaurant service on a train.

Lizzies (RS)
LM&SR 8P 4–6–2 locomotives, introduced

1933. After 'Princess Elizabeth', the second to appear.

LJR
Lowestoft Junction Rly, inc 1897, Lowestoft Line Junc near Yarmouth (Beach) to Gorleston (North) [N&SJR], opened 1903 as part of M&GNR.

LKT
Look-out (qv)

LL
Low Level.

Llanberis Lake
Llanberis Lake Rly, 1 ft 11½ in/597 mm gauge tourist line over part of the former Padarn Rly near Llanberis.

Lloyd Express
A *CIWL* service between Hamburg and Genoa, introduced 1907. Restored after WW1. Connection made with the sailings of Norddeutscher Lloyd liners between Genoa and the USA.

LLR
1. Lauder Light Rly, known locally as 'Auld La'der Licht', Fountainhall to Lauder, LRO 1898, opened 1901, worked by NBR. Part of L&NER 1923. Closed to passengers 1932, entirely 1958.
2. Llanberis Lake Rly (qv).

LM (Fr)
Limite de Manoeuvres, limit of shunt/working.

LMA
Locomotive Manufacturers' Association, formed 1875. Renamed LAMA (qv), 1956.

LM&SR
London, Midland & Scottish Rly, formed 1923, a grouping of L&NWR, Midland Rly, NSR, FR (*2*), CR (*1*), G&SWR, HR (*7*) and various minor and joint lines. Part of BR 1948.

LMR
1. *see* BR (LMR).
2. Longmoor Military Rly, Bordon–Woolmer–Liss, built and operated by the Royal Engineers and Army rly units; first sections opened 1906, 1907. Originally titled Woolmer Instructional Military Rly (WIMR). Renamed LMR 1935; latterly operated by RCT (qv) as their training ground for rly operation.

Closed 1969, training transferred to 79th Rly Squadron in Germany.

3. (LT) Lift Machine Room.

LMS

see LM&SR.

LMS Railway Magazine

Monthly staff and house journal of the LM&SR (qv) November 1923–September 1939. *See also Carry On, On Time.*

LN&RN

Locomotive News & Railway Notes founded and published by J.H. Fellows and mostly reporting current rly activities from its first issue on 10 March 1919. Retitled *Locomotive News and Railway Contractor*, 1922; publication ceased after the issue of 10 September 1923.

LNR

Leeds Northern Rly, a renaming of the Leeds & Thirsk Rly (which was extending to Stockton) in 1851. Absorbed into York, Newcastle & Berwick Rly and then the NER in 1854.

LO or L/O

Look-out (qv).

Loaders (RS) (obs)

Men employed to aid hard-pressed train crews at busy periods, also known as 'dispatchers'.

Load factor

The average use made of a train or service capacity. Usually calculated by dividing passenger miles (qv) by seat miles (qv).

Load/Loading gauge

1. The profile which must not be exceeded by anything moved over the rly, including locos, to ensure there is safe clearance between structures and passing trains on adjacent tracks. *See also* Berne gauge; Kinematic envelope; Structure gauge. The Network Rail (NR) loading gauge is a standard profile known as 'W6A', applying to all NR-controlled infrastructure; certain exceptions to it are allowed.

2. A metal frame suspended over a track to indicate the limits to which an open freight wagon may be safely loaded.

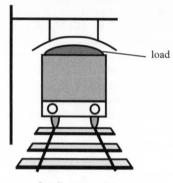

Loading gauge (2)

Loadhaul Ltd

Freight operating company of BR, previously Trainload Freight North East, reorganized for sale to private sector, 1994. *See* EWS.

Load unit

A generic term for both containers (qv) and swap bodies (qv).

Local Control Unit

A box at any automatic, cctv or remotely controlled level crossing which is opened up to work the crossing manually when required.

Local rly

Term used (mostly on the mainland of Europe) to describe any rly serving a limited area. Such lines are normally no more than about 20 to 30 m long and are usually of light rly (qv) type.

Local traffic (obs)

Traffic arising on a specific rly system, as distinct from that originating on 'foreign' (qv) rlys.

Locher system

A type of rack rly (qv) invented 1889 by the Swiss engineer Col. Eduard Locher-Freuler (1840–1910) for the 48 per cent (almost 1 in 2) gradient line up the Pilatus mountain.

Lock and block

A signalling system, incorporating mechanical and electrical safety and locking devices which are interconnected with the block instruments and signal levers positively to ensure that only one train at a time occupies a block section. System first patented by Edward Tyer in

1869 but the most commonly used version was introduced by W.R. Sykes from 1874. *See also* Release Key.

Locked up (RS)
Prevented from moving signal or points levers by the action of the interlocking mechanism or locking bar.

Locker First/Second/Third Composite
A coach containing passenger accommodation with a 'locker' (space for luggage and parcels, etc.) but no guard's accommodation or equipment.

Locking bar
A bar placed on the inside of the rails which is depressed by wheel flanges and prevents points being changed while a vehicle is passing over them.

Locking frame
see Interlocking.

Loco
Locomotive or, (RS), locomotive shed or MPD (qv), e.g. 'Kings Cross Loco'.

Locomotion
A periodical dealing with rly matters, established 1930 by R.M. Robbins and Jack Simmons (and R. Kidner from 1933). Quarterly from March 1931 (vol. II). Final issue June 1939.

Locomotiva (It)
A steam loco.

Locomotive Express
A monthly magazine for rly enginemen and others interested in steam locos, published 1947–5?.

Locomotive Magazine, The
see Moore's Monthly Magazine.

Locomotore (It)
An electric or diesel loco, as distinct from *locomotiva* (qv).

Loco spotter (RS)
Train spotter (qv).

Lodging turn (obs)
A duty which required enginemen and guards to spend a night away from home in a rly staff hostel or lodgings.

L of C
Line/s of Communication; a British Army term for any rly/s in military use, usually those linking a base or port with the railhead (qv).

Lok (Ger)
Abbreviation for *lokomotiv/e* (loco/s).

Lokalbahn
Austrian word for local rly (qv).

Lokey (NZ RS)
A loco.

Lollipop (RS)
A tool used by lengthmen for testing condition of sleepers. From its shape.

Lombardy Express
A service between Paris and Milan, introduced 1960.

London and South East Sector
A BR business sector formed 1982 to cover passenger facilities (other than InterCity) in London and SE England, reconstructed as NSE (qv) 1986.

London Area
The LPTB area (qv). *See also* Extended London Area.

London Commuter Area
Extended London Area (qv).

London Crosslink
See Crosslink.

London end
That end of a station, tunnel, etc. nearest to London.

London Lines
A TOC (2) owned by National Express Group (qv) combining C2C (qv), Silverlink Metro (*see* Silverlink Train Services) and WAGN (Great Northern) (qv) 2004–6.

London–Merseyside Express
A service between London (Euston) and Liverpool (Lime St.), introduced 1927, renamed Merseyside Express (qv), 1928.

London Necropolis Co.
Inc as the LN & National Mausoleum Co. in 1852, it operated funeral trains, using its own hearse vans, but with locos, passenger coaches and train crews provided by the L&SWR/SR, from a private station at Waterloo (resited and rebuilt in Westminster Bridge Road in 1902), using the L&SWR (later the SR) between Waterloo and Brookwood. At the latter, the funeral trains moved on to a line with two private stations inside the company's cemetery. This operation lasted from 1854 to 1941. Some Necropolis specials may have been worked

from Waterloo (SR) to Brookwood after 1941, but the tracks in the Brookwood cemetery were removed *c.* 1947.

London Smash 'em and Turn 'em over
Nickname for the LC&DR.

London Traffic Combine
A term used (mainly by politicians and journalists) for the UERL (qv).

London Travel Centre
see Travel centres.

London Underground Ltd
See LUL

Londres-Vichy Pullman
A *CIWL* all-Pullman First Class train (connecting with Folkestone–Boulogne sailings) 1927–30.

Lone wolf (USRS)
An employee who does not belong to a trade union (brotherhood).

Long and Narrow, The
Nickname for the L&NWR; from its initials and geographical shape.

Long Charleys (RS)
GWR eight-wheeled coaches with fixed wheelbase but some lateral play available to the wheels.

Long Drag, The (RS)
The Settle to Carlisle line.

Long link (RS)(obs)
Crews available only for normal duties. *See also* Fluffy link; Link.

Long rail/long welded rail
In Britain any rail longer than 36 m. London Underground uses shorter rails welded together or tight-joint fishplated together in lengths of 200–730 m.

Long Toms (RS)
1. (obs) Yorkshire coal.
2. GNR 0–8–0 coal traffic locos of 1901 (L&NER classes Q1, 2 & 3). From their sound, said to resemble that of the 'Long Tom' field gun used in the South African War, 1899–1902.
3. (obs) A tall tail lamp used on GWR slip coaches.

LonSLR
Lee on the Solent Light Rly, Fort Brockhurst to Lee on the Solent, inc 1893, opened 1894, worked by L&SWR from 1909. Part of SR 1923.

Look-out
A person trained to be alert to all approaching trains in order to give adequate warning to those working on the line by whistle, horn or by operating a remotely controlled 'Pee Wee' (qv) siren.

Loop/loop siding
A track with connection to main running lines at each end, allowing shunting and overtaking. *See also* Goods loop; Passenger loop; Platform loop.

Loop line
A rly broadly parallel to another line but serving territory at some distance to one side of it and connected to it at each end. *See also* Loop, The; Potteries Loop.

Loop, The (RS)
The March–St Ives–Cambridge line.

Loop, to (RS)
To put a train into a loop to allow a more important service to overtake it, hence 'to be looped', to be put into a loop.

Loose (USRS)
Rolling stock which has become detached from a loco or remainder of train.

Loose-coupled [freight/train] (obs)
A train of wagons and vans connected only by three-link couplings or instanter couplers (qv) in the extended position, i.e. without continuous braking, relying solely on the loco brakes and guard's handbrake. However on steep gradients some manual brakes on the wagons would be pinned down (qv).

Loose gang
A group of track maintenance staff not attached to a length (qv), but available for attending accidents, relaying work, etc.

Loose shunting
Shunting by propelling vehicles into a siding without coupling them up to the loco. *See also* Flying shunt.

LOR
Liverpool Overhead Rly, inc 1888, opened 1893, 1894, 1896 as a mainly elevated electric rly serving the docks area; closed 1956.

Lord of The Isles
A service between Edinburgh and Mallaig/Oban, so named 1989.

Lord's My Shepherd
Nickname for (LMS) LM&SR.

Lord Willoughby's Rly
Built by Lord Willoughby de Eresby
to connect his Grimesthorpe Castle,
near Edenham, with the GNR main
line at Little Bytham, opened in 1856.
Passenger and freight traffic was
carried but the former (begun in 1857) was
occasionally suspended owing
to poor maintenance of track and locos.
Horse traction was resorted to in the
line's last days and the line closed
c. 1882.

Lorelei
An express between Hook of Holland and
Basle/Lucerne 1953–74;
Hook/Amsterdam–Basle 1975–86;
Hook–Basle 1987; Hook–Cologne 1988,
renamed *Colonia Express* 1989.

Loreley
A Blackpool–Sheffield–Harwich diesel car
service in connection with Continental
sailings, ran only in 1988. Name used for
Birmingham/Liverpool–Harwich service,
1989. *See also* Britannia.

Loriot
GWR TC for well wagons carrying agricultural and other machinery (eighteen types).
Later a 20-ton flat wagon used by BR
engineers.

LOS
Limit Of Shunt; a sign or position light
signal marking the point where shunting
movements must cease on a track in the
wrong direction.

Lose 'em, Mix 'em and Smash 'em
Nickname for (LMS) LM&SR.

Lose its feet, to (RS)
Used of a loco suffering from wheel-slip
('She's lost her feet', etc.).

Lot, to give it/her the (LTRS)
To make an emergency brake application.

Lothian Coast Express
A summer service between Glasgow and
North Berwick/Gullane/Dunbar,
introduced 1914, restored 1922 to North
Berwick and Gullane only, to North
Berwick only from 1933, withdrawn at
end of 1933 season. Possibly the first

British train to carry its name on a loco
headboard.

Louse cage (USRS)
A caboose (qv).

Low elliptical roof
Another term for cove roof (qv).

Low-Fit (obs)
12 ton flat wagons designed to carry road
trailers loaded with gas to fill RAF barrage
balloons in WW2. These wagons travelled
in vacuum-braked trains at express speed.

Low Iron (USRS)
Sidings and yard lines, as distinct from
High Iron (qv).

Low leg/low rail
Inner rail of a curved track (even if higher
than the other rail).

Low Level Line, The
Ditton Junc–Warrington–Arpley–Timperley.

Lower quadrant
A semaphore signal whose arm, normally
horizontal, falls to about 45 degrees below
horizontal when pulled 'off'.

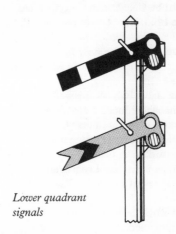

*Lower quadrant
signals*

LOWS
Look-out Operated Warning System; to
warn track workers of an approaching
train. *See also* Look-out; Pee Wee.

LPC
Locomotive Publishing Co., set up in 1900
to market photographs (mainly of locos)
some under the imprint 'F. Moore'. Also
published *Moore's Monthly Magazine* (qv)
and *The Locomotive Magazine* (qv).
Acquired by Ian Allan Ltd 1956.

LPTB
London Passenger Transport Board,
formed 1933. It included the rlys formerly
operated by the UERL (qv) and the
Metropolitan Rly and was replaced by LTE
(*1*) 1948. Popularly known as 'London
Transport' or 'LT'.

**LPTB or London Passenger Transport
Area**
The area controlled by the LPTB after 1933.
This extended from Wendover,
Tring, Luton and Bishops Stortford in the
north to Guildford, Horsham and
Edenbridge in the south; and from
Amersham, Slough and Chertsey in the
west to Brentwood, Grays and Sevenoaks
in the east, covering a total of 1,986 square
miles. This territory was also assigned
to the LPTB's immediate successors (i.e.
until 1970).

LR
1. Lanark Rly, opened 1854 as private line,
freight only, Cleghorn Junc–Lanark,
worked by Caledonian Rly, passenger
traffic 1855. Inc 1860 as part of CR.
2. Leslie Rly, inc 1857, Markinch–Leslie,
opened 1861, worked by Edinburgh,
Perth & Dundee Rly, part of NBR from
1872.
3. Lesmahagow Rly, Motherwell
(Lesmahagow Junc)–Lesmahagow
[Brocketsbrae]–Coalburn–Galawhistle
Pit/Spireslack, first section opened
1856, worked by Caledonian Rly,
passenger service to Lesmahagow
1858. Part of Caledonian Rly from
1881.
4. Leven Rly, inc 1853, Thornton to
Leven, opened 1854. Worked by
Edinburgh, Perth & Dundee Rly.
Amalgamated with EofFR as L&EofFR
1861, extended to Anstruther 1863,
part of NBR 1877.
5. Londonderry Rly, or Marquis of
Londonderry's Rly, rope-worked line
from Penshaw Collieries to Seaham
Harbour opened *c.* 1831. Extended
from Seaham to Sunderland, as
Londonderry, Seaham & Sunderland
Rly, opened 1854, passenger service

worked over NER into Sunderland
station, 1855. Part of NER 1900.
6. Lydd Rly, inc 1881,
Appledore–Lydd–Dungeness, opened
1881, 1883, extended to New Romney
1884. Part of SER 1895.
7. Lymington Rly, inc 1856,
Brockenhurst–Lymington, opened
1858, worked by L&SWR, part of
L&SWR 1879, extended to Lymington
Pier 1884.

LR&D
Llanelly Rly & Dock, Llanelly–Llandilo;
Pantyffynnon–Brynamman/Gwaun cae
Gurwen; Tirydail–Cross Hands, inc 1828
as Llanelli Rail-road & Dock Co. (dock &
colliery tramroad). Llanelly Rly & Dock
Co. 1835, opened 1833 (Dafen branch),
1839, 1840, 1841, 1857. Extended to
Llandovery by leasing Vale of Towy Rly
1858. Llandilo Junc–Carmarthen opened
1865, Pontardulais to Swansea and
Penclawdd branch 1867. These last two
lines inc 1871 as Swansea & Carmarthen
Rly, worked by L&NWR and name
changed 1877 to Central Wales &
Carmarthen Rly. Absorbed by L&NWR
1891. Rest of LR&D absorbed by GWR
from 1889.

LR&H
Lowestoft Rly & Harbour, rly inc 1845,
Reedham to Lowestoft, opened 1847,
leased by NR 1846, part of ECR 1848.

LR&TJ
Light Railway & Tramway Journal, founded
1899, renamed *Electric Railway & Tramway
Journal* 1914, *Electric Railway, Bus &
Tramway Journal* 1932, *Passenger Transport
Journal* 1938, later shortened to *Passenger
Transport.* Amalgamated with *Buses
Illustrated* as *Buses,* 1968.

LRC
1. Light Railway Commission, established
under the Light Railways Act, 1896
and empowered to make orders
authorizing construction of light rlys,
the orders to be submitted to the BoT
(qv) for confirmation (until this was
received, they were known as
provisional orders). Confirmation gave

the order the same status as an act of parliament. The LRC was wound up in 1922 when powers to make orders passed to the MoT (qv).

2. Light, Rapid & Comfortable, diesel push-pull, tilt-body, high-speed trains developed by a consortium of Canadian companies from 1967 onwards. First train delivered to Amtrak, 1980.

LR&MT

Light Rail & Modern Tramway, a retitling of *MT* (2) from January 1992. Retitled again 1998, *see T&UT*.

LRO

Light Rly Order: *see* LRC (*1*).

LRPC

London Regional Passengers' Committee, set up 1984; replaced TUCC for London. *See* CTCC. Replaced 2000 by LTUC (qv).

LRPHJC

Lots Road Power House Joint Committee, (London). Inc 1911 with representatives of MDR and LER, to acquire the Lots Road power station from the UERL and lease it to these statutory companies. Ceased to exist with formation of LPTB in 1933.

LRR

London Railway Record, quarterly magazine covering rlys in Greater London, published from 1994.

LRRS

London Railway Road Services, a BRB organization which formerly provided all cartage services (qv) within the London area for the London-based regions of BR.

LRT

1. Light rail transit (qv) or light rapid transit (qv).

2. London Regional Transport, formed 1984, under the London Regional Transport Act, 1984, to take the place of LTE (2) and remove control from the Greater London Council to the Secretary of State for Transport. Like its predecessors, it was soon popularly known as 'London Transport' and this subsequently became accepted officially. *See also* LUL; TfL.

LRTA

Light Rail Transit Association, founded as the Light Railway Transport League, 1938, name changed 1979. Devoted to the advocacy and study of light rail transit and tramways (*3*). Publishes *T&UT* (qv).

LRTF

Light Rapid Transit Forum, formed 2004 to represent the views of the private sector elements involved in light rail transit schemes within the UK.

LRTL

see LRTA.

LRV

Light Rail Vehicle, as operated on light rail transit systems (qv), normally electrically propelled, usually wider than conventional tramcars of tramways (*3*) and often incorporating special features such as variable-height platform access.

LStH&SLR

Liverpool, St Helens & South Lancashire Rly, inc 1885 as St Helens & Wigan Junction Rly, renamed LStH&SLR 1889, opened 1895, Lowton St Mary's to St Helens, to passengers 1900. Worked by MS&LR. Part of GCR from 1906.

LSL

Long Swing Link, *see* Swing link.

LT

London Transport. The abbreviated title for the various public transport authorities restless politicians have devised for London since 1933, i.e. LPTB, LTE (*1*), LTB, LTE (*2*) and LRT (and no doubt more to come). *See* TfL.

LTA/LTA Advertising

London Transport Advertising, established 1963 to sell sites on and in LT vehicles and on LT properties. Sold to private sector, 1994.

LT&SR

London, Tilbury & Southend Rly, inc 1852, eventually extending from London (Gas Factory Junc with GER, in Bow)–Southend–Shoeburyness via Tilbury and via Upminster; branches Upminster to Romford, Upminster to Grays and Stanford le Hope–Thames

Haven. Promoted jointly by L&BR (*3*) and ECR. First sections opened 1854, 1855, 1856, stock provided by ECR. Leased to contractors, Peto, Brassey & Betts, 1854. Partial independence achieved 1862 but GER and L&BR appointed two-thirds of the board of directors. Operated with GER stock from 1875, own rolling stock and locos introduced 1877–80. A fully independent company from 1882. Became part of Midland Rly from 1912 when there were 79¼ route miles of line.

LTB
London Transport Board, formed 1963 on the dissolution of the BTC, as an independent statutory undertaking reporting directly to the Minister of Transport. It was succeeded by LTE (*2*) (qv) at the beginning of 1970.

LTE
London Transport Executive. There were two bodies so named, the first LTE (*1*), which existed from 1948–62, was a subsidiary of the BTC and was replaced by the LTB (qv); the second, LTE (*2*), whose life extended from 1970–84, was formed under the Transport (London) Act, 1969, which transferred the overall policy and financial control of London Transport to the Greater London Council; it was succeeded by LRT (qv). Both bodies were popularly known as 'London Transport' or 'LT'.

LTI
An organization originally set up by LT in 1968 as the LT Consultancy Service, to provide advice on underground rly planning, construction, operation, etc. to overseas clients. Became LTI, London Transport International Services Ltd, a wholly owned subsidiary of LTE (*2*), in 1976. Dissolved 1992.

LTM
1. *London Transport Magazine*, replaced *Pennyfare* (qv), 1947. Ceased publication 1973, replaced by LTN (qv).
2. London Transport Museum, Covent Garden, London, opened 1980 in the former Flower Market building, replacing the London Transport Collection, Syon Park, Chiswick, opened in 1973. Interior rebuilt and rearranged 1994 and 2005–6. Title altered to London's Transport Museum in 2000 after formation of TfL (qv) which then became its parent body. *See also* Depot, The.

LTN
LT News, the LT staff newspaper, published fortnightly, 1973–84, renamed *LRT News*, 1984, published four-weekly from 1987, name reverted to *LTN*, 1990. Ceased 1995. *See OTM.*

LTP
London Transport Police, formed 1934 to assume duties of former Metropolitan Rly and MDR police. Part of BTCP, 1948.

LTPC
London Transport Passengers' Committee, formed 1970. Became LRPC (qv), 1984.

LTS Rail
A TOU (qv), 1994, operating services over lines of former LT&SR (qv). A TOC (*2*) (qv) 1996, branded as C2C (qv) from 1999.

LTUC
London Transport Users Committee; replaced LRPC (qv) from 2000, with remit to represent users of all forms of public transport and taxis in the Greater London area following formation of TfL (qv); funded by TfL.

Luas (Ire)
A light rail scheme for the Dublin area, first section opened 2004. (Luas = speed in Gaelic.)

Lufthansa Express
A special service for air passengers operated between Frankfurt Airport station and Düsseldorf 1982–93.

Luftseilbahn (Ger)
An aerial cableway (also known as a *Seilschewebebahn*). *See* Aerial Rlys.

Luggage First/Second/Third/Composite
Alternative term for locker (qv).

Luggage boxes (obs)
Containers for transporting passengers' luggage which could be transferred easily

between rly wagons and ships for rail-sea-rail journeys.

Luggage train (obs)
Early (1830s/1840s) term for a goods train.

Luigis (AusRS)
Australian rly track maintenance workers. From their predominantly Italian origin.

Luis de Camoes
A *TALGO* day express between Lisbon and Madrid, introduced 1989.

LUL
London Underground Ltd, formed 1985 as a subsidiary trading company of LRT, as required by London Regional Transport Act, 1984. Popularly known as 'the Underground' or (less correctly) as 'the Tube' (qv). Came under the control of the Mayor of London and TfL (qv) from 15 July 2003. *See also* PPP.

Lunar lights
A form of route indicator used in combination with colour-light signals at junctions, in which a series of white lights are aligned at 45, 90 or 135 degrees to left or right, according to the direction of divergence, to inform the driver which route has been set up by the signalman for his train. From their whiteness.

Lunatic line
The Uganda Rly (Mombasa–Lake Victoria) 1901, so-called from a reference in a verse by Henry du Pré Labouchère in his journal *Truth*: 'It clearly is nought but a lunatic line'.

Lune Valley line
Clapham–Kirkby Lonsdale–Low Gill.

Lung (USRS)
1. A drawbar.
2. The main line air hose.

Lung doctor/jerker/specialist (USRS)
A heavy-handed loco driver apt to strain or even pull out drawbars.

LUR
Lancashire Union Rlys, inc 1864, opened 1868, St Helens–Haigh Junc–White Bear [Adlington]/Wigan and Chorley–Cherry Tree [near Blackburn]. Passengers 1869. Part of L&NWR from 1883 but Boar's Head–White Bear and Chorley–Cherry

Tree were joint L&NWR and L&YR from opening in 1868 (under an Act of 1865) until 1921.

Lurry (obs)
A manually-propelled wagon used by platelayers to carry materials, etc.

LURS
London Underground Railway Society, founded 1961 for those interested in the history and operations of the LT rlys. Publishes UN (qv).

Lusitania Express
A night service between Madrid and Lisbon, introduced 1943.

Lusso, treno (It)(obs)
A luxury fast train with double supplementary fare.

Lutetia
An express between Geneva and Milan, introduced 1981. Name used for Paris–Lausanne (connections at Geneva for Milan) *TGV* 1984.

Luxe, trains de (Fr)(obs)
Important fast trains with superior accommodation, usually *CIWL* restaurant/sleeping/Pullman cars, and normally restricted to First class passengers.

Luxor Express
A *CIWL* train between Cairo and Luxor, introduced 1898.

LV
1. The Last Vehicle of a train. *See also* Last vehicle indicator.
2. A Luggage Van.

LVR
1. Lambourn Valley Rly, Newbury–Lambourn, inc 1883, opened 1898. Part of GWR 1905.
2. Llynvi Valley Rly, Nantyffyllon–Bridgend/Porthcawl, inc 1846. Acquired Duffryn, Llynvi & Porthcawl Rly (a 4 ft 7 in/1,397 mm gauge tramroad opened 1829) and Bridgend Rly (a 4 ft 7 in/1,397 mm gauge tramroad opened 1834, Bridgend to the former near Tondu). Re-inc 1855 with powers to operate as an ordinary steam rly. Opened as conventional steam rly (7 ft/2,134 mm gauge) 1861 (Tondu–Porthcawl was mixed broad and standard gauge, the

latter used by OVR trains); passengers 1865. Amalgamated with OVR 1866 to form L&OR (qv) and by 1868 mixed gauge track had been laid throughout on the former LVR.

3. (US) Lehigh Valley RR.

LWR/LWT

Long Welded Rails/Track, in which unit lengths, usually 60 ft/18.28 metres, are welded together in lengths of up to half a mile/0.8 km. *See also* CWR.

Lyntog

Lightning Trains. Diesel-electric expresses introduced by the Danish State Rlys in 1935.

Lynton & Barnstaple Rly

See L&BR (5).

Lyonnais, le

TEE Paris–Lyon, introduced 1969 with 3 h 47 min schedule. Lost *TEE* status 1976.

LZB (Ger)

Linienzugbeinflussung; an ATP (qv) system used on *DB* lines authorized for high-speed running.

L-Zug (Ger)(obs)

Luxuszug; a first class only luxury train on *DR*.

M

M

1. Motor car in a mu train set.

2. MTA (qv).

3. Worldwide symbol used on maps and signs, etc. for Metro (1) (qv).

Ma and Pa, The (USRS)

The Maryland & Pennsylvania RR (USA).

Mac (RS)

Machinery truck (qv).

Macarthur (US)

Term for a steam loco with 2–8–2 wheel arrangement, used in the WW2 (and named after the famous US general in preference to the Japanese term *Mikado* (qv)). Name also used for USA-built 2–8–2 locos supplied in WW2 to narrow gauge rlys in India and Far East.

Macaw

GWR TC for various kinds of bolster truck for carrying rails, timber, etc.

Machinery truck

A low-floor wagon for carrying agricultural and other machinery.

Machine-tender (Fr)

Tank loco.

Mackerel

A 17-ton hopper ballast wagon used by engineers.

MacRats (RS)

BR locos class 26/27.

Mac turbos (RS)

Class 170/4 demu (qv) introduced on Scotrail (qv) services, 1999.

Madhouse (USRS)

The loco foreman's office.

Madras Rly

See MSM.

Maggies (RS)

Magnetic brakes; actuated by magnetic attraction induced between the brake and rail surface, mainly used on tramways (3) (qv).

Magistral

Polish and USSR term for a high capacity main line, especially when newly built or newly upgraded.

Maglev

Magnetic levitation transit system. In use between Birmingham Airport and BR's Birmingham International station 1984–95. Under development for high-speed inter-city links in Japan. A 19-mile, 267 mph line between Shanghai and its airport was opened in 2003.

Magnets, to drop the (RS)

Sudden application of magnetic brakes on a tramcar, causing them to clamp quickly on to the rails.

Magnificent Seven (RS)

A crew of dining car stewards.

Magrini roof (obs)

A roof for double-deck tramcars (qv) with a cover which could be folded away entirely in good weather, converting the tram to the open-top design. Patented in 1902 by Bonomo Magrini of Liverpool.

Mahogany, on the (RS)

On the cushions (qv).

Maidens & Dunure

see M&DLR.

Mail Rail

Line name for PO Rly (qv).

Main, the (RS)

The principal through passenger line between any two points.

Main iron (USRS)

see Main line.

Main line

To a rlyman this term means any tracks
on which trains run between given points,
as distinct from sidings, yards, etc. In a
wider sense, it signifies the principal
tracks between major cities and towns,
on which the fastest trains run, as
distinct from other parallel tracks and
branch and suburban lines.

Main line company/rlys

Until 1948, a rly company/system handling
all types of business, passenger and freight,
on a significant scale, over, say, more than
100 route miles, e.g. the four 'grouped'
companies of 1923–47 LM&SR, L&NER,
GWR, SR.

Mainline Freight Ltd

A freight operating company of BR formed
from Trainload Freight South East,
preparatory to sale to private sector,
1994. *See* EWS.

Main pin (USRS)

A high-ranking rly official.

Main signals

Another term for Running signals (qv).

Main stem (USRS)

A principal trunk line, a main line.

Main tracker (USRS)

A long distance service, calling only at
principal stations.

Maintrain

A rolling stock maintenance co. under the
joint control of Midland Mainline and
Central Trains, and owned by National
Express Group plc (qv).

Mak (Ger)

Maschinenbau Kiel; a Krupp company
manufacturing rly locos.

Make a joint, to (USRS)

To couple wagons or coaches.

Make a road, to

Setting up points and signals over a certain
route for a train approaching a signal box
or signal control area.

Malles des Indes (Fr)

Indian Mail; the popular and unofficial
name for service from Calais (connecting
with Dover sailings) to Marseilles and later

to Brindisi (connecting with P&O Line
sailings at both the latter ports). Operated
from 1852, passengers carried from 1880.
Replaced by Peninsular Express (qv) 1890.

Mallet

A steam loco with a single boiler but two
sets of coupled driving wheels, the rear set
rigidly mounted to the main frame, the
other jointed to the main frame. At first
Mallets were usually compounds (qv) with
low pressure cylinders in the front unit.
The design was patented in 1884 by
Anatole Mallet (1837–1919) and was
highly-developed in the US, culminating in
the 540-ton Union Pacific 'Big Boy'
4–8–8–4 type, of 1941–4, the world's
largest and heaviest steam locomotives.

Maltese Cross train (obs)

The first partially fitted freight trains on
the L&NWR (qv), with a minimum fitted
head (qv) of four wagons. Introduced 1912
and so-called from the symbol used to
distinguish them in the working timetable
(qv). The classification continued under
the LM&SR (qv) and BR (1) until 1950.

MAN (Ger)

Maschinenfabrik–Augsburg–Nürnberg AG;
loco builders since 1840.

Manchester Pullman

Express between London (Euston) and
Manchester (Piccadilly) introduced 1966
with new purpose-built Pullman cars. By
1978 it was the last traditional Pullman
service in Britain. Ceased 1985, but the
cars were retained for charter service. The
Pullman name thereafter was applied by
BR to 'Executive' trains using standard
First class stock.

Manchurian Express

see Trans-Manchurian Express.

Mancunian

Express between London (Euston) and
Manchester, introduced 1927, restored
1949. Name dropped 1966.

M&BR

Manchester & Birmingham Rly, inc 1837,
opened Manchester–Stockport–Crewe,
1840, 1842, part of L&NWR 1846.

M&CR

Maryport & Carlisle Rly, inc 1837, first

section opened 1840, completed 1845; part of LM&SR from 1923.

M&DJR
Malton & Driffield Junction Rly, inc 1846, opened 1853, part of NER 1854, closed 1958.

M&DLR
Maidens & Dunure Light Rly, Alloway Junction (near Ayr)–Dunure–Girvan, LRO 1899, G&SWR, opened 1906, last section closed 1968.

M&DRJC
Metropolitan & District Rlys Joint Committee, managing joint section Mansion House to Aldgate/St Mary's, 1879–1932.

M&EE
Mechanical & Electrical Engineers' [Department].

M&ER
Midland & Eastern Rly, inc 1866, an amalgamation of the Spalding & Bourne and Lynn & Sutton Bridge Rlys. Leased Norwich & Spalding Rly, which it absorbed in 1877. Part of E&MR 1883.

M&G
Mountain & Gibson Ltd, Bury, manufacturers of tramcar trucks in the Elton Fold Works which had been set up in 1902 by McGuire Manufacturing Co. of Chicago, exploiting the McGuire designs. Also built complete works cars. Ceased production *c.* 1908, but Mountain & Gibson Truck & Engineering Co. Ltd continued to supply truck parts until *c.* 1915.

M&GNJC
Midland & Great Northern Joint Committee, inc 1893, to take over existing E&MR (qv). Bourne–Kings Lynn–Yarmouth; Peterborough–Sutton Bridge; branches to Norwich and Cromer from Melton Constable. Joint Midland and GNR 1893–1922, LM&SR & L&NER 1923–47. Worked by L&NER from 1936. BR (E) from 1948. *See also* N&SJRC.

M&MR
Manchester & Milford Rly. This company, inc 1860, aimed to complete a direct rail link between Manchester and the port of

Milford Haven by constructing a line between Llanidloes and Pencader, north of Carmarthen. An Aberystwyth branch was authorized in 1865 and the line between Aberystwyth and Pencader was opened in 1866 and 1867; this was leased to the GWR in 1906 and vested in the GWR in 1911. The remaining section of the 'main line', between Llanidloes and Strata Florida, completed only between the Mid-Wales line and Llangurig, was never used for public traffic.

M&SDR
Moretonhampstead & South Devon Rly, Moretonhampstead to Newton Abbot, inc 1862, worked by SDR, opened 1866. Part of GWR 1872.

M&SMR
Madras & Southern Mahratta Rly, India, formed 1852, taken over by Government 1907.

M&StJWR
Metropolitan & Saint John's Wood Rly, inc 1864, Baker St. to Finchley Road, branch Swiss Cottage to Hampstead authorized 1865 but never built. Opened 1868 and worked by Metropolitan Rly. Vested in Metropolitan Rly, 1882.

M&SWJR
1. Midland & South Western Junction Rly, Cricklewood to Acton Wells Junction, London; inc 1864 as Finchley, Willesden & Acton Rly (M&SW Junction), opened 1868, freight only, Cricklewood–Acton section only. Absorbed by Midland Rly 1874. Sometimes known as the 'old' M&SWJR, to avoid confusion with M&SWJR (*2*).
2. Midland & South Western Junction Rly, Andoversford–Cirencester–Swindon–Marlborough–Andover, inc 1884, first section opened (as Swindon, Marlborough & Andover Rly) 1881, part of GWR from 1923.

Mangle (RS)
A manual drilling machine.

Mankillers (RS)
GWR 47XX 2–8–0 locos.

Mania, The
see Railway Mania.

Manifest

List of vehicles in a train, also (USRS) a redball (qv).

Manifold Valley

see L&MVLR.

Manned conditional

A development of Q services (qv) in which locos and crews are booked for trains which run, as required by traffic, to one or more possible alternative destinations as shown in the working timetable.

Manned/Manual level crossings

A generic term for level crossings of roads at which the gate/s or barriers are operated locally by a signaller, crossing keeper (qv) or train crew. *See also* Local Control Unit; MCB; MG; TCO.

Manning Wardle

Manning, Wardle & Co. Ltd, Boyne Engine Works, Hunslet, Leeds, loco builders from 1858. Became part of Kitsons (qv), 1927. *See also* LH Plant Engineering Co.

Man of Kent

Express between London (Charing Cross) and Folkestone, Dover, Deal, Sandwich, and Margate, introduced 1953, ceased on electrification of the route, 1961.

Mansell wheel

A wheel consisting of a wooden disc or segments forced inside a heated iron or steel tyre by hydraulic pressure, patented 1848, 1862 and 1866 by R.C. Mansell, Carriage & Wagon Superintendent SER. Widely used in Britain, where it delayed the introduction of track-circuiting. Also loosely used for any type of solid, spokeless wheel.

Mansfield Rly

Kirkby (junction with GCR main line London to Sheffield) via Mansfield to Clipstone, junction with former LD&ECR Chesterfield–Lincoln line. Opened 1913–17, worked by GCR, part of L&NER from 1923.

Mansion House Tanks

L&NWR 2–4–2T of the 1880s used for services over the MDR and certain suburban lines.

Manta

A 14-ton unfitted wagon 62 ft long, used by engineers.

Man trap (RS)

Catch points (qv).

Manumotive (obs)

Hand-propelled rail trolley used by permanent way staff.

Manxman

Summer-only express between London (Euston) and Liverpool, in connection with sailings to and from Isle of Man, introduced 1927, restored 1951. Name dropped 1966.

Many Short Jerks & Always Ready; Many Short Jerks & Away

Nicknames for MSJ&AR.

Manzoni

EC service between Zurich and Milan via Gotthard route, introduced 1989.

Maple Leaf

Montreal–Chicago service of CNR, introduced 1927, ceased 1971. Name now used for Amtrak Toronto–Chicago service.

MARC (US)

Maryland Rail Corporation.

Marcher à vue (Fr)

To drive a train on sight only, vigilant for any obstructions on the line ahead. *See also* Permissive block, Permissive working, Smoking in.

Marches Line

BR brand name for Shrewsbury–Hereford–Newport services.

Marco Polo

Rome–Venice–Trieste/Udine service, introduced 1977.

Mare Nostrum

Day service between Port Bou and Valencia/Alicante, introduced 1966.

Margin

1. Time allowance required for a slower train to precede a faster one on the same track to avoid impairing the running of the fast train.

2. (obs) A term formerly used in north-east England for a wheel flange.

Margining

Regulation of train running by signal staff by reference to margins (qv).

MARIE

Mass Transit Rail Initiative for Europe. An EC-sponsored project supported by UITP (qv) and *UNIFE* (qv) investigating standardization, harmonization, etc. in mass transit (qv) products across Europe.

Markers (USRS)

Lamps or flags attached to the front (head) and the last vehicle of a train. White head end markers denote an extra train, green head end markers indicate that the train has been split and a second section is following.

Märklin

The pioneer commercial manufacturers of model rly equipment (from 1890). Based since 1900 at Göppingen, Germany.

Marlin

A 14-ton bogie wagon 67 ft long, used by engineers.

Marmara Express

Belgrade–Istanbul service, 1967–77, carrying through cars between Paris and Istanbul off the Direct Orient Express (qv) also through cars Munich–Istanbul off the Tauern Orient Express (qv).

Maroc Express

Paris–Algeciras–Casablanca rail/ship service, 1948–52.

Marquis of Londonderry's Rly

see LR (5).

Marshalling

The breaking up of freight train formations and the subsequent sorting of wagons into train loads for final destination, carried out in a marshalling or sorting yard.

Marshalling yard

A complex of sidings in which marshalling (qv) takes place. Usually divided into arrival sidings, main yard and departure sidings. The first was built at Edge Hill, Liverpool by the L&NWR, 1875–82. Later yards incorporated refinements such as humps (qv), control towers and wagon retarders/accelerators (qv).

Marshlink

Brand name for the Ashford–Hastings line.

Mars light (USRS)

An oscillating head end or tail end light.

Marston Vale Line

Brand name for the Bletchley–Bedford services of Silverlink (qv).

MARTA

Metropolitan Atlanta Rapid Transit Authority. An integrated bus and rail system within the boundaries of Atlanta (USA) and its adjacent counties.

Mary Rose, The

A London (Waterloo)–Portsmouth Harbour service, so named 1988–92.

Marys (RS) (obs)

Class 405 emus, originally known as 4-SUBs (qv). After the long-bodied RAF road vehicles known as 'Queen Marys' from the liner of that name in view of their great length.

MAS

Multiple-Aspect Signalling [scheme]. Area scheme for colour-light signalling, usually connected to one control centre. *See also* Multi-aspect signal.

Mass transit (US)

Urban/suburban public transport by rail and road.

Mast

The vertical pole supporting the trolley boom (qv) of a tramcar.

Master/Master of the Cars (USRS)

A conductor (*3*).

Master Cutler

Express between London (Marylebone) and Sheffield (Victoria), so named 1947, operated as an all-Pullman service from Kings Cross to Sheffield (Victoria) from 1958. Pullman service ceased 1968 and London terminus changed to St Pancras. Renamed Master Cutler Pullman, 1987.

Master Maniac (USRS)

A master mechanic.

Master Room

Accommodation on US long-distance trains from *c*. 1940, comprising an apartment with four movable armchairs for day use and two beds, one longitudinal, one transverse, also an en suite lavatory/wc and shower.

Mastodon

Originally a US term for steam locos with 4–8–0 wheel arrangement but later applied to those with 4–10–0 wheel arrangement.

Matchboxes (RS)

GWR 57XX 0–6–0 pannier tanks. From their appearance.

Match dials, to (USRS)

To compare or synchronize watches.

Match truck

1. A wagon with a dual set of buffers at each end which can be placed to run between two others having buffers and draw gear at varying heights.
2. Any wagon placed beneath an overhanging freight load or crane on an adjoining vehicle. *See also* Runner wagon.

Mate (obs)

Another word for ganger.

Mather & Platt

Suppliers of electric traction equipment, formed by William Mather and John Platt; limited co. 1892; now part of Wormald International.

Matisa ®

Brand name for a self-propelled tamping machine, *see* Tamp.

Matterhorn

EC service Frankfurt–Brig, introduced 1989.

Maul [her], to (USRS)

To work a steam loco at full stroke and full throttle.

Maurice Ravel

EC service Paris–Munich, introduced 1989.

MAV

Magyar Allamvasutak; Hungarian State Rlys. 7,608 km.

MAX

Light rail system in Portland (Oregon) USA; first part opened 1987.

Maximum traction truck

A type of tramcar truck which has one motored axle with large wheels and an unmotored pony axle with smaller wheels. A variation is the 'reversed maximum traction truck' with the smaller wheels facing towards each end of the car.

Mayflower

Express between London (Paddington) and Plymouth, introduced 1957. Name dropped 1965, revived 1970. Name dropped 1971, revived 1984, dropped 1985.

Mayfly

GWR TC for well truck used to transport large electrical transformers.

Maze, the (RS)

Clapham Junction.

M-bahn (Ger)

A version of Maglev (qv).

MB&MR

Macclesfield, Bollington & Marple Rly, inc 1864, opened 1869, 1870, 1871, 1873, vested jointly in MS&LR and NSR 1871, GCR & NSR 1897, L&NER and LM&SR 1923–47.

MBC

BR Motor Brake Composite coach.

MBCL

As MBC (qv) but with Lavatory.

MBM&MJR

Manchester, Buxton, Matlock & Midland Junction Rly, inc 1846, opened Rowsley to Ambergate 1849. Leased jointly by L&NWR and Midland 1852. Rowsley–Buxton completed by Midland 1863. Part of Midland Rly 1871.

MBRSM

Motor Brake Refreshment Standard class coach with Modular layout, BR.

MBS

Motor Brake Second/Standard class, BR.

MBSL

As MBS (qv) but with Lavatory.

MBSO

BR Motor Brake Second/Standard class Open coach.

MBTA

Massachusetts Bay Transportation Authority, controlling the rly passenger system in the Boston area (USA).

MC

1. Motor Composite (First and Second/Standard class) coach, BR.
2. Movement Control, British Army staff in charge of traffic forwarding, including rail traffic. *See also* RTO.

MCB

1. (US) Master Car Builders' Association, later the Mechanical Division of the AAR (qv).
2. A Miniature Circuit Breaker.
3. (US) A form of automatic coupler approved as a US standard by (*1*).
4. (US) A form of truck recommended by (*1*) for passenger stock. Known in Europe as the Pennsylvania bogie/truck.

5. Manually Controlled Barriers, a level crossing with manually worked gates moved across the roadway or across the railway.
6. Manually controlled full-width barriers/gates at a level crossing with manned signal box or a gate box (qv).

MCC

A MCB (qv) or MG (qv) level crossing equipped with cctv.

McGuire

McGuire Manufacturing Co., Chicago producers of car trucks/bogies from 1888, later builders of rly, tramway (3) and interurban cars and other rolling stock. Name changed subsequently to McGuire-Cummings Manufacturing Co., then Cummings Car & Coach Co. Vehicle production ceased 1930, parts business continued until 1943. *See also* M&G.

McKenzie & Holland

A Worcester firm manufacturing signalling equipment from the 1860s, absorbed J.F. Pease & Co.'s signalling interests in 1901, amalgamated with Westinghouse Brake Co. *c.* 1907 to form McKenzie, Holland & Westinghouse Power Signalling Co. *See also* Consolidated Signal Co.

MCL

As MC (1) (qv) but with Lavatory.

MCO

Mutual Change Over; a mutually agreed exchange of duties.

MCR

Midland Counties Rly, inc 1836, Nottingham to Derby, and Nottingham to Leicester and Rugby, opened 1839, 1840. Part of Midland Rly from 1844.

MCT

Maritime Container Terminal.

MCTA

Metropolitan Commuter Transportation Authority [for the New York area], formed 1965 to take over the Long Island RR and assume control of NYCTA (qv), the Manhattan & Bronx Surface Transit Operating Authority, the Triborough Bridge & Tunnel Authority and Staten Island Rapid Transit. MTA (qv), from 1968.

MCW

Metropolitan Carriage & Wagon Co., Saltley, Birmingham, originally established in 1835 by Joseph Wright, later known as Joseph Wright & Sons. MCW established 1862, renamed Metropolitan Amalgamated Railway Carriage & Wagon Co. 1902, after merger with Ashbury (qv), Brown, Marshalls (qv), Lancaster (qv) and Oldbury (qv). Renamed Metropolitan Carriage, Wagon & Finance Co. 1912. Wholly owned subsidiary of Vickers Ltd, 1919. Became Metro-Cammell (qv) in 1929. Builders of rly coaches, wagons and tramcars. *See also* MV.

MD&HB

Mersey Docks & Harbour Board; operated docks lines at Liverpool and Birkenhead which were also used by L&NWR and GCR (LM&SR and L&NER from 1923, BR from 1948). Last lines closed 1973.

MDET

Metropolitan District Electric Traction Co. Formed 1901 to erect and equip Lots Road Power Station, London, and supply funds for the electrification of the MDR. Largely US-financed; taken over by UERL (qv), 1902.

MDM (obs)

A form of route-setting (qv) with hydro-pneumatic powered interlocking (qv), mainly used in France from *c.* 1910, known by the initials of the names of the inventors, Moutier, Dumartin and Monard. The aim was to eliminate point levers in power signalling (qv) installations and to set complete routes (qv) by the operation of a single lever (*le minimum de manoeuvre avec le maximum de mouvement*).

M-door (LT)

Door at front of driving cab allowing access to track.

MDR

Metropolitan District Rly, inc 1864, first section South Kensington to Westminster Bridge, opened 1868. Extended to serve Hammersmith, Ealing, Putney, Hounslow and other western suburbs and owned Whitechapel & Bow Rly jointly with LTSR, which gave it access to Barking and Upminster. 28 route miles by 1914. Part of LPTB from 1933.

Meat run (USRS)
An express freight train for perishables.

Mechanical signalling
Signalling operated solely by movement of manual levers in a lever frame (qv).

Mediolanum
TEE Milan–Munich, via Brenner Pass, introduced 1957. Lost *TEE* status 1984. Replaced by Leonardo da Vinci (qv), 1987.

Medloc
Acronym for Mediterranean Line of Communication, British Army rail service between Italy, South of France and French Channel ports to carry returning servicemen from the Mediterranean countries and Middle East after both World Wars. After WW2, the trains were composed mainly of ex-*DR* and *FS* stock but some British coaches were also used. Name later transferred to Villach–Hook of Holland trains used by British Army of Occupation in Austria.

Medway Valley Line
BR brand name for Strood–Maidstone–Paddock Wood.

Meet/meet order (US)
A planned crossing of two trains at a loop on a long section of single line and the train order specifying this.

Mega-wedged (RS)
An extremely overcrowded train.

Meitetsu
Nagoya Rly (Japan).

MEL
see Merseyrail.

Melon
GWR TC for bogie or six-wheel brake van with Third class seating (six types).

Memling
TEE Paris–Brussels, 1974–84. Name used for EC service between Ostend and Frankfurt, 1987.

Mendip Rail
A pool of roadstone wagons and dedicated locos operated by Foster Yeoman Ltd and ARC (qv) from 1993. Operated as FOC (qv) from 2000.

Mentor
Mobile Electrical Network Tester and Observation Recorder, BR, 1972. A coach used to inspect overhead line equipment under operating conditions and to monitor performance of electric circuits in locos and emus.

Meon Valley
The former L&SWR line from Alton to Fareham.

MER

1. Manx Electric Rly, Douglas to Ramsey, inc 1893 as Douglas & Laxey Coast Electric Tramway Ltd, 3 ft/914 mm gauge, opened 1893, 1894, 1898 and 1899. Renamed Isle of Man Tramways & Electric Power Co. Ltd 1894. MER (inc 1902), took over the undertaking from the IMTEP liquidator. System includes the Snaefell Mountain Rly (SMR), Laxey to Snaefell Summit, electrically worked, 3 ft 6 in/1,067 mm gauge, with Fell (qv) centre rail, opened 1895. Purchased by Manx Government, 1957.

2. Millwall Extension Rly, authorized 1865, Millwall Junction (L&BR) to North Greenwich, opened 1871, 1872. Some sections were owned by Blackwall Rly, the remainder by dock companies. Passenger services ceased 1926. In 1929 the new lock entrance from Blackwall Reach severed the line. The southern part is now used by the DLR (qv).

3. Mersey Electric Rly, alternative title for MR (*7*).

Merchandise peddler [pedlar] (USRS)
Way freight train (qv).

Merchants Limited
Express between New York and Boston, introduced 1903 on 5 h schedule. 4 h 15 min in 1940. Coach class included from 1949. Now an Amtrak day train Boston–New York–Washington DC.

Merchants' Rly
Another name for the Portland Rly. *See* PR (6).

Merchant Venturer
Express between London (Paddington), Bath, Bristol and Weston-super-Mare, so named 1951. Name dropped 1965, revived 1984. Name dropped 1986.

Meridians
Class 221 dmu (qv) trains introduced by Midland Mainline (qv) 2005.

Merkur

TEE Stuttgart–Copenhagen, introduced 1974. Lost *TEE* status 1978, became IC Copenhagen–Karlsruhe; diverted to Frankfurt 1985, EC from 1987.

Merlin Rail

A TOC (2) (qv) without locos or rolling stock (these obtained on a spot hire basis) but employing train crews to operate charter (qv) train services. Merged with Fragonset (qv) 2004 to become FM Rail (qv).

Mermaid

TC for 14-ton tipping ballast wagon.

Merry-go-round

1. MGR (qv).

2. (USRS) A loco turntable.

3. (USRS) A telegraph circuit.

Merrymakers (obs)

BR (M) brand name for excursions, introduced 1971.

Mersey Loop and Link

Terminal loop opened 1977 beneath the centre of Liverpool, James St.–Moorfields–Lime St.–Central–James St. for the Mersey/Wirral lines together with a new underground link between Central and Moorfields for the Southport/Ormskirk/Kirkby–Garston–Hunts Cross electric services, with interchange at Central.

Merseyrail/Merseyrail Electrics Ltd

Merseyrail was the brand name introduced by BR in 1971 for the third rail electric local passenger services it operated for the Merseyside PTA (qv) in the Liverpool/Wirral area (Merseyside county). The operation became a TOU (qv) in 1994 and a TOC (2) (qv), Merseyrail Electrics Ltd, in 1997. Franchise held by Arriva Trains Merseyside 2000 (*see* Arriva). Franchise to new TOC formed by Serco (qv) 2003.

Merseyside Express

Service between London (Euston) and Liverpool (Lime St.), introduced 1928, a renaming of the 1927 London–Merseyside Express. Restored 1949. Name dropped 1966.

Merseyside Pullman

Partly Pullman service between London

(Euston) and Liverpool, introduced 1985, replacing Liverpool Executive (qv).

Merseytram

Light rail (qv) system for Liverpool area. First section City Centre–Kirkby (18.5 km) to open 2009.

Merseytravel

Brand name for Merseyside PTE (qv).

Met

Brand name of the electric urban and suburban rlys of Melbourne, Australia.

Met, The

Abbreviation semi-officially adopted by the Metropolitan Rly [London] about 1914, but see also Metro (*2*). Since 1933, the popular abbreviation for the Metropolitan Line of London Transport. Also an abbreviation for the Metropolitan Electric Tramways (London, 1902–33), but pronounced 'Emmetee' to avoid confusion with the Met Rly.

Metadyne

An invention of Professor Pestarini, involving a complicated system of traction motor control for electric trains, in which a rotary converter is arranged to supply current exactly equivalent to the effort required. Tested by the LPTB on ex-Metropolitan stock running on the Inner Circle in 1934–5, it eliminated resistances and thus saved wasted current. Deceleration was mainly effected by enabling the motors to return current to the line, thus saving brake wear. Fifty-eight two-car and nineteen six-car metadyne-fitted trains were placed in service on the Metropolitan and Hammersmith & City lines in 1937–8, but in the postwar period maintenance of this stock became very expensive and difficult due to shortage of skilled staff, and from 1955 the cars were converted to PCM control (qv).

Metal Mickey (RS)

An emergency speed restriction warning board. *See also* Zebra board.

Metals

Rails/track.

Met&GC Joint

Harrow to Chesham, Aylesbury and

Verney Junction. This section of the
Metropolitan Rly was leased to the
Metropolitan & GCR Joint Committee
1906–33. LPTB & L&NER Joint 1933–47,
became part of LTE 1948–50. Amersham
to Aylesbury passed to BR from 1961–2.

Met&L&NER Joint
Watford branch, opened 1925, L&NER
passenger trains withdrawn 1926. Became
part of LTE 1948–50.

Météor (Fr)
A new high-capacity underground rly
across the centre of Paris from south-east to
north-west, linking the Cité Universitaire to
la Porte Genevilliers, served by driverless
trains and totally automated. Opened
1998.

Meterspur (Ger)
1,000 mm gauge.

Met gang (RS)(obs)
The regular Metropolitan Link at Kings
Cross (GNR/L&NER/BR) depot,
responsible for working suburban services.

Methley Joint
Joint Committee of GNR, L&YR and NER
set up in 1864 to work a line between
Lofthouse GNR and Methley L&YR,
opened 1865, passengers 1869. Worked by
GNR. GNR, NER and L&NWR 1922.
LM&SR and L&NER 1923–47, BR 1948.

Metra
The operator of commuter rail services in
the Chicago region.

Métrazur
Métro Côte d'Azur, a regular interval
service between Cannes, Nice, Monaco
and Menton, introduced 1970.

Metro
1. In recent years this term (an
   abbreviation of 'metropolitan rly') has
   come to be accepted almost as *lingua
   franca*, for urban rail systems, normally
   'heavy' as distinct from light rail, usually
   including substantial underground
   sections and operating over a number of
   self-contained, elaborately-signalled
   lines, carrying the heaviest traffic and
   using rly-type rolling stock, although
   normally independent of conventional
   main line rail systems. Absolute ticket
   control at entry and/or exit is another
   distinguishing feature. Examples include
   London Underground, the Paris *Métro*,
   and the Moscow Metro. *See also U-bahn.*
2. An abbreviation officially adopted by
   the Metropolitan Rly [London] in 1920.
3. An abbreviation for Metro Trains (qv).
4. Brand name for West Yorkshire PTE
   (qv).

M-e-t-r-o-b-u-s
Light rail and bus network serving Rouen,
France, opened 1994.

Metro–Cammell
Name used after the 1929 merger of MCW
(qv) and Cammell Laird car building
activities as the Metropolitan-Cammell
Carriage, Wagon & Finance Co. Ltd. Full
title altered to Metropolitan-Cammell
Carriage & Wagon Co. Ltd, 1934,
Metropolitan-Cammell Ltd from 1965, with
car building concentrated at Washwood
Heath, Birmingham. Absorbed Cravens
(qv) 1965. Part of GEC-Alsthom, 1989.

Metro de Madrid
Madrid's underground rly system, first
section opened 1919. *See also MetroSur.*

Métro des Pyrénées, le (Fr)
see Cerdagne, la ligne de.

Metro gnome (LTRS)
Driver on LT Metropolitan Line.

Metro-land
A term officially adopted by the
Metropolitan Rly from 1915 to describe
the residential and country areas it served.
Popular use lingered after the formation of
the LPTB (qv) in 1933.

Metroliner
Fast emu service between New York and
Washington DC, introduced 1969.

Metrolink
1. Light rapid transit system in
   Manchester, first section
   Altrincham–Piccadilly–Victoria–Bury,
   partly in streets, but mostly over former
   BR lines, opened 1992. Extended to
   Eccles, 1999/2000.
2. A light rail system in the St Louis area,
   USA.

Métrolor (Fr)
Local electric service Nancy–Metz–

Thionville, introduced 1970. The pioneer *TER* (*1*) (qv) service.

Metronet

A consortium (Atkins, Balfour Beatty, Bombardier Transportation, Seeboard and Thames Water) accepted 2003 as Infraco (qv) under the PPP (qv) for the Bakerloo (qv), Central (qv), Victoria (qv), Waterloo & City (*see* W&CR), Metropolitan (*see* Metropolitan (1)), District (qv), Hammersmith & City (qv) and East London (*see* ELR (3)) lines of the London Underground.

Metro–North

Passenger rail operator in the Hudson, Harlem and Connecticut areas around New York, under contract to MTA (qv).

Metropolis

The *FS* (qv) subsidiary owning all real estate not in use for rly purposes.

Metropolitan

1. Metropolitan Rly [London], inc 1853 as North Metropolitan Rly, name changed 1854. First section opened 1863, Paddington–Farringdon Street, the world's first urban underground rly. Extended to South Kensington and Aldgate, operating the Inner Circle with the MDR, and also to Harrow/Uxbridge, Chesham, Amersham, Aylesbury and Verney Junction, 66 route miles by 1914. Operated freight and parcels traffic and claimed to be a main line company. Part of LPTB from 1933.
2. Metropolitan Railway Carriage & Wagon Co. Ltd: *see* MCW.

Metropolitan (Ger)

A special-fare luxury service between Köln and Hamburg, introduced 1999.

Metropolitan [City] Widened Lines

see City Widened Lines.

Metrorail

The operator of suburban rail services in Cape Town, Port Elizabeth, East London and three other urban areas in South Africa; subsidized by the government.

MetroSur

Self-contained wholly underground 28-station circle line of the Madrid Metro system, opened 2003.

Metro tanks (RS)

GWR 2–4–0T, originally introduced 1869. Fitted with condensing gear to enable them to be run over the Metropolitan (*1*), hence the name.

Metro Trains

BR services operated for West Yorkshire PTA.

Metrotramvia

Light rail (qv) services, partly over existing tram tracks, in Milan region from 2003.

Metrovias

Operator (with *Trainmet* (qv)) of suburban rly services in Buenos Aires. Also operator of *Subte* (qv).

Metrovick

see MV.

Mets (RS)(obs)

Freight and parcels trains working to and from main lines over the City Widened Lines between Kings Cross/St Pancras and Farringdon (London).

Mex

GWR TC for cattle wagon.

MEZ (Ger)

Mittel Europäische Zeit; Middle European Time.

MG

Manual Gates; a level crossing with gates manually operated by a rly employee. *See also* Manned/Manual level crossings; TCO.

MGB

Matterhorn Gotthard Bahn; a 2003 merger of *BvZ* (*Brig-Visp Zermatt Bahn*) and *FO* (*Furka Oberalp Bahn*), the route of the Glacier Express (qv).

MGR

Merry-go-round. A system of operating continuously moving permanently coupled block trains (qv) between collieries and electric power stations, ports, steel works, etc., using bottom door discharge hopper wagons loaded and emptied automatically as the train slowly passes through the installation. Introduced by BR 1965–70. Conceived and named by Gerard Fiennes, chief operating officer, BR and developed by R.T. Munns and others.

MGWR

Midland Great Western Rly (Ireland), inc 1845, Dublin to Mullingar and Longford, first section opened 1847. Subsequently extended to Athlone, Westport and Achill, Galway and Clifden, Sligo, Cavan, etc.; 538 route miles by 1914, all in central Ireland. Part of GSR from 1925.

MH&R

Morecambe Harbour & Rly, inc 1846, harbour at Morecambe and rly to Lancaster, opened to Lancaster (Green Ayre) 1848. Part of NWR (qv) 1846.

MHE&R

Muswell Hill Estate & Rlys, Muswell Hill to Alexandra Palace, promoted by the Muswell Hill Estate Co., inc 1866 and 1871, opened 1873, worked by GNR as part of its branch from Highgate. Renamed Muswell Hill & Palace Rly 1886, closed at various times since its fate was linked with the fluctuating fortunes of Alexandra Palace. Part of GNR from 1911.

MHR

see Mid-Hants.

MIC

Mutual Improvement Class/es (qv).

Mica

GWR TC for various types of meat van, some refrigerated.

Michelangelo

Day service between Munich and Rome, introduced 1988.

Michelines

Rubber-tyred petrol-engined railbuses introduced in France 1930. So called after Michelin tyre firm, sponsors of the prototype. Loosely used in France to describe any species of diesel or petrol-engined railcar.

Mickey (RS)

A Metal Mickey (qv).

Mickey Mouse or Mickey (RS)

Term applied severally to LM&SR Class 2 2–6–2T, Class 2 Ivatt 2–6–0, class 5 4–6–0 and BR Standard 2–6–4T locos. Also class 315 emu.

Microbes (RS)

NLR 4–4–0T locos.

Micro-buffet

BR term for an open saloon coach with a small counter from which an attendant serves refreshments carried on a standard catering trolley which has been loaded on to the train. Introduced 1979.

Midday Scot

Express between London (Euston) and Glasgow (Central)/Edinburgh (Princes St.), name officially introduced 1927 for a train which had run since 1889 (The Corridor, (qv)). Restored 1949, Euston–Glasgow (Central) only. Name dropped 1966.

Middlebere Plateway

Norden to Middlebere Wharf on Poole Harbour, 3 ft 9 in gauge, built by Benjamin Fayle for the transport of excavated ball clay, opened with horse traction 1806 and 1807. Abandoned *c*. 1867 after the construction of another line from Norden to Goathorn Pier (Fayle's Tramway, (qv)).

Middle Circle (obs)

London train service worked 1872–1905 by the GWR from Moorgate, later Aldgate, via Baker St., Kensington (Addison Road) [now Olympia], and Victoria to Mansion House; Earls Court–Moorgate only from 1900; Kensington (AR)–Moorgate only from 1905; Kensington (AR)–Edgware Road only from 1906 until 1940.

Middle man (USRS)

The second or middle brakeman on a freight train.

Middle road(s)

Line(s) at a station, between the platform roads, used for through running, or for shunting, or for engine run-round movements.

Middle Shift/Turn

Daylight hours shift between Early Turn and Late Turn.

Middleton

Middleton Rly, Hunslet, Leeds, to collieries at Middleton, a horse-worked wagonway, the first rly to be sanctioned by an Act of Parliament (1758). 4 ft 1 in/1,245 mm gauge; steam locos used from 1812 until 1835, then horse-worked again. Steam locos re-introduced 1866. Converted to standard gauge 1881 and connections made to Midland and GNR. By 1958 only Parkside GNR to Middleton Colliery remained. Hunslet Moor to Middleton Park taken over by Middleton Railway Preservation

Society, 1960, to become the first standard gauge preserved line.

Mid-Hants

Inc as Alton, Alresford & Winchester Rly 1861, name changed to MH Rly 1864. Opened 1865, worked by L&SWR and leased by that company from 1880. Part of L&SWR 1884. Alton to Alresford now operated as a preserved line, the Mid-Hants Rly, first section opened 1977.

Midi

Chemin de fer du Midi (France), jointly managed with *P–O* (qv) from 1934.

Mid-Kent

Lewisham (London) to Beckenham, inc 1855 as the Mid-Kent & North Kent Junction Rly, opened 1857, extended to Addiscombe Road 1864, part of SER from 1866. The seemingly misleading title arose because the promoters envisaged extension through the area later occupied by the LC&DR main line. Also Mid-Kent (Bromley & St Mary Cray) Rly, inc 1856, to extend from the WEL&CPR (qv) at the present Shortlands station to St Mary Cray. Opened Shortlands to Bickley 1858, leased and worked by SER as an extension of its Mid-Kent Line (qv). Linked at eastern end to LC&DR main line 1860, leased and worked by LC&DR 1863. Part of SR 1923.

Mid-Kent Line

Originally the SER/SR/BR services from London (Charing Cross/Cannon St.) to Beckenham Junction and Hayes/ Addiscombe/Sanderstead. Now to Beckenham Jc and Hayes only. *See also* Mid-Kent.

Midland

1. Midland Rly, inc 1844 by amalgamation of the North Midland, Midland Counties and Birmingham & Derby Junction Rlys. Subsequent extensions and absorptions brought the Midland to London, Birmingham, Bristol and Bath, Lincoln, Swansea, Leeds, Bradford and Carlisle, 2,169 route miles by 1914. Part of LM&SR from 1923.

2. Midland Railway Carriage & Wagon Co. Ltd, originally the Midland Waggon Co.,

rly wagon builders from 1853, renamed 1877. Main works at Shrewsbury, also at Birmingham (Washwood Heath) until 1912. Part of Cammell Laird (qv) from 1919. Name continued as the wagon-hire subsidiary of MCW (qv).

Midlander

Express between London (Euston), Birmingham and Wolverhampton, introduced 1950, name dropped 1966.

Midland Mainline

A TOC (2) replacing ICMM (qv), 1996, operating services between London (St Pancras), Leicester, Derby, Nottingham, Sheffield and Leeds.

Midland Metro

A light rail transit scheme for the Birmingham–Wolverhampton, conurbation; first line Birmingham (Snow Hill)–Wednesbury–Wolverhampton, 1999.

Midland Pullman

BR diesel-electric mu, all-First class air-conditioned six-car all-Pullman trains, painted blue, introduced 1960 between London (St Pancras) and Manchester/ Leicester, also St Pancras–Nottingham from 1961. Withdrawn 1966.

Midland Rly Butterley

Renaming from 2003 of Midland Rly Centre/Trust (qv).

Midland Rly Centre/Trust

Preserved line between Ironville and Hammersmith, Derbyshire, first section opened 1982. *See* Midland Rly Butterley.

Midland Scot

Express between Birmingham, Glasgow and Edinburgh, introduced 1970, name dropped 1975. Name revived for Birmingham–Glasgow service 1992. Name ceased to be used from 2 June 2002.

Midline

Brand name of passenger services operated by BR for West Midlands Passenger Transport Authority (Centro). Not used after 1991; *see* Centro.

Mid-Notts

Mid-Nottinghamshire Joint, LM&SR/L&NER line from Checker House near Retford to junction with former GCR line at Hucknall, north of Nottingham, inc

1926, opened 1931, but only from Ollerton to Farnsfield. Part of BR (M) 1948.

Mid-Suffolk

Mid-Suffolk Light Rly, Haughley to Laxfield and Cratfield, LRO 1901, opened 1904–6, passenger services 1908, sections closed 1912 and 1915, part of L&NER from 1924, BR from 1948, completely closed 1952.

Mid-Sussex & Midhurst Junc

see MS&MJR.

Mid-Sussex Line

[Dorking/Three Bridges]–Horsham–Arundel–Ford. *See also* MSR.

Mid-Wales

see MWR.

Mid-Wales Line

Shrewsbury–Newtown–Aberystwyth.

Mindbender (RS)

An instructor.

Mikado (US)

Term for steam loco with 2–8–2 wheel arrangement, used also in UK. Derived from the destination of the first ones built (Japan). *See also* Macarthur.

Mike

1. (RS) Any loco employed in a shunting yard or for moving other locos around in a depot (a shedturner's Mike).
2. (USRS) Mikado (qv).

Mikes (RS)

GER Holden 0–6–0T.

Milan–Ancona Pullman Express

CIWL service operated 1927–9.

Milan–Genoa–Livorno–Montecatini Express

CIWL all-Pullman summer service operated 1926–9.

Milan–San Remo–Nice[–Cannes] Express

The first all-Pullman train operated by the *CIWL*, ran 1925–35.

Milan–Venice Express

CIWL all-Pullman service, ran summer only, 1926, 1927 and 1929.

Mileage (obs)

1. Portion of fares or freight rates divided between rly companies according to the distance travelled over each and computed by the RCH (qv).

2. Sum received from a 'foreign' company for use of a vehicle on that company's lines.
3. Cash bonus paid to footplate staff working over 200 miles in one shift.

Mileage boy/hog (USRS)

A loco driver who uses his seniority to get the best-paid duties when these are paid on a mileage basis.

Mileage siding/yard (obs)

GWR (qv) term for any siding/yard with access for road vehicles and used for wagon-load traffic which could be loaded/unloaded for direct transfer between the two modes. Probably so named because rail transit charges were based on mileage carried rather than weight. *See also* Mileage traffic.

Mileage traffic (obs)

GWR term for full wagon-load traffic loaded direct from road vehicles into rly wagons and vans and unloaded into road vehicles brought alongside at the destination. *See also* Mileage siding/yard.

Military Marys (RS)

ROD (qv) 2–8–0 locos obtained from the government after WW1.

Milk & Soda Water (RS)

Nickname for M&SWJR (*2*).

Milk dock (obs)

A platform at a station set aside for loading and unloading milk in churns, or later, milk tankers.

Milk float (RS)

A derogatory description for emus.

Milking the tubes (LTRS)(obs)

A form of fraud practised by some booking clerks in which preprinted tickets were sold to passengers, out of numerical order, and taken from the middle of the 'tubes' or cylinders holding them, instead of in sequence from the base. The fares paid were pocketed by the clerk and the missing tickets remained undetected until all those below them were sold.

Milk van (RS)

A motored van marshalled in the centre of trains used on the extended electric services to Coulsdon North and Sutton introduced by the SR (qv) on 1 April 1925.

Based on the erroneous belief that they were converted from bogie brake vans.

Mill (USRS)

A loco.

Milnes

George F. Milnes & Co. Ltd, works at Birkenhead (closed 1902) and Hadley (Shropshire) (1900–4), tramcar builders, 1886–1904.

Milnes–Voss

G.C. Milnes, Voss & Co., established 1902 (public company 1906), builders of tramcars and electric rly cars, suppliers of tramcar equipment. Ceased production 1913.

Milta

GWR TC for milk tank wagon.

Milwaukee (US)

Chicago, Milwaukee, St Paul & Pacific RR. *See also* St Paul.

Mimara

EC (qv) Leipzig–Munich–Zagreb express, introduced 1996.

Mineral traffic (obs)

Low value goods other than coal and coke, not necessarily minerals, passing in bulk, and charged on the basis of what transport cost the commodity could bear.

Miners' Friends (RS)

LM&SR 'Royal Scot' 4–6–0 locos. From their heavy appetite for coal.

Minfits (obs)

Vacuum-fitted mineral wagons.

Mini[ature] buffet

BR term for purpose-built coach with small saloon areas at each end and counter section in centre for the serving of refreshments and hot drinks, but not hot food. Introduced 1958.

Miniature lever frame

An interlocking frame with very small levers, controlling power signalling.

Miniature rly

A passenger-carrying line of any gauge between 7¼ in/184 mm and 2 ft/609 mm, operated with locos which are models of real or imaginary full-size types from one-eighth full size upwards. Mostly built primarily for pleasure purposes but some operate a public service and some have been sanctioned as light rlys (qv).

Miniature warning lights

Small red and green lights at user-worked level crossings to indicate to users whether it is safe to cross the rly.

Mini-Gronks/Grunts (RS)

BR class 03 and 04 diesel-mechanical locos.

Ministry of Transport Act, 1919

This established the MoT (qv), which assumed most of the functions of the BoT (qv) relating to rlys and tramways (3).

Minitram

A form of Ultra Light Rail (qv) vehicle, normally battery powered, recharged en route as necessary, demonstrated in 1997 by Minitram Systems.

Mink

GWR TC for various types of covered freight wagon.

Minnow

A 14-ton wagon with fixed sides and ends used by engineers for carrying sleepers.

Mins (RS)(obs)

Mineral wagons.

Minute men (RS)(obs)

Work Study engineers.

MIP

Mobility Impaired Person/s, as in MIP lift, elevator, toilet.

Misery Pacific (USRS)

Nickname for Missouri Pacific RR.

Missouri

Missouri Pacific RR.

Mister Punch's Rly

Nickname for WLR (*1*), much lampooned in *Punch* soon after its opening.

Misto, treno (It)(obs)

A mixed train (qv).

Mistletoe men (RS)

Employees not belonging to a trade union, i.e. parasites.

Mistral

Express between Paris, Lyon and Marseilles, introduced 1950, extended to Nice, 1952. Fastest day train between Paris and Nice until 1982. *TEE* 1965. Became a two-class train, losing *TEE* status, 1981. Replaced by *TGV*, 1982.

Mite

GWR TC for twin timber wagon.

Mitropa
*Mitteleuropäische Schlafwagen und
Speisewagen Aktiengesellschaft*; Middle
European Sleeping & Dining Car Company.
Formed 1917, taking over all restaurant and
sleeping car services in Germany and
extending its workings to Austria,
Czechoslovakia, Denmark, Hungary,
Netherlands, Poland and Switzerland. Its
cars ran through to Istanbul, Turkey until
the end of WW2. Name revived by *DBAG*
(qv) for its on-board catering and its sleeping
car services, 1994.

Mixed gauge track
Track accommodating more than one
gauge of loco/train.

Mixed traffic loco
Any loco usable for both passenger and
freight train haulage.

Mixed traffic men (RS)(obs)
Same as Half Dirties (qv).

Mixed traffic train/Mixed train
A train containing both freight and
passenger vehicles.

MJR
Methley Joint Committee, GNR (originally
WYR), NER and L&YR, opened 1865,
Lofthouse–Methley. L&NER and LM&SR
1923–47.

MK&T
Missouri, Kansas & Texas RR.

ML
Main Line (qv).

MLR
Marland Light Rly, owned by North Devon
Clay Co. and opened 1880, 3 ft gauge,
Torrington to Peters Marland. Torrington to
Dunsbear abandoned when ND&CJLR
opened in 1925. Last section closed 1982.

MLRI
Multi-Lamp Route Indicator; an alpha-
numeric route indicator working with main
junction signals. *See also* Junction indicator;
Theatre-type indicator.

MLSLO Ltd
Main Line Steam Locomotive Owners Ltd;
assumed responsibility for all aspects of
main line steam loco operation from SLOA
(qv), 1996.

MLSO

BR Motor coach Standard class with Open
plan seating and Luggage accommodation.

MLV
Motor Luggage Van, non-gangwayed,
introduced 1959–61 for BR (S) boat trains.
Worked from batteries or third rail as
required, driving cab at each end. *See also*
GLV.

MM
Ministry of Munitions, formed June 1915,
wound up 1921.

MML
see Midland Main Line.

MMM
Moore's Monthly Magazine (qv).

MMR
Melbourne Military Rly. LM&SR line
between Chellaston Junction and Ashby-
de-la-Zouch, taken over in 1939 as a Royal
Engineers' Railway Training Centre and
bridging school to supplement the LMR.
Handed back to LM&SR 1945.

MMs
see Military Marys.

MNM&HJR
Marple, New Mills & Hayfield Junction
Rly, inc 1860, opened Marple to New
Mills 1865, leased and worked by MS&LR,
part of S&M Joint (qv) 1869.

MNR
Manx Northern Rly, first section Douglas–
St Johns opened 1879, 3 ft/914 mm gauge.
Part of IofMR (qv) from 1905.

MNR
Mongolin Tomor Zam; Mongolian Rlys,
1,815 km of 1,520 mm gauge.

MOB
Montreux–Oberland–Bernois Rly,
Switzerland.

Mobrail (TC) (obs)
Ammunition train.

Modules (USRS)
Dormitories provided for employees by the
railway company.

M of W/organization/staff (US)
Maintenance of Way (i.e. permanent way
(qv)).

Mogo
GWR TC for end-door van used for
carrying motor cars.

Mogul (US)
Term for steam loco with 2–6–0 wheel arrangement; also used in UK.

Mogul Forney (US)
A steam loco with 2–4–4 wheel arrangement.

Mohawk (US)
1. A steam loco with 4–8–2 wheel arrangement.
2. Chicago–Detroit service of Grand Trunk Western RR, ceased 1971. Name revived by Amtrak for New York–Syracuse service.

Molière
Renaming of Paris–Ruhr (qv), 1973 (Paris–Düsseldorf). Paris–Cologne from 1975. Lost *TEE* status 1979 and became IC. EC Paris–Dortmund, 1987.

Monday (RS)
A heavy hammer usable only by strong, fit men.

Money box (RS)
Mail train carrying registered packets, etc. containing money.

Money Sunk & Lost
Nickname for MS&LR. *See also* Gone Completely.

Money wagon (USRS) (obs)
Rly cars carrying staff pay, usually guarded by armed men and operated only in daylight; introduced *c.* 1870, last used 1960.

Mongolipers (RS)
SR N class 2–6–0.

Monitor roof
A car roof with raised central section running longitudinally from end to end and incorporating ventilators in its sides, i.e. a form of clerestory.

Monkey (USRS)
A brakeman.

Monkey, caught by the (USRS)
To be still at work after twelve hours' continuous duty. *See also* Bear law; Dog law; Hog law (qv).

Monkey money (USRS)
A staff pass affording free travel.

Monkey motion (USRS)
Walschaert or Baker loco valve gear.

Monkey Special (RS)
A train chartered for school outing; also

trains to Clifton Down, for Bristol Zoo.

Monkey tail (RS)
A door handle on mineral wagon.

Monmouthshire Rly & Canal
Monmouthshire Canal Company (inc 1792); narrow gauge tramroads dating from 1798 were converted to rlys by the Monmouthshire Rly & Canal Co., inc 1845. First rly opened, Newport to Pontypool, 1852; all were converted by 1855. By 1879 owned Newport–Blaenavon/Abersychan; Newport–Crumlin–Ebbw Vale/Nantyglo; Risca–Nine Mile Point. Worked by GWR from 1875, part of GWR from 1880.

Monorail
A form of rly mainly relying on a single rail, using the rail either as the principal means of suspension for its trains; or, by providing ancillary rails for guiding and stabilizing vehicles running astride a single central rail (*see* Lartigue system); or, by fitting gyroscopes, rubber-tyred road wheels or other means of achieving stability for vehicles astride a single rail. Although the term itself seems not to have entered into general use until the 1890s (OED), many ingenious proposals have been put forward by inventors since the early nineteenth century, with remarkably little practical outcome. In contrast to conventional rlys, there has been no widespread construction of monorail networks, merely a small number of isolated installations operating with varying degrees of success. Despite this long history of limited application, the general concept continues to enjoy some popular favour, notably among architects, journalists and futurologists.
See also L&BR (1), *Schwebebahn*.

Monster
GWR TC for bogie 50-ft theatrical scenery van.

Montaigne
Express between Paris and Bordeaux (4 h 5 min) introduced 1980, replaced by TGV 1990.

Mont Blanc
IC Hamburg–Geneva, introduced 1982,
EC from 1987.

Mont Cenis
Express between Lyons, Turin and Milan.
TEE from 1957. Lost *TEE* status 1972.

Moonlight merchant (USRS)
The night foreman at a loco depot.

Moore's Monthly Magazine
The pioneer illustrated rly periodical catering
for a popular, non-professional readership.
First published 1896, and concerned
primarily with loco matters. Renamed *The
Locomotive Magazine* 1897, *The Locomotive
Railway Carriage & Wagon Review*, 1916.
Ceased publication 1959, merging with *TI* (qv).

Moorgate protection
Safety measures adopted by LT after the
1975 Moorgate accident to automatically
slow down and stop trains entering a
terminal road.

Mopac (US)
Missouri Pacific RR.

Morel
GWR TC for three types of wagon
designed to carry ships' propellers.

Morning Talisman
Express between London (Kings Cross)
and Edinburgh, introduced 1957.
Renamed Fair Maid (qv) in that year.

Morpeth boards
Advance lineside warning of speed
restrictions, introduced following an
accident at Morpeth in 1969.

MoT
Ministry of Transport, formed 1919,
inheriting the rly responsibilities of the BoT
(qv). Renamed Ministry of War Transport
1941, MoT again 1946. Part of the Department of the Environment 1970, reconstituted
as DTp (qv) 1976, DETR (qv), 1997,
DTLR (qv) 2001, DfT (qv) 2002.

Mothballed
BR term for a line placed out of use and
not under maintenance but not dismantled
in any way. *See also* Blocked.

Mother Hubbard (USRS)
A camel loco (qv).

Motion [of a loco]
The pistons, connecting rods and valve gear.

Motor
Same as Rail motor (qv).

Motor car/coach
A rly car/coach with passenger
accommodation but also containing a
driving cab and power unit (usually electric
when this term is employed) hauling
trailers (qv). *See also* NDM; Railcar; Rail
motor [car].

Motorman
The driver of an electric multiple unit
train, electric railcar or tramcar.

Motorail
A brand name introduced by BR in 1966
for special services (car carriers, car
sleepers) operated since 1955 to carry
motorists, their passengers and their cars in
the same train. Ceased 1995, a victim of
'privatization'.

Motor Rail
Motor Rail [& Tram Car] Co. Ltd, Bedford,
builders of 'Simplex' locos and railcars.

Motor train
see Auto-train.

Motor trolley
A four-wheel petrol-engined rail vehicle
used by permanent way staff to transport
men and materials to and from work sites.

Mountain
US and, later, European term for steam
loco with 4–8–2 wheel arrangement.

Mountaineer
Vancouver–Chicago service, introduced
1920, ceased 1958.

Mountain pay (USRS)
Overtime payments.

Mountains of Mourne (RS)(obs)
Piles of ashes and clinker at loco depots.

Mourners (RS)
L&NWR Webb 0–6–2T locos. Painted in
unrelieved black livery.

Movable crossing
Track crossing with moving nose, providing
a continuous running rail and thus
allowing higher speeds at turnouts.

Movable platform
Same as Trolley bridge (qv).

Moving block
An electronic system designed to
overcome the inflexibility of the block

system (qv), with its fixed length sections and consequent constraints on frequency of service, by providing a block system with variable section lengths according to circumstances, the exact position of each train being known to the central computer.

Moving spirit (USRS)
A train dispatcher. *See also* Train order.

Mozart
A day train between Paris and Salzburg, introduced 1954, extended to Vienna 1964, EC 1987.

MPD
Motive Power Depot. In the UK this term began to replace the older usage 'engine shed/loco shed/loco depot' in the 1930s, led by the example of the LM&SR.

MPMV
Motor Parcels and Mail Van, BR self-propelled rail vehicle.

MPTA
Municipal Passenger Transport Association; a 1939 renaming of MTA (2) (qv). Became APTO (qv).

MPV
Multi-Purpose Vehicles, a term specifically applied in 1999/2000 to Railtrack (qv) motive power units with a cab at each end and a capacity to carry tanks or containers between the cabs. Designed to attack leaf mulch on rail surfaces, iced conductor rails and track weed growth. They can also be adapted to act as bridge inspection units and structure gauges and to carry out litter clearance and drain cleaning.

MR
1. Maenclochog Rly, or Narberth Road & Maenclochog Rly, authorized 1872, opened 1876, Clynderwen to Rosebush slate quarries, closed 1882, vested in NP&FR (qv) 1881.
2. Malmesbury Rly, Dauntsey Junction to Malmesbury, inc 1872, opened 1877, worked by GWR, part of GWR from 1880.
3. Mansfield Rly: *see* Mansfield Rly.
4. Margate Rly, inc 1859, Herne Bay to Margate, a renaming of the Herne Bay & Whitstable Rly; extension to

Ramsgate authorized 1861 and name changed to KCR (qv) [opened Herne Bay–Ramsgate 1863].
5. Marlborough Rly, Savernake (Low Level) to Marlborough (High Level), inc 1861, opened 1864, worked by GWR, part of GWR from 1896.
6. Mawddwy Rly, Cemmaes Road to Dinas Mawddwy, inc 1865, opened 1867, closed 1901 to passengers, to freight 1908. LRO 1910, reopened 1911 after rebuilding as light rly, worked by Cambrian Rlys. Part of GWR from 1923.
7. Mersey Rly, inc 1866, as Mersey Pneumatic Rly, but steam locos used when opened 1886, Liverpool to Birkenhead. Electrified 1903, LM&SR Wirral electric services ran over the MR from 1938. Part of BR from 1948.
8 Metropolitan Rly: *see* Metropolitan.
9. Middleton Rly: *see* Middleton.
10. Midland Rly: *see* Midland.
11. Milford Rly, Johnston Junction to Milford Haven, inc 1856, opened 1863, worked by GWR. Part of GWR from 1896.
12. Minehead Rly, Watchet WSR to Minehead, inc 1871, opened 1874, leased to and worked by B&ER and then by GWR. Part of GWR 1897.
13. *Modern Railways*; a 1962 renaming of TI (qv).
14. Moffat Rly, Beattock to Moffat, inc 1881, opened 1883, leased and worked by Caledonian Rly, part of CR 1889.
15. Mold Rly, Saltney Ferry to Mold, inc 1847, opened 1849, worked by Chester & Holyhead Rly and part of that rly 1849. [C&HR taken over by L&NWR 1858.]
16. Monmouth Rly, inc 1810, Howler Slade [Forest of Dean] to Coleford and May Hill, Monmouth, opened *c.* 1817 as a 3 ft 6 in gauge horse tramroad. Part of its course used by Coleford, Monmouth, Usk & Pontypool Rly, completed 1857, and the section from Wyesham to Coleford by the Coleford Rly, opened 1883.

17. Morayshire Rly, inc 1846, opened 1852 Elgin to Lossiemouth; Orton to Rothes and Dandaleith 1858, Elgin to Rothes 1862, Dandaleith to Craigellachie 1863. Worked by GNofSR from 1866, part of GNofSR 1880.

18. Mumbles Rly: *see* Mumbles.

MR&CC

see Monmouthshire Rly & Canal.

MR&FoDJR

Mitcheldean Road & Forest of Dean Junction Rly, Bilson to Drybrook and Speedwell, inc 1871, part of GWR 1880, opened 1885 Bilson Junc to Speedwell Siding, then to Drybrook Halt 1907. Remaining 2½ miles built but never opened.

MRC

1. Model Railway Club, founded 1910.

2. Myanmar Rlys Corporation; 3,955 km of metre gauge.

MRCE

Metropolitan Railway Country Estate Ltd, an associate company of the Metropolitan Rly [London], formed in 1919 to develop middle class housing estates in the rly's catchment area, using surplus rly-owned land and purchasing new sites. On the formation of the LPTB in 1933, this company was not taken over, becoming an independent organization dealing with all kinds of property development in all areas; it subsequently became the Metropolitan Estates & Property Corporation Ltd.

MRGB

Miniature Rlys of Great Britain Ltd, founded 1904 by Bassett-Lowke (qv) and R.P. Mitchell to supply, manage and operate miniature rlys (qv). First lines opened at Abington Park, Northampton and Blackpool, 1905. Succeeded by NGR (qv), 1911.

MRL

Mendip Rail Ltd (qv).

MRS

Military Rail Service (US).

MS

BR Motor car Second/Standard class.

MS&LR

Manchester, Sheffield & Lincolnshire Rly, formed 1847 by amalgamation of the Sheffield, Ashton-under-Lyne & Manchester Rly, Sheffield & Lincolnshire Rly, the Sheffield & Lincolnshire Extension Rly, the Great Grimsby & Sheffield Junction Rly and the Great Grimsby Docks undertaking. Various absorptions and extensions followed, including a line to London, opened 1899. Renamed GCR (qv) 1897.

MS&MJR

Mid-Sussex & Midhurst Junction Rly, Petworth to Midhurst, inc 1859, opened 1866, worked by LB&SCR, part of LB&SCR 1874.

MSCC

Malleable Steel Castings Co., Pendleton, Lancs., manufacturers of wagon parts, tramcar trucks, etc.

MSCR

Manchester Ship Canal Co. Rlys, inc 1885, opened 1894. Used its own locos and rolling stock. Provided connections between the canal docks, warehouses, etc. and main line rlys at Ellesmere Port, Runcorn, Warrington, Partington, Irlam, Barton, Manchester Docks, etc. Closed *c.* 1978.

MSDR

Manchester South District Rly, inc 1873, Manchester to Alderley and branches, part of Midland Rly 1876, opened 1880 from Heaton Mersey Junction (Stockport) to Chorlton-cum-Hardy and Throstle Nest Junc near Cornbrook, [CLC]. Section north of Chorlton Junc [Chorlton-cum-Hardy] became part of CLC 1891.

MSJ&A

Manchester, South Junction & Altrincham Rly, inc 1845, opened 1849, Altrincham to Manchester (London Rd). Jointly controlled by MS&LR & L&NWR, owned its own rolling stock but local trains were at first worked by MS&LR locos, also by L&NWR locos from 1899. After 1923 the LM&SR and L&NER as joint owners, took over full responsibility for alternate five-year periods. Electrified 1931.

MSL
As MS (qv) but with Lavatory.

MSLR
see Mid-Suffolk.

MSM
Madras [&] Southern Mahratta Rly, India; opened from 1852 as Madras Rly. Government-owned from 1907. Broad and metre gauge; became part of the Southern Rly of India 1951. *See* SR (6).

MSR
Mid-Sussex Rly, inc 1857, Horsham to Pulborough and Petworth [Coultershaw], opened 1859. Leased and worked by LB&SCR, part of LB&SCR 1864.

MSS
Maximum Safe Speed; a term used in ATP (qv).

MSW Line
Manchester–Penistone–Sheffield/Barnsley–Wath.

MT
1. *Modern Transport,* a weekly newspaper, founded 1919; acquired by Ian Allan Ltd 1963. Monthly publication from 1966–8. Revived as a quarterly magazine January 1978–April 1980.
2. *Modern Tramway & Light Rail Transit,* monthly organ of LRTA, founded as *Modern Tramway* in 1938. Became *LR&MT* (qv) January 1992.
3. *Mass Transit,* bi-monthly journal devoted to all forms of public road and rail transport, also people-movers. Published in the USA but international in its coverage.

MTA
1. Metropolitan Transportation Authority (New York). Formed 1 March 1968, also simply known as 'M'.
2. Municipal Tramways Association, founded 1903, inc 1911, renamed Municipal Tramways & Transport Association (MT&TA) 1926, renamed MPTA (qv) 1939.

MT&AR
see Head of Valleys Line.

MT&TA
See MTA.

MTR
Mass Transit Rly, heavy rapid transit system on Hong Kong Island and Kowloon, first section opened 1979.

Mtys (USRS)
Empty wagons.

MU
Multiple Unit (qv).

Mucho, to do a (LTRS)
To agree an MCO (qv).

Muck/Mud, Sludge & Lightning
Nickname for MS&LR.

Mucker (USRS)
A labourer engaged in excavation work.

Mud chicken (USRS)
A surveyor.

Mud digger (RS)
A loco with a tendency to derail.

Muddle, and Go[es] Nowhere
Nickname for M&GNJR.

Mud hen (USRS)
A loco without a superheater.

Mud hop (USRS)
A clerk employed in a yard.

Mud, Slush & Lumber
Nickname for MS&LR.

Mud sucker (USRS)
A choked injector on a steam loco.

Mule (USRS)
A brakeman.

Müller Lights
Small windows in the partitions between rly compartments, introduced by several companies following the murder (the first on a British train) by Franz Müller of a clerk named Briggs in a NLR compartment in July 1864.

Mullet
A 51-ton bogie wagon used by engineers for carrying rails.

Multi-aspect signal
A form of colour-light signal with separate lamps and lenses for each aspect, normally mounted one above the other, with red at the lowest (driver's eye) level.

Multifret
A freight wagon accommodating containers up to 2.74 m (9 ft) high, also capable of carrying a swap body (qv). Can be worked at speeds of up to 90 mph.

Multiple Unit/MU

An electric (emu) or diesel-electric powered (dmu or demu) train in which the motive power is distributed over a number of car axles instead of being concentrated in a loco or driving car. All motors can be controlled by the driver at the front of the train through a master controller connected to all equipments, irrespective of their location. Since the number of motored units can be varied and placed in any desired position in a train and trains can be driven from either end without reversal, mu formations are very flexible in use. The emu system was invented by the American Frank J. Sprague in 1897.

Multiple working

Electric or diesel-electric locos coupled together to enable the driver of the leading one to have complete control of power and braking in all of them. *See also* Tandem working.

Multi-Spad (RS)

A particular signal which becomes notorious for being overlooked by drivers due to poor visibility, unusual positioning, etc. *See also* SPAD.

Multi-up, to (RS)

To couple up locos to run in tandem/multiple and operate as a single source of motive power.

Mumbles

Mumbles Rly, Swansea to Mumbles Pier, inc 1804, as Oystermouth Railway or Tramroad, Oystermouth to Swansea, opened 1806, about 4 ft gauge, passengers carried (horse traction) from 25 March 1807, the earliest known date for regular carriage of passengers by rail. Closed to passengers *c.* 1827, passenger traffic resumed 1860. Steam traction introduced 1877. Extended to Mumbles Pier 1898. Leased to Swansea Tramways Co. (later South Wales Transport Co.) from 1899, electrified 1929, using large double-deck tramcar type vehicles. Closed 1960.

Murray's Timetables

Published in Glasgow monthly 1843–1966 and showing all Scottish rly, coach and steamer services.

Mushrooming

The widening and flattening of the head of a low rail (qv) that results from high traffic loading.

Music master (USRS)

A paymaster.

Mutual, to do a (LTRS)

To arrange an MCO (qv).

Mutual Improvement Classes

A voluntary spare time arrangement which allowed firemen to be instructed by drivers in the skills of handling steam locos.

Muzzle loading hog/muzzle loader (USRS)

A steam loco which has to be fired by hand.

MV

1. Metropolitan Vickers Electrical Co. Ltd, Trafford Park, Manchester, successors to Westinghouse (qv), formed 1919 and controlled by Vickers Ltd and MCW (qv). Vickers sold out their interest to the International General Electric Co. (US) in 1928. Became part of AEI, 1959.
2. (Fr)(obs) *Marchandises et Voyageurs*; a mixed train (qv).
3. (Fr) *Marcher à Vue* (qv).

MW&SJR

Much Wenlock & Severn Junction Rly, Much Wenlock to Buildwas Junc, SVR, inc 1859, opened 1862, worked by WMR and GWR, part of GWR 1896.

MWL

1. Miniature Warning Lights displaying red or green indications to road traffic at automatic level crossings which are worked by approaching trains. *See also* Automatic level crossings.
2. Miniature Working Lights (qv).

MWR

Mid-Wales Rly, Talyllyn Junc–Rhayader–Llanidloes, inc 1859. Talyllyn Junc to Three Cocks section acquired from Hereford, Hay & Brecon Rly. Opened 1864, worked by Cambrian from 1888, amalgamated with Cambrian from 1904.

Mystex (obs)

TC for an advertised excursion train worked to an unpublished 'mystery' destination.

MZ

Makedonski Zeleznici; Macedonian Rlys, formed from part of *JZ* (qv), 752 km.

MZA

Madrid, Zaragoza & Alicante Rly, absorbed by *RENFE* (qv) in 1941.

N

N
Nahverkehrszug (qv).

NA
National Archives, formed 2003 by
amalgamation of PRO (qv) and the
Historical Manuscripts Commission.

Nags (RS)
BR 350 hp diesel shunters with three
coupled axles.

Nahverkehr (Ger)
Local transport.

Nahverkehrszug (Ger) (obs)
Local train. Now RB (qv).

Name boards
Boards attached to the roofs or sides of rly
coaches bearing the starting point and
destination of the train and also the name
of the train, if any.

Namer (RS)
Train spotters' term for any loco with a
name on a nameplate.

N&BJR
Northampton & Banbury Junction Rly, inc
1863, opened Blisworth–Towcester 1866;
to Cockley Brake Junc (L&NWR), 1872.
Part of S&MJR, 1910.

N&BR
Neath & Brecon Rly, inc 1862, opened
1864, 1867. Part of GWR from 1922. *See
also* DVMR.

N&ER
Northern & Eastern Rly, inc 1836,
Stratford [London] to Bishop's Stortford,
opened, 5 ft gauge, 1840, 1841, 1842,
1843 with running powers over ECR into
London (Shoreditch). Converted to
standard gauge, 1844. Leased to ECR
1844, vested in GER 1902.

N&R Joint
Nantybwch & Rhymney Joint, L&NWR
and Rhymney Rly from 1867, LM&SR &
GWR from 1923–47.

N&SJRC
Norfolk & Suffolk Joint Rly Committee,
inc 1898, M&GNJC and GER: North
Walsham–Mundesley–Cromer, opened
1898, 1906, and Yarmouth–Lowestoft via
Gorleston, opened 1903. LM&SR &
L&NER 1923–47, BR(E) 1948. *See also*
M&GNJC.

N&SWJR
North and South Western Junction Rly,
Willesden L&NWR to Old Kew Junction
(with L&SWR) and branch South Acton
to Hammersmith & Chiswick, London,
inc 1851, opened 1853 and 1857, and
worked by the L&NWR and L&SWR,
passenger service provided by NLR
from 1853; jointly leased by L&NWR,
Midland and NLR 1871–1922. LM&SR
from 1923.

N&W (US)
Norfolk & Western RR. From 1959
included Virginian RR; from 1964 also
included Nickel Plate, Wabash &
Pittsburgh, and West Virginian Rly.
Acquired Erie RR 1968.

Napoli Express
Paris–Naples service introduced 1979.

NA Rly
North American Rly; an amalgamation in
2000 of BNSF (qv) and CN (qv), making
it the largest rly system in North America
in terms of mileage.

Narrow gauge
Any track gauge narrower than the

standard 4 ft 8½ in/1,435 mm. During the period when it had broad gauge (qv) lines, the GWR (qv) always referred to standard gauge track as 'narrow gauge'.

Nasmyth, Wilson

Nasmyth, Wilson & Co. Ltd, Patricroft, loco builders, 1838–1939.

National Express Group plc

A passenger road transport operator which acquired a number of UK rly operating franchises after BR (1) (qv) was privatized in the mid-1990s. *See* Central Trains, Gatwick Express, Midland Mainline, ScotRail, Greater Anglia, London Lines.

National Rail/Rlys

A convenient generic term adopted in 1996 to describe the whole national railway network of Great Britain after the introduction of the privatized regime. Officially used by LT from 1997. 'National Rail' was adopted by ATOC (qv) in 2000 as the brand name for the former nationalized network of Great Britain along with its supporting double arrow logo and the slogan 'Britain's train companies working together'. *See also* Network Rail.

National Sunday League/NSL Excursions

The NSL, founded in 1855 to support Sunday opening of museums and parks, extended its activities to the organization of rly excursions between London and the south coast resorts, particularly over the LB&SCR. It chartered complete trains, printed its own handbills and issued its own tickets. NSL excursions continued over the SR but ceased in 1939.

Nation Rail Supplies

Trade name of a supplier of track, signalling and electric traction parts for maintenance and replacement.

National Rail Timetable

Public single-volume timetable covering all National Rail (qv) services in Great Britain published by ATOC (qv), replacing the BR All system timetable (qv).

National Route Code

A numeric code identifying rly routes between junctions. Replaced by Engineer's Line References (qv).

NATM

New Austrian Tunnelling Method, in which quick-setting concrete is sprayed on to steel mesh or lattice steel arches provided to give it support; a permanent concrete lining is added later. It provides significant cost reductions over the traditional method of lining tube tunnels with metal or concrete segments or bricks. First used in Austria in 1954.

Navette (Fr)

A shuttle service (qv).

Navetteur (Fr)

A commuter.

Navigator

A navvy (qv).

Navvies' wedding cake (RS)

Bread and margarine.

Navvy

1. An abbreviation of 'navigator' which has become a word in its own right; a manual labourer, employed originally on canal and navigable waterway (inland navigation) construction (hence the name), and later on rly building and other maintenance and construction projects.

2. (US)(obs) A steam shovel.

Navvy King, The

Popular term for Thomas Brassey (1805–70), rly contractor, who employed up to 80,000 navvies (qv).

Navvy Mail (RS)(obs)

A train operated to transport rly and dock construction gangs.

NBDS

Noord Brabantsch Duitsche Spoorweg; North Brabant Rly Co. Concession 1869, first line opened 1873. Taken over by Netherlands State Rlys Co. 1919.

NBL

North British Locomotive Co. Ltd (qv).

NBR

North British Rly, inc 1844, first section, Edinburgh to Berwick and Haddington, opened 1846. By 1914 it operated over 1,375 route miles, mainly in central and eastern Scotland. Part of L&NER 1923.

NBS (Ger)

Neubaustrecken (qv).

NCB
National Coal Board.

NCC
Northern Counties Committee, formed 1903 to manage the B&NCR (Ireland) when it was acquired by the Midland Rly [of England]. Part of LM&SR from 1923, purchased by UTA from BTC 1949.

NCIT
National Council on Inland Transport, founded 1962.

NCL
National Carriers Ltd. Former Sundries Division of BR, established as a subsidiary of NFC under Transport Act, 1968. *See also* NFC.

NCR
1. North Cornwall Rly, inc 1882, first section, Halwill Junc–Launceston opened 1886, completed to Wadebridge 1895. Worked by L&SWR, part of SR 1923.
2. Northumberland Central Rly, inc 1863, Scotsgap to Rothbury, opened 1870. Part of NBR from 1872.

NCU (obs)
Non-Common User; a rly vehicle confined to system which owns it, to be loaded only for destinations on the owner's system.

ND&CJLR
North Devon & Cornwall Junction Light Rly, LRO 1914: a reconstruction to standard gauge of the 3 ft gauge Torrington & Marland with a new line thence to Halwill Junction. Opened 1925, worked by SR; BR from 1948, closed 1965.

N de M
National Railways of Mexico, formed 1908 by merger of the National Railroad of Mexico and the Mexican Central Rly. Other systems were subsequently acquired and by 1948 all main lines were converted to standard gauge (qv). Further acquisitions in 1987 resulted in *FNM* (qv).

NDM
Non-Driving Motor car in a mu set, i.e. a car with motors and control gear but no cab.

NDR
North Devon Rly, inc 1851, opened 1854 Crediton to Barnstaple, leased to L&SWR 1863, converted from 7 ft to standard gauge 1863, absorbed by L&SWR 1865.

NE
Abbreviation used by the L&NER on freight wagons, and from 1942–6, on locos. *See also* NER.

Near side
On the left of the train in the direction of travel.

Nearside car
A US design (1911) of tramcar in which passengers boarded and left by a large doorway at the front end. The conductor was stationed behind the driver to take the fares of passengers boarding and control the doors. Later many nearside cars were given a central exit. The name derives from the practice on some tramway (*3*) systems of locating stops on the near side of intersecting streets.

Nebenbahn (Ger)
A local rly (qv) of standard gauge.

Ned Train
Rolling stock services arm of NS (qv), undertaking consultancy functions, etc. in other countries.

Needle Noses (RS)(obs)
Auditors searching for paper evidence of unproductive paid time.

NEFR
North East Frontier Rly [of India], formed 1958.

Negative cant
A situation where the inner rail of a curve is raised above the level of the outside rail. *See also* Cant.

Neggy (LTRS)
The negative conductor rail.

NEHRT
New Europe Heritage Railway Trust, 1999. Works with FEDECRAIL (qv).

Neilson
Kerr, Mitchell & Neilson, loco builders, Glasgow, from 1843; Neilson & Mitchell 1845; Neilson & Co. 1855; Neilson, Reid & Co. 1898. Amalgamated with Sharp (qv) and Dübs (qv) to form North British (qv), 1903.

Nelson (RS)
Jim Crow (qv).

Nelsons (RS)

SR emu corridor stock introduced for the 1937 Portsmouth Direct electrification. Derived from the 'one-eyed' appearance of the front ends, with driver's window at one side of the corridor connection and route indicator at the other. *See also* COR and RES.

NE Magazine (LNER)/NE & Scottish Magazine(LNER)

Monthly staff and house journal of the north-east area of the L&NER (qv) January 1923–June 1924, renamed as shown from July 1924–December 1926, then became *L&NER Magazine* (qv) from January 1927.

Nene Valley

Peterborough–Wansford–Yarwell Junction; a preserved rly using part of former BR Peterborough–Market Harborough line. First section opened 1977.

NER

1. North Eastern Rly, inc 1854, an amalgamation of York, Newcastle & Berwick Rly, Y&NMR, Malton & Driffield Rly and Leeds Northern Rly. Newcastle & Carlisle Rly absorbed 1862, S&DR (qv) absorbed 1863. 1,249 route miles by 1914, mainly in Yorkshire, Durham and Northumberland, part of L&NER from 1923.

2. North Eastern Region, BR; merged with ER from 1 January 1967.

3. North Eastern Rly [of India], formed 1958.

NE Railway Magazine

Monthly staff and house journal of NER (1) (qv), published January 1911–December 1923.

Nerve Centre, The (RS)

Control Office; or, even more facetiously, the yard foreman's cabin.

NET

Nottingham Express Transit. Light rail scheme in Nottingham area. First line opened 2004.

Networker Express

BR class 365 electric stock, dual-voltage.

Networkers

BR dc emus classes 465 and 466.

Network Rail

A 'not for profit company' replacing Railtrack plc (qv) from 3 October 2002 with a £21 billion Government Guarantee; legal name Network Rail Infrastructure Ltd from 3 February 2003. It has broadly the same functions as its predecessor. Responsible for rly infrastructure in Great Britain, with over 16,536 km of route.

Network Rail Asset Territories

London North Eastern; Midlands & North West; Southern & East Anglia; Scotland; Western.

Network SouthCentral

A TOU (qv), 1994. A TOC (2) (qv), 1996; services covering London–Epsom/Guildford/ Dorking/Horsham, London–Brighton, London–Horsham– Littlehampton/Bognor, London–Lewes– Eastbourne/Hastings, Bournemouth–Brighton– Ashford; *see* Connex, South Central, Southern.

Network SouthEast

see NSE.

Neubaustrecken

Inter-city lines of *DB* built for fast running, and constructed from 1974 onwards.

Neutralisée, ligne (Fr)

A rly which is completely closed between two stations (exclusive in each case), thus severing through operation, but on which freight services still operate over the sections at each end.

Neverstop Railway

A transport system invented by Adkins and Lewis, in which the motive power is provided by a circular shaft laid beneath the track and fitted with a spiral metal band with which a mechanism on each car engages. The shaft is rotated at a uniform speed but the speed of the car is controlled by the pitch of the spiral band so that when passing through stations, the cars slow to 1–1.5 mph/1.6–2.4 km/h to allow passengers to board and alight. With the widening of the spiral, cars accelerate to 20 mph/32 km/h or more on leaving stations. The system, which obviates the need for signalling, since there is no possibility of collisions, enables cars to be spaced along the line so that there is always one in each station. After a demonstration in the grounds of the Kursaal at Southend-on-Sea in 1923, a line was provided for the 1924–5 British Empire Exhibition at Wembley, London. There have been no subsequent installations.

Newcastle Executive
Service between London (Kings Cross) and Newcastle, so named 1973. Name dropped 1986.

Newcastle hook (RS)(obs)
A shunting pole.

Newcastle Pullman
BR Newcastle–London (Kings Cross) service introduced 1991.

Newcastle [rail/wagon] road (obs)
A generic term current in the eighteenth and early nineteenth centuries for a gravity- or horse-operated wooden-rail waggon way (qv) linking coal mines with water transport. Such lines were particularly concentrated in Tyneside and Wearside but were also to be found in other parts of northern England, the Midlands and Wales.

New Haven
see NH.

New Line
1. Guildford New Line (qv).
2. Roade–Northampton–Rugby.
3. London (Euston)–Watford suburban lines, opened 1912–22.

News butcher (USRS)
A vendor of newspapers, confectionery, fruit, etc. on trains. Usually an employee of the Union News Company.

New Tokaido line
Shinkansen (qv) built parallel to Tokaido line (qv).

Nexus
1996 brand name for light rail, buses and ferries operated within Tyne & Wear PTE area (qv).

Nf (Fr)
Non-franchissable. A notice placed on a signal which may not be passed when the danger aspect is shown, i.e. permissive working (qv) is not applicable. Usually applied to *le carré* (qv).

NFC
National Freight Corporation; set up under the Transport Act, 1968, to exercise powers, in conjunction with BRB, to provide, secure or promote properly integrated services for carriage of freight by road and rail and secure that in the provision of such services, freight should be carried by rail whenever that was efficient and economic. The NFC was given power to operate road freight services and enter into arrangements with BRB for rail transport. Its business comprised the road freight and shipping facilities of the former THC, the sundries and medium weight business of BR handled by NCL, and 51 per cent of the business of Freightliners Ltd. In 1982, under the first Thatcher Conservative administration, the NFC was sold off to the management and staff.

NGR
1. Narrow Gauge Rlys Ltd, registered 1911, directors W.J. Bassett-Lowke (qv) and R.P. Mitchell; successor company to MRGB (qv). NGR installed and operated 15 in gauge miniature rlys at Southport and Rhyl and opened the R&ER and the Fairbourne Rly as 15 in gauge passenger lines in 1915–16.
2. Natal Government Rlys [South Africa], formed 1878, became part of SAR&H (qv), 1910.

NGRS
Narrow Gauge Railway Society, founded 1951.

NH
New York, New Haven & Hartford RR. Later known as the New Haven Co.

Niagara (US)
A loco with 4–8–4 wheel arrangement, also known as Northern or Pocono.

Nibble
Nickname of S&MJR.

Nickel Plate (US)
Nickname for New York, Chicago & St Louis RR. From the saying of Jay Gould, who entered a low bid for the purchase of this company but when challenged to raise it, replied he would not do so, even if the lines were nickel-plated.

Nicky Line
Nickname for Harpenden–Hemel Hempstead & Boxmoor branch.

Nidd Valley
see NVLR.

Nigger Chiefs (RS)
Nickname for L&YR 4–4–2 locos, 'Big, black and powerful'.

Niggerhead (USRS)
Steam dome or turret on a loco.

Nigger heaven (USRS)
The roofs of freight cars when used for illicit free rides.

Nigger track (USRS)
A little-used line.

Night Aberdonian
Service between London (Kings Cross) and Aberdeen, so named 1971. London terminal moved to Euston 1987.

Night Caledonian
Service between London (Euston) and Glasgow (Central), introduced 1970, ceased 1976. Name revived 1986.

Night Capitals
Sleeping car train between London (Kings Cross) and Edinburgh, so named in 1971, name dropped 1979.

Nightcaps (RS)
Fishplates (qv) held together with adjustable clamps to temporarily support defective welds and other rail defects.

Night Ferry
London (Victoria) to Paris and Brussels, with through *CIWL* sleeping cars carried on purpose-built train ferries Dover–Dunkerque, introduced 1936, suspended 1939–47, ceased 1980.

Night Limited
Service between London (Euston) and Glasgow (Central), introduced 1964, with Pullman lounge bar. Ceased 1988.

Night Mail
TPO (qv) service London (Euston)–Glasgow (Central) 1923–1993. Subject of a documentary film of this title, 1936.

Nightrider
London (Kings Cross)–Edinburgh/Glasgow–Aberdeen service with First class air-conditioned stock (dimmed lighting), all-night buffet and continental breakfast service. Introduced, with reduced fares, to meet road coach competition, 1982. London (Euston)–Glasgow (Central)

service added 1983, all services ran via WCML from 1988. Discontinued 1990.

Night Riviera
Sleeping car train London (Paddington)–Plymouth–Penzance. So named, with new cars, 1984. Diverted to London (Waterloo) for Eurostar connections, 1995. Returned to Paddington 1998.

Night Scot
Sleeping car service between London (Euston) and Glasgow/Edinburgh, so named officially 1927. Name dropped 1939. Name given to Plymouth–Glasgow/Edinburgh sleeping car service 1992–5.

Night Scotsman
Sleeping car services between London (Kings Cross) and Edinburgh/Glasgow/Perth/Aberdeen, so named officially 1927. Edinburgh only 1939. Name dropped 1968, revived 1971. London terminal moved to Euston, 1987.

Night West Countryman
Glasgow/Edinburgh–Plymouth sleeping car service 1992–5.

Niles (US)
Niles Car Co., Niles, Ohio, car builders, notably of interurban cars, inc 1901. Ceased car production, 1917.

Nineteen Order (USRS)
Train order requiring no signature which could be handed over on a hoop or delivery fork without stopping the train. From the form number.

Nipper
1. (RS) The junior member of any gang, obliged to run errands, make tea, etc.
2. (RS) The member of a track gang responsible for the supply to the work site of the required tools and for making sure they are collected upon completion of work; the nipper may also be responsible for ensuring any tools requiring attention from the blacksmith are delivered to him and collected after treatment.
3. (USRS) A brakeman.

NIR
Northern Ireland Rlys Ltd, formed 1967 to take over the running of the remaining rlys in NI after the dissolution of the

UTA/UTR (qv). 357 km of 1,600 mm gauge. *See also* Translink.

NI Railways
Brand name for NIR (qv), 1997.

Nishitetsu
Nishi–Nippon [West Japan] Rly.

NITHC
Northern Ireland Transport Holding Co.; owns and manages the immovable property required by NIR to operate its rail services.

Nith Valley Line
Dumfries to Kilmarnock.

NJT
New Jersey Transit, operating passenger rail services in and around Newark and Hoboken, NJ, US.

NLLR
North Lindsey Light Rly, inc 1900, Scunthorpe to Winterton and Thealby. Opened 1906, worked by GCR, extended to Winteringham 1907, to Whitton 1910. Part of L&NER from 1923.

NLR
1. North London Rly, inc 1846 as E&WID&BJR (qv), first sections opened 1850, 1851, renamed NLR 1853. Largely under the control and ownership of the L&NWR but existed until 1922 as a nominally independent concern with its own locomotives and rolling stock; senior management posts taken over by the corresponding officers of the L&NWR from 1909. Became a part of the L&NWR from 1922.
2. North London Rlys (qv).

NLU
The National Logistics Unit of Network Rail (qv), supplying materials for work on rail track and other infrastructure projects.

NMBS
Initials of the Flemish equivalent of *SNCB* (qv).

NMC
Network Management Centres; using digital radio, these disseminate instructions to trains for train movements at junctions and level crossings, and also transmit movement authorities and permitted speeds. *See also* TBS; TCS.

NMR
1. North Midland Rly, inc 1836, Derby to Leeds, opened 1840, became part of new Midland Rly, 1844.
2. North Metropolitan Rly; *see* Metropolitan.

NMT
New Measurement Train; an IC-125 (qv) set converted by Network Rail (qv) 2004 and equipped with state-of-the-art digital and laser technology systems providing full high-speed track geometry and gauge measurements which can be displayed at very low speed. The facilities also include video inspection of track and OLE (qv). *See also* Pandora.

NMVB
Initials of the Flemish name for the *SNCV* (qv).

NNR
North Norfolk Railway; a preserved rly using the former BR line between Sheringham and Holt. First services began 1975.

No-Bill (USRS)
An employee not belonging to the trade union (brotherhood).

No-block line
A line on which a signaller does not monitor the state of the block section.

NOC
National Operations Centres, from 2006. The NOC for rly radio telephones is at Didcot, that for fixed rly telecommunications at Stoke-on-Trent.

NOL
SR emu compartment stock two-car sets with NO Lavatories, converted from L&SWR non-corridor stock in 1934–6, 2-NOL.

NOMO
No-Man Operation; a proposed LT fully automatic system of train operation.

Non common user
A wagon excluded from the common user (qv) wagon pool.

Nondescript (obs)
Passenger stock with reasonably good seating standards and available for use by First, Second (old) or Third Class ticket holders according to operational requirements.

Nonker (RS)

Train spotters' term for a loco with only a number, no name. *See also* Namer.

Non stop

Strictly a train proceeding between two points without any intermediate stops for passenger purposes. The London Underground rlys, however, for many years used both noun and verb in a misleading fashion to denote trains merely omitting only one or some intermediate stops.

Non-token lock and block

A method of single line working devised by the Sykes' Interlocking Signal Co. and first used in 1905. The instruments are arranged so that no signal for a train to enter a single line section can be put to clear ('off') without the sanction of the signalman at the other end, and after that signal has allowed a train to enter, it is automatically restored to danger without the consent of the signalman in advance and cannot be altered until the train has left the single line section, this action releasing the instruments. The system met all contingencies except that of a train becoming divided while on the single line section, leaving to the human element (i.e. the signalman in advance) the task of checking that every train leaving the section was complete.

Nord

Chemin de fer du Nord; Northern Rly of France. Part of *SNCF* (qv), 1938.

Nord Belge

A subsidiary of *Nord* (qv) operating within Belgium. Became part of *SNCB* (qv) 1938.

Nord Express

CIWL service Paris/Ostend–Berlin–St Petersburg, introduced 1896. Suspended in WW1, curtailed at Riga, 1921; Hamburg and Copenhagen portion 1929. Also from 1920s, portions for USSR frontier with connection thence to Moscow, and for Bucharest via Breslau. Suspended in WW2, re-instated 1946 as Paris/Ostend–Hamburg– Copenhagen–Stockholm; Oslo portion from 1951. Became Paris–Copenhagen sleeping car service 1975. From 1986 Ostend–Aachen– Copenhagen only

(Paris–Scandinavia traffic was then transferred to new Viking Express (qv)).

Nord–Sud

A section of the Paris *Métro* formerly operated by an independent company, *Chemin de fer Électrique Souterrain de Nord–Sud*. Became part of *CMP* (qv) in 1930.

Nord–Sud (Brenner) Express

CIWL service Berlin–Munich–Rome– Naples via Brenner, introduced 1897. Cannes portion 1901.

Norfolk Coast Express

Service between London (Liverpool St.) and Cromer, with portions for Sheringham and Mundesley, Trimingham and Overstrand, introduced 1907, replacing Cromer Express. Withdrawn 1914.

Norfolkman

Express between London (Liverpool St.), Norwich, Cromer and Sheringham (the latter two in summer only), introduced 1948, name dropped 1962.

Normal Clear system

A signalling system in which the main running signals display a clear aspect at all times when it is safe for them to do so.

Normal Danger system

Signalling system in which all signals are kept at danger and indicate clear only as required for the passage of a train.

Normal position

The position in which signalling equipment lies when not set for the passage of a train.

Normals (RS)

Ordinary rly passengers as distinct from Gricers (qv), Train spotters (qv), and other rly enthusiasts. *See* also Berts.

Normandy Express

Boat train London (Waterloo)– Southampton Docks for Channel Islands and St Malo/Le Havre sailings, introduced 1952. Ceased 1964.

Norseman

Summer-only express between London (Kings Cross) and Newcastle (Tyne Commission Quay for Scandinavian sailings), introduced 1931, restored 1950. Name dropped 1965.

Norte
Northern Rly of Spain, absorbed by
RENFE (qv), 1941.
North & West Line
Newport (Mon)–Abergavenny–Hereford–
Shrewsbury–Crewe.
North Atlantic Express
Belfast–Portrush service, introduced by
NCC in 1934.
Northbound
see Eastbound.
North British
North British Locomotive Co. Ltd,
Glasgow, loco builders. Formed 1903 as an
amalgamation of Sharp (qv), Dübs (qv) and
Neilson (qv). Ceased production 1962. *See
also* LH Plant Engineering Co.
North Briton
Express between Leeds (City) and Glasgow
(Queen St.), so named 1949, terminated at
Edinburgh from 1965. Name dropped
1968, restored 1972 as Leeds–Edinburgh
service. Name dropped 1975.
North Country Continental
Unofficial name for GER Harwich–
Doncaster service 1882, later extended to
York and Liverpool and then re-routed
Harwich–Manchester. Replaced 1983 by
the European (qv).
North Devon
see NDR.
North Downs Line
NSE brand name for Tonbridge/Gatwick–
Redhill–Guildford–Reading services from
1989. Renamed Thames–Gatwick Line
1993, part of Thames Trains (qv), 1994.
North East
see Regional Railways North East.
North East Corridor
Boston–New York–Washington.
North Eastern
Express between London (Kings Cross),
Darlington and Middlesbrough, so named
1964, name dropped 1968. *See also*
Newcastle Executive.
Northern (US)
Steam loco with 4–8–4 wheel arrangement.
Northern Belle
A land cruise (qv) train for sixty passengers,
introduced by L&NER 1933, including

sleeping cars, lounge/writing room car, dining
car, shower and hairdressing facilities. This
train toured scenic lines, offering road and
water side trips, mainly in Northern England
and Scotland, over seven days, for an
inclusive charge of £20. It ran each year in
June until 1939 inclusive.
Northern City Line
Name for the Finsbury Park to Moorgate
tube service, when operated by LT. *See*
GN&CR.
Northern Heights, The
GNR publicity term for the residential zone
served by its lines to Edgware, High Barnet
and Alexandra Palace. The expression was
first used as the title of a book by William
Hewitt, published in 1869.
Northern Irishman
Boat train between London (Euston) and
Stranraer Harbour (for Larne sailings), so
named 1952, ran via Castle Douglas until
1965 then via Mauchline and Ayr. Name
dropped 1966.
Northern Line
Name adopted 1937 for LT tube service
Edgware/Highgate to Morden via London
Bridge and via Charing Cross. Applied to
subsequent extensions to High Barnet and
Mill Hill East.
Northern Rail
A TOC (2) (qv), 2004, replacing Arriva
Trains Northern (qv) and First North
Western (qv).
Northern Spirit Ltd
Renaming of RRNE (qv), TOC (2) (qv),
1998. Had contractual agreements with
West Yorkshire, Greater Manchester, South
Yorkshire and Tyne & Wear PTEs (qv).
Franchise awarded to Arriva Trains
Northern in 2000. *See* Arriva.
North Kent Line
London (Charing Cross and Cannon
St.)–Deptford (North Kent East Junc)–
Blackheath–Woolwich–Dartford[–Strood]
(or via Greenwich).
North Lindsey
see NLLR.
North London Line (obs)
London (Broad St.)–Gospel Oak–Willesden
(HL)–Kew Bridge/Richmond.

North London Lines

BR brand name, introduced 1989, for the Euston/Liverpool St.–Watford and the North Woolwich–Willesden Junction–Richmond electric services. *See also* North London Railways.

North London Railways

Brand name adopted 1994 for North Woolwich–Richmond; Euston–Watford Junction; Euston–Northampton; Gospel Oak–Barking; and Willesden Junction–Clapham Junction lines and services. A TOU (*qv*), 1994. A TOC (*2*), 1997, operating local services in north London over the former NLR (*qv*), also London (Euston)–Watford–Northampton–Birmingham and branches Watford–St Albans and Bletchley–Bedford. Renamed Silverlink Train Services (*qv*), 1997.

Northumbrian

Express between London (Kings Cross) and Newcastle, introduced 1949. Name dropped 1964. Revived 1988 for service between Poole and Newcastle via Birmingham. Name dropped 1990. *See also* Dorset Scot.

North Wales Land Cruise

see Land cruise.

North Warwick[shire] Line

Birmingham (Tyseley)–Henley in Arden–Bearley. *See also* BNW&SR.

North-West Dane

Blackpool–Manchester–Harwich service connecting with sailings for Esbjerg and connection for Copenhagen, so named 1987. Name dropped 1988. *See also* Loreley.

North West Regional Rlys/Trains

A TOU (*qv*), 1994. A TOC (*2*), 1997, operating services as North Western Trains in Lancashire, also Chester–Holyhead and branches; Crewe–Birmingham; Stafford–Stoke–Manchester; Preston–Windermere; Barrow–Whitehaven–Carlisle; Manchester–Sheffield; Clitheroe–Carlisle. Acquired by First Group 1998 and renamed First North Western; *see* FNW.

North Yorkshire Moors

see NYMR.

North Western

1. L&NWR (*qv*).
2. (US) Chicago & Northwestern RR.

North-West Express

Hook of Holland–Copenhagen service, extended to Stockholm in summer. Introduced 1952.

Norwest (RS)(obs)

The L&NWR, its locos, or its men.

Nose [of a crossing]

The point at which the outer rail of diverging line crosses inner rail of the line it is leaving.

Nose [of a loco] (USRS)

The head or front end.

Nosebag (RS)

Food carried to work and eaten while on duty.

Nosing (USRS)

An unpleasant and alarming oscillation sometimes appearing when railcars and interurban cars are driven at very high speeds.

Notation [of electric and diesel locos]

The most usual form is that in which a single motored axle is denoted by 'A', two coupled motored axles by 'B', and three by 'C' and so on. Carrying wheels in front and behind motored axles are shown by a numeral denoting the number of axles.

B

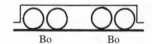

Bo   Bo

Co   Co

2   C   C   2

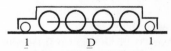

1   D   1

Notation of electric and diesel locos

Axles individually driven are similarly lettered but suffixed 'o'. Thus 1D1 = one pair of carrying wheels in front, four coupled motored axles and one pair of carrying wheels behind, Bo Bo = four axles, each individually driven.

A plus (+) sign indicates that the drawgear is mounted on the trucks/bogies and there is a coupling between the trucks/bogies to transmit the tractive effort. If such coupling is not present and the tractive effort is transmitted via the pivots through the main frames, a hyphen sign (-) is used instead.

Notation [of steam locomotives]
see Continental notation; Whyte's notation.

Notch, to give it/her a, (RS)
To apply power at first notch briefly, with brakes on, to call the guard's attention or to shake the train in the hope of dislodging a sticking air-door.

Notch up, to (RS)
To reduce the period in which steam enters the cylinders of a loco, or to increase power on electric trains and tramcars.

Notre Métier
The *SNCF* magazine, founded 1938. Since 1952 known as *La Vie du Rail* (qv).

Nottingham Express Transit
see NET.

Nottingham Pullman
Service between London (St Pancras) and Nottingham, introduced 1990.

Nottingham Suburban Rly/Line
Trent Lane Junction–St Ann's Well–Sherwood–Daybrook, 1889–1951.

Notworker (RS)
Facetious term for BR Network SouthEast class 442 Wessex electric emus and class 465. From their initial unreliability and late delivery.

Nought nought (RS)(obs)
Standard 95 lb bullhead rail.

Novatrans (Fr)
A subsidiary of *SNCF* which handles international and intermodal freight traffic.

Nozomi
A Tokyo–Osaka Shinkansen (qv) service. Introduced 1991, average speed 128.1 mph.

NP
National Power; operated own wagons and locos for power station traffic. Sold to EWS (qv), 1998.

NP (US)
Northern Pacific RR.

NP&FR
North Pembrokeshire & Fishguard Rly. Inc 1878 as Rosebush & Fishguard Rly, name changed to NP&FR 1884. Absorbed Narberth Road & Maenclochog Rly 1881, opened Clynderwen to Letterston 1895 (Clynderwen–Rosebush section reopened) and Letterston to Fishguard & Goodwick 1899, part of GWR from 1898.

NPCCS
Non passenger-carrying coaching stock, BR, (i.e. for parcels, mail, perishables, etc.).

NR
1. National Rail (qv).
2. Network Rail (qv).
3. Norfolk Rly, inc as Yarmouth & Norwich Rly 1842, opened 1844, amalgamated with Norwich & Brandon Rly and adopted title of NR 1845, leased by ECR, 1848, purchase completed 1850.
4. Northern Rly [of India], formed 1952.
5. Nigerian Rly, formed 1912. Became NRC (qv).

NRC
1. National Railway Corporation Ltd [Australia], formed 1991, jointly owned by Commonwealth, New South Wales and Victorian Governments.
2. Nigerian Rly Corporation, 1955. 3,557 km of 1,067 mm gauge.

NR CTRL
Network Rail CTRL Ltd; a company formed 2003 to manage the CTRL (qv) until completion of construction in 2007/8.

NRDC (obs)
Non Repairs Domestic Coal; a branding on old wooden coal wagons used by BR in the 1950s to augment coal stocks.

NRES
National Rail Enquiry Service. A central enquiry service providing route and timetable information to the public,

established as a telephone enquiry service 1996, operated by ATOC (qv) on behalf of all TOC (*2*) (qv).

NRHS

National Railway Historical Society Inc, founded 1935, incorporated in US 1937. Over 15,000 members in 1990.

NRM

National Railway Museum (York). An outstation of the Science Museum, established under Transport Act, 1968, opened 1975 and the inheritor of the former BTC and rly company collections (except for LT and waterways items).

NRN

National Radio Network, a VHF Band 3 radio system inaugurated by BR and continued by National Railways (qv). Used for drivers' on board (qv) to shore (qv) communication and also for communication between work gangs and their offices, etc. *See also GSM-R.*

NRPC

see Amtrak.

NRS

National Railway Supplies: a private company formed to maintain trackside fixtures, 1996. Also responsible for retail sales of surplus railway equipment, etc. Britain's largest independent supplier of rly infrastructure materials and services.

NRT [Great Britain]

National Rail Passenger Timetable, a 1999 retitling of GBPRT (qv).

NRZ

National Rlys of Zimbabwe, formed 1980. *See also* RR (*6*). 2,745 km of 1,067 mm gauge.

NS

1. *Nederlandse Spoorwegen NV*; Dutch State Rlys, formed 1938. 2,809 km, mostly electrified.
2. Newcomen Society for the study of the history of engineering and technology, founded 1920, inc 1961.
3. Norfolk Southern [Corporation]; a merger of N&W and SR (*5*) in 1982.

NSB

Norges Statsbaner; Norwegian State Rlys. 4,218 km.

NSE

Network SouthEast; a BR business sector covering all passenger services in London and south-east England not worked by InterCity. Established June 1986 to succeed L&SE sector (qv). Ceased to exist 31 March 1994, following reorganization of BR preparatory to 'privatization'.

NSKT

No Signalman Key Token; single-line working with the drivers responsible for operating token instruments remote from the controlling signal box.*See also* Train staff/tablet/token and ticket.

NSL

National Sunday League (qv).

NSR

1. North Staffordshire Rly, inc 1847, first section opened 1848 Stoke–Crewe, 220 route miles by 1914, centred around Stoke-on-Trent. Part of LM&SR from 1923.
2. North Sunderland Rly, inc 1892, opened 1898, Chathill (NER) to North Sunderland and Seahouses; managed and worked by L&NER from 1939, and by BR 1948, closed 1951.

NST

No Signalman Token system, a method of single line working in which there is a manned signalbox only at one end of a single line section.

NSWGR

New South Wales Government Rlys (Aus); from 1972 part of the Public Transport Commission of New South Wales.

Number cruncher (RS)

A fanatical type of rly enthusiast given to collecting or 'observing' locomotives and other vehicles and recording their numbers until all have been seen.

The gear carried often includes binoculars, personal tape recorder and camera.

The somewhat pointless obsession is in extreme cases carried over from childhood and adolescence into middle and old age and is almost exclusively confined to males.

Number grabber (RS)

Number cruncher (qv).

Number one (RS)
The outer home (qv) signal. *See also* Right the one.

Number snatcher (RS)
A freight wagon checker; also another word for number cruncher (qv).

Number takers (obs)
Outdoor employees of the RCH (qv), stationed at junctions between different companies' systems to record and report the movement of all vehicles and wagon tarpaulins between one company and another. These men were the rock on which the whole clearing system was established: 'It is to them in great measure that the efficiency of the Clearing House is due' – *The Times,* 26 January 1892. Before 1847, men had been employed by individual companies on the same task – they were also known as 'wagon tellers' at that time.

NUR
1. North Union Rly, inc 1834 as an amalgamation of the Preston & Wigan Rly and the Wigan Branch Rly (opened 1832). Wigan to Preston opened 1838. Amalgamated with Bolton & Preston Rly (completed 1843) in 1844. Joint L&NWR and L&YR 1846–1921. Part of L&NWR 1922.
2. National Union of Railwaymen, founded 1913 by amalgamation of ASRS, GRWU and UP&SS (qv). Initial membership 267,611. Became RMT (qv), 1990.

Nutcrackers (RS)(obs)
The original L&SWR electric mu motor cars, after the characteristic clicking of their cab-mounted electrical contactors.

NVBS
Nederlandsche Vereeniging van Belangstellenden in het Spoor-en Tramwegen; the senior Dutch society catering for those interested in rlys and tramways.

NVK
Nationale Vervoer-Korporasie Beperk; National Transport Corporation of Namibia 1988. 2,382 km of 1,065 mm gauge, physically connected to Spoornet (South Africa).

NVLR
Nidd Valley Light Rly, Pateley Bridge to Lofthouse and Angram Dam, built by Bradford Corporation. LRO 1901, opened 1907, public passenger service to Lofthouse ceased 1929, line closed 1936.

NVR
see Nene Valley.

NWMR
North Wales Mineral Rly, inc 1844, opened Ruabon–Saltney 1846, amalgamated with Shrewsbury, Oswestry & Chester Junction Rly 1846 to form Shrewsbury & Chester Rly.

NWNGR
North Wales Narrow Gauge Rly, 1 ft 11½ in gauge, Dinas Junction (L&NWR) to South Snowdon (Rhyd-ddu) and branch to Bryngwyn, inc 1872, opened 1877, 1878, 1881. Part of WHR from 1922.

NWR
1. North Western Rly, inc 1846, opened Lancaster to Morecambe 1848, Skipton to Ingleton 1849, Clapham to Lancaster 1850. Worked by Midland Rly from 1852, vested in Midland 1871. Known colloquially as 'The Little North Western' to distinguish it from the L&NWR.
2. North Western Rly [of India]. After the partition of India it became the NW Rly of Pakistan (NW or NWR).
3. North West Regional Rlys (qv).

NWT
See North West Regional Rlys/Trains.

NWSR
North Western State Rlys [India], formed 1886. Later NWR (2).

NX System
An entrance–exit system of route-setting in power signal boxes in which a route is set by one button or switch on the panel at the entrance to the route and by activating another at the exit.

NY&CR
North Yorkshire & Cleveland Rly, inc 1854, Picton–Grosmont, opened 1857, 1858, 1861, 1865; part of NER 1859.

NYC (US)
New York Central RR.

NYCTA
New York City Transit Authority, formed 1953 to operate and manage the bus, tramway (*3*) and local passenger rly systems in the NY City area. Part of MCTA (qv) 1968.

NYMR
North Yorkshire Moors Rly, preserved rly operating over the former BR line between Grosmont and Pickering since 1973.

NZASM
Nederlandsche Zuid Afrikaansche Spoorweg Maatschappij; a railway system in Transvaal, South Africa 1890–1900.

NZGR
New Zealand Government Rlys, formed 1876. Privatized 1993. *See* Tranz Rail Ltd.

O

OA&GB
Oldham, Ashton-under-Lyne & Guide Bridge, joint MS&LR and L&NWR 1862, LM&SR & L&NER, 1923–47, BR (M) 1948.

OAG Railguide
Formerly *ABC* (qv). Monthly timetables of rail services in Britain.

O&AT
Oxford & Aylesbury Tramroad, inc 1888; leased and worked WT (qv) 1894–1900, but did not build its proposed line from Brill to Oxford.

O&I
Otley & Ilkley Joint, Midland & NER 1865, LM&SR & L&NER 1923–47.

O&K
Orenstein & Koppel AG, established 1876, loco works at Potsdam, this becoming *VEB Locomotivbau Karl Marx* from 1948. Loco production ceased 1968. O&K now manufacture, inter alia, lifts, escalators and rly wagons.

O&R Rly
Oudh & Rohilkhand Rly; amalgamated with EIR (qv) 1923.

OAT
Overseas Ambulance Train, British Army. *See also* Ambulance train.

Oban bogies (RS)
Caledonian Rly 4–4–0 locos of 1882.

ÖBB
Österreichische Bundesbahnen; Austrian Federal Rlys, formed 1923–4. 6,123 km.

Oberland Express
Paris–Interlaken, introduced 1895. Calais–Interlaken winter sports train 1920–39. Through coaches for this route attached to other trains from 1946, but name dropped.

OBS
On Board Services, formerly InterCity OBS, became separate business 1994, responsible for on-train catering services. *See also* ERC; Rail Gourmet.

Observation car
A coach specially constructed with large windows, and end windows or open balcony, normally running as the last vehicle in a train, to provide passengers with the best possible views. Often furnished with special seating to facilitate enjoyment of the passing scenery. *See also* Vistadome.

Observatory tower (obs)
A structure erected above the line of a proposed tunnel from which open air sections of the planned rly alignment could be viewed by the surveyors; this facilitated accurate siting of the vertical shafts required for construction of the tunnel.

OC
1. Observation car (qv).
2. Open [level] crossing of a rly without barriers or signals; warning notices only. Usually an occupation crossing (qv) or a footpath crossing for pedestrians only.

Occupation crossing/level crossing
Crossing of a rly over a pre-existing private road or track. Not necessarily a public right of way. Facilities for crossing provided by the rly. *See also* OC (2).

Ocean Liner Express (obs)
A generic title used on roofboards of London (Waterloo)–Southampton boat trains.

Ocean Specials (obs)
Boat trains with restaurant cars and luxury

saloons operated by GWR and BR(W) between Plymouth Docks and London (Paddington) in connection with ocean liners, usually in the 'Up' direction only.

Ocean terminal

Facilities for interchange of traffic between ocean liners and boat trains to and from London (Waterloo) opened at Southampton Docks, 1950, including two reception halls, a VIP lounge, customs examination halls, etc. The 1950 building was demolished in 1983 but later terminal facilities remain in use.

OCEM (Fr)

Office Centrale d'Études de Matériel, French agency for standardizing designs. The all-steel coaches delivered to the French railways between the wars were an *OCEM* design.

OCS

1. On Company's Service; indicating that an item so marked travelled free.
2. One Control Switch; a route-setting signalling system (qv) with a single switch to control each route.

OCT

Open Carriage Truck (qv).

OCTI

Office Central des Transports Internationaux par Chemins de Fer, Central Office for International Rly Transport, the chief executive body controlling application of the international conventions concerning carriage of freight, parcels and passengers by rail (CIM and CIV), mediating and conciliating in disputes related to these conventions.

Octopus

A 65-ton bogie hopper wagon used by engineers.

ODTC

One Day Travelcard, allowing unlimited travel by NR (1), Underground, buses and trams around London within all or some specified zones. Also includes out and return journey from specified rly stations outside Greater London. *See also* Travel card.

Oerlikon stock

Popular name for the L&NWR electric saloon stock of 1915–23 for its London area services; from its 260 hp traction motors made by Maschinenfabrik Oerlikon, Switzerland. This stock was withdrawn in 1955–60.

OES

One Engine in Steam (qv).

OEZ

Ost Europäische Zeit; East European Time.

Off

1. *see* On/off.
2. (RS) Starting from, e.g. 'the 10.00 off Bournemouth' = the train starting from Bournemouth at 10.00.

Officer (RS)

A signalman. This term derives from the early use of policemen as signalmen.

Officer, Rly

see Railway officers.

Officers

See Railway Officers; RROA.

Official Guide

The Official Guide of the Railways and Steam Navigation Lines of the United States, Porto Rico, Canada, Mexico and Cuba. The North American equivalent of 'Bradshaw', first published 1867. It contains timetables and other particulars of all rlys in US and Canada, and is issued monthly. In modern times airline timetables have also been admitted.

Off sheet (LTRS)

An error in train register made by a signalman.

Off side

On the right of the train in the direction of travel.

Off the book (LTRS)

Train service running out of timetable order.

Off the front(s) (LTRS)

Employee demoted from motorman to guard after committing a disciplinary offence.

Off the pipes/road (RS)

Derailed.

OFQ

Organization For Quality. BR reorganization of 1990–2 abolishing regions and establishing 'profit centres', etc.

Ogmore Vale Extension Rly

Tondu–Margam–Port Talbot.

Ohio
TC for 'Send on with all speed to . . .'.
OHL
Overhead Line (carrying traction current).
Oil can (USRS)
A tank wagon for petroleum or other oil products.
Oiseau Bleu
TEE Paris–Brussels introduced 1957. Ceased 1984.
Oiseau Bleu Pullman
CIWL service Paris–Antwerp, introduced 1929, extended to Amsterdam 1936, ceased 1939, restored (Paris–Brussels) 1947–57 with *SNCF* stock, then replaced by a *TEE – Oiseau Bleu* (qv).
OLC
Open Level Crossing. A level crossing without signals to control road traffic.
Oldbury
Oldbury Railway Carriage & Wagon Co. Ltd, Oldbury, Birmingham, 1863–1902. Became part of MCW (qv).
Old head (USRS)
An experienced railwayman.
Old Line, The
Roade–Weedon–Rugby.
Old Reliable, The (US)
The slogan of the Louisville & Nashville RR.
Old Road, The
Chesterfield (Tapton Junc)–Killamarsh–Rotherham. Also used for the original line from Brockenhurst to Poole via Ringwood to distinguish it from the later route via Sway.
Old Worse & Worse, The
Nickname for the OW&WR (qv).
OLE
Overhead Line Equipment. The totality of wires suspended over an electric rly, including insulators, fittings and other attachments such as feeders, auto transformer feeders, overhead line switches, jumpers (5) (qv) and return conductors. *See also* Catenary; Contact wire; Dropper; Headspan; Knuckle.
OLGA
Overhead Line [Structure] Gauging train (qv).

OMC
Operating & Maintenance Centre (DLR).
Omnibus, train (Fr)/**omnibus, treno** (It) (both obs)
Train stopping at most but not necessarily all the stations on its route. *See also* Tramway, train.
OMO
One Man Operation. Now replaced by the 'non-sexist' OPO (qv).
OMS (obs)
Organization for the Maintenance of Supplies; formed 1925 to organize volunteers in the event of a major strike affecting the rlys and other essential transport.
ON
Overground Network; brand name for those National Rail services in the TfL (qv) area in which train frequency is four tph (qv) outside rush hours, Mondays to Saturdays (inclusive); inaugurated 2003, a partnership between the TOC (2) (qv) and TfL.
On board
Used to distinguish any equipment or features on trains from those located On shore (qv).
On/off
Block is said to be 'on' when the signal is at danger, or 'on'. When a train is accepted by the signal box in advance, the block is taken 'off' and the signal is pulled 'off'.
ONCFM (Fr)
Office National des Chemins de Fer du Maroc, Moroccan Rlys. 1,907 km.
ONE
Brand name 2004 for Greater Anglia (qv) services in East Anglia using Liverpool Street (London) station, all of which are Operated [by] National Express.
On or near the line
Network Rail define this as on the line itself, or within 3 m (10 ft) of the nearest rail of any line (unless the rail is on the other side of any intervening permanent fence or structure). Station platforms are excluded, unless a person is working within 1.25 m of the platform edge.

On Time

Monthly newspaper of LM&SR (qv)
Operating Department, published
December 1934–September 1939.

One arm bandit

1. (RS) AWS equipment.
2. (RS) Stock with a combined traction
   and brake controller handle.

One back, to go (LTRS)

Reversing the motors of an electric
train, especially for an emergency stop.
From the movement of the controller
handle.

One Engine in Steam

A method of working single lines
(usually dead end single line branches)
which restricted operation to one
train on the line at any given time. A
wooden staff for A to B or B to A was
carried to authorize each journey and
normal block working (qv) was
dispensed with. Any points at
intermediate locations or at the branch
terminus were worked from a
ground frame unlocked by a key
incorporated in the train staff. Now called
'One Train on Line'/OTL. *See also*
Annett's Key; Train staff/tablet/token
and ticket.

One on! (RS)

A shouted warning of a train approaching.

One rounder (LTRS)

Duty with only one round trip to be
worked.

One under (RS)

A person fallen under a train (normally at a
station and normally a suicide attempt).

On juice (RS)

A train picking up traction current.

Only Way, The

Slogan of the Chicago & Alton RR,
'The only way between Chicago and St
Louis'. From the title of a dramatization of
Dickens' *The Tale of Two Cities*, performed
in Chicago in 1899.

On shore

See Shore

On the Advertised (USRS)

On time, i.e. a train running precisely
according to the advertised timetable.

On the back (LTRS)

Working as a guard.

On the bells (RS)(obs)

A freight train under permissive working
(qv).

On the block (RS)

Held at a stop signal, line congested.

On the blocks (RS)

Against the buffer stops of a terminal road.

On the blood (RS)(obs)

At full steam pressure. From the red mark
on the pressure dial in the cab.

On the board (LTRS)

The appearance of a train on the train
describer/indicator board.

On the cars (US)

On the train.

On the cushions (RS)

Footplatemen and other uniformed
employees travelling in public passenger
accommodation while on duty. Also 'on the
mahogany' (RS).

On the deck/floor/ground (RS)

Derailed.

On the front(s) (LTRS)

Driving an electric train (usually used by
guard/motormen).

On the ham (RS)

Working overtime.

On the handle(s) (RS)(obs)

Driving an electric or diesel train as
distinct from steam loco driving.

On the juice (RS)

Running over electrified lines.

On the Panel (LTRS)

1. Off sick. Panel (obs)(S) = the pre-NHS
   appointed panel of National Insurance
   doctors.
2. On the trainers' panel, qualified to train
   other staff in the same grade.

On the pitch (LTRS)

A senior uniformed employee undertaking
duty on station platform.

On the point (USRS)

To ride at the leading end of a loco or wagon
to ensure safe movement (e.g. in a yard).

On the shovel (RS)(obs)

Firing a steam loco.

On the spot (USRS)

Time taken for refreshment and rest.

On the stops (RS)
Next to the buffer stops.
On Time
Monthly newspaper of LM&SR (qv)
Operating Department published
December 1934–September 1939.
Op (USRS)
A telegraph operator.
Open
GWR TC for various types of open
wagon.
Open Block
When the block system (qv) was first
introduced, a block section was regarded as
being clear for entry by a train, whether or
not one was due, provided there was no
train already in the section. After the Abbots
Ripton accident of 1876 this system was
replaced by 'closed' block, with the
associated procedure of offering and
accepting trains between adjacent signal
boxes. However, with the introduction of
track circuit block (qv) there was a return to
the open block system as signals cleared to
green once track circuits showed the section
of line in advance was not occupied.
Open carriage truck (obs)
A four- or six-wheeled open flat wagon
used for transporting road vehicles such as
horse-drawn carriages and vans, also
agricultural machinery, etc. Usually loaded
and unloaded at a carriage dock (qv).
Open coach
A passenger coach with a centre
gangway and seats either side and no
compartments.
Open [level] crossing
See OC (2).
Opening out
Digging out old ballast (qv) to expose
sleepers (qv), timbers or bearers for
inspection, relaying or respacing. *See also*:
Dinting.
Open line
A section of line in which signals are
normally left in the 'off' position.
Open point(s) (obs)
A movable point used on horse and steam-
worked tramways (3), with a tongue
frequently only one inch deep. When

passing through such points, tram drivers
pulled their animals halfway across the
road until the tramcar wheels were brought
to take the correct path.
Open station
A station without ticket inspection and
collection at the exit and entry to
platforms. Also 'open platform/s'.
Open the gate, to (USRS)
To switch a train into or out of a siding.
Open up, to
1. (LTRS) To open train doors.
2. (RS) To accelerate a train.
Open wagon/Opens
A freight or engineer's wagon with closed
sides but open at the top, designed to carry
coal, ballast and other 'minerals', as well as
timber and any general freight not liable to
damage in wet weather (or sufficiently
protected by tarpaulins).
Operator (US)
The official responsible for transmitting
and receiving by telegraph or telephone the
train orders (qv) issued by the dispatcher
and for passing train orders to train crews.
At small stations, this task was often
combined with other station duties.
OPO
One Person Operation; a train controlled
entirely by its driver, i.e. without any guard
or conductor.
Opposing trains
Trains moving towards one another over a
single track.
OPRF/OPRAF (obs)
Office of Passenger Rail Franchising. Set
up 1994 under Railways Act, 1993 to sell
rail franchises for TOC (qv) to private
sector bodies. Powers transferred to SRA
(qv), 2000.
Opsco
Operations Company under PPP (qv) scheme
for London Underground; operates train
services, collects fares, oversees engineering
standards and safety of passengers and staff,
replacing LUL (qv) in these roles, under
TfL (qv). Pays ISC (qv) to Infraco (qv).
OR
1. (obs) Owner's Risk parcel traffic
   handled at cheap rate.

2. Okehampton Rly, inc 1862, 1863, 1864, leased to L&SWR 1863, first section, Yeoford to North Tawton opened 1865. Name changed to D&CR 1865.

3. Oldbury Rly, inc 1873, as Dudley & Oldbury Junction Rly, Langley Green Junc to Oldbury, name changed to OR 1881, opened 1884, 1885, worked by GWR, part of GWR 1894.

4. Oxford Rly, inc 1843, Didcot–Oxford, opened 1844, part of GWR 1844.

5. Oystermouth Rly: *see* Mumbles.

Orange peel (RS)
A high-visibility vest (HVV). *See* HV clothing.

ORC

1. *Organisme Repartiteur Centrale Voitures-Lits*; European sleeping car pool.

2. (US) Order of Railroad Conductors; hence, a conductor.

Orcadian
A restaurant car service between Inverness and Wick/Thurso, so named 1936. Name revived 1962 but soon dropped, perhaps because connections with the Orkney sailings were not good. Name revived 1983, and later used for a BR 'Land Cruise' train.

ORCATS
Operational Research Computer Allocation of Tickets to Services. A system evolved by BR (*1*) (qv) as a basis for distributing ticket sales revenue among its constituent parts and still used under the privatized regime to determine how much is due to the TOC (*2*) (qv). 'Orcats raiding' involves engineering the train services provided to secure maximum revenue in return for minimum expenditure and low traffic levels. *See also* RSP.

Order board (US) (obs)
The post or location where train orders (qv) were placed to be grabbed by the crews of passing trains.

Order loop (US) (obs)
A metal rod and loop enabling an operator (qv) to pass a train order (qv) up to a member of the crew of a train not stopping at a station.

Ords (RS)(obs)
Long-distance services stopping at most

stations, featuring a variety of rolling stock and locos. A term mainly confined to the GCR (qv) and L&NER (qv); presumably derived from 'ordinary'.

ORE
Office de Recherches et d'Essais. UIC (qv) organization based at Utrecht, Holland and concerned with research and trials carried out by member rly administrations, studying costing and rationalization. Replaced 1990 by ERRI (qv).

Oresund Link
A fixed rail link using bridges and tunnels to cross the water gap between Denmark and Sweden, allowing through trains between Copenhagen and Malmø. Opened throughout 1 July 2000.

Orient Express
CIWL pioneer 'hotel train' service between Paris and Constantinople (Istanbul) via Munich, Vienna and Bucharest, composed of sleeping and dining cars, introduced 1883, with some sections by sea and river transport. Through rail coaches Paris–Istanbul from 1889 (then 67 h 35 min) reduced to 61 h (via Belgrade) by 1902, suspended 1914. Re-introduced 1919 as Paris–Vienna–Warsaw service. From 1921 this service provided through sleeping cars Paris to Bucharest and Istanbul, also a through sleeper Calais–Bucharest, in connection with sailings from Britain. Through sleeping cars between Ostend and Istanbul and Amsterdam and Bucharest were attached/detached at Linz. After WW2, the OE divided at Stuttgart, one portion running to Prague and Warsaw. The Paris–Bucharest through service was fully resumed in 1955. Discontinued east of Vienna, and beyond Prague 1961, extended to Budapest in summer 1964 and again to Bucharest 1965. Ceased 1987 and replaced by daily Vienna–Bucharest through sleeping car and one through ordinary coach between Paris and Bucharest. Through carriages to Bucharest and Budapest withdrawn June 2001.

ORR
Office of the Rail Regulator, set up 1994 under the Railways Act, 1993 to license rly

operators, improve access arrangements and protect the interests of all rail users under the privatization of the rlys of Great Britain. Some functions transferred to SRA (qv), 2000. Under the Railways & Transport Safety Act, 2004, the post of Rail Regulator was abolished and replaced by a nine-member Regulatory Board headed by a chairman appointed by the Secretary of State for Transport. This board, assisted by a chief executive, had the same functions as the former Regulator but also assumed the responsibilities for rail safety formerly resting with the HSC/HSE (qv). With this change, ORR then stood for the Office of Rail Regulation.

ORT
Oil Rail Terminal; a BR facility providing reception, storage and distribution facilities for trainloads of petroleum products for more than one oil company.

OS
1. (USRS) (obs) On [the] sheet; the recording of the passing or departure time of a train on the dispatcher's train sheet as reported by an operator (qv), hence 'O-sing' for the act of recording times of trains.
2. (USRS) On schedule, i.e. on time.

Osborne Judgement
Walter V. Osborne, a GER employee, secretary of the Walthamstow branch of the ASRS (qv), refused to pay the union's compulsory parliamentary levy to Labour Party funds and with support from the Conservative *Daily Express*, took legal action to restrain the union from using any of its funds for political objects. At this time MPs received no salary from public funds and the three railwaymen in parliament relied on the unions for their income and campaign expenses. In 1909 the House of Lords endorsed the Appeal Court's decision that Osborne was entitled to restrain the ASRS from raising the levy. The anomaly was removed by the Trade Union Act 1913, which allowed a trade union to spend money on political objects approved by a majority of members, with an option for individuals to contract out. Osborne, who

had continued his campaign up to 1914, was expelled from the NUR in that year.

OSE
Organismos Siderodromos Ellados; Hellenic Rlys Organization, a limited co. formed 1971, owned by the state, *See also CH*.

Osgood Bradley
Osgood Bradley Car Co., Worcester, Mass, US, established 1833, rly, tramway and interurban car builders. Absorbed by Pullman Standard (qv), 1930.

OsSShD
Organisation für die Zusammenarbeit der Eisenbahnen; Organisation for Railway Collaboration, operating in Eastern Europe and Asiatic communist countries from 1957.

Ostbahn (Ger)
Name used for rlys in German-occupied Poland, 1939–45. Under DRB (qv) from 1943.

Ostend–Cologne Pullman
CIWL service 1929–39 in connection with sailings to and from Britain. In its period, it provided the fastest surface link between Britain and Germany.

Ostend–Karlsbad Express
Introduced 1895, ceased 1914, restored after WW1, ceased finally in 1939.

Ostend–Vienna Express
CIWL service (via Brussels) introduced 1894 in connection with sailings to and from Britain. Revived after WW1 and again in 1950 (name restored 1951).

Ost–West Express
Through sleeping car train between Paris and Moscow, introduced 1960. Ceased 1994, replaced by un-named Moscow–Warsaw–Berlin–Brussels service.

OTDR
On Train Data Recorder; same as OTMR (qv).

OTL/OTOL
One Train on Line; modern term for One Engine in Steam (qv).

OTM
On the Move, monthly publication for all LRT (qv) staff from January 1996.

OTM/P
On Track Machines/Plant, self-propelled or capable of being moved on rails in a train; includes cranes and track relayers.

OTMR

On Train Monitoring and Recording, providing essential information about a train's speed, responses to signals, braking, power door operation and other safety parameters. Built to survive severe impacts and designed to assist in establishing the cause of accidents. The rly equivalent of the 'black box' fitted to passenger aircraft. Introduced by BR (1) (qv) 1987–9.

Ottley

A Bibliography of British Railway History by George Ottley, first published 1966, a definitive work. Second edition 1983 and also *Supplement*, 1989, covering publications 1964–80. Second Supplement published 1998 covering 1981–1995, also addenda and corrigenda; compiled by R&CHS (qv).

Otto Lilienthal

EC Berlin–Zurich, introduced 1991.

OTW

One train working. A modern version of One Engine in Steam (qv). *See also* OTL.

Ouest

Chemin de fer de L'Ouest; Western Rly of France. Part of *État* (State Rlys) from 1909.

Outer Circle (obs)

A London train service worked by the L&NWR, 1872–1909: Broad St.–Hampstead Heath–Willesden Junction High Level–Kensington (Addison Road)–Earls Court–Mansion House. A Willesden Junc–Earls Court remnant lasted until 1940.

Outer home signal

A home signal (qv) about ¹/₄ m on the approach side of what is then called the inner home signal. Provides additional overlap at busy points. On the LM&SR and BR (M) known as 'Home 1'. *See also* Home signal; Inner home signal.

Outer rail (LT)

Term used to describe track used by the London Underground Circle Line trains travelling in a clockwise direction. *See also* Inner rail.

Outfit car (US)

A coach fitted out for the feeding and accommodation of construction and maintenance men working on the rly.

Out of correspondence

Points not correctly set.

Out of gauge load/vehicle

A very wide load or vehicle which exceeds the loading gauge (qv) and may even foul adjacent tracks but is still capable of being handled on the rly under special working arrangements. *See also* Exceptional load.

Outrider

Crane stabilizing arm.

Outrider (RS)

An employee not belonging to the appropriate trade union.

Outside (obs)

The upper/top deck of a double-deck tramcar (qv), mostly without weather protection in the early years. However, use of the term persisted until the 1960s, long after top decks were roofed over and completely enclosed. *See also* Inside.

Outside edge

Back edge (of a rail) (qv).

Outside porter

Badge porter (qv).

Outside swingers (RS)

Locos with outside frames and outside cranks to the coupling rods.

Outward half

Half an Edmondson ticket applying to the outward journey. The other section is known as the 'return half'.

Overbridge

Any bridge over a rly, also known as an overline bridge.

Overend, Gurney failure

When the City of London finance house of Overend, Gurney & Co. failed on 11 May 1866, largely as a result of the speculative character of rly schemes in 1865–6, it brought the principal rly contractor, Sir Samuel Morton Peto, to bankruptcy and caused acute financial difficulties for rly companies, notably the GER, GWR, LB&SCR and NBR.

Overhead

Generic term for traction current wire and supporting cables over an electric rly or tramway (3).

Overland (US)
A steam loco with 4–10–2 wheel
arrangement.

Overland Express/Mail
see Peninsular Express.

Overland road
Light track laid over the surface of the
ground by contractors during rly
construction, used for removal of
spoil, etc.

Overland Route, The (US)
Slogan of the Union Pacific RR.

Overlap
In signalling, the distance in advance of a
stop signal which must be free from
obstruction before a movement is allowed
to approach that signal. The standard
British overlap beyond a home signal is
440 yd/402.3 metres although this is
modified in special circumstances.

Overlap track circuit
A short safety margin in advance of a signal
operated by track circuits (qv).

Over-rider
Locking bar fitted to draw gear of all
British post 1992-built stock to reduce
telescoping (qv) on impact.

Over the Alps (RS)
see Alps/over the Alps.

Overthrow
The extra overhang at the centre and ends
of a vehicle on curved and canted track
which must be taken into account when
assessing lateral clearances; it is dependent

Overthrow

on the radius of the curve and the length of
the wheelbase of the vehicle.

Over time
Delayed.

OVGS (obs)
Orange Free State Rlys.

OVR
Ogmore Valley Rly, inc 1863, opened
Tondu–Nantymoel 1865, amalgamated
with LVR and L&OR, 1866.

OW&WR
Oxford, Worcester & Wolverhampton Rly,
inc 1845, opened 1850, 1852, 1853, 1854,
1855, 1858, 1859, amalgamated 1860 with
Newport, Abergavenny & Hereford and
Worcester & Hereford Rlys to become
WMR (qv).

Owl (USRS)
A late-night train, or a night operator.

Owl car (US)
An all-night service tramcar.

Owl service (US)
An all-night rly or tramway (*3*) service.

Oxford Pullman
All-Pullman service introduced
1967 between London (Paddington) and
Oxford, ceased 1969.

Oxo Workhouse (LTRS)
Oxford Circus station; from its high level of
activity and traffic.

Oyster
1. TC for the civil engineer's ballast brake
   van.
2. A universal smartcard microchip card
   reader ticketing system involving prepaid
   'Oyster Cards' used by the passenger at
   entry points; adopted by TfL (qv) for
   use on London Underground rlys, the
   DLR (qv), buses and trams from 2003.

P

PA
Public Address [system].

PA (Fr)
Point d'Arrêt, stopping point.

Pablo Casals
EC *TALGO* sleeping car service between Barcelona and Berne, introduced 1989, extended to Milan 1989, Zurich portion added 1990.

Pacers
BR four-wheeled diesel railcars with bus type bodies introduced 1983 onwards (classes 140, 141, 142, 143 and 144).

Pacific
US and, later, also British term for steam loco with 4–6–2 wheel arrangement. From the rly first ordering this type – the Missouri Pacific RR.

Packers (RS)
Platelayers, track maintenance men. From packing (qv).

Packing
Forcing ballast under and around sleepers to strengthen the trackbed and on curves to raise the outer rail. Hence packers (qv).

Packing brake van
A brake van (qv) adapted to carry packing materials and forming part of a breakdown train (qv).

Packwagen (Ger)
Luggage van.

Paco
GWR TC for various types of horse box.

PACT
BR acronym for Paved Concrete Track, a form of construction that eliminates the necessity for routine maintenance such as tamping (qv) in difficult locations like tunnels.

PAD
see PA panels.

Padarn
4 ft/1,219 mm gauge rly built to carry slate from quarries around Llyn Padarn (near Llanberis) to Port Dinorwic. Opened 1843. Main line closed 1961, completely closed 1969. Part of route along Llyn Padarn reopened 1971, 1972 as *Rheilffordd Llyn Llanberis* (Llanberis Lake Rly).

Padded cells (obs)
Popular name for the original C&SLR cars, which had no windows apart from narrow toplights and were upholstered up to that level.

Paddle
1. (RS) An insulated tool for lifting a collector shoe (qv) clear of the conductor rail (qv).
2. (USRS) A semaphore signal arm.

Paddle boxes/boats (RS)
L&SWR Drummond T14 4–6–0 locos of 1911–12. From the shape and width of their driving wheel splashers, which resembled this feature of a paddle steamer.

Paddle wheel (USRS)
A narrow gauge loco with an outside frame. From the resemblance to a paddle steamer's wheels.

Paddy (RS)
1. A train which removes coal from a pithead.
2. The Irishman express.
3. Any train to and from Stranraer or other ports for Ireland.

Paddy Mail (RS)(obs)
Any train specially provided to carry navvies or colliers to and from their workplace.

Pagodas (RS)
The standard GWR corrugated iron passenger shelters used for halts (qv) and platforms (qv). From the inward curving shape of the roofs.

Pail hands (RS)
Carriage cleaners.

Pair, to do a (LTRS)
To adjust the disposition of crews on two trains.

Pair of wheels (RS)(obs)
The traditional type of two-wheeled hand barrow for use by platform staff. *See also* Sack truck.

Palace (USRS)
A caboose (qv).

Palatine
Express between London (St Pancras) and Manchester (Central), so named 1938, ceased 1939, name restored 1957, dropped 1966.

Palatino
Overnight express between Paris and Rome, introduced 1969.

Pallet van
A van with doors designed specifically for loading palletized traffic. *See also* Palwag.

Palwag/van
TC for wagon or van designed for traffic loaded on pallets.

PAN
SR six-car emu corridor set including one PANtry car (qv), for fast services, 1935, 6-PAN.

Pan
The uppermost section of a pantograph (qv) which carries the renewable carbon or copper strips collecting the traction current from the overhead (qv); also an abbreviation for pantograph (qv).

Panama Limited
Illinois Central RR express between Chicago and New Orleans, formerly the Chicago & New Orleans Limited. Renamed Panama Limited in 1911 on completion of the Panama Canal. Schedule of 21 h in 1926, 18 h in 1942. Now operated by Amtrak as City of New Orleans.

Pan catcher (RS)
A device which prevents pantograph-

equipped locos and cars from proceeding beyond the end of overhead traction current wires with their pantographs still raised.

Panda
Hamburg–Zurich ICE (qv) service 1992, the first international ICE.

P&C
Points (qv) and crossings (qv).

P&D
Preparation and Disposal; a term in use in motive power depots.

P&DSR
Paignton & Darmouth [Steam] Rly; preserved line dating from 1973 using former BR Paignton–Kingswear line. Previously titled Torbay Steam Rly and Torbay & Dartmouth Rly. *See also* Dart Valley Rly plc.

P&LJ
Preston & Longridge Joint, L&NWR and L&YR, 1867–1921.

P&N (US)
Piedmont & Northern Rly.

P&O Express
see Peninsular or P&O [Overland] Express.

P&O Punjab Express
An express between Bombay, Delhi and Peshawar, in connection with P&O liner sailings, introduced 1927.

Pandora (RS)
A bubble car (qv) converted in 2000 to a track recording and inspection vehicle fitted with video cameras and other recording equipment and GPS (qv). Used to compile a complete asset register of UK rly track and trackside features. Compiles input for manipulation by an on shore (qv) computer, and also records condition of the track, pitch, roll and heave and yaw, enabling bad patches to be pinpointed, using the GPS data. The video cameras are also used to check vegetation problems, signal sighting distances (qv), etc. *See also* NMT.

P&R
Park and Ride (qv).

Pandrol® clip
The trade name for a widely used FB rail-fastening spring steel clip which is hammered into position and extracted by

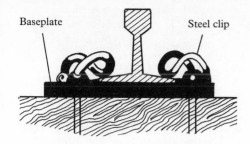

Baseplate · Steel clip

mechanized devices (Pandriver® and Pandrex®). Adopted by BR from 1959.

P&WJ
Preston & Wyre Joint, L&NWR and L&YR, 1849–1921.

P&WJR
Portpatrick & Wigtownshire Joint Rlys, Portpatrick–Newton Stewart–Castle Douglas formed 1885 from PR (*1*) and WR (*6*). Purchased jointly by CR (*1*), G&SWR, L&NWR and Midland Rly and operated as joint line 1885–1922. Then LM&SR.

Panel
Controls, indications and track diagram in a panel box (qv).

Panel box
A signal box or control centre with a panel (qv) employing buttons or switches as controls, as distinct from miniature levers. *See also* Power box.

Panhandle, The
St Louis, Cincinnati and Pittsburgh line of the Pennsylvania RR. From the slender (pan handle-shaped) northern part of West Virginia it traversed.

Panhandle line/service
A circular line or service (the pan) starting or finishing at different points, on lines diverging from the circle (the handles).

Pannier tank
A steam loco with its water tanks placed high up on the sides of the boiler, not resting on the frame plates. From the resemblance to the panniers on a pack horse.

Pannonia Express
Berlin–Budapest–Bucharest service, introduced 1958.

Pantagraph
Superseded alternative spelling of pantograph (qv).

Pantechnicon
See Lift Van.

Panto
Abbreviation for pantograph (qv).

Pantograph [collector]
A lightweight, self-adjusting framework raised and lowered by compressed air, which by means of springs maintains its collector pan and carbon strips in continuous contact at all speeds with the overhead wires carrying the traction current required to move an electric loco or train. It has the merit of operating without adjustment if the direction of travel is reversed.

Pantry cars (obs)
SR First Class cars introduced for the Eastbourne/Hastings electrification of 1935 which were equipped with a 'pantry' or servery staffed by the Pullman Car Co. (qv) from which were dispensed light refreshments and hot drinks but not cooked dishes. Service of teas, etc. at seats was extended along the whole train when conditions permitted. *See also* PAN.

Panzer link (RS)
Link (qv) allocated to tasks performed under instructions of Control (qv).

PA panels
Pre-assembled lengths of track, thus PAD = PA Depots.

Paper car (USRS)
A van carrying newspapers.

Paper ticket (obs)
Paper form with blank spaces for entering fare, destination, etc., used in place of normal ticket. Usually made out by booking clerk for destinations on another company's system. *See also* Blank card tickets, Excess fare receipt.

Paper weight (USRS)
A clerk.

PAR
Pakistan Rlys (Pakistan Western Rly 1947–74), 7,344 km, mainly 1,676 mm gauge. Physical connections to Indian Rlys. *See also* BAN.

Parachute crane
A form of water crane (qv) with a cylindrical tank fed from a centrally placed vertical pipe.

Paraffin burners (RS)
Diesel cars and locos.

Paraffin Junction (RS)(obs)
Any remote or exposed station or halt.
From the smell of the paraffin lamps used
for the lighting of such platforms.

Parallel rail (obs)
An early form of rail in which the upper and
lower flanges were of equal size, intended to
give a double life by turning. This proved
unsatisfactory in practice and the bullhead
rail (qv) was developed from it.

Parallel working
1. A four-track layout in which the two
   'Up' lines are on one side and the two
   'Down' lines on the other, so that a
   train may run from the main/fast line to
   the relief/local/slow line without fouling
   the path of traffic in the opposite
   direction.
2. A method of maximizing the use of flat
   junctions so that (e.g.) when the
   crossing is occupied by a train leaving a
   branch for the main line at a lefthand
   junction, a train in the opposite
   direction is allowed to proceed on to the
   branch from the main line. Use requires
   precise compliance with working
   timetables to be effective.

Parcel
GWR TC for parcels van.

Parcels Group
A BR business sector with its own board
from 1991. Divided into Red Star (qv),
Trainload and Track 29 (qv).

Parcels traffic
Any freight conveyed by passenger or
parcels trains in small consignments not
requiring the provision of special rail
vehicles.

Paris–Côte Belge–Pullman Express
CIWL Pullman services between Paris and
Knokke, ran in summer 1928 only.

Paris–Côte d'Azur
Paris–Ventimiglia couchette service, so
named 1957.

Parisienne
London (Waterloo)–Southampton service
connecting with overnight sailings for le
Havre and train to Paris, introduced 1981,

subsequently altered to operate via
Portsmouth Harbour. Name and through
rail bookings ceased 1983 but connections
remained available.

Paris–Madrid TALGO
Sleeping car service introduced 1981.

Paris–Ruhr
Service between Paris and Cologne (later
Dortmund), introduced 1954, *TEE* from
1957, terminated at Düsseldorf 1971,
renamed Molière (qv) 1973.

Paris–Scandinavia Express
Paris–Stockholm service introduced 1955.
Name dropped 1975.

Park and Ride/Park 'n' Ride
Provision of large car parks at stations to
encourage motorists to use rly services.
Parking is free or very cheap and access to
trains is made as easy as possible. *See also*
Kiss 'n' Ride, Railheading.

Parkway
A term coined by BR to describe a main
line station equipped with a very large car
park and within reasonable driving distance
or taxi/bus ride of a large city or town or
otherwise serving an important catchment
area. Some such stations are sited near
motorways. The first was Bristol Parkway,
opened in 1972.

Parliamentary fares/tickets/trains
Gladstone's 1844 Regulation of Railways Act
required all passenger rly companies to run
at least one train daily each way on all lines,
calling at all stations, at a fare not exceeding
one old penny (1*d*) a mile, the minimum
overall speed to be 12 mph, the accommodation to be protected from the weather.
Receipts from such trains were not liable to
passenger duty (qv). Although the Parliamentary
fare distinction virtually disappeared after
the passing of the Cheap Trains Act in 1883
(after which all Third class fares came down
to 1*d* a mile) most lines retained
'Parliamentary', all-stations services daily
until the early years of the BR era.

Parlor (USRS)
A caboose (qv).

Parlor Brakeman (USRS)
A freight train brakeman (qv) responsible
for protecting the rear of a train in an

emergency; from his right to travel in the relative comfort of the 'parlor', i.e. caboose (qv).

Parlor car (US)(obs)
A Pullman (qv) type passenger vehicle designed for daytime use.

Parlor maid/man (USRS)
Rear brakeman or flagman riding in the parlor (qv).

Parlor shack (USRS)
Rear end brakeman riding in the parlor (qv).

Parl(e)y (RS)(obs)
Parliamentary train (qv), but loosely used for any main line stopping train until the 1970s. Also for related fare and tickets.

Parmalee Transfer (US) (obs)
A pre-arranged and prepaid transfer by limousine between two Chicago terminal stations, primarily for the benefit of travellers between the East and West Coast centres, e.g. from New York to Los Angeles.

Parr
A 51-ton bogie wagon for carrying concrete sleeper track panels. Used by engineers.

Parrot wagon (TC)
A bogie wagon designed to make optimum use of the loading gauge (qv), for carrying aircraft parts or large packing cases containing small aircraft.

Parry People Mover
A form of ULR (qv) using small railcars/tramcars which are moved by a mechanical flywheel kept in rotation by periodical bursts of power from low voltage feeders sited at stopping places. First used for public services at Bristol Harbour 1998.

Parsifal
TEE Paris–Dortmund, introduced 1957, extended to Hamburg 1960. Became IC 1979, EC Paris–Cologne 1987.

Parsons & Prawns Line
London & Southampton, described in 1834 as likely to carry 'parsons and prawns – the one from Winchester, the other from Southampton'.

Parspex
TC for an unadvertised party special train.

Parthenon
Summer service Paris–Brindisi with ferry connection to Greece, so named 1978.

Partially fitted (obs)
A train in which only some wagons are fitted with continuous brakes (qv).

Parto
GWR TC for covered van with internal partitions.

Passante (It)
An underground rly affording through running connections across a city/town centre for conventional rail services (as at Milan and Turin). *See also* CrossRail; RER.

Passed cleaner (obs)
A steam locomotive cleaner who has been examined and passed out for firing duties on the footplate (qv).

Passed fireman (obs)
A fireman qualified to drive but not yet employed as a driver.

Passenger action
Term first adopted by LUL (qv), *c.* 1995, to describe any incident (qv) in which the smooth running of train services is disrupted by foolish/drunken/drugged/ violent or other unreasonable behaviour by individuals or groups.

Passenger Duty
A central government tax on passengers carried by rail, imposed from 1832 and collected by the British rly companies for the Inland Revenue. Introduced to compensate for the alleged loss of revenue caused by rly abstraction of road coach traffic, which had been taxed for many years. Removed from all fares up to and including 1*d* a mile by the Cheap Trains Act, 1883, effectively exempting most Third class fares. Removed from all fares by Finance Act, 1929.

Passenger full brake
See Full brake.

Passenger journeys
The number of throughout journeys made by passengers in a given period, return journeys counting as two.

Passenger loop
A BR term for an additional running line authorized for passenger trains, entry and

exit controlled from one signal box. *See also* Slow line.

Passenger mile

A measurement of traffic, the equivalent of one passenger travelling for one mile.

Passenger Service Agent

See PSA.

Passenger traffic

As well as passengers, the following were at one time all regarded as 'passenger traffic', suitable for carriage by passenger train and counted as passenger traffic for revenue purposes: bicycles, cars and motorcycles, bullion, horse-drawn carriages and vans, Government (armed forces) traffic, parcels, perishables (including milk), luggage, newspapers, birds & poultry, cattle, dogs, goats, horses, pigs, rabbits, sheep and other small animals, mail and railway letters (qv RLS). Also known as 'coaching traffic'.

Passimeter (obs)

A free-standing kiosk in a ticket hall of a station, designed to combine the facilities for issuing tickets on entry and checking them on exit and equipped with turnstiles operated by the booking clerk. First used in the US; introduced on the London Underground in 1921 and widely adopted by that undertaking between the wars. Also introduced by the Metropolitan Rly and the L&NER at suburban stations in the 1920s and 1930s. All Underground installations withdrawn as part of the UTS (qv).

PAT (LT)

Public Access Terminal; computer with touch screen providing timetable and route information for rlys, buses and trams in the London area, introduced at Hammersmith (H&CR), 1998.

Passing loop

Crossing loop (qv).

Patentee (obs)

A steam loco with 2–2–0 wheel arrangement.

Pates (RS)

LM&SR Patriot class 4–6–0 locos.

PATH

Port Authority Trans–Hudson; operated underground rlys beneath the Hudson River between New York and Jersey City and Newark (Hudson Tubes (qv)) from 1962. Now part of the MTA.

Path

Planned routing and timing of a train over specific lines relative to others using the same lines, i.e. a space for its unimpaired working without its interfering with other trains running ahead and behind it. *See also* Forcing a path.

Patrol length/route

The extent and route for a routine track and other infrastructure inspection and maintenance allocated to a patroller (qv).

Patrollers

Persons responsible for routine track safety inspections, looking for new and deteriorating defects in trackwork and structures, and carrying out minor maintenance tasks. Alternative titles: Patrolmen, Track Patrollers. *See also* Lengthmen; Patrol length/route; PLOD; Trackman, Track walker.

Paulin

US for tarpaulin.

Paved [concrete] track

Track without ballast or sleepers, the rails being fixed directly to a reinforced concrete slab through a continuous longitudinal pad. Also known as slab track.

Paxmans (RS)

BR class 29 locos; after the manufacturers.

PAYE

Pay As You Enter; system and vehicle design for tramways (3) and other road services, in which passengers pay their fare or show their ticket on entry. Originated in Montreal, Canada *c*. 1906.

Payload

Proportion of the total hauled weight of a train which is earning revenue.

PAYP

Pay As You Pass; system and vehicle design for tramways (3) in which passengers pay their fare or show their ticket as they pass the desk of a seated conductor. Originated in Peter Witt (qv) cars.

Pay-trains

BR term for local or branch line services in which tickets are issued/checked on the train by conductors. Introduced 1966.

PBA
Port of Bristol Authority.
PB&SSR
Portmadoc, Beddgelert & South Snowdon Rly, 1 ft 11¹/₂ in/597 mm gauge, inc 1901, partly built 1906–10, never officially opened. Acquired by WHR (qv) 1922.
PBC/PC
see Piggyback Consortium.
PC
Penn Central (qv).
PC (Fr)
Poste de Commandement, train control office.
PCC car
Presidents' Conference Committee [tram]car. Tramcar design for tramways (*3*), aiming to provide smooth acceleration, quiet running, good riding qualities and high traffic speeds, produced by a committee organized in 1929 by the presidents of the leading USA city transport undertakings. The first completed car was built by Pullman Standard and the first production orders were delivered in 1936. PCC cars were widely used in the US from that time and were also adopted in Canada, Europe and elsewhere.
PCM
Pneumatic Camshaft [Control] Mechanism. An improved light and compact type of electric train control gear incorporating cam-operated contactors with camshaft driven by an air-operated, oil-damped engine. Modified from a US design of *c.* 1928, it was introduced by LT on 1938 Tube and later Underground stock. Also used extensively on BR(S) electric mu stock from 1957.
PCV
Propelling Control Vehicle; driving trailer (qv) vans for working Post Office traffic, BR.
PD&SWJR
Plymouth, Devonport & South Western Junction Rly, inc 1883, opened from Lydford to Devonport via Tavistock 1890, leased and worked by L&SWR. Branch from Bere Alston to Gunnislake (ECMR) opened 1908. Part of SR from 1923.

PDWCL/PDS
Powell Duffryn Wagon Co. Ltd, absorbed Gloucester (qv) 1986 and Standard Wagon Co. Ltd 1989, becoming PDS – Powell Duffryn Standard, 1989.
PE/PER
Pakistan Eastern Rly, formerly the Eastern Bengal Rly.
Peak, the
Busiest periods of the traffic day, thus morning/evening peak, peak hours. *See also* Peak hour.
Peaked end, the (USRS)
The front or head end of a train.
Peak Express, The
Service between London (St Pancras) and Manchester (Central), so named 1938.
Peak Forest Line
Ambergate–Millers Dale–Chinley.
Peak Forest Tramroad
Inc 1794 in association with Peak Forest Canal, from Dove Holes quarries to the canal at Bugsworth (now Buxworth), in use from 1796. By subsequent legislation, the canal and tramroad eventually passed to the MS&LR and were vested completely in that rly in 1883. Operated by horses and gravity on flanged rails of 4 ft 2¹/₂ in/1,283 mm gauge, laid on stone block sleepers. Closed *c.* 1925.
Peak hour
The period in which the maximum number of passengers join or alight from trains at a city terminus or all termini, or use a metro/underground rly system.
Peak Rail
Peak Rail Society, Peak Rail Operations Ltd; a preservation project using the former BR line between Buxton and Matlock.
Peaks (RS)
BR Class 44/45/46 diesel locos. From the names originally carried by class 44.
Peanut roaster (USRS)
Any small loco.
Pêchot–Bourdon (Fr)
Articulated 0–4–0 + 0–4–0 locos designed in 1900s by two French artillery officers of these names for hauling heavy guns over 60 cm gauge military rlys.
Peck (USRS)
A twenty-minute meal break.

Peckett
Originally Fox, Walker & Co., loco
builders, Atlas Works, Bristol, from 1864;
became Peckett & Sons Ltd, 1880. Loco
production ceased 1968.

Peckham
Peckham Motor, Truck & Wheel Co., New
York, manufacturers of tramcar motors,
wheels and trucks. Licences were granted
to various European firms permitting them
to manufacture Peckham tramcar trucks in
the period 1908–48.

PED
Platform Edge Doors; introduced on the
Leningrad Metro in the 1970s, on urban
rlys in Lille and Singapore in the 1990s and
also adopted for the eight underground
stations of the Jubilee line (qv) extension to
Stratford, London, opened in 1999.

Peddle (USRS)
A local freight train.

Peddle, to (USRS)
To set out freight wagons.

Pedestal frame
The framework holding the shelf of block
instruments in a signal box.

Pee Wee
A system at the work site operated remotely
by a look-out (qv) stationed at a suitable
distance in the rear to give track workers
adequate warning of an approaching train.

Peg (RS)
A semaphore signal, hence 'pegged'
meaning a signal is in the off position.
From to peg-up (qv).

Peg number (RS)
The unique alpha-numerical identification
given to every signal controlled by a
particular signal box/signalling centre.

Peg-up, to (RS)
To move a block instrument from 'Line
Blocked' to the 'Line Clear' or 'Train on
Line' position, the preliminary to pulling-
off signals.

Pelican pond, the (RS)(obs)
The concentration of ooze and slime on the
ground in a steam loco yard arising from
the blowing out of boilers.

Pembroke Coast Express
Service between London (Paddington) and
Pembroke Dock, introduced 1953, ceased
1963. Name revived (as Pembroke Coast
Holiday Express) in summer only, 1985.

Pendelzug (Ger)
A push and pull train.

Pendolino
A tilt body train developed by Fiat. The
first emu design entered public service in
1976.

Pendulaires (Fr)
Swiss term for commuters.

Pendular suspension
A system which allows coach bodies to tilt
on curves.

Pendulum truck (obs)
A tramcar (qv) truck with axles capable of
moving laterally and independently of the
frame. Developed in an effort to adapt the
motion of the vehicle to irregularities in the
track.

Peninsular or P&O [Overland] Express
The popular and unofficial name for the
service between Calais (connecting with
sailings from Dover) and Brindisi via Turin
and Bologna, introduced 1890 for
passengers on the P&O line sailings to
India and the Far East. In 1898 when the
P&O liners started to call at Marseilles, an
additional service, known as the P&O
Overland Express ran between there and
Calais. Between the wars, the two trains
were known as P&O Marseille and P&O
Brindisi, but the latter was withdrawn in
the 1930s, after which the survivor became
known as the P&O Express, with a 22 h
timing between Calais and Marseille. This
service was not re-introduced after WW2.
The Indian and Far East mails were carried
by the same routes in separate non-
passenger trains ('Overland Mail') until
transferred to air.

Penn-Central
Penn Central Transportation Co., formed
1968, a merger of the Pennsylvania RR and
NYC. The co. absorbed the NH in 1969.

Pennsy (obs)
Nickname of Pennsylvania RR (US) and
also the Pennsylvania terminal station in
New York City, erected in 1910 and
demolished in 1963–4.

Pennsylvania
1. (US) A steam loco with 6–4–4–6 wheel arrangement.
2. (USRS) Coal.

Pennsylvania bogie/truck
see MCB (*4*).

Pennsylvania Limited
An overnight express between New York and Chicago, introduced 1881 as the New York and Chicago Limited, renamed PL 1891. Replaced by Broadway Limited in 1902 (qv).

Pennyfare
Staff magazine of LT (qv), formerly *TOT Staff Magazine*, 1934–47. The penny fare was at this time the main source of LT revenue. *See also LTM*, TOT.

Penrhyn
Penrhyn Rly, built to carry slate from Penrhyn quarries near Bethesda to Port Penrhyn, opened 1801, 1 ft 11$^5/_8$ in/ 585 mm gauge; re-routed and adapted for steam traction on 1 ft 11 in/584 mm gauge, 1875–6. Main lined closed 1962, completely closed 1965.

PEP
BR (S) prototype high density emu set of 1971–2 with automatic sliding doors (the first appearance of this feature on BR (S)). Originally designated PER (Prototype Electro-Rheostatic) but recoded for presentational reasons.

Percentage cut-off
see Cut-off (*1*).

Perch
A 60-ton bogie train wagon used by engineers.

Periodical ticket (obs)
Another term for season ticket (qv).

Peripheral station
BR term for an outer suburban station designated for main line stops, to save passengers travelling to and from a city terminus, e.g. Watford, Wilmslow.

Perishable
Nickname for 12.15 Penzance–Glasgow van train, also for Penzance–Paddington van train, 1975.

Périurbain (Fr)
Rail services from city centres to suburbs

and other outlying communities usually by tram-trains (qv).

Permanent way
Rly track; rails, sleepers, fastenings and ballast; so called to distinguish it from the temporary way laid during rly construction.

Permissive block
A system of signalling, usually with special block instruments, allowing more than one train to be in a block section at any one time; used only on freight lines, or for freight trains on passenger lines, or where platform lines in a block section are required to accommodate two or more trains at the same time.

Permissive signal (LT)
Original name for a draw-up signal.

Permissive working
A system in use on certain freight-only lines whereby trains are allowed to follow one another, within sight of each other, at low speeds. *See also MV*, Permissive block, Smoking-in.

Persecuted minority (RS)
Employee over age sixty-five and still at work.

Personal Rapid Transit
see PRT.

Perpot
GWR TC for special trains carrying Channel Islands perishables from Weymouth.

Personenzug (Ger)(obs)
A stopping passenger train.

Persuader (USRS)
A blower on a steam loco.

Perth (General) Station Committee
Committee of representatives of CR (*1*), NBR and HR (*7*), formed 1863 to administer this jointly-owned station. LM&SR & L&NER 1923–47.

Pertis
An acronym for Permission to Travel ticket machine.

Peru Rail
Organization controlling and operating the southern and south eastern rlys in Peru from late 1999; a partnership of Peruval Corporation and Sea Containers Ltd.

Per way
Permanent way (qv).

Peter Witt
A front-entrance, centre-exit tramcar designed in 1917 by Peter Witt, a Cleveland St. Rly Commissioner. Widely adopted in US and Canada and also in Milan, Italy. The conductor was positioned in the centre of the car by two side doors ('front centre' and 'rear centre'), the entire front section forming an internal platform for passengers waiting to pass him and pay their fare. Passengers had the choice of dropping their fare in a box and walking to the rear, leaving by the 'rear centre' door, or paying as they left by the 'front centre' door. There was a modification in which passengers could also enter by one of the centre doors, paying as they passed the conductor.

Petite Vitesse (Fr)
Ordinary freight traffic, as distinct from *Grande Vitesse* (qv).

Petticoat (USRS)
A shield which guides steam into the throat of a loco chimney.

PFI contracts
Private Finance Initiative contracts, in which a contractor or consortium of contractors undertakes responsibility for construction, use, maintenance and management of physical assets including rolling stock; a feature of the PPP scheme (qv).

Physical
Physical needs relief; allowance in working timetables to allow train crews to use lavatories.

Physical connection
A connection between the tracks of two separately worked lines, or two different companies' lines, enabling through running, as distinct from a 'walk-over' connection, in which passengers have to detrain and cross to another platform or, on a tramway (3) or interurban, walk from one vehicle to another.

Picc/Piccy (LTRS)
Piccadilly Line (qv).

Piccadilly/Piccadilly Line
The LT tube line from Cockfosters via Piccadilly Circus to Heathrow and Rayners Lane, originally GNP&BR (qv).

Picking-up (RS)
1. Train skidding on braking or acceleration, usually due to wet rails.
2. Train crew taking over a train.
3. Track circuit re-energizing after passage of a train.
4. Giving a signalman emergency release.

Picking the wheels up (RS)
Skidding.

Pick-up goods (obs)
A freight train calling at each goods yard along a stretch of line to leave and collect wagons.

Pick-up services (obs)
Freight routes radiating from a primary marshalling yard.

Picnic saloon (obs)
A carriage, usually third class, designed for hire by private parties. Previous notice given, these vehicles could be marshalled into scheduled services or excursion trains. Seating was usually arranged longitudinally, facing a long table, at which any refreshments brought on board by the party could be consumed.

PICOP
Person In Charge Of a Possession (qv).

Picture, going to see the
(RS)(obs)(GWR)
A disciplinary interview held in the company boardroom. The offender faced a full-length portrait of Charles Russell, chairman of the co., 1839–55.

PID
Passenger Information Display, showing time of next train(s), destination, intermediate stops, etc.

Pie card (USRS)
A ticket entitling the holder to a meal.

Pig (USRS)
A loco.

Pig iron (USRS)
A loco.

Piggery (RS)
Staff canteen or messroom.

Piggyback
A freight system in which loaded heavy road trucks and road trailers (usually the

latter) are carried by rail on specially adapted low-loader flat wagons. Developed from 1937, but principally in the 1950s, in the US. *See also* Road-Railer, TOFC.

Piggyback Consortium

A group comprising local authorities, shippers, freight operators, SNCF (qv), Eurotunnel (qv), and Railtrack (qv); formed with the object of promoting the use of the Piggyback (qv) freight transport system. Replaced by BIG (qv), 1999.

Piggyback railpack (USRS)

A long flat wagon used for carrying road freight vehicles or containers.

Piglet

Acronym for Piggyback Innovative Gauge-Limited Equipment. A type of Piggyback (qv) system using small diameter wheels for both road and rail vehicle, allowing Piggyback operation on restricted loading gauge routes in the UK.

Pig mauler (USRS)

A loco driver.

Pig pen (USRS)

A loco depot.

Pigs (RS)

Clodhoppers (qv).

Pig's ear (RS)

A small side light in a colour-light signal which enables a driver drawn right up to it to see a change in aspect.

Pigtail

1. (LTRS) The braided copper lead on a dc electric loco or motor car which connects the collector shoe to the power cable.
2. (LTRS) Electrical connection from the conductor rail shoe of a rly car.
3. Corkscrew-like fitting which guides the trolley-rope of a tramcar.
4. (RS) A Pandrol clip (qv).

Pike

A 31-ton ballast and sleeper wagon used by engineers.

Pike (USRS)

Any particular rly line or system.

Pike's Tramway

see Furzebrook Tramway.

Pilchard

TC for civil engineer's flat wagon.

Pilchers

Nickname of Manchester Corporation 4-wheel tramcars built 1930–32. After the general manager, R. Stuart Pilcher.

Pilot

1. (US) Term for the front end of a loco.
2. Pilotman (qv).
3. (obs) Early term for train staff (qv).
4. (US) Fender (qv) of loco or tramcar.
5. (RS) A shunting loco.

Pilot engine

1. (obs) A loco carrying the pilotman (qv), designated to haul every train in either direction over a single line section.
2. (obs) A light engine which until *c.* 1914 ran ahead of royal or other very important trains to ensure the line was clear.
3. A loco allocated to standby, shunting, banking assistance or other special duties at particular locations or to work between two specific points, e.g. station pilot, bank pilot.
4. Any loco assisting the train engine. The usage is condemned by purists who prefer 'assisting engine'.

Pilot light

A small indicator light in drivers' or guards' compartments to show that all sliding doors on the train are properly closed.

Pilotman

1. An employee wearing a distinctive cap or armband and allocated to a section of single line, or, more usually, double track temporarily under single line working, who accompanies a train on the single line section, no train being allowed to proceed over it without him on board, or without his authority. Formerly he travelled on the pilot engine (qv).
2. A driver familiar with the route who joins a train or engine crew to give guidance and warnings.

Pilot plow (US)

Cowcatcher (qv).

Pimple (RS)

Hump (qv).

Pimps (RS)

Material used for lighting a loco fire. From eighteenth-century colloquial usage – faggots used to 'introduce the fire to the coals'.

Pin (USRS)
Coupler.
Pin, to (USRS)
1. To couple cars together.
2. To complete a day's work.
Pinch bar
Long wooden bar with metal end; with the
rail as a fulcrum, it was used to move
vehicles in yards, etc. when no loco or
horse was available.
Pinch point (LTRS)
Heavily congested location on LT Rlys.
Pin down, to (obs)
To operate the hand brakes on individual
wagons, e.g. before a loose coupled train
descended a gradient.
Pine
TC for a train terminating short of its
scheduled destination.
Pines Express
Service between Manchester (London
Rd)/Liverpool (Lime St.) and
Bournemouth via Bath and S&DJR. So
named 1927, restored 1949, diverted via
Oxford 1962, ceased 1967. Name revived
for Manchester–Bournemouth–Poole HST
(qv) service, 1991 (Manchester–
Bournemouth, 1992). Name ceased to be
used after 2 June 2002.
Pinhead (USRS)
A brakeman (qv). From his handling of
pins (qv).
Pink City Express
Service between Delhi and Jaipur.
Pin lifter (USRS)
A pointsman or yard brakeman. From pin
(qv).
Pin puller (USRS)
A shunter. From his handling of pins
(qv).
Pioneer Rlys
Alternative term for Children's Rlys (qv).
Pioneer Zephyr
The first US streamlined lightweight
diesel-electric three-car set, worked
between Chicago and Denver from 1934,
originally called the Burlington Zephyr
(qv). Withdrawn 1960.
Pipe (LTRS)
A tube (qv) tunnel.

Pipe (RS)
Tunnels between main line and
Underground (GNR to Metropolitan City
Widened Lines) at King's Cross, London.
Piped wagon/piped only (obs)
An unfitted (i.e. loose-coupled) wagon or
other vehicle equipped with through pipes
which allowed continuous train brakes to
be applied elsewhere on the train.
Pipe-fitted (RS)
Train or vehicle fitted with continuous air
or vacuum brakes. Also, from this, the
traditional rlymen's question to a new
father: 'Is it pipe-fitted [male] or common
user [female]?'
Piping
Longitudinal splitting occurring inside any
part of a steel rail, caused by an
imperfection in the steel ingot.
Pips (RS)
BR diesel locos class 31.
PIRATES
Passenger Information, Reservations,
Accounting & Ticketing Computer System
for Europe.
Piss and Vinegar
Nickname for M&SWJR (2) (qv). From
the odour of its carriages, which were
much used by drunken soldiery.
Pitch-in (LTRS)
Collision between trains.
Pixie/PIXC
Acronym for 'passengers in excess of
capacity' under the limits set for the TOC
(2) (qv) by the OPR/OPRAF (qv) or SRA
(qv).
Pixies
Passengers in excess of capacity.
PJKA
Perusahaan Jawatan Kereta Api; Indonesian
State Rlys Corporation. 6,458 km of 1,067
mm gauge.
PK
Pullman Kitchen car, BR.
PKP
Polski Koleje Państwowe; Polish State Rlys.
23,420 km mostly standard gauge.
PKTM
Pentadbiran Keretapi Tanah Melayu;
Malayan Rlys. *See KTM (B).*

PLA

1. (obs) Passengers' Luggage in Advance. A system started in the 1900s in which, for a low inclusive charge, a passenger's luggage was collected, carried to destination and delivered to hotel or other holiday accommodation or residence to await arrival; similar arrangements were made for its return journey.
2. Port of London Authority. *See also* PLA Rlys.

Plaice

A 22-ton wagon used by engineers for carrying sleepers.

Plain line/plain line, to

A stretch of track without special work (qv)/ to convert a length of rly to this form.

Plaisir, train de (Fr)(obs)

An excursion train: 'their cheapness is more than counterbalanced by their discomfort' – Baedeker.

Plandampf (Ger)

A timetabled service of steam trains operated for tourist/enthusiast purposes.

Planet

1. A steam loco with 2–2–0 wheel arrangement.
2. Trade name for internal combustion (petrol, paraffin, crude oil) and petrol-electric locos manufactured by F.C. Hibberd & Co. Ltd.

Plank (obs)

The size of an open wagon was formerly designated by the number of planks of wood in its sides, e.g. 'a three-plank wagon'.

Plant, The (RS)

Doncaster Works, GNR/L&NER/BREL, RFS Industries. Wabtec Rail.

PLA Rlys

Port of London Authority dockside rlys; the PLA operated rlys with its own fleet of locos, and connected to the main system, at its London and Tilbury dock complexes. The London system closed in 1970 and PLA operations at Tilbury ceased in 1972.

Plasser (RS)

A track tamping machine. From the name of a firm manufacturing this equipment.

Plastic pigs (RS)

BR Wessex electric emu sets class 442. Most internal fittings were plastic and 'pig' relates to the high rate of initial failures.

Plastics (RS)

Generic term for any BR second-generation dmus (qv).

Plate/Plates (obs)

Flanged iron plates of L-section used to form a tramroad (*1*) (qv). Also thin strips of wrought iron fixed to the top surface of wooden rails to diminish friction

Plate, to/plated

To fix an official plate to a rly vehicle or loco denoting its owners and appropriate numbering and date of manufacture.

Plate frame

The normal foundation for a British-built steam loco, comprising two parallel iron or steel plates (main frames) reinforced by flanges to prevent distortion and cross-braced to provide a rigid structure.

Platelayer (obs)

Surfaceman or track maintenance worker, inspecting and laying permanent way. From the laying of cast iron angle plate rails on plateways.

Plateway (obs)

A line formed of plates (qv), also known as a tramroad (*1*) (qv).

Platform

Apart from the normal meaning, the GWR used this term to denote a station, usually staffed, of sufficient length to accommodate a short train, i.e. an intermediate category between a halt (qv) and a standard fully appointed passenger station. The Highland Rly used the term to denote any unstaffed calling place.

Platform hustler

see Hustler.

Platform lines/roads

Tracks serving a passenger platform.

Platform loops

BR term for lines serving platforms at stations where the main lines have no platforms, with loop entry and exit under the control of one signal box.

Platform safety pit (LT)

Formal name for suicide pit (qv).

257

Platform starting signal
A stop signal at the departure end of a station platform.

PLB
Possession Limit Board; a red sign and red light marking the beginning of a possession (qv). Also known as a stop board.

PLD
Passenger Load Determination. On-board (qv) equipment incorporating a computer which can measure passenger loadings at given points on a train journey.

Pliers (USRS)
A ticket punch used by a passenger train conductor.

PLM
Compagnie de chemins de fer de Paris à Lyon et à la Méditerranée. Part of the *SNCF* from 1938.

PLOD
Patroller's Lock Out Device, which can be used on a single line by the patroller, with a signaller's permission, to prevent the signalled movement of trains in one direction only when the patroller would otherwise be exposed to serious danger from an oncoming train.

Plonker (RS)
An extremely dirty loco requiring heavy work in removing encrusted filth before cleaning. Probably from plonk (S), meaning mud.

Plough
Shoe and mounting fitted to tramcars to pick up traction current from conduit track (qv).

Ploughshift (obs)
The changeover point between conduit and overhead wire current collection on a tramway (3) with a facility enabling the plough (qv) to be inserted or removed from beneath a tramcar (qv). Known on LCCT (qv) as change pits (qv).

Plow (US)
Same as plough (qv).

PLS
Position Light Signal (qv).

Plug (USRS)
Throttle of a loco.

Plug puller (USRS)
A steam loco driver. From plug (qv).

Plug run (USRS)
A local train.

PlusBus
A ticket offering for a small supplementary payment a day's unlimited bus travel at either or both ends of a rail journey, introduced September 2002; proposed to be extended to cover every major town in UK.

Plush/Plush haul/Plush run (USRS)
A passenger train/working.

Plym Valley
Marsh Mills–Yelverton; preservation project on former GWR/BR (W) Launceston branch.

PMR
The former company-owned Pekin–Mukden Rly (China).

PMV
A parcels and miscellaneous van, BR; fitted with side and end doors, and not gangwayed.

PN (Fr)
Passage à Niveau, level crossing.

PNB/PNR
see Physical.

Pneumatic railway
A rly employing a system of propulsion involving compressed air or a vacuum. *See also* Atmospheric rly.

Pneumonia cab (RS) (obs)
A steam loco cab with curved side-sheets offering the enginemen only minimal protection in cold or wet weather.

Pneumonia Junction (RS)
Any station where waiting for trains is rendered uncomfortable by lack of adequate shelter.

PNR
Philippine National Rlys. Formed in 1964 to operate all the rlys on the main island. 429 km of 1,067 mm gauge.

PO
1. Pullman Open, BR First class IC 125 Mark 3 coach.
2. Private owner wagon (qv).

P–O
Compagnie de chemins de fer de Paris–Orléans, jointly managed with *Midi* (qv) as *PO–Midi* from 1934. Part of *SNCF* from 1938.

Poached eggs (LTRS)

1. External door indicator lights on trains. From their colour.
2. (RS) Gold braid on uniforms. From its appearance.

Pocatello Yardmaster (USRS)

A fraud or a liar. From the false claims made by boomers (qv) of having experience as yardmasters at Pocatello, or wherever.

Pocono (US)

A steam loco with 4–8–4 wheel arrangement.

Poggy (RS)(obs)

Another version of Puggy (qv).

Point (USRS)

The front or head end of a train. *See also* Peaked end, the.

Pointe du matin/Pointe du soir (Fr)

Morning/evening peak hour (qv).

Point detector

A device for proving that points are correctly set, allowing a clear signal to be given for a train to pass over them.

Point heater

An electric or Calorgas heater to melt snow or ice that might otherwise impede correct operation of points.

Point lock

A bolt fitted to facing points in passenger lines, operated by a locking lever in the signal box, ensuring that the point blades are securely held in the correct position. The associated signals cannot be cleared until the bolt is fully home.

Point machine

Apparatus which changes the position of points by use of compressed air or electric power.

Points

The moving parts of a turnout (qv) which control the route to be followed, consisting of a pair of switch or tongue rails each tapered to fit a stock or side rail. A right hand set of points will turn a train to the right of a person facing the points, a left hand set to the left. Points are described as facing or trailing according to whether the train passes over them from toe (qv) to heel (qv) of a switch, or heel to toe respectively. The term is also

used as an alternative to turnout (qv). *See also* Catch points; Dummy point; Open point; Switches.

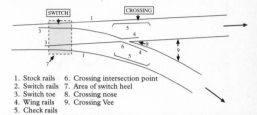

1. Stock rails
2. Switch rails
3. Switch toe
4. Wing rails
5. Check rails
6. Crossing intersection point
7. Area of switch heel
8. Crossing nose
9. Crossing Vee

Point shifter/turner

Electrically worked point-changing mechanism for tramways (*3*), usually operated by a setting on the driver's controller (qv).

Pointsman (obs)

An early term for a signalman.

Point to point ticket

A ticket allowing no break of journey.

Point wedges

Wedges, worked from a signalbox, which hold facing points in position to reduce the risk of an accident.

POIS

Passenger Operating Information System; a BR computer system.

Pole, to (USRS)

1. To run light engine (qv).
2. To move a wagon on a parallel track by using a pole against the buffer beam of the loco.

Pole pin (USRS)

A telegraph superintendent.

Pole shunting (obs)

Use of a pole mounted on a loco to move wagons on an adjacent track, particularly on the NER. *See also* Pole, to.

Police (obs)

1. Signalmen. Rly signalling was originally entrusted to sworn constables (rly police); the use of this term and police type uniform continued for some time after the introduction of specialized signalmen and mechanical signalling. *See also* Bobby Officer.
2. A loosely styled term for other traffic staff carrying out purely rly duties

formerly performed by sworn constables. These included 'booking constables' (booking clerks) and ticket collectors.

Policeman (LTRS)

1. A blind train stop not associated with a signal.
2. A signal halfway down a platform, especially a 'creeper' (qv).
3. (RS)(obs) An employee of the rly carrying out duties formerly the responsibility of sworn constables.

See also Police (*1*) and (*2*).

Pollen

GWR TC for various types of girder-carrying truck. Pollen 'E' was also used as a gun-carrier.

Pollock

A 31-ton wagon used by engineers for carrying ballast and sleepers.

Polmont route, The

Edinburgh (Waverley)–Falkirk (High)–Glasgow (Queen St.).

Polonez

A Moscow–Warsaw service, introduced 1973.

Polonia

A Warsaw–Budapest–Sofia service, introduced 1963.

PO(L) Rly

see PO Rly.

Pom-Poms (RS)

GCR 0–6–0 locos of 1901 (9J/J11). From the sharp sound of their exhaust beat, supposed to resemble that of the quick-firing 'Pom-Pom' guns used in the South African War, 1899–1902.

POMS (LT)

Acronym for Passenger Operated ticket MachineS.

Ponderosa (RS)(obs)

A word used by steam loco crews to describe a line inadequately provided with water columns, particularly London (Kentish Town) to Barking. A reference to a fictional ranch in the 1950s TV series *Bonanza*.

Pony truck

A single axle truck placed before or behind the driving wheels of a steam loco.

Pool

See Traffic pool; Wagon pool.

Pop, to (USRS)

To release a loco safety valve and reduce boiler pressure.

Po phone (LTRS)

The external, as distinct from the rly, telephone. From Post Office (now British Telecom) telephone service.

Pop safety valve

Manufactured by R.L. Ross & Co., Ltd, Stockport, and designed to release a large volume of steam from the moment it lifts, the blowing-off starting very suddenly (with a 'pop') and ending equally suddenly. These valves release steam at the exact pressure to which they are set.

Pop-up (LTRS)

A signal which lights up as a train approaches.

PO Railway

Post Office [Tube] Rly, London, 2 ft/609 mm gauge, authorized 1913, opened 1927 between Paddington rly station, Paddington District Office (now Paddington Letter Office) and Eastern District Office (now North East Letter Office), Whitechapel Road, via Mount Pleasant and Liverpool St. station. Fully automated, it latterly carried only letter post and since 1987 was known as Mail Rail. Closed May 2003.

Porpoise

A 14-ton bogie wagon used by engineers.

Porridge bowl/box (RS)(obs)

Royal Scot express (qv).

Portable railways

The lightest possible form of rly, in use since 1870s for construction projects, industrial, military, and agricultural purposes, employing prefabricated track which is easily dismantled and re-used. Manual, animal, steam, electric battery or petrol/diesel engine traction may be used in combination with light tip wagons, etc. *See also* Decauville track; *Feldbahn*; Jubilee track.

Portage Rlys/RR

See Ship rly.

Porter (obs)

A person employed on general manual

duties at passenger and freight stations, cleaning, closing train doors, assisting passengers, loading and unloading trains, handling luggage, parcels, freight, etc. Now known as a railman/railwoman.

Porterbrook Leasing Co. Ltd
A ROSCO (qv).

Portillon Automatique (Fr)
A solid, heavy gate or door installed at stations on the Paris *Métro* system, designed to prevent passengers from delaying departure of trains, blocking off latecomers from the platforms by closing automatically across entry subways as a train came into the station. Not now in general use.

Portion
A part of a train reserved for a particular destination or place of departure, detached from or attached to the main train at some intermediate point.

PORTIS
Portable Ticket Issuing System (BR); used by conductors on rural and local services. *See also* SPORTIS.

Port Road, The (RS)
Carlisle–Dumfries–Stranraer.

Portrush Flyer
A Belfast–Portrush service introduced 1934.

Portsmouth Direct [Line]
Woking–Guildford–Havant.

Ports to Ports Express
The unofficial name for a Newcastle–Sheffield–Banbury–Cheltenham–Cardiff–Barry service, introduced by the GWR and GCR in 1906. Ceased 1915. Restored 1920 and extended to Swansea. Ceased 1939.

POS
Post Office Sorting van, BR.

Position Light Signal/PLS
A signal controlling movements other than normal through running. Fixed on the same post as a running signal (qv) or a separate ground signal (qv).

Positive rail
Rail which carries the traction current in third-rail and fourth-rail systems to be picked up by shoes (qv) on multiple unit trains and locos.

Possession
Period in which a section of line is taken over by the civil engineer for maintenance, renewal or alteration; can be 'partial' or 'absolute'. *See also* White period.

Possession trains
Trains moving material and/or equipment to and from sites where engineering work is in progress; also known as Engineer's trains. These trains may include track-borne machinery, *See also* Infrastructure traffic.

Possum belly (USRS)
Toolbox slung beneath the frame of a caboose.

Possy (pronounced *pozzy*) (RS)
Positive rail on an electrified track.

Poste (Fr)
A signal box.

Post Office (London) Rly
see PO Rly.

POT
Post Office Tender, BR; an open van for the stowage of mailbags.

Pot (RS)
An insulator holding a conductor rail (qv).

Potato Cans (RS)
L&SWR 2–2–0T of 1906, later converted to C14 0–4–0T locos.

POTIS
Acronym for Passenger Operated Ticket Issuing [machine].

Pots (RS)
Same as Coffee pots (qv).

Pot sleepers
Circular iron supports like large inverted saucers used in some countries, without much success, as an alternative to transverse sleepers, to give track stability in sandy soil or to prevent destruction by termites.

Potter (RS)(obs)
An employee who walked along the coach roofs towards dusk, dropping lit oil lamps into the lamp recesses to illuminate the interiors.

Potteries Loop
NSR line Etruria–Hanley–Burslem–Kidsgrove. Arnold Bennett's 'Loop Line'.

Potts, The
Nickname for PS&NWR, also carried over to S&MLR.

Pounded (RS)
Shunted into a siding to allow another train to pass.

Pourrie (RS)
An oil can with an elongated spout.

POW
Private Owner Wagon (qv).

Power box
A signal box in which all signal and point movements are controlled by, and routes set by, electrical power. Miniature levers, thumb switches or push buttons are used in combination with electrical interlocking.

Power cars
Traction units (in effect locos) normally forming an integral part of a train set, as in HST (qv), TGV (qv), and Eurostar (qv).

Power frame
The interlocking signal frame in a power box (qv).

Power signalling
The operation of signals and points by compressed air, hydraulic power or electricity.

Pozzy
see Possy.

PP (LTRS)
Penalty Payment; extra pay, e.g. for working a rest day.

PPE
Personal Protective Equipment; worn by track workers or those otherwise officially permitted to be on the rly. It includes HV clothing (qv), safety footwear and safety helmets. Additional items may be required for specified tasks.

PPI (Fr)
Passe Partout International, Berne gauge (qv).

PPM
Public Performance Measure; introduced in 2000 by the SRA (qv) to provide improved indication of the performance of the privatized rail services in Great Britain. A combination of statistics of punctuality and reliability for every period of seven days.

PPP
Public Private Partnership/s. A system introduced by the New Labour administration from 2003 to attract private money and management over a period of 30 years for the modernization and maintenance of the London Underground system's existing infrastructure and renewal and maintenance of its rolling stock, but not for construction of any new stations or extensions. TfL (qv), as the operator and freeholder, remains in the public sector but the 'infrastructure companies' (Infraco (qv)) are private-sector consortia, currently entitled Metronet (qv) and Tubeline (qv). These companies receive payment (from fare revenue, subsidies and public funds) mainly based on the amount of time passengers would save as a result of the investment, by improving operational performance and the capacity of the system. PPP needed almost £500m in consultants' fees and other costs to set up and required an annual subsidy from public funds of around £1bn.

PR
1. Portpatrick Rly, inc 1857, Castle Douglas–Stranraer–Portpatrick, opened 1861, 1862, worked by Caledonian Rly 1864, amalgamated with WR (6) 1885 to form P&WJR (qv).
2. Peebles Rly, inc 1853, Hardengreen (near Dalkeith)–Leadburn–Peebles, opened 1855, worked by NBR; leased by NBR 1861, part of NBR 1876.
3. Pentewan Rly, 2 ft 6 in/762 mm gauge, St Austell–Pentewan, opened 1829, worked by gravity and horses. Converted to rly using steam locos, 1874–5, closed 1918.
4. Portsmouth Rly, or Direct Portsmouth Rly, inc 1853, Godalming–Havant (LB&SCR), opened 1859, leased by L&SWR, amalgamated with L&SWR 1859.
5. Palestine Rlys; operated under the British mandate, 1920–48. *See also* IR.
6. Portland Rly, inc 1825, 4 ft 6 in.gauge Portland (Dorset) (Castletown Pier)–Priory Corner. Built to carry stone from the quarries to ships. Opened 1826 at first with horse traction and a cable-worked incline. Closed 1939. Unofficially known as the Merchants' Rly.

Prairie (US)
A steam loco with 2–6–2 wheel arrangement.

Prawn
TC for S&T 30-ton wagon.

PRCI (Fr)
Poste à Relais à Commande Informatique, signal box using programmed circuits and computer technology.

Precaution signal
A fishtailed semaphore signal, usually with ring on centre of arm which, when at danger, indicates that a platform line is already partly occupied and stopping short will be necessary.

Preliminary caution
see Double yoke.

Pre-métro
A Belgian term (1966) for an electric tramway using shallow subways, which could easily be converted to a full 'heavy' metro (qv). The term *semi-métro* was used in the same sense earlier.

Premier Line, The
Self-styled title of the L&NWR.

Preserved line/rly
Term used to describe sections of BR or other abandoned rlys which have been restored and reopened by enthusiasts, who operate train services with restored steam and diesel locos and rolling stock. Services are usually seasonal, and oriented towards tourist/pleasure riding rather than providing a useful year-round, full day public transport facility. There is a heavy dependence on volunteer labour. Many such lines have associated static museum exhibits and other 'sideshow' features.

Presflo
Sealed BR hopper wagon with a compressed air discharge system, used for carrying powders in bulk, e.g. cement or fly-ash.

Prestige
Acronym for Provision of Revenue Services, an integrated revenue collection service for London bus, rail and tram services, embracing ticket machines, universal entry/exit gates at Underground stations, tills and contact-free smart cards, introduced by LT from 1998.

PRG (Fr)
Poste tout Relais à câblage Géographique, signal box with route-setting buttons on track diagrams.

Priam
A steam loco with 2–2–0 wheel arrangement.

PRIDE
Passenger Rail Information Display Equipment: A system providing train information to passengers by monitors linked to satellite receivers placed on roofs of stations. Installed on LTS (qv) line, 1992.

PRIMA
Professional Rail Industry Management Association. *See also* RP (*3*).

Primary yard (obs)
BR term for a marshalling yard in which the originating traffic received its initial marshalling to form up trains for other yards and which served a local area of collection and distribution.

Priming
Term used to describe the situation in which water from an over-full boiler passes with the steam into the cylinders of a loco.

Primrose Line
Nickname for Kingsbridge (Devon) branch. Brand name for Dart Valley Rly (qv), 1990.

Prince of Wales (RS)(obs)
Loco steam blowing off through safety valve. From the resemblance to Prince of Wales feathers.

Print out
List of passing times and incidents taken from a train describer (qv) recorded through the controlling computer. Replaces the former manually compiled train registers (qv).

Prinz Eugen
TEE Bremen–Vienna (10 h 29 min), introduced 1971; ran Hannover–Vienna from 1976, lost *TEE* status 1978, became EC service 1987.

Priv (RS)
A privilege ticket (qv).

Private car
1. A rly car luxuriously fitted out for the exclusive use of one wealthy individual

and guests, or of the company's president or owner, or senior officials. Such cars, which were usually attached to scheduled trains, included kitchens, lounge, dining and sleeping accommodation, bathrooms, lavatories, etc. Some were made available for private charter use. There were similar private interurban cars and less elaborate private cars were operated on some tramways (3).

2. (US) A private owner wagon (qv).

Private owner wagon
A freight wagon or van provided for or by a particular customer of the rly, at the customer's expense, to be used exclusively for their traffic and painted with the user's name. Most were hired, not owned; a more accurate term would be 'trader's wagon'.

Private right of way/track
Sections of tramway (3) or interurban away from public roads.

Private siding
A siding provided for the exclusive use of a particular customer of the rly, at the customer's expense, on the customer's property, connected to but normally gated-off from the running lines.

Private station
A definable stopping place not normally usable by the general public and not normally shown in the public timetables. The costs involved in erecting and maintaining any buildings or platforms would not be met by the rly undertaking.

Private varnish (USRS)
A private car (1) (qv).

Privatization of BR
see Railways Act, 1993, and Transport Act, 2000.

Privilege cab
A cab licensed to ply for hire on rly premises.

Privilege ticket
A ticket issued at a heavily discounted fare to rly and RCH employees and their families.

Prize length
A length (qv) for which the responsible track gang has been awarded a prize in recognition of their high standards of maintenance.

PRM
Passenger Rail Management, published ten times a year from June 1993 to report developments in rly and light rail (qv) passenger vehicles, services and infrastructure, including ticketing.

PRO
Public Record Office. Became NA (qv) 2003. *See also* BTHR.

Procar 80
A high capacity motor car transporter wagon introduced by Procor in 1979.

Procor
Procor Engineering (UK) Ltd, established 1970 in Wakefield. Designers, builders, repairers and hirers of freight rolling stock. Acquired the Standard Railway Wagon Co. fleet of wagons, 1971, BRT (1) (qv), 1974 and Roberts (qv), 1974. Part of Bombardier Inc (Canada), 1990 and renamed Bombardier Prorail Ltd.

Programme machine
A signalling system introduced by LT in 1958, in which the appropriate routeing through interlocking machines was remotely controlled by machines activated by a roll of punched plastic tape on which the train service for the day was stored. The operation of the machines was monitored from a Central Regulating Room, whose staff could take over operation of the signalling if required.

Progress
Berlin–Prague midday service, introduced 1974.

Propel a train, to
To push a train from the rear.

Propping (RS)(obs)
Pole shunting (qv).

Protection [measures]
Prescribed actions to be taken by staff to protect a train stopped by an emergency or failure, to prevent it being run into by following trains; also, if derailed, by trains coming in the opposite direction.

Protection of trains
This is normally achieved by keeping the aspect (qv) of stop/stopping signals (qv) at danger; placing detonators on the track in advance of an approaching train; using

track circuit operating clips (qv); or by showing a red flag or red lamp.

Provincial/Rlys (obs)

A BR business sector established in 1982 covering all passenger services other than NSE, InterCity and those provided for PTAs. Renamed Regional Rlys (qv), 1990.

PRS (Fr)

Poste tout Relais à transit Souple, power signal box with route setting.

PRT

Personal[ized] Rapid Transit; a rapid transit system (qv) with very low capacity vehicles running at close headways, capable of being summoned to a designated point to pick up, and of running to a designated point to set down, computer-controlled and generally designed to offer a close approximation to taxi-type service. None yet built in the UK.

PRW

Private Right of Way (qv).

PS

Private Siding (qv).

PSA

Passenger Service Agent; an employee of the DLR (qv) carrying out the duties formerly titled Train Captain (qv); in use from 1999.

PS&NWR

Potteries, Shrewsbury & North Wales Rly, inc 1865, opened Shrewsbury–Llanymynech 1866 with branches to Breidden (Criggion) and to Llanyblodwel. Closed 1866, reopened 1868, closed again 1880. Llanyblodwel branch reopened 1886 and worked by Cambrian Rlys. Taken over by Shropshire Rlys 1888, acquired by S&MR (qv) 1909.

PSB

Power Signal Box.

PSO

Public Service Obligation; a central government block grant made to BR from January 1975, under the Railways Act, 1974, to compensate for losses arising from meeting general obligations in respect of passenger services which are imposed by the government.

PSR

1. Permanent Speed Restriction.
2. Passenger Service Requirement; the minimum standard of services to be provided by TOC (2) (qv) under the privatized regime for British rlys, sometimes below BR services as at 1994, and against which no appeal is possible.

PSTA

Public Service Transport Association; a 1939 renaming of T&LRA/T&LRTA (qv). Became CPT (qv).

PT

1. Privilege Ticket (qv).
2. Pannier Tank (qv).

PTA/PTE

Passenger Transport Authorities/ Executives. Originally set up under the Transport Act, 1968. The PTEs are responsible for implementing the local transport policies made by the PTAs, which are, in England, the corresponding Metropolitan County Councils, and in Scotland, Strathclyde Regional Council. There are seven PTA/PTEs in all: Greater Manchester (formerly south-east Lancs and north-east Cheshire), Merseyside, South Yorkshire, Strathclyde (formerly Glasgow & Clydeside), Tyne & Wear (formerly Tyneside), West Midlands and West Yorkshire. Under the Railways Act, 2005, subsidies for local rail services became the sole responsibility of the DfT (qv), which alone defined the basic service provision and budget; however, the PTE could raise or reduce the level of service, provided it bore any extra cost of improvements itself. The Act also allowed PTEs to initiate rail closures, and if closure were put into effect the PTE could introduce Quality Contracts for the replacement bus services. The 2005 Act also gave the English PTEs powers to become co-signatories to rail franchise agreements, specifying and contracting for the rail services required of the TOC (2) (qv).

PTC

Positive Train Control; a US computerized system from Union Switch & Signal involving on-board computers and GPS (qv), designed to signal, police line speeds, enforce TSR (qv), prevent accidents and protect track workers over long stretches of track. First used in Alaska from 2007.

PTR&D
Port Talbot Rlys & Docks, inc 1894, opened 1897, 1898, Port Talbot–Maesteg–Pont y Rhyll; Port Talbot–Pyle/Cefn Junc; and Port Talbot–Whitworth/Blaenavon. Part of GWR 1922.

PTSO
Pantographed Trailer coach Standard class, with Open plan seating, BR.

PUD (US)
Pick Up and Delivery service.

Puddle Jumper (USRS)
A shunting loco.

Puerta del Sol
A through overnight sleeping car service between Paris and Madrid, introduced 1969. Withdrawn 1996.

Puffler (RS)
A foreman, ganger (ex-miners' S).

Puggies (RS)(Scots)(obs)
Any small shunting loco.

Puggy (RS)
GCR or GCR employee or train.

Pugs (RS)
L&YR 0–4–0ST dock locos; also a general term for contractors' locos and for small shunting locos of any type in Scotland. *See also* Puggies.

PUL
SR six-car corridor emu set including one PULlman car for fast services, 1933 (6-PUL, and later, 4-PUL).

Pull and push train
see Push and pull train/unit.

Pull-down, to (LTRS)
To stop a train by using the passenger-operated emergency brake valve; hence a pull-down, to be pulled-down.

Pullman
1. In Britain this term was normally used for the specially-appointed 'parlor' (obs) or lounge cars, originally of US design, in which passengers were served at their armchair seats with drinks, light refreshments and full meals and given

other attendance by the Pullman Co.'s staff in return for payment of a supplementary fare and gratuities. The first P cars ran on the Midland Rly in 1874 and on the GNR in 1879, and the first all-Pullman train (Pullman Limited Express (qv)) on the LB&SCR in 1881. Between 1875–1908 some British rlys also operated US-built P sleeping cars. After 1908, all P cars operated in Britain were built in the UK by or on behalf of the Pullman Car Co. Ltd (qv), which also staffed and operated the service. BR continued to operate P services after the Pullman Car Co. became a wholly owned subsidiary in 1963 but its own catering staff eventually replaced the former P employees. From 1985 BR applied the brand name 'Pullman' to a facility offering high quality service of meals and drinks at seats in its normal First class Inter-City coaches, some of which were given names, in the P tradition. P cars were also operated in North America by Pullman USA (qv) and by the *CIWL* (qv) in mainland Europe (until 1971) and Egypt. The word derives from George Mortimer Pullman (1831–97), the US inventor of this concept of luxury rail travel and designer (in 1859–68) of the original P sleeping, dining and 'parlor' cars.
2. (RS)(obs) Shunting truck, GWR, BR (W).

Pullman Car Co. Ltd
Established in Britain 1882 as the Pullman Co. Ltd, purchased by Davison Dalziel in 1907, re-formed in 1915 as the PC Co., taken over by BR, partly in 1954, and wholly in 1963.

Pullman Co./Pullman Inc. (US)
Formed as Pullman's Palace Car Co. 1867, name changed to P Co. 1899. The company built and operated most sleeping and dining cars in North America and Mexico for many years. Tramcars were also built from 1891. At the height of its operation in the 1920s, it boasted itself as 'The World's Grandest Hotel' with some

100,000 guests sleeping nightly in its cars. Manufacturing facilities (Pullman Standard Car Manufacturing Co. since 1934) remained under the Pullman parent corporation along with the car services until 1947 when ownership of the latter was transferred to a group of US rly companies. The existing independent services organization was, however, retained. From the beginning of 1969 all North American rlys cancelled their Pullman operating contracts and began to operate their own services. Production of rail vehicles by Pullman in Chicago ceased in 1979.

Pullman gangway
A gangway (qv)/corridor connection used on British Pullman (qv) cars which was more spacious than the standard type. Projecting in front of the buckeye (qv) coupler, it was clipped up under compression to its counterpart on the next car by the use of springs.

Pullman Limited Express
All-Pullman service between London (Victoria) and Brighton, introduced 1881, the first such in the UK.

Pullman Pup (RS)(obs)
Six-wheeled battery vans for providing lighting power in some British Pullman Co. cars.

Pullman truck
A six-wheeled bogie/truck of US design.

Pull off, to (RS)
To place a signal in the 'Off' position.

Pull-offs
Fitting used on curves for supporting and/or retaining in position the trolley/contact wires of tramways (3).

Pull the air, to (RS)
To apply brakes from a valve on the train.

Pull the back one, to (RS)
To set the distant signal in the 'Off' position.

Pull the handle, to (LTRS)
To use the passengers' emergency brake handle.

Pull the pin, to (USRS)
To uncouple; hence to leave the railway service, make any major change, to die.

Pull the plug, to (USRS)
To drive a loco.

Pull the string(s), to (RS)
To release vacuum or air brake valves manually.

Pump (LTRS)
The air compressor on a train.

Pumping
A state in which wet subsurface materials, i.e. ballast and sand, appear around the sleepers; caused by vertical movement in wet conditions, often when track is laid over impermeable clays. The point where it occurs is known as a 'wet spot'.

Pumping/pump, to (RS)
A movement applied where route cancellation has to be carried out by a signalman/woman after the passage of each train past a controlled (but not semi-automatic) signal. To avoid having to restore the signal to 'On' at the appropriate time and then subsequently returning to the entrance button when the controls allow the route to be re-set, both operations are carried out in one movement at any time after the signal has returned to red by the action of the track circuit (qv). When the appropriate controls are clear, the 'pumped' signal will change to 'Off'. Introduced with BR (S) resignalling of Kent Coast Lines 1959–62.

Pump trolley
A rail trolley used by permanent way and other staff which is moved along the track by working the long handles up and down in a pumping action which operates a crank on the axle.

Pump up, to (RS)
To recharge the air reservoirs in a train.

Punching turn (LTRS) (obs)
A duty restricted to supervision of entry barriers, not involving imposition of excess fares.

Punch up, to (LTRS)
1. To operate a lift manually in event of failure.
2. To transmit a train's description by depressing the button on the train describer.

Punctuality Parkes
Charles Henry Parkes, chairman of the GER 1874–93.

Punjab Limited
An exclusively First class boat train between Bombay and Peshawar, introduced 1927 for the sole use of passengers to and from Europe.

Pups (USRS)
Small four-wheel shunting locos.

Purbeck Line
Wareham to Swanage. Heritage operation of the former BR Swanage branch.

Purlin/purline
The longitudinal roof members extending over carlines (qv), and with them, forming an anchor for the roof.

Push and pull train/unit
A train capable of being driven from either end. When a steam loco was used, the usual arrangement was to have controls connecting with the driver's brake valve and the regulator in the driving compartment at the end opposite to the loco (or in the two driving compartments if the loco was in the centre of the train). There was also some form of audible warning operable from the remote driving compartments and some means of communication with the fireman on the footplate.

Push back, to (LTRS)
To propel a train, or the act of so doing.

Push down, to (RS)
To close gaps between wagons in sidings.

Pushers (RS)
BR class 33 locos, which are capable of pushing trains from the rear.

Push-in trains (LTRS)
Additional trains injected into the rush hour services at suitable intermediate points to provide extra capacity.

Push out, to (LTRS)
To give assistance to a defective train by pushing it with another train in rear.

Put back, to/putting back
Another term for Set back, to (qv).

Put back, to (LTRS)
To return a signal to danger, usually by putting lever in normal position.

Put [it] away, to (RS)
To stable a train.

Put [it/him] inside, to (RS)
To signal a train into a loop or siding to allow another train to overtake it.

Puzzle switch (USRS)
Four levers in one position which will throw four sets of points in a yard.

PW
Permanent Way (qv).

P Way
Permanent Way (qv).

PWD
Permanent Way Department.

PWF
Private Wagon Federation.

PWI
The Permanent Way Institution, founded 1884, inc 1908.

PWR
1. Permanent Way Repairs/Restriction; a speed restriction imposed during or immediately after track repairs or replacement or after damage to the formation by subsidence, earth fall, etc.
2. Pakistan Western Rly, formerly the North Western Rly [of India].

PWS
Permanent Way Slack; *see* PWR (*1*) (qv).

Pyrénées–Côte d'Argent Express
A *CIWL* service between Paris and Hendaye/Pau, introduced 1911, restored after WW1 as a night train Paris–Irun–Tarbes. Replaced by Iberia Express (qv), 1957.

Python
GWR TC for van used for private horse carriages or motor cars.

Q

Q, The (US)
Chicago, Burlington & Quincy RR.

Q-Jump
A 24-hour, 7-day telephone call centre
issuing rail tickets and providing timetable
and fare information, in operation from
2002, acting as an agent for all TOC (qv).
Merged with Trainline (qv) 2004.

Q-paths/services
Trains for which paths (qv) are allocated
but which only run as required by traffic or
operational needs. Locos and crews are not
specifically allocated but are found as
required by Control from reserve capacity
or cancelled booked services. *See also*
Manned conditional.

Q Train
A special train manned by British Transport
Police officers and supported by other police
in radio contact travelling in road vehicles in
the vicinity of the train. The train can be
stopped at any time, at the direction of the
officer in charge, to enable the police to
deal with any incidents of vandalism,
trespass or other crimes encountered on the
journey. Introduced *c.* 1983.

Quad-arts
Articulated suburban stock of 1914–24
designed by Nigel Gresley for the GNR and
L&NER, consisting of sets of four
compartment coaches mounted on five
four-wheel trucks/bogies, two four-coach
sets being coupled to make an eight-car
train, in which the two sets (each with a
different arrangement of accommodation)
were close-coupled with short buffers at the
inner ends. Similar sets were also built for
the L&NER from 1924. Withdrawn 1966.

Quads (RS)(obs)
Bolster wagons (qv) with four bolsters,
designed to carry long steel girders, steel
bars, etc.

Quarry Line
LB&SCR line opened 1899–1900 between
Coulsdon and Earlswood to by-pass
congestion at Redhill and over the original
SER and LB&SCR joint line between
Coulsdon and Redhill.

Quarter lights
Fixed windows in passenger coaches,
originally those either side of the doors of
passenger compartments, so-called because
their shape initially resembled a quarter-
circle. On tramcars, the term denotes the
small horizontal windows above the large
fixed panes along the car sides. These
occupy about a quarter of the combined
height of the window and are hinged at the
lower edge of the frame, or slide sideways,
for ventilation.

Queen Mary (RS)(obs)
Vacuum-braked, long-wheel-base freight
guard's van, larger than older types. From
the RMS *Queen Mary* (1936).

Queen Marys (RS) (obs)
1. An alternative term for Queen of
   Shebas (qv) after their straight-backed
   seats, reminiscent of Queen Mary's
   upright, well-corseted stance.
2. An alternative term for Marys (qv).

Queen of Scots
Pullman train between London (Kings
Cross), Edinburgh and Glasgow, so named
1927. Restored 1948, name dropped when
partly replaced by White Rose Pullman
(qv) 1964.

Queen of Shebas (RS)(obs)
SR four-car suburban emu sets with six-a-side seating, first introduced 1941; SUB (qv). 'She came to Jerusalem with a very great train' – I *Kings* x, 2.

Queen points (RS)
The second pair of points in the sequence leading from the hump (qv) of a marshalling yard to the sorting sidings. *See also* Jack points; King points.

Queenposts
The vertical components of the central trussing of a wooden rly coach or tramcar.

Queenslander
An air-conditioned express between Brisbane and Cairns, introduced 1986.

Queen Street route, The
Edinburgh (Waverley)–Falkirk (High)–Glasgow (Queen St.).

Quick, The (RS)
The fast lines.

Quike (LTRS)
A four-wheel rail-mounted cycle used for track inspection in tube tunnels. A combination of QUeer and bIKE.

Quill (USRS)
A loco whistle.

Quill drive
A form of drive for electric locos which uses a hollow sleeve or 'quill' which is connected to the driving wheels by springs.

Quilling
1. (RS)(obs) The process of picking out wealthy-looking passengers, and offering to handle their luggage (usually performed by an off-duty employee). Also a verb – to quill. From earlier (S) usage of same word meaning to curry favour.
2. (USRS) Manipulation of loco whistle to play tunes or make other distinctive sounds. From quill (qv).

Quint-arts
Similar to quad-arts (qv) but in five-coach sets which could run coupled together or separately. They were allocated to former GER suburban services by the L&NER when provided from 1924 onwards.

Quintinshill
Britain's worst rail disaster, 1915, in which 226 died.

Quints (RS)(obs)
Bolster wagon (qv) with five bolsters, designed to carry very long steel girders or bars, etc.

R

(Fr)
Ralentir, slow.

RA
1. 'Right Away!' The signal to start a train from a station or other stop. Given by hand, or bell signal through the train, to the driver and at some places with a curved platform repeated by 'RA' or 'R' on an indicator visible to the driver. *See also* Baton; Ding-ding and away.
2. Route Availability, followed by a number; no loco may work on a route of lower numbered RA than that of its RA classification.

RA (Fr)(obs)
Regime accéléré, a fast freight service.

RA
Railway Archive; a quality illustrated journal devoted to British rly history, published three times a year from July 2002.

Rabbit (USRS)
Catch points (qv).

Rabbits (RS)
Short distance passengers, also fare dodgers with an 'alibi' ticket.

Race track (USRS)
Section of line safe for high speed running and used for such.

Race trains
Special trains run to stations at or near horse race courses on race days.

Rack railway
Line using a mechanical system (Abt, Riggenbach, Strub or Locher) which features arrangements of steel teeth set continuously along the track to engage pinion wheels or cogs in the specially equipped locos or motor coaches.Such systems enable trains to climb very steep gradients up to 1 in 2.

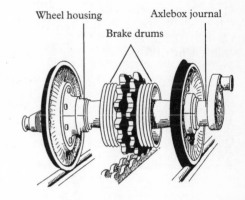

Rack railway (Abt system)

Radial axle
An axle and wheel set which is able to move within a fixed radius.

Radials (RS)
LB&SCR E4 0–6–2T locos.

Radial tank (obs)
Tank loco in which the carrying wheels move in radial guides to enable it to negotiate sharp curves. Applied in particular to L&SWR Adams 4–4–2T, built from 1882.

Radial truck (obs)
A four-wheel truck (usually on tramcars) in which the axles can move freely relative to the truck frame to adjust more closely to track curvature.

Radio train

A special train for tourists in which a commentary on passing scenery or points of interest is given through radio loudspeakers in each coach. The first was operated by CIE in 1950. BR adopted the concept in 1953. *See also* Land cruise.

Raffaello

An EC service between Basle and Rome, introduced 1989.

Raft (RS)

Two or more wagons coupled together, usually during shunting.

Rafter (RS)

A fully loaded train.

Ragtimes/Ragtimers (RS)

GNR '1630' 2–6–0 locos of 1912 (L&NER class K1) – from the appearance of their outside Walschaerts motion, which was associated with the movements of a contemporary dance music craze. 'We believe this slang description is applied . . ., it is neither dignified nor appropriate, and is certainly not worthy of perpetuation' – *The Railway Magazine*, January 1922.

Rag waver (USRS)

Flagman.

RAI

Rahahane Djomhouriye Eslami Iran; rlys of the Islamic Republic of Iran, 7,201 km, much of recent construction; physical connection with Turkish rlys (*see TCDD*).

RAIB

Rail Accident Investigation Branch of DfT (qv); established in 2005 to investigate accidents and incidents on rlys in Great Britain, including the UK portion of the Channel Tunnel, light rail systems and metros (1) (qv), to determine their root causes and contributory factors, and to report to the Secretary of State for Transport.

Rail

1. A nineteenth-century alternative for 'railway'.
2. (USRS) A rly employee.

Rail

A twice-monthly magazine dealing with current rly developments, first published in 1981 as *Rail Enthusiast*; renamed 1988.

Rail a train, to (LTRS)

To move a train, using overhead trolley lead, from the unelectrified depot tracks to the electrified line outside.

Rail bender (RS)

A driver who thrashes his loco.

Rail bond

A device to maintain electrical connection between one rail and another across a rail joint, ensuring conductivity for track circuits.

Rail brakes

Lengths of machined rail fitted on the inside of running rails; when switch/points are set in the clear road position, these move away from the running rails, allowing the train wheels to pass over freely, but if the road is not clear, the rail brake is positioned close to the running rails, thus retarding the movement of the train by side pressure, so reminding the driver of a SPAD (qv).

Rail buff (US)

Term for any person interested in rlys. This expression has gained some currency in the UK in recent years but is mainly used by journalists and others lacking such interest.

Railbus

A lightweight low-capacity diesel or petrol railcar with bus or bus type body, usually on four wheels, used for passenger services on branch and other lightly trafficked lines.

Railcar

A passenger-carrying car, running singly or with others, propelled by an integral light steam engine, a petrol or diesel engine, or by electric traction.

Railcard

An identification card sold by BR to enable particular categories of passenger (e.g. senior citizens, young persons) to obtain discounted fares, introduced 1975.

Railcare

A 1995 alliance of Siemens (qv), Babcock (qv) and the former BR Wolverton and Springburn (Glasgow) carriage and wagon works. Acquired by Alstom (qv), 2001.

Rail creep

The tendency of rails to move very slowly out of position longitudinally, in the direction of traffic, as a result of braking action by trains.

Rail Crown
The topmost point of the rail head (2) (qv).
Rail Drive
A self-drive car hire service for BR
passengers, introduced 1969.
Railed road
see Rail road/railroad.
Rail Europ Junior
Discounted fares applying to international
journeys within Europe and available for
persons under twenty-one, introduced 1970.
British and Irish rlys included from 1973.
Railex
see RLS.
Railfan (US)
Term for a person interested in rlys.
Railfan & Railroad (US)
First published May 1979, a merger of *Railroad
Magazine* (*see* RM (3)) and *Railfan* (1974–9).
Rail ferry
NZ for train ferry (qv).
rail4chem
German open-access operator from 2001,
providing through international rail freight
services in Europe, including Great Britain
via the Channel Tunnel.
Railfreight
A BR business sector devoted to freight
movement, formed 1982, but the term was
in fact in use before that time to describe
BR's freight activities. Became Railfreight
Distribution (qv) in 1988.
Railfreight Distribution
BR freight organization, resulting from a
merger of Freightliner (qv) and Speedlink
(qv) in 1988. Bulk business separated off as
Trainload freight (qv) in 1990. By 1994
concentrating on automotive, Channel
Tunnel and intermodal business. *See* EWS
International.
Railfuture
Campaigning name adopted by RDS (qv)
2001.
Rail Gourmet/Rail Gourmet (UK) Ltd
1998 successor to ERC (qv), offering rail
catering services in UK. Parent co. SAir
Group (SwissAir).
Rail grinder
A vehicle equipped with the means of
smoothing out imperfections and

irregularities in rail surfaces, usually by
means of carborundum blocks.
Rail head
1. The nearest rly facilities to any given
   location. In military usage, this term
   denotes the nearest point to the combat
   zone to which troops, equipment and
   ammunition may be brought by rail.
2. The top part of a rail, including the
   running surface.
Railheading/to rail head
Use of private motor cars by commuters
and others to reach a station providing a
faster or more reliable rail service than that
available at the nearest one.
Railion
A 1999 merger of *Cargo AG* (qv) (94 per
cent) and initially its Dutch equivalent (6
per cent), a multinational rail freight
operator in mainland Europe. Its
components subsequently rearranged as
the former freight divisions of *DB* (qv) (98
per cent) and *DSB* (qv) (2 per cent).
Rail motor [car] (obs)
A combination of a steam engine and
coach. *See also* Railcar.
Rail-mounted machines/plant
Machines/plant capable of moving along
rly track and operating from running lines.
Railnet
1. The totality of rail lines in a given
   country or other specified area.
2. System introduced by Royal Mail in
   1996 in which mail is handled in
   containers carried by dedicated trains
   and specially designed rolling stock
   between 'Distribution Centres' and
   provincial 'hubs' served by road vans.
Railnews
BR newspaper for staff, established 1963.
Separate regional editions published until
1971. Last issue October 1996. Revived as
an independent monthly with same title,
covering the whole of the British rly
network, first issue March 1997.
Railophone (obs)
A system of telephoning to and from trains
in motion introduced in 1911.
Railpax (US) (obs)
National Railway Passenger Corporation. A

273

federally subsidized rail passenger system, introduced 1971. Superseded by Amtrak (qv).

Rail Regulator
See ORR.

Rail road/railroad
1. (obs) Used from seventeenth century as a generic term for any form of surface rly but from *c*. 1790 applied principally to edge rail (qv) lines, all others being described as tramroads (*1*) (qv).
2. Originally an alternative term for 'railway' in UK and other English-speaking countries but by the late nineteenth century this usage became largely confined to North America, though 'railway' is also current there, especially in company titles, the two forms proving useful for making legal distinctions.

Railroad bull (USRS)
A policeman or detective employed by a rly company.

Railroad Development Corporation
See RDC (3).

Railroad Magazine
see RM (*3*).

Railroadman's Bible (USRS)
The rly company's rule book.

Railroadman's Magazine
See RM (4).

Railroad roof
see RR roof.

Railroad Stories
See RS.

'Railroad that went to sea, The'
see Flagler's Folly.

Rails (obs)
Rly company stocks (e.g. Home Rails).

Rail Safety & Standards Board
Established 1 April 2003, a not for profit organization owned by the rly industry, providing health & safety leadership for the rly industry in Britain.

Rail scooters
Rail-mounted manually propelled equipment used in pairs or larger numbers to move rails along the track during maintenance work.

Rail skate
A device with two rail wheels which is used by track workers to assist in moving heavy items along the track.

Rail table
See Running surface.

Rail tensor
Hydraulically powered machine which stresses and restresses lengths of LWR (qv).

Railtrack
Initially a subsidiary of BR (1), Railtrack became an independent plc in 1994. Set up under the Railways Act, 1993, it was a key feature of the privatization of the former BR (1) (qv) rly network in Great Britain. With the exception of the Island Line (qv), it became owner of all rly lands, tracks and other infrastructure, responsible for timetabling, for operating signalling systems and for all infrastructure maintenance and new investment. Its income was derived from 'access charges' imposed on the TOC (2) (qv) and from rentals for stations leased to those companies (apart from a group of 14 major stations, directly managed). Following a major financial crisis, Railtrack was replaced by Network Rail (qv) from 3 October 2002.

Rail tractive effort
Net tractive effort at the rail of a loco power plant after taking account of all internal losses but excluding resistance forces met by the train. *See also* Tractive effort.

Rail trolley
See Pump trolley; Trolley (2).

Rail turning
Turning a rail so that the existing back/outside edge (qv) becomes the running edge (qv).

Rail 2000 (Swiss)
A 1999 renaming of *Bahn 2000* (qv).

Rail Way (obs)
Same as Rail road/railroad (*1*) (qv).

Railwayac (obs)
A term current from *c*. 1890 to *c*. 1925 to denote a person interested in rlys.

Railway Accident Reports
Reports of the RI (1)(qv) on railway accidents, published by HM Stationery Office.

Railway Acts [of Parliament]
These fall into four groups:

1. *General Acts,* laying down general conditions for rly operation (e.g. the Railways Clauses Consolidation Acts, 1845 and 1863).
2. *Private Acts,* authorizing private rly companies to construct new works including new rlys, extending time for completion of new works previously authorized and sanctioning other specific powers. Such Acts incorporated the relevant provisions of (*1*).
3. *Transport Acts* (qv).
4. *British Railways Acts* and *London Transport Acts,* essentially the same as (*2*) but applying to the nationalized undertakings.

Apart from major or special schemes such as the CTRL (qv) which are made the subject of specific Acts, new rly works (including light rail) are now authorized by the system laid down in the Transport & Works Act, 1992 (qv).

Railway & Canal Commission (obs)
This was established in 1873 (reconstituted 1888), to regulate rlys and canals, giving judgement on disputes arising between companies and to arbitrate between companies. Abolished by the Railway & Canal Commission (Abolition) Act, 1949, and its functions transferred to the High Court (England and Wales) and Court of Session (Scotland).

Railway & Travel Monthly
see R&TM.

Railway Chronicle, The
See RC.

Railway Clearing House
See RCH.

Railway Club
see RC (*1*).

Railway Commission/Board
Constituted under an Act of 20 August 1846 (a) to ensure the rly cos did not contravene the provisions of their special Acts of parliament or any general statutes and (b) to report to parliament if so directed upon any pending rly Bills. Part of the board's functions were assumed by the Board of Trade (qv) in 1848, and the remainder in 1851 when it ceased to exist.

Its period of authority lasted from 9 April 1846 to 10 October 1851.

Railway Directory & Year Book
see RYB.

Railway Dog (obs)
see Dog Collector.

Railway Engineer
see RE (*2*).

Railway Executive (RE)
Established as a corporate body under the policy-making BTC (qv) in 1947 to undertake detailed management and, through its regional organization, operation of the newly nationalized rlys (BR). In 1953 a Conservative Government abolished the RE and the rlys were then directly managed by the BTC and the BR regions. Not to be confused with the Railway Executive Committee (REC (qv)).

Railway Fly Sheet
see RFS.

Railway Forum
An organization formed 1999 to discuss and promote matters of mutual concern and interest to the TOC (*2*) (qv), Railtrack (qv), rail freight companies and the rly manufacturing industry.

Railway Gazette
see RG (*1*).

Railway Group
A grouping of over 50 companies comprising the duty holders of rly safety cases (qv), including Railtrack (qv), LUL (qv), the TOC (*2*) (qv) and some rly contractors.

Railway Herald
see RH.

Railway Heritage Committee
A national statutory body established by the Railway Heritage Act, 1996, as amended by the Transport Act, 2000. It designates those rly artefacts requiring retention for posterity. *See also* RHT.

Railwayist (obs)
Another version of railwayac (qv) and contemporary with it. Preferred by the RM (*2*) (qv) and used by it as late as 1934.

Railway King, The
George Hudson (1800–71). Involved, not always honestly, in promotion and financing of numerous rly schemes and amalgamations, mostly in the north and

midlands. Others sometimes suggested for this title include Sir Edward Watkin (1819–1901), the German Dr Barthel Heinrich Straussberg (1823–84) and the American William Henry Vanderbilt (1821–85).

Railway Letter [Service]
see RLS.

Railway Magazine
see RM (*1*) and (*2*).

Railway Mania
A period (1844–7) in which large numbers of rly proposals, many of them ill-founded and unwise speculations, were submitted for parliamentary approval.

Railway News
see RN.

Railway Newsletter
See RN (2).

Railway Observer
see RO (*2*).

Railway observer
Genteel term for one who notes down locomotive and rolling stock numbers, their locations and their movements.

Railway of Death
A Japanese project to connect Burma and Thailand by rail in WW2, on which British and other prisoners of war were employed in appalling conditions. Completed in October 1943, but the section north of Nam Tok was abandoned soon after WW2.

Railway officers (obs)
Management grade employees of the pre-1948 British rly companies and LT. Use of the term persisted into the nationalized undertakings. There was a class distinction from other employees, with separate messes, etc., as in the armed services. *See also* RROA.

Railway Official Gazette
see RFS.

Railway Pictorial
see RP.

Railway Post Offices (obs)
An early term for TPO (qv), renamed Railway Sorting Carriages 1914 and from 1928 TPO (qv).

Railway Procurement Agency
See RPA.

Railway Ramblers
A club founded 1976, devoted to the exploration on foot of disused rly lines and to encourage their conservation as public walking routes. It publishes *Railway Ramblings* four times a year.

Railway rambling
Walking along the alignments of abandoned rlys. A term coined *c.* 1975.

Railway Record
see RR (*1*).

Railway Reflections
See RR.

Railways
Illustrated monthly for amateurs and (initially) modellers. First published December 1939. Name changed to *Railway World* (*see* RW) from September 1952.

Railways Act, 1993
Statute passed under a Conservative administration 'privatizing' the national rly system of Great Britain (BR) by breaking up a vertically integrated publicly owned structure into 27 privately owned passenger train operating companies (TOC (2) (qv)), some five privately owned freight businesses (FOC (qv)), a plc with seven 'zones' owning and maintaining the infrastructure (Railtrack (qv)), and three major private companies with some smaller fish owning and leasing-out motive power and rolling stock (ROSCO (qv)). Such central administration and control as was deemed necessary was allocated to a Franchising Director (OPRAF (qv)) and a Rail Regulator (ORR (qv)). Significant changes were made by the Transport Act, 2000 (qv) and the Railways Act, 2005 (qv).

Railways Act, 2005
This Act abolished the Strategic Rail Authority (qv), moving many of its responsibilities, including rail strategy, into the DfT (qv). It also amended the duties of the ORR (qv) and those of Network Rail (qv), changed the funding of transport by the PTA/PTE (qv) and allowed these to propose rail closures and control replacement bus services. Another section abolished the RPC (qv) in the English regions. Other SRA functions were transferred as appropriate to

the Scottish Parliament, Welsh Assembly and the Mayor of London (TfL (qv)).

Railway Safety Case
See Safety case/s.

Railway Safety Principles & Guidance
Issued by HMRI (qv).

Railway Services Representative (obs)
BR (qv) euphemism for canvasser (qv).

Railways Illustrated
see RI (*2*).

Railway Sorting Carriages (obs)
Used officially from 1914 to describe what became TPO (qv) in 1928.

Railways South East
see RSE.

Railway Times
see RT.

Railway World
See RW.

Railway World
see Railways; *T&RW*.

Railway Year Book
see RYB.

Rajdani Express
Name used for fast trains between Bombay, Calcutta and New Delhi.

Rake
A set of coaches, normally kept together and usually semi-permanently coupled.

Ram (USRS)
The injector on a steam loco.

Ram a shot of air under the wheels, to (USRS)
To brake a train or loco.

Rame (Fr)
A set of coaches, often permanently or semi-permanently coupled together, one or more of which sets make up a complete train, or a push-and-pull unit (qv).

Ramp
See Side ramp.

Ramp wagons
Flat-bed rly wagons from which one wheel slot can be removed to form a ramp for loading and unloading armoured fighting vehicles.

R&CHS
Railway & Canal Historical Society; founded 1954 to raise the standard of original historical research and to foster and maintain historical investigation and research, also to indicate and record where information may be found. Publishes a *Journal* three times a year.

R&CT
Rye & Camber Tramways Co. Ltd, operating a 3 ft/914 mm gauge light rly opened 1895, Rye to Rye Golf Course; extended to Camber Sands, 1908. Public service ceased 1939, dismantled 1948.

R&ER
Ravenglass & Eskdale Rly, Ravenglass to Boot, 3 ft/914 mm gauge, inc 1873, opened freight 1875, passengers 1876. Closed 1908, reopened 1909, closed 1910, reopened 1911, closed again 1913. Converted to 1 ft 3 in/381 mm gauge miniature rly by NGRL (qv) and reopened 1915. The Ravenglass–Murthwaite section had mixed standard gauge and 15 in gauge track to allow through working of quarry traffic from 1929–53.

R&KFR
Rowrah & Kelton Fell Rly, inc 1874, opened 1877. Disused by late 1920s, track removed 1934.

R&LHS
Railway & Locomotive Historical Society Inc. (USA), founded 1921, inc 1926.

R&L&NWR Jt
Rhymney & L&NWR Joint line, Rhymney to Nantybwch, inc 1867, opened 1871; LM&SR & GWR Joint 1923–47.

R&RA
Road & Rail Association, formed 1959 to encourage effective use of the internal UK freight transport facilities, roads, railways, waterways and coastal shipping, taking into account economic and social factors.

R&SBR
Rhondda & Swansea Bay Rly, inc 1882, Treherbert–Aberavon–Swansea, etc., first section opened 1885, worked and managed by GWR 1906; part of GWR 1922.

Randstad Rail (Dutch)
Conventional rail, light rail, tramway (*3*) and metro improvements and integration planned for completion in 2000–2010 for the *Randstad* (the area around and between Rotterdam–The Hague–Amsterdam).

R&TM
Railway & Travel Monthly, founded 1910, renamed *T&TM* (qv), 1920.

Ranger ticket
BR term for a ticket providing unlimited travel within a specified area, usually valid for one day only. *See also* Rover ticket.

Ransomes
Ransomes & Rapier Ltd, Ipswich, founded 1868, manufacturers of rly cranes, hydraulic buffer stops, signalling equipment, etc. Production ceased 1987. (Not to be confused with Ransomes, Sims & Jeffries, also of Ipswich, manufacturers of agricultural machinery, steam and electric road vehicles and trucks.)

Rapid (LTRS)
Rapidprinter ticket issuing machine, or the ticket it produces.

Rapide, train (Fr)(obs)
The fastest category of train, some of them First class only, often carrying mail.

Rapidi, treni (It)
Supplementary fare expresses, with restaurant cars, in the period when three passenger classes existed they were confined to First and Second class only.

Rapid transit (US)
Term, in use since *c.* 1885, to describe an urban public passenger transport system operating over segregated routes, normally an electric underground, elevated or surface rly, or a mix of these. Not always living up to its name (hence the quip 'Transit it is, rapid it isn't'). *See also* Light rapid transit.

Rapier
Code name for the special train used by the Commander-in-Chief Home Forces 1941–5 for which rolling stock was supplied by the L&NER (qv).

Rapilège (Fr)
Light weight block trains (*2*) (qv) transporting between 500 and 800 tonnes of freight.

Rap the track, to (USRS)
To run a loco at high speed.

RAR
Royal Arsenal Rlys; an internal system in the Royal Arsenal, Woolwich, London, 1 ft 6 in/457 mm and standard gauge, opened 1870–6. Closed 1965.

RAS
Railway Air Services; formed by the four grouped British rly companies in 1934, in an attempt to control the development of competition from internal air services. Ownership transferred to British European Airways Corporation in 1947.

RAT
Rail Adhesion Train, LT; trains of converted passenger cars used to distribute Sandite (a compound of sand and stainless steel particles) on the surface of rails to improve adhesion and electrical contact when these are impaired by the slime generated from falling leaves.

Rat (USRS)
A freight wagon.

Rat hole (RS)
The Waterloo & City line (*see* W&CR).

RATP
Régie Autonome des Transports Parisiens; Paris Transport Authority, controlling public passenger transport systems in the Paris region, established 1948.

Rats (RS)
BR diesel locos classes 24 and 25. From the frontal appearance.

Rattle her hocks, to (USRS)
To drive a loco (i.e. an 'iron horse') very fast.

Rattler (USRS)
A freight train.

Ratty
Nickname for R&ER (qv).

Raves
A GWR and SE&CR term for the slightly projecting shaped steel plates at the top sides of a tender which help to retain piled-up coal.

Rawhider (USRS)
A disciplinarian, any supervisor who drives his men hard.

Razor gang (RS)
Audit staff, or any visiting staff from headquarters looking for economies.

RB
BR buffet car with kitchen and twenty-three seats at tables.

RB (Ger)
Regionalbahn, regional services of *DBAG* (qv) other than RE (*4*).

RBI

Railway Benevolent Institution, founded 1858.

RBR

BR buffet car which has been refurbished.

RBS

Regionalverkehr Bern–Solothurn. A network of electric metre gauge interurban light rlys around Berne formed by the merger of the *SBZ* (*Solothurn–Zollikofen–Bern*) and *VBW* (*Vereinigte Bern–Worb–Bahnen*).

RC

1. The Railway Club, founded 1899. The oldest-established club catering for those interested in rlys, professional and amateur. It has a central London clubroom and an extensive library.
2. A misleading abbreviation formerly used in British rly timetables to signify *any* form of on-board refreshment service.

RC

The Railway Chronicle, a journal of traffic, shares and engineering, published weekly from 20 April 1844 to 29 December 1849.

RCA (obs)

1. Railway Companies' Association, formed 1869.
2. Railway Clerks' Association. The original body of this name was formed in 1865 but proved to be a failure. A new association was founded in 1897 and survives today under the name adopted after nationalization – the TSSA (qv).

RCAF (obs)

Restaurant/cafeteria car, BR.

RCB (obs)

Railway Conciliation Boards, set up, at the suggestion of Lloyd George, in 1907. These boards, composed of trade union and company representatives, endeavoured to settle questions of pay and working conditions without recourse to formal arbitration. A revised scheme followed the 1911 strike and a complete scheme of local and national negotiating machinery was established by the Railways Act, 1921. *See also* RSNC, RSNT.

RCEA

The Railway Civil Engineers' Association.

RCF

Rolling Contact Fatigue (qv).

RCH

1. Railway Clearing House; an organization established in 1842 (and inc in 1850 and 1897) to deal with questions relating to through traffic passing over the lines of different rly companies, apportionment of receipts, etc. The RCH also laid down standards and organized most other matters of mutual concern and interest, offering neutral ground for discussion and negotiation by the participating companies. Its statutory existence ceased in 1954 together with its separate identity and independence, but the name and a residual organization continued under the BTC until it was finally disbanded in 1963. 'The RCH' also came to mean the RCH headquarters offices in Seymour (now Eversholt) St., Euston, London NW. *See also* Number takers.
2. The initials RCH were adopted by BR to denote standard items and designs.
3. Railway Convalescent Homes. First home established 1901. After privatization of BR, access was thrown open to non-rly patients, title reduced to initials RCH and number of Homes reduced from seven to two (Dawlish and Llandudno).
4. The Railway Clearing House, resurrected 1995 by Torvale Engineering, to provide central services after privatization of British rlys.

RCL

Railway Conversion League; founded 1957 by Brig. T.I. Lloyd to advocate total conversion of rlys into segregated motor roads, an idea mooted as early as 1928. Latterly known as Railway Conversion Campaign.

RCS

Rail Charter Services Ltd, formed 1996, owners of loco-hauled passenger stock used for chartered trains and providers of chartered train services.

RCT

Royal Corps of Transport; a corps of the British Army formed in 1965 to take over the transport functions of the RASC and the rly and port operating and movement control responsibilities of the RE (*1*) (qv). Now RLC (qv).

RCTS
Railway Correspondence & Travel Society, founded 1928. One of the largest British organizations for rly enthusiasts, primarily catering for those obsessed by the fine detail of day-to-day operations, particularly by the locos, trains and rolling stock, their movements and their numbering. Now has about five thousand members. Publishes the monthly *Railway Observer* and very detailed and well-regarded locomotive histories. Affectionately known as 'The Royal Corps of Train Spotters'.

RD
Railway Digest: condensed and illustrated extracts from worldwide railway periodicals, published from summer 1947. Ceased publication 19??

RD (TC) (obs)
Message received.

RDA
Railway Development Association; founded in 1951 to advocate retention, modernization and extension of rly facilities in Britain. Amalgamated with the Railway Invigoration Society to form the RDS (qv), 1978.

RDC
1. (LTRS) Rest Day Cover.
2. Rail Diesel Car; a diesel railcar, carrying passengers, mail, baggage, etc. Applied mainly to diesel-hydraulic cars built by Budd in the 1950s.
3. Railroad Development Corporation (USA); operating rly services in Argentina, Estonia, Guatemala, Peru, Malawi, Mozambique and the USA.

RDS
Railway Development Society; formed 1978 from the RDA (qv) and the Railway Invigoration Society. *See* Railfuture.

RE
1. Corps of Royal Engineers; the part of the British Army which until 1965 was responsible for rly operating and workshops as well as rly construction and maintenance. Since 1965 it has

been concerned only with rly and port construction and maintenance. *See also* RCT; REME; RLC.
2. *The Railway Engineer*; a periodical devoted to rly construction and engineering, founded 1880. The first modern rly technical journal. Came under the control of RG (*1*) (qv) in 1919; separate publication ceased and merged into RG (*1*), 1935.
3. The Railway Executive (qv).
4. Regional Express, fast limited-stop regional services of *DBAG* (qv).

REA (US)
Railway Express Agency formed in 1928 to handle nationwide express (qv) business.

Reading (US)
1. A steam loco with 4–4–4 wheel arrangement, the first being supplied to that company.
2. Philadelphia & Reading RR, eventually officially known as the Reading Co.

Real estate (USRS)
A facetious term for poor coal.

Rear, in the
In the context of signalling, this term denotes anything on the approach side of a given point when facing the direction of travel. Anything beyond that point is described as 'in advance' of it.

REC
1. Railway Executive Committee; formed 1912 of the managers of eleven leading rly companies under the nominal chairmanship of the President of the BoT (qv), to control and manage the rlys as a unit in the event of a national emergency. This control was operated throughout WW1 under the direction of professional rly officers. The REC was disbanded at the end of 1919 but was re-appointed by the MoT (qv) in 1938 with representatives of the four main line companies and the LPTB. It acted as the Minister's agent and as a channel of communication between the Government and the rlys during the period of Government Control in WW2, when it again facilitated the management and operation of the

company-owned networks as a unified system throughout the period. Disbanded in 1947. (Not to be confused with the Railway Executive (qv).)

2. Railway Enthusiasts' Club, founded 1953.

Receiving office (obs)
Premises operated by a rly company, usually in the commercial centres of large cities, at which parcels and goods were received for transmission by rail, rly passenger tickets were issued and information about rly services dispensed. In London several were on the sites of historic coaching inns. The term became obsolete in the period between the wars when the rly companies rationalized their in-town enquiry and ticket offices.

Reception road/siding/track
Tracks designated and signalled to receive trains moving from running lines into a yard or depot.

Recovery margin/time
Extra time built into the working timetable timings of a train over unrestricted sections of line, providing a margin above its standard point to point running time, usually approaching the end of its journey. This allows drivers to recover punctuality after passing over those parts of the route liable to engender minor delays because they are congested, subject to speed restrictions, etc. Introduced generally in Britain in the 1940s and 1950s.

RED
Railway Engine Driver; British Army term, used to avoid confusion with drivers of other types of vehicle.

Red Arrow [*Krasnaya Strela*]
A fast night service between Moscow and Leningrad, introduced 1938. Interrupted by German Army's advance in 1941; service resumed 1944.

Redball (USRS)
A fast freight train.

Red board (USRS)
A stop signal.

Red Caps (obs)
Officially used term for baggage porters at major US and Canadian stations. From their headwear.

Red cards, red carding
The procedure of placing a red card into the card holder on a wagon, van or coach to denote that it is faulty and must not be used. *See also* Green card.

Red Devils (RS)
Midland Rly compound 4–4–0 locos.

Red Dragon
An express between London (Paddington) and Carmarthen, so named 1950, name dropped 1965. Name revived for Swansea–London service, 1984, became the Red Dragon Executive in 1986 and, in 1988, the Red Dragon Pullman.

Red engine (also blue/yellow) (obs)
GWR colour code which denoted the axle load of a loco. Used on signs, etc., e.g. 'Red engines must not pass this board'.

Red eye (USRS)
A stop signal.

Red-eyed Devil/Monster (LTRS)
The Line Controller. From the red light which shines on telephone switchboards when the LC is calling.

Red onion (USRS)
A rly refreshment room.

Redpath Frauds
The fraudulent creation of GNR stock by one of its employees, Leopold Redpath, who was sentenced to transportation for life in 1856–7. The company lost about £244,000 at 1857 values.

Red Rose
An express between London (Euston) and Liverpool (Lime St.), so named 1951. Name dropped 1966.

Red Star
The BR express 'to be called for' registered parcels service, introduced 1963, designed to secure certainty and speed in transit, using the first and fastest trains available to provide a same day or overnight service. In 1991 it became a profit centre of the Parcels Group (qv). Sold to management, 1995. Bought by Lynx 1998. Rail use ceased 2001.

Reefer (RS) (USRS)
A refrigerated wagon or container. From the first syllable.

Ref (RS)

A list of loco numbers, usually separated into types or classes and drawn up by the owning train spotter (qv). From reference book.

Réfectoire (Fr)

Staff canteen.

Refectory car (US) (obs)

Early term for restaurant/buffet car.

REFER

Rede Ferroviaria Nacional. Portugese Rlys Infrastructure Authority, 1998.

Refuge

An alcove in a tunnel, viaduct or retaining walls to allow track workers to shelter safely from passing trains.

Refuge siding

A siding, entered through a trailing connection, which provides temporary accommodation for slow non-passenger trains out of the way of fast traffic. The term was first used by the GWR (qv).

Regelspur (Ger)

Standard gauge (qv).

Regenerative braking

An arrangement which enables an electric loco or train to reduce its energy consumption by feeding back into the traction supply power generated by the motion of the train when it is descending a gradient. In effect while this is happening the traction motors are temporarily converted into dynamos. Where the substation equipment is not designed to receive regenerated power, the controlled electric braking is similarly arranged but the generated energy is dissipated as heat in the starting resistances instead of being returned to the traction supply. This alternative is known as *rheostatic braking.*

Regionali

Regional stopping services in Italy.

Regionalbahn (Ger)

see RB.

Regional Express

see RE (*4*).

Regional Railways (obs)

A 1990 renaming of BR Provincial Sector Rlys (qv). Ceased to exist 31 March 1994.

Regional Rlys North East

A TOU (qv), 1994. A TOC (*2*), 1997,

operating services in the area bounded by Liverpool, Manchester, Chesterfield, Lincoln, Cleethorpes, Hull, Scarborough, Whitby, Sunderland, Newcastle, Chathill, Carlisle, Lancaster and Blackpool. Renamed Northern Spirit (qv) 1998.

Régional, train (Fr)

see Train Régional.

Regionalzüge (Swiss/Ger)

Stopping trains.

Regulation [of passenger traffic]

A system (first introduced in 1918–19 by the L&YR, for peak traffic periods in and out of Blackpool and Southport), in which passengers were required to book in advance for the outward journey and were then given tickets to travel by a specific numbered train, thus allowing the operators to plan a regulated service of appropriate capacity, in punctual, evenly loaded trains, while assuring the passenger a seat. On arrival at the destination, the passengers were given another special ticket bearing the number of a specific train on their chosen day of return. The special tickets used were known as Regulation tickets and no extra charge was made for the facility. An analogous system, introduced in 1904 by the GWR, and still used by BR at busy periods, is that of requiring all passengers on specified ('controlled' or 'limited') trains to have a numbered reserved seat ticket or 'boarding card', obtained in advance.

Regulator [handle]

The valve which allows the driver to control the quantity of steam admitted to the steam chest from the boiler; when the regulator is in the position known as 'fully open', the maximum amount of the steam available is being used.

Regulator/Traffic Regulator (obs)

An official, usually without supervisory status, posted at strategic points on tramways (*3*) to control loading of vehicles and operation generally.

REHAP

BR (S) emu sets, rebuilt from NOL sets (qv).

Reichsverkehrsgruppe Schienenverkehr (Ger)

A state-sponsored body exercising

coordination of tramways (*3*) and light rlys in WW2.

Relayer (RS)

A section of line which has been, or is about to be relaid, and which requires a reduction of speed.

Relay interlocking

Interlocking (qv) between signals and between signals and points/switches, activated by track circuits (qv) and panels (qv).

Relays

see Track circuits.

Release key

A key provided to enable a signalman to release the plunger lock on a lock and block (qv) system, thus overriding the mechanical and electrical safety devices built into the system. The key is necessary for use if a fault develops in the train-actuated treadle release or when a train is offered forward and then cancelled. It should only be used when there is no train in the relevant block section. Misuse of this key has been the cause of several serious accidents.

Relief

Staff allocated to replace others whose duty hours have expired but are not in position to sign off; also staff replacing others due for meal breaks, etc.

Relief lines

A term for Slow lines (qv) used by the GWR (qv) from 1880.

Relief siding

Refuge siding (qv).

Relief train

A train not shown in the public timetable but operated in a suitable path (qv) to carry passengers who cannot be accommodated on the scheduled train.

Rembrandt

TEE Amsterdam–Munich introduced 1967. Amsterdam–Stuttgart 1980. Lost *TEE* status 1983. IC Amsterdam–Frankfurt, 1983–4, Amsterdam–Chur, 1984, became EC 1987.

REME

Royal Electrical & Mechanical Engineers; that part of the British Army which took over the RE (qv) rly workshop responsibilities in 1965.

'Remember Abermule'

see Abermule.

Reminder appliances

Various devices installed in mechanical signal boxes to alert signallers that sections of tracks unprotected by track circuits (qv) are occupied by trains or rolling stock.

Remit (RS) (obs)

The daily cash receipts at a station.

Remorque (Fr)

A trailer (qv).

Remote interlocking

Interlocking (qv) equipment located outside signal boxes or control centres but linked to them by various means.

Remus

A Vienna–Rome service, introduced 1977.

RENFE

Red Nacional de los Ferrocarriles Españoles; Spanish National Rlys, formed 1941. 12,646 km of 1,668 mm gauge. Since 1992 new high-speed lines have been constructed to standard gauge (*see AVE*). See also GIF.

REP

BR (S) emu corridor unit with Restaurant/buffet car and Electro-Pneumatic brakes, for Bournemouth electrification, 1967. Two motor cars Second/Standard class, one trailer brake. First, one buffet car. Capable of working as a tractor unit with one or two TC (qv) sets, 4-REP.

Repeater

An electrically-worked indicator in a signal box which shows the position of a semaphore signal, usually one not visible from the box; also shows whether the signal lamp is alight.

Repeater [signal]

Signal arms co-acting with the main arm and placed at a lower point on a signal post. Adopted in situations where the main signal cannot be clearly seen in sufficient time (e.g. when starting). *See also* Banner repeater.

REPTA

Railway Employees' Privilege Ticket Association.

Reptile (USRS)

A yard brakeman.

RER (Fr)

Réseau Express Régional; Regional Express

Railway Network. Underground and surface electric rlys, financed by the state and local authorities, running through the centre of Paris and into the suburbs either side, linked with existing rlys, and providing communication between all zones of the city region via the central area. First section opened 1969.

RES

SR four-car corridor emu set with kitchen and REStaurant cars for Portsmouth Direct electrification, 1947, 4-RES.

Res

Rail Express Systems, a trainload division of BR Parcels Group, including trunk haul parcels, light freight and Royal Mail traffic, 1991. Now EWS (qv).

RESA (Fr)

A combined supplementary fare and seat reservation charge applied on a variable basis for TGV (qv) and other premium services. *See also Resarail.*

Resarail (Fr)

International rly seat reservation system covering Europe and Channel Tunnel.

RESCO

Railway Engineering & Supply Co., Woolwich.

Reserved track

A section of tramway (3) laid off public roads, or in the centre or at the sides of public roads in a 'reserved' alignment, not available to other traffic. When away from roads altogether, sometimes also known as 'private tracks'.

Reshaping/Reshaping Report

see Beeching.

Residential expresses/traffic (obs)

A late Victorian and Edwardian term for medium to long distance commuter traffic and services.

Resi (obs)

Abbreviation for residential traffic (qv).

Resilient wheel

A wheel containing a rubber section sandwiched between tyre and centre plate and used to reduce running noise in tramcars.

Restall's tours/trips

Frederick J. Restall was a pioneer organizer of half-day rail trips from Cambridge (in 1885) and (beginning in 1894) from London, largely at first for the benefit of shop staffs on early closing days. First using the LB&SCR from London, his activities soon spread to other companies and, by 1913, over 400 trips a year were being organized. The last of these trips ran in 1939. 'Rest-all and be thankful' – G.R. Sims.

Restroke, to (LTRS)

To put back, and then immediately pull off a signal lever.

Retarders, wagon

Rail-mounted brake to slow down and stop wagons moving by gravity into sorting sidings from a marshalling yard hump (qv). Remotely operated from the control tower or manually worked. A refinement also accelerated wagons moving too slowly (wagon accelerator/ retarder). First used on DR (3), adopted at Whitemoor, March, L&NER, 1929.

RETB

Radio Electronic Token Block; a system which combines a microprocessor and a mobile radio, designed to work lightly used single lines, replacing staffs, tablets, tickets and tokens. It provides direct radio communication between the driver and the signalman. First adopted on BR on Dingwall–Wick/Thurso line in 1984–5.

Retention tanks

Tanks holding waste from water-closets on trains until emptied at a suitably equipped depot.

Return half

The half of an Edmondson ticket which the passenger retains for the return journey.

Reverse

In the context of points/turnouts this denotes the position contrary to the normal one.

Reverse(d) curve

Track curving in contrasting directions in succession, i.e. in an 'S' or reversed 'S' conformation.

Reversed stairs (obs)

Stairs on a double-deck tramcar (qv) rising in a clockwise spiral from the platform; adopted from 1900, partly as a safety measure to prevent passengers on the stairs from being thrown forward when the vehicle stopped suddenly.

Reversible working/line
A section of track signalled for working in either direction according to traffic requirements.

Reversing station
A location on rlys constructed to ascend very steep gradients by using a zig-zag alignment at which trains are reversed. *See also* Switchback.

Reversing triangle
see Triangle.

Revue Générale (Fr)
La Revue Générale des Chemins de Fer; rly engineering journal founded in 1878.

REW
Railway Engineering Workshop, LT.

RF
BR Restaurant car, First class, with kitchen and twenty-four seats at tables.

RFB
Refreshment Car First Class, with Buffet section, BR.

RfD
Railfreight Distribution (qv).

RFF (Fr)
Réseau Ferré de France; rail infrastructure authority in France, 1997.

RFFSA
Rede Ferroviaria Federal SA. Holding co. for most of the publicly owned rly undertakings in Brazil from 1957. 30,129 km, mostly metre and 1,600 mm gauge.

RFI
A *FS* (qv) subsidiary responsible for all Italian rly infrastructure; formed 1 July 2001.

RF[L] (obs)
Railway Finance Ltd, a financing consortium established by the BRB (qv) in 1971 as a means of circumventing Government investment limits and increasing cash flow. Abolished at the behest of HM Treasury, 1973.

RFG
Rail Freight Group, an organization representing the rly freight industry, promoting rail freight to potential users and putting the industry's interests and concerns to policy makers. *See also* BIG.

RFM
BR Restaurant [car] First [class] Modular.

RFO (obs)
BR Restaurant car, First class, with loose chairs.

RFS
1. *Railway Fly Sheet*, organ of the RBI (qv), first published April 1870, retitled *Railway Fly Sheet & Official Gazette* 1882, merged with *RN* (qv), 1914.
2. Rail Freight Services.

RFS Industries
An engineering firm formed 1987 to take over part of Doncaster rly works from BREL (qv). Passenger rolling stock business sold in 1994 to Bombardier Pro Rail (qv), remainder retitled RFS(E), sold to Westinghouse Air Brake (USA) (WABCO), 1998; renamed WABTEC Rail Ltd, 2000. *see* WABTEC; Westinghouse Brake.

RG
1. *Railway Gazette* title of a weekly newspaper published in November and December 1835.
2. Same title used by *Bradshaw's Railway Gazette* (qv) 1846–72.
3. Same title used by *RSJ* (qv) 1872–84.
4. Same title used from 1905 by new weekly journal, founded as *Transport*, 1892, renamed *Transport & Railway Gazette* 1904. Renamed *Railway Gazette*, 1905. Published twice monthly from January 1964, monthly from October 1970 as *Railway Gazette International*.

RG
BR griddle car with kitchen, bar and buffet counters and seating at tables. *See also* Griddle car.

R/G
An automatic level crossing with red and green warning lights for road traffic.

RG&RR
Reading, Guildford & Reigate Rly, inc 1846, 1847, first section opened 1849, worked by SER, purchased by SER 1852.

RGI
Railway Gazette International, see *RG (4)*.

RGP (Fr)
Rame de Grand Parcours; express diesel railcar units introduced by the *SNCF* in 1955.

RGS&SS

Railway Guards', Signalmen's and Switchmen's Society of the United Kingdom, formed 1866, lasting only one year.

RH

1. *Railway Herald* published 1845–7.
2. *Railway Herald*, first published 1887 as a weekly for rly employees which also contained articles of general rly interest. Circulation boosted in 1888 by prize competitions and free insurance against accidents. Also published *Railway Herald Locomotive Album* (1897–8), *Railway Herald Station Album* (1900?) and *Railway Herald Magazine* (monthly, 1895–8). Publications ceased 1903.

RH&DR

Romney, Hythe & Dymchurch Rly, 1 ft 3 in/381 mm gauge miniature pleasure and public service line from Hythe to Dungeness, LRO 1927. First section opened 1927.

RHC

see Railway Heritage Committee.

Rheingold

A Pullman-style Mitropa day train between Hook of Holland (connecting with Harwich sailings), Amsterdam and Basle, so named 1928. Ceased 1939. Revived 1951; new rolling stock 1962, including vistadome cars which were withdrawn in 1976. *TEE* 1965, Amsterdam–Geneva/Amsterdam–Chur/Hook of Holland–Milan. Hook of Holland coaches ran only to Geneva, 1973 and Hook portion ceased in 1979. In 1980–2 the train ran Amsterdam–Berne/Zurich; in 1982–3 Amsterdam–Basle only; in 1983–6 Amsterdam–Basle/Salzburg. Ceased 1986. In 1987 the southbound working was replaced by the Rembrandt (qv), the northbound by the Erasmus (qv).

Rhein–Main

Diesel railcar set between Frankfurt and Basle, introduced 1949. *TEE* Amsterdam–Frankfurt, introduced 1957. Renamed Van Beethoven 1972 (qv).

Rheinpfeil

Rhine Arrow; express Amsterdam–Basle 1951–3. Name revived 1958 for

Dortmund–Munich service, exchanging coaches at Duisburg with the Rheingold. *TEE* 1965–71. IC 1971. EC Hannover–Chur, 1987.

Rheostatic braking

see Regenerative braking.

Rhinelander

Service between Manchester and Harwich (Parkeston Quay) in connection with sailings to Hook of Holland, introduced 1987 in replacement of the European (qv), replaced 1988 by the Loreley (qv).

Rhodanien

TEE Paris–Marseille, so named 1971, lost *TEE* status 1978. TGV from 1981, name then dropped.

Rhodesia Express

A service between Capetown (connecting with Union Castle Line sailings) and Bulawayo (connections to Congo, etc.). In 1932 it covered 1,354 m in 48 h 20 min on 3 ft 6 in/1,067 mm gauge.

RHP

Rail Horsepower.

RHT

Railway Heritage Trust; an independent trust, formed 1985 with the objective of preserving and enhancing Britain's rly buildings and structures of architectural and/or historical importance (both those in use and those no longer required for BR purposes). Also encourages public enjoyment of this heritage. *See also* Railway Heritage Committee.

Rhymney

Rhymney Rly, inc 1854, Cardiff–Caerphilly –Hengoed–Rhymney. First section opened 1858. By means of joint lines with GWR and L&NWR, eventually also reaching Dowlais, Merthyr and Nantybwch, 62 route miles including joint lines. Part of GWR from 1922. *See also* R&L&NWR Jt.

RI

1. The Railway Inspectorate, established 1840. At first part of the BoT, then MoT, etc. (qv). Until 1982 most of the inspectors were officers of the RE (*1*) (qv). Their duties included inspection of new rlys and tramways, also reporting on accidents and safety, etc. The

Inspectorate was transferred to the HSC/HSE (qv) and retitled HMRI (qv) in 1991. It became part of the DfT (qv) in 2005. *See also* Blue Book; Railway Accident Reports; RAIB.

2. *Railways Illustrated*, founded 1908, merged with RN (qv) 1908.

3. *Rail Infrastructure*, specialist magazine for the rly infrastructure industry, published six times a year from 1998.

RIA
Railway Industry Association of Great Britain. A 1971 renaming of LAMA (qv).

Rialto
Name originally used 1957 for a Milan–Venice service, adopted for a Venice–Geneva service 1985. Latter renamed Monteverdi in 1987. *Rialto* again used, for a Venice–Paris service, 1990.

Ribbons (USRS)
Tracks.

RIC
Regolamento Internazionale Carrozze; International Carriage & Van Union, regulates dimensions and operating requirements of vehicles (other than wagons) used on international services. Established at Lucerne, 1921. *See also RIV*.

Riddling (obs)
Manual ballast cleaning, in which ballast was shovelled into riddles (sieves) to remove dust and other fine material and then returned to the track.

Ride high, to (USRS)
To travel on the roofs of box cars.

Rider (RS)
An engineman accompanying a loco being hauled by another.

Ride shotgun, to (RS)
To act as second man (qv).

Ride the bars, to (S)
To travel on a moving train by clinging to external handles, usually for the length of a station platform, a juvenile/adolescent amusement originating in London *c.* 1988.

Ride the point, to (USRS)
To ride on the loco. *See also* Point, the.

Ride the rods, to (USRS)
The hobo practice of travelling on the truss rods of wagons and vans.

Riding van
A brake van (qv) adapted to carry the crew of a breakdown or engineer's train.

Riff (USRS)
A refrigerated wagon.

RIGA (Ger)
Reisezugwageninstandhaltung in Ganzügen, passenger cars maintained and operated as complete semi-permanent train sets.

Riggenbach
A form of rack rly (qv) in which a driven cogwheel on the loco or railcar engages with a ladder-type strip securely fixed halfway between the running rails; patented in 1863 by Nikolaus Riggenbach (1817–99).

Right Away!
see RA.

Right hand side, on the (USRS)
The US rly driver's position in the cab, hence his status, thus 'Herb's now on the right hand side'.

Right-side failure
A fault which does not reduce the amount of protection given by signalling equipment.

Right the one! (RS) (obs)
Fireman's call to his driver on seeing the outer home signal (qv) indicating 'Line clear'. *See also* Number one.

RII
Railway Infrastructure Insight, published six times a year from 1997, covering developments and policy relating to the fixed structures of the European rail system, including electrification.

Rijeka Express
A summer service between Ostend and Rijeka, so named 1969, and replacing the Dalmatia Express. Cut back to Villach and name dropped, 1975.

Ringer (RS)
A crowbar.

Ringmaster (USRS)
Foreman or yardmaster.

Ring out/ring off (obs)
A bell signal given to the adjacent signal box by the crew of a loco waiting to leave a loco shed/MPD (qv), indicating they were ready for departure and also their next destination.

Rio Grande Zephyr
A service with vistadome cars between Denver and Salt Lake City (with bus link to Ogden), introduced 1971. Replaced by California Zephyr (qv), 1983.

Rio Tinto
British-owned rly between the Rio Tinto copper mines in southern Spain and the port of Huelva.

RIP (US)
Repair, Inspect and Paint; letters seen on wagon or car in need of attention.

Riprap
An embankment of large stones to protect a formation against erosion by water action.

Rip track (USRS)
Track on which damaged or faulty vehicles are parked to await repair or scrapping; it may include a repair facility. From RIP (qv).

Rip van Winkle money (RS)
Pay earned whilst sleeping or resting (e.g. when returning to home depot 'On the cushions' (qv)).

RITC
Rail Industry Training Council.

RIV
Regolamento Internazionale Veicoli; International Wagon Union, regulates dimensions and operating requirements of wagons used on international services. Established at Stresa, 1921. *See also RIC.*

Riverside branch/loop, The
Newcastle–Walker–Carville–Percy Main.

Rivet counter (RS)
A person showing an excessive (and obsessive) interest in the smallest details of rlys and their equipment (usually locos and rolling stock).

Riviera Express
CIWL service Hamburg/Amsterdam/ Berlin–Nice, introduced 1900; reintroduced 1934 as Amsterdam/Berlin–Ventimiglia with Cologne portion. Ceased 1939. Reintroduced 1957 Cologne–Ventimiglia.

RJC
Railway Joint Council, a forum for discussion of major pay and conditions questions between trade unions and management, replaced RSNC (qv) 1992.

RJIS
Rail Journey Information Service; journey information system introduced by ATOC (qv) for ticket and enquiry offices and travel agents from 1999. Computer-based, with interactive tv and train screens and also internet displays. Provides complete data on all public transport services (rail, tram and bus), also on fares, engineering works and other disruptions to services.

RK
BR Kitchen car, with kitchen only.

RKB
BR Kitchen/Buffet car, no seats.

RLC
Royal Logistics Corps, successors to RCT (qv) from 1993.

RLO
BR Restaurant open lounge car.

RLS
Railway Letter Service; a facility introduced in 1891 by which for postage and a supplementary charge, letters could be handed in at rly stations for conveyance by the next train and any necessary onward connections to the station nearest the destination, where they could be called for, or alternatively posted from the station. Express facilities (called Railex from 1934) were also available in which letters were taken to the departure rly station by Post Office messenger and immediately delivered on arrival at the destination station. This service was discontinued in 1984, except for special occasions.

RLTU
Rail Lifting Transportation Unit, LT.

RM
1. *Railway Magazine*, monthly, founded May 1835, renamed 1836 under new ownership (John Herapath) as *Railway Magazine & Annals of Science*. Renamed *Railway Magazine & Commercial Journal*, 1839; became a weekly, *Herapath's Railway Magazine*, 1841 (*see* Herapath).
2. *Railway Magazine*, founded 1897, the first periodical covering *all* aspects of rlys and catering for the popular, non-professional readership. Published monthly, no connection with (*1*).

3. *Railroad Magazine,* popular US rly, tramway and interurban journal, including fiction with a rly background. Published December 1937–April 1979, then became *Railfan & Railroad* (qv).

4. *Railroadman's Magazine* (US) published October 1906–December 1918 (First Series) and December 1929–November 1931 (Second Series). Became *Railroad Stories. See RS.*

RMB

BR Miniature Buffet (qv) car Second/Standard class with a small serving counter and forty-four to forty-eight seats.

RME

Railway Mechanical Engineer; a professional journal published in New York.

RMMM

Rail Mounted Maintenance Machine.

RMT

National Union of Rail, Maritime and Transport Workers. Formed 1990, an amalgamation of the NUR (qv) and the National Union of Seamen.

RN

1. *Railway News,* founded 1864, merged with RG 1918.

2. *Railway Newsletter,* a monthly bulletin distributed to editors of newspapers and other periodicals by the British Railways Press Bureau (qv) from January 1929.

RNCFC

Régie National des Chemins de Fer du Cameroun; Cameroun National Rlys, 1,006 km of metre gauge.

RO

1. An open merchandise wagon.

2. *Railway Observer,* the organ of the RCTS (qv), founded 1928 as *Railway News* renamed RO 1929.

RO (Fr)

Régime Ordinaire; a normal-speed freight service, *SNCF. See also RA.*

ROA (LT)

Railway Operating Apprentice; later used to denote any junior trainee.

Road

Term for a specific rly track (i.e. one set of rails), thus 'No. 2 Road', 'Through Road'; also for a specific rly route, thus 'learning

the road', etc. On LT, the official meaning is any track other than a running line but staff use it of all lines. In the US the term is synonymous with railroad.

Road & Rail Association

See R&RA.

Road bed

Another term for formation (1) (qv); can also be used for the totality of material supporting the track (i.e. including the ballast). Also known as the track bed.

Road box/truck/van/wagon

see Station truck (*2*).

Road engine (US)

A loco available for through/long distance workings as distinct from shunting or local trips.

Roader shed (obs)

A small lock-up goods shed usually found on a passenger platform, particularly on the SER.

Road foreman (US)

Motive power department official responsible for the immediate supervision and control of loco crews.

Road Railer/Ro Railer/Ro Rail

Types of passenger and freight vehicles and infrastructure plant/machinery equally able to operate on roads or rlys.

Road Railer (US)

A piggyback (qv) system but consisting only of the road vehicle chassis supported by a conventional rly truck. Requires a shorter trackside loading platform since train length shortens as trailers return to road mode.

Road/roadside station

Any small intermediate station.

Road vehicle truck

A wagon designed to carry road freight transport vehicles.

Roarers (RS)

BR class 81 electric locos.

Roaring rails

Another term for corrugation (qv).

Roberts

Charles Roberts & Co. Ltd, Horbury Junc, Wakefield, rly carriage and wagon builders, also manufacturers of tramcars and hirers of wagons. Established 1856. Acquired

Hurst, Nelson (qv), 1958. Became part of Procor (qv) 1974.

Robert Stoltz
An EC service between Munich and Graz, introduced 1989.

Robin Hood
An express between London (St Pancras) and Nottingham (Midland), so named 1959. Name subsequently dropped. Re-introduced 1990 for London (St Pancras)–Leicester–Nottingham Pullman service, subsequently extended to Sheffield.

Robin Hood Line
Former BR lines reopened for passenger services from 1993: Nottingham–Newstead–Mansfield–Shirebrook–Worksop [–Retford].

Rock and Roll (USRS)
Excessive lateral movement of locos and rolling stock associated with low speeds and poorly-maintained jointed track.

Rock and Rollers (RS)
BR (S) Hastings line diesel electric mu sets. From their somewhat wild riding qualities at speed.

Rocker panel (obs)
The lower side panel of a tramcar (qv) of waisted side construction.

Rockets (RS)
L&SWR 2–2–0T of 1906 and later conversions to C14 0–4–0T. A facetious reference to their feeble power.

Rocket, The
Toronto Metro & Rapid Transit system.

Rocking chair (USRS)
Retirement with pension.

Rocking horse (RS)(obs)
A freight guard's van offering a bumpy ride.

Rock Island (US)
Chicago, Rock Island & Pacific RR.

ROD (obs)
Railway Operating Division; a division of the British Army Royal Engineers, largely recruited from staffs of British rly companies, which controlled and operated standard and narrow gauge rlys and repaired and overhauled locomotives behind British fronts in France, Belgium, Greece, Egypt and Russia during WW1. Formed in 1915. The total number of men in the ROD had reached twenty-four thousand by 1918.

RODs (RS)
GCR Robinson 2–8–0 locos, as used by the ROD.

ROeEE (Ger)
Acronym for *GySEV* (qv).

Rola
Roll-on, roll-off piggyback (qv) facility for road trucks which are carried on very low-floor rail wagons. Promoted by Okombi (Austria). *See also Rollende Landstrasse.*

Roland
A Bremen–Basle service, introduced 1957. *TEE* Bremen–Milan, introduced 1969, included Milan portion of *Rheingold* south of Basle. Withdrawn 1980. Name used for *TEE* Bremen–Stuttgart, 1980.

Roland the Rat (LTRS)
The RAT (qv). After the TV character.

Rollböcke (Ger)
A set of narrow gauge trucks forming part of four-wheeled standard gauge wagons to allow the wagons to move over narrow gauge (750–1000 mm) rlys and tramways (3) (qv). Known as the Langbein system, the special wagons could traverse curves as sharp as 15 m radius, and when fully loaded could be moved over narrow gauge tracks at a safe speed of 13 mph/21 kph. *See also Rollwagen.*

Roll by (USRS)
Slow movement of a passing train providing an opportunity for a lineside observer to detect possible defects. *See also* Walk the train.

Rollende Landstrasse (Ger)
Moving highway, a German Rly intermodal system in which roll-on, roll-off road tractor and trailer rigs are carried on small-wheeled rail wagons.

Rollerman (RS)(obs)
A criminal who travels on trains to break open and rob unguarded luggage.

Rolling contact fatigue (RCF)
Rail fatigue leading to cracks and even fracture of rails caused by the deteriorating quality of the interaction between vehicle and loco wheels and rails. Following the

formation of a privatized fragmented rly by the Railways Act, 1993 (qv), which broke up the wheel/rail interface existing under the earlier rly regimes in Britain, it was discovered after the Hatfield accident of 2000 that RCF was occurring at much higher levels than expected. *See also* Gauge corner cracking; WRISA.

Rolling stock
Generic term for all types of rly vehicle other than locos, which are usually referred to separately.

Rollschemeln (Ger)
A variation of *Rollwagen* (qv) in which a framework of narrow gauge wheels accommodates each standard gauge wagon or vehicle.

Rollwagen (Ger)
A method of transporting standard gauge rail vehicles over a narrow gauge rly by using flat wagons fitted with standard gauge track. *See also Rollböcke.*

Roma–Milano Express
An all-sleeping car *CIWL* service introduced 1924. Still runs, but now un-named.

Roma–Napoli–Palermo Express
An all-sleeping car *CIWL* service, introduced 1925.

Roma–Napoli Pullman Express
A *CIWL* Pullman service, ran only in 1929.

Roma–Torino Express
An all-sleeping car *CIWL* service introduced 1925.

Roma–Venezia/Trieste Express
An all-sleeping car *CIWL* service introduced 1925.

Rome Express
A *CIWL* service between Calais (connecting with UK sailings), Paris and Rome, introduced 1890, running in winter only. Ran from Paris only from 1902, by 1913 ran all year round, Paris–Rome 26 h 20 min. Reinstated after the WW1, as all-year-round working, with through coaches to and from Boulogne (connection for London (Victoria)) from 1924. By 1935 Paris–Rome timing was reduced to 22 h 35 min. Reintroduced 1951 as Paris–Rome (20 h 35 min), no longer exclusively a

CIWL service. Extended to Naples 1979 and renamed *Napoli Express.*

Romulus
An express between Vienna and Rome, introduced 1969.

Roof garden (USRS)
The assisting loco on a mountainous section of line.

Roomette (US)
Term for cabins or compartments on a long distance train, entirely enclosed each side of central gangway, each forming a small day room, at night convertible for sleeping with a longitudinal bed lowered from the wall. A private lavatory is provided. Windows are necessarily on the outer side only.

Rooters (RS)
1. LB&SCR Stroudley A1 0–6–0T of 1872. *See also* Terriers.
2. (RS) A large hook attached to a wagon hauled by up to three locos, used by German army engineers in WW2 to rip up rly tracks during withdrawals before Allied Forces. The German name was *Schienenwolf.*

Rope runner (obs)
A man whose duty it was to hitch wagons on to the rope used to haul them up steep inclines worked by rope and stationary steam engine.

Ropeway
see Aerial rlys/ropeways.

ROSCOs
Rolling Stock Companies (Angel Train Contracts, HSBC Rail (UK) Ltd, Porterbrook Leasing Co. Ltd and some minor players). These are all private companies formed following the Railways Act, 1993 (qv), to lease out motive power and passenger rolling stock to TOC (2) (qv). Initially ROSCOs took over almost all BR passenger train and loco fleets, but later new stock was purchased, usually with a maintenance liability accepted by the manufacturers. Otherwise ROSCOs are responsible for heavy overhauls, but TOC (2) have to carry out running maintenance and day-to-day repairs.

Rosenkavalier
An express between Munich and Vienna, introduced 1969.

Roses Line, The
[Leeds/Bradford/Halifax–] Burnley–
Blackburn [–Preston–Blackpool].
The name dates from 1984. Also known over part of the way as the Copypit Line (qv).

Rosette
A wall mounting for the overhead span wires of tramway (*3*). From its shape. *See also* Span wires.

Rossiya
[Russia]; a service between Moscow and Vladivostok.

Rosslare Express
A Cork–Rosslare boat train, ceased 1967.

Roster
Notices to show individual employees which diagrams (qv) they are to work and what duties they are to perform.

Rotank
GWR TC for a flat wagon used to carry road milk tankers.

Rotary block
A system adopted by the Midland Rly in which the block instruments are movable only in rotation from 'Normal' through 'Line Clear' to 'Train on Line' back to 'Normal'. To cancel a 'Line Clear', adjacent boxes must both agree to press a cancelling button simultaneously. The 'Train on Line' indication release button can only be activated by breaking the glass covering that protects it.

Rotary coupler
A coupler designed to allow wagons to be turned upside down for unloading without uncoupling.

Rotary snow plough [plow (US)]
A snow plough patented in Canada by Orange Jull in 1884. It uses a fan at the head end, equipped with two sets of blades rotating in opposite directions, and was originally powered by steam; propelled by one or more locos, these ploughs can force a passage through very deep or compressed snow at a speed of 6–8 mph.

Rough (RS)
Unsorted wagons.

Roughnecks (USRS)
Specifically applied in the rly context to freight train brakemen – a tough breed.

Rough turn (RS)
A period of duty with a high proportion of train working.

Roundabout, The
L&SWR timetable term for its services London (Waterloo)–Wimbledon–Kingston–Twickenham–Waterloo and vice versa. Sometimes also referred to as the 'Kingston Roundabout'.

Rounder (RS)
A round trip.

Roundhouse
A building, originally circular in plan, in which locos are accommodated on tracks radiating from a central turntable. The name was first used for the shed opened at Camden, London in 1847. It came to be applied to any loco shed with tracks fanning out from a turntable, even if not circular in plan. In the US it was used for any loco shed or depot.

Round the benders (LTRS)
Additional automatic signals installed on curves in tube tunnels after the 1953 Stratford (Central Line) accident, ensuring that the driver always has a signal in sight.

Roustabout (USRS)
A duty for loco crews which involves a number of short trips.

Route
In a signalling context, this noun implies a path along the section of track between two successive signals.

Route bells
Electric bells in signal boxes on which signalmen in adjacent boxes describe the class and destination of an approaching train by means of an audible code. *See also* Train describer/indicator.

Route crime
A generic term for trespass, graffiti spraying and other acts of vandalism on the rly and rly property.

Route indicator

1. A device on a signal at a junction exhibiting a stencil letter or number code corresponding to the designation of the route to be taken by an approaching train.
2. Information displayed on the front of a loco or train which informs signalmen and others of its route, destination, etc. *See also* Train describer/indicator.

Route km/miles

A measurement of length of rly/rlys disregarding the number of parallel tracks, i.e. the geographical distance covered by the line or lines. *See also* Track miles/km.

Route number

In the context of tramways (*3*) this is usually the number exhibited on the vehicle to inform the public and staff of the route which will be followed between the two termini. On the LCCT (qv) and some other undertakings, however, the term signified the service number (qv).

Route relay interlocking

Route control of electrically interlocked points and signals by use of thumb switches.

ROUTES

Acronym for Rail, Omnibus and Underground Travel Enquiry System, a computer-based public information system introduced by LT in 1994.

Route-setting signalling

A system of power signalling which automatically sets the points and signals over a section of a route selected by a signalman, following movement of a single lever at a control panel.

ROV (obs)

Railway Owned Vehicles, a term used by the Pullman Car Co. (qv) and others to distinguish between cars owned by a rly co. but manned by Pullman staff and Pullman cars proper.

Rover ticket

BR term for a ticket allowing unlimited travel within a specified area for periods longer than one day. *See also* Ranger ticket, Travelcard.

Royal clerestory

A design in which the clerestory (qv) is sloped down to merge with the roofline at each end of the coach.

Royal Duchy

An express between London (Paddington) and Penzance, so named 1957, name dropped 1965. Revived 1987, with 4 h 46 min timing.

Royal Highlander

A sleeping car express between London (Euston) and Aberdeen/Inverness, introduced 1927. Later to and from Inverness only. Ceased 1939, name restored 1957. Has at various times enjoyed the dubious distinctions of being the most unpunctual train on BR and one of the longest trains in the UK.

Royal Road

Nickname for the L&SWR, first used by (Sir) Sam Fay in his 1882 book of this name.

Royal Scot

An express between London (Euston) and Glasgow (Central)/Edinburgh (Princes St.), introduced 1927 as name for a day train that had run since 1848. Name dropped 1939, restored 1948. Timing 7 h 30 min in 1936, 7 h in 1938, reduced to 4 h 52 min with electric traction by 1989. Name ceased to be used after 2 June 2002 but was restored for London (Euston)–Glasgow (Central) *Pendolino* (qv) service from 27 September 2004 (4 h 42 min Up, 4 h 52 min Down).

Royal trains

Trains made up of special stock, provided as required for journeys made by the Royal Family and their Household staff. Now financed directly from the Exchequer. Stringent safety and operating instructions apply to the working of these trains and the crews are specially selected experienced staff. However, in recent years, unlike some Ministers of the Crown, the Royal Family also travel in specially reserved coaches attached to normal public services.

Royal Wessex

A service between London (Waterloo) and Swanage/Weymouth, so named 1951.

Ceased 1967. Name revived for an electric service between London and Weymouth introduced 1988.

RP

1. *Railway Press*, 1888–98. Began as another edition of *RH* (qv), then became a monthly news journal, from 1891 listing principal rlys and their officials.
2. *Railway Pictorial*, founded 1946, retitled *Railway Pictorial & Locomotive Review* 1949, a high-quality, well-illustrated magazine. Ceased publication 1950 (incorporated in *Railways* (qv)).
3. *Rail Professional*, monthly magazine of PRIMA (qv), first published January 1997.

RPA

Railway Procurement Agency; formed 2001 to channel private-enterprise funding into rly development in the Republic of Ireland. Has powers to acquire land by compulsory purchase and has full authority for the development of all rail transport in the Dublin area, including light rail. It may allow private-sector participation in the design, construction, financing and operation of rlys anywhere in the Republic.

RPAC

Railway Passengers' Assurance Co., founded 1849. By payment of a nominal sum at the ticket office at the time of booking, a passenger could obtain a RPAC policy in the form of a ticket, providing accident cover relating to that particular journey, over and beyond any legal liability of the rly undertaking to pay compensation.

RPC

Rail Passengers Council; a non-departmental public body funded by the SRA (qv) and supported by eight Regional Committees, handling complaints from passengers, responding to representations made by passengers and keeping under review passenger and station services, including objections to rail closure proposals; negotiating with TOC (2) (qv) and other relevant bodies. A renaming in 2000 of the CRUCC (qv) and its related RUCC (qv). The supporting Rail Passenger Councils in the English regions

were however abolished by the Railways Act, 2005 (qv). *See* also LTUC

RPI

Revenue Protection Inspector. Modern (from 1980s) term for ticket inspector.

RPO

Railway Post Offices (qv).

RPO (US)

Railroad Post Office. The US equivalent of TPO (qv).

RPP

Rail Passenger Partnerships; schemes launched from 1999 to assist in modal shift from road to rail transport and foster integration of transport modes. Schemes were initially approved and funded by the SRA (qv).

RPS

Railway Photographic Society, founded 1922.

RPSI

Railway Preservation Society of Ireland.

RR

1. *Railway Record*, founded 1844, merged with RN 1901.
2. (US) Abbreviation for railroad.
3. Redditch Rly, Barnt Green–Redditch, inc 1858, opened 1859, worked by Midland Rly, part of Midland Rly 1874.
4. Ramsey Rly, inc 1861, Holme to Ramsey, opened 1863, worked by GNR, part of GER, 1875, leased to GNR 1875, part of L&NER 1923.
5. Richmond Rly, from what is now Clapham Junc–Richmond, inc 1845, opened 1846, part of L&SWR 1846.
6. Rhodesia Rlys, formed 1899. Beira Rly, Mashonaland Rly & Rhodesian Rlys amalgamated as RR 1927, purchased by Rhodesia Government 1947. Lines north of Victoria Falls became Zambia Rlys, 1967. Renamed NRZ (qv) 1980.
7. Regional Railways (qv).

RR

Railway Reflections published in 28 issues 1980–5. 'A wholly pictorial steam nostalgia magazine' (Robert Humm).

RRI

Route Relay Interlocking (qv).

RRNE

Regional Rlys North East; a TOU (qv),

1994. A TOC (*2*) (qv) 1997, renamed Northern Spirit (qv).

RROA
Retired Rly Officers Association, founded 1901.

RR roof
Railroad roof, the US term for clerestory (qv).

RRT
Railway Rates Tribunal. *See also* TT.

RRV
1. Road Rail Vehicles; vehicles capable of moving under their own power on roads or rly track. *See also* Road Railer.
2. Rail Response Vehicles; four-wheel-drive road vehicles used by Network Rail to move key staff to a serious incident on the rly which are then capable of transformation to a control point for directing operations and handling communications.

RS
Railroad Stories published December 1931–November 1937.

RSA
Railway Study Association, founded 1909 as the Railway Students' Association of the London School of Economics & Political Science (University of London), for the purpose of furthering the study of rly transport. Receives official support from bodies and firms within the rly industry.

RSAB
Rolling Stock Acceptance Board (Railtrack).

RSB
1. BR Second/Standard class Buffet coach.
2. Railway Shops Battalion, US Army.

RSB (Ger) (obs)
Regional Schnellbahn, fast regular interval services within a defined region providing links with the long-distance services. Now RB (qv).

RSC
1. Railway Signal Co. Ltd; formed 1881, works at Fazakerley, Liverpool. Became part of Westinghouse Brake & Signal Co. after WW2, works closed 1974.
2. Railway Safety Case. *See* Safety case.

RSE
Railways South East, illustrated magazine devoted to historical and current rly

matters in London and south-east England, 1987–94.

RSI
Rolling Stock Inspector.

RSJ
Railway Supplies Journal, founded 1872 as *Railway Gazette*, retitled *c.* 1884, ceased *c.* 1898.

RSL
1. Railway Sites Ltd, a company formed by the L&NER in 1937 to develop land, inactive after formation of BTC (qv). Name used for new company formed by BTC 1961 to exploit surplus rly land and property. Moribund by 1965. *See also* BRPB.
2. Rolling Stock Library. A system linked to TOPS (qv) containing details of all rolling stock (qv) approved by Network Rail (qv) for operation within its infrastructure constraints.

RSNC
Railway Staff National Council, consisting of representatives of BR and the rly trade unions, set up 1956 to consider major issues of pay and conditions. Superseded by RJC (qv), 1992. *See also* RSNT.

RSNT
Rail[way] Staff National Tribunal, established 1956, consisting of a member selected by BR, another nominated by the rly trade unions and a chairman approved by agreement between BR and the unions. Its duty was to hear and decide upon issues agreed by RSNC (qv) to be of national importance and the final arbiter in all such matters.

RSO
BR Restaurant car, Second/Standard class, Open; no kitchen.

RSP
Rail Settlement Plan. Computer systems which monitor all ticket sales and distribute a share of the total revenue (£3.3bn in 1999–2000) to each TOC (*2*) (qv). *See also* ORCATS.

RSSB
Rail Safety & Standards Board Ltd; a not for profit body formed 2003 and owned by

the rly industry in the UK to provide a forum and focus for the development of improved safety measures for rly passengers, rly workers and 'neighbours' of the rly system.

RSUASS
Railway Signalmen's United Aid Sick Society, founded 1865. Subsumed by UP&SS (qv).

RT
Railway Times, founded 1837, merged with RG (qv) 1914.

RTA (US)
Regional Transportation Authority.

RTC
Railway Technical Centre, BR, Derby.

RTCC
Rail Traffic Control Centre; first used for Saltley RTCC, 2002. *See also* ICC.

RTD
Returned To Duty.

RTG (Fr)(obs)
Rame de Turbine à Gaz; the second type of *SNCF* gas turbine train, 1973.

RTO
Railway Transport Officer; a British Army officer (colonel, major or captain) specifically designated to supervise and organize the movement of troops, horses and military equipment by rail in conjunction with rly officials, and to report these movements appropriately. RTOs wear the uniform of their regiment, but are distinguished by a white armband bearing these initials and worn on the left arm.

RTR
Ramsgate Tunnel Rly; an electric rly, 2 ft/609 mm gauge, from Dumpton Park to Ramsgate Harbour, mainly using the former LC&DR tunnel leading to Ramsgate Harbour station. Opened 1936, closed during WW2, reopened 1946, closed 1965.

RU
1. BR Restaurant car, Unclassified, open with kitchen.
2. Regular User.

RUB
BR Restaurant/Buffet car, Unclassified, with kitchen.

Rubber (USRS)
Recovery time (qv). *See also* Take the rubber out of them, to.

Rubberneck car (USRS)
An observation car (qv). From US (S) rubberneck = tourist.

Rubens
TEE Paris–Brussels, introduced 1974, lost *TEE* status 1984. Name used by an EC in 1987 (Ostend–Frankfurt).

RUCC
Rail Users' Consultative Committees; replaced TUCC for all areas outside London, 1994. Became RPC (qv). *See also* CRUCC; CTCC; LRPC; TUCC.

Rudd
A 20-ton ballast wagon used by engineers.

RUG
Railfreight Users' Group, formed 1990.

Rugby bedstead, The (RS) (obs)
An unusually large and elaborate signal gantry erected on the London side of Rugby station in 1895. All signal arms were repeated, the higher ones being intended for long-distance sighting. Dismantled 1939.

RUK
BR Restaurant car, Unclassed, with Kitchen.

Rule Book (obs)
A pocket-size book of Rules & Regulations variously described as 'for the guidance of the officers and men' or 'for observance by employees'; issued by the pre-1948 British rly undertakings and by BR (1), covering operating procedures, staff conduct, etc. *See* Working Reference Manual.

Rule 55
If a train is held at a signal more than two minutes (three before 1950) after giving audible indication of its presence, this rule requires a member of the train crew to go to the signal box to remind the signalman of the presence of the train in his block section. Once there, he signs the train register book (qv) and does not leave until the signalman gives the train a clear signal or until he has seen lever collars (qv) placed in position to protect his train. The rule is usually waived where lines are track-circuited or there is

some means of communicating with the signalman from the lineside. Nowadays, with modern signalling installations operated remotely from widely dispersed signal control centres, large areas of track-circuiting, and virtually all signals equipped with telephones, the rule is a much less important factor in rail safety than formerly. *See also* Stop and Proceed.

Rule G (US)
Forbids possession or consumption of alcohol or narcotics when on rly duty.

Rule One car (USRS)
A freight car running on the rly to which it belongs.

Rules of the Route
An agreement and document between Network Rail and the relevant TOCs (2) showing when possessions may be taken of a section of rly for engineering work and the duration and severity of subsequent speed restrictions. *See also* Blockade.

Ruling gradient
The steepest gradient of significant length on a given stretch of line, which determines the load a given loco can haul at a given speed over that route. In some cases the ruling gradient may not be the steepest but a section with a lesser gradient limiting the capacity of a line for other reasons, e.g. liability of exposure to strong crosswinds or a vulnerability to presenting slippery rails.

Rumney
Rumney Railroad or Tramroad; horse-drawn tramroad built for carriage of iron from the Rhymney Ironworks to Newport, inc 1825, opened 1836, reconstituted as a rly company 1861, purchased by B&MR (qv) 1863, opened as a rly 1865, 1866.

Run (obs)
A section of a waggonway over which wagons could travel downhill.

Run a board, to (USRS)
To ignore a signal, accidentally or deliberately. *See also* SPAD (qv).

Run & Shove Behind
Nickname for R&SBR.

Runaway
A train, loco or vehicles moving along a running line out of control.

Runaway points/siding
see Catch points.

Run-in (USRS)
A collision.

Runner
1. *see* Guard truck (qv).
2. (RS) A platform inspector.
3. (USRS) A loco driver.

Runners (RS) (obs)
A 24-hour service of coal and steel trains between Annesley yard and Woodford Halse, GCR (*1*).

Runner, Shunters' (RS)(obs)
A 4-wheel rail wagon with low steps and hand rails provided for the use of shunters, GWR, BR(W). *See* Shunting truck.

Runner wagon
A wagon marshalled at one or both ends of a wagon carrying a load which projects beyond its ends, to allow the loaded wagon to be coupled up in a train without the projecting load fouling the neighbouring wagons. *See also* Match truck.

Running band
Contact strip (qv).

Running edge
The inside face of the head (qv) of a rail when it is in position on the track. Also known as the gauge face or the running face.

Running face
See Running edge.

Running gear
Wheels, axles, axleboxes, springs and vehicle frame.

Running-in boards
Boards erected alongside platforms to exhibit the names of stations and halts to passengers in trains. Beneath the name other information may be shown, such as 'Alight here for . . .' or 'change for . . .'.

Running light
Light engine (qv).

Running line
Tracks for through train movements as distinct from sidings, bays, docks and yards.

Running powers
A formal arrangement by which one or more 'foreign' companies could exercise a

right to operate trains over the owning company's lines in return for a rental payment.

Running rooms
Indian term for accommodation provided at rly stations for guards and enginemen who have worked trains out of their headquarters station and require rest before making the return trip to base.

Running round [a train]
The process of releasing a loco from the front of a train at the completion of a journey and moving it to the other end of the train ready for the return run. Hence a run-round layout.

Running shed (obs)
A depot to house the locos in daily use on a particular stretch of line, possessing only minimal maintenance and repair facilities.

Running signals
Signals protecting movements on running lines.

Running surface
That part of the railhead (qv) in contact with the wheel tyres, extending from the gauge corner to the back edge corner. Also known as the rail table or the running table.

Running table
See Running surface.

Running wires
That part of the overhead (qv) of tramways (3) (qv) which carries the traction current fed to the cars by the trolley (qv), bow collector (qv) or pantograph (qv) on the tram.

Run-round
A track arrangement, usually at a terminus, to enable a loco to run round its train, ready for a return journey or to take it into sidings.

Runt (USRS)
A dwarf signal. From runt, meaning an undersized or inferior person.

Run-through [of points]
An incident involving a train running through a set of trailing points (qv) not set in the correct position for the movement.

RUS
Route Utilization Strategy; laid down by SRA (qv) or, from 2005, by Network Rail (qv). Under this, each route or franchise was required to establish its own integrated control centre (*see* ICC (2)), staffed by representatives of the TOC (2) and Network Rail.

Rust (USRS)
Rly tracks.

Rustle/rustle the bums, to (USRS)
To search along a train for hobos taking illicit free rides.

Rusty rail (USRS)
A rlyman with very long service.

RV&HJR
Rhondda Valley & Hirwain Junction Rly: inc 1867, a colliery line at Blaenrhondda, opened 1878 (never completed to Hirwain [now Hirwaun]). Leased by TVR, part of TVR 1889.

RVAR
Rail Vehicle Accessibility Regulations; governing design features to assist MIP (qv).

RVO
BR Restaurant car, unclassed, open, no kitchen.

RVR
Rother Valley Rly: *see* K&ESR.

RW
Railway World; a renaming of the monthly *Railways* (qv) from September 1952. Replaced by *RI* (2) (qv) March 2003. *See also*: T&RW.

RYB
Railway Yearbook, first published 1898, now known as *Railway Directory & Year Book*.

RZBL (Ger)
Rechnerunterstützte Zentrale Beitriebsleitung. A system of central control covering the whole of the German rail network, supervising all passenger trains and the more important freight services. Located at Frankfurt am Main and introduced 1997.

RZD
Russian State Rlys, formed after dissolution of the Soviet Union in 1991, replacing *SZD* (qv). *Rossiye Zhelezniye Dorogi*. Became Russian Rlys Co., with all shares owned by the state, 2003, *c.* 150,000 km of 1,520 mm gauge.

S

S
1. Station.
2. (obs) BR Second/Standard class non-gangwayed compartment coach.

S (Fr)
Sifflez, sound whistle.

Sack truck
A barrow, mainly of wooden construction, used to move luggage and freight at rly stations and freight depots. Fitted with two handles at the top and a right-angled metal support and two small wheels at the base.

SACM (Fr)
Société Alsacienne de Contsructions Mécaniques; Belfort and Graffenstaden. Manufacturers of locos, etc.

Sacred ox (USRS)
A very powerful loco.

Saddlebacks (RS)
L&SWR 0–6–0ST of 1876.

Saddle tank
A tank loco with water tank curved over the top of the boiler in the manner of a saddle on a horse. In Whyte's notation, abbreviation ST follows wheel arrangement, e.g. 0–6–0ST.

SAFB
Société Anglo–Franco–Belge; loco carriage and wagon builders.

Safe cess
Hard standings, safe paths, recesses, barriers, etc. to allow safe walking use of the cess (qv) by authorized staff.

Safety case/s
A document available for public inspection which embraces information about the holder's activities, details of their related organization, safety management systems, technical specifications, risk assessments and other material relevant to safety. Its object is to instil confidence that the holder has the ability and resources properly to control safety risks and it provides a check list showing that the relevant safety systems have been put in place and continue to operate as originally intended. Safety cases apply to any body in control of rly infrastructure and must be scrutinized and accepted by the ORR (qv) (which has powers to require revision) and also by other authorities, e.g. in the case of operators by those controlling the particular infrastructure over which the operator's trains run. Safety cases can be a feature of legislation and were extended to rlys under the Railways (Safety Case) Regulations, 1994.

Safety points
Catch points (qv). Originally used to describe any trap points (qv) worked from a signal box.

SAGA (Fr)(obs)
Société Anonyme de Gérance et d'Armement, former operator of French flag maritime service between Calais and Dover, in connection with British/French rly services.

SAI
On a lineside sign: Stop and Await Instructions (from a signaller or yard controller).

Saint David/Executive/Pullman
A HST between London (Paddington), Cardiff and Swansea, so named 1984. Added 'Executive' 1986, 'Pullman' 1989.

St Louis
St Louis Car Co., St Louis (US), inc 1887.

Builders of rly, interurban and tramcars;
the only US builders of the last two vehicle
types to survive WW2.

St Louis–San Francisco (US)
St Louis–San Francisco Rly System.

Saint Mungo
Express between Glasgow (Buchanan St.)
and Aberdeen, introduced 1937, restored
1949.

Saint Paul (US)
1. A steam loco with 4–6–2 wheel
   arrangement. From an order by
   Chicago, Milwaukee & St Paul RR.
2. Chicago, Milwaukee & St Paul RR.

**Saint Petersburg–Nice–Cannes
Express**
A *CIWL* service introduced 1899.

Sairseal
A Limerick–Dublin service, introduced
1969. Name dropped 1975.

SAL (US)
Seaboard Airline Rly Co.

Salmon
TC for civil engineer's 50-ton bogie flat
wagon.

Salmon tins (LTRS) (obs)
1920 MDR all-steel cars. *See also* Tank
stock.

Saloon
1. In rly parlance this term can be used for
   a complete vehicle, e.g. family saloon
   (qv), invalid saloon (qv), picnic saloon
   (qv) and any open coach (qv). It can
   also be applied to the open section of
   any coach which additionally features
   compartments (qv) or one or more
   coupés (qv).
2. (obs) The enclosed section of the
   lower deck of a double-deck tramcar
   (qv).

Salts, give the Old Girl a dose of, to
(USRS)
Dust her out, to (qv).

SAM
Switch Actuation Mechanism, an electro-
mechanical switch actuator, controlled
electronically, which detects and monitors
the relative positions of switch and stock
rails (qv), checking them against a
predetermined datum.

SANAL
*Société Anonyme de Navigation Angleterre
Lorraine Alsace*. A French company in
which BR held a financial interest,
operating short sea services out of
Dunkirk to Tilbury and later Folkestone,
also the Dunkirk–Dover train ferries.

Sand blanket
See Blanket.

S&BR
Shrewsbury & Birmingham Rly, inc 1846,
opened 1849, 1854 (section between
Wolverhampton and Birmingham not
built). Shrewsbury to Wellington was joint
GWR & L&NWR/LM&SR, remainder
part of GWR from 1854.

S&C
1. Switches and Crossings.
2. Settle & Carlisle line.

S&CER
Swindon & Cheltenham Extension Rly, inc
1881, opened 1883, 1891, amalgamated
with SM&AR as M&SWJR 1884.

S&CLER
Southport & Cheshire Lines Extension Rly,
inc 1881, 1882, Aintree–Birkdale–
Southport, opened 1884, worked by CLC,
part of BR 1948.

S&CR
1. Shrewsbury & Chester Rly, inc 1846.
   Main section opened 1848. Part of
   GWR from 1854.
2. Sutherland & Caithness Rly, inc 1871,
   Thurso–Wick; Helmsdale–Georgemas
   Junction, opened 1874, part of HR (*7*)
   1884.

S&DJR
1. Somerset & Dorset Joint Rly, Bath to
   Wimborne with branches from
   Evercreech Junction to Burnham-on-
   Sea and from Glastonbury to Wells.
   Formed 1862 by amalgamation of
   SCR and DCR; leased jointly by
   Midland Rly and L&SWR 1876, vested
   in LM&SR and SR 1923, to BR (S)
   1948.
2. Salisbury & Dorset Junction Rly, inc
   1861, Adderbury Junction to West
   Moors, opened 1866, worked by
   L&SWR, part of L&SWR 1883.

S&DR
Stockton & Darlington Rly, first section
opened 1825; part of NER from 1863.
First public rly to open with steam locos.

Sand drag
A means of slowing down and stopping
trains which have overrun and are
approaching the end of a track. Sand or
other material with retardation properties
is held in place over the rails by boards or
steel plates. Alternative methods of
achieving the same result are frictionally
controlled buffer stops or friction-type train
arrestors. *See* Buffer stops.

S and E
Signal & Electrical Engineer/ing, LT.

S&GE Rly Signal Co
See SGE Signals Ltd.

S&H Joint
Shrewsbury & Hereford Rly inc 1846,
opened 1852, 1853, leased to L&NWR,
GWR and WMR 1862, jointly vested in
GWR & L&NWR from 1870, LM&SR &
GWR from 1923, to BR (W) 1948.

Sand Hutton
see SHLR.

San Diegan
A diesel-electric streamline train set
running between Los Angeles and San Diego,
introduced 1938, schedule 2 h 30 min.
Name revived by Amtrak over same route.

Sandies (RS)
L&NER B17 4–6–0 locos; abbreviation of
the class name (Sandringhams).

Sandite
A gritty, jelly-like substance containing sand
and metal particles, developed by BR in the
1980s. It is applied to rail surfaces in the leaf
fall season to maintain proper adhesion
between wheels and rails and also to ensure
efficient operation of track circuits (qv).
Application is made after leaf debris has
been blasted from the track by water cannon.

S&K Joint
Swinton & Knottingley Joint, Midland Rly
and NER from 1879, LM&SR & L&NER
from 1923.

S&K Line
Swinton–Moorthorpe–Knottingley
(Ferrybridge).

S&MJL
Sheffield & Midland Joint Lines
Committee, Hyde to New Mills; New
Mills–Hayfield, (opened 1865), inc 1869,
MS&LR and Midland Rly, GCR and
Midland Rly, L&NER & LM&SR from
1923–47.

S&MJR
Stratford-upon-Avon & Midland Junction
Rly, formed 1908, an amalgamation of the
E&WJR, ER&SJR and Stratford-upon-Avon,
Towcester & Midland Junction Rly. N&BJR
purchased 1910. Part of LM&SR 1923.

S&MLR
Shropshire & Montgomeryshire Light Rly,
Shrewsbury to Llanymynech and branch to
Criggion. A refurbishment and reopening
in 1911–12 of PS&NWR (qv). Passenger
service ceased 1933, requisitioned by the
Army 1941: some passenger services
worked during and immediately after
WW2. Under dual military and BR
administration (BR ownership) from 1948,
main section closed 1960.

S&MR
1. Stratford & Moreton Rly, Moreton-in-
   Marsh to Shipston-on-Stour and
   Stratford-on-Avon, inc 1821, 1825,
   opened 1826, 1836 as 4 ft gauge horse
   tramroad. Leased to OW&WR 1845
   and partly relaid 1853. Moreton–
   Shipston converted to conventional rly
   and worked by GWR with locos from
   1889. Closed to passengers 1929, to
   freight 1960. Shipston–Stratford section
   finally lifted 1918, although the
   northern section was disused from some
   time before then.
2. Swansea & Mumbles Rly: *see*
   Mumbles.

S&SJR
Surrey & Sussex Junction Rly, inc 1865,
Croydon–Oxted–Groombridge, part of
LB&SCR 1869, construction started but
works abandoned. Eventually built by
LB&SCR and SER, jointly owned between
Selsdon Road, Oxted and Crowhurst
Junction, LB&SCR owned Crowhurst
Junc–East Grinstead and Hurst Green
Junction–Groombridge. The joint section

was administered by the Croydon, Oxted and East Grinstead Railways Joint Committee, formed 1884. Opened 1884, 1888. Part of SR, 1923.

S&ST&LR

Schull & Skibbereen Tramway & Light Rly, 3 ft gauge, inc 1883 as West Carbery Tramways & Light Rlys Co. (S&S branch), opened 1886, name changed to S&ST&LR 1886, part of GSR 1925, closed April 1944, reopened December 1945, finally closed at end of 1946.

S&T

Signals & Telegraphs/Telecommunications [department/engineers].

Sandwich train (RS) (obs)

A train in which the loco was positioned in the centre. *See also* Auto train (*1*); *Cages à Poules*.

S&WR

Shrewsbury & Welshpool Rly, inc 1856, opened 1862, purchased by L&NWR 1864, vested jointly in GWR and L&NWR (LM&SR from 1923) from 1865.

S&WR&C/S&W Joint Rly

Severn & Wye Rly & Canal Co. inc 1809 as Lydney & Lydbrook Rly, renamed S&WR&C Co. 1810. Part of rly (a 3 ft 8 in gauge horse-worked plateway) opened 1810, the rest of the main line 1812, the harbour 1813. A 7 ft gauge rly Lydney–Wimberry alongside plateway 1868, converted to standard gauge from 1872. Amalgamated with SBR (qv) 1879; purchased jointly by Midland and GWR (Severn & Wye Joint Rly) 1894. LM&SR and GWR 1923–47. Part now a preserved line (*see* Dean Forest Rly).

Sandy

see Sandies.

San Francisco Overland Limited

All-Pullman 'hotel train' service between Chicago and San Francisco, including, in the 1920s, a library car, observation car, showers, ladies' dressing room and maid service, gentleman's valet and barber service, a club car, lounge cars, dining and sleeping cars.

San Francisco Zephyr

Amtrak daily each way service between Chicago and San Francisco (Oakland),

2,390 m in 48 h, with double-deck observation coaches, introduced 1971, renamed California Zephyr 1983.

San Marco

A summer weekend overnight service Vienna–Venice, introduced 1963.

Sante Fe (US)

1. Atchison, Topeka & Sante Fe RR, later amalgamated with Gulf, Colorado & Santa Fe RR and the Panhandle & Santa Fe Rly Co. as Santa Fe Lines. *See* BNSF.

2. A steam loco with 2–10–2 wheel arrangement. The first one was used on the AT&SF RR.

Santa Fe Chief

AT&SFRR service Chicago–Los Angeles, introduced 1926, renamed Super Chief (qv), 1936.

SAP

1. BR (S) HAP (qv) emu downgraded to Second/Standard class status for suburban service in 1976. Second class And electro-Pneumatic brakes, 2-SAP.

2. (USRS) A brake club (qv).

Saphir

An express between Ostend, Brussels, Cologne and Dortmund, introduced 1954. *TEE* from 1957, extended to Frankfurt 1958. Brussels to Frankfurt from 1966. Lost *TEE* status 1979. IC 1979. Re-extended to Ostend 1981. Replaced by Memling (qv), 1987.

Sap up binders, to (USRS)

To set the handbrakes on a freight train. *See also* Binders; SAP (*2*).

SAR

1. South Australian Government Rlys. *See also* ANR.

2. St Andrews Rly, inc 1851, Milton Junction, Leuchars, to St Andrews opened 1852. Part of NBR 1877.

SAR[&H]

South African [Government] Rlys [& Harbours] Administration. Formed 1910 from CSAR (qv), CGR (qv) and NGR (qv). Rlys in former German South West Africa included from 1922. Privatized 1990. *See* SARCO; SATS; Spoornet;

Transnet Ltd.

SARCO
South African Rail Commuter
Corporation; 2,616 km of 1,067 mm
gauge. *See also* SATS; Spoornet.

SAS
Initials of the Afrikaans title of the SAR
[&H] (qv).

Sassnitz Express
A Stockholm–Berlin–Munich service.
Stockholm–Berlin only from 1973.

Satellite interlocking
Same as remote interlocking (qv).

SATS
South African Transport Services; the
holding company for the SAR[&H] (qv),
South African Airways, etc., denationalized
1990 and operated by Transnet Ltd (qv).

SA(TS) (LT)
Station Assistant (Train Service). Their
presence is indicated to drivers by a board
with a white square bearing the letter S. If
present, they can give a driver the right to
depart.

Saundersfoot Rly
See SR&H Co.

Saut de mouton (Fr)
A flyover (literally 'sheep's leap').

Saxby & Farmer
Saxby & Farmer Ltd, manufacturers of
signalling equipment at Kilburn, London
from 1863. Acquired by Consolidated
Signal Co. (qv) 1901–2. The name
continued in use from the new owners'
Chippenham Works.

Saw-by (USRS)
A shunting operation at a siding on single
track to allow one train to pass another
when the siding is too short to allow a
single movement.

SBAFB
Société Belgo–Anglaise des Ferry Boats. Co.
in which BR has a financial interest, which
operates the train ferry port installation at
Zeebrugge (Belgium) and owns rail ferry
vans.

S-bahn (Ger)
Schnellbahn; urban rail or light rail services
with average journey length of $7^1/_2$–$12^1/_2$ miles
and frequency of 30 min. or less operating in

the cities and conurbations. May operate over
segregated tracks or alongside main lines
(qv).

SB&CR
Surrey Border & Camberley Rly,
$10^1/_4$ in/260.4 mm gauge passenger line
(originally called Farnborough Miniature
Rly). Opened 1934, eventually extended
from Farnborough Green (near Frimley
SR) to Camberley. Closed 1939.

SBB
Schweizerische Bundesbahnen; Swiss Federal
Rlys formed 1902. *See also* CFF, FFS, SFF.

SBR
Severn Bridge Rly, inc 1872 to bridge the
Severn Estuary at Sharpness, opened 1879,
part of S&WJR 1879.

SBZ
See RBS.

SC
1. A self-cleaning smokebox which blows
   most of the fire ash up through the
   chimney.
2. Sleeping Car, an abbreviation mainly
   used in Bradshaw (qv).
3. Sorting Carriage, a rly vehicle specially
   designed for sorting mail en route, so
   named officially in 1904 but in use
   much earlier. Renamed TPO (qv),
   1928.

Scalp, to (RS) (obs)
The fraudulent device of splitting an out-
of-date Edmondson (qv) ticket and
replacing the back portion with that of a
ticket bearing a current date.

Scalpers (USRS)
Agencies selling rly tickets at less than
regulation rates.

Scandinavian
A summer-season express between London
(Liverpool St.) and Harwich (Parkeston
Quay) in connection with sailings to
Esbjerg and rail connections beyond.
Originally named the Esbjerg Continental.
Introduced 1930, restored 1945, name
dropped 1975.

Scandinavian–Swiss Express
CIWL service Stockholm–Chur,
introduced 1948, renamed
Scandinavia–Italy Express, 1949, through

cars Stockholm/Copenhagen–Rome, renamed *Schweiz Express*, 1960.

Scarborough Flier/Flyer
Summer-only express between London (Kings Cross), York and Scarborough, so named 1927, Whitby portion included from 1934, 3 h 55 min London to Scarborough in 1935. Restored 1950. Ceased 1963.

Scarf (RS)
A foreman – 'always on the necks of his men'.

Scarifying
A process of breaking up existing compacted ballast before laying new track on old ballast.

SCAT (LT)
Speed Control After Tripping. *See* Train stop; Tripped.

SCC
Signalling Control Centre.

SCD
Short-Circuiting Device.

SCETA
Société de Contrôle et d'Exploitation des Transports Auxiliares; an *SNCF* (qv) subsidiary responsible for various auxiliary activities.

SCFB
Société des Chemins de Fer de Bourkina; co. operating the 622 km portion of the metre gauge line to Abidjan (Ivory Coast) lying within the Democratic Republic of Burkina Faso. *See also SICF.*

Scharfenberg coupler
An auto-coupler with a central buffer, designed to permit complete simultaneous coupling and uncoupling of air pipe, mechanical and electrical connections and all connections from the driver's cab. A patented design of LHB (qv).

Schedule
A list of the passing and stopping times of a particular train on one journey. In the US, a timetable.

Scheme ticket (obs)
A system in which the ticket issued to the passenger covered travel to any one of a group of stations to which the same fare applied; a list of the furthest stations to which the ticket was valid was printed

vertically. Adopted by London Underground in 1911 and last used in 1971.

Schienenwolf (Ger) (obs)
See Rooter (2).

Schindler Waggon
Rly rolling stock builders and component manufacturers based at Pratteln and Altenrhein, Switzerland. Rolling stock sector taken over by ADtranz (qv), 1998.

Schmalspurbahn (Ger)
A narrow gauge rly.

Schnellfahrstrecke (Ger)
High-speed line.

Schnellzug (Ger)(obs)
A fast train.

School, The (LTRS)
White City Railway Training Centre.

Schumann
A Luxembourg–Brussels service, introduced 1973.

Schwebebahn (Ger)
A rly in which the train is suspended from an overhead running rail, as at Wuppertal.

Scissor bill (USRS)
Yard brakeman.

Scissors crossover
Connections between two parallel tracks in both directions, the two connections crossing each other diagonally at their centres. In plan it resembles an open pair of scissors, hence the name.

Scissors crossover

SCL (US)
Seaboard Coast Line RR Co.; a 1967 merger of SAL and ACL. P&N absorbed in 1969. L&N wholly owned from 1972.

Scoff (RS)
Food.

Scoop (obs)
1. (USRS) A fireman's shovel.
2. The means of taking up water into a loco tender from water troughs (qv).

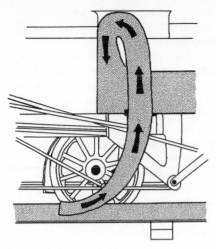

Scoop (2)

Scoot (USRS)
A shuttle (qv) working.

Scorpion
GWR TC for open truck used for carrying road carriages by passenger train (five types).

Scotch Arthurs (RS)
SR King Arthur 4–6–0 locos built by North British Locomotive Co. in 1925.

Scotch blocks
Wood blocks, fixed in frames and pivoted at one end, the other end when in use projecting across a rail to prevent vehicles running down an incline, or on to another track. Sometimes worked from signal box and interlocked with signals. A substitute for catch points (qv).

Scotches
Triangular wooden blocks placed in front of wheels to stop movement when stabled. Also used in unmechanized yards to bring wagons to a stand by skidding.

Scotchmen (RS)
LC&DR 0–4–2T of 1866, named after Scottish rivers and islands; also LB&SCR B4 4–4–0s, made in Scotland by Sharp, Stewart.

ScotRail/Rlys
BR brand name for Scottish Region services, introduced 1984. Became a division of Regional Rlys (qv) upon the dissolution of the Scottish Region in 1991.

ScotRail Rlys, a TOU (qv), 1994. A TOC (*2*) (qv), 1997, ScotRail Rlys Ltd, operating most national services within Scotland and the Anglo-Scottish sleeping car services. Receives subsidy from Strathclyde PTE (qv) for services in that region. Franchise to First Scotrail (qv) 2004.

Scottish Pullman
BR Pullman service Edinburgh/Glasgow–London (Kings Cross), introduced 1991.

SCR
1. Somerset Central Rly, inc 1852, Highbridge–Glastonbury, opened 1854, 1858, 1859, 7 ft gauge, worked by B&ER. Part of S&DR 1862.
2. Scottish Central Rly, inc 1845, opened Perth–Castlecary 1848, part of CR (*1*) 1865.
3. South Central Rly [of India], formed 1966 from parts of CR (*6*) and SR (*6*).

Scrambled eggs (LTRS)
1. Gold braid on hats of senior uniformed staff; and the wearers.
2. Poached eggs (qv).

Screening
The separation of fine particles from ballast by riddling (qv) or by use of a mechanical ballast cleaner.

Screw coupling
see Coupling screw.

Screw down (RS)
To secure a train by applying handbrakes, especially when stabling (qv).

Screw jack
A device for lifting locos and rolling stock vertically (and often also moving them horizontally) in event of derailment. Usually carried on locos and in brake vans.

Scud (RS)
1. BR class 158 dmu, after the missile.
2. A travelling ticket inspector. From (S) scud = a fast mover.

Scuds (RS)
BR class 158 dmus; after the missile.

SCV (obs)
Special Cattle Van.

SD&LUR
South Durham & Lancashire Union Rly, inc 1857, Spring Gardens Junc (West

Auckland) to Tebay, first section opened 1861, part of S&DR 1862.

SD&TR
South Devon & Tavistock Rly, inc 1854, opened 1859, Plymouth–Tavistock, worked by SDR (*1*). Part of SDR (*1*) 1865.

SDR
1. South Devon Rly, Exeter to Plymouth, Newton Abbot to Torquay, inc 1844, 1846, first section opened 1846, Exeter to Teignmouth. Worked by GWR 1876, part of GWR from 1878.
2. South Devon Rly, name adopted 1990 for preserved rly on part of former GWR Totnes–Ashburton branch, formerly known as the Dart Valley Line (qv).
3. Sheffield District Rly, inc 1896, Treeton Junc–Tinsley–Brightside, opened 1900, 1903; worked by LD&ECR, GCR, part of L&NER from 1923.
4. Snailbeach District Rly, Pontesbury–Snailbeach, gauge 2 ft 3¾ in/2 ft 4 in (704.8 mm/711.2 mm), inc 1873, opened 1877. After a period of closure reopened 1923. Finally closed 1963.

SDS
Signalling Display System. A panoramic display in a signal box showing the whole of the track layout controlled, with all the trains occupying it. Equipped with buttons and switches for setting up routes, also train description apertures.

SDT
A Self-Discharging Train, carrying aggregates, solid fuels, etc.

SE (Ger)
Stadt Express, services in German conurbations, or outer suburban services averaging 15–31 miles in length, at speeds up to 87 mph, calling only at main stations in inner city.

Seaboard
see SAL; SCL.

Seacow
TC for ballast wagon. Now a name for 40-ton hopper ballast wagon used by engineers.

Seahare
31-ton ballast wagon used by engineers.

Sealink
Brand name, introduced 1970 for BR

Shipping and International Services Division with its shipping services linking Britain with Ireland and continental Europe, including joint operations with French cross-Channel services, also BR harbours and the rly-operated lake steamer services. Sealink became an independent subsidiary company of BR in 1979 and in 1984, in conformity with the Conservative government's policy, was sold by BR for £66m to British Ferries Ltd, a wholly owned subsidiary of Sea Containers. The non-shipping activities then became BR International while the French assets remained state-owned until the formation of *SNAT* (qv).

Sealion
40-ton bogie hopper ballast wagon used by engineers.

SE&CDR
Abbreviation used in its early years by the SE&CR (qv).

SE&CR
South Eastern & Chatham Rly. A managing committee formed by the SER (qv) and LC&DR (qv) 1899 to operate the rlys of both companies as a single entity. 637 route miles in 1914. Part of SR from 1923.

Seandun
Cork–Dublin service, introduced 1969, name dropped 1975.

Seapigs (RS)
LM&SR Fowler 2–6–4T; a reference to their ugliness.

Searchers (obs)
Staff employed in carriage sidings and sheds to walk through coaches returned from revenue service, looking for lost property, damage, etc.

Searchlight signal
A form of colour light signal with a single lamp and lens behind which a sliding spectacle plate with appropriately coloured glasses moves to give the aspect.

Seashore (USRS)
Sand in a loco sand dome.

Season ticket
A ticket providing unlimited travel between two given points over a week, month, quarter, or a year and sold at a discount.

Seaspeed
Brand name given to BRH (qv) services
from 1968. Became Hoverspeed after
merger with Hoverlloyd Ltd in 1981. Sold
off to the management in 1984.

Seat miles
A measure of capacity provided, the
equivalent of one passenger seat moving
over one mile.

Seat regulation
see Regulation [of passenger traffic].

Sea urchin
A low sided 24-ton ballast wagon used by
engineers.

Secondaire, chemin de fer (Fr)
A secondary rly (qv).

Secondary rly
Any rly not of major importance in the rly
system of a country, whether or not built to
main line standards.

Secondary sorting sidings (obs)
Additional sidings in a marshalling yard
which were allocated to local distribution.

Secondary track (US)
A track on which train movements may be
made without conforming to the timetable
or train order (qv) and which is not
controlled by signals.

Secondary yard (obs)
A yard which received traffic for second
and subsequent marshalling into trains for
other yards, fulfilling a staging function.

Second class
Originally the intermediate class between
First and Third, provided on most rlys,
beginning with the Liverpool &
Manchester Rly on its opening in 1830.
Abolished in Britain between 1875 and
1925 except on boat trains and the
L&NER's former GNR and GER London
suburban services. Withdrawn on London
suburban services in 1938 ahead of
electrification. This old Second class totally
disappeared in Europe (except in Spain
and Portugal) in 1956 with a general
renaming of Third class as Second at that
time (Spain converted 1965–73, Portugal
in 1963). BR renamed its Third class as
Second class in 1956 and this in turn
became Standard class in 1987.

Second driver (obs)
Former steam loco firemen, so named
1970–87 but not authorized to drive.
Assisted driver in observance of signalling
and available to act in an emergency.

Second mess room (LTRS)
A public house or bar room.

Section
The line between two stop signals,
irrespective of whether these signals are
within the control of the same signal box.

Sectional Appendix
A Network Rail publication giving details
of running lines, their infrastructure
features, junction layouts, distances and
permissible speeds, etc.

Section boxes/pillars
See Feeder boxes/pillars.

Section insulator
A device for dividing a contact/trolley wire
(qv) into electrified sections whilst
maintaining mechanical continuity and a
continuous path for current collection by
tramcars and electric locos and trains.

Sectionmen
Track maintenance workers.

Section signal
A stop signal (qv) controlling entry to a
block section or an intermediate block
section (qv); a starting signal (qv).

Section 12 station (LTRS)
See Subsurface station.

Sector table
A form of turntable not describing a full
circle and used to give access to a part-
roundhouse; also formerly used at termini to
move locos and vehicles from one track to
another.

See Mum Immediately (LTRS)
SMI (qv) or a summons to see the SM (qv).

Seilbahn (Ger)
Any type of cable rly.

Seilschwebebahn (Ger)
A suspension or aerial cableway,
synonymous with *Luftseilbahn*. *See* Aerial
rlys.

Sekon
Pseudonym of George Augustus Nokes
(1867–1948), rly author, first editor of the
RM (*2*) (qv) (1897–1910), editor of the

R&TM (qv) (1910–22) and pioneer of popular rly and transport journalism.

Selby Diversion

A 14-mile double-track, high-speed diversion of the ECML between Temple Hirst, south of Selby, and Colton, north of Ulleskelf, avoiding Selby. Constructed to allow the NCB to exploit coal seams under the old line. Opened in October 1983.

Self-acting incline

An incline worked by ropes or cables, on which the weight of descending vehicles provides the power to haul up others on adjoining track.

Self-trimming tender

A tender in which the coal slides down towards the cab on a sloping surface, maintaining an even level.

Self-weighing tender

A steam loco tender design introduced in 1942 incorporating a device that weighed the coal, allowing fuel consumption to be measured during special test runs.

SELNEC

South-East Lancashire and North-East Cheshire Passenger Transport Authority/Executive. Became Greater Manchester PTA/PTE in 1974.

SELTRAC

A moving block (qv) system developed by Standard Electrik Lorenz AG (SEL). Provided by SEL Canada for Skytrain (qv) and DLR (qv). Three computer systems are employed; a systems management centre under a human operator; a vehicle control centre with responsibility for safe train movements communicating with each train and receiving instructions from the management centre; and a vehicle onboard computer receiving and verifying commands.

Semaphore (Fr)

A section signal (qv), which may be passable when showing danger aspect, in an area of manual block signalling.

Semaphore signal

An obsolescent form of signal, in use from 1841, normally operated mechanically by wires from levers in a signalbox, which gives an indication by the angle of its arm or board to the vertical. At night the position of the arm allows a lamp on the post to shine through the appropriately coloured spectacle plate (red, yellow or green). *See also* Lower quadrant; Somersault; Upper quadrant.

Semi-direct (Fr)(obs)

A train calling at many but not all stations on its route.

Semi/semi-automatic

A semi-automatic signal, i.e. one normally worked by track circuits (qv) but which can be controlled by a signalman as necessary.

Semi-métro

see *Pre-métro*.

Semis (RS)

LM&SR Duchess class 4–6–2 locos with streamlined casing removed or built in non-streamlined form.

Senior Conductor

see Conductor (*3*); Train manager.

Sens impair (Fr)

Equivalent of Down (qv) in UK, i.e. proceeding away from Paris, trains given odd numbers.

Sens pair (Fr)

Equivalent of Up (qv) in UK, i.e. proceeding towards Paris, trains given even numbers.

Sentinel

Alley & McLellan Ltd, marine engine builders, produced steam road vehicles at Glasgow from 1904, going on to build a new works at Shrewsbury in 1915 and using the product name Sentinel.

This works became the Sentinel Waggon Works (1920) Ltd, also manufacturing locos and railcars. Now part of Rolls Royce Ltd.

Sentinel Track Safety Card

This card (or a temporary Sentinel Certificate) must be carried by all who work on or near rly tracks; the card shows which tasks the holder is competent to perform and which equipment they are trained to use.

SEPTA (US)

South Eastern Pennsylvania Transportation Authority, operating rail passenger services in and around Philadelphia.

Sequential locking

A type of signal box locking frame which

ensures that signals can only be pulled 'off'
(qv) in the correct sequence.

SER

1. South Eastern Rly, inc 1836, first
   section opened 1842, London Bridge to
   Tonbridge via L&CR. Expanded greatly
   through East Sussex and Kent, often in
   fierce competition with LC&DR. 430
   route miles by 1898. Working union
   with LC&DR 1899. *See also* SE&CR.
2. South Eastern Rly [of India], formed
   1955 from part of ER (5).
3. (LT) Signal Equipment Room.

SERCO

Serco Rail Test Ltd, a privatized section of
the former BR Research Department,
Derby, providing testing, instrumentation
and data management services, also track
and other infrastructure assessment. A
licensed TOC (2) (qv), owning test and
Sandite (qv) trains. *See also* Merseyrail.

Serene & Delightful

Nickname for S&DJR.

SERMA (Fr)

*Société d'Études pour la Réalisation des
Chemins de Fer Métropolitains Anonymes*;
combining with *SGTE* (qv) from 1948 to
seek contracts to plan, build and operate
urban underground/metro (qv) systems
outside France.

Serpent

GWR TC for goods truck designed to
carry furniture removal vans and other
large road vehicles.

Service

A rail service can be expressed either as a
frequency (e.g. 5 t.p.h) or as a *headway* (e.g.
every 12 min).

Service application/rate

A gradual slowing of speed caused by use
of air brakes throughout the train at a rate
slower than an emergency application (qv).

Service Braking Distance

Distance at which, at any given speed, a
train of any type is able to come to a stop
without causing passenger discomfort or
alarm or without damaging freight.

Service cadencé (Fr)

Train service running at regular intervals of
time.

Service number

The running number of a specific tramcar
operating on a particular service on
tramways (3). On the LCCT (qv), this
term signified the route number (qv). *See
also* Route number.

Service slack

A reduction in speed permanently imposed
on sharp curves, in congested areas, etc.

Service Time Book/Timetables (obs)

Working timetable (qv).

Sesselbahn (Ger)

A chairlift.

SET

South Eastern Trains; an interim operation
of the former Connex South Eastern
franchise services by the SRA (qv) from
January 2004. Returned to private
franchise 2006. *See also* Connex Rail Ltd;
South Eastern Trains Co.

Set

1. A bend made in a rail which ensures
   that the head (qv) continues to be
   adequately supported by the web (qv)
   over the full length of the rail.
2. A combination of coaches or other rolling
   stock kept together on a semi-permanent
   basis for a particular purpose.
3. (obs) Two or more wagons using a rope-
   worked incline.
4. (obs) Total number of open wagons (qv)
   a navvy (1) (qv) would be expected to fill
   manually in one working shift, usually
   given as seven, say 20 tons lifted per man.
5. (RS) The crew of a loco: driver and
   fireman, or driver and second man (qv).

Set back, to

1. To reverse a train into a bay or side platform.
2. To reverse a train which has overshot a
   platform, or has started out from a
   station, after permission from signallers
   who have blocked the line in the rear.
3. To make a shunting movement back
   towards the shunter.
4. To move a loco backwards on to a train.
   See also Back down, to.
5. To make the very short reversing
   movement necessary before a steam
   loco can move forward after stopping at
   dead centre (qv).

Set down, to
To unload passengers; thus a timetabled stop may be designated 'to set down only'.
Set number (LT)
The train running number.
Set of Huns (RS)
see Huns.
Settebello
A luxury emu service between Milan and Rome, introduced 1953 (5 h 55 min). Name adopted officially 1958. *TEE* 1974–84. Became Colosseum (qv).
Settle & Carlisle, The
Hellifield–Appleby–Carlisle.
Severn–Tyne
A service between Weston-super-Mare and Newcastle, introduced 1970, running that year only.
Severn Valley
Severn Valley Rly, Shrewsbury to Hartlebury, inc 1853, opened 1862, 1878. Leased to WMR 1860, part of GWR from 1870. Bridgnorth to Bewdley and Kidderminster reopened from 1970 onwards as a preserved line, using this name.
Sewer (LTRS)
LT Northern Line tube. Unloved by staff for its long section of tunnel running.
Sewer rat (RS)
A London Underground Rlys train driver.
SFE
Sexy Front End. Originally coined by Gatwick Express (qv) for its class 460 trains introduced 2000, but soon adopted for any frontal configuration immediately identifiable from a distance which gives an impression of speed and modernity.
SF
Santa Fe Lines: *see* AT&SF; Santa Fe (*1*).
SFF
Strade Ferrate Federali; the title of Swiss Federal Rlys in Italian-speaking area of Switzerland 1901–44. Replaced by *FFS* (qv). *See also CFF; SBB.*
SFM (Sp)
Serveis Ferroviaris de Mallorca; operator from 1981 of all rail services on Mallorca/Majorca except those between Palma and Soller.

SGE Signals Ltd
A 1961 retitling of the Siemens & General Electric Rly Signal Co. Ltd with works at Wembley, Woolwich and Lewisham, London. Now part of GEC (qv).
SGR
Sudan Government Rlys. *See* SRC.
SGRO
Saudi Government Railroad Organization. *See* SRO.
SGTE
Société Générale de Traction et d'Exploitation; *c*. 1948; reconstitution of the *CMP* (qv). It acquired 55 per cent of *SERMA* (qv), working jointly with it to plan, build and operate urban underground/metro systems outside France.
Shack (USRS)
Brakeman, as in 'head shack', 'swing shack', 'rear shack'.
Shackle
1. The link of a chain coupling placed over the drawbar hook of the adjoining vehicle.
2. The link which connects signal wires to the chain of the signal box manual levers, or the crank at base of a semaphore signal post.
Shakespeare Express
A summer service between London (Paddington) and Stratford-upon-Avon, introduced 1928, ceased 1931.
Shakespeare Route, The
Brand name adopted by the S&MJR.
Shamrock
An express between London (Euston) and Liverpool (Lime St.), connecting with sailings to Belfast and Dublin, introduced 1954. Ceased 1966.
SH&DR
see WR (*1*).
Shanty
1. (RS) A staff mess room.
2. (USRS) A caboose (qv).
Shark
1. TC for civil engineer's ballast train brake van, usually fitted with a plough to level off tipped ballast.

2. (RS) A ticket inspector. From (S) shark = a swindler, a pilferer, a person who snaps up whatever comes up, like a shark.

Sharks (RS)(obs)

A link (qv) of men willing to take any kind of job that comes along. From (S) shark – see Shark (2).

Sharp

Sharp, Roberts, loco builders, Manchester, from 1833; became Sharp Brothers, 1843 and Sharp, Stewart, 1852. Moved works to Glasgow, 1888, taking over Clyde Locomotive Co. Ltd and becoming Sharp, Stewart & Co. Ltd. Amalgamated with Neilson (qv), and Dübs (qv) in 1903 to form North British (qv).

Sharpies (RS)

Locos built by Sharp (qv).

Shay

Steam loco with two or three sets of wheels all driven by bevel-toothed gearing from a shaft along one side, powered by a vertical engine alongside the boiler. The shaft is in sections, jointed to allow each section to move independently.

She

In colloquial usage locos (especially steam locos) and trains, like ships, have traditionally been awarded the feminine gender, thus 'Here she comes', 'She's running late'. '. . . for they make these curious little fire-horses all mares' (Fanny Kemble, 1830). Also applies in the US.

Shebas (RS)

Another version of Queen of Shebas (qv).

Shed, to

To return a loco to its home depot or to denote mpd allocation of a loco (e.g. 'No. 3456 is shedded at X').

Shed bash (RS)

A visit (usually unofficial) to a loco depot for the purpose of noting/spotting/gricing/copping the numbers of the locos seen there, a process normally accomplished at great speed. Hence *shedbasher.*

Sheds (RS)

Class 66 GM (EMD) (qv) locos; suggested by the corrugated configuration at the sides.

Sheffield and Manchester Pullman

An all-Pullman train from London (Kings Cross) to Sheffield (2 h 57 min) and Manchester (Central) (4 h 7 min), introduced in summer 1925. It failed to attract traffic, and was diverted in September 1925 to become West Riding Pullman (qv).

Sheffield Pullman

An all-Pullman train between London (Kings Cross), Nottingham and Sheffield, introduced 1924 (3 h 15 min). It did not attract sufficient custom and became Sheffield & Manchester Pullman in 1925. Re-introduced 1958, running via Retford. Ceased 1968.

Sheffield trolley

A pump trolley (qv), after its manufacturer, George S. Sheffield & Co.

Sheppey

Sheppey Light Rly, Queenborough to Leysdown, LRO 1899, opened 1901, worked by SE&CR, SR and BR (S), closed 1950.

Shin

Fishplates (qv).

Shiner (USRS)

A rlyman's lamp.

Shining time (USRS)

The departure time; time for use of the shiner (qv).

Shinkansen

Direct high speed standard gauge passenger rlys and trains of Japanese National Rlys. The first line (*Tokaido*) was opened between Osaka and Tokyo in 1964. Colloquially known in the west as 'Bullet trains' from their shape. Two types of service are provided; fast limited-stop trains (*Hikari* = Lightning) and fast stopping trains (*Kodama* = Echo).

Ship rly (obs)

Also known as portage rly. A combination of canal and rly transport, in which canal vessels were placed on rly flat wagons for haulage over steep gradients. In Britain, in 1826 boats on the Bude Canal were fitted with small iron wheels and moved up and down seven inclined planes over two lines of rails. They were lifted by an endless chain worked by two tanks alternately filled with water and descending into wells. In Pennsylvania USA passengers and goods were conveyed in boats from Philadelphia to Pittsburgh partly overland on portage railways and partly on canals. This system included the 36½ mile 1833 Allegheny Portage RR with its ten rope-worked inclined planes linked by level sections worked by locos. A similar overland boat portage system operated in the 1830s in conjunction with the Morris & Essex Canal in New Jersey USA. *See also* Canal haulage rlys.

Shirt button (RS)(obs)
The GWR logo/monogram introduced late in 1934 in which the company's initials were shaped to be enclosed in a circle.

SHLR
1. Sand Hutton Light Rly; opened 1910 as 15 in gauge miniature line in grounds of Sand Hutton Hall near York, LRO 1920, converted to 18 in gauge light rly, serving estate farms, etc. and providing a passenger service. Closed 1932.
2. Surrey Heights Light Rly; Orpington to Sanderstead, proposed 1925; widely publicized, but never built.

SHMD
Stalybridge, Hyde, Mossley & Dukinfield Tramways & Electricity Joint Board, operating tramways (*3*), 1905–45.

Shocvan
GWR TC for van fitted with shock-absorbing body.

Shoeboxes (RS)
BR class 73 electro-diesel locos; from their shape.

Shoofly (USRS)
A temporary track around an obstruction.

Shooting a speed (RS)
The fixing of a detonator to rails to cause drivers to reduce speed in an emergency or where a temporary speed restriction has been imposed without due notification.

Shooting, shoot, to (RS)
To place detonators on the rails. *See also* Shots.

Shooting galleries (RS)
NER Raven 4–6–2 locos. From the length of their boilers. Also known as skittle alleys for the same reason.

Shop, to/shopping
The overhaul/heavy repair of locos and rolling stock.

Shore
Any part of the rly other than a moving train. From naval usage. *See* On board.

Shore rlymen
Staff employed at stations, etc., as distinct from those who work on trains. *See also* Shore.

Shore supply
A fixed facility to supply electricity for heating and air conditioning to a stationary train lacking its motive power.

Short flag, to (USRS)
To use flags or lamps at the rear of a stopped train in an endeavour to protect it but at a point which does not allow an approaching train on the same track an adequate distance in which to stop.

Shorting bar
A wood and metal tool used to cause a short circuit and so remove traction current from conductor rails in an emergency.

Short line (US)
A small rly undertaking, often one connecting a small town to a main line. Normally under 100 m long and handling only freight traffic.

Short of puff (RS)
A loco which is steaming badly.

Shorts (RS)(obs)
Wagons destined for local stations which were shunted out of freight trains at marshalling yards.

Short tail (USRS)
A rail worker who does not belong to a trade union (brotherhood).

Shots (RS)
Detonators fixed to railheads (qv). *See also* Fog signal; Shooting a speed.

Shoulder
Ballast heaped up against ends of sleepers to check lateral distortion of the track.

Showing the white feather (RS)
A steam loco emitting a wisp of steam from its safety valve.

Shrimp (RS)
Tamper; tamping machine. *See* Tamp.

Shuffle, to (USRS)
To shunt.

Shunt ahead signal
A subsidiary signal fixed below the signal controlling the entrance to a block section. When 'off' it authorizes a driver to proceed for shunting purposes only.

Shunter's pole (obs)
A long pole with a specially shaped hook at one end, introduced from *c.* 1880 to enable shunters to couple and uncouple loose-coupled vehicles from the lineside without standing between the rails. Use of these poles helped to reduce the many deaths and serious injuries sustained by shunters endeavouring to fasten and unfasten couplings by hand. *See also* Spar.

Shunters' Runner
see Runner.

Shunt frame
Similar to Ground frame (qv), frequently replacing a signal box.

Shunting
1. The process of moving rolling stock from one line to another for the purpose of arranging vehicles in a certain order, or to place certain vehicles in a desired position in a train, or to place them at the point of discharge or loading. Hence shunter, shunting yard, shunting locomotive. Sometimes also called marshalling or sorting.
2. The withdrawal of a train from the main line into a siding or loop to allow another to overtake it.

Shunting frame
A manned control point for shunting movements; only available when released by the related main signal box.

Shunting movement
A restricted short-distance movement on a running line.

Shunting neck/spur
BR term for a line on which shunting may proceed without movements affecting through lines. *See also* Headshunt.

Shunting pole (obs)
See Shunter's pole.

Shunting/Shunters' truck (obs)
A four-wheeled truck hauled around yards by a shunting loco. It enabled shunters to move more quickly and in greater safety around their workplaces than the alternative method of standing on the steps of a loco or brake van, holding on with one hand, while grasping a shunter's pole (qv) in the other. The truck accommodated shunters' poles in relative safety when not in use, while also offering mobile storage for tools, spare lamps and poles, re-railers and sprags (qv). The GWR and its successor BR(W) were the major users of this accessory but a smaller number were employed in LM&SR yards.

Shunt movement
Usually to set back (qv) through points controlled by position light signals (qv).

Shuttle/shuttle service
A service which simply operates frequently between two points, usually not far apart. BR services between Edinburgh and Glasgow so-named 1991. *See also* InterCity shuttle.

Shuttle, le
Anglo-French name for the trains operated by Eurotunnel (qv) carrying road vehicles, including cars, and their drivers and passengers through the Channel Tunnel. Official usage of the term ceased in 1998 after objections from French linguists.

SI (obs)
BR invalid saloon.

Siberia Express
A *CIWL* service between Moscow and Irkutsk, introduced 1899. *See also* Trans-Siberian Express.

SICA
Signalling Infrastructure Condition Assessment.

SICF
Société Ivoirienne des Chemins de Fer; Ivory Coast (*Côte d'Ivoire*) Rlys, 660 km, metre gauge. *See also* SCFB.

Sick (RS)
Used of a wagon or coach in need of repair.

Sick and Tired (RS)
S&T Department (qv).

Sick, Lame and Lazy (LTRS)
The paper work required for staff taking time off. Adopted from the British Army slang term for a sick parade.

Side bay caboose (US)

A caboose (qv) with bay windows on each side instead of a cupola (qv), to allow observation of the train.

Side chains (obs)

Additional couplings formerly used between passenger vehicles to prevent severance should screw couplings fail, they were placed one on each side of the drawbar, between it and the buffers, and when connected, hung loose to allow for play on curves.

Side door Pullman (USRS)

A box car used by tramps (hobos) to steal free rides (qv).

Side lamps (obs)

Lamps placed on each side of a freight brake van when this was attached to an unfitted (loose-coupled) freight train.

Side lights

The windows along the sides of a rly carriage.

Side ramp/Positive side pick-up ramp

A metal ramp fixed to conductor rails (qv) at points/switches which facilitates efficient transition of the shoes collecting traction current.

Siderodromophile/ia

A lover of/love of rlys and rail travel; the opposite of siderodromophobe/ia - *OED* notes the latter as 'irrational fear of rail travel'.

Side swipe (RS)

A sideways-on collision.

Side tank

The conventional water tank arrangement for a tank loco, rectangular in shape and resting on the frames either side of the boiler.

Side track (US)

Any siding not used for passing trains on a single line.

Side winder

1. (RS) A diesel railcar or dmu set with starter button at side of body.
2. (USRS) A Shay (qv) loco.

Siding

Any track which is not a running line (qv), and on which vehicles may be loaded,

unloaded, stabled, shunted or marshalled. In the US, a passing loop on a single line (any other siding in the US is a side track). *See also* Cripple siding; Holding siding; Private siding; Reception road; Stowage siding.

Siding switch

A switch controlling the passage of traction current between the OLE (qv) of running lines (qv) and that in sidings (qv) and yards.

Siding traffic

Freight traffic which is normally loaded or unloaded by the customer's own staff and despatched from or received at private sidings (qv).

Siemens

The German firm of Siemens & Halske (later Siemens AG) was established in 1847 by Werner (von) Siemens (1816–92). Initially supplying electric telegraph equipment, it entered the electric traction field after demonstrating the world's first passenger-carrying electric rly at the Berlin Trades Exhibition of 1879. The English branch, Siemens Bros. & Co., was established at Woolwich in 1864 and headed by a younger brother, Carl Wilhelm S. (1823–83). The electrical machinery side of the Siemens Bros. was taken over by Siemens Bros. Dynamo Works Ltd, operating from a new works at Stafford, in 1903. Acquired by DK (qv), 1918. Siemens Bros. & Co. part of AEI (*1*) (qv) 1955. Siemens Ltd, formed 1965 is part of Siemens AG, Munich. *See also* SGE Signals Ltd.

SIFA (Ger)

Sicherheits-Fahreinrichtung; a vigilance control system.

Sighting distance

The extreme distance from which a signal is visible to the driver of an approaching train.

Signal box panel

A panel diagram inside a signal box showing the total track layout controlled from the box.

Signal box register

Same as Train register (qv).

Signal cabin

Term used by some rlys (e.g. GCR (*1*) (qv)) as an alternative to the more usual signal box.

Signaller

A 'politically correct' term, introduced by Railtrack (qv) in 1995 to describe those formerly known as signalmen/women.

Signalling centre

A power box (qv) controlling signalling, train movements, level crossings, etc. over a very large area and long distance of route, even a complete line between major population centres.

Signalman (US)

An employee responsible for maintaining rly electrical systems and undertaking electronic engineering tasks. [The US equivalent of the British usage signalman/signaller is tower man/woman (*see* Tower).]

Signal number

See Peg number.

Signal post replacement key/switch

A key-operated switch which will turn an automatic or semi-automatic (qv) colour light signal to show a red aspect (qv) until the key is used again.

Signal warning boards

see Warning boards.

Signing the Book (RS)

Obeying Rule 55 (qv).

Silent death (RS)

An electric train. From its fast and comparatively noiseless approach to anyone on the tracks.

Silent partner (RS)

Second man (qv).

Silk hats (USRS)

Rly officers, senior officials.

Silk trains (US)

Trains worked in the 1920s to give the fastest possible transit times between US West Coast ports and inland silk mills for perishable raw silk imported from the Far East. The Seattle–St Paul line of the GN (qv) offered the shortest route and easiest grades and secured most of the traffic. Running times of the GN's steam-hauled Silk Trains, which had priority even over

named expresses, were comparable to those of modern diesel-hauled trains on the same route.

Sillon (Fr)

A path (qv).

Silver Arrow

A combined road, rail and air service between London and Paris, cheaper than direct air flights, introduced 1956 via Lydd (Ferryfield) and Le Touquet airports. In 1959 this facility was reorganized as London (Victoria)–Margate (rail), Manston airport–Le Touquet airport (air) and Etaples–Paris (rail), the complete journey taking about 6 h each way. The air journey was altered to Gatwick–Le Touquet in 1962. With a rail branch into the latter airport opened in 1963 and express *SNCF* railcars, the overall time was eventually reduced to 4 h. The introduction of hovercraft services and faster rail services in France resulted in the discontinuation of the service in 1981.

Silver bullets

1. (LTRS)(obs) Unpainted aluminium tube cars, especially when they were a new feature in the late 1950s and early 1960s.
2. Steel wagons used on Burngullow–Irvine workings.

Silver Fern

A day train between Auckland and Wellington, NZ.

Silver Jubilee

A supplementary fare express between London (Kings Cross), Darlington and Newcastle (4 h), introduced 1935 (the silver jubilee year of King George V). Britain's first streamlined train, it was given specially designed 4–6–2 locos and articulated coaches. Ceased 1939. Name revived for a London (Kings Cross)–Edinburgh train 1977, discontinued 1978.

Silverlink Train Services Ltd

Renaming of North London Rlys (qv), September 1997. Services divided into 'Silverlink County' (long and medium distance) and 'Silverlink Metro' (north London local services and Clapham

Junction–Willesden Junction). *See* London Lines.

Silver Meteor

A Seaboard Coast Line streamlined diesel train between New York and Miami, introduced 1939 (25 h in 1940). Still operated as an Amtrak service.

Silver Princess

A prototype stainless steel coach produced by Budd; built in the US in 1947 and operated on BR. Scrapped in 1966.

Silver Standard

A BR InterCity package for full fare Standard Class passengers aimed at 'middle-management' businessmen and women, and introduced 1988. Included at-seat service of hot meals and refreshments and complimentary tea or coffee and snacks.

SIMBIDS

Acronym for Simplified Bi-Directional Signalling, in which only selected locations, such as level crossings and crossovers, are signalled, to allow limited train service while the other line of a double track is being repaired or renewed.

Simple engine

A loco in which the steam passes through the cylinders only once, in contrast to a compound (qv).

Simplex (R)

Trade name of Motor Rail (qv).

Simplon Express

A *CIWL* service between Paris and Venice/Trieste, introduced 1906, became Simplon–Orient Express (qv) after WW1. Name revived 1962 for a Paris–Zagreb service, altered to run Paris–Belgrade 1969. From summer 1992 the service worked from Geneva Airport station with through coaches for Venice, Trieste, Zagreb and Belgrade.

Simplon–Orient Express

A *CIWL* service introduced 1919, Paris–Lausanne–Milan–Venice–Zagreb–Belgrade–Sofia–Istanbul/Athens. Through sleeping cars Calais–Trieste–Istanbul and Paris–Bucharest–Athens/Istanbul, giving a 76 h London–Istanbul timing in 1927. Paris–Cairo connection provided 1928 (Tripoli–Haifa covered by road coaches).

Revived 1949, Paris–Istanbul only. Athens portion from 1951. In that year London–Istanbul was covered in 80 h. Renamed Simplon Express 1962 and withdrawn east of Zagreb.

Single

A steam loco with one pair of driving wheels, usually of large diameter.

Single driver

see Single.

Single iron (USRS)

Single track.

Single lead junction

A single track link between two sections of double track or between double track and a single line, to reduce the complication and cost of pointwork. Adopted by BR as an economy measure from the 1960s.

Single line/track

One track, used for movements in both directions. Crossing places or loops are provided when such lines are of more than two or three miles in length and their spacing is related to the frequency of the service.

Single-line gantry

A crane on wheels which run on rails temporarily laid outside the sleeper ends. Used in pairs to remove track panels and install new sleepers, it operates within loading gauge allowing normal traffic to pass along the other track at slow speed.

Single-line spoil handling train

A train of specially designed wagons incorporating a conveyor belt which can be loaded from one end.

Single line working

Movement of trains in either direction over a single track. Controlled by one of the following systems: (a) one engine in steam (qv); (b) pilotman (qv); (c) train staff/tablet and token and ticket systems (qv); (d) tokenless block (qv); (e) train order (qv); (f) non-token lock and block instruments (qv); (g) RETB (qv). *See also* Wrong line working.

Single-phase

A system of electrification using high voltage alternating current (ac) at industrial frequency (usually 50 Hz). First satisfactorily used for rly traction in Hungary in 1923. Since *c.* 1950 superseded by the use of industrial frequency, 25 kV, 50 Hz ac, rectified on the locos or emus for supply to their direct current traction motors.

Single slip
A connection between two tracks when one crosses the other at an angle.

Single stick (USRS)
A single camshaft on a diesel-electric loco.

Siphons
1. GWR TC for milk/poultry/fish vans used in passenger trains (nine types).
2. (RS) BR diesel locos class 37.

SIR
1. Surrey Iron Rly, inc 1801, opened with horse traction 1803 from Wandsworth Basin to Croydon, closed 1846. *See also* CM&GIR.
2. South Indian Rly, formed 1890, taken over by Government 1891. Part of SR (*6*), 1951.

Sirhowy
Sirhowy Rly, Sirhowy and Tredegar to Nine Mile Point, inc as Sirhowy Tramroad 1802, opened about 1805, gauge 4 ft 2 in, name changed to Sirhowy Rly 1860, converted to standard gauge rly by 1863, opened to passenger traffic 1865. Leased and worked by L&NWR from 1876.

SISD (obs)
Shipping & International Services Division of BR, formed by merging the Continental Departments of BR (S) and BR (E). Became Sealink (qv).

Six Bells
Signalmen's block telegraph code for 'obstruction danger'.

Six-foot [way]
Space between any two adjacent parallel rly tracks, measured between the outsides of the adjacent rails, in fact usually about 6 ft 6 in/1,981 mm. *See also* Ten-foot.

SJ
Svenska Statens Järnvägar; Swedish State Rlys. Sometimes irreverently referred to as *Societas Jesu* (Jesuits). Privatized from 1993. Operates rly services on business terms and must put any services it

considers unprofitable out to tender for private operation. *SJ* owns almost all rly rolling stock in Sweden. *See also*: *BV*; Oresund Link.

SJR
Solway Junction Rly, inc 1864, 1867, Kirtlebridge–Annan–Bowness–Brayton (running powers over NBR Silloth line). Opened 1869, 1873. Vested in Caledonian Rly by acts of 1873 and 1895. Traffic over Solway viaduct ceased 1921. Part of LM&SR 1923.

SK
BR corridor Second/Standard class compartment coach.

Skate
1. A 31-ton bogie wagon for skip storage used by engineers.
2. A device consisting of a cradle and two rollers used for moving a rail vehicle whose wheels have broken or are locked on a restricted site (e.g. in tunnels) where lifting is not possible.
3. A four-wheeled rail trolley operated manually or by kerosene motors, sometimes illegally used (e.g. on PNR (qv)) for carriage of passengers and freight.

Skateboard (LTRS)
A trolley (not rail-mounted) which is used for removing baskets of rubble from tube tunnels during maintenance work.

Skater (LTRS, rhyming S)
Escalator.

Skin (RS)
Driver's report form. *See also* Blister.

Skinheads (RS)
BR diesel locos class 31/0. From their appearance – the lack of indicator boxes resulting in a bare look.

Skipper (USRS)
A conductor (*3*). From (S) skipper = master, boss, captain.

Skippers (RS)
Name given to Class 142 (Pacers (qv)) dmus when used in Devon and Cornwall.

Skittle Alleys (RS)
NER Raven Pacific locos. A reference to the length of the boiler. Also known as *shooting galleries* for the same reason.

Skodas (RS)
BR class 90 locos.
Skye line
Dingwall–Kyle of Lochalsh.
Skye Rly
Dingwall & Skye Rly, Dingwall–Kyle of Lochalsh, first section opened 1870, completed 1897. Part of HR (7) from 1880.
Skyliner (RS)(obs)
A steam loco in which the boiler fittings are enclosed in an aerodynamic casing.
Sky Rail
A people-mover link between Birmingham International railway station and Birmingham Airport, opened 2003.
Sky Rockets (USRS)
Red hot cinders ejected through a loco chimney.
Sky Train
Name of a fully automated light rail system opened in Vancouver 1986. Uses linear induction motors, SELTRAC control (qv) and steerable axle trucks.
Skytrain
1. Brand name for London (Liverpool St.)–Stansted Airport services, 1996.
2. Brand name for Bangkok elevated electric rly system. *See* BTS.
SL
1. *Storstockholms Lokaltraffik AB*; the Greater Stockholm Transport Co.
2. Thus written in Japanese text to denote a steam loco.
Slab track
Rails set into a concrete or asphalt base without sleepers or ballast. *See also* Paved track.
Slack
A speed restriction.
Slacker
A device for damping down dust in coal wagons, using a water spray.
Slainte
A service between Dublin and Cork, so named 1960. Name dropped 1975.
SL&NCR
Sligo, Leitrim & Northern Counties Rly, (Ireland), Enniskillen to Collooney thence over M&GWR to Sligo Quay, inc 1875,

opened 1879, 1880, 1881, 1882. Closed 1957, when it was the last privately owned rly service in Ireland.
SLC
BR Sleeping Car First and Second/ Standard class, the latter with double berths.
SLE
BR Mark III sleeping car, either class.
Sleeper
1. A form of support placed between the rails and the ballast. Originally the rails rested on stone blocks and later longitudinal wooden sleepers were used. Transverse creosoted softwood sleepers then became general for many years but iron, steel, hardwood and concrete transverse sleepers have all been tried; the latter are now becoming general in Britain.
2. (RS) A second driver in the cab of a diesel or electric loco/train.
3. A berth in a sleeping car, a sleeping car, or a complete sleeping car train.
Sleeper bonker
A machine used to test the integrity of sleepers on site.
Sleeper track
A section of tramway (3), usually away from public roads, or on reservations at the side or in the centre of roads, in which rly type track is used. *See also* Private right of way/track; Reserved track.
Sleeping partner (RS)
Second driver (qv).
Sleet car (LTRS)
Electric sleet loco (ESL).
SLEP
A BR convertible sleeping car, i.e. adaptable for either class, with single- or double-berth compartments. For Mark 3 stock this code was used to designate SLE (qv) fitted with a pantry.
Slew, to (sometimes spelled slue)
To move track back to its correct alignment or a short distance from its original position.
SLF
BR Sleeping Car, First class, with single-berth compartments.

SLG
Sri Lanka Government Rly, 1,459 km,
mainly 1,676 mm gauge.

Slim Jims (RS)
BR class 33/2 diesel-electric locos built
with narrow bodies for use on the formerly
substandard loading gauge line between
Tonbridge and Hastings.

Slim Lines (RS)
Slim Jims (qv).

Sling van
See Lift van.

Slip car (USRS)
A loaded banana van.

Slip coach (obs)
A coach capable of being detached
from the rear of a moving train.
Controlled by its special guard, it was
'slipped' to travel under its own
momentum until braked at the platform of
its destination station, thus eliminating the
delay entailed in stopping the main train.
Some expresses included up to three slip
coaches. Slip coach operation in Britain
ceased (at Bicester) in 1960. The
reverse process defied the ingenuity of
inventors.

Slipper boy (obs)
A youth employed to unhook horses from
vehicles when these were used for shunting.

Slipper brake (obs)
Brake shoes which the driver of a tramcar
(qv) could bring to bear down on the rails
by operating a handwheel from the driving
position.

Slips
Short connections between two sets of rails
crossing over one another. *See also* Double
slip; Single slip.

Slip working
The parking of an unpowered MGR
(qv) train ready to be loaded at a later
time.

SLM
Swiss Locomotive & Machine Works,
Winterthur.

SLO
BR Second/Standard class open coach with
centre gangway (3 + 2 seating) and
lavatory in the centre.

SLOA
Steam Locomotive Operators' Association.
An organization concerned with the
operation of preserved steam locos on BR
and other lines. Wound up 1996; its
functions and responsibilities were then
passed to MLSLO Ltd (qv).

Slotted post (obs)
A design of semaphore signal which had
three aspects – arm at horizontal = danger;
45° downward = caution; arm dropped
vertically and hidden inside the post = clear.

Slotted signals
Two signals on one post (home and distant
or starter and distant) each worked by a
signalman in separate, closely spaced
boxes. Mechanical or electrical slotting
equipment prevents one signalman
changing his signal to 'off' unless the other
has withdrawn his slot, thus ensuring that a
train does not move forward into the next
block section until the signalman in charge
of that section has allowed it to do so.
Either signalman can put both signals to
danger at any time.

Slough, in the (RS)
Derailed at catch points.

Slovakia
A service between Moscow and Vienna via
Košice and Bratislava.

Slow & Dirty
Nickname for the S&DJR.

Slow & Doubtful
Nickname for the S&DJR.

Slow, Dirty and Jerky
Nickname for the S&DJR.

Slow, Easy & Comfortable
Nickname for the SE&CR.

Slow lines
Term for a second pair of running lines
authorized for passenger train working,
with entry and exit controlled by separate
signal boxes. *See also* Passenger loop, Relief
line.

Slow, Mouldy and Jolting
Nickname for the S&MJR.

Slow order
A written instruction to drivers requiring a
speed restriction to be observed at a
particular location.

SLR

1. South Leicestershire Rly, Nuneaton and Hinckley, inc 1859 as N&HR, name changed to SLR 1860, opened 1862, worked by L&NWR. Vested in L&NWR 1867.
2. (Aus) Sydney Light Rail; light rail (qv) system in Sydney, New South Wales, first section opened August 1997.
3. (obs) Sierra Leone (Government) Rly, 2 ft 6 in. gauge. First section opened 1899, whole system abandoned 1974.

SLS

Stephenson Locomotive Society, formed 1909 as the Stephenson Society, a splinter group from RC (1) (qv) comprising those members whose interest lay mainly in steam locos. Renamed the SLS 1911. A pioneer in preservation, the SLS purchased the LB&SCR 0–4–2 *Gladstone* in 1927.

SLSTP

BR sleeping car, Second/Standard class, with pantry.

SLU

Standard Length Unit; a measure of a siding or loop length, in use since the 1930s. Originally defined as the overall length of a wagon on a standard 17 ft 6 in underframe, later fixed at 21 ft (6,405 mm).

Slue, to

To reposition a rly track laterally.

Slug (USRS)

A poor fire in a loco.

Slugs (RS)

Class 37 diesel-electric locos.

Slurried ballast

Ballast (qv) saturated with fine wet material (slurry), often originating from the underside of the formation (qv).

Slurry spot

An accumulation of slurried ballast (qv).

SLW

Single Line Working (qv).

SM

Stationmaster, and more recently, Station Manager. Now obs in Great Britain.

Smalls

1. (obs) Traffic conveyed at small consignments (normally under one ton) scale of charges, later combined with sundries (qv).
2. Small items used by track workers such as bolts, pads, fishplates, nuts and washers.

SM&AR

Swindon, Marlborough & Andover Rly, inc 1873, opened 1881, 1882, 1883, amalgamated with S&CER (qv) as M&SWJR (2) (qv), 1884.

Smash board (USRS)

A semaphore signal.

Smash 'em and turn 'em over

Nickname for the LC&DR.

SMI (LT) (obs)

Station Manager's Instructions – a duty in which the crew worked according to instructions issued by a SM.

SMJR

Scottish Midland Junction Rly, inc 1845, Perth to Forfar, opened 1848, merged with Aberdeen Rly to form SNER, 1856. *See also* S&MJR.

Smoke/Smoke agent (USRS)

A loco fireman.

Smoke board/plate (obs)

A fitting attached to the underside of gantries and overbridges to reduce damage from smoke and steam.

Smokebox

The front section of a steam loco, forming an extension of the boiler and containing the main steam pipes to the cylinders, the blastpipe and the chimney.

Smoke deflectors

Metal plates fixed either side of the smokebox or either side of loco chimney to deflect the smoke upwards and prevent it from blowing down over the cab and restricting the engine crew's vision of the line ahead.

Smoke orders (USRS)(obs)

Running on a single line without train orders, relying only on visual indication of any opposing train (qv).

Smoker (USRS)

A steam loco; also the firebox.

Smokestack (US)

Term for loco chimney. 'The term locomotive chimney seems weak and effeminate to an American' – *Railway Mechanical Engineer*, USA, 1938.

Smoking 'em (USRS)(obs)
Taking a chance, completing a run in less than the scheduled time. From smoking in (qv).

Smoking in (USRS)(obs)
Moving cautiously along a single line, without a train order, looking out for the smoke of any opposing train (qv).

SMR
1. Snaefell Mountain Rly: *see* MER.
2. South Manchuria Rly. Built by the Chinese Eastern Rly Co. in 1900–1 to connect the Chinese rly system with the Trans-Siberian Rly. Following the Russo-Japanese war, the rly was ceded by Russia to Japan in 1905. The Japanese converted it from 5 ft/ 1,524 mm gauge, first to 3 ft 6 in/ 1,067 mm and then to standard gauge, reopening it with the latter as the SMR in 1907.

SMT
Snowdon Mountain Tramroad/Rly, Llanberis to Snowdon summit, 2 ft 7¹/₂ in/800 mm gauge. Abt rack system, inc 1894, opened 1896.

Smudge/Smudger (RS)(obs)
A loco cleaner.

Snagger (RS)(obs)
An inspector of finished work in a main works.

Snails (RS)
Young people travelling by train around Europe, etc. at concessionary fares, bent under very large backpacks.

Snake
1. GWR TC for passenger brake van (five types).
2. (LTRS) Insulated, ribbed multicore cable. From its appearance.
3. (USRS) A shunter. From his movements when busy.

Snakehead (USRS)(obs)
A rail worked loose from the track, rising up to penetrate the floor of a wagon or coach.

Snap (RS)
Packed food, hence snap tin, to snap off (to take a break for a snack). From the snap fastening of box lid.

Snapper (RS)
1. A ticket collector.
2. An assisting loco.

SNAT
Société Nouvelle d'Armements Trans-Manche. Formerly the French arm of Sealink (qv).

Snatcher/s (RS) (obs)
Conductors employed by LCCT (qv) to move from one tram to another at busy periods to collect fares.

SNCB
Société Nationale des Chemins de Fer Belges; Belgian National Rlys, formed 1926. Also expressed in Flemish and abbreviated *NMBS. See* B-Rail.

SNCF
Société Nationale des Chemins de Fer Français; French National Rlys, the nationalized system, formed 1938 from all main line rly undertakings, state and company-operated, existing at that time. 32,682 km.

SNCFA
Société Nationale des Chemins de Fer Francais Algériens; formed 1960. *See* SNTF.

SNCFT
Société Nationale des Chemins de Fer Tunisiens; Tunisian National Rlys. 2,219 km of standard and metre gauge.

SNCRDC
Société Nationale des Chemins de Fer du République Démocratique de Congo; Rly authority of the Democratic Republic of Congo. 6,000 km mainly 1,067 mm and 600 mm gauge.

SNCS
Société Nationale des Chemins de Fer du Sénégal; 906 km, metre gauge.

SNCV
Société Nationale des Chemins de Fer Vicinaux; National Local Railways Company, formed 1885, grew into an extensive undertaking, operating light rlys and some tramways (*3*) throughout Belgium. The Flemish title was abbreviated *NMVB.* In 1991 it became *VVM* (qv) and *SRWT* (qv). The *SNCV* was formally dissolved on 30 December 1991.

SNCZ
Société Nationale des Chemins de Fer Zairois, See SNCRDC.

SNDM

Special Non-Driving Motor Car in an LT emu set (with guard's position).

Sneck (RS)

Points/switch (qv).

Sneltram

Light rail transit (qv) system at Utrecht, Holland, opened 1983.

SNER

Scottish North Eastern Rly, formed by amalgamation of Aberdeen Rly and SMJR (line Perth–Forfar–Aberdeen). Part of CR (*1*) from 1866.

Snifting valve (obs)

This device, mounted on the smokebox behind the chimney, admitted air to cool the superheater elements of a steam loco when the steam was shut off during running. Later designs of superheaters were able to stand intense heat and the sv was rendered superfluous.

Snip (RS)

A ticket collector.

Snipe (USRS)

A track worker.

Snip turn (LTRS)

An easy duty.

Snoozer (USRS)

A sleeping car.

Snow blower

A snowplough fitted with a powered fan which, when used together, removes large quantities of drifted snow blocking the track.

Snow brooms

1. (obs) Brooms attached to guard irons (qv) of locos or tenders to sweep snow from rail surfaces.
2. A tramcar (qv) purpose-built or adapted to sweep snow from tracks of tramways (*3*). Usually fitted with axle-driven rotary brooms at each end to push the snow to the near side.

Snowbucking (USRS)

An attack on a deep snow drift with a bucker plow (qv) propelled by a loco, in which a run is taken at the drift at high speed. In steam days up to eight locos would be used to propel the plough into the drift.

Snowdonian

A summer service Rhyl/Llandudno to Llanberis (for Snowdon mountain), operated 1956–62. Name used for a London (Euston)–Pwllheli summer service introduced 1987.

Snow dozer (USRS)

Snow plough.

Snowflaker (USRS)

A newly recruited worker.

Snowman (RS)

A track worker required to clear snow from points/switches and crossings, signal wires and pulleys, point rodding, etc.

Snow shed

A roofed structure (usually wooden) erected over tracks to prevent accumulation of snow on the line; normally sited on hill or mountain sides.

SNR

Shanghai–Nanking Rly; 195 mile main line completed 1908 by a British co. Now part of Chinese Rlys.

SNTF

Société Nationale des Transports Ferroviaires; Algerian Rlys, 3,898 km, mostly standard gauge, with physical connections to the Morocco (*see* ONCFM) and Tunisia (*see* SNCFT) systems. Separate bodies are responsible for infrastructure and construction of new lines.

Snuff dipper (USRS)

A steam loco burning lignite. From its snuff-coloured stain.

SO

1. Saturdays Only.
2. BR Second/Standard class Open coach with centre gangway and 2 + 1 or 2 + 2 seating, no gangway connections.

Soap & towel (RS)

Bread and cheese.

SOCRATE

Système Offrant à la Clientele la Reservation d'Affaires et de Tourisme en Europe; a Europe-wide computer-based seat reservation, ticket sales, hotel booking and general information service introduced by the *SNCF* in 1992.

Soda jerker (USRS)

A loco fireman.

SOE
Simplon–Orient Express (qv).

Soffit
Underside of a sleeper (qv), timber or beam.

Sofrerail (Fr)
A rly consultancy service subsidiary of *SNCF* and *RATP* (qv).

Soft belly (USRS)
A wooden-framed wagon or coach. Easily damaged in an accident.

Soft class
On certain overseas rlys, notably those of Russia and China, this accommodation, with its fully upholstered seats, is the superior class. *See also* Hard class.

Soft plug
A fusible plug in the crown sheet of a steam loco.

Soft spot
See Slurry spot.

Sole
A 12-ton unfitted ballast wagon used by engineers.

Sole bar
The longitudinal outer side member of the underframe (qv) of a wagon or coach, usually braced to afford additional rigidity and strength.

Solent & Wessex (obs)
NSE brand name (1990) for the Hampshire and Dorset services.

Solent Link (obs)
NSE brand name for the electric services introduced in 1990 between Portsmouth and Southampton and between Portsmouth and Eastleigh.

Sole plate
A component fixed on the sleeper under the rails at facing points to hold the rails to gauge. The point locking mechanism is fixed to it.

Solid car, a (USRS)
A fully loaded wagon.

Solum
Scottish term for subgrade (qv).

Somersault signal
A form of semaphore signal with a balanced centrally pivoted arm which is connected through a linkage to the light spectacle casing, which is also pivoted to the outside of

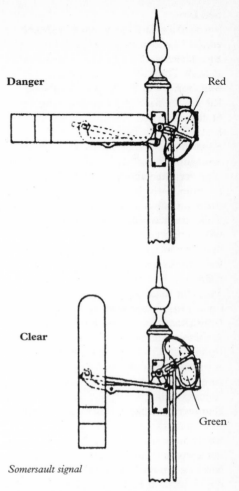

Danger   Red

Clear

Green

Somersault signal

the post. The arrangement eliminates the possibility of ice or snow falsely holding down the semaphore arm to give a spurious 'off' aspect. This problem was highlighted by the Abbots Ripton accident of 1876, which caused the GNR to adopt the somersault design, a few examples of which survived in Britain until the late 1990s. These signals were also used in Australia, supplied by Mackenzie & Holland.

Sonderzug (Ger)
A special train.

Sonia/Sonya(s) (LT) (RS)
The voice of the recorded announcements made to passengers in London Underground trains (after listening to them many times over it *get Sonya nerves*).

Soo Line
Minneapolis, St Paul and Sault Ste Marie
Rly Co., a subsidiary of the CPR. From an
approximation of the French pronunciation
of Sault. From 1961 the Co. merged
with the Duluth, South Shore & Atlantic
RR and the Wisconsin Central RR to
form the Soo Line RR Co. in which
Canadian Pacific held 56 per cent of
ownership.

Soot blower
A device fitted above the firehole of a
steam loco which diverts a jet of steam to
the boiler tubes to remove soot and ashes
while the loco is moving. It is normally
used at approximately hourly intervals
while the loco is in motion. *See also* Ash
blower; Blower.

SOR
Save Our Railways. A pressure group set
up in 1993 to campaign against the
Conservative government's rly privatization
proposals. Merged with Transport 2000
(qv) in 2000. *See also* Trainwatch.

Sorting carriage
see SC (3).

Sorting sidings
A group of sidings for the principal sorting
of wagons and their assembly into trains,
forming the major part of the main yard in
a marshalling yard.

Sorting tender (obs)
see ST (2).

Sorting yard
see Marshalling yard; Sorting sidings.

SOS (RS)
Short of Steam.

South American
A boat train between London (Waterloo)
and Southampton Docks, connecting with
Royal Mail Line sailings, introduced 1953.
Ceased 1969.

Southbound
see Eastbound.

South Central
TOC (2), a subsidiary of Govia Ltd, which
took over following the withdrawal of
Connex South Central franchise (*see*
Connex Rail Ltd) from 26 August 2001.
Renamed Southern (qv) 25 May 2004.

South Eastern, The
SER (qv).

South Eastern Trains
See SET.

South Eastern Trains Co.
A TOU (qv), 1994, operating services in
south-east London and Kent, also
Tunbridge Wells–Hastings and London–
Redhill–Gatwick Airport/Tonbridge. TOC
(2) (qv) 1996 as Connex South Eastern
Ltd, *see* Connex Rail Ltd.

Southern
A TOC (2), the trading name of the New
Southern Rly Ltd, a wholly owned
subsidiary of Govia Ltd (qv), 2004. *See also*
South Central.

Southern Belle
A Pullman service between London
(Victoria) and Brighton, introduced 1908.
Ceased 1916, re-introduced 1919. All-
Pullman from 1921. Renamed Brighton
Belle (qv) 1934.

Southern Crescent
see Crescent Limited.

Southerner
An express between Christchurch (NZ),
Dunedin and Invercargill, introduced
1970. 10 h in 1989.

Southern Pacific (US)
A steam loco with 4–10–2 wheel
arrangement. The first one was supplied to
that rly.

Southern Railway Magazine, The
House and staff journal of SR (1),
published monthly January
1923–December 1947.

South Hams
South Hams Light Rly, Yealmpton to
Newton Ferrers and Noss Mayo; construc-
tion begun 1906, never completed.

South London Line
London (Victoria), Clapham, Peckham
Rye and London Bridge. First section of
the LB&SCR to be electrified, known as
'The South London Elevated Electric' on
its introduction in 1909 and for some years
afterwards.

South London Link
Brand name for South London Line (qv)
from 1991.

South London Metro
Brand name introduced by Connex Rail Ltd (qv) in 1996 for a frequent train service in and around the triangle London (Victoria)/London Bridge–Croydon.

Southpaw, The (US)
Nickname for the Chicago & North-western RR, the only rly in the US to adopt left-hand running (southpaw is US (S) for a left-handed person).

South Staffordshire Line
see SSR.

South Tynedale
South Tynedale Rly, a 2 ft/609 mm gauge tourist line on part of the former BR Alston branch, first section reopened 1984.

South Wales & Bristol Direct
Wootton Bassett–Patchway, opened by GWR 1903.

South Wales & West Rly Ltd
A TOU (qv), 1994. A TOC (*2*) 1996, *see* Wales & West.

South Wales Pullman
Service between London (Paddington) and Swansea, introduced 1955; dmu 'Blue Pullman' sets used from 1961, ceased 1973.

South Western Gazette/Magazine, The
The first enduring rly staff magazine, published monthly from June 1881. It started as a private charitable enterprise by three L&SWR clerks (including Sam Fay), who secured official approval but no financial support. Renamed *The South Western Magazine* from January 1916, it was taken over by the L&SWR from January 1918 and produced monthly by the company's Publicity Department, becoming *The Southern Railway Magazine* (qv) from January 1923.

South Western Lines (obs)
NSE brand name for former L&SWR suburban area services.

South West Trains
A TOU (qv), 1994. A TOC (*2*) 1996, oper-ating suburban services in south-west London and Surrey and also medium- and long-distance services from London (Waterloo)–Portsmouth, Southampton, Bournemouth, Weymouth, Salisbury and Exeter.

Southwold
Southwold Rly, 3 ft/914 mm gauge, Halesworth GER to Southwold, inc 1876, opened 1879, closed 1929.

South Yorkshireman
An express between London (Marylebone) and Bradford (Exchange) introduced 1948. Ceased 1960.

South Yorkshire Supertram
Light rail transit scheme for Sheffield area, opened from 1994.

Sou'West (RS)
The G&SWR (and that company's lines from 1923)

Soviet (US)
A steam loco with 4–14–4 wheel arrangement.

SP
1. Signalmen's code for 'urgent and important'.
2. (US) Southern Pacific RR, now SP Lines. Absorbed D&RGW from 1988.

Space ships (RS)
BR standard 9F 2–10–0 steam locos.

SPAD
Signal(s) Passed At Danger.

SPAD Indicator
A signal placed in advance (qv) of high-risk stop signals which, whilst normally dark, will show three red lights (centre constant, top and lower flashing) to warn any driver who has passed a red stop signal in its rear. Introduced in Britain *c.* 1995.

Spam cans (RS)
SR Bulleid Pacific locos, Merchant Navy, West Country and Battle of Britain classes. From their streamlined outer casing.

Span wire
A stranded wire, usually of steel, extending between supporting structures (poles, masts, towers, rosettes (qv)), which supports and retains the correct lateral position of the contact/trolley wire (qv) in tramway (*3*) overhead.

SPAP
Siderodromoi Piraeus–Athenae–Peloponnesus; Peloponnesian Rlys. *See also OSE.*

Spar (USRS)(obs)
A shunter's pole (qv).

Spark/sparker/sparkler (RS)
An emu (qv).

Sparks (USRS)(obs)
A rly telegrapher.

Sparks effect
The additional traffic, not abstracted from other services, or arising from any other identifiable cause, which usually follows the electrification of a rly. A term coined by BR in the 1960s.

Spate indicator
An indicator placed above a TSR (qv) warning board to show that the TSR is not in force.

Spa Valley Line
A preserved rly based on the former BR Tunbridge Wells (West)–Groombridge–Eridge line. Opened 1996. *See also* TWERPS.

Special, The (RS)
A royal train.

Special carriages
See Family saloon; Invalid carriage.

Special duties (LTRS)
Unofficial evasion of work.

Special stop order
A written instruction (usually authorized by Control) to the driver of a train to stop at one or more stations at which his train is not scheduled to call, e.g. when other trains have been cancelled or service has been temporarily interrupted.

Special traffic
Trains additional to those appearing in the public and working timetables (qv), providing for the requirements of the armed forces and to meet the demands of those attending major sporting events, naval and military reviews, air and motor shows, etc. On a less demanding scale, trains to cater for notables including heads of state from other countries; trains for ramblers, school and firms' outings, and for society weddings and funerals. *See also* Chartered train; Excursion [trains]; Royal trains; Special train.

Special train
A train hired, often at short notice, for the convenience of one individual or a private party.

Special work
Points and crossings.

Spectacle plate
The motion plate beneath the boiler of a steam loco through which the connecting rods pass. Also the weatherboard, i.e. the front of the loco cab, containing the spectacle windows through which the enginemen may view the line ahead. Purists accept only the first of these definitions. Also used for spectacles (qv).

Spectacles
The frame on a semaphore signal which moves in front of the lamp. It contains the coloured glasses which give the signal indications at night.

Speed boards
Lineside indicators showing the maximum speed which may be used on the section ahead.

Speeder (USRS)
A light motorized inspection trolley used by track workers, a *Draisine* (qv).

Speedfreight (obs)
1. BR overnight express freight service carrying 10-ton containers between London and Manchester, introduced 1963. The prototype Freightliner (qv) working.
2. A wagon load freight service (registered wagon system), introduced by BR (M) 1969–70.

Speedlink
BR name for its air-braked wagon-load freight services, assisted by TOPS (qv). Introduced 1972. Maximum loading was reached in 1986 when just under seven million tons were carried. Merged with Freightliner (qv) as Railfreight Distribution (qv), 1988. Speedlink services were generally withdrawn from BR in 1991.

Speed whiskers (RS)(obs)
Painted curved lines on the front of early BR dmus.

Speedy (USRS)(obs)
A call boy (qv).

Speller Amendment [Legislation]
A 1981 amendment to the 1962 Transport Act (moved by an MP called Speller) which

allows BR to reopen a line experimentally for passenger traffic without the burden of going through the statutory closure procedures should it prove a failure.

Spen Valley Line
Huddersfield–Bradley–Gomersal–Farnley–Leeds.

Sperry car
A track recording railcar manufactured by Sperry Rail Service Inc, USA.

Speyside Line
Craigellachie–Boat of Garten.

Spider (RS)
1. Signal apparatus between the rails.
2. The metal component, reminiscent of the shape of a spider which slides between the two steel horizontals of the crosshead of a steam loco motion.

Spiers & Pond
Catering, hotel and restaurant contractors to various rly companies until *c.* 1940 including Metropolitan, L&SWR, LC&DR, SER (*1*), Midland, FR (*2*), and SR (*1*).

Spike
The heavy nail of square section which holds a flat-bottomed rail to a sleeper. Screw spikes with threads are also used, and, in recent years, patented clips (e.g. the Pandrol (qv) clip).

Spill (USRS)
A station.

Spindryers (RS)
BR class 323 emus; from their noise pattern.

Spinners (RS)
Midland Rly Johnson 4–2–2 locos. From a propensity to suffer from wheel slip.

Spirit of Capricorn
An electric (ICE = Inter-City Electric) service between Brisbane and Rockhampton, introduced 1989, with speeds up to 75 mph on 3 ft 6 in gauge.

Spiv days/spiv turn (RS)
Rest days. From (S) spiv = a person who does not like hard work but lives by craftiness.

Spiv link (RS)
Rest day relief drivers' link. *See also* Spiv days/spiv turn.

Spivs (RS)
Nickname for Blackpool tramcars series 304–328 of 1952–3.

Splash, to give it/her a (RS)
To apply the air brake.

Splice bar (US)
Term for fishplates (qv).

Splits/Split turns
A very unpopular arrangement in which duties are broken into two sessions, separated by two or more hours, e.g. 5 h in morning and 3 h in the evening.

Splitting distants
Normally only one distant signal is provided in the rear of a junction, worked only for the direct route, but in some cases where the speeds are the same on more than one route, distants are arranged in bracket form to correspond with junction stop signals. They are then called splitting distants.

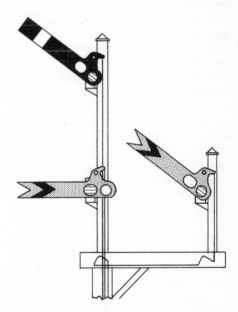

Splitting distants indicating line clear for right-hand diverging route at next signal box

Spoil bank/heap
Unwanted or unsuitable material excavated in rly construction or alteration formed into a heap or bank.

Spoornet
Brand name for South African Rlys, introduced 1990. *See also* Transnet. Together with SARCO (qv), the South African rlys have some 23,000 km of 1,067 mm gauge.

SPORTIS
A portable version of APTIS (qv), developed from PORTIS (qv).

Sports Centre (LTRS)
Signal Engineer's Report Centre.

Spot, to
1. (US) To shunt; to place a wagon in its designated position.
2. (RS) To see a specific loco/traction unit/vehicle for the very first time. *See also* Train spotter.

Spotter
1. (RS) *see* Train spotter (qv).
2. (USRS) A company checker or inspector.

Sprag (RS)(obs)
A freight train guard. From sprags (qv).

Sprags (obs)
Pieces of wood placed between the spokes of wagons to prevent or slow down movement; also the men who performed this operation.

Spragues (RS) (Fr)
Generic term applied to all electric multiple-unit (qv) stock on the Paris *Métro* system built before 1940. *See* Sprague trains.

Sprague trains
Generic term for electric multiple unit trains in the early years of their use, after their US inventor, Frank Julian Sprague (1857–1934).

Sprat & Winkle
see Crab and Winkle (qv).

Spray Express (RS)
A weed-killing train (qv).

Spread the track, to
Action of pushing rails further apart, e.g. by working a loco with a long rigid wheelbase over a sharp curve.

Spring
The place at which the moveable and tapered switch or tongue rail of points ends up against the stock or side rail.

Springbok
A boat train between London (Waterloo) and Southampton Docks in connection with Union Castle Line sailings to South Africa. Introduced as Union Castle Express 1953, renamed 1957. Name dropped *c.* 1971.

Spring points
Unworked trailing points which return to the normal position under spring load after the passage of a train.

Sprinters
1. NS two-car emu type SGM of 1974–7. With high acceleration, capable of making many intermediate stops without delaying long distance trains.
2. BR diesel railcars, classes 150, 151, 153, 155, 156 and 158.

SPT
A Signal Post Telephone.

Spudler (RS)
A person who causes trouble indirectly.

Spur
Very short section of line branching off another, hence shunting spur.

Spurt
Self-Propelled Ultrasonic Rail Tester; used on Indian Rlys to detect rail condition and faults. *See also* Ultrasonic rail flaw detection.

Sputnik (LTRS)(obs)
An all-motor car (and therefore fast-running) six-car COP stock train. Named after the first man-made satellite, launched by the USSR in 1957.

Square span
An overbridge (qv) crossing a rly at right angles to the track.

Square wheel (RS)
A wheel with one or more flats. *See* Flat (3).

Squeezer (USRS)
A wagon retarder. From its action.

Squid
A 31-ton general materials wagon used by engineers.

Squirrel, to (USRS)
To climb up a wagon.

Squirter (RS)
An injector on a steam loco.

SR

1. Southern Rly, formed 1923, a grouping of the L&SWR, LB&SCR, and the SE&CR. Part of BR from 1948.
2. Stourbridge Rly, inc 1860, 1861, first section Stourbridge–Cradley Heath opened 1863, amalgamated with GWR 1872.
3. Stratford-upon-Avon Rly, inc 1857, Hatton to Stratford-upon-Avon opened 1860. Part of GWR 1883.
4. Strathspey Rly, Dufftown to Craigellachie, inc 1861, opened 1863, part of GNofSR 1866.
5. (US) Southern Rly System.
6. Southern Rly [of India], formed 1951.
7. ScotRail (qv).

See also Southwold; Stocksbridge.

SRA

1. State Rly Authority [of New South Wales].
2. Strategic Rail Authority (qv).

SR&H Co.

Saundersfoot Rly & Harbour Co. colliery rly. Reynalton–Saundersfoot–Stepaside, (Pembrokeshire), 4 ft ¾ in gauge, inc 1829, first section opened 1833–4, closed 1939.

SRC

Sudan Rlys Corporation; 5,516 km of 1,067 mm gauge.

SRJ&P

Society of Rly Journalists & Photographers, founded 1999.

SRPS

Scottish Railway Preservation Society, founded 1961.

SRM

Southern Railway Magazine (qv).

SRO

Saudi Rlys Organization. Riyadh to Ad-Dammam by two routes, first section opened 1951, second (direct) line 1985, total length 1,392 km. Extension to serve Al Jubayl port to open 2005–6. 'Land bridge' line Riyadh–Jeddah planned.

SRT

State Rlys of Thailand. 4,071 km, metre gauge, physically connected to the rlys of Malaysia (*KTM (B)* (qv)), Singapore and Kampuchea (Cambodia).

SRWT

Société Regionale Wallonne du Transport; Wallonne Regional Transport Co., the Wallonne section of the former *SNCV* (qv), independently managed from 1991. *See also VVM.*

SSC

Slow Speed Control.

SSF

Slow Speed Fitment, a driving cab safety device operating electronically through the speedometer feed. It controls speed to a preset low level (around 7 mph) if the loco or train moves away when its master switch has been left in the neutral setting.

SSI

Solid State Interlocking, in which signalling and points interlocking is carried out centrally by one or more microcomputer interlockings, their number depending on the size and complexity of the control area. First installation by BR at Leamington 1985; superseded by WestLock (Westinghouse Interlocking) (first trials 2005–6).

SSL

1. Short Swing Link: *see* Swinglink.
2. (LT) The sub-surface lines of the London Underground system (District, East London, Hammersmith & City, Inner Circle and Metropolitan) when it is necessary to distinguish these from the deep-level tube lines with their smaller-size tunnels and rolling stock. *See also* Subsurface stations; Tube (1).

SSM&WCR

South Shields, Marsden & Whitburn Colliery Rly, opened by Whitburn Colliery Co. 1879, passenger service from 1888. Operated by Harton Coal Co. from 1891, vested in National Coal Board 1947, passenger service ceased 1953, closed 1968.

SSR

South Staffordshire Rly, Wichnor Junction (with Birmingham & Derby Rly, later Midland Rly) to Lichfield, Walsall and Dudley, inc 1846, opened 1847, 1849, 1850, 1854, worked by L&NWR from

1852, leased by L&NWR 1861, vested in L&NWR 1867.

ST

1. Saddle Tank (qv).
2. Sorting Tender, a rly carriage specially designed for sorting Royal Mail en route, introduced 1838, renamed Sorting Carriage (*see* SC (*3*)), 1904. *See also* Railway Post Offices; TPO.

Stab (USRS)

A delay faced by a train.

Stable, to

To put a train away in its shed, depot, sidings, etc. after work.

Stack music (USRS)

The sound of a steam loco working full out.

Stack of rust (USRS)(obs)

A steam loco in an advanced state of neglect.

Stadtbahn (Ger)

City rly; usually operated as an independent entity by a local transport undertaking and normally of conventional heavy rly (qv) type construction, underground and/or surface. There are two exceptions: in *Berlin*, the *Stadtbahn* is the four-track (long-distance and local services) cross-city line of the national rly system (*DBAG* (qv)), mostly on viaduct, with 11 stations; in *Vienna*, it is a unique hybrid of underground rlys and an electric tramway (*3*). The term should not be confused with *S-bahn* (qv).

Stadt Express (Ger)

see SE.

StadtTicket (Ger)

Ticket introduced by DB (qv) in 1997, giving unlimited travel on most public transport services in principal German cities.

Staff

see Train staff/tablet/token and ticket.

Staff of ignorance (USRS)(obs)

A brake club (qv).

Stageworks

Execution of major alterations to track layout in stages, each a complete task, often carried out over a weekend, interrupted by normal or near-normal train working.

Staggered platforms

A station arrangement in which the side platforms serving the 'Up' and 'Down' lines are not placed opposite one another but with one end of one somewhat set apart from the opposite end of the other, thus virtually doubling the length of the station site. Its adoption often reflects site considerations: the physical difficulty (and therefore extra expense) of building platforms to the conventional plan; the position of sidings and level crossings; or the site of the passenger exit. Also, by placing the platforms either side of a road crossing on the level, obstruction to road traffic could be minimized. Some nineteenth-century engineers apparently considered staggering would save the cost of footbridges and subways since passengers could cross on the level in relative safety, using the clear space which could always be maintained between the ends of two trains standing at the staggered 'Up' and 'Down' platforms. This argument, however, is flawed, since it overlooks the possibility of a train passing through the station in the opposite direction without stopping while passengers are still moving between a train and the exit.

Staggers Act (US)

US legislation of 1980 which removed almost two-thirds of all rly rates from the control of the ICC (qv) and deregulated all inter-modal transport activity.

Stainmore Line, The

Darlington–Barnard Castle–Kirkby Stephen–Tebay/Penrith, passing over Stainmore summit.

Stairway to the stars (RS)

The ladder up a signal post.

Stake (USRS)(obs)

A pole attached to a wagon in front of a loco and used for shunting.

Stake driver (USRS)

A surveyor or civil engineer's employee.

Stall (USRS)

A compartment in a van.

Stammstrecke (Ger)

The original (historic) line after another line has been built between the same two points.

Stanchion

A solid round or hollow tube used to retain loads.

Standage

See Standing.

Standard class

Former BR Second class (qv), so renamed 1987. The term was first used on the CIE.

Standard gauge

The most widely used rail gauge, 4 ft 8½ in/ 1,435 mm. In Britain, the choice was determined by a Royal Commission in 1845–6. Currently in the UK the measurement must lie within the range 1,432 mm to 1,438 mm inclusive.

Standard length rail

Formerly the normal maximum length produced and capable of being handled and transported was 60 ft.(18.288 m). It is now 120 ft (36.676 m). Referred to colloquially as a 'length'.

Standedge Line, The

Leeds–Manchester via Huddersfield and Stalybridge, through Standedge Tunnel.

Standing

A measure of clear space available in a siding, loop line or terminal road, e.g. 'Standing for 12 cars', 'Standing for 20 wagons'.

ST&MJR

Stratford-upon-Avon, Towcester & Midland Junction Rly, Towcester to Ravenstone Wood Junc and spur to L&NWR at Roade, inc 1879, opened 1891. Part of S&MJR 1909.

Standseilbahn (Ger)

A funicular rly.

Stanhopes (obs)

Box-like open wagons, often without seats, provided for the lowest class of passenger traffic in the early days of rlys. Rather unfairly they took the name from the light, open, road vehicles called after the Hon. and Revd Fitzroy Stanhope (1787–1854), for whom these were first made.

Stanier Black

see Black Stanier.

Stanislas

TEE Paris–Nancy–Strasbourg (3 h 47 min), introduced 1971. Lost *TEE* status 1982.

Stansted Express

Fast service between London (Liverpool Street) and Stansted Airport station, from April 2004 operated as part of the ONE (qv) Greater Anglia franchise.

Starbuck

George Starbuck, Birkenhead, builders of tramcars from 1862. Limited company 1871. Became Milnes (qv), 1886.

Starfish

A 10-ton unfitted ballast wagon used by engineers.

Stargazer (USRS)

A brakeman failing to attend to his duties.

Star guard (LTRS)

Guard-motorman, i.e. one trained to perform both guard's and driver's jobs.

Starlight Specials

Very cheap-fare summer weekend night services between London (St Pancras) and Glasgow (St Enoch) and between London (Marylebone) and Edinburgh (Waverley), introduced 1953 to counter road coach competition. Ceased in 1962.

Star of Egypt Express

CIWL sleeping car service between Cairo, Luxor and Aswan, introduced 1929.

Star Ships (RS)

BR class 323 emu; from the noise made by the underfloor electrical equipment.

Starter

Starting signal (qv).

Starting signal

A stop signal (qv) placed in advance of a signal box and the home signal, usually at the front end of a station platform, controlling the entrance to a block section. On the LM&SR and BR (M) known as Home no. 3. *See* diagram overleaf. *See also* Advanced starter.

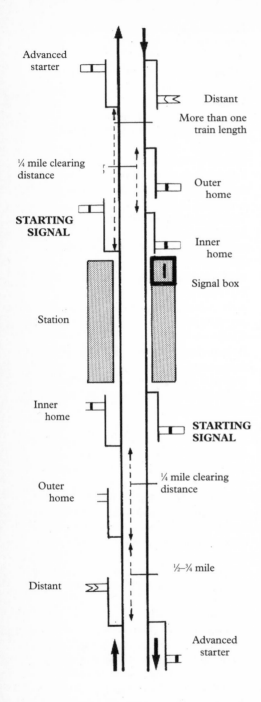

Advanced
starter

Distant

More than one
train length

¼ mile clearing
distance

Outer
home

**STARTING
SIGNAL**

Inner
home

Signal box

Station

Inner
home

**STARTING
SIGNAL**

Outer
home

¼ mile clearing
distance

½–¾ mile

Distant

Advanced
starter

Starting signal

Star-21

Abbreviated name for 'Superior Train for Advanced 21st Century Rly', a 350–400 km/hr train set design proposed for *Shinkansen* (qv).

Starved/ing lion (RS)(obs)

A facetious term for the BR emblem adopted in 1949.

State room (obs)

A segregated section of a US Pullman sleeping car, usually with three berths and lavatory en suite, affording privacy and obtainable by payment of a supplementary fare.

Statesman

A boat train between London (Waterloo) and Southampton Docks in connection with sailings of *SS United States*, introduced 1952. Ceased 1969. Later a privately owned luxury charter train.

Static

When used in connection with rail or track condition, this implies a complete absence of load, i.e. of vertical or lateral forces. When used in connection with a rail vehicle it implies the dimensions measured while at rest on a straight track.

Station Agent (US)

A person in charge of a small station, obs. in Britain after late 1800s but current much later in the US, there usually a person also acting as operator (qv), baggage man, etc. *See also* Agent.

Station limits

Section between the outermost stop signal (qv) of one box and the last stop signal under control of the same box, containing a station. Within these limits, the signalman is able to make some train movements without referring to the adjacent boxes, and there can be more than one train within them if the appropriate signals exist. Where an intermediate block signal is controlled from the box, station limits cease at the last stop signal in the rear of the intermediate stop signal; the space in advance from that point to that signal is known as the intermediate block section. Where power boxes (qv) exist, station limits are defined as being the section of line between two specified stop signals.

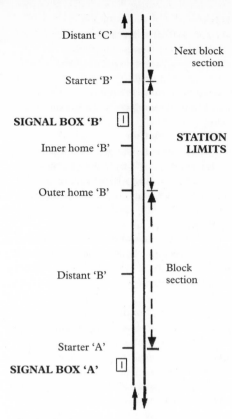

Station limits

Station traffic/station to station traffic
(obs)
Traffic conveyed by rail to and from
stations without collection and delivery by
rly road vehicles at each end.

Station trucks (obs)
1. Two-wheeled hand barrows for goods,
   or four-wheeled trucks for passengers'
   luggage and large items. Generally
   superseded by BRUTES (qv).
2. On the GWR, a 'station truck' was a rly
   wagon carrying small quantities of
   freight, usually over branch lines,
   picking up and delivering at each station
   as required, when there was insufficient
   traffic for a wagon to be worked to each
   station. Other companies referred to
   this variously as a road box, road truck,
   road van, or road wagon.

Station working
The rules governing movements within
station limits (qv).

Statutes, railway
see Railway Acts; Transport Acts;
Transport and Works Act.

STCRP
*Société des Transports en Commun de la
Région Parisienne*; Paris Region Public
Transport Company, formed 1921 to take
over the management and operation of all
tramways (*3*) and motorbuses in and
around the French capital. Replaced by
RATP (qv) in 1948.

Stealth bombers (RS)
BR class 91 locos and (later) GNER (qv)
IC (*1*) (qv) trains. After the US military
aircraft.

Steam Banana (obs)
A van heated by steam pipes to ripen
bananas while in transit.

Steaming (S)
A crime in which a gang of youths move
through a train, terrorizing and robbing
passengers at knife-point. This was first
practised on the London Underground
in the 1960s. From the rapid movement
of the operation (cf. 'in a steaming
hurry').

Steam keys
Shut-off valves for the main steam
manifold of a loco.

Steam Navvy (obs)
A steam-powered digger or steam
shovel, invented in the US *c.* 1840 but
not adopted in Britain for rly
construction until *c.* 1880. *See also*
American devils.

Steam pig (RS)(obs)
A person or thing which cannot be easily
identified or defined.

Steamroller (LTRS)
Line Controller (rhyming S).

Steam rollers (RS)
L&SWR 380 class 4–4–0 locos of 1879;
from the appearance of the disc wheels
used in their bogies.

Steam tender
A tender driven by steam from a loco boiler
and fitted with coupled wheels, cylinders

and motion, the object being to increase hauling power of the loco. First used on the GNR (qv) in 1863–6. *See also* Booster.

Steamtown

Steamtown Rly centre; a depot and maintenance centre for preserved steam locos based on former BR mpd at Carnforth, Lancs, established 1969. Closed 1997.

Steam winder (USRS)

1. Car fitted with nothing but a screw-down handbrake.
2. Climax geared loco.

Steel gang (USRS)

A rail-laying gang.

Steeple cab

A centrally placed cab, enabling a loco to be driven without difficulty in either direction without reversal. *See also* Camels (1) and (2).

Steiermark Express

A service between Ostend, Graz and Rijeka, introduced 1955. Replaced by Dalmatia Express (qv).

Stem (USRS)

A rly right of way, trackage.

Stencil indicator

An alpha-numeric route indicator used for shunting operations.

Stendhal

A Paris–Turin–Milan sleeping car service, introduced 1983.

Stephensons

Robert Stephenson & Co. Ltd, loco builders, founded in Newcastle 1823, works transferred to Darlington 1902. Merged with Hawthorn, Leslie to form Robert Stephenson & Hawthorns Ltd, 1937. Part of EE (qv) from 1955.

Stephenson valve gear

A form of steam loco valve gear or link motion with two eccentrics for each valve fitted to the crank axle to give a reciprocating motion through eccentric rods to a slotted expansion link.

Stepping distance

The distance between the passenger step of a coach and the outer edge of a station platform.

Stepping up/back (LTRS)

Obtaining quick turnrounds at termini

in peak hours by requiring the driver and guard of an arriving train to 'drop back' and take over the next arriving train, assuming the correct positions on the platform ready to take up their posts as soon as it arrives, instead of 'changing ends' on the same train.

Step-plate junction

A trumpet- or cone-shaped junction of two tube (qv) lines made by using circular linings of increasingly larger diameter from the normal running tunnel size to one large enough to accommodate two tracks.

Step rail

An early form of rail for tramways (3) of L-shaped section, the lower level between the outer flanges providing a hazard to other road traffic.

Stevens

Stevens & Sons, Southwark, London, manufacturers of signalling equipment from the 1840s until *c.* 1901.

Stick

1. (RS) A signal.
2. (USRS) A train staff (qv).

Stick to stick running (RS)

Stopping at all signals.

Stick trouble (RS)

Defective working of signals.

Sticky door (RS)

Air doors not closing properly.

Stinger (USRS)

A brakeman.

Stingray

A 40-ton ballast hopper wagon fitted with a generator and used by engineers.

Stink bombs (RS)(obs)

Capsules placed in the hollow crank pin of the middle big ends of certain L&NER locos, designed to evaporate when the bearing was running hot, releasing a strong smell to warn the enginemen to take appropriate action.

Stink buggy (USRS)(obs)

Rlymen's contemptuous term for a motor bus or coach. Also used of petrol- or diesel-powered railcars.

Stinker

1. (RS)(obs) A wagon much delayed, and

held in a yard. From the smell of decaying perishables therein.

2. (USRS) A hot box (qv).

Stitch wire

A wire suspended from the catenary (qv) wire from which the contact wire (qv) is suspended.

STN

Special Traffic Notice. Instructions to operating staff notifying timing, etc. of special traffic (qv) workings. *See also* Typos.

Stock car (US)

Cattle wagon.

Stockholder (USRS)

1. A rly employee who is always overly conscientious, always concerned to work for the company's interests.

2. Anyone riding on a free pass or at reduced rates.

Stock pen (USRS)

A yard office.

Stock rails

The lengths of fixed running rail against which the blades of the switch rails bear. *See* points.

Stocksbridge

Stocksbridge Rly, branching west from Deepcar near Sheffield to serve a steel works, inc 1874, opened 1876–7. Passenger services operated until 1931. Now owned by Stocksbridge Engineering Steels.

Stock train (US)

Term for a train composed entirely of cattle wagons.

Stoker (obs)

A steam loco fireman.

Stone/s (RS)

Ballast (qv).

Stood down (RS)

Suspended from duty.

Stoot/stute (RS)

Institute (qv).

Stop and proceed [rule] (LT)

Rule G 7 enables a driver to pass a defective automatic signal at danger after re-setting a tripcock (qv) which has been knocked off by the related train stop. The train may then be moved very slowly, with its driver ready to stop at any obstruction, not resuming

normal speed until a clear signal is reached. *See also* Apply the rule, to.

Stop board

A board indicating that all trains must stop while crews obey prescribed instructions such as opening gates, obtaining tokens, etc.

'Stop, look, listen'

Wording first used in 1912 for warning notices at level crossings in the USA.

Stop order

see Special stop order.

Stopper puller (USRS)

A brakeman or shunter.

Stopping the job (RS)

Interrupting the train service. *See also* Job.

Stop signal

Any type of signal capable of displaying danger ('on') and clear ('off') indications, and which must not be passed when 'on'.

Stores train (obs)

A train running regularly over a rly system, distributing requisitioned stores of all kinds to stations, signal boxes, yards, etc.

Storm sheet

A waterproof tarpaulin erected as required between the cab roof of a steam loco and its tender to protect the enginemen in severe weather.

Storno (RS)

Driver to controller telephones. From the name of the suppliers, Storno Ltd.

S to S (obs)

Station-to-Station rate of charge for freight (coal, bricks and other low-class traffic) or parcels brought in by the sender and collected by the consignee.

Stour Valley

Birmingham (New St.)–Dudley Port– Wolverhampton (HL)–Bushbury; originally promoted in 1846 by the Birmingham, Wolverhampton & Stour Valley Rly.

Stour Valley Line

Ashford (Kent)–Canterbury West–Minster (–Ramsgate).

Stove piping (USRS)

Shop talk among rly workers.

Stowage siding
A siding (qv) in use exclusively for storing temporarily unwanted wagons.

Straightback (RS)
A loco lacking a steam dome, notably those of the H&BR.

Straight road
The main or primary route through a set of points, not always in a straight line. *See also* Through road, Turnout road.

Strapontin (Fr)
A tip-up seat, usually located in the vestibule area of rly car and available if not too many passengers are standing.

Strapper (RS)
A beginner, usually a youth.

Strappers (obs)
Rly employees whose duty it was to strap luggage on to the roofs of passenger coaches.

Strap rails (obs)
Wooden rails with iron strips laid on top to reduce wear.

Strassenbahn (Ger)
Tramway (*3*).

Strassenroller (Ger)
Same as *Culemeyer* (qv).

Strata-Domes (US)
Vistadomes (qv) equipped with powerful searchlights to sweep the night scenery, introduced in 1952 by the Baltimore & Ohio RR.

Strategic Rail Authority (obs)
Established by the Transport Act, 2000, the SRA functioned fully from January 2001. Funded by a mix of grants and loans from the Exchequer, it was tasked to promote the use of the privatized British rly system for passenger and freight traffic; to secure development of the rly network; and to ensure its contribution to an integrated system of transport. The SRA had powers to provide rail services if it considered them desirable and to operate them itself; it could be guided by the DETR (qv) in forming its strategies. Residuary functions of the BRB (qv) were assumed. OPRAF (qv) was taken over, as were some of the functions of the ORR (qv). After a further review of rly policy, the SRA was abolished by the Railways Act, 2005 (qv).

Strathearn Express
Service between Glasgow and Crieff, introduced 1911.

Strathspey Railway
Preserved rly on former BR line between Aviemore, Boat of Garten and Grantown, on the former BR Aviemore–Forres line. First section opened 1978.

Strawberry patch (USRS)
The rear end of a train, with red lights shining in the night, also a yard at night with many red signal lamps visible.

Straw boss (USRS)
Foreman of a track gang.

Straw hat (USRS)
A rlyman not inclined to work in extreme climatic conditions.

Streaker (RS)
A fast train.

Streak of rust (USRS)
Rly tracks.

Streaks (RS)(obs)
Streamlined locos, mainly the LM&SR and L&NER 4–6–2s.

Streetcar/street car (US)
Tramcar (qv).

Street railway (US)
Tramway (*3*) (qv).

Stressing [rails]
Use of hydraulic machinery to adjust the length of LWR/CWR (qv) during installation to eliminate stress at a specified rail temperature.

Stretch 'em out, to (RS)
To take out the slack in the drawbars and couplings of a train.

Stretcher
The bar which connects the two tongue rails or switch blades of points and holds them in the required position in relation to the stock rail and the track gauge.

String (USRS)
A cut (qv) of wagons or cars.

Stripping the road
Removal of old track and ballast in preparation for relaying.

Strip tickets (obs)
Tickets covering up to six or more journeys, issued at a single transaction, often at a discount.

Strong arm (USRS)(obs)
A steam loco not equipped with mechanical stoker.

Strowger
See: Hudd system.

Strub system
A form of rack rly (qv) invented by the Swiss engineer Emil Viktor Strub (1858–1909), first used on the Jungfrau rly. In this system the teeth of the rack are formed in the head (qv) of a flat bottom rail fastened to the sleepers (qv).

Structure gauge
The profile into which trackside features and rly infrastructure must not encroach. It usually requires a clear space of some 5 ft (1.52 metres) each side of the running lines. *See also* Kinematic envelope.

Structure gauging train (OLGA)
A train equipped to measure the structure gauge (qv) profile along any route it uses.

Stub
Any short dead-end siding or line.

Stub switch
Points without tongue rails (blades) which secure the change in direction simply by lateral movement of the running rails. Used in early rly practice and still to be seen on portable rlys.

Sturgeon
A 50-ton bogie wagon for carrying rails and sleepers used by engineers. Suffixed 'A' if bolsters (qv) fitted.

SU
BR (S) Single [electric, motor brake] Unit.

SUB
SR and BR (S) SUBurban emu sets of 1941, 1944, 1945, and 1946–51. Early examples were compartment stock, but in subsequent production open-saloon design predominated, 3-SUB, 4-SUB. *See also* Queen of Shebas.

Sub (RS)
A substation (qv).

Sub, The
South Suburban Loop Line, Edinburgh.

Subgrade
Ground beneath the formation (1) (qv).

Subscriber's ticket (obs)
Season ticket (qv).

Subsidiary signal
A signal mounted at track level to control shunting and other low-speed movements.

Substation
A building containing the machinery (originally rotary converters but later rectifiers and transformers) which converts the industrial electricity supply to low voltage direct current for traction purposes.

Subsurface lines
see Surface lines.

Sub-surface station
A term used in Home Office Regulations made in 1989 under Section 12 of the Fire Precautions Act, 1971 which covers any rly station with passenger platforms below surface level, at whatever depth. Also known as 'Section 12 stations'.

Subte
Buenos Aires underground rlys.

Subway (US)
Any type of urban underground rly, apparently picked up from the use of this term in the early (1868–87) legislation for London tube rlys (*see* Tube (*1*)) which, for convenience, was sometimes vague as to what would be put in the 'subway' after it was built. In Britain, this rather specialized application of the word had ceased by the end of the nineteenth century.

Sud Express
CIWL service Calais/Paris, Bordeaux, Biarritz, Irun and Madrid and Lisbon, introduced 1887 (with a change of trains at Irun owing to gauge difference). Daily from 1900. Revived after WW1, all-Pullman from 1926. Ceased 1939. Revived 1946 as Paris–Lisbon/Madrid, but no longer all-Pullman. Pullman cars withdrawn 1971. Madrid portion withdrawn, 1973. Ceased 1994 and replaced by Lisbon–Hendaye sleeping car service connecting at Hendaye with Paris TGV (qv).

Sugar (USRS)
Sand.

Sugar puffs (RS)
BR Class 03 six-wheeled diesel-mechanical locos. From the resemblance of their chimneys to those of locos illustrated on packets of Sugar Puffs cereal.

Suicide pits (LT)
Pits placed between the running rails for the full length of the platforms at London tube tunnel stations to frustrate suicide attempts and afford some measure of protection from serious injury to anyone falling on to the track. Installed from 1926 onwards following the extreme difficulty encountered in extricating from beneath trains the bodies of those committing or attempting suicide at such stations. Officially known as 'Platform Safety Pits'.

Suisse–Arlberg–Vienne Express
A *CIWL* service introduced 1924.

Sulzers (RS)
Any BR loco equipped with Sulzer diesel engines, particularly class 26/27.

Summer uniform (RS)
Waterproofs and leggings.

Sunbuckle (USRS)
Rails distorted by the heat of the sun.

Sunday Pullman Limited
A LB&SCR service between London (Victoria) and Brighton, introduced 1898. A description rather than a train title.

Sunday Scotsman
The Sunday version of Flying Scotsman (qv) until 1939.

Sundries [traffic] (obs)
Consignments of less than one ton which did not require exclusive use of a wagon and were carried at the lower rates charged for freight train transport.

Sunflower (RS)
The BR AWS (qv) visual indicator in driving cabs; from its appearance.

Sunny South Express
A service between Liverpool (Lime St.)/Manchester (London Rd) and Brighton/Eastbourne/Ramsgate, so named 1927. Name dropped 1939.

Sunny South Sam
SR (*1*) publicity figure, a smiling, smartly uniformed, idealized passenger guard, 'always at your service', conceived by the SR publicity department in 1930 and featured in posters and advertisements, etc.

Sunset Limited
Southern Pacific RR express between New Orleans, Los Angeles and San Francisco,

introduced on a weekly basis with a 75 h journey time in 1894. The longest through passenger working in the US (2,480 m) in 1911. Daily service started in 1913. Restored by Amtrak but between Los Angeles and New Orleans only. Extended to Miami in 1993, the first regular train service to traverse the USA from coast to coast.

Sunset Route, The
Slogan of the Southern Pacific RR.

Sunshine Express
Winter season *CIWL* Pullman service between Cairo and Luxor, introduced 1928, ceased 1939.

SuO
Sundays Only.

Super Chief
The flagship of the AT&SF RR, the first high speed diesel-hauled service between Chicago and the Pacific Coast (Los Angeles), introduced in May 1936, 2,228 m in 39 h 45 min. Conveyed Los Angeles sleepers from New York off the Twentieth Century Limited and the Broadway Limited, with similar facilities eastbound. In 1936 it was the world's fastest train, covering the 202.4 m La Junta–Dodge City in 145 min (average 83.7 mph). Operated from 1937 with streamlined diesel sets, the first diesel-powered all-Pullman streamlined sets. Revived by Amtrak in 1971, 2,222 m in 40 h, name dropped 1974, now called the South West Chief.

Super Clauds
GER Claud (qv) locos, with Belpaire firebox.

Super-Continental
A CNR service between Toronto, Montreal and Vancouver, introduced in 1955 with a schedule of 72 h 5 min eastbound.

Superelevation
See Cant.

Super Gronks/Grunts (RS)
BR class 09 locos.

Superheater
An apparatus which raises the temperature and volume of the steam leaving the boiler of a loco.

Superliners
Amtrak double-deck coaches introduced on long-distance services in 1979.

Super Mountain (US)
A steam loco with 4–10–2 wheel
arrangement.
Superpointe (Fr)
A weekend which coincides with a public
holiday, causing a major traffic peak.
Super-rapido (It)
A high-speed emu train with
supplementary fare.
Super Scuds (RS)
BR class 159 dmus; after the Scud missile.
Super Sprinters (RS)
BR class 155/156 dmus.
Supertram
South Yorkshire Supertram (qv).
Surface contact (obs)
A system of current collection for tramways
(3) in which the traction current was taken
up from studs in the road surface between
the rails by a magnetic contact skate on the
vehicle. Once the vehicle had passed, the
studs retracted and the electric current was
cut off (in theory, not always in practice).
Surface lines
Term used by LT to distinguish the
Metropolitan, Hammersmith & City,
Circle, District, and East London lines,
with their 'full size' loading gauge from the
smaller deep level *tube* lines. Sometimes
also referred to as the sub-surface lines.
Surfaceman
A track maintenance worker, repairing and
checking the permanent way.
Surface Raiders (RS)(obs)
BR Southern Region emus. From the
initials.
Surfing (S)
A 'thrill game' in which juveniles and
adolescents ride on the roofs and sides of
trains, standing upright and dodging
overhead wires and structures. Originated
in Rio de Janeiro in the 1980s.
Susie Q
see Suzy Q.
Suspended joint
A connection between the ends of two rails
by fishplates when they project beyond the
ends of the last supporting chairs.
Sussex Scot
A BR service between Glasgow and

Brighton via Reading, introduced in 1988.
Edinburgh–Oxford–London–Brighton
service 1992.
Suzy Q (US)
Nickname of the New York, Susquehanna
& Western RR.
SV
BR IC 225 coach (Service Vehicle), with
kitchen, and buffet/bar/dining area.
SV (It)
Società Veneta, operating local rlys in
Veneto province.
SVR
1. Swansea Valley Rly, inc 1847, opened
   Swansea–Glais 1852, renamed Swansea
   Vale Rly 1855, opened Swansea–
   Pontardarwe 1860, leased by Midland
   Rly 1874, part of Midland Rly 1876.
2. Severn Valley Rly (qv).
SW (on a lineside board)
Instruction to drivers to sound whistle.
SW (Ger)
see Schindler Waggon.
Swammies (RS)
L&NWR four-cylinder compound 0–8–0
locos, also L&NER large-boilered 2–8–0s
(Big Swammies).
Swanage Rly
Swanage Rly Co., a preserved line using
the former BR Wareham–Swanage branch,
first section reopened 1979.
SW&W
South Wales & West Rlys (qv).
Swan necks (RS)
L&SWR Beattie 2–4–0T. From their tall
slim chimneys.
Swansea District Line
Neath–Felin Fran–Llandeilo Junc.
Swansea Pullman
A service introduced in 1967 between
London (Paddington) and Swansea, using
Midland Pullman (qv) mu sets. Ceased
1973.
Swap body
Demountable freight containers which can
be lifted on and off road trucks, rail wagons
and ships. Swap bodies must conform to
European standards, usually those laid
down by the *UIC* (qv). They carry a coding
plate giving details of gauge profile and a

code number indicating height and width in millimetres.

SWB wagon
A Short Wheelbase (four-wheel) wagon.

Sweat box (RS)
A slewing or alignment jack requiring much muscular effort.

Swedey/Sweedie (RS)(obs)
The GER, its trains, its locos, or its staff.

Swedish Scrubber (RS)
A former newspaper van converted in Sweden in 1991 by Mähler & Söner into a rail-cleaning unit for use on BR mainly in the leaf-fall season.

Swellhead (USRS)
A conductor (3). Fully in charge of the train, and therefore often apt to put on airs.

Sweltrack
South West London Transport Conference, concerned with improvement of public transport provision in south-west London area, including surface access to London Airport (Heathrow).

Swept envelope
See Kinematic envelope.

SWIFT
South Wales Integrated Fast Transit; a consortium of six local authorities in the Cardiff/Glamorgan area working 'in partnership' with TOCs (2) (qv), Network Rail (qv) and local bus operators to improve public transport in the area by end 2007.

Swift & Delightful
Nickname for S&DJR.

Swing (USRS)
1. A brakeman stationed in the middle of a train.
2. Additional staff allocated to very long trains or other difficult workings.

Swing a bug, to (USRS)
To brake.

Swing bolster
A bolster (qv) able to swing laterally in relation to the bogie/truck to reduce lateral blows and shocks transmitted to the body of the vehicle and also to cushion the body momentum action on the truck frames and the wheel flanges.

Swinger
1. (RS) An additional coach on a train.
2. (RS) Any vehicle (usually unbraked) at the back of a fully fitted train.
3. (LTRS) A collector shoe of a car when out of alignment.
4. (LTRS) The bracket supporting cables which are suspended from the lineside compressed air main on open air sections.
5. (LTRS) An unbraked unit on a train following a defect.
6. (RS)(obs) A heavy and long loose-coupled train.

Swinging window (LTRS)
A hinged car window not correctly seated in its catch.

Swing link
Part of the suspension system of many types of truck/bogie, consisting of a metal bar, pivoted at each end.

Switch, to (US)
To shunt.

Switches
Alternative term for points (qv) (hence Switchman (qv)), originating in US but increasingly becoming the generally accepted form (preferred in BSI glossary). *See also* Points; Switch engine; Switching; Switch rails; Turnout; Heel; Toe.

Switchback
1. A rly in mountainous area laid out in zigzag pattern to minimize gradients. At the end of each gradient is a 'reversing station' where the train is 'switched back' or reversed in direction ready to tackle the next gradient.
2. A rly constructed with alternate steep ascents and descents so that momentum achieved in descents provides enough, or almost enough, power to negotiate the ascents.

Switch engine/switcher (US)
A shunting loco.

Switch heel
see Heel.

Switch hog (USRS)
A yardmaster.

Switching (US)
Shunting. Hence switching yard.

Switching company (US)
An undertaking principally or solely engaged in providing shunting or terminal facilities.

Switching out
Linking block instruments either side of a signal box and closing it down. More than one box may be switched out at the same time to provide a very long block section between the two boxes remaining open. Also 'switching in', for the reverse process.

Switch line/railroad
Switching company (qv).

Switchman (US)
A yard brakeman.

Switch monkey (USRS)
A shunter or switchman.

Switch rails
The rails in points (qv) or switches (qv) which move in relation to the stock rails (qv) to secure a change in direction by the train. *See also* Points.

Switch toe
see Toe/switch toe.

Switzerland Express
A *CIWL* service Calais–Lucerne, introduced 1890.

SWMR
South Wales Mineral Rly, inc 1853, Glyncorrwg to Briton Ferry, opened 1860–2, worked by GWR from 1908, part of GWR 1923.

SWR
1. South Wales Rly, Grange Court Junction near Gloucester to Cardiff, Swansea, Carmarthen and Neyland, inc 1845, first section opened 1850. Amalgamated with GWR 1863.
2. Saffron Walden Rly, inc 1861, 1863, Audley End–Saffron Walden–Bartlow, opened 1865, 1866. Part of the GER, 1877.

SWT
South West Trains (qv).

SX
Saturdays excepted. Not always understood by passengers reading station time sheets; rly officials are sometimes asked 'Where is platform 3 SX?'

Sybic
Acronym for synchronous bi-current, an electric loco fitted with synchronous traction motor for operating with two voltages.

SYD&GR
South Yorkshire, Doncaster & Goole Rly, inc 1847, 1848, Barnsley–Swinton–Doncaster and branches. Opened 1849, Swinton to Doncaster and Mexborough to Elsecar, 1850. Retitled SYR&RDN (qv) 1850.

SYJR
1. South Yorkshire Junction Rly, inc 1890. Conisborough to Wrangbrook Junc (with H&BR), opened 1894, worked by H&BR. Part of NER 1922.
2. South Yorkshire Joint Rly, Kirk Sandall Junc (with GCR)–Tickhill–Dinnington/ Firbeck Colliery. Inc 1903, opened 1909, 1926, 1929. Passenger service (Shireoaks–Doncaster) 1910–29. GCR, L&YR, GNR from 1909, LM&SR & L&NER from 1923–47.

Sykes
see Syx.

Sykes' lock and block
see Lock and block.

Syphons (RS)
BR class 37 diesel-electric locos.

SYR
South Yorkshire Rly: *see* SYD&GR; SYR&RDN.

SYR&RDN
South Yorkshire Rly and River Dun [Don] Navigation, inc 1850, new title of SYD&GR (qv). Extended to Barnsley 1851, to Thorne 1856 and to Keadby 1859. Operated by and leased to MS&LR 1864. Part of MS&LR 1874.

SYTRAL
The public transport authority of the city of Lyon, France, operating metro, trams (3), buses and trolleybuses.

Syx
Trade mark of W.R. Sykes' Interlocking Signal Co. Ltd, Clapham, London, manufacturers of rly signalling equipment, founded by W.R. Sykes, 1899.

SZ
Slovenske Zeleznice; Slovenian Rlys, formed from part of *JZ* (qv).

SZD
USSR Rlys, now *RZD* (qv).

T

T

1. Trailer car.

2. Tank engine.

T2

CIWL sleeping car containing small two-berth compartments on two levels.

T3

CIWL sleeping car containing three-berth (upper, middle and lower) compartments.

TA

Training Allowance.

TAA (Fr)

Train Autos Accompagnés; equivalent of day Motorail (qv) services, introduced 1957. *See also TAC; TAJ*.

Table

A turntable (qv).

TAC (Fr)

Train Auto Couchettes; Motorail type service with sleeping accommodation. Renamed *Auto-Trains* (qv), 1994. *See also TAA; TAJ*.

Tache ovale

This French term meaning 'oval spot' is now in use in Britain to describe a fatigue crack in the railhead (qv). Similar kidney-shaped fatigue cracks may also appear elsewhere on the rail profile and are then sometimes described as of '*tache ovale* type'.

Tackhead (USRS)

A yard clerk.

Tacot (Fr)

A ramshackle local train. *See also Tortillard*.

TACV (obs)

Tracked Air Cushion Vehicle; developed by THL (qv).

Tadpole

1. GWR TC for open fish truck.

2. (RS)(obs) BR (S) demu sets class 206, type 3R, made up from DMB and TC of the narrow Hastings line conformation, and DTS of standard width, the whole giving the appearance of a tadpole.

TAF (Sp)(obs)

Tren Automoteur Fiat; express diesel railcar sets used in Spain and Portugal in the 1950s and 1960s.

Taff Bargoed Joint

Inc 1867, opened 1875, 1876, Nelson & Llancaiach to Dowlais, GWR and Rhymney, part of GWR 1922.

Taff Vale Judgement

When its employee members of the ASRS were on strike in 1900, the TVR was granted an injunction against the Union, which was reversed by the Court of Appeal but upheld by the House of Lords in 1901. This established that a trade union could be sued and legally restrained from picketing and offering violence to those employees who remained at work. As a result, the TVR recovered £24,000 damages from the ASRS. The law was subsequently altered.

Taffy

Nickname for the L&NWR.

Tag, The (US)

Nickname for Tennessee, Alabama & Georgia RR (formerly the Chattanooga System). From the initials.

Tail end Charlie (RS)

Freight train guard.

Tail lamp

Invariably carried on the last vehicle of a train, day and night, to indicate the train is complete.

Tail over her back (USRS)(obs)
A full head of steam, with a plume of steam blowing back like a tail from the safety valve.

Tail rope (obs)
A rope with hook at each end used for moving wagons when the shunting engine was working on a parallel track; also called a tow rope/chain. The term was also used to denote the lower rope of a counterbalance incline or funicular when the winding equipment was at the lower end of the line.

Tail, to (RS)
To attach coaches, wagons or vans to the rear end of a train.

Tail traffic (RS)
Non-passenger-carrying vehicles, mainly milk vans, luggage vans, newspaper vans and horse boxes, attached to the rear end of a passenger train. *See also* Passenger traffic.

Tail wag (RS)
Sideways motion at the rear of a train.

TAJ (Fr)
Train Auto Jour; day Motorail (qv) type trains, introduced 1967, now *TAA* (qv). *See also TAA; TAC*.

Taj Express
A day service New Dehli–Agra–Gwalior.

Take the dolly, to (RS)
To make a movement authorized by a shunt signal.

Take the rubber out [of them], to (USRS)
To pull out or disconnect brake air hoses.

Take minutes, to (USRS)
To stop for lunch.

Taktfahrplan
Introduced on Swiss Rlys in 1982, a regular-interval, patterned, symmetrical timetable in which fast and stopping trains connect with one another and as far as possible with buses, to provide a seamless through journey. This resulted in a half billion increase in the number of rail users. The Swiss system has since been copied in Germany (Rhine Palatinate), France (Toulouse region) and Italy (Piedmont region).

Talbot
Waggonfabrik Talbot, based at Aachen, Germany; rly carriage, wagon and tramcar builders. Controlled by Duewag (qv) from the 1960s.

TALGO (Sp)
Tren Articulado Ligero Goicoechea–Oriol. An ultra-lightweight articulated train design with short and low-slung car bodies, each body resting on a single pair of independent steered half-axles, the other end carried on the axles of the adjoining car. Invented by an army engineer, Alejandro Goicoechea, and sponsored by Sr Oriol. Prototype tested in Spain in 1941. ACF (qv) built the first complete trains in the US in 1949 and these ran regularly in service between Irun and Madrid from summer 1950. In 1969, *TALGO* trains began to run internationally in Europe, following the development of devices to facilitate gauge change at the Spanish frontier. *See also Barcelona TALGO; Catalan TALGO*; Pablo Casals; *Paris–Madrid TALGO*.

Talisman
An express between London (Kings Cross) and Edinburgh, introduced 1956 to replace the Coronation (qv). Pullman cars included until 1965. Name dropped 1968, revived 1972.

Tallowpot (USRS)(obs)
A steam loco fireman. It was one of the fireman's duties to draw and use a supply of tallow for cleaning and lubricating purposes.

Talyllyn
Talyllyn Rly, 2 ft 3 in/686 mm gauge, Tywyn to Abergynolwyn and Nant Gwernol, inc 1865, opened 1866 principally for slate but also carrying passenger traffic. Closed 1950 at end of summer season, reopened 1951 as Britain's first preserved line.

Tamp, to
To compact ballast under the sleepers, hence tamping machine.

Tanat Valley
Porthywaen Junction to Blodwell Junction and Llangynog, LRO 1898, opened 1904, worked by Cambrian, part of GWR from 1922.

T&BR
Tenbury & Bewdley Rly, inc 1860, opened 1864, worked by GWR, part of GWR from 1869.

T&CLR
Timoleague & Courtmacsherry Light Rly, Ireland, Ballinascarthy to Courtmacsherry, inc 1888, opened 1890, 1891, 5 ft 3 in/1,600 mm gauge, part of GSR from 1924, CIE 1945, regular passenger services ceased 1947, closed 1961.

T&DLR
Tralee & Dingle Light Rly, Ireland, 3 ft/914 mm gauge, inc 1888, Tralee to Dingle and branch to Castlegregory. Opened 1891, part of GSR 1925, CIE 1945. Closed to passengers 1939, closed entirely 1953.

Tandem working
Two locos coupled together with power applied separately, a driver in each, both drivers able to apply brakes throughout the train. *See also* Multiple working.

T&FGR
Tottenham & Forest Gate Rly, inc 1890, South Tottenham (T&HJR) to Woodgrange Park (LT&SR), jointly owned by Midland and LT&SR, opened 1894. Midland from 1912, LM&SR 1923.

T&HJR
Tottenham & Hampstead Junction Rly, inc 1862, Tottenham North Junction (GER) to Highgate Road and Gospel Oak (HJR), opened 1868. Jointly vested in Midland and GER 1902, LM&SR/L&NER 1923–47.

T&LRA/T&LRTA
Tramways & Light Rlys Association founded 1897, renamed Tramways & Light Railways & Transport Association (T&LRTA), 1930, became Public Service Transport Association 1939. *See* PTA.

T&MLR
Torrington & Marland Light Rly, 3 ft gauge, 8 m, opened 1880 and operated by the North Devon Clay Co. No public passenger or freight traffic carried. Part of its length was used for the ND&CJLR (qv) and was then converted to standard gauge. The remaining operation, with a standard gauge siding and diesel traction on both gauges, continued until 1982.

T&NDR
Tiverton & North Devon Rly, Tiverton to Morebath Junc, inc 1875, opened 1884, part of GWR from 1894.

T&RW
Tramway & Railway World, founded as *Railway World* 1892, and soon renamed *T&RW*. Renamed *Transport World* 1934. Mainly concerned with tramways (*3*), and trolleybuses and (in later years) motor buses.

T&TM
Transport & Travel Monthly, a renaming of *R&TM* (qv) in 1920, merged with *RM* (qv) from January 1923.

T&UT
Tramways & Urban Transit, a retitling of *LR&MT* (qv) from January 1998.

T&V
Trespass and Vandalism. *See also* Route crime.

Tanfield Waggonway
Opened 1725, horse-hauled over wooden rails, to carry coal from Tanfield collieries to Dunston staithes on the river Tyne at Gateshead. Converted to a rly by 1839 including inclines operated by steam winding engines and self-acting rope inclines. Part of NER, 1854. Sunniside to Causey Arch section operated as a preserved line from 1977.

Tangos (RS)
GNR 2–8–0 locos of 1914 (L&NER O1/O2). From the contemporary dance craze.

Tank
1. (US) A loco with 4–6–6 wheel arrangement.
2. (USRS) Loco tender.

Tank engine
A steam loco carrying its water supply in tanks placed around the boiler and with a small supply of coal in a bunker behind the footplate, rather than in a separate hauled tender. Designated T in Whyte notation (qv). *See also* Pannier tank; Saddle tank; Side tank; Well tank; Wing tank.

Tanker (US)
Tank wagon (qv).

Tankflat
A form of Warflat (qv) with shorter length and fishbelly side girders.

Tank stock (LTRS)
MDR 'F' stock trains (1920). Also known as 'Salmon tins' (qv).
Tank, The (RS)(obs)
The GCR Works at Gorton, Manchester. From a high water tank which was a prominent feature.
Tank town (USRS)
A community built around a point where steam locos could take on water. (e.g. Las Vegas). *See also* Jerkwater town.
Tank transporter
A wagon adapted to carry army tanks.
Tank wagon
A vehicle with a large container for carrying liquids or gases.
Tanner-oner (RS)
A GWR 2–6–2T of the 61XX series. From 'tanner', slang for sixpence (6*d*).
Tanzam
3 ft 6 in/1,067 mm gauge line between Kapiri Mposhi, Zambia, and Dar-es-Salaam, Tanzania (1,154 m/1,857 km). Opened 1975. Also known as the Great Uhuru (Freedom) Rly or the TZR. Administered by TAZARA (qv).
Tap line (US)
Alternative term for a short line (qv); it 'taps' a main line, giving access between it and industrial, military, etc. complexes.
Tapper (RS)(obs)
A C&W examiner. From wheel tapper (qv).
TAR
Trans-Australian Rly; Port Augusta–Kalgoorlie.
Target (RS)
A device giving a visual indication of the direction in which a pair of points has been set.
Tariff van (obs)
A freight train brake van (qv). The usage reflects the fact that it was a vehicle earning revenue, as distinct from a brake van on work trains (qv) or breakdown trains (qv).
Tarka line
BR brand name for Exeter–Barnstaple line, 1989.
Tartan Arrow
A road haulage firm which began to operate

company trains of containers and parcels traffic between London and Glasgow in 1967, constructing special depots at Kentish Town and Bridgeton, Glasgow. Road journey times were cut by half. The operation was nationalized into the THC (qv) in 1967 and became part of NFC (qv) in 1969. The service ceased in 1976.
Tasmanian Government Rlys
see TGR.
Tauern Express
A service between Ostend (connecting with sailings to and from UK), Munich, Klagenfurt and Ljubljana, with through portion to Belgrade, introduced 1950. Ceased 1987.
Tauern Line
[Salzburg]–Schwarzach–St Veit–Spittal–[Villach–Trieste–Belgrade].
Tauern Orient Express
A service between Munich and Belgrade, with through coach to Istanbul. Ceased 1979.
Taurus/Toros Express
A *CIWL* restaurant and sleeping car service between Istanbul (Haydarpasa), Aleppo and Baghdad/Cairo. Introduced 1930, as an extension of the Simplon–Orient express, using road and air transport to cover rail gaps in the Middle East. Re-routed via Ankara, 1935. All-rail service to and from Baghdad, 1940. Revived after WW2, Istanbul–Baghdad, connecting at Istanbul with the Paris service (Simplon Orient, (qv)). Subsequently confined to Turkish territory owing to political disputes. *See also* Baghdad Rly.
TAV (It)
Treno Alta Velocità; high-speed train. Also the initials of a co. owned by *FS* (qv) and certain financial institutions which controls the Italian high-speed rail network.
Taw Valley
see NDR.
Taxis (RS)
GWR 0–6–2T class 66XX.
TAZARA
Tanzania–Zambia Rly Authority. *See also* Tanzam.

T-bana
Tunnel-bana, Stockholm Underground
Rlys.
TBCF
see TCF.
TBCK
BR Trailer Brake Composite coach.
TBF
BR Trailer Brake First class, brake coach
with some First class seating.
T-board
Board marking the termination of a temporary speed restriction. *See also* C-board.
TBS
1. BR Trailer Brake Second/Standard class,
   passenger brake coach in a dmu set with
   some Second/Standard class seating.
2. Transmission-based Signalling, in which
   a micro-processor on the train
   communicates with a central computer,
   registering the train's position and
   speed. 'Advice' is then signalled back to
   the train regarding its continuing
   progress within the margins of its safety.
TBS/TBTCS
Transmission Based Train Control System,
using shore (qv) radio to transmit
signalling data to on-board (qv) displays,
eliminating the need for trackside signals.
See also TCS; NMC.
TBSK
BR Trailer Brake Second/Standard class
with corridor and compartments.
TBSL
TBS (*1*) with Lavatory.
TBSO
BR Trailer Brake coach with open-plan
seating.
TC
1. Trailer Composite – BR dmu trailer with
   First and Second/Standard class seating.
2. Traffic Circular: LT equivalent of
   Working Notice (qv). Originally called
   Joint [Weekly] Circular.
3. BR (S) control trailer corridor sets for
   Bournemouth electrification 1967, two
   driving trailer Second/Standard class
   and one brake coach Second/Standard
   class, 3-TC; also the same plus a First
   class trailer car, 4-TC; also six-car

trailer corridor units formed of 4-COR
cars – two driving brake Second/
Standard class, three trailer cars
Second/Standard class and one trailer
composite car, 6-TC.
4. Transportation Corps (US). *See* USATC.
5. Through Coach/Carriage (qv).
TCC
Traffic Control Centre. A refinement of
CTC (qv), introduced in US *c.* 1957,
allowing one man to control signalling on
up to 100 m of single track line. By
pressing the appropriate buttons, the
controller makes all the necessary point
and signal movements at chosen locations.
TCDD
*Türkïye Cumhuriyeti Devlet Demiryollari
Isletmesi*; Turkish State Rlys. 8,439 km.
TCF
To be Called For; parcels consigned to be
collected by consignee at destination
station.
TCK
TC (*1*) with corridor and compartment
seating.
TCL
TC (*1*) with Lavatory.
TCO
Train Crew Operated level crossing; at
which the train stops and the driver or guard
descends to operate the gates or barriers.
T-COD
Track Circuit Operating Device, which can
can be placed on the track to operate the
track circuit (qv), holding a signal at
danger to provide protection for a disabled
train, hand trolley, emergency engineering
work, etc. *See also* Track circuit [operating]
clips, Track circuits.
TCS
1. Train Control System; a moving block
   (qv) signalling system incorporating
   digital radio communication between
   NMC (qv) and train cabs via balises
   (qv) in which on board computers (qv)
   receive signalling data and instructions,
   process them and inform drivers via
   control panels in the cabs. The
   responses of drivers are monitored to
   ensure compliance with safe working of

trains. ETCS (European Train Control System) is proposed for interoperability in Europe but its high cost may delay implementation.

2. Transportation Control System; a computer-based system recording real-time information regarding locos, wagons and services, linkable with rail customers' own computer systems. Operated by UP (qv).

TCSOL
TC (*1*) with a mix of open-plan and compartment seating and with Lavatory cubicle.

TCV
BR Tiered Car Van; an end-door car carrier with space for two motor cars in the well between the bogies and up to four on an intermediate hydraulically raised floor.

TD
Train Description [number], the number allocated to a specific train, usually identifying its category, destination, route and serial number.

TDM
Time Division Multiplex; a control system for the remote working of traction power units in push/pull formations, introduced by BR in 1979. Also used in mu operation of locos.

TDZ
Turkmenistan Rlys; 2,440 km of 1,520 mm gauge.

Tea kettle (USRS)
An elderly loco.

TEB
Telephone Enquiry Bureau (BR).

TEC
Transports Européens Combinés; European container services operated under the auspices of Intercontainer (qv).

Teddy Bears (RS)
GNR 0–6–2T, introduced 1907. After the children's teddy bears which first appeared in that year. Also Ivatt 2–6–2T and BR class 14 diesel-hydraulic locos, some of which were eventually sold to the NCB.

TEE
Trans-Europ Express. A network of supplementary fare, all-First Class luxury trains, with on-board customs and immigration facilities, introduced in 1957 to run in and between France, Belgium, Luxembourg, Italy, West Germany, Switzerland and Holland. Conceived by F.Q. den Hollander, president of NS (*1*). Managed by *SNCF, SNCB, CFL, SBB* and NS (*1*) (and *RENFE* when Spanish workings were added from 1969). In decline from 1982–5, virtually abandoned with the cessation of the last international workings in 1988. Replaced by the EC network (qv).

TEEM
Trans-Europ Express Marchandises; fast international freight services, introduced 1961.

Tees–Thames Express
A service between Saltburn and London (Kings Cross), calling at principal stations to York, introduced 1959, replacing Tees–Thames Link (Middlesbrough–Doncaster (connection to London)), an 'Up' dmu headboarded train introduced October 1958. Name very soon discarded.

Tees–Tyne Pullman
An all-Pullman train between London (Kings Cross) and Newcastle, introduced 1948, ceased 1976. Relaunched as a 3 h 12 min HST service in 1985.

Teifi Valley
Pencader–Newcastle Emlyn, former BR branch partly reopened as 2 ft/609 mm gauge tourist/pleasure line, 1986.

Teign Valley Line
Heathfield–Christow–Exeter (City Basin Junc). *See also* TVR (*2*).

Teleferica (It)
Aerial cableway/ropeway. *See* Aerial rly/ropeway.

Téléphérique/Transport téléphérique (Fr)
Aerial rly/ropeway (qv).

Telescoping
The manner in which a rly coach was apt to force itself into the adjoining one in a serious collision, resembling the action of closing a telescope. Likelihood much reduced by modern methods of coach construction.

Télésiège (Fr)
Chairlift.
Telltales (USRS)
Strips of material hung in front of bridges and tunnel mouths, etc. to warn men on the roofs of wagons.
Telpher/way
Aerial rly/ropeway (qv).
TEN
Trans-Euro Nacht/Nuit/Night; name used from 1980 for the pool of *DSG* and *CIWL* sleeping cars leased to West German, French, Swiss, Italian, Belgian, Dutch, Austrian, Danish and Luxembourg rlys for international services. The pool, which was financed by the rly administrations involved and *Eurofima* (qv), was formed in 1971–2; the first services were operated in 1974 and new stock was added subsequently. Ceased 1994.
Tenbury
Tenbury Rly, Woofferton Junction to Tenbury Junction, inc 1859, opened 1861, worked by S&H, transferred to L&NWR and GWR 1869, LM&SR and GWR from 1923–47.
Tenby & Carmarthen Bay Express
Summer service between London (Paddington), Tenby and Pembroke Dock, introduced 1928.
Tench
A 50-ton bogie wagon with doors used by engineers for carrying rails and sleepers.
Tender-cab
A cab similar to that on the loco, built on the forward end of a tender to provide shelter to the engine crew when the loco is moving tender first or shunting. Adopted by the Midland Rly 1908, also used on some overseas rlys.
Tender dip (obs)
The pick-up scoop used for raising water from water troughs (qv). *See* Scoop (*2*).
Tender engine
A steam loco hauling its supply of coal and water in a separate vehicle (tender).
Tender first
A steam tender loco running backwards, with its tender in front.
Tenderlok[omotive] (Ger)
A tank engine.

Ten foot
The space between parallel sets of double tracks, which is approximately this width (i.e. 3.05 metres). Also any other space between tracks which measures substantially more than 6 ft/1.83 metres.
Tennants (RS)
NER 2–4–0 locos of 1884–5 built when the co. was temporarily without a loco superintendent and the general manager, Henry Tennant, was in charge of the loco department.
TEN-T
Trans-European Networks. Key rail passenger and freight routes across Europe declared 'of European interest' and supported financially by the EC.
Ten wheeler (US)
Term for a steam loco with 4–6–0 wheel arrangement.
TER
1. (Fr) *Transport Express Régional*: co-ordinated *SNCF* rail or road local services sponsored by the Departmental or Regional Authority. Identifiable by distinctive liveries and logos. *See also Métrolor*.
2. (Sp) *Tren Español Rapido*; express diesel railcars, successors to *TAF* (qv).
TERFN
Trans-European Rail Freight Network; launched March 2003, giving EC rail freight operators access and planning rights to the European rail network; also launching negotiations to establish common technical and safety standards and promoting operation of rail freight services between all EC member-states.
Terminal company (US)
Switching company (qv).
Termination indicator
Sign marking the conclusion of a TRS/TSR (qv).
Terminator (RS)
Normally used in combination with a station name to denote a train which will terminate at that station.
Termite
GWR TC for a Third class coach (nine types).

Terra firma, on (RS)
A derailment at catch points.
Terriers (RS)
LB&SCR Stroudley 0–6–0T, introduced 1872. *See also* Rooters.
TESCOs
Train Engineering Service Companies. Four organizations set up to service rolling stock after the privatization of British rlys under the Railways Act, 1993.
Tevan
GWR TC for Mica (qv) converted to carry tea traffic.
Texas (US)
Term for a steam loco with 2–10–4 wheel arrangement. The first was built for the Texas & Pacific RR.
Texas Eagle
A St Louis–Dallas–San Antonio service of the Missouri Pacific RR, introduced 1948. Renamed Aztec Eagle 1958 and extended to El Paso with through cars St Louis–Mexico City from 1962 until 1969. Now Texas Eagle again and operated by Amtrak between Chicago, Dallas and El Paso.
TF
Trailer First; a BR First class trailer with side-corridor and compartments.
TfL
Transport for London. Executive body responsible from 2000 under the Mayor of London and Greater London Authority (established by Greater London Act, 2000) for implementing London's transport strategy. Its remit embraces highways, Underground, local rail, light rail, bus, taxi and Thames river services. Replaced LRT (qv) and LUL (qv). After political delays over acceptance of the PPP (qv), TfL assumed full control of London Underground from 15 July 2003.
TFM
Trackside Functional Modules. Modules which provide increased reliability for signal equipment in areas subject to a high level of traction current interference. Incorporating an interface with ATP (qv).

TFOLH
A TF (qv) with Open plan seating, Lavatory and Handbrake.
TGR
Tasmanian Government Rlys, formed 1872, part of ANR (qv), 1976. 3 ft 6 in/1,067 mm (and originally also 2 ft/609 mm) gauge. All regular passenger services ceased 1978.
TGS
BR Trailer Guard Second/Standard class; HST trailer with guard's accommodation and parcels area.
TGV
Trains à Grand Vitesse; the *SNCF*'s very high speed electric trains and train services, travelling for the greater part of their run over purpose-built rlys. Introduced 1981. *TGV–PSE* = Paris–Lyon; *TGV–A* (Atlantique) = Paris–Le Mans/Tours; *TGV–Nord* = Paris–Channel Tunnel/Brussels. *TGV–Sud* = Lyon–Marseille; TGV–Est = Paris–Alsace (under construction).
THALYS
Four-voltage *TGV* (qv) type train sets for Paris–Brussels–Amsterdam–Cologne service, 1997.
Thames (obs)
NSE brand name introduced 1989 for services between Paddington–Reading–Oxford/Bedwyn; branches Henley, Marlow, Bourne End; and Oxford–Bicester/Banbury. *See also* Thames Trains.
Thames–Clyde Express
A service between London (St Pancras) and Glasgow (St Enoch) introduced 1927. Restored 1949. Name dropped 1975 when it ceased to run from and to London.
Thames–Forth Express
A service between London (St Pancras), Leeds and Edinburgh (Waverley), introduced 1927. Ceased 1939. *See also* Waverley.
Thames–Gatwick
Brand name for Reading–Guildford–Gatwick Airport services (some to and from Oxford), from 1993.
Thameslink Rail Ltd
Brand name for dual-voltage emu services

linking stations north and south of London (Bedford/Luton–Brighton/Sevenoaks/Guildford, etc.) using the reopened Farringdon–Blackfriars line, introduced from 1988. Thameslink Rail Ltd, TOU (qv) from 1994. A TOC (2) (qv), 1997, operating services between Bedford/Luton and Gatwick Airport/ Brighton, also local services between Luton and south-west London via the Wimbledon–Sutton line. Expansion of services proposed after infrastructure improvements – *see* Thameslink 2000. Franchise to include the former services of WAGN (qv) into Kings Cross station from 2006.

Thameslink 2000
Expansion of Thameslink services including a new tunnel at Kings Cross, to serve Hertford, Welwyn Garden City, Stevenage, etc., first proposed in 1988.

Thames Trains Ltd
A TOU (qv), 1994. A TOC (2) (qv), 1996, operating suburban services in west London and the Thames valley, also Reading–Oxford–Stratford upon Avon/Worcester–Hereford; Oxford–Bicester; Oxford–Bristol; Reading–Basingstoke; Reading–Newbury–Bedwyn; and Reading–Guildford–Gatwick Airport. Part of First Group under the brand name First Great Western Link from April 2004. See First Great Western.

Thames Valley Rly/Line
Strawberry Hill–Shepperton, inc 1862 as Metropolitan & Thames Valley Rly, opened 1864, part of L&SWR from 1865.

Thanet Belle
An all-Pullman summer service between London (Victoria), Margate and Ramsgate, introduced 1948, renamed Kentish Belle (qv) 1951.

Thanet Pullman Limited
An all-Pullman First Class only Sunday service London (Victoria), Margate, Broadstairs and Ramsgate, introduced 1921. As an independent train, it ran in summer only and ceased in 1928.

THC
Transport Holding Company; a statutory company set up under the Transport Act, 1962 to own and manage all transport investments of the former BTC except those transferred to BRB, LTB, BTDB and British Waterways Board. Following the Transport Act 1968, its bus businesses were vested in the National Bus Co. or the Scottish Transport Group, and its road haulage and shipping interests in the NFC. The residue of travel and tourism interests were subsequently also sold off, including Thomas Cook & Son Ltd (in 1972). The residual BR activities of the BTA (qv) became a wholly owned subsidiary of the BRB, retaining the name BTA Ltd.

Theatre-type indicator
Indicator used in conjunction with colour-light signals, showing the platform, line number or letter designation of the route set up by the signalman (e.g. ML = Main Line). From the device placed by the stage of a theatre to indicate the number of the scene or turn in progress.

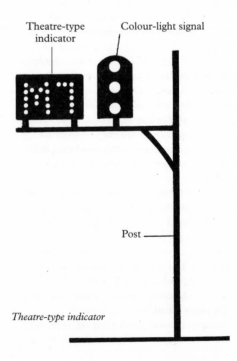

Theatre-type indicator | Colour-light signal

Post

Theatre-type indicator

Thermit weld
An alumino-thermic process for welding rails together to form a continuous surface.

Thick as a bag (RS)
Very foggy.

Thick work (RS)
Points (qv) and crossings (1) (qv); Special work (qv).

Thin oil engine (RS)(obs)
A diesel loco.

Thin red line (RS)(obs)
The marking on loco steam pressure dials indicating a full head of steam.

Third class
In Britain (apart from the rare examples of Fourth class (qv)) the cheapest class of passenger accommodation. Renamed Second class, 1956, further renamed Standard class, 1987. Third class was withdrawn on west European rlys (except in Portugal and Spain) in 1956; in Portugal in 1963; and in Spain between 1965 and 1973.

Third rail
The conductor rail carrying the positive dc traction current. Usually placed to one side of and slightly above the running rails. The loco/train collector shoe may make its contact with the top (most usually), side or lower surface of this rail. The latter two methods provide greater reliability in ice and snow.

Thirty (USRS)(obs)
The end of a telegraphed message.

Thirty one order (US)
Train order (qv) requiring a signature to acknowledge that it is received and under-stood, and therefore causes the train to stop.

THL
Tracked Hovercraft Ltd; a subsidiary of the National Research Development Corporation which, with government financial support, undertook trials of a high-speed magnetically levitated vehicle propelled by a linear motor on an experimental track at Earith, Cambridgeshire between 1970 and 1973.

Thomas Cook
Thomas Cook & Son Ltd, formed in 1924 to take over the travel agency founded by Thomas Cook (1808–92) in 1841. Controlled by *CIWL* from 1928. Taken over by the four British main line rly companies in 1942 after the *CIWL* had become 'enemy property'. On the nationalization of the British rlys in 1948, the ownership of Thomas Cook was vested in the BTC. With the dissolution of the BTC imminent, it became part of the THC in 1962. In 1972 the undertaking was sold to a consortium of the Midland Bank, Trust Houses Forte and the Automobile Association. Purchased by *Westdeutsche Landesbank*, 1992. *See also* Cook's Timetable.

Thomas the Tank Engine
A blue-painted Hudswell-Clarke 1945 0–6–0T of the British Sugar Corporation, Peterborough, bought in 1973 by the Nene Valley Rly and adopted as a character in the highly popular children's rly stories written by the Revd W. Awdry.

Thomson-Houston
Thomson-Houston Electric Co., formed in US 1881 from AEC (2) (qv). Suppliers of electric traction equipment. Merged with Edison General Electric Co. in 1892 to become GE (2) (qv).

Thousand-miler (USRS)
A very dark-coloured working shirt which can allegedly be worn by engine and train crews for 1,000 m before requiring re-laundering.

THR
Tendring Hundred Rly, inc 1859, Hythe (Colchester)–Wivenhoe, opened 1863, worked by GER; extended to Colchester (St Botolph's) 1866, and to Walton-on-the-Naze 1867. Part of the GER, 1883.

Thrall Car/Thrall Europa
Chicago-based rly rolling stock manufacturer. Thrall Europa took over BR York Carriage & Wagon Works, UK, 1997.

Three-bagger (USRS)
Three locos on a train.

Three Counties Line
BR brand name for Bletchley–Bedford services 1990–3.

Threepenny-bitting (RS)
A section of track which appears to be laid in a series of angles rather than a smooth curve.

Three-phase
A system of electric traction using high voltage alternating current and two overhead wires per track, the asynchronous induction or constant speed motors on the locos and trains taking power directly from the generating station or via transformer substations and usually operating at line voltage. Regenerative braking (qv) is possible. First used on certain Swiss mountain rlys but employed on main lines, principally in northern Italy, from 1902 until 1972. Still survives on some mountain rlys. *See also* Single-phase.

Three-throw points
Points working three sets of rails diverging at the same place.

Three-valve sets (RS)
SR 3-cylinder 2–6–0 locos (N1 and U1) of the 1920s. From the popular contemporary radio sets.

Throat
The complex tracks at the approaches to a terminus or other large station.

Thrombosis (RS)
Traffic apprentice – 'a bloody clot wandering round the system'.

Throttle, throttle lever (US)
Regulator, regulator handle.

Throttle artist/jerker/puller (USRS)
A steam loco driver.

Through, [to go] (RS)
Overshooting a platform, e.g. 'two cars through' means that the driver has overshot by two car lengths.

Through coach (obs)
A coach shunted and attached to two or more trains during its journey, allowing its passengers to travel through to their destination without the chore of changing trains or crossing London.

Through lines
A pair of tracks passing through a station between the local or slow lines and therefore not served by platforms.

Through pipe/d
see Piped wagon.

Through road
Same as Straight road (qv).

Through siding (obs)
A siding without signalling but usable for through movements under the control of a shunter or other authorized person.

Throw
See Overthrow.

Throw-off points
Catch points (qv).

Throw-over
see Overthrow.

Thumpers (RS)
BR class 205 demus. From their characteristic sound. Later the term was applied to all demus.

Thunderbirds (RS)
A term coined in 1993 to describe stand-by locos used to rescue trains disabled by failure of motive power; after the television puppet series. *See also* Drag.

TI
Tramways Institute 1890, an association of the general managers of tramway (3) company systems; superseded by T&LRA (qv).

TI
Trains Illustrated, founded 1946, and at first largely directed at juvenile train spotters (qv); monthly publication from February 1950. Gradually altered to cater for professional as well as amateur rly interests and covering all aspects of contemporary rly engineering, operation, administration and politics; accordingly renamed *MR* (qv) from January 1962.

TIA
Traitement Intégrale Armand; an invention of Louis Armand, one time president of the *SNCF*, a device for the chemical processing of steam locomotive feed water to neutralize those ingredients which encourage scaling and boiler and firebox corrosion.

Tichies (RS)
GWR 0–4–2T and 2–4–0T. From children's (S) for small.

Ticino Express
TEE Zurich–Milan, introduced 1961. Ceased 1974.

Ticket agent
A person/firm selling passenger tickets on behalf of ATOC (qv). Also current in US.

Ticket grabber (USRS)
A conductor (*3*).
Ticket office (US)
Term for booking office, now generally adopted in UK.
Ticket platform (obs)
Special platforms erected outside large stations, at which ticket collectors took up tickets from passengers on incoming trains, and used for no other purpose. Some conveniently sited public stations with very light traffic (e.g. Holloway for Kings Cross) were also mainly given over to this role.
Ticket snapper (RS)
A ticket collector.
Tickhill
Tickhill Light Rly, Bawtry–Haxey, LRO 1901, part of GNR 1907, opened 1912.
Tiddly Dike Rly
Nickname for M&SWJR (*2*).
Tie (US)
Sleeper. Sometimes expressed as a cross tie (i.e. transverse sleeper), as distinguished from a switch tie (supporting points) or a bridge tie.
Tie bar/rod
A metal bar placed across the roadbed to keep rails to gauge at places where side pressure is high, or when rails are laid on a flat concrete base, e.g. in a roadway.
Tie ['em] down, to (RS)(obs)
To set handbrakes.
Tie ['em] off, to (RS)
To uncouple.
Tie on, to (RS)
To couple up.
Tie plate
A flat piece of steel with flanges on one side, used on light rlys (qv) and tramways (*3*). Attached to the upper side of wooden sleepers (ties) to support the rail, it prevents the rail cutting into the wood and also helps to preserve true gauge.
Tie up, to (USRS)
To pause for sleep or eating.
Tightlock
An automatic coupler, a refinement of the Buckeye (qv) coupler, adopted in Britain after trials in 1976. It virtually eliminates any tendency to ride up vertically.

Tilbury, The
LT&SR (qv).
Tilt bar
A bar or rod placed above the centre of a wagon from end to end to carry a canvas cover.
Time and Time (RS)
Punctual arrival and departure of a train.
Time bill (US)
A poster-size timetable.
Time freight (USRS)
A fast freight train.
Time interval system/working
A crude method of signalling in which a train is allowed sufficient time to clear a section ahead after which a second train is admitted to the section. In general use in the early days of rlys.
Timkenized (USRS)
A wagon or car equipped with (Timken) roller bearings.
Tingalairy (RS)
A manually operated auger.
Tinies (RS)
1. L&YR Aspinall 4–4–2 locos.
2. GCR 0–8–0 locos (L&NER class Q4).
Tin lizard/lizzie (USRS)(obs)
A streamlined train or loco.
Tin opener (LTRS)
A device erected in LT depots to remove snow from roofs of cars stored in the open. So called because it has occasionally begun to remove the car roofs as well.
Tinsel string (USRS)(obs)
A circus train (qv).
Tin tabs/tabernacles (RS)(obs)
L&YR iron-sided brake vans. From the corrugated iron chapels and churches, known as tin tabernacles.
Tinto Express
A 1911 renaming of the Upper Ward Express (qv).
Tip (RS)
1. A tippler wagon.
2. Advice passed by hand signals to a pointsman.
3. (RS) The indication given by platform staff to the guard and by the guard to the driver that a train is ready to start.
Tip-out, tipping 'em out (LTRS)
Detraining passengers, especially when a

defective train has to be taken out of service.

TIS (obs)

Three-car set of former LT tube stock refurbished in 1967 for working the BR Ryde Pier–Shanklin service, 3-TIS. Operated with the associated four-car VEC (qv) sets, combining as VECTIS, the Roman name for the Isle of Wight.

Tishies (RS)

L&NWR Prince of Wales inside-cylinder 4–6–0s fitted with outside Walschaerts valve gear. From a racehorse named Tishy which had a reputation for getting its legs crossed.

Tissue (USRS)

A train order (qv).

TIV

Track Inspection Vehicle (qv).

Tizzie/Tizzy (RS) (obs)

Used by SR staff for 1920s electric trains, possibly from 'tin lizzie' (S) for a cheap motor car, or perhaps from tizzy = nervous agitation.

TLF

Trainload Freight (qv).

TLV

Trailer Luggage Van (gangwayed), BR (S).

TM&WER

Tooting, Merton & Wimbledon Extension Rly, inc 1864, vested in L&SWR and LB&SCR 1865, opened 1868, Streatham Junction to Wimbledon, part of SR from 1923.

TMD

Traction Maintenance Depot (BR).

TML

Trans-Manche Link. The consortium of contractors responsible for building the Channel Tunnel.

TMO

Same as TCO (qv).

TMS

Tramway Museum Society, founded 1955. It owns and operates the National Tramway Museum, Crich, Derbyshire, opened with horse operation 1963, electric working from 1964.

TO

1. Tourist Open coach (BR).
2. (LT) Train Operator (qv).

Toad

1. GWR TC for freight brake van with large balcony at one end only.
2. BR TC for any type of freight brake van.
3. (USRS) A rolling stock repair man.
4. (USRS) A derailing device.

Toadfit

BR TC for a fitted freight brake van.

Toastrack

An unroofed tramcar with open body sides and crossbench seating entered from the footboards at the sides. From its vague resemblance to its namesake.

TOC

1. Train Operating Centres; sited at Wembley, Crewe, Dollands Moor, Mossend and Doncaster and designed for marshalling freight trains using the Channel Tunnel.
2. Train Operating Company/ies. Private sector businesses taking over from TOUs (qv) under the Railways Act, 1993.

TOD

Tourist Open Disabled coach. BR IC 225 coach with wheelchair space and lavatory designed for use by the disabled. Marshalled next to a catering vehicle.

TOE

Tourist Open End. BR IC 225 coach, marshalled next to the loco. Corridor connection at one end only.

Toe [of points]/switch toe

The tapered end of a switch or tongue rail, fitting against the stock rail (qv). *See* Points; Switches.

Toe boards (USRS)

Walkway on roofs of freight wagons.

Toe path (USRS)

1. The running board of a loco.
2. Toe boards (qv).
3. The cess (qv).

TOFC (US)

Trailer on Flat Car. An intermodal system in which road trailers are carried on rail flat wagons. *See also* Piggyback.

Toffee apples (RS)

1. (obs) Casks of asphalt or pitch.
2. BR diesel locos class 31/0. From the shape of the control handles.

Tokaido line

The 3ft 6 in gauge main line from Tokyo to Osaka via Nagoya and Kyoto. *See also* New Tokaido line.

Tokenless block

Block instrument, with electrical interlocking, suitable for single lines, giving the same safety as train staffs, tablets or tokens (qv); introduced on BR in 1965. After a train has been accepted by the box in advance, signals at both boxes are released to allow it to pass through the single line section. A further release can only be obtained when it arrives at the entrance to the passing place in advance, actuating a track circuit and an electric treadle. *See also* Non-token lock and block.

Token working

see Train staff/tablet/token and ticket.

Tolstoi

A Helsinki–Moscow service, so named 1982.

TOM

1. Ticket Office Machine, LT.

2. Train Operations Manager, LT.

Tommy (RS)

1. A ground disc signal.

2. Any BR class 76 loco after NS (*1*) (qv) had so named class 76 no. 26000.

Tommy Dodd (RS)

A calling-on or ground disc signal.

Tom Puddings (RS) (obs)

Large steel containers used to transport coal by both rail and waterways/sea successively.

Toms' Express, The (RS) (obs)

The 00.05 London (Victoria)–Brighton train, much patronized by ladies of easy virtue plying for business at the end of the nineteenth and early twentieth centuries. (Tom = prostitute (S)).

Tongue rails/switch blades/rails

The moveable rails in a turnout (qv) which incorporate the 'sharp' end to guide the wheels of a train.

Tonk (USRS)

Carriage and wagon fitter (i.e. a carman (qv)).

Ton-mile

A unit measuring the movement of one ton of freight over one mile.

Tonnage hound (USRS)

An official who loads up trains to the point of straining their motive power.

Tool train (USRS)

A breakdown train with re-railing equipment.

Toonerville [trolley] (USRS)

A very small (i.e. with approximately one to five short routes) electric tramway (*3*) system in US. After a comic strip, *The Toonerville Trolley that meets all the Trains*, by Fontaine Fox, begun in 1908 and syndicated in newspapers throughout the US.

Toot and Bunny

Nickname for Reading–Hungerford line.

Toothpaste (RS)(obs)

NSE's initial red, white and blue livery.

Top (RS)

The top of the track formation; rail level.

TOP/TOp (LT)

Train Operator (qv).

Top, to (RS) (obs)

To double-head (qv) a train. Also to position coaches at the front end of a train already standing at a platform.

Top and tail (RS)

A train with a loco at each end.

Top ballast

The upper layer of ballast (qv) which is available for tamping (see Tamp), also known as Boxing-in ballast. *See also* Ballast; Bottom ballast.

Top dresser drawer (USRS)

The upper bunk or berth in a caboose or sleeping car.

Tope

A 21-ton ballast and spoil wagon used by engineers.

Toplights

The openable section at the top of a coach window, or a small window above main light, often in a door, to allow a standing passenger to see out.

Top link

see Link.

Topo, el (Sp)

The Mole; name for the line between Hendaye and San Sebastian with its numerous tunnels.

Topping the road (RS)
Correcting rail height by packing.
TOPS
BR computer-based Total Operations
Processing System of freight information
and transit control, introduced 1973–5
and copied from that used by the SP (qv).
Every event concerning freight traffic is
transmitted, as it happens, to a central
computer to form a comprehensive and
up-to-the-minute picture of the freight
traffic situation over the whole British rly
system. Details of the deployment of all
freight rolling stock, locos, services, depots
and yards are stored on the central
computer. The data bank also holds details
of all non-mu passenger stock and its
location.
Tops gen (RS)
Information gained from the TOPS (qv)
computer printouts or screen displays.
Top Shed (RS)(obs)
Kings Cross Loco Depot.
Tops, oiling the (RS)
Attending to the oiling points of a steam
loco along the foot framings and under the
boiler, just behind the smokebox (qv) and
the inside valve spindles.
Top station (LT)
That part of a London Underground
station at or immediately below street level.
Torbay Express/Limited
A service between London (Paddington),
Torquay and Paignton (to Kingswear in
summer), introduced 1923, restored 1946,
name dropped 1968. Relaunched 1984 as a
summer service to Paignton only. In
1988–90 the Mondays to Fridays train was
renamed West Country Pullman (qv) but
the Saturday working retained the earlier
name. From 1991 the Torbay Express ran
six days a week in summer only. Winter
operation was introduced in 1996/97 but
lasted for that season only.
Torbay–Tyne
An express between Paignton, Torquay and
Newcastle, introduced 1970, ran that year
only.
Toros Express
see Taurus/Toros Express.

Torpedo (USRS)
A detonator.
Torpedo wagons (RS)
Wagons designed to carry molten steel.
From their shape.
Torquay Pullman Limited
A service between London (Paddington),
Torquay and Paignton, the first all-Pullman
service on GWR, introduced 1929, ceased
after 1930.
TORR
Train-Operated Route Release. A device at
the exit point which automatically
releases/cancels a route set up on a power box
signalling panel as the train passes out of it.
Tortillard (Fr)
Popular name for train on a secondary line,
or the line itself; literally 'twister' or
'shuffler'.
Torvill & Deans (RS)
BR class 141 dmus. From their propensity
to skid, like the ice skaters, Torvill & Dean.
TOT
Train-Omnibus-Tram, title of an official
Underground Group (qv UERL)
publication for the information of the
public 1913–14. Transferred to the staff
magazine, 1914, which was then renamed
TOT Staff Magazine from 1922 until
replaced by *Pennyfare* (qv) 1934. TOT was
also used for the through tram/bus/
Underground tickets and facilities of the
various undertakings in the UERL.
Totem
GWR TC for twelve-wheel wagons to carry
45-ton loads, originally designed to carry
armour plating.
TOU
Train Operating Units, the 25 'Stand-
alone' businesses formed within BR to
operate specific groups of passenger rail
services in preparation for 'privatization' of
the rlys under the Railways Act, 1993 (qv).
Touch, to get a (LTRS)
To receive an electric shock from a live rail.
Tourist, The
Summer through service between Ventnor
and Freshwater, Isle of Wight, 1934–9,
revived 1951. Ceased 1953 with closure of
Freshwater branch.

Tourist car (obs)
An inferior type of US Pullman sleeping car available at half the normal Pullman fare.

Tourn
GWR TC for 36-ft bogie open truck to carry 25-ton loads.

Touropa (Ger)
A holiday tour company owning couchette cars (*Liegewagen*).

Tower (US)
Signal box, or the control cabin in a marshalling yard.

Tower buff (USRS)
A rly enthusiast.

Tower Subway
A deep level tube tunnel beneath the Thames from Tower Hill to Tooley Street, inc 1868, opened 1870. Since it briefly contained a 2 ft 6 in/762 mm gauge cable-worked rly, it was in effect the first passenger tube (qv). However, rail service lasted only a few months although the subway remained open for pedestrians until 1896.

Town Halls (RS)
BR standard class 5 4–6–0 locos. From the prominent steps at the front of the frame.

Towns Line (RS)
The GNR direct line between Doncaster and London via Grantham and Newark.

Tow-roping (obs)
A practice (made illegal by parliament in 1900) involving shunting (qv) by means of ropes fastened to a loco running on a track adjacent to the siding containing the wagons to be moved.

TOWS
Train Operated Warning System. An audible warning for track workers which, when switched on, is operated by an approaching train.

Toy rly (obs)
Used up to *c*. 1940 to describe any UK passenger-carrying narrow gauge or miniature rly.

Toys (RS)
BR IC 125 (qv) train sets.

Toy trains (LTRS)
Name given by Metropolitan Line crews to the (small size) tube stock running to Stanmore.

Tph
Trains Per Hour; a unit of frequency on intensive services.

TPH
Track Paralleling Hut (qv).

TP hut
Track Paralleling hut; used on the electrified third rail lines of SR and successors, these contain equipment designed to reduce voltage drop between substations. They also allow speedy isolation of a substation in the event of a fault.

TPO
Travelling Post Office; a train exclusively devoted to the carriage of Royal Mail, in which letters are sorted during the journey to save time. Although the term Travelling Post Office dates only from 1928, the system was introduced in 1838. It still continues today but the lineside apparatus which enabled mail to be taken up into the train or dropped from it at speed was finally taken out of use in 1971. Last TPO service withdrawn January 2004. *See also* Railway Post Offices; SC (*3*); ST (*2*).

TPWS
Train Protection [and] Warning System: on-board equipment which detects if a train is approaching a signal at danger at too high a speed, triggering an emergency brake application. It will also apply brakes to a train started against a red signal.

TPWS+
Extension of TPWS (qv) to make it operate at speeds up to 100 mph.

TR
1. Thameslink Rail (qv).
2. Talyllyn Rly (qv).

TRA
Taiwan Rly Administration; 1,108 km of 1,067 mm gauge.

Trac Gopher
A self-propelled excavator which can remove (but not screen) ballast from the shoulder and from under plain track and special work (qv), then load it into trucks standing on an adjacent line.

Track
1. The running lines and sidings, etc. of a rly or tramway.

2. (RS) A track circuit [section] (qv); hence 'track failure', which is not what it may seem to the untutored when announced as a cause of train delays.

3. (US) Station platform (usually with the associated numeral).

Track access charges
Sums paid to Network Rail by TOCs (2) (qv) and FOCs (qv) for use of the infrastructure and related services.

Trackage rights (US)
Running powers (qv).

Track basher (RS)
One who indulges in track bashing (qv).

Track bashing (RS)
Travel by gricers (qv) and others over rarely used or unusual stretches of line, difficult or impossible to cover in ordinary passenger trains, with special emphasis on travelling to the very limits of such lines ('buffer-kissing'); also the pursuit of an ambition to travel over *all* lines in use in the UK or in some other defined area.

Track bed
Track formation (1) (qv); the term is also used of the ballast surface on which the rails and sleepers are laid.

Track chargeman
The leader of a track maintenance team.

Track circuit block
A method of working sections of line by equipping them with continuous Track circuits (qv) and multi-aspect colour-light (qv) signals.

Track circuit [operating] clips
Two metal spring clips connected by a wire band, carried in all BR driving cabs for use in emergency. Clipped to the running rails, they close the track circuit in the same way as the train, putting all automatic signals to danger to prevent any train running into a derailment or incident affecting the parallel track. *See also* T-COD.

Track circuits
A valuable safety device invented by the American William Robinson in 1872. It involves the passing of a low voltage electric current through one of the running rails of a section of line (the rails have to be bonded and insulated joints made at each end of the section), then via a track relay and back through the other rail, thus completing the circuit. Should a train or part of a train be on the line, however, this signal current will take the shorter path through its wheels and axles, thus demagnetizing (de-energizing) the track relay. Should there be an electrical failure or accidental short circuit, the relay is also de-energized, thus 'failing safe'. By this means signalmen can be informed on track diagrams of the presence and progress of a train on any section, and if track circuiting is continuous, automatic signalling is made possible, since signals in the rear of a train can be made to remain 'on' by the opening of the track relay while a train is in the section in advance. Track circuits also enable points to be secured against movement under or in front of an approaching train and, where manual signalling is in use, permit signals or block instruments to be locked or controlled so that signals cannot be moved to 'off' while a train (or part of it) is on the section and closing the circuit in the rear of the relay. The introduction of track circuits in the UK was much delayed by the widespread use of Mansell (qv) wheels but the device was universally adopted for London's Underground from the early 1900s, both on new tube lines and on existing lines when these were electrified. The system is now widely used in Britain. *See also* Overlap track circuit; Track circuit block; Track circuit clips.

Tracked hovercraft
see THL.

Tracker ball
Computer ancillary similar to a Microsoft 'mouse' used by signallers in IECC (qv) to set routes.

Track failure
see Track (2).

Track geometry
The horizontal and vertical alignment of the rails, taking account of cant (qv).

Track Inspection Vehicle/coach
A saloon coach converted for assessing track condition and riding quality;

equipped with measuring instruments, etc. On Network Rail now replaced by Pandora (qv) and NMT (qv).

Track man/woman
A member of a track maintenance team. *See also* Patrollers.

Track miles/km
The total length of all track in any specific rly system or country, i.e. the route miles/km (qv) multiplied by the number of parallel tracks on the routes concerned, plus track miles/km in sidings, stations, yards, depots, etc.

TrackMon
AEA Technology system for monitoring track conditions which can be fitted to a bogie (*see* Truck (3)) on an ordinary service train and, by means of an on-board computer, will supply an analysis of track quality. The data obtained can then be transmitted from the train to a central computer.

Track panel
A prefabricated assembly of rails, sleepers and fittings ready for positioning on the required site.

Track pans (US)
Water troughs (qv). In use in the USA 1870–1956.

Track paralleling hut
A building containing unattended equipment which connects electrically through circuit breaker sections of conductor rail (qv), enabling any sections to be isolated (switched out) by the ECR (qv) in an emergency or during track maintenance. These installations are located on direct current electrified rlys at intermediate points between substations (qv).

Track Relaying/Renewal Machine
An on-track multi-vehicle machine suitably equipped to relay track in one quick operation in conjunction with purpose-built sleeper wagons.

Track Relaying/Renewal Train
A train with all the necessary equipment and facilities to enable track relaying to be undertaken speedily. It includes gantries to handle sleepers, purpose-built sleeper wagons, a fastening vehicle, a handling

vehicle, beam wagon and a clipping unit. Introduced in Britain by Railtrack (qv) 1999.

Track stop (US)
A Train stop (qv).

Track 29
A former profit centre of BR Parcels Group (qv) specializing in the heavier consignments. From a line in the song *Chattanooga Choo Choo* referring to the track (platform) from which that train departs.

Track walker
A track man/woman who walks along the line (usually daily) to check for defects and adjustments needed. *See also* Patrollers.

Traction (RS)
Generic term used by enthusiasts for electric, diesel and diesel-electric locos.

Traction current/supply
The flow of electricity to locos, multiple units, light rail vehicles, trams, etc. through the overhead (qv), conductor rail (qv) or trolley wire (qv) and passing back through the rails or other return circuit.

Traction pole/standard
Steel poles at the side of a rly, interurban or tramway (3) which are used to suspend the overhead traction current wiring.

Traction unit
A generic term embracing locos, multiple units (qv), diesel railcars, tramcars/light rail vehicles, self-propelled rail vehicles and road/rail vehicles moving on rails. *See also* Vehicle.

Tractive effort
The maximum force developed at any given time at the rim of a loco's driving wheels while working itself and its train. Its value always exactly balances the net resistance forces met by the train and it is not by itself a measure of power. *See also* Drawbar pull; Rail tractive effort.

Tractor
British Army term for a petrol-driven loco.

Tractors (RS)
BR diesel-electric locos, class 37.

Traffic apprentices (obs)
A scheme in which promising youngsters were selected and trained for management positions on the rly, originally adopted by the NER following the initiative of Sir G.S.

Gibb in 1897. Superseded by the BR
Management Training Scheme.

Traffic Circular
see TC (*2*).

Traffic Movement
A measure of rail and road traffic at a level
crossing.

Traffic pool
An arrangement between competing
companies/undertakings under which
receipts from specified traffic flows are
shared in agreed proportions.

Traffic Regulation
Control exercised over the movement of
traffic for a particular destination or
consignee in circumstances where
conditions demand a departure from
normal planned movements. *See also*
Regulation [of passenger traffic].

Traffic Regulator
A supervisor employed in large signal
boxes to decide local priorities in train
working and give directions to the
signalmen. The TR is not concerned with
'traffic regulation' (qv).

Trafford Park
Rlys in the Trafford Park Industrial Estate,
Manchester, opened 1900.

Trail boss (RS)(obs)
A stationmaster.

Trailer
Any passenger vehicle without a power
unit of its own, usually those in dmu or
emu sets. Also any non-powered unit
hauled by a tramcar or dummy (*1*) and (*2*)
(qv).

Trailing load
The gross weight of passengers and freight
and the rolling stock pulled by the power
unit, expressed in tons.

Trailing points
Points where lines converge in the direction
of running, passed over by the train from
the heel to the toe of the switch; the
opposite of facing points (qv).

Trailing points

Train
In demotic speech and writing, this word is
often used outside the accepted, dictionary
definition. Thus locomotives or any
traction unit (qv) is referred to as a 'train'.
It is also employed as a substitute for
'railway', as in 'train line', 'train station'
(qv), 'train bridge' or 'train tunnel'. The
practice may have its origins in retained
kiddie-talk.

TRAIN
Acronym for Telerail Automated
Information Network, a computerized
freight car information system operated in
the US, Mexico and Canada by the AAR
(qv). Introduced 1971, 1974.

Train Bleu, le
see Blue Train.

Train call (obs)
A notice posted in a theatre to inform a
touring company of actors of the details of
their rail journey to the next engagement.

Train captain
1. (obs) An employee in charge of an
automatically-operated train on the
DLR (qv). The duties include checking
tickets and taking over manual control
when normal working is interrupted or
inexpedient. Renamed PSA (qv) 1999.
2. Used by Eurotunnel (qv) for official in
charge of a train working *le Shuttle* (qv).

Train car (US)(obs)
An early term for caboose (qv).

Traincare centre/depot
A facility for maintaining and servicing
coaches, including multiple-unit (qv) stock.

Train control
Supervision of train running exercised by
Control (qv). Not to be confused with
traffic regulation (qv).

Train de luxe (Fr)(obs)
A First class only luxury train.

Train de neige (Fr)
A special train for winter sports traffic.

Train describer/indicator
An apparatus by which the description of a
train (type and route) are passed from one
signalbox to the next or provided on a
panel on power box track diagrams. The
term 'train indicator' was used for the early

forms of electrically-operated apparatus serving this purpose. With the development of computers and electronics, train describers have been adapted to trigger route-setting, together with associated signal and point movements and also to operate indicators (now normally vdus) to show passengers the destinations, etc. and sequence of trains due to arrive at a station.

Train description

Digit, letter and two digits allocated to every train in the working timetable (qv) and displayed on train describers (qv) in signal boxes and control centres.

Train dispatcher/runner

see Train order.

Train document

A list containing information necessary for the safe operation of a specific freight train, prepared by TOPS or manually.

Train doors (US)

The doors at each end of a car which give access via step flaps to the next car. Also in use on LT.

Train engine

The loco hauling a given train as distinct from any assisting or banking engine.

Train Ex

A term first used in 1969 for exhibition trains (qv). Title of a limited company formed in 1973, with BR participation, to provide a complete service for design, construction, management and operation of trains for travelling exhibition purposes.

Train express (Fr)(obs)

A fast train with all three classes of accommodation.

Train ferry

A purpose-built ship fitted with rly tracks, which, in combination with suitable ramps on shore, enable rail vehicles, including complete trains, to be moved across water gaps. Among the through passenger and freight rail services operated by this means are those between Germany, Denmark and Sweden; between European and Asiatic Turkey at Istanbul; and (until the opening of the Channel Tunnel) between Britain and France. *See also* Night Ferry.

Train graph

A graphical representation of train movements over a section of line in terms of time and distance. Used in planning timetables, etc.

Train indicator

see Train describer/indicator.

Train in distress warning

A continuous series of long blasts on the loud tone of the cab horn.

Train length limit

The maximum number of vehicles which may be formed into a train passing over a given section of rly.

Train line

The complete system of brake pipes through a train.

Trainline, The

Formed 1999 by ATOC (qv) to provide on-line information and rail ticket booking. Merged with Q-Jump (qv) 2004–5.

Trainload

The formation of a train, taking into account train load and length limits.

Trainload Freight (obs)

A separate BR business sector formed in 1990 to manage the bulk load freight business. Subdivided into Trainload Coal [solid fuels and nuclear flasks], Trainload Construction [aggregates, cement and refuse], Trainload Petroleum [oils and petrol], and Trainload Metals [steel and aluminium]. All other rail freight activity remained a responsibility of Railfreight Distribution (qv). Broken up into three businesses (Loadhaul, Transrail, Mainline Freight) in 1994 in preparation for sale to private sector. *See* EWS; FOC.

Trainload limit

The maximum tonnage which may be conveyed by a given class of train and/or hauled by a loco over a route.

Train Manager

Virgin Rail (qv) term for Senior Conductor (qv), 1998.

Train master (US)

The official in charge of a terminal, directly responsible for the supervision and control of conductors (*3*) (qv), also for arranging train schedules and allocating duties.

Trainmet
Operators (with *Metrovias* (qv)) of
suburban services in Buenos Aires.

Train mile
A measurement representing the
movement of one train over one mile.

Train omnibus (Fr)(obs)
See Omnibus, train.

Train operator
Person in sole charge of a London
Underground train; in use after
introduction of OPO (qv) in 1984. *See also*
TOC (2).

Train order
Telegraphed instructions given by a train
dispatcher as to the exact operation of
trains over long unsignalled and lightly
used sections of single line in the US and
elsewhere outside the British Isles. These
orders give details of locations and times
for the train to cross others coming in the
opposite direction, etc. Responsibility for
observing a train order is shared by the
conductor and the engineer, who both have
to sign for restrictive train orders. In
theory, written train orders are only
necessary for extra trains or when late
running is occurring, since trains otherwise
proceed according to the planned
timetables and recognized running
priorities, but with the dispatcher always in
overall control. In the USA, written train
orders were replaced in the mid-1980s by
DTC (qv) and TWC (qv).

Train path
See Path.

Train pipe
The pipe through a train with flexible
connections between wagons or coaches
used in connection with automatic air and
vacuum brake systems. *See also* Train line.

Train protection bar
A locking bar to prevent a signalman taking
off a home signal while a train remains in
the station.

Train ready to start plunger
see TRS (2).

Train Régional (Fr)
A term used in France and Switzerland to
denote a local stopping train.

Train register
The written record kept in a signalbox of
the actual times when the approach of a
train is advised; when it passes; when it is
warned on to the next box; the minutes it is
late or early, and any unusual state such as
open door, tail light not visible, etc. The
primary purpose of the register is to
remind the signalman of the position of the
trains he is dealing with at any given time.
See also Booking lad; Print-out.

Train regulation
The work of Control (qv) or of a traffic
regulator (qv).

Train regulator (LT)
An operator stationed in a signalling control
centre, who continually supervises the
working of a whole line, aided by mimic
diagrams, vdus, etc., intervening to manage
local regulation and make minor
adjustments of the train service as required.

Train runner
Train dispatcher: *see* Train order.

Train shed
An overall roof covering all tracks and
platforms at a through or terminal station.

Train signal book
SR (qv) term for Train Register (qv).

Trains Illustrated
see TI.

Trains Magazine (US)
A magazine for rail enthusiasts published
monthly from November 1940. Renamed
1962, *see MR*(13).

Train spotter
A term introduced *c.* 1945 for a breed that
had existed for at least seventy years without
a name – those (mostly juvenile and male)
addicted to lineside or station observation for
the purpose of recording in a notebook
('copping') the numbers of locos when first
seen. The word 'spotter' was borrowed from
the rather more purposeful aircraft spotters of
WW2, and the Ian Allan 'Spotters' Club' was
formed in 1945; its name was changed to
'Ian Allan Locospotters' Club' in 1948. The
term was subsequently adopted by media
hacks and others as a mildly derogatory label
for anyone interested in rlys. By the 1990s it
was in general usage to describe any obsessive

behaviour over detail, in any sphere, 'the train-spotter mentality'. *See also* Foamer.

Train staff/tablet/token and ticket

Train staffs are a visible token of a driver's authority to enter a single line section between crossing places. Before a train can enter, this staff must be held by the driver, and since only one exists for each section, working is thus restricted to alternate trains moving in opposite directions. A refinement is the *train staff and ticket* system in which drivers of the first trains through the section are shown the staff (to demonstrate the section ahead is clear) and given a paper form or metal ticket. These tickets are kept in signal cabins or booking offices in boxes which can only be opened and closed by use of the key in the train staff. Removal of the staff relocks the box. By this means two or more trains can pass through the section in the same direction, only the last of the group carrying the staff. No trains can pass in the opposite direction until the staff has arrived at the other end of the section. Normal block working applies. A further refinement is the *electric token or tablet* system, in which the 'visible authority' (staffs, tokens or tablets, unique to their section) is contained in electrically controlled and interlocked instruments which allow only one to be released at a time. When this authority is placed in the instrument at the other end of the section, a second staff/tablet can be taken from the instrument at the beginning of the section, allowing a second train to pass through, and so on. Tokens or tablets are usually placed in a leather pouch attached to a metal hoop to facilitate exchange between signalman and train crews.

Train station (US)

Term for a rly station, adopted by the UK media and others from the 1980s. Until then, in the UK, the word 'station' had, for around 150 years, always been taken to denote a rly station, the other types (police station, bus station, etc.) being given their full title.

Train Stop

A device at the trackside, usually at a signal, which automatically stops a train attempting to pass the signal when it is at

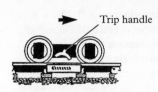

Signal at green, Train Stop arm lying down

Signal at red, Train Stop arm sticking up, knocks back trip handle on train, so applying brakes

danger since, when that is the case, the arm is raised and held vertically in a position in which it knocks open the tripcock (qv) on the offending train or loco.

Train tramway (Fr)(obs)

see *Tramway, train.*

Trainwatch (obs)

A scheme set up in 1993 by SOR (qv) to monitor and publicize the impact of rly privatization in Great Britain.

Trakrat

A diesel-powered 4-wheel rail vehicle for transporting maintenance crews and their equipment. Suitable for carriage by road vehicle when required. In use from 1999.

Tram

1. (obs) Any vehicle, but usually a wagon, used on a tramroad (*1*) (qv).
2. A shortened form of tramcar (qv).
3. (RS) A mildly derogatory term for an electric train, which was more widely current when steam trains were ubiquitous and provided a much more interesting object for the activities of the average train spotter (qv).

Tram basher (RS)

A fanatical type of enthusiast who indulges in haulage bashing (qv) on electric rlys. *See also* Undergricing.

Tramcar

Used from *c.* 1860 for vehicles working over tramways (*3*), usually passenger-carrying, and since *c.* 1898 (earlier in the US), usually electrically powered. Often abbreviated to tram and, until *c.* 1950, to 'car'.

Tram engine (obs)
A steam tank engine with enclosed motion suitable for running on tramways (*3*) and (*4*), or on sections of rly laid in the roadway. *See also* Dummy.

Tramlink
A light rail transit system for south London [Wimbledon–Croydon–New Addington/ Elmers End/Beckenham] opened in 2000.

TRAMM/GP-TRAMM
Track Renewal And Maintenance Machine or General Purpose Track Maintenance Machine, originally introduced by BR (1). A self-propelled rail vehicle fitted with a lifting arm which can supply hydraulic power for tools, etc. used by track workers. Also used to carry materials to and from work sites.

Trammie (S)
A tramway (*3*) driver or conductor.

Tram pinch
Wording of a road sign warning motorists that tramway (*3*) track swerves close to the edge of the roadway ahead.

Tramplate/tram plate (obs)
Another term for plate (qv).

Tramroad/Tram road (obs)
1. Term current from *c.* 1790 for a rly of flanged iron plates or angle rails of L-section, accommodating vehicles with flangeless wheels; sometimes also known as a plateway (qv).
2. A term used occasionally in the late nineteenth and early twentieth centuries in the formal titles of undertakings operating tramways (*3*). By that time few tramways (*1*) existed and the word was a convenient way of distinguishing lines or systems which included sections not laid on public roads. The term was revived at the end of the twentieth century to describe those parts of a light rail transit system (qv) not on a public road.

Tram-Trains
Use of 'heavy' trams/LRV (qv) capable of operating seamlessly on both conventional rly tracks to reach outlying areas and over street tracks in cities and towns, using diesel or electric traction or both. A system adopted

from the early 1990s at Karlsruhe and Saarbrucken (Germany) and recommended for the UK by ACoRP (qv), 2004.

Tram walloper (S) (obs)
A pickpocket specializing in the tramcar side of the business.

Tramway
1. (obs) Term used from mid-eighteenth century to describe light industrial rlys on which wagons or trams (*1*) were moved over wooden planks or iron plates (qv) by manual or animal power in underground locations (mines and quarries).
2. Term used from *c.* 1830 to distinguish light industrial rlys employing any form of motive power from the emerging public passenger and freight rlys using steam locomotives. From the mid-nineteenth century the word was haphazardly used by the Ordnance Survey to describe *any* kind of industrial or minor rly irrespective of gauge, use or ownership.
3. A term used in Britain from *c.* 1860 to describe a tracked system, wholly or mainly used for the carriage of passengers within urban and suburban areas, or linking up such areas within a conurbation, its tracks mostly laid along the centre or at the side of streets and roads but possibly with some sections segregated on a central or side reservation, on private right of way off roads, or in shallow subways. Originally animal, cable and steam traction were the main forms of motive power, but since *c.* 1898 (*c.* 1888 in the US), virtually all such systems have been electrically worked, usually with traction current taken from an overhead line by trolley wheel, skid, bow, or pantograph. *See also* Light rail [transit]; Light rly.

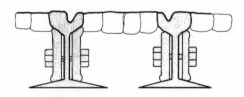

Cross-section of track for tramway (3)

4. (obs) A form of light rly, usually alongside or on public roads, connecting two or more towns, a town and nearest rly station, or a city with a satellite community. Usually worked initially with steam tram engines or steam tramcars and carrying freight as well as passengers.

5. (US) An aerial cable rly with suspended cars (aerial tramway). *See* Aerial rlys/ropeways.

Tramway & Railway World
see T&RW.

Tramway Museum Society
see TMS.

Tramway, train (Fr)(obs)
A local stopping train not conveying heavy luggage or parcels traffic.

Transalpin
An express emu service between Vienna and Zurich, introduced 1958, became an EC 1987.

Transalpino
A limited company, formed in 1952 to organize discount fare rail travel for adults under twenty-five. Ceased in 1989.

Trans-Andine
Rly from Buenos Aires to Valparaiso, completed 1910. Destroyed by floodwaters in 1934, rebuilt and reopened 1944. Journey time about 36 h. Closed again by a landslide, 1984. Service at present interrupted.

Transatlantique, trains (Fr)(obs)
Boat trains between Paris (St Lazare) and Le Havre (Gare Maritime) in connection with Transatlantic liner sailings.

Trans-Australia Express
Service between Port Pirie and Kalgoorlie with connections at these break of gauge points, to provide a Perth–Melbourne journey. The timing in 1938 was 29–30 h. The connecting Perth–Kalgoorlie service (The Westland) was timed at approx 15 h and the Port Pirie–Melbourne connection at 17 h 5 min. At this period, the 2,690 m from Perth to Sydney could be covered in 85 h 45 min westbound and 88 h 15 min eastbound. The line is now standard gauge throughout and the Sydney–Perth journey

has been reduced to about 64 h, travelled in the same train. *See also* Indian Pacific.

Trans Balt Zug (Ger)
A company jointly owned by *DBAG* (qv) and *RZD* (qv) set up in December 2004 to provide through passenger rail services between Germany and Russia.

Trans-Canada Limited
CPR all-sleeper service between Montreal, Toronto and Vancouver, introduced 1919, 93 h 30 min westbound, 92 h 15 min eastbound.

Trans-Europ Express
see TEE.

Transfer
1. A method of applying inscriptions, coats of arms and other insignia, logos, etc. after the completion of coach painting.
2. (obs) A type of ticket issued on some tramways (*3*) which allowed the holder to transfer at specified points to cars on other lines to reach a specified destination.

Transfer Agent (US)(obs)
Term for an official who walked through long-distance trains as they approached major stations, undertaking the delivery of passengers' luggage and giving receipts in exchange for the baggage checks. Transfer Agents also undertook delivery of luggage to rly stations and its transfer between stations in the large centres. *See also* Baggage master; Check system; Parmalee transfer.

Transfers (RS)(obs)
Wagons to be exchanged between sidings, lines or companies.

Transfer table (US)
Traverser (qv).

TRANSFESA (Sp)
Transportes Ferroviarios Especiales SA; Special Railway Transport Co. Formed 1943 to facilitate the operation of through running freight cars between Spain and other European countries.

Tranships (obs)
Freight loaded into one wagon for various destinations when traffic to these is insufficient to justify a through wagon. Hence tranship wagon/van. *See also* Station trucks.

Transition beam
Connecting unit to be placed between
conventional and slab track (qv).

Transition curves
Forming the entry to a main curve out of
straight track, a transition curve begins
with a very flat curve, gradually
sharpening until it attains the radius of the
main curve. Superelevation on transition
curves increases from zero until it reaches
its greatest angle at the beginning of the
main curve. Transition curves are also used
to link curves to curves where the hand of
the curves or their radii (or both) are
different.

Translink
Citybus, NIR (qv) and Ulsterbus,
operating together as an integrated system
from 1995–7, instead of competing with
each other as formerly.

Trans-Maghreb Express
A service between Tunis and Algiers,
introduced 1975. Political disputes have
prevented its planned extension to serve
Casablanca.

Trans-Manchurian Express
A *CIWL* service Harbin and Changchun,
introduced 1906. Restored after WW1,
ceased 1935.

Transmark
Transportation Systems & Market
Research Ltd, BR subsidiary advising and
assisting overseas authorities on rly
matters. Formed 1969, began trading
1970. Sold to private sector, 1993.
Renamed Halcrow Transmark (qv).

Transnet Ltd
The private operators of South African
Rlys from 1990.

Trans-Pennine
BR dmu services between Liverpool
(Lime St.) and Leeds/Hull, introduced 1961,
name dropped 1969. The title survived
tenuously as a general brand name for
services Liverpool/Manchester to Leeds/Hull/
Newcastle for another twenty years until
their integration into the new Provincial
Sector Express services. Name re-
introduced for all express workings via
Huddersfield, 1993.

TransPennine Express
A TOC from 2004 owned by
FirstGroup/Keolis providing trans-Pennine
services Liverpool–Manchester–Leeds–
York/Hull/Sheffield/Newcastle formerly
operated by Arriva Trains Northern and
partly by First North Western. *See also*
Arriva; First North Western.

Transponder
A trackside transmitter/receiver which
transmits signals electronically and
automatically to or from train drivers when
actuated by pre-determined signals.

Transport
see RG (4).

Transport Acts
A general title adopted for legislation
affecting BR, LT and other public transport
operations, beginning with the 1947 Act,
which nationalized public transport and set
up the BTC (qv). Further structural and
policy changes were made by the Transport
Acts of 1953, 1962, 1968, 1969 (London),
1980, 1981, 1983 and 1985. *See also*
Railways Act, 1993; Transport Act,
2000; TfL.

Transport Act, 2000
A statute passed under a New Labour
administration, revising the scheme of
'privatization' introduced by the Railways
Act, 1993 (qv). A major change was the
setting up of a central Strategic Rail
Authority (SRA (qv)) which, inter alia,
took over the powers of OPRAF (qv).

Transport & Travel Monthly
see T&TM.

Transport & Works Act
This 1992 legislation replaced the private
bill procedure (*see* Railway Acts) for
authorizing construction of new rlys, light
rlys and tramways (3) which were in future
to be sanctioned by orders made by the
Secretary of State for Transport following a
Public Inquiry. The 1992 Act repealed the
Light Railways Act, 1896 (*see* Light Rly)
and the Tramways Act, 1870.

Transport 2000
An organization formed in 1973 to bring
together all groups concerned about the
future of public transport services. It calls

for a co-ordinated national policy to avoid wastage of rail and other public transport assets, the improvement and modernization of these assets, and control of the increasing environmental damage caused by the relentless growth of road transport.

Transport World
see T&RW.

Transrail Ltd
A freight operating business of BR, previously Trainload Freight West, reorganized 1994 preparatory to privatization. See EWS.

Transrapid
Trade name for Maglev (qv) system.

Trans-Siberian Express
A *CIWL* service between Moscow and Irkutsk, introduced 1898 as Siberia Express, extended to Harbin (Kharbin) and Vladivostok 1904 and so named. See also Rossiya.

Trans-Siberian Rly
Connects Moscow and Vladivostok; completed 1891–1904. An all-Russian route via Khabarovsk was completed in 1916, and the line was laid with double track throughout from 1928. Now electrified throughout.

Transtrack
IE (qv) overnight parcels and groupage services using wheeled pallets loaded into containers.

Tranz Rail Ltd
Private co. operating the New Zealand rly system from September 1993. 4,273 km of 1,067 mm gauge.

TRAP
Tracking Railway Archives Project. Begun in 2001, this initiative set out to provide a listing of all rly archive material in the UK on the worldwide web, together with a guide to all British record repositories holding such items.

Trap points
Safety points provided in a line to prevent unauthorized movements on to another line.

Traps (RS)
Guard's equipment, or any equipment normally carried on duty by any rlyman.

Travan (TC)
Large covered freight van.

Travel agent
A private individual or firm selling rly passenger tickets on behalf of ATOC (qv) in return for a commission.

Travelator
Alternative spelling of Travolator (qv).

Travel card
A ticket allowing unlimited travel by rail, underground, trams and buses in one or more zones within the Greater London area for one day or longer periods; introduced 1984 by the Greater London Council. Passengers making one return rail journey from many stations outside the Greater London area were also able to purchase this facility (initially under the name 'Capital card') from 1985. See also ODTC.

Travel centres
Offices established at principal BR stations in the 1960s and 1970s to advise passengers on BR travel facilities and sell tickets and seat reservations for journeys to any destination. The name had an earlier origin: the BR London Travel Centre in Lower Regent St. was opened in June 1953, serving a similar function and replacing several smaller ticket and enquiry offices in central London.

Travelers' Aid
A US social agency formed in 1907, to give assistance to travellers in difficulties, notably children, immigrants and old people. TA staff man booths or desks at rly stations which are marked by a blue and white globe.

Traveling card (US)
A card issued by a trade union (brotherhood) to a member in search of rly employment.

Travellers-Fare
Brand name for BR catering outlets, adopted 1973. Separated from BTH (qv) as a free-standing division of BRB, 1982. Sold to management 1988, BR retaining freehold of station sites.

Travelling College
A BR train of thirteen coaches, including sleeping accommodation, shop, meeting room and classrooms, launched 1989. Ceased trading 1991.

Travelling crane
A crane mounted on a truck, used for minor breakdowns and accidents and also for loading and unloading in sidings, etc. where no fixed crane exists. The term is also used for workshop cranes moving along fixed overhead tracks.

Travelling porter (obs)
A man who rode on a hooded seat at the back of loco tender to observe the train, ensuring that all was well. The practice lasted from 1847 until 1861.

Travel on one's basket, to (obs)
Free travel in the guard's van for minor or junior members of a theatrical party sitting on the basket containing their personal gear. An unofficial but apparently tolerated extension of free trucking (qv).

Traverser
A powered platform with a short section of rly track, running across the ends of depot, etc. tracks and used to transfer vehicles or locos one at a time to and from parallel roads. Also a feature of tramcar depots.

Traversias (Sp)
Track sleepers.

Traversing jacks
Pairs of jacks, linked by a crossbeam containing a screw thread and used for re-railing vehicles.

Travolator
A form of escalator or moving walkway without steps, on which passengers are conveyed on the level or up or down a gradient by a continuously moving belt on which they may stand or walk. The first rly use was at Bank station, W&CR (qv) in 1960.

Trax
Abbreviated form of Traxcavator (qv) and of Traxcavating (qv).

Traxcavating/Traxing (RS)
Reballasting using a Traxcavator (qv); also to describe any form of reballasting using machinery other than ballast cleaners.

Traxcavator
A form of skid shovel.

TRB
BR Trailer Buffet.

TRC
Tanzanian Rlys Corporation; owns and operates former EAR (qv) lines in Tanzania. 2,600 km of metre gauge. *See also* Tanzam.

Treacle toffee (RS)(obs)
Welsh coal.

Treadle
A device attached to a rail in which electrical contacts are operated by the passage of a train. Used for example to prove that a train has left a block section.

Treenail or Trenail
A hardwood plug used with track spikes for fastening chairs to sleepers.

Tren de Sierra
A service between Lima and Huancayo over the world's highest main line rly, reaching 15,694 ft/4,783.5 metres above sea level.

Treni populari (It)
Excursion trains available at a 20 per cent discount on standard fares.

Trenitalia SPA (It)
The state-owned rail transport operator in Italy from June 2001, a subsidiary of *FS* (qv). It has three divisions, covering passenger services, freight transport, and regional/metropolitan passenger transport.

Trent Valley Line
Rugby–Tamworth–Stafford.

Trespass guard
Another term for cattle guard (qv).

TRFB
BR Trailer, First Class, with Buffet.

TRFBL
TRFB with Lavatory.

TRFK
TRFB with Kitchen area.

TRFM
BR Trailer, Refreshment car, First class, Modular layout.

Triangle
An arrangement of facing and trailing points leading into and out of a spur which enables loco to be turned without use of a turntable.

Triangulation lighting
An additional front-end light centrally positioned above the driving cab window/s of modern locos and stock; now a standard requirement in Britain.

Tri-Bo
Locos used on *le Shuttle* (qv).
TRIBUTE
BR ticketing system with terminals linked to central data bases, issuing ticket documents of airline type detailing fare, train time and seat reservation. Introduced 1994.
Trick (USRS)
A shift or duty.
Tricomposite/compo (obs)
A coach with seating for First, Second and Third class passengers.
Trimmer (USRS)
A shunting loco assigned to recovering misdirected wagons in a hump yard.
Trip
1. A local train movement of a small lift of freight wagons or vans between freight terminals/private sidings/marshalling yards, etc., hence tripping, trip engine, trip working.
2. (LTRS) A tripcock (qv).
3. (RS)(obs) The annual holiday outing of employees at Swindon Works.
Tripcock/trip handle
A valve attached to a train or locomotive which, if activated by an erect train stop arm (qv), releases compressed air from the train pipe, causing an immediate emergency brake application.
TRIPlanner
Computer terminals with touch screens installed at key locations, which after receiving from travellers indication of their starting point, destination and date of journey, indicate a route with timings. This data can also be printed out and taken away for later reference. Introduced in Hampshire by a public/private partnership, 1995.
Triple crown (RS)
A loco exhibiting three headlamps.
Triplet restaurant cars/set (obs)
Articulated stock (qv) set consisting of restaurant car, kitchen car and a second restaurant car, carried on four bogies.
Trip past, to (LTRS)
Apply the rule, to (qv).
Tripped, to be (LTRS)
A train brought to a halt by the action of a train stop (qv) and tripcock (qv).

Tri-Rail (US)
An organization formed in 1989 and sponsored by three counties to operate a passenger rail service between West Palm Beach and Miami, southern Florida.
TRM
Track Relaying/Renewal Machine (qv).
TRN (Fr)
Trains Rapides Nationaux. Brand name for main line services in France other than *TGV* (qv), 1993.
Trolley
1. The current collection gear of an electric tramcar or other simple electric rail vehicle, consisting of trolley pole, trolley head, grooved trolley wheel or skid, and base.
2. A light manually operated or motored vehicle used for inspection of rly tracks or transport of track workers and their tools.
Trolley Bridge
A movable platform which can be positioned across rly tracks to supply a level surface between two station platforms, permitting easy transfer of heavy items such as loaded barrows (and formerly, milk churns). Normally interlocked with signals to prevent trains moving into the track it temporarily blocks.
Trolley [line/system] (US)
Term for a tramway (*3*) operated by electric cars; hence trolley car, sometimes shortened to 'trolley'.
Trolley freight (US)
Term for any freight service operated by electric locos or cars powered through an overhead line and trolley (qv), interurban and otherwise.
Trolley retriever
A device fitted to tramcars to restrain a trolley pole which has left the trolley wire (qv). It consists of an enclosed spring-loaded drum on to which is wound one end of a light cable attached at its other end to the trolley pole. Extra cable is paid out under gentle tension and any slack cable is wound in but the sudden jerk arising from a dewirement of the trolley causes the spring to wind in the cable until the trolley pole assumes a horizontal position.

Trolley reverser
A triangular layout of tramway (*3*) trolley/contact wires fitted with an automatic frog (qv) at each angle and installed at sites where cars need to be reversed. If the tramcar is stopped beyond the triangle and reverses slowly, the trolley pole and wheel follow one side of the triangle and then the other, so turning the trolley pole in the trailing direction ready for the return trip and eliminating manual swinging round of the trolley pole and replacement of the trolley wheel on the trolley wire.

Trolley wagon
A long flat bogie (qv) wagon for carrying large forgings, turbine castings, aircraft propellers, etc.

Trolley wire
A round or grooved section wire supplying traction current to an electric train, loco or tramcar. Also known as the contact, conductor or traction wire.

Trouble card (LTRS)
A form provided in driving cabs for reporting train defects.

Trout
A 25-ton unfitted hopper ballast wagon with centre and side discharge used by engineers.

TRP
TOPS (qv) Reporting Point.

TRS
1. Temporary Restriction of Speed. *See also* TSR.
2. Train Ready to Start indicator/plunger. Installed at busy stations; operation of a push button or plunger by platform staff causes an indicator in the signal box to show that the train at a specified platform is ready to start.

TRSB
BR Trailer Second/Standard class with Buffet.

TRSBL
TRSB with Lavatory.

TRT
1. Turn-Round Time. The time allowed at the terminus or end of a working to turn a train or loco round, service it as necessary and start the next run, possibly including a rest period for the crew.
2. (obs) Turn Round Time. The time from the start of one loaded journey of a freight wagon to its next.
3. Track Relaying Train (qv).
4. Track Recording Train/Trolley.

TRUB
Trailer Unclassed Buffet/restaurant car with kitchen in a BR HST set.

Truck
1. Any open wagon.
2. A fixed, rigid undercarriage to a rail vehicle, incorporating axles and wheels and, in electrically powered cars, the motors.
3. A four- or six-wheeled undercarriage attached to a loco or vehicle by means of a king-pin or pivot, thus allowing an easier passage round curves than is afforded by (*2*) and also permitting a vehicle of greater length. In electric vehicles the trucks incorporate the traction motors. This type of truck has long been known in the UK as a 'bogie' (except in the case of tramcars and some electric rly cars) but the word truck is also used, as it has always been used in the US, for both (*2*) and (*3*). *See also* Bissell; Commonwealth; Peckham; Pony.
4. (obs) The GWR endeavoured to establish usage of this word for a fitted (qv) vehicle to distinguish it from an ordinary wagon equipped only with manual brakes. In practice staff did not always comply with this directive.

Truck/s
Demotic term for wagon/s (qv).

Truck train
A demu (qv) or dmu (qv) formation adapted for movement of small to medium freight loads, 1997.

TRUK
Trailer Restaurant Unclassed [with] Kitchen in a BR HST set.

Trumpet (LTRS)
A loud hailer.

Trunk haul (obs)
The main part of a freight transit, usually from the initial to the final marshalling point.

Trunk line

A rly system serving an extensive area.

Truss bars

The heavy cross-members of a bogie/truck (qv).

TRUST

Train Running System; a BR computer system.

TS

1. Trailer Second/Standard class in a BR dmu or HST set.
2. Target Speed; used on London Underground in connection with ATP (qv).

TSDB

Train Service Data Base. A computer system holding details of all BR scheduled passenger services. Based at York.

TSG

Transport Supplementary Grant. A central government grant paid to local authorities in respect of public transport expenditure carried on local budgets. Introduced 1975.

TSL

BR TS (qv) with Lavatory.

TSM (LT)

Train Services Manager.

TSO

BR Tourist Open Second/Standard class coach, with 2 + 2 seating.

TSOD

A TSO adapted for use by disabled passengers.

TSOL

A TSO with Lavatory.

TSOLH

A TSOL with Handbrake.

TSOT

A TSO with accommodation for a refreshment Trolley.

TSR

Temporary Speed Restriction. Also TRS (qv).

TSSA

The Transport Salaried Staff Association; founded 1897 as Railway Clerks' Association and renamed in 1951 after the formation of the BTC.

TSSG

Track Safety Strategy Group.

TT

1. The Transport Tribunal. Established under the Railway Act, 1921 as the Railway Rates Tribunal and so renamed by the Transport Act, 1947 which conferred upon it jurisdiction over rates and charges for public transport facilities.
2. The Transport Trust, a registered charity founded in 1964–5 to encourage the permanent preservation through affiliated organizations, or directly, of representative items of the UK transport heritage, land, sea and air. The Trust gives financial assistance and advice to transport preservation projects, and maintains a register of such projects.
3. Thames Trains (qv).

TT (Fr)

Tête des Trains, marking the place where the front of a train will be found.

TTI

Travelling Ticket Inspector.

Tub (RS)

A brake.

Tube

1. Strictly an underground rly using tunnels driven at deep level by means of a tunnelling shield, or the trains which operate on such lines, notably in London, thus, the tube, tube rlys, tube stations, tube trains, etc. The word 'tube' was first used *c.* 1885 to describe the special type of tunnel, but by 1890 the expression 'tube rly' was current. The special meaning was maintained for over sixty years and is respected in this dictionary, but since about 1950 loose journalistic use ('Tube Chaos' made a snappy headline) has increasingly led to its being employed to describe *any* type of underground rly, particularly in London, whether of tube or cut and cover construction. Sadly, from *c.* 1978 London Transport gave this sloppy custom its official blessing by misusing the word in its own publications, notably in the title of its newspaper for Underground staff, *Tubeline*.
2. (obs) A booking office ticket container for Edmondson (qv) card tickets.

Tubeline
News sheet for LT Underground rly staff (not only tube staff), 1986–94.

Tubelines
A consortium (Amey, Jarvis and Bechtel Field) accepted as the Infraco (qv) under the PPP (qv) for the Jubilee (qv). Northern (qv) and Piccadilly (qv), lines of the London Underground.

Tubes, loco
The horizontal pipes carrying smoke and burning gases from the firebox to the smokebox, heating the boiler water which surrounds them, thus producing the steam.

TUCC (obs)
Transport Users' Consultative Committees. *See* CTCC.

Tumblehome
A contraction in body width of a rly coach or tramcar below the waistline.

Tunbridge Wells Fargos (RS)(obs)
Old-style Pullman cars used on BR (S) Hastings service via Tunbridge Wells. From the 1938 film, *Wells Fargo*.

Tunnel
A rly tunnel was defined by BR civil engineers as any structure that carries the rly through or under a *natural* obstruction, anything else being considered a 'bridge' or 'covered way'. By this definition some passages through man-made obstructions were longer than short tunnels. According to the PWI *Track Terminology*, 2004, an overline bridge covering more than 50 metres' length of rly is now regarded as a 'tunnel'.

Tunnelbana/Tunnelbanenätet Metro
(Swedish)
Metro system in Stockholm.

Tunnel miners
Specialist labourers employed on the construction of tube rlys and similar tunnels.

Tunnel motor (RS)
GWR 0–6–0 PT loco fitted with condensing gear for working over the Metropolitan and Circle lines of the London Underground.

Tunnel rats (LTRS)
Trainmen/women working on London tube rlys.

Tunnel tigers
Nickname for tunnel miners (qv).

Tunny
A 20-ton unfitted ballast wagon with fixed ends used by engineers.

Tuppenny Tube
Nickname bestowed on the CLR by a journalist. When opened in 1900, it had a uniform 2d fare for all journeys.

Turbo Expresses (RS)
BR class 166 turbo-charged demus.

Turbomotive
LM&SR 4–6–0 built in 1935 to the designs of W.A. Stanier and equipped with a turbine drive instead of the usual cylinders. Rebuilt as a conventional steam loco in 1952, it was destroyed in the serious accident at Harrow & Wealdstone later that year.

Turbos (RS)
BR class 165 turbo-charged dmus.

Turbostar
ADtranz (qv) name for family of dmu (qv) introduced in 2000, including classes 168 and 170.

Turbot
A 34-ton ballast and sleeper wagon with drop sides, used by engineers.

Turbotrain (obs)
A French gas turbine train design, usually with auxiliary diesel engines, exported to Egypt, Iran, USA and Canada. *See also* ETG; RTG.

Turin–Nice–Cannes Pullman
A *CIWL* service, ran summer 1927 only.

Turin–Venice Pullman
A *CIWL* service, ran summer 1928 only.

Turksib
A major Russian rail project of the period between the two world wars, connecting the Trans-Siberian line (qv) with Turkestan in the far south. Opened 1931, and the subject of a film of this title.

Turn
The daily duty or shift for uniformed and ticket office staff.

Turnback link (obs)
The link (qv) of enginemen which relieved incoming crews at the end of a journey, taking the loco to the depot and preparing it for the return run.

Turnbuckle

A screw component of the trussing of a rly coach which may be adjusted to pull or push the underframe into shape by lifting the central part above the rest so that it levels out when bearing the weight of the body.

Turner, engine (obs)

An employee at an engine shed whose duties were to move locos around the yard and turn them on the turntable.

Turnout

The total assembly of trackwork involved in 'turning out' one line from another by means of a pair of switches, a crossing and a reverse curve running in the direction of the second line, with or without an intermediate section of straight line. Strictly *not* synonymous with points, but often so used. *See* Points.

Turnout road

The secondary road through a set of points or turnout (qv) as opposed to the Straight or Through road (qv).

Turnover working

An arrangement in which the loco of the previous train is attached to the rear of the next arrival at a terminus to secure a rapid turnround.

Turnplate (obs)

A small turntable for moving wagons and short coaches from one line to another.

Turn-Round Time

see TRT.

Turntable

A revolving table over a pit, fitted with a central pivot and carrying a section of track. Used to turn a vehicle or loco around or move it from one line to another. Manual operation was usual but as the weight of locos increased, mechanical refinements and vacuum or electric power were introduced.

Turn-under

Another term for Tumblehome (qv).

TUT (obs)

Terminal Utilization Time; the time between the arrival of a particular wagon at a depot until its despatch, loaded or empty.

TV

Trent Valley (qv), Tanat Valley (qv). *See also* TVR.

Tvärbanan (Swedish)

Cross-line; Stockholm orbital light rail transit (qv), first section opened 2000.

TVLR

see Tanat Valley.

TVR

1. Taff Vale Rly, Cardiff to Merthyr/Aberdare/ Maerdy/Treherbert, etc., inc 1836, first section opened 1840. 124 route miles by 1914. Part of GWR from 1922.

2. Teign Valley Rly, Christow–Heathfield, inc 1863, opened 1882, worked by GWR. Part of GWR from 1923.

3. Tees Valley Rly, inc 1865, from near Barnard Castle to Middleton-in-Teesdale, opened 1868, worked by NER, part of NER 1882.

4. Trent Valley Rly, Stafford–Tamworth–Rugby, inc 1845, opened 1847, acquired by L&NWR (qv) 1846.

TW/TWD

Trench Warfare Dept, WW1.

TWC (US)

Track Warrant Control; an operating system used on long stretches of dark track (qv) under which train crews receive (and repeat back) train orders (qv) by on-board (qv) radio.

Twelve wheel loco (US)

A loco with 4–8–0 wheel arrangement.

Twentieth/20th Century Limited

An overnight NYC express between New York and Chicago, introduced 1902 with a time of 20 h. Affectionately known as 'The Century', it had become 'a national institution' by 1926. Journey time reduced to 18 h in 1932. Timing became 16 h in 1938, with new stock, and all sleeping accommodation in rooms. The 16 h schedule was resumed in 1946, and had been reduced to 15 h 30 min by 1954. The consist remained all-Pullman until 1957. Ceased to run on 2 December 1967.

Twenty-four-hour clock

A system in which p.m. times are distinguished by adding 12, e.g. 3 p.m. = 15.00. Adopted by Indian rlys 1864–70; Italian rlys *c.* 1890; Belgian and Spanish rlys in the 1900s; French and Portuguese rlys in 1912; the British Army in 1918; Cook's Timetables (qv) in 1919, and by most European rlys other than those mentioned in the 1920s. BR moved to the system in 1965; LT in 1964–5.

TWERPS
Tunbridge Wells (West)–Eridge Rly Preservation Society, initial title of group restoring this former BR line. *See* Spa Valley Line.

Twilight zone (RS)(obs)
The waiting period experienced by a fireman before promotion to driver.

Twin-block sleepers
Separate concrete blocks supporting each rail of a track and linked to their opposite number by a metal tie. Lighter in weight than concrete sleepers of traditional conformation they offer improved resistance to lateral forces as four faces are in contact with the ballast instead of two.

Twin Rover (obs)
A ticket formerly available for one day's unlimited travel on most of London Underground and central area buses and trolleybuses on Saturdays, Sundays and Bank Holidays, introduced 1958.

Twirly (RS)
A pensioner using a concession ticket/free pass, or the ticket itself. Usage of these facilities is normally restricted to the period after the morning peak and the origin of the term is the question frequently asked by holders uncertain whether the hour for its use had been reached: 'Am I *too early?*'.

Twist
A change of cant.

Twisters (USRS)
Hand brakes.

TWM
Travel West Midlands, operator of Midland Metro (qv).

Two crows for a banker (RS)(obs)
The whistle code exchanged between train engine and banker when ready to move.

Two labour gains (RS)
see Labour gain[s].

Twopenny Tube
see Tuppenny Tube.

Two rooms and a bath
A colloquialism for an articulated tramcar set in which two cars are connected by a small flexible central entrance section in which the conductor is seated.

Two-two-two (RS)(obs)
222 Marylebone Road, London, the former headquarters of the RE (*3*), BRB and BTC.

Two Woodbines and an aspirin (RS)(obs)
The engine driver's breakfast; Woodbines were a very cheap cigarette.

Tyne & Wear Metro
The prototype British light rail transit system (qv), largely based on former BR tracks in the Newcastle area and serving Whitley Bay, Gateshead, Jarrow and South Shields. First sections opened 1980.

Tyne Enterprise
Stranraer–Ayr–Carlisle–Newcastle service, so named 1992.

Tynesider
A sleeping car express between London (Kings Cross) and Newcastle, so named 1950. Name dropped 1968.

Tyne Trader
Girvan–Ayr–Carlisle–Newcastle service, so named 1992.

Tyne Valley Line
Newcastle to Hexham and Carlisle.

Typo/s (RS) (obs)
Stencilled typewritten sheets sent to the staff concerned, notifying detailed instructions, timings, etc. in relation to special traffic (qv) when insufficient time was available for normal printing. *See also* STN.

Tyre (US = tire)
The flange and tread profile of rly/tramway wheel.

Tyrol Express
A *CIWL* service [Calais] Paris–Zurich–Innsbruck–Salzburg, introduced 1932.

TZR
Tanzania–Zambia Rly; *see* Tanzam.

U

U
Unclassed vehicle, BR.
U-Bahn (Ger)
Untergrundbahn, underground rly within an urban/suburban zone, not part of the main German rly system and synonymous with Metro (qv). May include elevated or surface operation.
Überleitstelle/Üst (Ger)
A crossover (qv) or running connection between different tracks of a double track line which is situated outside a station zone.
U-boats (RS)
SR U class 2–6–0 locos.
UCC
Union Construction Company; the manufacturing subsidiary of the UERL (qv), registered 1901. Reconstituted as Union Construction & Finance Co. Ltd, 1929. Built and rebuilt tramcars and tube cars at Feltham, Middlesex, 1925–32. Wound up in 1933 following the formation of the LPTB.
UEC
United Electric Car Co. Ltd, Preston, rly and tramway vehicle builders. Inc 1898 as ER & TCW (qv), a subsidiary of DK (qv); renamed UEC 1905, after purchase of the assets of the BEC (qv) and Milnes (qv). Became part of EE (qv), 1919.
UEG
Union Elektricitäts Gesellschaft, manufacturers of electrical equipment under US licences. Merged with *AEG* (qv), 1903.
UERL
Underground Electric Railways Company of London Ltd. Popularly known as the Underground Company or, with its subsidiaries, as the Underground Group.

Also known (mainly among politicians) as the London Traffic Combine. Formed in 1902 to take over the MDET (qv), and held a controlling interest in the MDR (qv) and the three tube rlys which became the LER (qv). Absorbed the London General Omnibus Co. in 1912, and the CLR (*1*) (qv) and the C&SLR (qv) in 1913. Also acquired control of the company-owned tramways in the London area and the North Metropolitan Electric Power Supply Co. Its transport interests became part of LPTB from 1933. 'The mysterious American Corporation' – RM, 1906.
UIC
Union Internationale des Chemins de Fer; International Union of Railways, formed at Paris 1922 to standardize and improve rly equipment and operating methods, with special regard to international traffic. Since 1950 the UIC has been responsible for ensuring co-ordination and unity of action in international rly organizations.
UIC gauge
see Berne gauge.
UITP
Union Internationale des Transports Publics; International Union of Public Transport, founded 1885 as the *Union Internationale des Tramways*. The present name dates from 1939. The Union's object is to pool the experience of urban and interurban public transport undertakings for joint study and research and to promote the technical and economic development of the industry.
Ukeleles (RS)
Class J39 0–6–0 locos L&NER.

UKRAS
United Kingdom Railway Advisory Service; formed in 1959 to provide an advisory and consultancy service to rlys overseas and to sponsor the training of overseas rly staff on BR. Reconstituted as UKRAS Consultants Ltd, 1966. Wound up 1969 and superseded by Transmark (qv).

ULR
Ultra Light Rail (qv).

Ulster Express
A service between London (Euston) and Fleetwood connecting with Belfast sailings, name introduced 1927, diverted to Heysham 1928. Name re-introduced 1949; service ceased 1975 with the withdrawal of the Heysham–Belfast service.

Ultra Light Rail
A low-cost form of Light Rail (qv), using small lightweight cars travelling over shallow trackbeds constructed with minimal disturbance to existing sewers and other services under roadways. Suitable for short distance transport in congested urban centres and car-free zones or for special purpose point-to-point applications, e.g. between car parks and retail/entertainment complexes. *See also* Minitram; Parry People Mover.

Ultrasonic rail flaw detection
Use of sound waves at a predetermined frequency to locate and assess rail defects.

U Magazine
Magazine for London Underground staff, replacing *Tubeline* and first published August 1994. Ceased after December 1995; replaced by *OTM* (qv).

UMLER
Acronym for Universal Machine Language Equipment Register; a computerized inventory of US rly rolling stock.

UMTA
Urban Mass Transportation Administration, subsidizing US urban public transport projects from the Federal budget.

UN
Underground News. The monthly publication (since December 1961) of the LURS (qv). From 1961 to December 1974 it was known as *UndergrounD; The Journal of the London Underground Railway Society*.

Unbalanced working
A duty without provision for return to depot or other starting point.

Unbooked route
A route different from that shown in the WTT (qv).

Unclassed/unclassified
BR terms for a coach available for use by both First and Second/Standard class passengers.

Uncoupling (LT)(obs)
The practice of providing short trains for off peak services by dividing up full-length trains.

Uncle Sam (USRS)
A Post Office employee working on a mail train.

Underbridge
A bridge carrying line over a road, canal, river or another rly, i.e. an underline bridge.

Underframe
A wood or metal framework carrying the main body structure of a vehicle.

Undergricing (RS)
Track bashing (qv) on underground rlys. Also undergricer, one who indulges in undergricing.

Underground [the]
The brand name since 1908 for all London underground rlys, deep tube and subsurface, including those not controlled by the UERL (qv) but (until 1994) excepting the W&CR (qv). Often displayed on signs and publicity as U-*N-D-E-R-G-R-O-U-N*-D. Use of the term persisted through and beyond the LPTB era but in more recent years it has to some extent given way to 'tube' (qv).

Underground hog (USRS)
1. A senior driver.
2. Chief engineer in charge of track maintenance.

Undermen (obs)
Men working on track under a ganger (qv).

Under the arm (RS)
Not up to standard.

Under the hammer (RS)
A train accepted at caution by a signalman.

Under the wire(s) (RS)
Travelling over or working on an electrified line with OLE (qv).

UNDM
Uncoupling Non-Driving Motor car in a mu set.
Undums (LTRS)
Colloquialism for UNDM (qv).
Unfitted
A wagon or other vehicle not fitted with continuous brakes (qv).
Unfitted tail (obs)
Unfitted (qv) vehicles marshalled at the back of a train to ensure braking force was maximized behind the loco.
UNIFE
European Rail Industry Association.
UNILOG
Universal Logistics & International Forwarding, a joint undertaking of Railfreight Distribution (qv) and *SNCB* (qv) (including the subsidiaries Ferry-Boats and Inter Ferry) to market Channel Tunnel freight services between Benelux countries and the UK, 1992.
Unimog
A four-wheel drive diesel-engined vehicle capable of operating on roads, across country or using rly tracks, developed by Mercedes-Benz in the 1960s.
Union
US term for a steam loco with an 0–10–2 wheel arrangement; first used on the Union RR, USA in 1936.
Union Castle Express
see Springbok.
Union Express/Limited
A boat train service between Johannesburg and Capetown, First Class only, connecting with Union Castle Line sailings; 956 m in 28 h 23 min on 3 ft 6 in gauge in 1926. Superseded by the Blue Train (2) (qv).
Union Pacific (US)
A steam loco with 4–12–2 wheel arrangement. The first was ordered by the UP.
Union Pacific RR
see UP.
Union Railways
Union Railways Ltd, a BR subsidiary agency formed 1992 to prepare, develop and manage the proposed direct rly between London and the Channel Tunnel and to assist with other new projects,

including the Heathrow Express (qv). Transferred to private ownership 1996 and tasked with overseeing construction of the CTRL (qv) from 1998. *See also* CTRL; L&CR (2).
Union station (US)(obs)
Term for large rly station shared by two or more companies. At St Louis (Missouri), no fewer than twenty-one companies used the Union station.
Union switch[er] (US)
Term for a steam loco with 0–10–2 wheel arrangement.
Unit train (US)
A high-tonnage train chartered for carrying a single bulk product, not requiring any marshalling between departure and destination points.
Unload, to (USRS)
To jump from a moving train.
Unterpflasterstrassenbahn (Ger)
U-strab (qv).
Unworked points
A set of points/switches (usually in sidings or yards) which are not under the control of a signaller or ground frame (qv). *See also* Hand points.
UP (US)
Union Pacific RR; absorbed Mopac, 1982, and MKT, 1988. Largest mileage of any North American system until formation of NA Rlys (qv) in 2000.
Up
1. The running line to or in the general direction of London, or (less usually) of the company's headquarters, or, for lines wholly in Scotland, of Edinburgh, and on the TVR (qv) up from the South Wales coast to inland destinations, the other direction being known as 'Down'. These terms were taken over from road coaching and in the London area and other urban locations have to some extent given way (notably on LT Rlys) to the more readily comprehensible US terms, eastbound, northbound, southbound and westbound. On rlys worked by the British Army, the Up lines are those used to reach the railhead (qv).*See also* Down (1).

2. (RS) Used of a train running early, e.g. 'four up', meaning four minutes early against the timetable. *See also* Down (2).

UP&SS

United Pointsmen's & Signalmen's Society, founded 1880, amalgamated 1913 with the ASRS and GRWU to form the NUR.

Uplift [tickets], to (USRS)

To collect tickets. *See also* Lift [tickets], to.

Uplighters

Lighting columns placed between escalators or in circulating areas which directed their illumination towards the ceiling, producing a soft and even reflected glow. Used widely in the 1930s architecture of the London Underground but subsequently mostly displaced by less atmospheric fluorescent tube lighting.

Upper quadrant

A semaphore signal with an arm which moves into the upper quadrant when 'off'. Adopted from US practice and used on some British lines, particularly the Underground, LM&SR and L&NER. Early types incorporated three positions horizontal (red light) = danger; 45° (yellow light) = caution; vertical (green light) = clear/proceed, *or* two positions, horizontal = danger; 45/50° = clear/proceed. The latter became general.

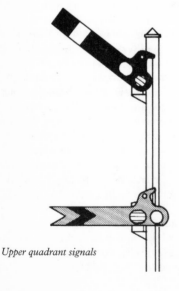

Upper quadrant signals

Upper Ward Express

A service between Glasgow and Moffat, introduced 1904, renamed Tinto Express 1911.

Ups and downs (RS)(obs)

GWR men used this term for ECS (qv) workings in and out of Paddington, London and the associated light engine runs.

Up siding

A siding trailing off an 'Up' (qv) line.

Up the hole (LTRS)

In a tube tunnel dead end siding.

Up the madhouse (RS)(SR)

London.

Up the road, to go (LTRS)

To see a manager regarding a misdemeanour.

UR

1. Ulster Rly, inc 1836, Belfast to Armagh, first section opened 1839, 6 ft 2 in/ 1,879.6 mm gauge, converted to 5 ft 3 in/1,600 mm, 1849, part of GNR (I) from 1876.

2. Uganda Rly; metre gauge, completed from Mombasa to Kisumu, Lake Victoria, 1901. Renamed Kenya & Uganda Rlys 1927 (*see* K&UR). Separate undertaking again 1977 (*see* URC).

URC

Uganda Rlys Corporation; formed 1977 to operate all rlys in Uganda. *c.* 1,200 km of metre gauge, physically connected to KR (qv).

URF

International Union of Railway Road Services.

URL

Union Railways Ltd (qv).

USA

Freight services operated by private companies, passenger services by Amtrak (qv), a public corporation; *c.* 195,000 km, almost all standard gauge.

USATC

United States Army Transportation Corps. Army rly battalions of the USATC functioned in all theatres of war in WW1 and WW2. In 1945 there were 43,306 officers and men engaged in USATC rly activities.

USRA
1. United States Railroad Administration; formed in 1917 by the US government to operate the main rly systems in wartime. USRA functioned in this role from 1 January 1918 until 1 March 1920. There was no similar state takeover in WW2 in the US.
2. United States Railway Association; a federal agency, formed in 1973 to plan and direct the reorganization of bankrupt private rly companies. *See also* Conrail.

Üst (Ger)
Überleitstelle (qv).

U-strab (Ger)
Subways used by tramways (*3*).

U-Strassenbahn (Ger)
Subways used by tramways (*3*); also *Unterpflasterstrassenbahn* or *U-strab* (qv).

UT
Conférence Internationale pour l'Unité Technique des Chemins de Fer. International Conference for the Technical Uniformity of Rlys. Established at Berne, 1882, with increased national representation from 1886 and the objective of securing uniformity across Europe in mechanical matters related to rly rolling stock. Based in Berne, Switzerland and known informally as 'The Berne Conference' or 'The Berne Convention'. *See also* Berne [Convention] gauge; Berne key; Berne rectangle.

UTA
Ulster Transport Authority; formed 1948, a merger of the Northern Ireland Road Transport Board, the NCC and the B&CDR. Took over GNR (I) (qv) assets in Northern Ireland from the GNR (I) board in 1958. Became UTR (qv), 1966.

UTI
Urban Transport International, English language periodical published in Paris covering urban public transport developments worldwide.

UTM
Urgent Train Message; a written communication sent by passenger train.

UTR
Ulster Transport Rlys; took over the rlys formerly operated by UTA (qv), 1966, became NIR (qv) 1967.

UTS
Underground Ticketing System. A system involving ticket-checking entry and exit gates, self-service automatic machines issuing magnetic-coded tickets and secure wall ticket and enquiry offices for staff, installed at London Underground stations 1987–90.

UTX
Under-track crossing. *See also* Cattle arch.

UVW
United Vehicle Workers; an amalgamation in 1920 of the AAT (qv), and L&PLW (qv), catering for workers on tramways (3).

UW
User-worked; prefix of codes for various types of level crossing worked by users: UWC: barriers operated by user; UWCM: miniature red and green warning lights operated by user; UWCT: User-worked crossing with telephone access to signallers; UWG: Gate crossing, gates operated by user.

UZ
Ukrainska Zaliznitsa; Ukraine Rlys, 22,500 km of 1,520 mm gauge.

V

VAB (obs)

A singleton BR(S) (qv) eight-car unit consisting of two VEPs (qv) of 3,000 hp with restaurant car, normally coupled to another VEP for working services between London (Waterloo) and Bournemouth. Now withdrawn.

Vacuum brakes

A braking system in which the brakes are held off by maintaining a vacuum in an operating cylinder on each vehicle and applied by partially destroying the vacuum by controlled admission of air. Normally arranged as continuous brakes (qv). Abolished in Great Britain 1987.

VAL (Fr)

Véhicule Automatique Légère; light automatic vehicle. A light rapid transit system (qv) developed by the firm of Matra, using automated rubber-tyred driverless trains running along concrete tracks and guided by horizontal rubber wheels bearing on concrete guideways. Introduced in Lille, 1983.

Valance

1. Reinforcing angle to loco footplate.
2. Decorative board work suspended from the edge of a platform canopy.

Valencia Express

A summer service between Paris and Port Bou, introduced 1966, with connecting service to and from Valencia from 1968. Name dropped after 1976.

Vale of Clwyd

Inc 1856, Foryd–Denbigh, opened 1858, worked and managed by L&NWR, part of L&NWR, 1868.

Vale of Glamorgan

Barry–Bridgend, inc 1889, opened 1897, worked by Barry Rly, part of GWR1922.

Vale of Llangollen

Ruabon–Llangollen, inc 1859, opened 1861, 1862, worked by GWR, amalgamated with GWR 1896.

Vale of Neath

Neath to Aberdare/Merthyr/Cwmamman, inc 1846, first section opened 1851, amalgamated with GWR 1865.

Vale of Rheidol

Vale of Rheidol Light Rly, Aberystwyth–Devil's Bridge, 1 ft 11$\frac{1}{2}$ in/597 mm gauge. Inc 1897, opened 1902, absorbed by Cambrian Rlys 1913, part of GWR 1922, closed 1939, reopened 1945. Part of BR 1948, sold in 1989 to Brecon Mountain Railway Ltd.

Vale of Teifi

Vale of Teifi Narrow Gauge Rly, 2 ft/609 mm gauge tourist/pleasure line over part of the former BR Newcastle Emlyn branch, opened 1985.

Vale of Towy

Llandovery Junction–Llandeilo. Inc 1854, opened 1858, vested in L&NWR 1884 but Llanelly Rly & Dock Co. (absorbed by GWR 1889) had power to lease. GWR & L&NWR Joint 1889–1922, GWR & LM&SR joint 1923–47.

Valley Lines

Brand name for commuter and other local services operated out of Cardiff Central and Queen St. stations by Cardiff Rly Co. (qv): Cardiff–Cardiff Bay/Penarth/Barry Island/Treherbert/Aberdare/Merthyr Tydfil/Coryton/Rhymney; also the Cardiff 'City Line' loop via Ninian Park.

Valve gear

The apparatus for controlling the steam

distribution valve in the cylinder steam chest of a loco.

Van (Canadian RS)

A caboose (qv).

Van Beethoven

TEE Amsterdam–Bonn, introduced 1972, replacing *Rhein–Main* (qv), extended to Frankfurt 1976. Lost *TEE* status 1979.

Vanderbilt tender

A cylindrical coal tender. After the inventor, Cornelius Vanderbilt Jr (1873–1942).

Vangölü Express

A service between Istanbul (Haydarpasa) and Tehran introduced 1971 using train ferry on Lake Van.

Van portion

That part of a Brake First/Second/Third (qv) reserved for the guard, parcels, luggage, etc.

Varnish, the (USRS)(obs)

A passenger train; strictly applicable only to old wooden stock. Also string of varnish, varnished boxes, varnished job, varnished shot, varnished wagons.

Vauxhall

see Voksal.

VBW

See RBS.

VDV (Ger)

Verband Deutscher Verkehrsbetriebe, a merger of *VÖV* (qv) and *BDE* (qv), 1991. Subsequently renamed *Verband Deutscher Verkehrsunternehmen*, the Association of German Local Transport Operators.

VEC (obs)

Four-car emu set of LT tube stock refurbished 1967 for BR service between Ryde Pierhead and Shanklin, 4-VEC; ran with TIS (qv), making VECTIS (the Roman name for the Isle of Wight).

VEG (obs)

BR (S) four-car emu sets; Vestibule, Electro-pneumatic brakes Gatwick, converted for Gatwick Airport–London (Victoria) service, 1978, 4-VEG.

Vehicle

In current rly terminology, this noun covers either (a) any unit of rolling stock forming part of a freight or passenger train

which is incapable of independent traction or (b) any self-propelled unit capable of carrying a load (such as those used for engineering purposes). *See also* Traction unit.

Vehicle gauge

The maximum profile not to be exceeded when a vehicle is built, which includes the limitations imposed by end and centre throw (*see* Overthrow) and the load/ing gauge (1) (qv) of the rlys it is to use.

Velocipede (obs)

A pedal-driven rail trolley used for track inspection, etc. capable of carrying up to four men.

Vélo-rail (Fr)

Pedal-driven rail trolley used by maintenance staff. Hired out for public recreational use on some disused lines in France and Belgium from the mid-1990s.

Vente ambulante (Fr)

A *CIWL* facility providing drinks and light refreshments from a trolley moved along the corridors and gangways of a train.

VEP

BR (S) four-car corridor emu sets of 1967–74; Vestibule, Electro-Pneumatic brakes; two driving trailer composites, one motor brake Second/Standard class coach and one trailer Second/Standard, all seating in open cars 2 + 3; 4-VEP.

VER

VR (*1*) (qv).

Verband (Ger)

Tramcar designs developed by *VÖV* (qv).

Versailles

A Paris–Geneva *TGV* service, introduced 1983.

Vestibule

An enclosed space at each end of a rly carriage giving access to the seating areas and also to adjacent coaches.

Vestibuled [train/coach]

A train or coach with vestibules and gangways enabling passengers to move between one coach and another. The term originated in the US in 1887. *See also* Corridor.

Vesuvio

TEE Milan–Naples 1973, lost *TEE* status 1986.

VFE (Fr)
Voyages France-Europe. The main inter-city services of *SNCF* (qv).

VFIL (Fr)
Compagnie Générale des Voies Ferrées d'Intérêt Local; a grouping of French secondary rlys.

VFR
Visiting Friends and Relatives; term used by BR to describe this class of passenger traffic. Adopted from air lines and travel trade usage.

VGR
see VR (*3*).

VIA Rail
A Canadian organization formed in 1977 (CNR had used VIA as a brand name from 1976) to take over the CPR and CNR passenger service marketing functions. From 1978 VIA became an independent corporation contracting with the federal government to manage all rail passenger services, acquiring the CPR and CNR passenger rolling stock and locos. Canada has approximately 50,000 km of rly route including freight-only lines.

VIBT
Vehicle Inspection and Brake Test.

Vic (LTRS)
Victoria Line, London Transport (qv).

Vichy Pullman Express
see London/Londres–Vichy Pullman.

Vicinal/Vicinaux
see SNCV.

Vickers
see MCW; Metro–Cammell; MV.

Vicrail
see VR (*3*).

Victoria Line
LT Tube rly from Walthamstow to Brixton via Oxford Circus and Victoria, connecting with most other Underground lines. The first of London's second generation of tube rlys, opened in sections 1968–71.

Victory
A London (Waterloo)–Portsmouth express, so named 1989–1992.

Vie du Rail, la
The title assumed by the *SNCF* magazine in 1952, formerly *Notre Métier* (qv). A

unique blend of well-illustrated and authoritative historical, technical and news items covering not only French rlys and tramways but those of the whole world, together with television, film, fashion and other pages for the family.

Vienna–Tyrol–Cannes Express
A *CIWL* service introduced in 1913.

View finder (RS)
Second driver (qv).

Vigilance device
Any arrangement which requires a driver to take positive action at frequent intervals to prevent the train from coming to a halt.

Vignoles rail
Flat-bottomed rail, introduced 1837 by the engineer Charles Blacker Vignoles (1793–1875).

Vignoles rail

Viking Express
A service between Stockholm, Copenhagen and Hamburg, introduced 1968. Name subsequently dropped, then revived for a service between Paris and Stockholm (24 h) introduced 1986, incorporating sleeping cars between Paris and Helsingør, which replaced the Paris coaches of the Nord express (qv).

Village, the
A two-storey office block completed in 1920 between platforms 15 and 16 at London (Waterloo). Demolished 1991 in connection with the construction of the London Channel Tunnel Terminal.

Vincent van Gogh
A Harwich–Liverpool/Birmingham service, so-named 1992.

Vindobona
An express between Berlin, Prague and Vienna, introduced 1957.

Virgil
GWR TC for 30-ton bogie freight van.

Virgin CrossCountry/CrossCountry Trains Ltd
A TOC (*2*) (qv) awarded the Cross Country Trains (qv) franchise in 1997, operating services connecting the south and south-west of England and Swansea with the Midlands, north-west and north-east England and Scotland. Connections between routes can be made at Birmingham (New St.). *See also* Voyager.

Virgin Trains [Group]
see VRG.

Virgin West Coast/West Coast Trains Ltd
A TOC (*2*) (qv) awarded the InterCity West Coast (qv) franchise in 1997, operating services London (Euston)–Birmingham–Shrewsbury; London (Euston)–Manchester/Liverpool/Holyhead/Blackpool; London (Euston)–Glasgow. *See also* Voyager/Super Voyager; WCML.

Virtual quarries
Stockpiles of ballast for rly use regularly fed from a quarry or port and designated for use in a defined area.

Visière (Fr)
see Capuchon.

Vistadome
An observation saloon occupying part of a passenger coach roof space, introduced on the Burlington RR (US), 1945. Full length dome cars followed in 1953.

V/Line
Public transport corporation of the state of Victoria, Australia.

VofGR
see Vale of Glamorgan.

VofLR
see Vale of Llangollen.

VofNR
see Vale of Neath.

VofRR
see Vale of Rheidol.

VofTR
see Vale of Towy.

Voiding
A state in which there is unsupported space beneath sleepers following displacement of ballast (qv), caused by traffic loading. The affected sleepers are described as 'hanging' or 'voided'.

Voksal (Russian)
The Russian word for a rly station, probably derived from the fact that the first rly in Russia (1837, St Petersburg–Pavlovsk) served gardens at Pavlovsk remodelled by Catherine the Great on the pattern of London's Vauxhall Gardens. (London's Vauxhall station did not open until 1848.)

VOL
Vehicle On Line indicator (in a signal box).

Volk's Rly
see VR (*1*).

Voltaire
A Paris-Geneva *TGV* service, introduced 1983.

Vomit Special (RS)
Any late night train patronized by inebriates.

VOP/4-VOP
Vestibule Open Plan, class 423, a modified VEP (qv) emu (qv) 1999–2000.

VÖV (Ger)
Verband Öffentlicher Verkehrsbetriebe, a voluntary association of light rly and tramway (*3*) operators with the object of coordinating and standardizing design, operations, etc. Renamed *VDV* (qv) 1991.

Voyager/Super Voyager
High speed Pendolino (qv) tilting (140 mph) (Super Voyager) and non-tilting diesel trains built 2000–2002 by Fiat Ferroviaria, Alstom (qv) and Bombardier Eurorail (qv) for Virgin West Coast (qv) and Virgin CrossCountry (qv) services.

VR
1. Volk's Rly, along Brighton seafront, opened by Magnus Volk (1851–1937), the electrical engineering pioneer, with electric traction in 1883, 2 ft gauge; the first enduring electric rly in the UK. Extended and converted to 2 ft 9 in gauge 1884; still operating in the summer season.
2. *Valtionrautatiet*; Finnish State Rlys. 5,850 km of 1,524 mm gauge, with

physical connections to the Russian Rlys
(*see* RZD).

3. Victorian [Government] Rlys
[Australia].

VRG

Virgin Rail Group Ltd (qv), Virgin Cross
Country (qv), Virgin West Coast (qv) and
part interest in L&CR (qv).

VRR (Ger)

Verkehrsverbund Rhein-Ruhr, established
1978. Europe's largest passenger transport
federation, with a 12,000 km network of
rly, bus and tramway (*3*) routes between
Dusseldorf and Dortmund.

VS&PR

Victoria Station & Pimlico Rly, inc 1858,
opened 1860, absorbed into SR 1923.

VSOE

Venice Simplon–Orient Express; a luxury
tourist train operation, using restored
traditional British Pullman Co. stock
between London (Victoria) and Folkestone
and restored *CIWL* restaurant, sleeping
and Pullman cars between Boulogne, Paris
and Venice, introduced 1982. Later also
ran to Vienna in summer. Some runs made
to Budapest from 1991. The British cars
are also used for day luxury excursions
under the same brand name, mostly in
south-east England. Owned by Sea
Containers Ltd.

Vulcan

1. Vulcan Foundry Co. Ltd, Newton-le-
   Willows, Warrington, loco builders,

founded 1830. Part of EE, 1955.

2. (US) Vulcan, a loco building firm,
   based at Wilkes Barre; no connection
   with (*1*).

Vulcans

LB&SCR 0–6–0 goods locos built by the
Vulcan Foundry Co.

Vulkan (Ger)

A loco building firm, at Stettin. No
connection with Vulcan (*1*) or (*2*).

Vulnerables

Traffic vulnerable to theft (wines and
spirits, tobacco, clothing, etc.).

Vulture (LTRS)

A retirement pensioner travelling free or at
concessionary fares.

VUT (Fr)

Voie Unique Temporaire, temporary single
line working.

VVM

Vlaamseveervoer Maatschappij; Flemish
Transport Company. The Flemish section of
the former *SNCV/NMVB* (qv),
independently managed from 1991. *See also*
Lijn, De; *SRWT*.

V/VSIC

Vehicle/Vehicle System Interface
Committee, set up 2005 by the RSSB (qv)
to 'investigate every aspect of rail vehicles
and how they react with the environment
and railway infrastructure'. Replaces
WRISA (qv).

VXC

Virgin Cross Country (qv).

W

Wabash (US)
Wabash, St Louis & Pacific Rly, latterly known officially as the Wabash Rly Co.
Wabash, to (USRS)
To drive a train with skill and speed. Also (sarcastically) to corner (qv). The Wabash was a company famed for its high standards of training.
WABTEC/WABTEC Rail Ltd
Wabtec Corporation, a 1999 merger of the Westinghouse Air Brake Co. (USA) (WABCO) and Motive Power Industries. In the UK, Wabtec Rail Ltd, formed in 2000, includes RFS(E), (*see* RFS Industries).
Wagenstandanzeiger (Ger)
A platform display board showing all long distance trains in diagrammatic form, indicating the exact sequence of coaches with their class of accommodation and seat reservation numbers, in relation to marked sections of the platform.
Waggon road/way (obs)
An early form of surface rly designed for vehicles with flanged wheels. Rails were usually wooden but towards the end of the eighteenth century it became usual to face the wood with iron and in time wholly iron rails were used. The term was mainly confined to north-east England (elsewhere 'rail way' or 'rail road' were normal); it fell out of use after *c.* 1830 with the spread of loco-worked rlys.
WAGN
West Anglia & Great Northern Rlys, a TOU (qv), 1994. West Anglia Great Northern Rly Ltd, a TOC (*2*) (qv) 1997, operating services London (Kings

Cross)–Peterborough/Cambridge/Kings Lynn; London suburban services from Kings Cross and Moorgate to Hertford, Stevenage and Welwyn Garden City ; also London (Liverpool St.)–Stansted Airport. West Anglia franchise (Liverpool Street services) to Greater Anglia (ONE) 2004 (qv); GN (Kings Cross services) to London Lines (qv) 2006.
Wagner Palace Cars
Pullman type cars operated by the 1882 Wagner Palace Car Company, owned by Webster Wagner and the Vanderbilts. The WPC Co., which originated in 1865 as the New York Central Sleeping Car Co., was acquired by the Pullman Co. (qv) in 1899.
Wagon
Generic term for any freight vehicle. On British rlys, after *c.* 1830, so spelled, i.e. *not* 'waggon', and universally used instead of 'truck'.
Wagon chaser (RS)(obs)
A brakesman or shunter in a shunting or marshalling yard. The duties including running after a moving wagon to pin down its brakes.
Wagon hoist (obs)
Machinery for lifting a rly wagon vertically between two levels, in a freight depot, etc., both the hoist and each level being provided with tracks.
Wagon length (obs)
The length of track which will accommodate a four-wheeled wagon. Used as a rough measurement for sidings, etc.
Wagon-lit (Fr)
A sleeping car. *See also CIWL; Couchette.*

Wagon load/wagonload

A consignment of one ton or more, charged at wagon load rates. The modern meaning is a single wagon of freight.

Wagon pool

A group of wagons allocated to a specific use or traffic (from the 1970s). *See also* Common user (1).

Wagon teller

see Number takers (qv).

WAGR

Western Australian Government Rlys.

Waist

Usually the middle part of a rly coach or tramcar at a point just below the windows; normally the widest section of the bodywork.

Wakers (RS)(obs)

Facetious term used by GWR and BR (W) employees for sleeping car trains.

Wales & Borders Rly

TOC (2) (qv) 2001 (formerly Cardiff Rly Co. (qv)) with an expanded area of operation covering all services within south, west and central Wales as well as Cardiff–Bristol/Manchester/London (Waterloo). Became Arriva Trains Wales 2003.*See* Arriva.

Wales & West Passenger Trains Ltd

New name for South Wales & West (qv) TOC (2) (qv), 1997. Provides inter-urban, commuter and branch line services in south-west England and Wessex; south, mid- and north Wales and as far north as Liverpool, Manchester and Birmingham; also Bristol to Brighton and London to Salisbury and the west. Franchise to Wessex Trains (qv) 2001.

Walk against the gun, to (USRS)(obs)

To drive a steam loco up a steep gradient with the injector on.

Walker

Walker Brothers (Wigan) Ltd, manufacturers of diesel-mechanical railcars and power bogies.

Walking the length (RS)

The daily track inspection.

Walk-on rly/service

A rly service arranged so that passengers may rely on turning up at a station without reservation, with a good chance of finding a seat either immediately or after a short interval of standing. In Britain, this was traditionally the case until the 1980s, with a reserve of rolling stock maintained to meet peak demands, but from that time, with increasing financial pressures imposed by central government, some parts of BR, and InterCity in particular, could no longer be regarded as offering a walk-on service.

Walk the dog, to (USRS)

To drive a freight train so fast that the high wagons sway violently from side to side.

Walk the train (USRS)

To walk alongside a train from the rear to the end to check for possible defects. *See also* Roll by.

Wall of Death, the (RS)

The steeply graded line between Wimbledon and Sutton (particularly at the Sutton end), built in 1929 to be operated by electric rather than steam trains. From the fairground sideshow in which motor cyclists ride round the inside of a circular wall.

Wall Street notch (USRS)

see Company notch. From Wall Street, New York City, where rly shares are traded.

Walking stick (RS)

A flange-wheeled framework specifically designed for use with ultrasonic rail flaw detection equipment.

Walrus

TC for civil engineer's 40-ton hopper ballast wagon. Term still in use.

Walschaert's valve gear

A form of steam loco valve gear (qv) invented in 1844 by the Belgian engineer Egide Walschaerts (1820–1901) and widely adopted around the world, not least in Britain.

Waltzing Matilda (RS)

Track tamping machine; it appears to be dancing when in use.

W&B (RS)

Works and Bricks [the building department] (qv).

W&B Joint

Whitechapel & Bow Rly, London;

Whitechapel MDR to Bow (Campbell Road Junction with LT&SR), inc 1897, opened 1902, joint MDR (LPTB from 1933) and LT&SR (LM&SR from 1923), part of LTE from 1948.

W&CIR
see W&KR.

W&CR
Waterloo & City Rly, an isolated electric tube rly from Waterloo station, London, to the Bank without an intermediate station. Inc 1893, opened 1898, part of L&SWR from 1907, SR from 1923, part of BR (S) 1948, LT 1994.

W&KR
Waterford & Kilkenny Rly (Ire), inc 1845, first section opened 1848, renamed Waterford & Central Ireland Rly 1868, part of G&SWR from 1900.

W&LLR
Welshpool & Llanfair Light Rly, Welshpool–Llanfair Caereinion, 2 ft 6 in/762 mm gauge, LROs 1899, 1901, opened 1903. Constructed and worked by Cambrian Rlys; part of GWR 1923, BR (W) 1948. Passenger service ceased 1931, freight 1956. Restored and reopened as preserved line from 1963.

W&MER
Wrexham & Minera Extension Rly, Brymbo–near Llanfynydd. Inc 1865, opened 1872, vested jointly in GWR and L&NWR 1866, GWR and LM&SR 1923, BR 1948.

W&MR
Wrexham & Minera Rly, Wrexham–Brymbo. Inc 1861, opened 1862, vested in GWR 1871.

W&PR
Weymouth and Portland Rly. Inc 1862, opened 1865, leased to and worked by GWR and L&SWR; GWR & SR 1923–47, BR (W) 1948.

W&SCR
Woodside & South Croydon Rly, Woodside SER–Selsdon Road Junction. Inc 1880, jointly vested in SER and LB&SCR 1882, opened 1885.

W&SJR
Wellington & Severn Junction Rly, inc 1853, 1854, Wellington (Salop)–Ketley–

Coalbrookdale–Lightmoor, opened 1857, part of GWR 1892.

W&SS
Wolverton & Stony Stratford: originally promoted as the Stony Stratford & District Tramways Co.; a steam tramway (*4*), 3 ft 6 in/ 1,067 mm gauge, inc 1883, name changed to WSS and District Light Rlys Co. 1886. Opened 1887, freight traffic begun 1888, extended from SS to Deanshanger 1888. Name changed to W&SS District Tramroads Co. 1889, closed 1889. W to SS reopened 1891, name changed to W&SS District New Tramway Co. 1893. Purchased by L&NWR 1919, part of LM&SR 1923, closed 1926.

W&TR
Waterford & Tramore Rly (Ire), 5 ft 3 in/ 1,600 m gauge. Inc 1851, opened 1853, GSR 1924, CIE 1945, closed 1960. Not physically connected to the rest of the Irish rly system.

W&UT
Wisbech & Upwell Tramway. Inc by GER Act of 1881, steam tramway (*4*), opened 1883, 1884, owned and worked by GER, L&NER and BR. Passenger service ceased 1927, completely closed 1966.

Wankers (RS)
LB&SCR Marsh class I 1x 4–4–2T, as rebuilt by R.E.L. Maunsell.

Wantage
Wantage Tramway, steam tramway (*4*) between Wantage town and Wantage Road station GWR, with physical connection to GWR. Inc 1873, opened 1875, passenger service ceased 1925, completely closed 1945.

Ward coupler
An automatic mechanical coupler; replaced by Wedglock (qv) couplers.

Wardrobes (RS)
BR Class 20 locos.

Warflats
Bogie flat wagons designed to carry heavy and/or bulky military equipment and vehicles, first used in WW1 and still used for Ministry of Defence traffic.

Warner
Term used on Indian rlys for Distant signals (qv).

Warning arrangement

Rule 5, modifying absolute block working (*see* block working) to allow a signaller to accept a train from the box in the rear with the line clear only to the home signal (qv) and not to the clearing point (qv). Used only in specified conditions and subject to warning being given to train crew. *See also* Warning Signal.

Warning boards

1. Boards exhibiting stripe or bar markings to warn drivers they are approaching a distant signal. First used in Belgium in 1907, also adopted in Germany and France. Copied by the British MoT/DTp to warn road traffic to slow down at the approach to a traffic roundabout, etc.
2. Yellow boards illuminated at night and during fog or falling snow, installed on the lineside at a minimum of half a mile before a temporary speed restriction. *See also* C&T indicators.

Warning indicator

A sign consisting of an inverted triangle with yellow border and speed figure, used on high speed routes in combination with AWS (qv) equipment and sited at a suitable braking distance from a PSR (*1*) (qv).

Warning signal

A semaphore arm bearing a 'W' to inform the driver that the train has been accepted under the warning arrangement (qv) by the next signal box ahead. Alternatively a green flag or lamp may be held steadily at a window by the signaller as the train approaches the signal box.

Warnkreuze (Ger)

A fixed red and white warning signal in the form of a cross installed at the road approaches to level crossings, widely used in Europe.

WARS

1. Waterloo Area Resignalling Scheme; completed 1991 and controlled from Wimbledon.
2. Initials of the PKP sleeping and restaurant car organization.

Warships (RS)

BR class 42/43 diesel-hydraulic locos (named after warships).

War well (obs)

Military well wagons (qv) designed to carry tanks and other armoured fighting vehicles (AFV). Originated in WW1 and also used subsequently.

Wash (LTRS)

Train washing machine.

Washing machines (RS) (obs)

Signal box frames made by Ransomes & Rapier.

Wasps (RS)

People wearing high visibility jackets seen walking on the track.

Wasteels

Belgian agency which charters international trains to carry migrant workers on visits home to see their families.

Water boiler (RS)(obs)

A steam loco fireman.

Waterburys (RS)

NER Worsdell 2–4–0 locos class G of 1887–8, converted into 4–4–0s from 1900 onwards. From the name of a watch.

Water crane

A lineside appliance fed from a water tank or cistern and fitted with flexible hose (or bag) for filling steam loco water tanks. Usually located at the forward end of a station platform.

Watercress Line

Brand name adopted by the preserved rly using the Alton–Alresford section of the former BR Alton–Winchester line. First section opened 1977. *See also* Mid Hants.

Water Level Route

The New York Central RR's name for its main line between New York and Chicago via Cleveland.

Water scoop

see Scoop (*2*).

Water troughs (obs)

Narrow and lengthy troughs placed between the rails from which water could be scooped up into the tender tanks of steam locos travelling at speed (optimum uptake was achieved at around 40 mph). Invented by John Ramsbottom, loco superintendent of the L&NWR and first installed on that rly in 1860.

Watford tanks (RS)
L&NWR 0–6–2T.
Wath Daisies (RS)
see Daisies.
Watteau
TEE Paris–Tourcoing, introduced 1978.
With *Faidherbe* (qv), the last of the *TEE*s.
Wattman (Fr)(obs)
A tramcar or electric train driver.
Waveney Valley
see WVR.
Waverley
An express between London (St Pancras)
and Edinburgh, so named 1957, ceased
1964, re-introduced as summer-only
service 1965, renamed Waverley Express
1968, ceased 1968.
Waverley route
Carlisle–Hawick–Galashiels–Edinburgh.
Way car (US)(obs)
Early term for a caboose (qv).
Way freight (US)(obs)
A pick-up goods (qv).
Way switching (US)
Shunting operations carried out en route.
Way train (US)(obs)
A slow or local train.
WBR
The Wansbeck Valley Rly, Reedsmouth–
Morpeth. Inc 1859, first section opened
1862, part of NBR, 1863.
WC (obs)
Wagon Control.
WC&ER
Whitehaven, Cleator & Egremont Junction
Rly, Morehouse Junction, near Whitehaven
to Moor Row, Rowrah and Marron
Junction; Ullock–Parton; Moor Row–
Egremont–Sellafield. Inc 1854, first section
opened 1857. Paid a 15 per cent dividend
in 1863, becoming one of the most
prosperous rlys in Britain. Leased to
L&NWR and FR 1879, part of LM&SR
1923, BR 1948, last section closed 1980.
WC&PR
Weston, Clevedon & Portishead Tramways
Co. Inc 1885, opened 1897, 1907. By act
of 1899 status changed from a steam
tramway to a light rly, and name changed
to WC&P Light Railways Co. Closed 1940.

WCJS
West Coast Joint Stock; rolling stock for
WCML services jointly owned by L&NWR
and Caledonian Rly.
WCML
West Coast Main Line, London (Euston)–
Crewe–Carlisle–Carstairs–Glasgow. A £6bn
upgrading programme (1999–2003) by
Railtrack was designed to allow higher
speeds and to increase the capacity of this
busy route as well as renew ageing
infrastructure.
WCR
1. West Clare Rly (Ire), Ennis to Kilrush/
   Kilkee, 3 ft/914 mm gauge, opened
   1887 to Miltown Malbay, extension to
   Kilrush/Kilkee constructed by South
   Clare Rlys Co., inc 1884, opened 1892,
   worked by WCR. Part of GSR 1925,
   closed 1961. Subject of a song by Percy
   French, *Are Ye Right There, Michael, Are
   Ye Right?*
2. West Cornwall Rly, Truro to Penzance,
   etc., inc 1846, first section opened
   1852, leased to GWR, B&ER and SDR
   1865, part of GWR from 1878.
3. West Cheshire Rly, inc 1861,
   Northwich–Helsby, part of CLC 1867,
   opened 1869, 1870.
WCRTCC
West Coast Rail Traffic Control Centre
(Saltley).
WCTC
Wisconsin Central Transportation
Corporation; a US co. with rly interests in
USA, Canada, Jordan (*see* ARC), New
Zealand and Great Britain. Purchased by
CNR (qv) 2001. *See* EWS.
WDLR (obs)
War Department Light Rlys. UK military
rlys, up to and including WW1.
WDR
West Durham Rly, from collieries near
Crook to Hunwick/Burnhouse Junc
(Bishop Auckland–Spennymoor line). Inc
1839, first section opened 1840, part of
NER from 1870.
Wear [the] blue, to (USRS)
To be delayed by a wagon, coach or loco
fault. From the blue flag displayed on parts

of trains on which men are working. *See also* Blue light/flag.

Weardale Railway Co.
Heritage operation of major part (Bishop Auckland–Eastgate) of the Weardale Line (qv); first section, Stanhope–Walsingham, opened 2004.

Weardale/Wear Valley Line
The Wearhead branch, NER. Originally the Wear Valley Rly, inc 1845, first section opened 1847, leased to S&DR 1847, purchased by S&DR 1858. Wear Valley Extension Rly (Stanhope to Wearhead) inc 1892, absorbed by NER 1894, opened 1895.

Wear [the] green, to (USRS)
To run a train in more than one section. From the colour of the flags and lamps shown on such trains.

Weasel
1. (LTRS) A dmu.
2. (RS) A tip from a passenger. *See also* Weasel, to/weaseling.

Weasel, to/weaseling (RS)(obs)
To race along an arriving train seeking out passengers wanting their luggage carried to the cab/taxi rank; to go all out for tips; to deprive another porter of his tip by getting in first. Probably from the weasel's alleged ability to suck out the contents of an egg without breaking the shell.

Weather board (obs)
The screen around the back of the firebox of steam locos originally forming the only weather protection for the enginemen.

Weave
Diversion of train services around an engineer's possession (qv) of one or two tracks on a four-track route.

Web [of a rail]
That part between the head and the base (or foot) of a rail.

Webbed foot/ed fusilier (RS)(obs)
A fussy steam loco driver unable to pass a water crane without topping-up water tanks of his loco.

Wedglock® coupler
A type of centre coupling which gives an instantaneous linkage between cars of all electrical and mechanical connections.

Wee bogies (RS)
G&SWR Smellie 119 class 4–4–0 locos.

Weed-killing train
A train fitted with spray equipment to eject liquid chemical solutions onto the track and cess (qv) strips to control vegetation.

Weekly Operating Notice
A listing of engineering and signalling work and other local instructions for each week (00.01 Saturday to 23.59 Friday following) for a given area. Also known as Weekly Engineering Notice or colloquially as 'Glossies'.

Weight/weighted treadle bar
See Clearance/depression bar; Fouling bar.

Weir Committee
A government committee on main line electrification, chaired by Lord Weir. It reported to the Minister of Transport in March 1931.

WEL
Western Enterprises Ltd (qv).

WEL&CPR
West End of London & Crystal Palace Rly. Inc 1853, opened 1856, Crystal Palace to Wandsworth Common, worked by LB&SCR, extended to Pimlico terminus on south bank at Battersea Bridge 1858 and to Bromley (now Shortlands) in 1857 and 1858. The Crystal Palace–Battersea section became part of the LB&SCR in 1859, remainder passed to LC&DR 1860.

Wells Fargo
Express freight (qv) operation using rlys, founded in 1851 by William G. Fargo, Henry Wells and others. Purchased the Overland Mail Co. (formed in 1857 by Fargo and others to carry US mails) in 1861.

Wells Fargo (RS)
Old style Pullman cars with US features.

Well tank
A type of steam loco in which the water is stored in a tank slung between the frames, often under the footplate, providing a useful low centre of gravity, increasing stability on light or poorly laid track.

Well wagon
A bogie wagon with a dip in the central section between the bogies which enables

high loads to be carried without fouling the loading gauge.

Welsh Chieftain
see Land cruise.

Welsh Dragon
A summer service between Rhyl and Llandudno introduced 1950; 17¼ m, with a pull and push set, in 31–39 min. Dmu sets were used from *c.* 1960 and it ceased soon afterwards. Name revived for London (Euston) to Holyhead service introduced 1987 (journey time 4 h 34 min). Name ceased to be used after 2 June 2002.

Welsh Highland Rly
See WHR.

Welsh Land Cruise
see Land cruise.

Welshman
A summer service between London (Euston), Prestatyn (first stop), Llandudno, Bangor/Holyhead, and Pwllheli/Portmadoc. Introduced 1927, revived 1949. Ceased 1966. Name revived 1987 for a Holyhead–Cardiff service, name dropped 1988.

Welwyn Control
A signalling modification widely adopted after the Welwyn accident of 1935, in which track circuits in the rear and in advance of a home signal were interlocked with the block instruments, thus preventing the signalman from accepting a following train until all the track circuits were cleared.

Wensleydale Line
Hawes–Northallerton. Passenger services operated by Wensleydale Rly Association from 2003; full restoration Northallerton–Garsdale proposed.

WES
BR (S) class 442 emu sets for the Weymouth electrification of 1988, 5-WES. An abbreviation of Wessex.

Wessex Electrics (obs)
NSE brand name introduced 1989 for London (Waterloo)–Southampton–Bournemouth–Weymouth and Southampton/Eastleigh–Portsmouth electric services.

Wessex Line
BR brand name for Portsmouth–Bristol–Cardiff service.

Wessex Scot
A service between Poole and Glasgow/Edinburgh via Oxford, introduced 1986. Bournemouth–Glasgow/Edinburgh from 1992. Name ceased to be used from 2 June 2002.

Wessex Trains
A TOC (2) (qv), 2001, formerly Wales & West (qv), supplying regional services in the west of England, as well as from 2003 the former South West Trains (qv) services London (Waterloo)–Exeter and beyond and Reading–Portsmouth/Brighton. Part of Greater Western (qv) franchise from 2006.

Wessie/ey (RS)(obs)
The L&NWR, or its locos or employees.

West Anglia & Great Northern
see WAGN.

Westbound
see Eastbound.

West Coast Corridor Express
With the introduction of corridor stock and dining cars in 1892, this became the unofficial name for the afternoon express between London (Euston) and Glasgow (Central) with coaches for Knutsford, Whitehaven, Edinburgh and Aberdeen, which had been introduced in 1889. The 1909 journey time was 8 h 20 min. *See also* Midday Scot.

West Coast Postal
The unofficial name for North Western Night TPO Down, Euston–Aberdeen, an all-mail train introduced July 1885.

West Coast Route, the
WCML (qv).

West Coast Trains Ltd
see Virgin West Coast.

West Country Pullman
A London (Paddington)–Paignton service, introduced 1988. Summer only. Ceased after 1990 season. *See also* Torbay Express.

Western Enterprises Ltd
A company formed jointly by the GWR and the Provident Mutual Life Association in 1936 to develop rly lands. Wound up by the BTC.

Westerns (RS)
BR class 52 diesel-hydraulic locos. From their names, which were all prefixed 'Western'.

Western Valleys
see Eastern & Western Valleys Lines.

West Highlander
BR IC land cruise train from London to Oban, Fort William and Mallaig. Also a sleeping car train between London (Euston) and Fort William, so named 1992.

West Highland Rly/Line
Craigendoran to Fort William and Mallaig. Inc 1889, 1896, opened 1894 to Fort William, 1901 to Mallaig, worked by NBR. Part of L&NER 1923.

Westinghouse
1. Westinghouse Electric Co. of London, formed 1889, became British Westinghouse Electric & Manufacturing Co. Ltd, 1899 with works at Trafford Park, Manchester. Manufacturers of electric traction equipment for rlys and tramways. Became MV (qv), 1919. See also Westinghouse brake.
2. Westinghouse Electric Corporation (US): manufacturers of lifts, escalators, automated rapid transit equipment and people movers.

Westinghouse brake
A compressed air automatic braking system invented by the US engineer George Westinghouse (1846–1914) in 1872–3. Much improved in 1886–7, and subsequently adopted by the Caledonian Rly, GER, LB&SCR, NBR and NER. A works to manufacture this brake was established at Kings Cross, London in 1879 (rebuilt 1889) and the English Westinghouse Brake Co. Ltd was inc in 1881. Amalgamated with McKenzie & Holland (qv) c. 1907 to form the McKenzie, Holland & Westinghouse Power Signalling Co. Name changed to Westinghouse Brake & Saxby Signal Co., 1920, after control had passed to the Consolidated Signal Co. (qv) and its Chippenham works. Name changed to Westinghouse Brake & Signal Co., 1935. Part of Hawker Siddeley Group, 1979. Westinghouse Air Brake Co. (USA) was merged with Motive Power Industries in 1999 to become WABTEC (qv). The UK Westinghouse Brake business was acquired by Invensys (qv) in 1999 and by *Knorr-Bremse AG* (qv) in 2000. *See also* Air brake.

Westkurier (Ger)
A Vienna–Bregenz overnight service.

West Line, The
Newcastle–Hexham–Carlisle.

West London Line
Willesden Junc–Kensington (Olympia)–Clapham Junc. *See also* WLER; WLR.

West Midlands Executive
An express between London (Euston) and Shrewsbury, introduced 1987. Name dropped 1988.

Westrail
Brand name for WAGR (qv).

West Riding Limited
Supplementary fare streamlined steam-hauled express between London (Kings Cross), Leeds (Central) and Bradford (Exchange), introduced 1937. Re-introduced as West Riding, 1949 but without streamlined stock. Ceased *c*. 1963.

West Riding Pullman
An all-Pullman service between London (Kings Cross), Wakefield, Leeds, Bradford and Halifax, so named 1927, renamed Yorkshire Pullman (qv) 1935.

West Somerset
West Somerset Rly, Norton Fitzwarren to Watchet. Inc 1857, opened 1862, leased and worked by B&ER, part of GWR from 1922. Name adopted for the preserved line between Minehead and Norton Fitzwarren (former BR Minehead branch), first section restored 1976. *See also* WSMR.

West Sussex Rly
See HofM&ST.

West Yorkshire Executive
A service between London (Kings Cross) and Leeds, so named 1984. Name dropped 1989.

Wet mole in the firebox, a (USRS)(obs)
A condition arising from incompetent firing of a steam loco.

Wet spot
see Pumping.

WEZ (Ger)
West Europäische Zeit; West European Time.

Whack (USRS)
A carman (qv).

Whale
A 50-ton bogie hopper ballast wagon used by engineers.

Whale body (USRS)
A wagon with a bottom hopper.

Wharf
A freight platform or loading dock. Adopted from marine and canal usage. *See also* Dock.

Wharncliffe Meeting (obs)
A meeting of shareholders (usually held at the same time as the regular half-yearly meetings) specifically to consider any bill seeking additional powers for a co. Approval by a minimum of three-fifths of the shareholders was necessary before such a bill could be presented to parliament. Required from 1846 by Standing Orders of the House of Lords, drawn up at the instigation of the first Lord Wharncliffe.

'Wheatley's Road'
Girvan–Portpatrick, after W.T. Wheatley, a former general manager of the line.

Wheel, to (USRS)
To drive a train at high speed.

Wheel arrangement
A method of identifying locomotive types by the arrangement of the driving and other wheels: *see* Continental notation [steam locos]; Notation [of electric and diesel locos]; Whyte's notation [steam locos].

Wheelbase
The distance between the points at each end of a vehicle where the tyres of the wheels rest on the rail. If the vehicle has trucks/bogies, the *overall or outer wheelbase* is the distance between the resting points of the outermost wheels. The measurement from the centre of one truck to the centre of the other is known as *distance between truck centres*, or in Fr, *l'entr'axe des bogies*.

Wheel burn
Damage to the running surface of a rail caused by a driving wheel spinning on a stationary or slow-moving vehicle. Wheel burns may conceal more serious defects arising from the excessive heat produced by wheel spin.

Wheel flange lubricator
See Flange lubricators.

Wheel flat
See Flat (3).

Wheel monkey (USRS)
A carriage & wagon inspector.

Wheel set
A pair of wheels mounted on their axle.

Wheel tapper (obs)
A C&W examiner specifically employed to check the wheels and axleboxes of trains in service when they stopped at the larger stations. From the tapping of the hammer used to confirm there were no defects in the wheels.

Whelk
A 42-ton bogie plate wagon used by S&T staff.

Whelley Line
Bamfurlong Junc–Standish Junc, avoiding Wigan.

WHH&R
West Hartlepool Harbour & Rly Co. Inc 1852, an amalgamation of the WH Harbour & Dock Co. with Stockton & Hartlepool Rly and Clarence Rly. Part of NER 1865.

Whipsnade
Whipsnade & Umfolozi Rly, 2 ft 6 in/762 mm gauge, Whipsnade Park Zoo, Bedfordshire, opened 1970.

Whirlybird (RS)
A Matisa ballast tamper.

Whiskers
1. (RS) Exhaust pipes bent up over the cab ends of BR diesel railcars (class 122, etc.). *See also* Speed whiskers.
2. (USRS) A very senior rlyman; seniority.

Whispering baritone (RS)
A garrulous, noisy person, a barrack-room lawyer.

Whispering death (RS)
A dmu. From its quiet approach to anyone on the track.

Whistle board
A white circular sign with blue edge and black 'W' in centre or 'SW' in white letters on a black background, warning drivers to sound whistle or horn at the approach to footpath or accommodation level crossings.

Whistle off, to (USRS)
To give two short blasts on the whistle as a warning the train is about to move.

Whistle out a flag, to (USRS)

To give one long and three short blasts on the whistle, indicating that the brakeman must protect the rear of the halted train with a flag or lamp. Or to give three short and one long blast, indicating that the brakeman must protect the head of the halted train with a flag or lamp.

Whistle pig (USRS)

A loco driver.

Whistlers (RS)

1. BR diesel locos class 40. From the sound emitted when starting.
2. BR Class 312 emus. From the aerodynamic noise when in motion.

Whistle signals

Signals given on a mouth whistle by signalmen, guards and shunters to start or stop a train and control shunting movements. Also sounded on loco whistles by accepted codes to warn of approach, start, clearance of points, confirm route required at junction, etc.

Whistle stop

A very minor station which trains approach with a whistle signal, not calling unless a flag or lamp is displayed. *See also* Flag stop.

Whistle stop tour

A full-scale tour of the US by presidential candidates, in a train using private cars (qv), during which stops were made at many small communities (whistle stops (qv)) for the candidate to address the crowd from the platform of the rear car. Harry S. Truman was the last presidential candidate to undertake a full whistle stop tour, in 1948. Some others have undertaken abbreviated tours subsequently, e.g. Jimmy Carter in 1976.

Whistling post (US)

A white post at the trackside warning that a level crossing is ahead and a whistle should be sounded.

White feather (USRS)(obs)

A plume of steam over the safety valve of a steam loco. Hence to carry a white feather, to run with a full head of steam.

White Hope (RS)

A steam loco cleaner filthy with grease, oil and dirt after work.

White period

A period of total occupation by the civil engineers, when no trains of any kind are allowed on a section of line.

White ribbon (USRS)

A white flag carried by an extra train.

White Rose

An express between London (Kings Cross), Leeds (Central) and Bradford (Exchange), introduced 1949, later Leeds only, name dropped 1964.

White Rose Pullman

An all-Pullman train between London (Kings Cross), Leeds (Central), Bradford and Harrogate, introduced 1964. Ceased 1967. Name re-introduced 1991 for a First class Pullman express between York and London (Kings Cross).

White shirt (USRS)

A rly officer or manager. Sufficiently remote from manual labour to be able to wear a white shirt.

White space (RS)

The white space in timetable diagrams indicating possible room for a path (qv) for an additional train or a path left for contingencies.

Whitewash coach/van (obs)

A vehicle equipped with a device which deposited whitewash on the track at any point where defects were sensed, to mark them for subsequent investigation.

Whiting

A 14-ton wagon used by engineers for carrying rails and sleepers.

WHR

Welsh Highland Rly, Portmadoc–Dinas Junction, 1 ft 11½ in/597 mm gauge, LROs 1922, 1923, acquired NWNGR and PB&SSR. Opened 1922, 1923, leased by FR 1934–42, closed to passengers 1936, to freight 1937. Partially reopened as preserved line from 1980. Further sections on original alignment reopened from 2000, whole line to be restored. This project has also included a new 1 ft 11½ in gauge line over the former standard gauge BR alignment from Caernarvon to Dinas Junc. station.

Whyte's notation

A method of classifying steam locos, invented by F.M. Whyte (1865–1941), one time general mechanical engineer, New York Central RR. Introduced in the USA 1900, in UK from *c.* 1903. The notation enunciates from left to right (i.e. from the front of the loco to the back) the total number of *wheels*, the central number(s) referring to the coupled driving wheels and the first and last to the leading and trailing uncoupled wheels. Thus 0–6–0 indicates three pairs of driving wheels and no others, 4–4–2, a four-wheeled leading truck, two pairs of coupled driving wheels and a two-wheeled trailing truck. The suffix T, e.g. 0–6–0T, indicates a tank loco; PT, a pannier tank; WT, a well tank; ST, a saddle tank. *See* diagram opposite. *See also* Continental notation.

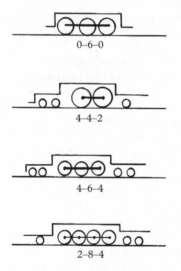

0–6–0

4–4–2

4–6–4

2–8–4

Examples of Whyte's notation

WICC

Wessex Integrated Control Centre; the first combined TOC (2) (qv) and Network Rail (qv) control centre, Waterloo station, London, directing operations over 600 route miles.

Wicket gate

A gate at a level crossing which can be locked from the signal box to prevent pedestrians from crossing the line when a train is approaching.

Wickham

D. Wickham & Co. Ltd, Ware, manufacturers of railcars, mu diesel sets and powered rail trolleys. Ware works closed 1991.

Wide gauge

The US term for broad gauge (qv).

Widen, to (USRS)

To open the throttle of a steam loco to increase speed.

Widened Lines

City Widened Lines (qv).

Wide space/Wide way (RS)

Ten foot (qv).

Widows and Orphans (RS)

A term used to describe the unsafe practice of walking along a running line with one's back to approaching traffic.

Wiener Walzer

A night service between Basle and Vienna, introduced 1959, extended to Bucharest 1962 (Budapest in winter).

Wiggly wire

1. (RS) A wavy band of stainless steel set in the top of the running rails to assist the conductivity of low tension current on little-used sections of track-circuited lines.
2. A system of AWS (qv) with a cab display showing the indication of the last signal passed.

Wig-wag (USRS)

A signal at a level crossing. From the action of its swinging arms.

WIIC

West India Improvement Co.; operator and owner of Jamaican rlys 1890–1900.

Wild cat (USRS)

A loco moving without a driver on board.

William Shakespeare

Summer express between London (Paddington) and Wolverhampton/Stratford-upon-Avon, so named 1951; ran that summer only.

William Tell Express

A summer service (two and sometimes three trains each way) between Boulogne and Lucerne (also Lugano, when traffic warranted), with all seats reserved by

British travel agencies, introduced by CTAC (qv) in 1934. Connecting trains were also chartered by CTAC to carry clients between London and Folkestone/Dover.

Willie (USRS)
Waybill for a loaded wagon.

Will it move rly (RS)
Woolmer Instructional Military Rly. *See* LMR (2).

Willmott Group
Harry Willmott and his son, Russell, who took up interests in unsuccessful railways, managed them and sought to improve their fortunes. Their achievements were much lauded in the Edwardian RM. At various times they managed or controlled the E&WJR, IofWCR, LD&ECR, Sheffield District, SDR (2), S&MJR, Edge Hill Light, and N&BJR.

Willoughby, Lord
See Lord Willoughby's Rly.

Wimbling (RS)
1. Any drilling operations by track maintenance staff.
2. The use of a manually operated auger.

WIMR
see LMR.

Wind (USRS)
Brake air/air brakes.

Windcutters (RS)(obs)
Locos incorporating a primitive and early form of streamlining in which features such as cabs and smokeboxes were modified in shape to decrease wind resistance. *See also Coupe-vent*; Windsplitters.

Windjammer
1. (RS) A blocked airpipe on a diesel engine.
2. (USRS) An air compressor used in a rly brake system.

Windowhang, to (RS)
To lean out of a window of a moving train for a protracted period.

Window music (USRS)
Attractive scenery.

Windsor Lines
Tracks between London (Waterloo) and Barnes used by Windsor and Reading services.

Windsplitters (obs)
US term for streamlined locos and diesel sets. Adams' 'Windsplitter' train, with flush-sided cars, was introduced in the US in 1900.

Wind up, to (LTRS)
To move the handle of the master controller of a train from the off position to a motoring position.

Wing her, to (USRS)
To set the hand brakes on a moving train.

Winging (RS)
Rail turning (qv).

Wing rails
Guide rails at the open spaces in crossings, which prevent derailment.

Wing tank
A design of industrial tank loco in which the main water tank forms a cradle for the boiler and smokebox.

Winkle
A 22-ton plate wagon used by S&T staff.

Wiper (USRS)
A loco cleaner.

Wipe the clock, to (USRS)
To make an emergency brake application (qv), sending the needle right round the dial.

Wire tapper (USRS)
A rly telegraph operator.

Wirral
see WR.

Wirral lines
Liverpool (Central LL) to New Brighton/ West Kirby.

Wisconsin
WCTC (qv).

Wisdom box (USRS)
A facetious description of a yardmaster's office.

Wise guy (USRS)
A station agent.

Wissington
Wissington Light Rly, an agricultural system connected to the GER Stoke Ferry branch at Abbey & West Dereham, first section opened 1905, latterly operated by the British Sugar Corporation, closed 1982.

Withered Arm
A name coined in 1967 by the late T.W.E.

Roche for the former L&SWR/SR lines west of Exeter after Beeching (qv) had done his work.

Wizzos (RS)
BR class 52 diesel-hydraulic locos.

WL
A shortened form of *CIWL* (qv).

WL&WR
Waterford, Limerick & Western Rly (Ire), Waterford–Limerick–Sligo with branches to Killaloe, Foynes, Tralee and Thurles, inc as Waterford & Limerick Rly 1846, first section (Limerick–Tipperary) opened 1848. Renamed WL&WR 1895. Part of GS&WR from 1901.

WLER
West London Extension Rly, from a point just south of the present Kensington (Olympia) station to Longhedge and Clapham Junctions with the L&SWR, LC&DR and LB&SCR. Inc 1859, opened 1863. GWR, L&NWR, L&SWR and LB&SCR Joint; GWR, SR and LM&SR joint from 1923. BR from 1948.

WLR
1. West London Rly, from North Pole Junction (with GWR and L&NWR), near Old Oak Common, to near the present Kensington (Olympia) station. Inc as Birmingham, Bristol & Thames Junction Rly 1836, named changed to WLR 1840, opened 1844, vested in GWR and L&NWR, 1854; GWR and LM&SR 1923, BR 1948.
2. West Lancashire Rly, Southport to Preston, inc 1871, first section opened 1878, part of L&YR from 1897.

WM&CQJR
Wrexham, Mold & Connah's Quay Junction Rly, inc 1862, opened 1866. Purchased by GCR 1905.

WMR
1. West Midland Rly; an 1860 amalgamation of the OW&WR, the Worcester & Hereford Rly and the Newport, Abergavenny & Hereford Rly. Part of GWR from 1863.
2. Woolmer Military Rly: *see* LMR.

WNJR
West Norfolk Junction Rly, Heacham–

Wells, inc 1864, opened 1866, worked by GER, merged with Lynn & Hunstanton Rly to become Hunstanton & West Norfolk Rly, 1874. Part of GER 1890.

WO
Waiting orders, goods on hand awaiting the consignor's instructions.

Wolds [Coast] Line
Brand name for BR Hull–Scarborough line and services.

Wolf (USRS)
see Lone Wolf.

Wolves (RS)
GNR large Stirling 0-4-4T. From their distinctive bark.

Womble (LTRS)
An elderly person, especially one travelling on a concessionary or free ticket.

Womming (RS)
Rail turning (qv).

Wood, The (RS) (obs)
The suburban platforms at Euston station, London.

Woodhead Line/Route
The former GCR Manchester to Sheffield line via Guide Bridge, Woodhead Tunnel and Penistone. Closed to through passenger trains, 1970, to freight, 1981.

Wood Line (LTRS)
The Metropolitan line from Baker Street to Uxbridge/Watford/Chesham and Amersham. From the name of the original section, the Metropolitan & St John's *Wood* Rly.

Woolworths (RS)
2–6–0 locos built in the early 1920s at Royal Arsenal, Woolwich, or 2–6–0 locos assembled from parts made there.

Wootten
A wide firebox for steam locos to provide a large grate area for slow combustion of anthracite, originated by US engineer John E. Wootten, who also patented designs for loco chimneys, steam gauges and rly car heaters.

Work a car, to (USRS)
To unload freight from a wagon.

Work(s) cars/work equipment
Rolling stock designed specifically for rly and tramway (*3*) construction and maintenance or used solely for those purposes, hence 'work trains'.

Working Notice
The weekly bulletin covering all engineering and signalling work, signalling changes and other occurrences affecting the operation of the rly (or sections of it) and also including other important information for train crews and operating staff.

Working Reference Manual
The modern equivalent of the Rule Book (qv).

Working timetable
The timetable produced for the use of rly staff showing all the trains on each line, passenger, freight, light engine movements, etc., their order of running, lines they shall use and also the exact time to the nearest half minute of passing, stopping and departure at stations, etc. Paths for trains run 'as required' are also shown. The times of passenger trains printed in the working timetable may differ from those given in the public timetables. Also known as the Service Time Book/Timetables.

Workmen's fares and trains (obs)
Cheap tickets for those travelling daily to and from work in the early morning, only available by stipulated trains or at stipulated times for travel from specified stations. They were required by various private railway acts, beginning with the LC&DR Metropolitan Extensions Lines Act, 1860. This act fixed the times such trains were to be run and the fares to be charged (the lines concerned were opened from 1865). The Metropolitan Railway had however voluntarily offered such facilities from May 1864. General and obligatory introduction of workmen's fares dates from the Cheap Trains Act of 1883. The workmen's facilities were replaced by the 'Early Morning Fares' in 1950 but these were withdrawn after 1961.

Works and Bricks (LTRS)
LT Works and Buildings Department and its staff. Dissolved 1987.

Work station
A position within the control room of an IECC (qv) devoted to the signalling and operation of a specific area and the interface with signal boxes still open on the edges of that area.

Work the yards, to (USRS)
To shunt.

Work through, to (LTRS)
To work through the middle of a split turn (qv).

Work train
A train carrying materials to lay or repair track or track formation, to repair or erect bridges, etc.

World Railways
See Janes' World Railways.

Worm (USRS)
A streamlined train.

Worm diagram (LTRS)
A sectional drawing showing the disposition of the tunnels and passenger subways at tube stations.

Worsborough branch
Wombwell–Worsborough–Silkstone.

Worth Valley
Keighley–Oxenhope. *See also* K&WVR.

WP (US)
Western Pacific RR.

WR
1. Wirral Rly, West Kirby to Liverpool ferry terminal at Seacombe and to Birkenhead Park/New Brighton, inc 1863 as Hoylake Rly and opened Hoylake to Birkenhead Docks 1866, closed 1870. Reopened by Hoylake Rail and Tramway Company from 1872, renamed Seacombe, Hoylake & Deeside Rly 1881. Wirral Rly Company inc 1883, opened Birkenhead Docks to Birkenhead Park 1881. Reconstituted and amalgamated with Seacombe, Hoylake & Deeside Rly Co. as the Wirral Rly, 1891. Part of LM&SR from 1923.
2. Wycombe Rly, Maidenhead to High Wycombe and Aylesbury also Princes Risborough to Thame and Kennington Junction (Oxford), inc 1846 (Maidenhead to High Wycombe), opened 1854, 1862, 1863, 1864, part of GWR from 1867.
3. Wenlock Rly, inc 1861, opened Coalbrookdale–Presthorpe 1864, to

Craven Arms 1867. Worked by GWR.
Part of GWR 1896.

4. Witney Rly, inc 1859 Yarnton to
Witney, opened 1861, part of GWR
1890.

5. Woodstock Rly, inc 1886, Kidlington to
Blenheim & Woodstock, opened 1890,
worked by GWR. Part of GWR 1897.

6. Wigtownshire Rly, inc 1872, Newton
Stewart–Whithorn and branch to
Garliestown, first section opened
1875–6. Amalgamated with PR (*1*) to
form P&WR (qv), 1885.

7. Western Region of BR.

8. Western Rly [of India], formed 1951.

9. *Wagon-restaurant*, restaurant car.

WR&GJC
West Riding & Grimsby Joint Rly,
Wakefield–Stainforth/Doncaster, inc 1862,
opened 1866, vested in MS&LR & GNR
1866 as WR&G Joint Rly, L&NER from
1923.

Wreck crew (USRS)
Breakdown gang.

Wreck train (USRS)
A breakdown train (qv).

Wrington Vale
Wrington Vale Light Rly, Congresbury
Junction to Blagdon, LRO 1898, opened
1901. Constructed, worked and financed
by the GWR.

WRISA
Wheel Rail Interface Systems Authority
Ltd, founded 2001 by companies
representing the rly industry: Railtrack
(qv), the rly operators, rolling stock leasing
companies and the RIA (qv). A systems
authority forming 'a focus for
understanding wheel and rail', WRISA
recommended actions 'which will ensure
that the industry will strike the right
balance between the technical and
economic factors affecting this vital
interface'. Wound up 2005 and replaced by
V/VSIC (qv). *See also* Gauge corner
cracking; Rolling contact fatigue.

WRM
Working Reference Manual (qv).

Wrong iron (USRS)
Wrong line/road (qv).

Wrong line/road
A reversal of the normal direction of
working on a rly. *See also* Wrong line
working; Wrong line orders.

Wrong line orders
Forms authorizing movement of a train
over the wrong line (qv) during
emergencies. Four types of form exist to be
completed, according to the circumstances:
guard to signalman; driver to signalman;
guard to driver; and signalman to driver.
Each move requires a separate form. *See
also* Wrong line working.

Wrong line working
When one line of a double track section is
obstructed or under maintenance, and there
is no system of bi-directional signalling, locos
and trains may be allowed to proceed wrong
line (qv), by the introduction of single or
wrong line working, using a pilotman (qv)
between one signal box and the next, as
arranged by a station manager, district
inspector or other responsible official who
completes special single line working forms
addressed to the pilotman, signalmen and
station managers in the area affected. *See also*
Wrong line orders.

Wrong one off (RS)
A signal cleared to the off mode, but for an
incorrect route.

Wrong side failure
The opposite of Fail-safe (qv). A failure in
track circuits (qv) or other signalling
equipment which does not leave signals
showing the danger aspect.

WRUR
West Riding Union Rly, inc 1846, an
amalgamation of the WYR and the Leeds
& West Riding Junction Rly, part of L&YR
1846. Bradford–Halifax–Sowerby Bridge;
first section opened 1850.

WS&WR
Wiltshire, Somerset & Weymouth Rly,
Salisbury–Westbury–Thingley Junction/
Bathampton/Devizes, Westbury–Weymouth,
Frome–Radstock. Inc 1845, opened 1848,
1850, 1851, 1854, 1856, 1857, part of
GWR from 1851.

WSF
see Wrong side failure.

WSMR
West Somerset Mineral Rly, Watchet to Gupworthy and Brendon Hills iron ore workings, inc 1855, opened 1859, passenger service 1865 (officially to Combe Row only). Closed 1898. Partially reopened 1907, closed 1909.

WSR
West Somerset Rly (qv).

WT
1. Wotton Tramway, also known as the Brill Tramroad or Tramway; Quainton Road to Brill, with branch from Wotton Underwood to Kingswood Lane Wharf; opened without parliamentary sanction 1871, 1872. Horses used initially, steam locos later. Passengers and freight carried. Leased and worked by Metropolitan Rly 1899 (Met & GC Joint Committee from 1906), under a 'temporary' arrangement. Closed 1935. *See also* O&AT.
2. A well tank locomotive (qv).
3. Initials used by GEC (qv) (Witton Works) to avoid confusion with GE (2) (qv).

WTT
Working timetable (qv).

WVER
Wear Valley Extension Rly: *see* Weardale/Wear Valley Line.

WVLR
Wrington Vale Light Rly: *see* Wrington Vale.

WVR
1. Waveney Valley Rly, Tivetshall–Beccles, inc 1851, 1853, first section opened 1855, worked by ECR. Part of GER, 1863.
2. Wear Valley Rly: *see* Weardale/Wear Valley Line.
3. Wye Valley Rly: *see* Wye Valley.

WWW&DR
Waterford, Wexford, Wicklow & Dublin Rly: *see* D&SER.

Wye (US)
A reversing triangle. From its 'Y' shape. *See also* Triangle.

Wye Valley
Wye Valley Rly, Chepstow to Monmouth, inc 1866, opened 1876, worked by GWR, part of GWR from 1905.

WYPTA/WYPTE
West Yorkshire Passenger Transport Authority/Executive.

WYR
West Yorkshire Rly, title assumed in 1863 by Bradford, Wakefield & Leeds Rly (Wakefield–Leeds, worked by GNR from its opening in 1857). Part of GNR 1865. *See also* MJR.

Wyvernrail
Operator of the Wirksworth branch as a preserved rly (qv) from 2003.

X

X (USRS)
An empty wagon.

Xmundifier (obs)
Maltese term for rly, a corruption of the
Fr *chemin der fer*. The Maltese also
called their rly *il vapur-tal-Art* = the land
steamer.

XP/XP Regulations (obs)
An XP marking on a vehicle identified it as
suitable for running as part of a passenger
train. The XP Regulations, 1938 set out
the requirements which made such use
permissible.

XP 64 (obs)
Prototype BR express passenger coaches in
blue and grey livery introduced on the
Talisman (qv) in 1964.

XPT
An Australian high-speed train with diesel
power units at each end, a version of BR
IC125 trains adapted to Australian
conditions, the first of which entered
service in New South Wales in 1982.

X 2000
A tilting electric train capable of 200 km/h,
proposed for Swedish Rlys/*SJ*.

Y

Y
An abbreviation for a wye (qv).

Yam-yams (RS)
Diesel multiple units. From the noise made by the engines when idling.

Y&NMR
York & North Midland Rly, York to Castleford and junctions with NMR, inc 1836, first section opened 1839. Later extended to serve Harrogate, Scarborough, Filey, Bridlington, Pickering, Market Weighton and Knottingley, etc. Part of NER from 1854.

Y&NNR
Yarmouth & North Norfolk [Light] Rly, Great Yarmouth–Stalham. Inc 1876, first section opened 1877 as Great Yarmouth & Stalham Light Rly. Renamed Y&NNLR 1878 (authorized to extend to North Walsham, which was reached in 1881). Part of E&MR (qv) 1883.

Yankees (RS)
Highland Rly P class 4–4–0T, originally built by Dübs & Co. for use in Uruguay, which someone must have thought was in the USA; also used of others built to the same design.

Yanks (RS)
1. General Motors diesel locos of the IE.
2. Class 59 locos; from their US origin.

Yard (LTRS)
1. A car depot.
2. (RS) (obs)LCCT (qv) staff colloquialism for depot or car shed.

Yard Bull (USRS)
A rly policeman/woman. *See also* Cinder Dick; Gumshoe.

Yard geese (USRS)
Shunters; always moving hither and thither round the rly yards.

Yard goat (USRS)
A small shunting loco.

Yardmaster/yard manager
The official responsible for the control of all operations within a shunting or marshalling yard and its effective working, directing inspectors, foremen, shunters, goods porters, checkers, etc.

Yardmen (US)
Shunters.

Y-drain
A Y-shaped incision in the side of a cutting or embankment filled with broken stone or rubble to drain off excess water.

YDR
Yorkshire Dales Rly (qv).

Yellow Engine
see Red engine.

Yellow eye (USRS)
A signal showing the caution indication.

Yellow Perils (RS)
Special printed notices, similar to TC (2) (qv), regarding signalling arrangements (especially on LT) or (generally) any operating notices issued to staff and printed (or originally printed) on yellow paper. From yellow peril, a fear raised in the 1890s/1900s in Europe that the Chinese and Japanese would before long terrorize and over-run the white races and their civilization.

Yellowstone (US)
A Mallet (qv) steam loco with 2–8–8–4 wheel arrangement.

Yellow whisker (RS)(obs)
Speed whiskers (qv).

Yerkes Tubes
Those London tube rlys (Bakerloo, Piccadilly and Charing Cross, Euston & Hampstead) originally built and controlled by the syndicate headed by the US financier Charles Tyson Yerkes (1837–1905).

YM
Yardmaster/manager (qv).

York, the (RS)(obs)
No. 9 platform in the old London (Euston) terminus, originally provided for trains to the Midlands and York.

Yorkie (RS)
A nickname for GNR, its employees or its locos.

Yorkshire
Yorkshire Engine Co. Ltd, Meadowhall Works, Sheffield, loco builders, inc 1865. Acquired by United Steel Companies 1945–8. Diesel loco manufacture started 1949. Last steam locos produced 1956. Taken over by Rolls Royce Ltd 1965 and loco production transferred to that company's Sentinel (qv) works.

Yorkshire Dales Rly
1. Skipton to Grassington, inc 1897, opened 1902, worked by Midland Rly, part of LM&SR from 1923.
2. Original name of ESR (5) (qv).

Yorkshireman
An express between London (St Pancras), Sheffield and Bradford (Exchange), so named 1927. 4 h 1 min timing in 1937.

Yorkshire Pullman
A renaming in 1935 of the West Riding Pullman (qv). All-Pullman service in three sections running between London (Kings Cross), Hull/Harrogate/Bradford (Exchange) and Halifax. Restored 1946, separate Kings Cross–Hull section, using Midland Pullman diesel units, 1966. Ceased to run as a Pullman service in 1978 and name dropped. Revived 1985 as a London (Kings Cross)–Leeds/Bradford service with a 1 h 59 min journey time London–Leeds in 1990.

Z

Zahnradbahn (Ger)
A rack or cog-wheel rly.

Zander
A 26-ton ballast wagon used by engineers.

ZASM
The usual abbreviation for *NZASM* (qv).

ŽBH
Željeznice Bosne i Hercegovine; Bosnia-Hercegovina State Rlys, formed out of *JZ* (qv).

Zebra boards (RS)
Emergency speed restriction warning boards. *See also* Metal Mickey.

Zero point
The point from which the mileage of a rly is measured.

Zone ticket
A ticket allowing unlimited journeys in a specified area for a short period, usually a week.

Zoo box (RS)
A mess van used by gangs working on the line.

Zoo keeper (RS)
A rlyman or woman checking tickets, etc. at station barriers.

ZR
Zambia Rlys, part of RR (qv) until 1967. 1,273 km of 1,067 mm gauge. *See also* Tanzam.

ZRS
Zeleznice Republike Srpske, the Serbo-Croat rly administration in Bosnia. *See also* ZBH.

ZS
Zeleznice Srbije; Serbia-Montenegro Railways, 2003, from the rump of *JZ* (qv). International code CS.

ZSR
Zeleznice Slovenakiy Republiky, Slovak Republic Rlys, part of *ČSD* (qv) until 1993. 3,664 km, mostly standard gauge.

Z stop
A comfort stop arranged for passengers travelling in a train not fitted with lavatories.

Zulu
1. (obs) The unofficial name for the 15.00 express from London (Paddington) to Plymouth and the corresponding return working, introduced in 1879 (during the Zulu War). The usage was current until around 1914.
2. (USRS) (obs) An immigrant rail passenger on US/Canadian rlys on the way to settling in his new home. Hence Zulu train and to travel Zulu style, i.e. with all portable household possessions and farm equipment.

Zulu Warrior
Nickname of the prototype Deltic (qv) now in the NRM. From its livery.